Statistical Reasoning in Law and Public Policy

Volume 1

Statistical Concepts and Issues of Fairness

This is a volume in
STATISTICAL MODELING AND DECISION SCIENCE

Gerald L. Lieberman and Ingram Olkin, editors
Stanford University, Stanford, California

Statistical Reasoning in Law and Public Policy

Volume 1

Statistical Concepts and Issues of Fairness

Joseph L. Gastwirth

Department of Statistics
George Washington University
Washington, DC

ACADEMIC PRESS, INC.
Harcourt Brace Jovanovich, Publishers

Boston   San Diego   New York
Berkeley   London   Sydney
Tokyo   Toronto

ACADEMIC PRESS, INC.
1250 Sixth Avenue, San Diego, CA 92101

United Kingdom Edition published by
ACADEMIC PRESS INC. (LONDON) LTD.
24-28 Oval Road, London NW1 7DX

Library of Congress Cataloging-in-Publication Data

Gastwirth, Joseph L.
  Statistical reasoning in law and public policy.

  (Statistical modeling and decision science)
  Includes bibliographies and indexes.
  Contents: v. 1. Statistical concepts and issues of
fairness—v. 2. Tort law, evidence, and health.
  1. Forensic statistics—United States. 2. Statistics.
I. Title. II. Series.
KF8968.75.G37 1988   349.73′021   87–33367
ISBN 0–12–277160–5 (v.1)   347.30021
ISBN 0–12–277161–3 (v.2)

Printed in the United States of America
88 89 90 91   9 8 7 6 5 4 3 2 1

Preface

Statistics originally referred to the organization and summarization of large amounts of data collected for purposes of the government. Modern day statistics, while still concerned with the collection and summarization of data, emphasizes methods of analysis and interpretation of data. This book introduces the reader to the concepts of statistics and applies them to a wide variety of data sets which arise in the context of legal and public policy decisionmaking. It is designed to serve as a textbook for students of law and public policy as well as a resource for individuals who are engaged in the planning, analysis and interpretation of statistical studies or in the assessment of the validity of the results of such studies.

In order to indicate the increased need for careful analysis of data in the legal area, we contrast the statistics examined by the Supreme Court in *Yick Wo v. Hopkins* 118 U.S. 356 (1886) with the data in the jury discrimination case *Castenada v. Partida,* 430 U.S. 482 (1977). In *Yick Wo* the Court considered the fairness of the San Francisco Board of Supervisors' administration of a law requiring permission for the operation of a laundry in a wooden house. The data showed that over 200 Chinese were refused permits, while about 80 persons, *none* of whom were Chinese, were given permits. Indeed, discrimination by the board was admitted and the Court stated that such discrimination violated the equal protection clause and the Fourteenth Amendment. In *Castenada,* the Court had to assess whether the proportion (39%) of Spanish surnamed persons summoned to grand jury duty was sufficiently far from their proportion (79%) of the adult population of Hidalgo country to indicate deliberate under-representation. The Court relied on a statistical test, which indicated that the jury lists were not representative.

The book is designed so that a reader who masters the concepts in the first five chapters can skip to topics of primary interest. For example, readers interested in equal employment might emphasize Chapters 6, 7, 8, and 11, while those concerned with health policy might study Section 6.5, Chapters 7, 8, 10, 11 and emphasize Chapters 13 and 14. Chapter 9 on sampling will be of interest to almost all readers. Chapter 12 on Bayesian inference presents an area of statistics seeing greater use and provides insight into issues of the validity and weight of scientific evidence.

Like many statistics texts we use formulas, however, we urge the reader not to spend too much time on calculation. An informative statistical analysis typically agrees with common sense. In any particular application, examine the data and consider it in the context of the application. The formal analysis should be consistent with the relevant facts of the case and legal or scientific background. For example, we will often assess the data and analysis in light of the appropriate time frame. Thus, whether the data refers to the time period before or after a case was filed or whether a person with a disease was exposed to an alleged carcinogen during a period consistent with the known latency period (time required for the disease to manifest itself) are important factors that will be considered. We mention that we include comments on interesting aspects of the data which may also involve nonstatistical issues. This is inevitable, as a good statistical analysis should be integrated with the subject matter. Finally, we indicate some problems with an asterisk (*). These should be read and thought about, as they are intended to add further insight.

Acknowledgments

This book grew out of the author's involvement as a statistical consultant to the Office of Management and Budget (OMB) and expert witness in a variety of legal cases, as well as his research in statistical methods for measuring inequality. It is a pleasure to acknowledge the help and support I received from many friends and colleagues, which aided immeasurably in bringing the book to fruition. Professors Herman Chernoff, Zri Griliches, Fred Mosteller and Phyllis Wallace, along with Christopher De-Muth, former Associate Director of OMB, encouraged my research and writings on statistical problems arising in law and public policy for many years.

A fellowship from the Guggenheim Foundation enabled me to devote the time needed to organize a wide variety of issues and topics into a coherent whole. Indeed, the book took its ultimate form while I was a Visiting Scholar in the Division of Statistics at the University of California at Davis during the 1985–86 academic year. No author could ask for a more supportive and encouraging host institution. Professors Jessica Utts and Neil Willets read over several chapters, provided computational assistance and made a variety of helpful suggestions. Professors P. K. Bhattacharya, Wesley Johnson and Jane-Ling Wang, who collaborated on joint research arising from my work on the book, also read and commented on some chapters. Dean Bartosic of the law school kindly arranged for me to have convenient access to the resources of the law library. The office staff of the statistics division—Aelise Houx, Colleen Christe and Cathy Grindheim—provided me with superb assistance.

I am grateful for the many valuable suggestions I received from Prof. Ingram Olkin, editor of the series, as well as the improvements suggested by the editorial staff of Academic Press. In addition to the editor and my colleagues at Davis, Professors Peter Bickel, Samuel Greenhouse, Tapan Nayak and Mrs. Ellen Lawsky provided me with helpful suggestions. Other students and professional colleagues who assisted me in a variety of ways include Dale Barone, Robert Blodgett, Dan Christman, R. Paul Detwiler, Richard Epstein, Ranjan Harikar, Robert O'Neill, Marvin Podgor, Ann Sigafoos, Sameena Salvucci and Dante Verme.

Special thanks go to Prof. Ralph Bunker, Mr. Jeffrey Fitter and Dr. Neil Willets, who created the preliminary version of nearly all the illustrations from various computer packages. In particular, Prof. Bunker developed a special program for the graphing of statistical functions and devoted substantial effort to ensure that the graphics needed would fit into his general system. Excellent typing and proofing assistance was provided by Colleen Christe and Janis Lopez in Davis and Owi Jayanan, Bickie Pham, Lilliam Sandoval and Anita Stearns in Washington. Finally, I wish to thank Mr. Ezra C. Holston, Production Manager of Academic Press, for the careful and efficient manner in which he guided the book through the production process.

Author's Involvement with Some of the Data Discussed in the Book

A number of data sets used in the book came from the author's experience as an expert witness or consultant. While I have tried to present the data accurately and utilize proper statistical methodology, there is always the possibility that unconscious bias enters into an analysis. Thus, the reader should be aware that I was an expert witness in the following cases, which are cited in the book.

Davidson v. Baird	(Unfair Tax Assessment—Plaintiff)
Berger v. Ironworkers	(Civil Rights—Plantiff)
Capaci v. Katz and Besthoff	(Civil Rights—Plaintiff)
Fort Belknap Indians v. U.S.	(Indian Claims—Defense)
Hogan v. Pierce	(Civil Rights—Plaintiff)
Johnson v. Perini	(Civil Rights—Defense)
Minnis v. Brinkerhoff	(Civil Rights—Defense)
Valentino v. U.S. Postal Service	(Civil Rights—Plaintiff)

In addition, I also use data (or modifications of data) that came from my participation in arbitration hearings or other consulting activities. My consulting with the Office of Information and Regulatory Analysis in OMB dealt with the planning and interpretation of epidemiologic studies. In particular, the material in Chapter 10 on the need for a careful analysis of the expected power of a study stemmed from my work there.

Introduction

During the last decade, civil cases have had to resolve complex issues such as alleged discrimination against minority groups in employment and housing opportunities, regulation of the environment and safety, and consumer protection against misleading advertisements in which quantitative arguments play a role in determining legal liability as well as the appropriate amount of compensation. This book is designed to introduce statistical concepts and their proper use to lawyers and interested policymakers and help them to avoid some of the common pitfalls occurring in the use of data. We emphasize that our purpose is not to make lawyers into statisticians or vice versa. If we facilitate meaningful communication between the two disciplines, our major goal will be achieved.

1. The Nature of Statistics

The discipline of statistics is concerned with the collection, summarization, and interpretation or analysis of data used in making decisions. One of the advantages of the subject is that a common body of methodology can be applied in a variety of areas. For example, the data one needs to determine whether women and men are paid the same for a job is similar to the data needed to determine whether a new drug cures a disease faster than a currently used one. In both situations, one needs data on the two groups being compared, which contains background data on relevant factors, e.g., seniority in the equal pay case and age (or general health) of the subjects in the drug study. Thus, the basic statistical methods developed for use in medicine, engineering and social science can often be used in the legal area. Sometimes, however, the methods may require modification in order to take into account special nuances occurring in a specific legal application.

Typically, statistical methods are used to deduce the characteristics of an entire population (e.g., voters in a state, employees of a firm) from a representative sample of the population, and statisticians are concerned with proper methods of drawing such samples. After obtaining a sound sample, one is concerned with drawing inferences about the whole population from the sample. Usually, one is interested either in estimating a parameter of the population, such as the proportion of voters who intend to vote for the incumbent in the next election, or in testing an hypothesis about the population, e.g., the promotion rates of male and female employees of a firm are equal against the alternative or competing hypothesis that the rates differ.

Almost all statistical inferences are expressed in terms of probabilities. In the problem of estimating the percentage of voters who favor the incumbent from a sample, both the percentage in the sample supporting the incumbent, say 60%, and a statement of its accuracy should be reported. The accuracy of the sample estimate is expressed in terms such as, the probability is .95 (95%) that the estimate is in error by less than 2%, and means that if *many similar* samples are taken, in approximately 95% of them the sample percentage will be within 2% of the true percentage. Hence, one can be 95% confident that the sample estimate is within 2% of the true value.

Hypothesis testing is concerned with checking the validity of a theory or hypothesis by assessing the consistency of the results of a data set with what the theory predicts. This is accomplished by computing the expected value of the average or other characteristic of the data, assuming the theory is true, and then calculating the probability of observing a result *at least as far* from the expected value as occurs in the actual data. If this probability, computed under the assumption that the hypothesis is true, is *small* (usually less than 5%), then we have observed data that are unlikely to occur if the hypothesis tested is true, so we doubt its validity (technically speaking, we reject the hypothesis). A common use of hypothesis testing occurs in analyzing jury selections. Suppose one suspects that women are being improperly excluded from jury panels in a county[2] and upon examining two jury panels, each consisting of 24 persons, one notices that only two women were among a total of 48. Assuming that women form half of the population qualified to be jurors, the probability of two or fewer females among the 48 is 4.18×10^{-12}, which is extremely small, so we must reject either the hypothesis that women form half the population of eligibles *or* the assumption that the jury panels were a representative sample of the eligible population. An advantage of this approach is that the plausibility of an explanation can also be tested. If the defendant county asserted that more women exclude themselves from jury duty due to the nature of their jobs (e.g., more women than men are teachers), one could exclude all persons in such occupations and compute the corresponding female fraction of eligible jurors. Suppose this fraction equaled one third. A new calculation assuming that women form one third of the population of potential jurors shows that the probability of two or fewer females out of 48 is 1.1×10^{-6}, approximately one in a million, so the reason offered does not fully explain the small number of female jurors. On the other hand, if the new female fraction of eligibles turned out to be .1 (10%), the probability of observing two or fewer females out of 48 selections would be .129, which is more than 10%, so the observed data are not especially rare and not ordinarily considered as being statistically significant.[3]

2.   Some Special Problems Occurring in Legal Applications

In order to calculate the margin of error of sample estimates, the data should be a random sample from the relevant population. In court cases, however, one sometimes must rely on whatever data is available from administrative files. While the data are supposed to encompass the entire population (as employee records may be), often some items of information are missing from the individual records, or records for employees who left the firm are no longer available. Quite often, the omissions are approximately random and standard techniques can be used. If, after checking for randomness, one feels that the omissions might cause a serious bias, then some special statistical techniques may need to be used or the data may be deemed irrelevant.[4] Since no large data set is perfect and since courts have sometimes noted a few observations (out of a thousand or so) that seemed in error and have thrown out the entire data set,[5] this is an important topic. A related issue that occurs in actual cases is whether the proportion of the entire population represented in the data is adequate for statistical analysis. Courts have used[6] and thrown out[7] data consisting of less than 50% of the population or the desired sample. The statistical concern is the representativeness[8] of the data, rather than the proportion of the population covered. We discuss the adequacy of samples in Chapter 9.

Another special problem occurring in data used in the legal and regulatory setting is that the passage of an act (e.g., the Civil Rights and Clean Air Acts) is intended to cause socially beneficial changes. Thus, pre-act and post-act data may be considered statistically as being from two distinct populations, even though the same quantity (minority proportion of employees in a firm or amount of a pollutant in the air over Los Angeles) may be measured in both periods. Although one would like to be able to analyze data from each period separately, often the actions taken in the pre-act period continue to have an effect in the post-act era. Sometimes it is possible to make a statistical adjustment for these pre-act effects; however, the problem is difficult and occurs often in the analysis of wage data in equal employment cases[9] where seniority typically is related to pay.

The use of the results of epidemiologic studies in the regulatory arena has subjected them to more critical review than is usual in medical and scholarly literature. Indeed, the Fifth Circuit in *Gulf South Insulation v. Consumer Product Safety Commission*[10] disregarded over 10 studies concerning a possible link between cancer and exposure to formaldehyde. As a result of this and similar regulatory issues, government-sponsored epidemiological studies are receiving careful review prior to being carried out in order that the sample size is sufficiently large to withstand questioning of the intrinsic accuracy and reliability of the data and results by an interested party. We discuss some of these considerations in Chapters 11 and 13.

3. Plan and Purpose of this Book

The elements of probability and statistical analysis and their use in a variety of applications are presented in the first 9 chapters. Several important but somewhat specialized topics are treated in remaining chapters.

Since the purpose of the book is to help the reader become aware of statistical concepts and their potential applicability to a wide variety of legal and public policy issues, rather than turn the reader into a professional statistician, less emphasis is placed on discussing a large number of special statistical procedures. Thus, the normal approximation to a statistical method is often used with the caveat that its accuracy may need to be verified in a particular application relying on a small number of observations. Also, chi-square tests are not discussed in detail.

On the other hand, we have tried to emphasize the need to present statistical tables, graphs and measures summarizing the data that focus on the specific question at issue. Thus, summary measures of the inequitable allocation of seats in a legislature, of the grade levels received by recently hired minority and majority members, or of the increased risk of cancer due to exposure to a chemical or drug are emphasized.

The two areas we stress that usually are given less emphasis in most statistical textbooks are measures of relative or comparative inequality and statistical methods for combining the results of several related statistical studies. The first area is important because many legal cases are concerned with issues of fairness or equal treatment. The special significance of the second topic arises from the fact that legal decisions and public policy often must be made from existing administrative records (personnel or health records of employees) or currently available studies, and a new carefully designed sample survey or further research cannot be undertaken. For instance, one may need to combine the results of several studies of the effect of exposure to a chemical or workers employed in different plants, because the number of employees at one plant (which is primarily determined by economic conditions) is too small for a reliable study. A similar problem occurs in Equal Employment Opportunity (EEO) cases where one needs to combine hiring data in a variety of occupations,[11] and in regulating drugs or chemical food additives whose safety may first be tested on several species of mice and a decision is reached by utilizing the results of all the studies.

NOTES

1. In equal employment cases, for example, the effect of legal pre-act discrimination has to be considered when the racial composition of a firm's work force is compared to census data. Thus, in *Hazelwood School District v. U.S.*, 433 U.S. 299, 97 S.Ct. 2736 (1977), the Court emphasized that post-act hiring data should be compared to the pool of teachers available for hire in the local labor market area.

2. The method discussed is based on the binomial model which was adopted by the Supreme Court in *Castenada v. Partida*, 430 U.S. 482, 97 S.Ct. 1272 (1977) and will be discussed later in Chapters 3 and 4.

3. The probability of the occurrence of all outcomes at least as far from what would be expected as the observed data is called the significance level of a test and is described in Chapter 3. In most social science applications, researchers require that the data reach the

5% level before they reject the hypothesis being tested, although this should not be rigidly adhered to in all applications.

4. For a thorough discussion of missing data, see *Vuyanich v. Republic National Bank*, 505. F.Supp. 224 (N.D. Texas 1980). In *Gulf South Insulation v. Consumer Product Safety Comm.*, 701 F.2d 1137 (5th Cir. 1983), the Court disregarded data on the formaldehyde levels in homes because a substantial portion of the sample homes were chosen from persons who complained about formaldehyde-related problems, so the homes studied by the CPSC were not representative of all homes with insulation containing formaldehyde.

5. In *Valentino v. United States Postal Service*, 24 EPD 31, 425 (D.D.C. 1980), affirmed 674 F.2d 56 (D.C. Cir. 1982), the judge disregarded the exhibits showing that at each educational level (e.g., high school graduate) women employees were in lower average grade levels than males because two males whose records indicated that they only had an elementary school education held high-level positions so that the data were likely to be incorrect. It should be mentioned that the defendants who asserted that the educational data was unreliable used it later in their regression analysis, which was accepted by the trial judge.

6. In *Chrysler v. Environmental Protection Agency*, 631 F.2d 865 (D.C. Cir. 1980), the court accepted tests on 20 vehicles, of which 18 violated the emissions standards despite the high non-response rate of owners. This was reasonable in light of EPAs attempt to obtain a proper sample and the very high rate (90%) of violations in the vehicles examined.

7. See *Equal Employment Opportunity Commission v. American National Bank*, 652 F.2d 1176 (4th Cir. 1981).

8. Quite often, a carefully designed sample consisting of a small proportion of the entire population can yield quite accurate results. Indeed, the national unemployment rate is determined on the basis of a sample of 50,000 households, which is less than 1% of all households.

9. For further discussion of this point, see *Segar v. Civiletti*, 508 F.Supp. 690 (D.D.C. 1981) and *Trout v. Hidalgo*, 517 F.Supp. 873 (D.D.C 1983), *vacated and remanded* 104 S.Ct. 1404 (1984).

10. 701 F.2d 1137 (5th Cir. 1983).

11. Indeed in *Vuyanich v. Republic National Bank*, 505 F.Supp. 224 (N.D. Tex. 1980) at 376, Judge Higginbotham noted that "in many job families zero black hires fell within the randomness range so that statistical significance could never be present," and therefore he aggregated the data for related job groups. The need to combine the results of statistical analyses of hiring in different occupations was noted by the Fourth Circuit in *Equal Opportunity Employment Commission v. American National Bank*, 652 F.2d 1176 (4th Cir. 1981) at 1194 and by Arthur Smith Jr. and Thomas G. Abram (1981). Quantitative Analysis and Proof of Employment Discrimination. *University of Illinois Law Review 1981*, 33–74.

	Using Statistical Tables
	and Summary
Chapter 1	Descriptive Statistics

1. An Illustrative Example of the Use of Statistical Tables in the Legal Setting

Before discussing formal statistical methodology, it is useful to see how organizing data into a few tables and charts helped to highlight the major issue in an actual case. In 1975, a farmer in Mississippi felt that he was paying far more in taxes than he should have to because the agricultural value of land was not incorporated in the formula used for land assessments. At that time, land in the county was classified into three categories: I (most fertile), II (middle quality) and III (lowest quality). For assessment purposes, the county used $375, $325 and $275 as the market values for the three categories. In 1974–1975, the assessed value of a property in Sunflower County was supposed to be 12% of the market value and the tax (or mill) rate equaled .005. The assessed values of the acreage, by category, and the corresponding total tax and share of that total paid by owners of the different classes of land at the time the case was brought are presented in Table 1.1.

The core of the claim was that the market values used for the three classes of land did not vary as much as the true values did. This led to many property owners having assessments significantly larger than 12% of the true value of their land. In particular, the farmer asserted that the most fertile land was worth more than twice what the lowest quality land

1

TABLE 1.1.   The Share of Revenue Paid by Owners of Various Types of Land Under the Present Valuation System

Type	Number of Acres	County Values	Total Value	Assessed Value at 12%	Net Revenue (.005) × Assessed Value	Share of Revenue
I	93,457	375	35,046,375	4,205,565	231,306	26.27
II	115,102	325	37,408,150	4,488,978	246,893	28.05
III	221,564	275	60,930,100	7,311,612	402,139	45.68
Total	430,123		133,384,625	16,006,155	880,338	100.00

Source: Author's copy of exhibits submitted by the plaintiff.

was worth, so owners of lower quality land paid far more than their fair share.

In order to demonstrate the unfairness of the tax system in operation at the time of the trial, two different land appraisers presented their opinions of the land's value. The first expert valued the three types of land at $687, $437 and $104, respectively, while the second appraiser appraised the three classes of land at $715, $430 and $262 per acre. Statistical tables were designed in order to emphasize the following aspects:

(a) Under both of the alternative appraisals, owners of class III land pay far more than their fair share.

(b) The plaintiff, Davidson, was truly affected by nonuniformity of the system.

(c) The total revenue that the county would receive would not be significantly affected by using the proper market values.

Tables 1.2 and 1.3 summarize what the effect of using the alternative appraisals would be on the share of revenue paid by owners of the three

TABLE 1.2.   The Share of Revenue Paid by Owners of Various Types of Land Using Values Given by Appraiser A With a 5.33 Mill Rate

Type	Number of Acres	A's Values	Total Values	Assessed Value at 12%	Net Revenue (5⅓%)	Share of Revenue
I	93,457	687	64,204,959	7,704,595	410,886	46.68
II	115,102	437	50,299,574	6,035,949	321,897	36.57
III	221,564	104	23,042,656	2,765,119	147,464	16.75
Total	430,123		137,547,189	16,505,663	880,247	100.00

Source: Author's copy of exhibits submitted by the plaintiff.

TABLE 1.3. The Share of Revenue Paid by Owners of Various Types of Land Using Values Given By Appraiser B With a 4.2 Mill Rate

Type	Number of Acres	B's Value	Total Value	Assessed Value at 12%	Net Revenue (4.2 mill)	Share of Revenue (Percent)
I	93,457	715	66,821,755	8,018,611	336,782	38.32
II	115,102	430	49,493,860	5,939,263	249,449	28.39
III	221,564	262	58,049,768	6,965,972	292,571	33.29
Total	430,123		174,365,383	20,923,846	878,802	100.00

Source: Author's copy of exhibits submitted by the plaintiff.

classes of land. Note that the mill rates were slightly modified in order to show that the same total revenue could be obtained when the more realistic alternative valuations were used.

In order to emphasize the fact that the owners of the lowest quality (type III) land pay far more than their fair share, while holders of the highest quality land (I) pay substantially less, we summarize the share of revenue paid by holders of the different types of land in Table 1.4.

The degree of overpayment of taxes by owners of Type III land presented in Table 1.4 can also be represented pictorially by pie charts. In each chart the pie or disc is split into three subareas, each representing the share or revenue paid by owners of each of the three categories of land. Since a circle has 360°, to create the chart one allots the sector representing a category the same fraction of 360° as its share of total revenue. Thus, in the first pie chart in Figure 1.1, which is *based* on the present system, owners of Type I land are represented by region I, whose angle from the center is $.2627 \times 360° = 94.57°$, while the sectors representing owners of Type II and Type III land are represented by sectors with angles of $.2805 \times 360° = 100.98°$ and $.4568 \times 360° = 164.45°$, respectively.

TABLE 1.4. The Share of Revenue Paid by Owners of Various Types of Land

Type	Present System	Assessor A's Value	Assessor B's Value
I	26.27	46.68	38.32
II	28.05	36.57	28.39
III	45.68	16.75	33.29

Source: Author's copy of exhibits submitted by the plaintiff.

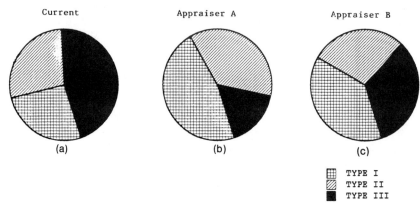

FIGURE 1.1.   Pie charts representing the share of the total real estate tax paid in
Sunflower county by owners of land of each quality category.
Chart (a) reflects the assessments at the time of the trial. Charts (b)
and (c) reflect the land values of the two appraisers.

Although the results in Table 1.4 demonstrated that the assessment
methods in use at the time of the trial discriminated against owners of
farmland consisting mainly of Type III land, the plaintiff also desired to
illustrate its impact on owners of the same value of land. This was done by
computing the assessed values and taxes for $100,000 worth of farmland
of each class under the current system and under the values given by
appraisers A and B. The results are summarized in Tables 1.5a and 1.5b
and show that owners of $100,000 worth of Type I land pay far less in
taxes than owners of an equivalent value of Type III land. The last
column reports the actual assessment ratio, i.e., the proportion of the true
value (based on the appraiser's valuation) that the land was currently
being assessed at. The values in the last column vary not only among
themselves but are also far from the supposed 12% standard in the
county. Notice that the ratio of the taxes paid by owners of the *same*
value of land of each type equals the ratio of the corresponding
assessment ratios. For example, in Table 1.5b, the ratio of taxes
(692.75/346.35 = 2) equals the ratio of their assessment ratios (.126/
.063 = 2).

Finally, in order to emphasize the reality of the problem, the true assessment ratios for the plaintiffs farm, for one of the best farms and for
one of the class III farms was presented (Table 1.6). It shows that the
plaintiff is paying nearly four times (24.7/6.8) what the owner of the best
quality farm was paying.

TABLE 1.5a. Impact of Sunflower County Assessment Ratio Discrimination on Owners of $100,000 Worth of Land (Valued by Appraiser A)

	Value A	County Value	County Assessment (12%)	Tax (.055)	Actual Assessment Ratio
Type I	$100,000	54,585	6,550.20	$ 360.26	.0655
Type II	$100,000	74,370	8,924.40	$ 490.85	.0892
Type III	$100,000	264,423	31,730.76	$1745.15	.3173

Source: Author's copy of exhibits submitted by the plaintiff.

TABLE 1.5b. Impact of Sunflower County Assessment Ratio Discrimination on Owners of $100,000 Worth of Land (Valued by Appraiser B)

	Value B	County Value	County Assessment	Tax	Actual Assessment Ratio
Type I	$100,000	$52,448	$ 6,293.76	$346.35	.063
Type II	$100,000	75,581	9,069.72	$498.84	.091
Type III	$100,000	104,962	12,595.44	$692.75	.126

Source: Author's copy of exhibits submitted by the plaintiff.

We hope that these exhibits convince the reader of the three assertions made earlier. In particular, we demonstrated that owners of the poor quality land pay more than their fair share and that the plaintiff's farm was severely overassessed relative to the supposed 12% county standard and especially in comparison with the best quality farmland.

TABLE 1.6. Impact on Plaintiff of County Assessment Discrimination

	True Value Per Acre	Actual Assessed Value Per Acre	True Assessment Ratio
A class III Farm	$104	30.36	29.0
Plaintiff	$130	32.10	24.7
Best Farm	$675	45.00	6.8

Source: Author's copy of exhibits submitted by the plaintiff.

Problems

1.   Using assessor B's values, construct a table analogous to Table 1.6 to illustrate the impact on the plaintiff.

2.   Under what conditions, if any, could the inaccurate valuations used by the county still yield the result that every landowner could still be paying his fair share?

3.   Consider the three sets of land values (275, 325, 375), (104, 437, 685) and (262, 430, 715). Which aspect of the way they differ caused the property tax inequality?

4.   In Table 1.6, the heart of the matter is shown by the wide variation among the assessment ratios (i.e., the ratio of the assessment to the true value). If you desire to study the uniformity of property tax assessments in your own area, what type of data would you collect? Where might you obtain it?

5.   In our discussion of the tables presented in *Davidson v. Baird*, the lawyer asked the statistician to modify the mill rates so that the total revenue obtained by the county would be unchanged.

   (a) Is this feature of the tables essential to demonstrating that owners of Type III land pay more than their share?

   (b) If your answer to (a) was no, why did the lawyer make this suggestion?

6.   The pictorial representation of the share of a *total amount* going to each of several exclusive categories by a pie chart can be an effective way of representing the concentration of minorities in low-paying jobs in employment discrimination (EEO) cases or market shares in antitrust cases. Similarly, they can be used to demonstrate changes over time in order to substantiate progress of minority employees in EEO cases or the dynamic nature of a market in antitrust cases.

   (a) Make pie charts for the following data for the liquor industry to illustrate the changes in consumer tastes that occurred during the period 1970–1980.

	Consumption in Gallons	
	1970	1980
Whiskey	219.2	240.8
Other hard liquor (e.g., gin, rum)	232.8	129.1
Wine	476.0	267.4

Source: *Business Week*, April 20, 1981.

Note: Since one ounce of hard liquor contains more alcohol (by a factor of about three) than wine, one might wish to express the data in terms of alcohol content.

(b) Try to find an opinion in a Civil Rights or antitrust case which reports sufficient data for you to draw the appropriate pie chart or charts.

Answers to Selected Problems

2. As long as the valuations used were in *proportion* to the true values, owners would pay their fair share. Thus, if the true values of the land categories had been 750(I), 650(II) and 550(III), all land would have been assessed at the same percentage (6%) of true value and the challenged system would have been a fair one.

3. The ratio of the value of high quality to low quality land is much greater in the appraisors' valuations than in the county's valuation. Thus, the owners of better quality land were really taxed at a lower percentage of true value than the owners of lower quality land.

4. You need data on assessments and recent sales of property in the area.

5. (a) No.
    (b) The plaintiff's lawyer wanted to make it easy for the judge to reach a conclusion favorable to his client by showing that the unfairness could be remedied without loss of revenue to the county.

2. The Ogive and Histogram

When one has a substantial amount of data (e.g., the Census Bureau surveys about 50,000 households each month to determine the state of the labor market), it is important to summarize it with a few measures and some tables and graphs that portray its essential features. A standard method is to classify the data into groups or classes and report the number of *data points* or *observations* that fall in each group. When one works with numerical data, e.g., height, income or wage, size of firm, one must select a set of class intervals and place each observation in its class.

Let us consider the following data (Table 1.7) on earnings in 1980 of full-time male workers in the U.S.[1] The data are classified into 14 intervals, each of which is well defined, since any income (which was rounded to the nearest dollar) can belong to only one class. Notice that the lengths (in terms of dollars) of the intervals vary from $1000 to $15,000. The second column gives the number of earners in the interval. The fraction of

TABLE 1.7.   Earnings of Male Full-Time (Year-round) Workers in 1980

(1) Earning Class	(2) Number of Males	(3) Fraction of Males in Class	(4) Fraction of Male Workers Earning Less Than the Lower Limit of the Next Class
1,999 or less	723	.0173	.0173
2,000 to 4,999	772	.0184	.0357
5,000 to 6,999	1288	.0308	.0665
7,000 to 8,499	1698	.0405	.1070
8,500 to 9,999	1588	.0379	.1449
10,000 to 12,499	4809	.1148	.2596
12,500 to 14,999	3557	.0849	.3445
15,000 to 17,499	4847	.1157	.4602
17,500 to 19,999	3724	.0889	.5491
20,000 to 24,999	7550	.1803	.7294
25,000 to 29,999	4671	.1115	.8409
30,000 to 39,999	3812	.0910	.9319
40,000 to 49,999	1294	.0309	.9628
50,000 and over	1546	.0369	.9997
Total	41,879	.9997	

Source: Adapted from Table 57 of *Current Population Survey, 1980*, CPS Report Series P-60, No. 132.

all male workers whose earnings fall in each interval are reported in column 3. These fractions are also called the class or group frequencies. The fraction of all workers earning less than or equal to the upper limit of the interval is given in column 4 and is obtained by *adding* all the previous fractions in column 3 to the fraction of the data (column 3) in the interval.[2]

The fractions in columns 3 and 4 are the basis of two graphical ways of presenting data: the *histogram* and *ogive*. For both, one uses graph paper and writes on the horizontal (x) axis the *limits* of the class intervals (in Table 1.7, they are $2000, $5000, $6000, $8500, etc). The *ogive* is a graph made by plotting the corresponding fractions in column 4 on the vertical (y) axis above the limits of the class intervals and connecting the points by a straight line. It is drawn in Figure 1.2 and was constructed by plotting .0173 above $2000, .0357 above $5000, etc. and then connecting the vertical points by straight lines. The ogive (Figure 1.2) of the data in Table 1.7 appears to start out slowly, rise at a steady rate between $10,000 and $30,000, and then increases at a slower rate. This suggests that the bulk of the distribution lies in the income range $10,000–$30,000. As 84.1% of the males earned less than $30,000, while only about 14.5% earned less than $10,000, we realize that the $10,000–$30,000 region contains 84.09 − 14.49 = 69.6%, or nearly 70% of the total population of full-time male workers, confirming our visual impression.

Because Table 1.7 does not report an upper limit for earnings greater than $50,000, we cannot plot the final point (1.000) on the ogive. This would be reached at the largest income, as nobody receives more than that amount.

The *ogive* enables us to find (approximately) the *fraction* of the data below any number, e.g., the fraction of male workers earning less than $14,000. The method of approximation assumes that the data are spread evenly throughout the interval. For example, to estimate the fraction of males earning less than $14,000, we note from column 4 of Table 1.7 that .2956 is the fraction earning less than $12,500, and the interval from $12,500 to $15,000 contains the fraction .0849 of the total. Since $14,000 is at the three-fifths point of the interval, i.e.,

$$\frac{14,000 - 12,500}{15,000 - 12,500} = \frac{1500}{2500} = \frac{3}{5} = .6,$$

we assume that six tenths of the data in the interval are in the range $12,500 to $13,999. Hence, we add six tenths of .0849, or .6 × .0849 = .0509, to .2956, obtaining .3645 as the estimated fraction of males earning

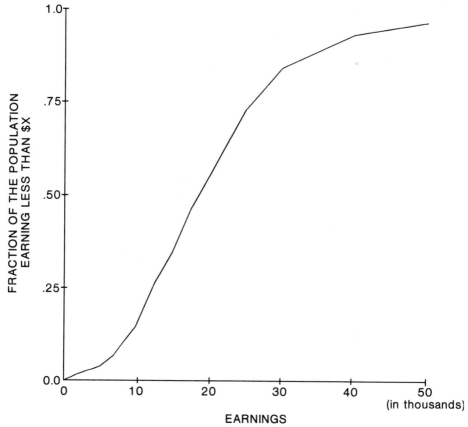

FIGURE 1.2.   The ogive summarizing the earnings data given in Table 1.7. The
value of the ogive at any value of x (thousands of dollars) denotes
the fraction of the sample who received less than $x. This ogive
stops at $50,000 so the maximum value is .963. The complete ogive
would reach 1.0 at the maximum earned income (which was not
given in the data).

less than $14,000. This method is called linear interpolation in the mathe-
matical literature.

The ogive is quite useful in comparing similar data sets,[3] e.g., earnings
of male and female workers (see problem 1). When one group is *better*
paid, its *ogive* will be *below* the other group because the fraction of the
higher paid group earning *less than a given salary* will be *smaller* than the
corresponding fraction of the lower paid group.

The *histogram* is a series of rectangles, one over each class interval,
constructed so that the *area over an interval represents the proportion of*

all the data that lies in that interval. The areas for each interval are given in Column 3 of Table 1.7; however, the height of the rectangle must be calculated by dividing the area by the length of the interval (chosen in suitable units, e.g., $1000 for income data).

We now describe how the histogram for the data in Table 1.7 given in Figure 1.3 was constructed. For the first interval going from 0 to $2000, the height h must satisfy $2 \times h = .0173$, $h = .0173/2$ or $h = .0087$. For the second interval of length *three* thousand, h must satisfy $3h = .0184$ or $h = .0061$. The heights over the next few intervals are 5000 to 6999, $h = .0154$; 7000 to 8499, $h = .0405/1.5 = .027$; 8500 to 9999, $h = .0379/1.5 = 0.253$; and 10,000 to 12,499, $h = .1148/2.5 = .0459$. The reader should verify a few other values of h given in the histogram in Figure 1.3. The histogram tells us where most of the data lie, as each unit on the x-axis represents the same amount of income ($1000). In particular, we see that the interval $15,000 to $17,499 contains the greatest *density* of incomes, *not* the interval $20,000 to $24,999, which a superficial look at the fractions in Table 1.7 might suggest. Although the $20,000–$25,000 interval contains about 18% of the data, its width is twice that of the interval from $15,000–$17,500, which contains about 11½% of the data.

The histogram of the earnings data looks different than the usual bell curve or normal distribution of school grades with which the reader is familiar, which has a bell or mode about a central or typical grade. There appear to be two modal (most frequent) income intervals, $10,000–$12,500 and $15,000–$17,500, in place of a single mode or bell. Also, the income data are not symmetric or evenly distributed about a central point, which might be about $17,500, as no one earns less than $0, but many people earn much more than twice $17,500. Indeed, we know from the data in Table 1.7 that 6.8% of the males earned more than $40,000 during 1980.

When broad income categories are used in Figure 1.3, the histogram may not give a realistic picture of the way incomes are spread. For example, it is unlikely that there is a sharp drop-off or rise in the frequency of incomes around the endpoints of each interval. More sophisticated approaches to graphing frequency or count data like that in Table 1.7 are available, but all have the basic property of the histogram, namely, the *area* over an interval represents the *proportion* of the data that lies in that interval.

A simple graphic device that does not display sharp jumps at the ends of each interval is the *frequency polygon* which is constructed by connecting the *midpoints* of the histogram over each interval by straight lines. For the

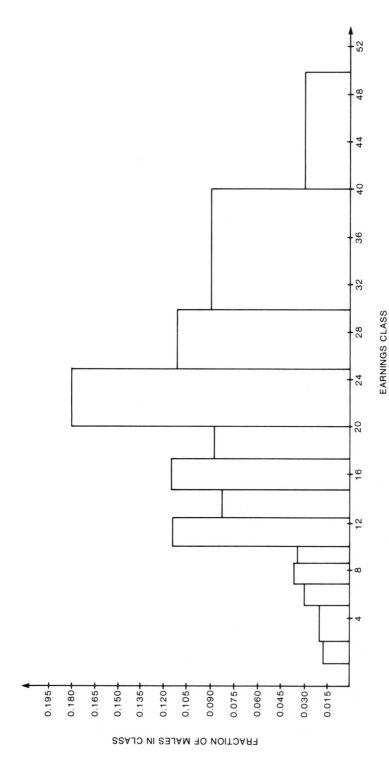

FRACTION OF MALES IN CLASS

EARNINGS CLASS

FIGURE 1.3.   Histogram of the earnings data in Table 1.7 for males earning $50,000 or less.

data in Table 1.7 the midpoint of the first interval, 0 to under 2000, is the point $x = 1000$, $h = .0087$; the midpoint of the second interval is $x = 3500$, $h = .0061$, etc. In order to complete the frequency polygon, one needs to extend the first and last intervals to ensure that the area under each region represents the fraction of the data in that region. This is accomplished for the first interval by connecting its midpoint to the x-axis at a *point one half* the width of the first interval. For the data in Table 1.7, this point is at $x = -1000$ as the interval had the width 2000. The last interval is treated similarly. The frequency polygon of the data is given in Figure 1.4.

Both the histogram and frequency polygon are easy to construct when the class intervals used to report the data have the same width (or length). However, many interesting data sets, such as earnings, are not conveniently summarized in that form, as the density of the data varies greatly across the intervals. The reader will see this clearly by looking at the histogram for the regions $5000–$7000 and $40,000–$50,000, both of which contain about 3.1% of the population of full-time male workers.

Problems

1.   (a) For the 1980 earnings data for female year-round workers given in Table 1.8, find the percentages needed to draw the histogram and ogive of the data.
    (b) Draw the histogram and ogive of the female earnings data.
    (c) Plot the ogives of the male and female earnings data on the same chart (use graph paper). What important implication can you draw from this plot?

2.   An alternative way to demonstrate point (c) in problem 1 is to consider the *fraction* of *persons* making at least $x,000, i.e., one cumulates the data in Table 1.7 from the bottom of column 3 up. Hence, 3.70% of the males make $50,000 or more, etc. Plot these curves[4] for the male and female earnings data. Would they be easier to explain than the ogive plots?

3.   One is often interested in estimating the midpoint, M, (called the median) of a distribution, which is characterized by the property that half the population earns less than M and half more. From the ogive in Figure 1.2, can you estimate the median? Similarly, the 75th (or 25th, etc.) percentile of a distribution is that point, $p(.75)$ such that exactly 75% (or three fourths) of the population receives less than it. From the ogive, estimate the 75th, 90th, 33rd and 25th percentiles of the earnings data in Table 1.7.

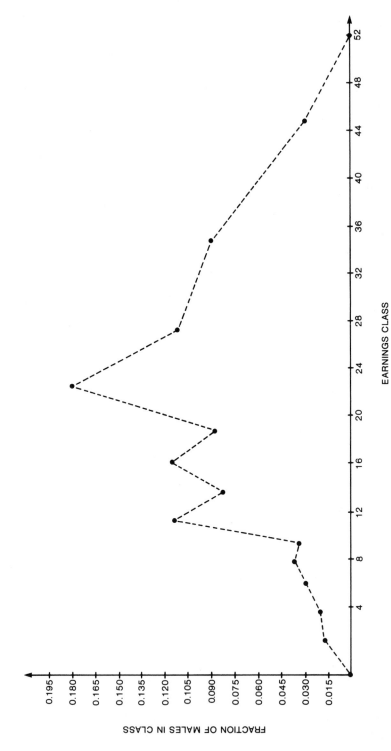

FIGURE 1.4. Frequency polygon describing the earnings data in Table 1.7 for men who earned $50,000 or less.

TABLE 1.8.   Earnings of Female Full-time (Year-round) Workers

(1) Earning Class	(2) Number of Females	(3) Fraction of Females in Class	(4) Fraction of Female Workers Earning Less Than the Lower Limit of the Next Class
1,999 or less	385	.0168	.0168
2,000 to 4,999	891	.0390	.0558
5,000 to 6,999	2106	.0922	.1480
7,000 to 8,499	3002	.1314	.2794
8,500 to 9,999	2504	.1096	.3890
10,000 to 12,499	5310	.2324	.6214
12,500 to 14,999	2779	.1216	.7430
15,000 to 17,499	2451	.1073	.8503
17,500 to 19,999	1240	.0543	.9046
20,000 to 24,999	1414	.0619	.9665
25,000 to 29,999	375	.0164	.9883
30,000 to 39,999	297	.0130	.9959
40,000 and over	96	.0017	1.0001
Total	22,850		

Source: Adapted from Table 57 of *Current Population Survey, 1980,* CPS Report Series P-60, No. 132.

Answers to Selected Problems

1.   (c) Female year-round workers earn *less* than male workers, as their ogive lies above the ogive in Figure 1.2 of male earnings.

3.   The median lies in the interval $17,500 to $19,999 and is about $18,800. The 75th percentile is determined by finding the point on the x-axis where the ogive intersects the horizontal line with height .75. This occurs near the beginning of the $25,000–$30,000 interval, so the 75th percentile is about $26,000.

3.   Statistical Measures that Describe the Main Characteristics of a Data Set

A primary purpose of statistics is to describe the essential characteristics of a large body of data by a few summary measures and possibly a few diagrams. Consider the problem of summarizing the distribution of wages. First, we are interested in obtaining a measure of what the typical worker earns. Statisticians use two measures of a central value, the median and the average or mean.

The median is the value m such that half the workers earn less than m and half more. The mean is the average value, i.e., the sum of the wages divided by the number of workers. As an illustration, consider the following five wages: 100, 125, 150, 185 and 200. The median is 150, while the mean is

$$\frac{(100 + 125 + 150 + 185 + 200)}{5} = \frac{760}{5} = 152.$$

Since we often work with fairly large sets of numbers, a shorthand notation for the sum of a set of n numbers $x_1, x_2, ..., x_n$ is useful. Specifically, we denote the sum of the n numbers by

$$\sum_{i=1}^{n} x_i,$$

where the numbers are *indexed* or labeled by i. Thus, in our example, $x_1 = 100$, $x_2 = 125$, $x_3 = 150$, $x_4 = 185$ and $x_5 = 200$. The mean of the numbers is denoted by $\bar{x}$ and is their sum divided by n. In symbols, the mean is expressed as

$$(1.1) \qquad \bar{x} = \frac{(\sum x_i)}{n}.$$

The median is calculated by first ordering the numbers (often called observations or data points) with the smallest being the first and the largest the last (n^{th}). In our example, the wages are already in order and the third largest (150) is the median. When there are an *even* number of observations (e.g., $n = 8$), the median is the average of the middle pair of observations (if $n = 8$, it is the average of the fourth and fifth ordered observations).

The mean has an interesting physical interpretation as the point about which all the observations are balanced. This can be seen in Figure 1.5, where the *distances* between each of the five points and the mean, $\bar{x} = 152$, are drawn. The *total* distance of all the points above the mean from the mean equals the total distance below the mean of all the observations less than the mean. Algebraically, this is derived as follows: as $\bar{x} = (\sum x_i)/n$, $n\bar{x} = \sum x_i$ or $\sum x_i - n\bar{x} = 0$, which implies that

(1.2)
$$\sum_{i=1}^{n}(x_i - \bar{x}) = 0,$$

as $\bar{x}$ is substracted from each one of the n observations (x_i).

A simple way to check the validity of (1.2) is to check it on some sets of few numbers ($n = 2$ or 3). For example, consider the two numbers, 100 and 200. Their average is 150 and the first 50 units less than the mean (150), while the second is 50 units greater than the mean, so the sum of their deviations from the mean is zero.

Whether the *mean* or *median* is the better summary measure depends on the particular application and the nature of the data. While both measures are readily understood, the numerical value of each observation enters into the calculation of the mean, while only the relative order of the observations is involved in calculating the median. Thus, when some observations may be *unusually large* (or small), the mean may not be as useful a measure as the median, as these observations may dominate the calculation. For example, suppose the largest observation in our set of five wages had been 600, instead of 200. Then the mean, $\bar{x}$, would equal $(150 + 125 + 150 + 185 + 600) = 1160/5 = 232$, substantially larger than any of the remaining four observations. Indeed, one might suspect that the large observation (600) might be somewhat unusual or atypical, so one would not wish to place much weight on it in estimating the central or typical value of the numbers. In contrast to the mean, the numerical value of the *median* would remain equal to 150, even if the largest observation had been 600. Thus, the median is a more stable measure of the central value of a set of numbers than the mean because it is not sensitive to a few

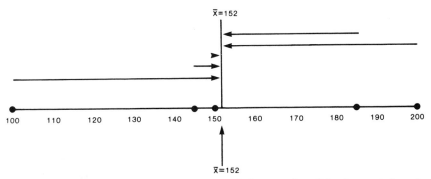

FIGURE 1.5. The mean ($\bar{x}$) as the center or balance point of the data set given in the text. The distances between each observation (x_i) and $\bar{x} = 152$ are drawn above the x axis.

extremely large or small observations. Because of this property, the median is used to summarize income data, since one is usually interested in how a typical family is faring economically and does not want the result to be affected by the accidental inclusion (or exclusion) of a few very rich families.

On the other hand, the mean has an advantage over the median when several means need to be combined. Suppose we have a data or wages paid to male and female computer programmers, e.g., the mean wage ($\bar{x}_1$) of n_1 males is \$400 and the mean wage ($\bar{x}_2$) of the n_2 females is \$350, then the *mean* wage of all programmers is

$$(1.3) \qquad \frac{\text{total wages}}{\text{total sample}} = \frac{n_1\bar{x}_1 + n_2\bar{x}_2}{n_1 + n_2} = \frac{n_1(400) + n_2(350)}{n_1 + n_2}$$

$$(1.4) \qquad\qquad\quad = \frac{n_1(400)}{n_1 + n_2} + \frac{n_2(350)}{n_1 + n_2}.$$

Formula (1.4) can be interpreted as a *weighted* average, i.e., the male salary is weighted by the fraction $n_1/(n_1 + n_2)$ of programmers who are male, and the female average is weighted by the female fraction of the total number of workers. If $n_1 = 100$ and $n_2 = 50$, then the average wage (1.4) becomes

$$\frac{2}{3}(400) + \frac{1}{3}(350) = 266.67 + 116.67 = 383.34.$$

Because two thirds ($100/150 = 2/3$) of the workers are male, the weighted average is closer to the average male salary than to the average female salary. Unfortunately, there is no way to obtain the median of the total sample of $n_1 + n_2$ observations from the *median* of each subgroup.

Moreover, the concept of a *weighted mean* or *weighted average* is useful when some observations are more important than others. If one had last year's *profit rate* data for the four major U.S. automakers, a weighted mean, weighting the profit rate of each firm by the fraction of all cars sold, would yield a better summary measure of the profitability of the auto industry than the ordinary mean or median of the four profit rates.

In summary, the median and mean are both statistically sound measures of the center of a set of numbers. The special characteristics of the data set and area of application determine which is more appropriate. With modern computers, both can readily be calculated and compared.

In addition to a measure of average wage, we are interested in how much variation or spread there is in the wages paid. There are several possible measures of the *spread* or *variability* of a set of numbers. The simplest ones are defined in terms of the distances between the observations (numbers) and the mean (or other central value). To define the distance between x_i and $\bar{x}$ carefully, we note that some x_i's are larger than the mean $\bar{x}$, while others are less than it. Therefore, we denote the arithmetic *difference* between an observation x_i and $\bar{x}$ by d_i and the *distance* between x_i and $\bar{x}$ by $|d_i|$ or $|x_i - x|$. The lines, | |, mean that one disregards the *sign* (positive or negative) of the difference between x_i and $\bar{x}$. The mean deviation from the mean,

$$(1.5) \qquad \text{M.D.} = \frac{1}{n} \sum_{i=1}^{n} |x_i - \bar{x}|,$$

is the average distance between the observations and their average value. In our example, the individual $|x_i - \bar{x}|$'s are 52, 27, 2, 33, 48 and the M.D. = 1/5 (162) = 32.4. The mean deviation can be visualized as the average of the *lengths* of the arrows (distances) in Figure 1.5.

In order to simplify the mathematics and avoid possible error due to the fact that the sign of the difference, d_i, is ignored in the calculation of the M.D., statisticians often measure the variability of a set of numbers about their mean in terms of the average squared distance, called the variance, which is defined by

$$(1.6) \qquad s^2 = \frac{1}{n - 1} \Sigma(x_i - \bar{x})^2.$$

The reason that the sum of squared differences in (1.6) is divided by $n - 1$ rather than n is due to relationship (1.2),

$$\Sigma(x_i - \bar{x}) = 0,$$

which implies that once the $(n - 1)$ differences $d_i = x_i - \bar{x}$ are known, the last difference can be determined from equation (1.2). Thus, we really have only $(n - 1)$ unrelated measurements of the spread of numbers (x_i) about their average, $\bar{x}$.

In order to measure the spread in units that are comparable to the observations themselves and their mean value, the square root, s, of the variance, s^2, is used. It is called the standard deviation of the observations x_i. In our example,

$$s^2 = \frac{1}{4}(52^2 + 27^2 + 2^2 + 33^2 + 48^2) = \frac{6830}{4} = 1707.5,$$

and

$$s = \sqrt{1707.5} = 41.32.$$

Some other measures of spread are also useful. If one replaces the mean, $\bar{x}$, by the median in formula (1.5), one obtains the mean deviation about the median. It is denoted by AD and is formally defined as

$$(1.7) \qquad\qquad \frac{1}{n} \sum_{i=1}^{n} |x_i - m|.$$

It is used when the median, m, is a better indicator of the center, or typical value distribution (or set of numbers), than the mean.

The last measure of spread we describe is the mean difference, Δ, of a set of numbers. It is obtained by computing the distance $x_i - x_j$ between *each* pair, x_i and x_j, of the numbers and calculating their average. For example, the mean difference of the numbers 1, 3 and 7 is $= \frac{1}{3}[(3 - 1) + (7 - 3) + (7 - 1)] = (2 + 4 + 6)/3 = 12/3 = 4$.

Until the computer era, Δ was quite tedious to calculate, as there are $n(n - 1)/2$ possible ways to select a pair of numbers from a set of n, and all these pairs enter into the calculation of Δ. One advantage of the mean difference as a measure of spread is that it does *not use* the distances from a central value, so it does not depend on specifying a measure (mean or median) of the center of the data. Thus, it is an intrinsic measure of the average distance between the observations.

Comment. The variance can also be defined without determining a central value. Essentially, it is one half the average *square* distance between two randomly chosen members of the population. As this is a cumbersome way to compute s^2, most text books define it as we did.

Problems

1. (a) Compute the mean, median, standard deviation, mean deviation and mean difference of the wages of four employees of a firm: $12,000, $16,000, $18,000, and $35,000.
    (b) Which measure best describes the wage of the typical employee?
    (c) Which measure best summarizes the spread of the wages among employees?
    (d) Which measure was the most difficult one to compute?

2.   A firm assigns its newly hired employees to one of three types of jobs, clerical, sales or managerial trainees. The respective salaries of the positions are: clerical $15,000; sales $20,000; manager trainee $25,000. The firm hired 100 recent high school graduates and assigned 50 to clerical, 30 to sales and 20 to manager trainee positions.

(a) Find the average (mean) salary earned by the 100 new hires.

(b) Find the standard deviation of the distribution of the salaries the newly hired employees received.

(c) Calculate the mean difference of the salary distribution.

3.   Why is the weighted mean of the profit rate of the four American auto producers described in the text superior to the ordinary arithmetic mean of the profit rates? Can you think of other appropriate weights to use in place of car sales? Do you think your weights would differ substantially from those suggested in the text?

4.   The Environmental Protection Agency places limits on the amount of a chemical that may be contained in the exhaust fumes of an automobile model. One standard that has been used is based on measuring the content of the exhaust of several, e.g., 10, cars and seeing how many of them emit more than the permissible level, say 50 parts per million (ppm) of the gas in question. For example, if at least eight of the cars in question emit less than 50 ppm, the cars pass the test; however, if three or more autos tested emit more than 50 ppm the tested model fails.

(a) Suppose that a person's likelihood of developing a health problem depends on their total exposure. Is this simple rule as sensible as one based on the sample mean being less than a fixed number (e.g., 40 ppm)?

(b) Suppose that there is absolutely no health risk to people when they are exposed to exhaust fumes which contain less than 50 ppm of the chemical at issue. Is the simple EPA rule more reasonable than a rule using the sample mean?

(c) Suppose as in (b) that there is no health risk to the public if the exhaust fumes contain no more than 50 ppm of the gas in question, but that the risk increases with exposures higher than 50 ppm. For example, the risk a person exposed to 70 ppm has of getting sick is twice that of a person exposed to 60 ppm etc.

(1) Is either standard a good criteria?

(2) If your answer to (1) is no, what type of criteria would you propose? Hint: What other descriptive measure might be relevant?

4. Measures of Relative Inequality and Their Use

The measures of variation or spread discussed in Section 3 may not convey the full meaning or implication of the variation among a set of numbers. For example, consider the following pair of family incomes:

(a) $5000 and $10,000,
(b) $95,000 and $100,000.

Although the value of s and Δ in both pairs (a) and (b) is the same (s = 2500, Δ = 5000), it is intuitively clear that the families in (b) are nearly equally well off, while the first member of (a) really is poorer than the second. What is relevant here is the ratio of the measure of spread to the average value. Two common measures of relative variation are the coefficient of variation (CV) defined by CV = $s/\bar{x}$, the ratio of the standard deviation to the mean, $\bar{x}$, and the Gini index, which is one half the ratio of the mean difference to the mean, i.e.,

$$(1.8) \qquad\qquad GI = \frac{\Delta}{2\,\bar{x}}.$$

For the pair (a) of incomes the CV = 2500/7500 = .333, while GI = 5000/ 15000 = .333. For pair (b) CV = .0256 and GI = .0256, so both measures reflect our intuitive notions of equality. The fact that they were numerically equal resulted from the simplicity of our example and is not true for most data sets.

Two other measures of relative variation or relative inequality are the ratio of the mean deviation to the mean (or twice the mean) and the ratio of the mean deviation from the median, to the median, called the coefficient of dispersion.

Measures of relative variation have been used by courts to study issues of equal representation and equal expenditures of school funds. Let us study the data used in the *Baker v. Carr*[5] one-person one-vote decision. In 1900 there were 33 districts ranging in population from 9466 to 19,992 (see Table 1.9), but in 1960 the populations ranged from 25,190 to 131,971 (see Table 1.10). Letting P_i denote the population in the ith district, the average population of the n (here n = 33) districts in 1900 was

$$\bar{P} = \left(\sum_{i=1}^{n} P_i\right), \qquad n = 14772.7,$$

TABLE 1.9.   Apportionment of the Tennessee Legislature in 1900

District	Population	Percent of Population In the District (q_i)	Cumulative Percentage $L(i/n)$
27	9466	1.942	1.942
14	10814	2.218	4.160
18	10830	2.222	6.382
19	10830	2.222	8.604
13	10992	2.255	10.859
2	11251	2.308	13.167
31	11627	2.385	15.552
24	11677	2.396	17.948
21	12629	2.591	20.539
23	12662	2.598	23.136
9	13320	2.733	25.869
12	14114	2.895	28.764
5	14130	2.899	31.663
6	14130	2.899	34.562
22	14269	2.927	37.489
11	14293	2.932	40.421
20	14318	2.937	43.359
29	14566	2.988	46.347
15	14986	3.074	49.421
25	15178	3.114	52.535
10	16645	3.415	55.949
16	16656	3.417	59.366
17	16656	3.417	62.783
8	16892	3.465	66.249
30	16938	3.475	69.724
32	16938	3.475	73.198
33	16938	3.475	76.673
28	17007	3.489	80.162
26	18604	3.817	83.979
7	18846	3.866	87.845
3	19604	4.022	91.867
1	19654	4.032	95.899
4	19992	4.101	100.000

Notes: The population in the state in 1900 was 487,452 and the legislature consisted of 33 districts. The cumulative percentage is the percent of the total state population contained in the district and all other districts with a smaller population.

TABLE 1.10.   Apportionment of the Tennessee Legislature in 1960

District	Population	Percent of Population In the District (q_i)	Cumulative Percentage
13	25190	1.273	1.273
23	26204	1.324	2.598
19	26380	1.333	3.931
21	26925	1.361	5.292
31	27511	1.390	6.682
27	29832	1.508	8.190
18	30478	1.540	9.730
14	31468	1.590	11.321
20	31680	1.601	12.922
24	31937	1.614	14.536
12	37641	1.902	16.439
22	38958	1.969	18.408
9	39954	2.019	20.427
28	42703	2.158	22.585
15	42740	2.160	24.745
29	44151	2.231	26.977
11	45172	2.283	29.260
26	47329	2.392	31.652
10	47414	2.396	34.049
25	53835	2.721	36.769
7	56834	2.873	39.642
3	63436	3.206	42.848
2	72612	3.670	46.518
4	81167	4.102	50.620
1	99355	5.022	55.642
5	102726	5.192	60.834
6	102726	5.192	66.026
16	105965	5.356	71.382
17	105965	5.356	76.737
30	109430	5.531	82.268
32	109430	5.531	87.799
33	109430	5.531	93.330
8	131971	6.670	100.000

Notes: The geographic boundaries of the 33 districts were the same as the 1900 apportionment. The state's population in 1960 totaled 1,978,549.

and the standard deviation was

$$s = \sqrt{\frac{1}{n-1}\Sigma(P_i - \bar{P})^2} = 2883.02.$$

The corresponding values for the 1960 apportionment (Table 1.10) are

$$\bar{P} = 59{,}956 \qquad \text{and} \qquad s = 33{,}144.$$

Notice that the coefficient of variation (CV) increased from .195 to .553. A calculation of the Gini index also reflects the greatly increased relative inequality of the district populations as it rose from .1124 to .3051 in the 1900–1960 period.

The degree of relative inequality of population data (or any set of positive numbers) can be described graphically by the Lorenz curve, which is made as follows: First, order the districts according to their populations (smallest to largest) as done in Table 1.9 and compute the proportion (fraction, q_i) of the total population in each district (column 3). Next, cumulate the fractions, q_i, for the ith district and all districts with smaller populations. This percentage $L(i/n)$ is the proportion of the total population living in the i smallest (of n) districts. Note that if all n districts had equal populations, each q_i would be $1/n$ and $L(i/n)$ would be i/n. The Lorenz curve graphs the values $(i/n, L(i/n))$, i.e., the value corresponding to $x = i/n$ is $L(i/n)$. For the data in Table 1.9, $L(1/n) = .01942$, $L(2/n) = .01942 + .02128 = .04160$ etc. The values of $L(i/n)$ are given in the last column of Table 1.9, and the curve is plotted in Figure 1.6. When all populations are equal, the Lorenz curve is the straight line joining $(0, 0)$ to $(1, 1)$ called the line of equality. The distance between the curve and this line also reflects the degree of inequality.

The Gini index of inequality can also be derived from the Lorenz curve by comparing the area A between the curve and the line of equality (the region of inequality) to the total area under the line of equality, which is $1/2$. This ratio is twice A and can be shown to equal the Gini index, $\Delta/(2\bar{x})$, defined earlier.

Generally, courts have not used the entire Lorenz curve but have relied on a single point of the curve, the minimum population percentage required to elect a majority. Since the Lorenz curve cumulates the percentage of the whole population residing in each district, arranged from smallest to largest district, the fraction of the whole population, $L(.50)$ belonging to the 50% of the districts with the smallest populations is the minimum population percentage having a majority of the legislative votes. Referring to the data in Table 1.9, there were 33 districts, so the minimum

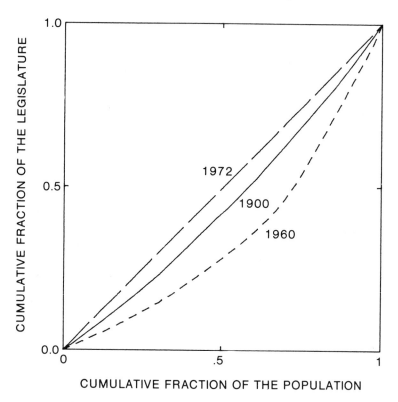

CUMULATIVE FRACTION OF THE POPULATION

FIGURE 1.6.   Lorenz curves describing the apportionment of the Tennessee legislature in each of the years 1900, 1960 and 1972.

population percentage required to elect a majority would be the fraction of the population in the 17 smallest districts, which is 43.36%. By 1960, however, the percentage of the total population residing in the 17 smallest districts had fallen to 29.26%. The data in Table 1.11 give the population in each district after the legislature was reapportioned to comply with the decision. Notice that the 17 smallest districts now contain 51% of the state's population.

Another criterion courts have used is to set a limit (e.g., 10%) for the *maximum percentage deviation* from the average. Thus, if the average district is 100,000 in size, then the smallest population permissible is 90,000 and the largest is 110,000. This measure is the larger of $(P_1 - \bar{P})/\bar{P}$ and $(P_n - \bar{P})/\bar{P}$, where P_1 is the population of the smallest district, P_n the population of the largest and $\bar{P}$ is the average population of all n districts. Notice that this is a *relative* measure, as the difference between the popu-

TABLE 1.11. The 1972 Reapportionment of the Tennessee Legislature Subsequent to the *Baker v. Carr* Decision

	Population	Cumulative Population	Cumulative Percentage
Dist. 21	116,807	116,807	.0298
17	117,477	234,284	.0597
19	117,550	351,834	.0897
5	117,564	469,398	.1197
14	117,597	586,995	.1496
27	117,639	704,634	.1796
32	117,669	822,303	.2096
16	117,759	940,062	.2396
20	117,942	1,058,004	.2697
22	118,186	1,176,190	.2998
6	118,259	1,294,449	.3300
7	118,351	1,412,800	.3602
25	118,369	1,531,169	.3903
13	118,377	1,649,546	.4205
26	118,383	1,767,929	.4507
9	118,401	1,886,330	.4809
24	118,434	2,004,764	.5111
8	119,142	2,123,906	.5414
4	119,262	2,243,168	.5718
2	119,310	2,362,478	.6022
11	119,381	2,481,859	.6327
25	119,410	2,601,269	.6631
18	119,436	2,720,705	.6936
10	119,560	2,840,265	.7240
30	119,654	2,959,919	.7545
29	119,816	3,079,735	.7851
1	119,889	3,199,624	.8157
33	119,928	3,319,552	.8462
3	120,211	3,439,763	.8769
32	120,460	3,560,223	.9076
15	120,519	3,680,742	.9383
12	120,879	3,801,621	.9691
28	121,191	3,922,812	1.0000

Note: The population of the state in 1972 totaled 3,922,812.

lation of the largest and smallest districts and the *average* population is compared with the average population, $\bar{P}$.

Recently the Supreme Court in *Karcher v. Dagett*[6] decided that any deviation from equality required justification as furthering a legitimate neutral state objective. Considering that an 11.9% maximum deviation from equality had been allowed in *Abate v. Mundt* (1971), while a disparity of 5.9% was voided in *Kirkpatrick v. Preisler* (1969), it is difficult to determine a permissible level of inequality in the apportionment of a legislature without considering possible reasons for it. In *Brown v. Thompson*[7] the Court allowed an apportionment of the Wyoming House of Representatives which had an average deviation from equality of 16% and a maximum deviation of 89%, because the state desired to preserve the integrity of counties, a reason deemed a legitimate objective in *Reynolds v. Sims*.

Statistical measures, such as the coefficient of variation, Gini index and the Lorenz curve, are useful in the analysis of other issues. Some government programs allot money on the basis of population or the population in poverty or the number of unemployed persons in a jurisdiction. One can measure the fairness of the resulting distribution of funds by arranging the eligible areas in order of the funds received per capita (where the whole population or relevant sub-population is the denominator of the calculated per-capita income received) and then calculate the Lorenz curve and summary measures.

The equity of school expenditures (per pupil expenditures) can be studied similarly. The Lorenz curve has also been used to measure the integration of minorities in schools. Here the schools are ordered by increasing the order of the minority fraction in them (see the book by Alker (1965) in the references for further details).

The criteria used to measure compliance with equal treatment is different in the two applications—tax assessment equity and one person equals one vote—we have discussed. While one can divide the total population, as given in the census, into virtually equal districts, the assessment of a property is more subjective. To measure the equity of property assessments, the U.S. Bureau of Census obtains data on the sales prices (S_i) of a sample of homes and their assessed values (A_i), and studies the variation of the ratios, $r_i = A_i/S_i$ about the *median* ratio. The measure of relative inequality used in the tax assessment literature is the ratio of the average deviation of the assessment-sales ratios from their median to the median ratio.

This measure is called the *coefficient of dispersion* (CD), and the tax assessment literature considers a CD of .20 as reasonable, although some specialists believe a CD of .10 should be the goal. Even if the CD of assessment-sales ratios equals .10 or 10%, a sizeable proportion of the properties may be over- or underassessed by more than 10%. Thus, the allowable difference from equality is greater in assessment studies than the more stringent criteria used in one-person, one-vote cases that discuss the *maximum* deviation from equality rather than an *average* measure.

In actual court cases, the complaining property owner usually is required to show that their property is overassessed relative to the median assessment-sales ratio. Thus, the treatment of the specific property may be more important than the overall inequality of assessment-sales ratios.

We close this section with two short lists, for the interested reader, of cases involving the one-person, one-vote cases and tax inequality.

ONE-PERSON, ONE-VOTE CASES

Reynolds v. Sims, 377 U.S. 533-632 (1964);
Maryland Commission for Fair Representation v. Tawes, 377 U.S. 656 (1964);
Baker v. Carr, 369 U.S. 186 (1962);
Borns v. Richardson, 384 U.S. 73 (1966);
Wesberry v. Sanders, 376 U.S. 1 (1964);
Gray v. Sanders, 372 U.S. 433 (1965).

CASES DEALING WITH MAXIMUM ALLOWABLE DEVIATION

Abate v. Mundt, 403 U.S. 182 (1971)—allowed an 11.9% maximum deviation;
Kirkpatrick v. Preisler, 394 U.S. 526 (1969)—voided a maximum deviation of 5.9%. The redistricting plan which had a maximum deviation of 63% was approved 341 F.Supp. 1158 (W.D.Mo.) *affirmed* 407 U.S. 901 (1972);
Mehan v. Howell, 412 U.S. 315 (1973)—upheld a 16.4% maximum deviation because it insured political fairness by measuring the voting strength of minority groups;
Swann v. Adams, 388 U.S. 440 (1967)—voided a maximum deviation of 30%;
White v. Register, 412 U.S. 755 (1973)—upheld a maximum deviation of 9.9%;
White v. Weiser, 413 U.S. 783 (1974)—voided a maximum deviation of 4.4%;
Chapman v. Meier, 420 U.S. 1 (1974)—voided a maximum deviation of 20%.

TAX INEQUALITY CASES

Siouz City Bridge Co. v. Dakota County, 260 U.S. 441 (1922);
Hillsborough v. Cromwell, 326 U.S. 620 (1946);
Baldwin Construction Co. v. Essex County Board of Taxation, 16 N.J. 329, 108 A.2d 598 (1954);

Gibraltor Corrugated Paper Co. v. Township of North Bergen, 20 N.J. 213, 119
  A.2d 135 (1955);
Switz v. Township of Middleton, 23 N.J. 580, 130 A.2d (1957);
In the Matter of Kents, 34 N.J. 21, 166 A.2d 763 (1961);
Bettigole v. Springfield, 178 N.E.2d 10 (Mass. 1961);
In re Brooks Building, 391 Pa. 137, A.2d 273 (1958);
Deitch Co. v. Board of Property Assessment of Allegheny County, 417 Pa. 213
  (1965);
Hamm v. State, 255 Minn. 64, 95 N.W.2d 649 (1959).

Problems

1.   Look up the *Reynolds v. Sims* case and plot the Lorenz curve for the
apportionment that caused the suit. Do the Lorenz curve and maximum
deviation from equality reflect the unevenness in the basic population
data?

2.   The theme of this section is the measurement of relative inequality.
When we examine the cases that relied on the maximum deviation, there
seems to be an inconsistency in the use of this measure by courts. Courts
often distinguish between the apportionment of congressional seats and
the apportionment of state and local legislatures. The reason underlying
the observed deviation from equality then becomes the issue. Develop
this theme in a report and assess whether there is a relationship between
the amount of inequality tolerated and the justification offered.

3.   It would be interesting to learn how far the assessment sales ratio of a
particular property has to be from the median ratio (in percentage terms)
in order for courts to decide that the owner is being over-assessed. Look
up some of the cases listed, as well as others, to get an idea of the
deviation courts have tolerated. Compare your results to the criteria used
in one person equals one vote cases.

5.   Measures of Monopoly Power or Concentration Viewed as Measures of Relative Inequality

Monopoly power is the power to control prices or exclude competition in
a market. The definition of the relevant market is an important topic,
since it depends on the nature of the product and the geographic area;
however, it is more of an economic and business question than a statisti-

cal one. Once the relevant market has been defined, statistical measures are useful in showing that one or several firms possess the ability or power to dominate it.

In a market consisting of n competing firms, we can order their respective fractions or shares of the market as

(1.9) $$f_i = \frac{x_i}{T},$$

where the total value of the market is $T = \sum_{i=1}^{n} x_i$, and x_i is the total sales of the ith firm, $i = 1, \dots n$.

Earlier we defined the Lorenz Curve in terms of the share or proportion of a total held by the possessors of the *smallest* i of a total of n shares. Monopoly power has often been expressed in terms of the share of the total market held by the *largest* k firms, where k is sometimes chosen as 3, 4 or 6. This share is called their concentration ratio and is denoted by CR-k. Since the share of the largest k firms is *one* minus the share of the $n - k$ smaller ones, CR-k can be calculated from the Lorenz Curve as

(1.10) $$\text{CR-}k = 1 - L\left(\frac{1-k}{n}\right) = \frac{\left(\sum_{i=n-kn}^{n} x_i\right)}{T} = \sum_{i=1}^{n} f_i.$$

A difficulty with using a particular CR-k, e.g., CR-3, is that the total number, n, of firms in the market does not enter into the calculation. Although one could use the entire Lorenz Curve or the Gini index as a summary measure of the inequality in the market shares of the competing firms, recent guidelines for mergers adopted by the Department of Justice[7] are expressed in terms of the Herfindahl index, which is the sum of the squares of the individual firm shares, f_i, i.e.,

(1.11) $$H = \sum_{i=1}^{n} f_i^2 = \sum_{i=1}^{n} \left(\frac{x_i}{T}\right)^2.$$

Notice that if all the firms have an equal share of the market, i.e., all $f_i = 1/n$, so that

$$H = \sum_{i=1}^{n} \left(\frac{1}{n}\right)^2 = n \times \sum \left(\frac{1}{n}\right)^2 = \frac{1}{n}.$$

Thus, the smallest value H can possibly have is the reciprocal of the number, n, of firms in the market. If the largest firm possessed virtually all the market, its share, f_n, would essentially equal *one*, while the other shares would be close to zero and H would nearly equal 1. Thus, a value of H of 1 indicates a total monopoly.

In order to illustrate the calculation of H, consider the following data on the number of cars produced in America during the period January 1 through January 10, 1984. Summing the squares of the shares, given in column 4 in Table 1.12 yields a Herfindahl index of .438, which is indicative of a fairly concentrated market. Notice that CR-3, the share of the largest three firms, is .927. Of course, the data only concerned cars produced in America, so imported cars were excluded. This highlights the importance of properly defining the *relevant* market before calculating statistical measures. If imported cars were included, the numerical values of both measures, H and CR-3, would be smaller.

Although the Herfindahl index appears to be different than the Lorenz curve, it is defined in terms of the proportions or shares, f_i, of a total which were the components of the Lorenz curve, and it is related to the coefficient of variation, a measure of *relative* inequality discussed earlier. This can be seen as follows:

$$(1.12) \qquad H = \Sigma \left(\frac{x_i}{T}\right)^2 = \frac{\Sigma_i x_i^2}{T^2} = \frac{\Sigma(x_i - \bar{x})^2 + n(\bar{x})^2}{(n\bar{x})^2},$$

as $T = n\bar{x}$ and $\Sigma(x_i - \bar{x})^2 = \Sigma x_i^2 - n(\bar{x})^2$. Dividing the numerator of the right side of formula (1.12) by the denominator yields

$$(1.13) \qquad H = \frac{1}{n} \left\{ \frac{\frac{1}{n}\Sigma(x_i - \bar{x})^2}{(\bar{x})^2} + 1 \right\}.$$

TABLE 1.12.   Calculation of the Herfindahl Index for Automobiles Produced in America

Firm (1)	Number of Cars (2)	Share (3)	Share Squared (4)
GM	91,488	.613	.37577
Ford	32,673	.219	.04796
Chrysler	16,935	.114	.01300
AMC	3,925	.026	.00018
Amer. Honda	2,876	.020	.00004
Volkswagen	1,239	1.009	.00006
Total	149,136		.43797

Source: *Wall Street Journal*, Monday, January 16, 1984.

As the sample variance (1.6) is $\Sigma(x_i - \bar{x})^2/(n - 1)$, the first term in the parenthesis in formula (1.13) is essentially $s^2/(\bar{x})^2$, the *square* of the coefficient of variation. (It actually is $n/(n - 1)$ times s^2/x^2, but for reasonably large n, $n/(n - 1)$ is nearly 1.0.) Thus, H can be thought of as being given (approximately) by

(1.14) $$\frac{1}{n}\{(CV))^2 + 1\}.$$

Formula (1.14) shows the Herfindahl index depends on the number of firms in the market and on the coefficient of variation (CV) measure of the relative inequality of their sales (x_i) in the market. Thus, the same degree of relative inequality as measured by the CV indicates less power in a market with a large (n) number of competitors than in one with few competitors.

Comments. (1) The 1982 U.S. Department of Justice guidelines[8] for horizontal mergers are expressed in terms of the Herfindahl index multiplied by 1000. Thus, the guidelines state that if the H index is in the range 1000 to 1600 (i.e., $.10 < H < .16$) and if the proposed merger would increase the index by 100 (.01), then it might be challenged on antitrust grounds. Of course, the H index is not the only factor to be considered in assessing the potential monopoly power of a few firms. The volatility of the shares, and the time trend (increasing or decreasing) of the H index or CR-4 should be considered as well as economic factors such as the difficulty a new firm would face in entering the market (barriers to entry) and the availability of readily substitutable goods (which implicitly enlarges the product market).

(2) The reader may wonder why several measures of relative inequality have been developed and used in the different applications. One reason is that the underlying issue in each application differs. In measuring the potential of a few firms to monopolize a market, one stresses the firms which are much larger than average. As the variance, s^2, depends on the squares of the differences between the observations and the average, it places greater weight on the large deviations than the mean difference or mean absolute deviation. Thus, the square of the coefficient of variation, $s^2/(\bar{x})^2$, is more sensitive to large values than the other measures and is more appropriate in summarizing market power. On the other hand, in applications where one may question the validity of the extreme observations[9] or where special circumstances may justify one or two deviations from average (e.g., in examining school expenditure data by district,

some differences from the average may be due to variation in the need for each district to provide for special services), the Gini index may be more appropriate.

(3) Another area where the quality of the data influences the choice of measure occurs in measuring the equity of real estate assessments. Ideally, if A denotes the assessed value of a house and S its current market value (e.g., sales price), all homes should have the same ratio A/S as long as all similar property is assessed at the same fraction of true value, i.e., the assessments are fair. The concept of *maximum* deviation from equality would appear to be the most useful criteria; e.g., no person should pay more or less than a fixed percentage, say 20%, over a set norm such as the median A/S ratio in the locality. As a statistical summary measure, however, the maximum deviation is very sensitive to the largest and smallest values of the assessment sales ratios studied. Although in assessment-sales ratio studies, sales between close friends, business associates and relatives are supposed to be excluded. Such transactions may be difficult to detect, e.g., a sale from parents to a married daughter and son-in-law. Thus, the maximum deviation from equality computed from a data set might be affected by an unusual observation, so the *coefficient of dispersion* is used.

Problems

1.   In addition to the 1984 data reported in Table 1.12, data for the corresponding time period in 1983 was provided. At that time, Honda did not produce cars in the U.S., so the shares were: GM (.644), Ford (.201), Chrysler (.113) AMC (.033) and Volkswagen (.009).

(a) Calculate the Herfindahl index for this data.

(b) Compare the results for both years. Why did the H index decline in 1984?

(c) What feature of the 1983 and 1984 share is *not* reflected in the H index but should be considered in assessing market power?

2.   In measuring the population of legislative districts, the U.S. Supreme Court said that any deviation from equality requires justification. In tax assessment equity cases, only relatively small deviations from equality are acceptable to the public. In antitrust cases, however, near-perfect equality of market shares is not the desired aim, rather competitive markets should be preserved.

(a) How are these differences in the legal application of the measures reflected in actual cases and government guidelines?

(b) What numerical aspect of the data is far more important in measuring the competitiveness of a market than in measuring the fairness of the allocation of seats in a legislature?

3. Verify that

$$\sum_{i=1}^{n} (x_i - \bar{x})^2 = \sum_{i=1}^{n} x_i^2 - n(\bar{x})^2,$$

either by a formal proof or by considering a small data set.

4. Assuming that assessors were doing their best to be accurate, why might one expect to observe a greater variability in the assessment-sales ratios in a city than in the allocation of seats in the city council.

Answers to Selected Problems

1. (a) .469.
   (b) n increased by one.
   (c) The ranking of the firms was virtually identical in both periods and the shares were similar. Larger variation in the market shares from year to year would suggest a greater degree of competition.

2. (b) The number, n, of firms in a market plays an important role, while the number of seats in a legislature should not affect the goal of equal representation.

4. Legislative districts can be drawn so that the difference among the populations in each district is quite small. Moreover, the population count changes slowly in a few years. In contrast, housing prices can change by 10% in one year, so assessments made of very similar houses made several months apart could differ by 5%. Other factors such as the interest rate or the assumability of a low rate mortgage or owner financing can also affect the sale price. It is difficult to obtain detailed data on these factors.

6. The Relationship between Variables

We often read statements like "education improves one's earnings ability" or exposure to a substance (e.g., cigarette smoke, cholesterol) increases the likelihood of getting a disease (lung cancer, heart failure) or "the death penalty deters crime." These statements are qualitative rather

than quantitative, and it is important to assess the strength of the relationship between the variables. If the only motivation a person has for continuing their education is the potential for increasing their lifetime earnings,
then their decision to continue should be based on comparing the expected increase in lifetime earnings with the costs[10] of continuing their
education. Similarly, whether someone changes their smoking or eating
habits depends on the degree of the relationship between smoking and
illnesses such as lung cancer and how much they enjoy the habit. In this
section, we shall describe some ways of describing the manner in which
variables or characteristics are related, but defer to Chapter 8 the formal
definition of the correlation coefficient, which measures the strength of a
relationship.

By making a bar chart (Figure 1.7) of the median earnings by educational achievement, one can visualize the relationship between earnings
and education. Notice that the data is not available in yearly categories,
e.g., males who had some high school but did not complete it are treated

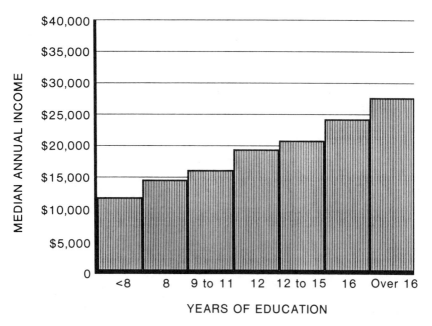

FIGURE 1.7.   Bar chart of the median total money income for males by educational level. The median income (in thousands of dollars) from
Table 1.13 is plotted over the corresponding educational level
(years of school completed).

as a common group. The data indicate median earnings do not increase at a constant rate; they jump sharply at the years corresponding to the completion of high school, college and postgraduate education.

The data suggest that a high school diploma increased a man's annual income by about $5,000 relative to elementary school graduates and that college education had a similar effect compared to males who just completed high school. Men who had completed some college (about two years on average) earned more than those who had only finished high school, but did not receive close to half the increased income received by those who completed college. Thus, the increased earnings reflected in the data may not totally be a result of the extra education. Perhaps the completion of an educational program indicates motivation or ability to stick to a task, as well as the knowledge gained in school, and this trait is also valued by employers and is reflected in the labor market. It is important to emphasize that the statistical relationship indicated in Figure 1.7 between education and earnings does not necessarily imply that education caused these income differences. Indeed, the more talented and ambitious members of the population may seek admission to higher education at a higher rate than others. Similarly, children of rich parents have a greater chance of going to college, as they don't require financial aid and may often have greater access to a high-paying job through family contacts than other young people.

In deciding whether to place a limit upon the amount of a chemical a worker may be exposed to on the job, the Occupational Safety and Health Administration uses laboratory studies of the effect of exposure on mice as well as epidemiologic studies on actual employees. Before a substance

TABLE 1.13.   Education and Median Total Money Income for Year-round Full-Time Workers—Male Workers of Age 25 and Over

	Educational Level (Years of School Completed)						
	Less than 8	8	9 to 11	12 (H.S)	Some College	College Graduate	Post-graduate
All Males	11,753	14,674	16,101	19,469	20,909	24,311	27,690
White Males	12,205	15,064	6,890	19,857	21,262	24,811	27,795
Black Males	10,337	11,771	11,804	15,658	16,740	17,861	23,715

Source: Table 51 of Money Income of Households, Families and Persons in the U.S.: 1980 Current Population Reports Series P-60, No. 132, U.S. Bureau of the Census.

is considered harmful (e.g., carcinogenic), evidence of a dose-response effect is usually required, i.e., the greater the amount of exposure (dose in a laboratory experiment) the greater the harm and disease rate should be.

The results of animal studies are usually summarized by reporting the *proportion* of animals exposed at various dose levels that develop the disease. When these proportions increase with dose level, the desired dose-response has been observed. In Chapter 8, we describe procedures for appropriate statistical tests, while use of such data in policymaking is discussed in Chapter 14. At this point, we want to mention that studies on human subjects need to account for both the *level* and *duration* of exposure and thereby introduce the need to relate the variable of primary interest to several factors.

One study considered by government agencies in their analysis of the toxicity of gases containing arsenic relied on the ratio of the *mortality rate* of exposed workers to the national rate. Technically, one considers the standardized mortality ratio (SMR), which compares the observed mortality rate of workers to that of a group of persons in the nation with the same age-sex distribution so that age and sex variables do not play a role in the comparison.

In Table 1.14, we report the standardized mortality ratios for respiratory cancers for workers exposed to a low and high amount of arsenic by number of years (duration) of exposure.

TABLE 1.14.   Respiratory Cancer Deaths and SMRs by Duration And Intensity of Exposure, Tacoma Smelter Workers

| | Intensity Estimate | | | | | |
| | Low | | | Highest | | |
Duration of Exposure Years	No. at Risk	Observed Deaths	SMR	No. at Risk	Observed Deaths	SMR
<10	687	15	169.9	824	25	203.9
10–19	149	7	268.2	168	11	321.6
20–29	225	10	278.6	717	16	577.6
30	159	9	302.0	165	11	347.0

Source: Table 12 from Enterline, P. E. and Marsh, G. M. (1982). Cancer Among Workers Exposed to Arsenic and Other Substances in a Copper Smelter. *American Journal of Epidemiology* **116**, 895–911.

Notice that for each of the exposure levels, the SMR generally increases with duration, as one would expect if arsenic were a harmful substance. If one had not considered the data separately for each exposure level, one would have examined the data as summarized in Table 1.15.

Notice that Table 1.15 is essentially a weighted average of the data for the two exposure levels. If one used the data in Table 1.15 instead of the data in Table 1.14, one would overestimate the risk for workers of low-level exposure for a short duration (i.e., 191.95 is larger than 169.9) and underestimate the risk to workers of long-time exposure to high levels of arsenic. Further illustrations of stratifying a data set into several more comparable subsets and combining the results into a summary result are given in Chapters 5, 6, 7 and 10.

One way of graphically representing the data in Table 1.14 is given in Figure 1.8, which represents the SMRs for each duration period of the two exposure categories by bars whose height is proportional to the SMR. In this way, we can see that for each period of duration of exposure, workers exposed to the higher amounts of arsenic had higher mortality rates than workers exposed to lesser amounts and that increased duration of exposure generally increases the risk of death (SMR) at either exposure level. Notice that each bar in Figure 1.8 is composed of two shadings, the lighter part represents an SMR of 1.0, i.e., the expected mortality rate of males of the same age composition as the employees studied. The darker part represents the *excess* mortality rate in each exposure and duration category.

In Chapter 8, we will discuss some ways of formally describing the relationship of one variable with respect to one or more other variables. If

TABLE 1.15.   Cancer Data in Table 1.14 Combining High and Low Exposure Categories

Duration	Number at Risk	Observed Deaths	SMR
<10	1511	40	191.95
10–19	317	18	301.5
20–29	396	26	408.3
30+	344	20	325.5

Source: Data derived from Table 12 of the Enterline and Marsh study cited in Table 1.14.

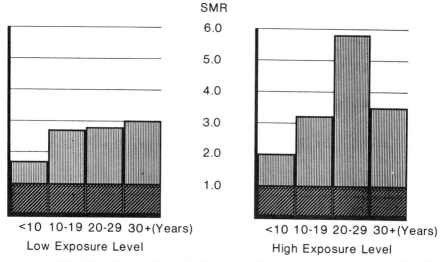

FIGURE 1.8.   Bar charts of standardized mortality rates and excess mortality of
smelter workers exposed to low and high amounts of arsenic. The
basic data is given is Table 1.14. The excess mortality rate is the
portion of the SMR in the vertically shaded region. The normal or
expected rate (1.00) is the darker portion of the SMR.

one variable typically has large values when another also has large values,
they are said to be *positively* related or associated. In our example, income was positively related to educational achievement, and the mortality rate of workers exposed to arsenic was positively related to the
amount of exposure and the duration of exposure.

   Other examples of positively-related variables are grades in law school
(or other graduate school) and scores in the LSAT (or graduate admissions test), height and weight, and salary and seniority. Of course, characteristics can be negatively or inversely related, e.g., an employee's
chance of being laid off is inversely related to their length of employment
(seniority) or the amount of betacarotene in a person's diet is negatively
related to their likelihood of developing lung cancer.

   In describing and using the existence of a relationship between characteristics and variables, one should keep in mind the following caveats:

   (a) Two variables may be related in general (that is what correlation
technically means), but the relationship does not inevitably apply to every
case. This is one reason why some students with high aptitude scores turn
out not to be especially successful.

   (b) The fact that two variables are correlated does not necessarily imply that one causes the other. It is possible that another variable causes both.

(c) If two variables are shown to be related, one should make sure that any other variable that is suggested as the common explanatory characteristic is also related to both of the original variables. Indeed, in order for a third variable to completely explain an observed relationship, it will have to be more highly related to at least one of the variables than the observed relationship between the original variables studied.

At this point, the above observations are somewhat imprecise; they set the stage for some of the refinements of the basic statistical methods that are needed to analyze data arising in many applications. For example, we will need to subdivide data into appropriate groups (e.g., males and females by educational background) in order to assess whether they receive fair treatment (e.g., equal pay).

Sometimes policymakers and lawyers may expect too much from an established relationship, while at other times the mere mention that another factor might possibly explain the data has led to disregarding relevant data rather than giving it less weight. These ideas will be important in our discussion of the use of data in equal employment cases and health policy. In Chapters 5 and 6 we will utilize a result of Cornfield to evaluate whether it is possible for another factor to explain a sound statistical association between exposure to a chemical and a disease. On the other hand, if an important variable is not measured accurately, policymakers may request that a new study be undertaken. This occurred in an epidemiologic study of Reyes' syndrome, a rare children's disease, where early studies indicating a link between the illness and prior ingestion of a medication containing salicylate also noted that the children who became ill had a higher fever during their previous illness. The new study which confirmed the association is described in Chapter 11.

Problems

1. Since smoking is known to be related to lung cancer, one would have liked to know the smoking habits of the workers in the arsenic study. Do you think that

(a) The fraction of workers who smoked differed significantly from the fraction of a comparable age-sex group taken from the nation as a whole?

(b) The smokers would have been assigned more frequently to high-exposure jobs so that the increased mortality due to exposure was really a result of smoking habits of the workers?

(c) Workers exposed to high levels of arsenic might have left the plant, causing the observed decrease in the SMRs from the 20–29 year duration period to the over 30-year period?

2. The data in Table 1.13 also reports data by racial category.

(a) On the same sheet of graph paper, make a chart similar to Figure 1.6 of white and black median earnings by education level.

(b) Do black college graduates appear to gain as much from completing college as whites? Compare their earnings to males who just completed high school.

(c) From your answer to part (b), can you conclude that college-educated blacks face more discrimination than those who just finished high school? Hint: What other factors might influence income?

3. The data for full-time year-round female workers corresponding to the male data in Table 1.13 is given below.

(a) Does education have a positive relationship to earnings for females of both races?

(b) Does the data suggest that black females gain about as much from completing college as white females?

(c) What might explain why the answer to part (b) differs from your answer to part (b) of the previous question?

(c) Does education appear to increase or decrease the gap between male and female earnings? What other factors might you wish to study before making a major decision relying solely on the above data?

Answers to Selected Problems

1. (a) Not likely.

(b) Not likely.

(c) More plausible. This could be examined by studying worker histories.

TABLE 1.16. Median Earnings for Full-Time Year-round Female Workers

	Less Than 8	8	9 to 11	12 (H.S.)	Some College	College Graduate	Post-graduate
All females	7,742	8,857	9,676	11,537	12,954	15,143	18,100
White	7,643	9,101	9,801	11,636	13,182	15,231	18,084
Black	8,036	—	9,119	11,008	11,828	14,912	18,479

Note: The omitted entry occurred because the sample included too few persons in the category.

2. (b) No.

(c) As blacks have not had even a rough equivalence in access to higher education until relatively recently, one should study the question for males of similar ages. Indeed, it is known that seniority plays an important role in wage determination. Also, the data reported in Table 1.13 includes interest, dividends, etc., in addition to earned income. The interested reader might check the 1980 census report on earned income to see whether the data by age is available.

3. (a) Yes.

(b) Yes.

(c) Traditionally women have gone into jobs such as teaching, which have salaries set by a governmental unit. Also, all women have historically been subject to discrimination, especially in the type of job they held. Thus, few women of either race were employed in high-paying blue collar jobs requiring only a high school education.

(d) Increase. One might wish to study the effects of occupation and seniority (women's participation in the labor force has risen sharply over the last two decades) as well as family responsibility on the earnings process underlying the data before attributing the entire increase in the income differential, as education increases, to labor market discrimination.

7. Some Basic Concepts and an Introduction to the Interpretation of the Results of Statistical Studies

In this chapter, our primary concern has been with summarizing data and drawing rather clear conclusions from these descriptive measures, rather than with assessing the logical strength or validity of the inferences made or the soundness of the procedures used to collect the basic data. In order to discuss these fundamental topics, we need to formally define some basic concepts that we have implicitly used already.

The *population* or *universe* to which the data refers is the totality of individuals, objects or measurements having some common property of interest.

A *variable* is a characteristic or measurement which may take on different values for different members of the population.

A *sample* is a *subset* of a population or universe with a measurement or observation on the variables of interest for each member of the population contained in the subset.

These ideas are readily understood in the context of a few specific examples which follow:

(1) Politicians are concerned with the set of registered voters (the population) and their party preference (the variable). The variable may be denoted by a 0 (Democrat) and a 1 (Republican) or vice versa.

(2) The earnings data in Table 1.7 dealt with the variable income of the population of men who worked full-time during the entire year (1980).

(3) The data concerning the apportionment issue referred to the *population* of *legislative districts,* and the *variable* or *characteristic* of interest was the number of persons living in each district.

In the third example, notice that the count of the human population in each district is the variable, while the *statistical population* is the set of *legislative districts.*

Sometimes the data set we use will contain information on the variable of interest for all members of the population. For example, the data in Table 1.12 reported the number of cars for each member of the population of U.S. automakers. In employment discrimination cases, one may have data on all employees, from which one may study the issue of equal pay. In many applications, however, it is feasible only to obtain data for a sample of the population of interest. This occurs in public opinion polls or census surveys of the nation, as the cost of obtaining the information from all citizens is prohibitive. Often, the most accurate and readily available data will be for a sample of the population. Indeed, the easiest way to study the issue of equity of real estate assessments is to use data on the prices and assessments of homes that were sold in a recent time period.

In order to conduct a proper study, one must carefully define its objectives at the outset. Then the suitable population must be delineated, and proper measurements of the variables of interest gathered on the entire population or a sample. Once the data and statistical calculations are made, we wish to reach conclusions about the population. This process is called *statistical inference,* as typically we infer characteristics of an entire population on the basis of a sample. The same concepts of inference, fortunately, are also useful in assessing data for a whole population.

The statistical summaries we have discussed so far were quite clear. Therefore, it was unnecessary to use formal statistical methodology. For example, it was easy to see that there was a significant increase in the relative inequality of the population counts of the legislative districts in *Baker v. Carr* or to realize that owners of low quality land were overassessed relative to owners of better quality land in Sunflower County.

Nevertheless, it is highly desirable to have scientifically sound techniques to make decisions and to numerically evaluate the logical strength of inferences made from data. Both basic summary statistical measures and indicators of the validity or strength of statistical inferences are useful in assuring *horizontal equity* in legal decisions and public policy, i.e., persons or firms in similar situations should receive similar treatment.

An additional important use of statistical reasoning arises in the process of weighing the evidence provided by the available data. As we mentioned in the introduction, the mere existence of a statistical difference from equality, say in tax assessments, does not mean that it arose from improper conduct. On further analysis, one may find that another factor caused the observed difference. In the assessment situation, suppose one found a *larger* difference or variation from fair tax assessment of single family homes in a county now than what was found in the 1977 census survey. While this may be due to an inefficient assessment process, e.g., updating assessments only once every 10 years or not obtaining data on home improvements, it may have arisen because of the sharp increase in mortgage rates, which has caused a wider variety of financing arrangements. Since the price of a home now includes a factor not closely related to its value, e.g., the seller giving the buyer a below-market-rate second mortgage, just looking at the variation of the assessment-sales ratios of recently sold homes about their median ratio cannot capture the effect of creative financing. Thus, more sophisticated methods, adjusting the sales price for below-market loans to the buyer, should be used.

On the other hand, a statistical study should not be totally ignored because some factor was not considered, unless it can be demonstrated that the factor was significant enough to explain the data. If the Sunflower County data had been taken in 1984, the interest-rate effect could not explain why the low quality land was overassessed, as everyone would be affected by the higher rates. While the owners of the better land might be in better financial condition and, therefore, could lend potential purchasers money at a discount from the market rate, it is illogical to believe that this could explain the data indicating that the plaintiff was assessed at a rate nearly *four* times that of the owner of the best quality land. The magnitude of any disparity, as well as the degree of its statistical significance (to be defined in Chapter 3) should be used to evaluate the likelihood that a suggested new factor could explain the disparity.

This problem arises quite often in employment discrimination cases when defendants criticize statistical findings without producing a more refined analysis. For instance, in the hiring aspect of *Capaci v. Katz and*

Besthoff,[11] the defendant tried to explain the fact that *no* females were hired into a manager trainee position out of about 250 as a result of women's not wanting to work at night (among other reasons). The District court accepted this answer, although women worked at night as clerks. Indeed, the opinion virtually required the plaintiff to use data that were not available. The appellate decision reversed the lower court on these aspects of the case. Of course, plaintiffs have also used unsound methods. In their study of equal pay in *Vuyanich v. Republic National Bank*,[12] plaintiffs used age of an employee in place of their seniority (length of time employed). The bank demonstrated that this biased the results, as male employees of the same chronological age as female employees typically had about two years more seniority.

Another useful method of substantiating the findings of a study is to relate them to similar studies. A fine example of this occurred in epidemiology. A multi-nation study was made to assess the influence of the age of a woman at the time she had her first child on her risk of subsequently having breast cancer. The data is reproduced in Table 1.17 and shows a clear positive (though small) increase in the chance of having breast cancer as age at first birth increases. Because of the variety of nations included in the study and the consistency of the relationship, factors such as diet and possible exposure to byproducts of an industrial society are unlikely alternative explanations of this finding. Hence, the relationship between age at parity and a woman's risk of having breast cancer later in life is generally accepted in the health area.

Two recurring issues in the use of data in the legal and regulatory areas are the validity of the measurements on the variable of interest and the representativeness of the sample from which inferences are made. These topics will be discussed later in Chapter 9, however, we mention that the most reliable method is to take a random sample of the population. This gives each member of the population the same chance of being in the sample.

In order to carefully define the ideas such as "the same chance," we need to discuss the concept of probability, which is the subject of the next chapter. These basic probabilistic concepts are also the logical foundation of statistical inference, as we will pay more attention to data indicating that an outcome (such as very few minorities receiving a promotion or workers exposed to a particular chemical on the job having a higher incidence of a specific disease) had a low probability of occurring by chance. If an event is unlikely to have occurred by chance, then some other factor, most likely, is responsible for it. In the promotion example,

TABLE 1.17.   Estimates of Relative Risk of Breast Cancer, By Age at
               First Birth

Centre	Nulliparous	Parous, age at first birth (years):				
		<20	20–24	25–29	30–34	35+
Boston	100	32	55	76	90	117
Glamorgan	100	38	49	67	73	124
Athens	100	51	71	79	106	127
Slovenia	100	81	74	94	112	118
Sao Paulo	100	49	65	94	84	175
Taipei	100	54	45	37	89	106
Tokyo	100	26	49	78	100	138
All places	100	50	60	78	94	122

Source: Taken from Table 3 of MacMahon, B., Cole, P., Lin, T. M., Lowe, C. R., Mirra,
A. P., Ravnihar, B., Saller, E. J., Valaoras, V. G. and Yuasa, S. (1970). Age at First Birth
and Breast Cancer Risk. *Bulletin World Health Organization* **43,** 209–221.
Note: The risks are relative to a risk of 100 for the nulliparous and were adjusted for age at
diagnosis.

if the minority employees have qualifications similar to those of the majority, one concludes that discrimination is likely to be the cause of the
outcome. In the chemical exposure setting, one concludes that the chemical either causes the disease directly or indirectly (i.e., it reinforces the
toxic effect of other substances), unless it can be shown that the workers
in the plant were atypical in that they had a greater degree of prior exposure to other harmful substances than most individuals.

Problems

1.   The following data reports the distance (in miles) between home and
the bank for all ten tellers employed by the bank:

$$1, .5, 2.2, .3, .7, 1.5, 1.8, 1.6, 1.9, 2.5$$

Find the mean and median, variance and standard deviation of these
distances.

2.   The commuting distance of the five senior officers of the same bank
are:

$$3.7, 9.4, 11.2, 13.8, 8.6$$

(a) Find the mean, median and standard deviation of the commuting distance of the bank officers.

(b) If one were studying commuting patterns of bank employees, does it make sense to *consider* the 15 commuting distance of all the employees of the bank as being from the same population and use the *mean* or *median* of the 15 distances as a summary measure?

(*Hint:* In addition to statistical considerations, think of the salaries of the positions.)

3. What is the population or populations on which data should be obtained to shed light on the following questions? What type of data (i.e., which variables) would be helpful?

(a) The government wished to investigate whether a merger of the third and fourth largest domestic manufacturers of automobile tires will diminish the competition in that market.

(b) Suppose that you learned that the merger candidates in (a) were the only pair of sellers in several states. Should this fact affect the decision to allow or refuse the companies to merge?

(c) A woman lawyer is denied partnership in a firm after serving as an associate for the same amount of time (about six years), as the seven male associates who became partners that year did.

(d) A bicycle manufacturer wishes to show that another firm is infringing on its trademark. It engages a market research company to survey the population to see whether people confuse the competitor's label or trademark with the manufacturers.

Answers to Selected Problems

3. (a) One could define the population either as all domestic manufacturers or all manufacturers competing in the tire market. Which is most appropriate might depend on the antitrust statute. One should obtain data on the number of tires and dollar value sold by each market participant.

(b) Yes, since the relevant population can be the tire market in a region of the nation.

(c) The two populations are the male and female lawyers employed by the firm for several years (perhaps as many as six or seven) prior to the decision about the complainant. Measures of ability and productivity, such as billable hours, outcome of cases (or settlements) and client satisfaction, as well as data on the types of tasks assigned to the different lawyers, would be relevant. Data on the success of women associates for several years prior to the complaint would be enlightening.

(d) Ideally, one should survey the population of purchasers or potential purchasers of bicycles. This might be determined from asking retail stores or from demographic data the manufacturer collected on a form giving a warranty.

NOTES

1. Adapted from Table 57 of *Money, Income of Households, Families and Persons in the U.S. 1980.* U.S. Bureau of the Census CPS Reports Series P-60, No. 132.

2. The total is very slightly less than 1.0 due to rounding of the original fractions.

3. When one compares data for two groups, one must be sure to define the groups carefully. Since a higher fraction of women work part-time or only for part of the year, we use data for full-time workers in problem 1.

4. In medical studies, one is primarily concerned with finding treatments which increase the fraction of patients who live. This fraction equals one *minus the ogive* at x, and the plot of these fractions is called the survival curve.

5. 369 U.S. 186 (1962).

6. 462 U.S. 725 (1983).

7. 462 U.S. 835 (1983).

8. The guidelines were issued on June 14, 1982 and are reprinted in *Trade Regulation Reports*. Commerce Clearing House, 99, 4500–4505.

9. In studies of the distribution of income or wealth, the inclusion or exclusion of one very rich family in the sample can seriously affect the result, since the total income can change drastically. Furthermore, an error in one observation can seriously distort the results. Recently, the Federal Reserve Board had to recall a study of the distribution of wealth, because a family worth $2 million had been recorded as having $200 million. Since these studies are often based on samples of a few thousand families, one can realize the impact of this error by calculating the share of the total wealth held by this particular family, assuming there were 999 other families in the sample whose average wealth was $50,000.

10. These calculations are the basis of cost-benefit analysis, which is also used to assess the impact of various regulations. References are given in Chapter 14. We note that these calculations require quite a few assumptions, since estimating the lifetime income of a college graduate involves predicting the economy for 40 years into the future.

11. 515 F.Supp. 317 (E.D.La. 1981) affirmed in part, reversed in relevant part, 711 F.2d 647 (5th Cir. 1983).

12. 505 F.Supp. 224 (N.D. Tex. 1980) *vacated and remanded* (on nonstatistical issues), 723 F.2d. 1195 (5th Cir. 1984).

REFERENCES

Formal Statistics Textbooks

DERMAN, C., GLESER, L. J. AND OLKIN, I. (1980). *Probability Models and Applications*. New York: MacMillan.

FREEDMAN, D., PISANI, R., AND PURVES, R. (1978). *Statistics.* New York: Norton.

HILDEBRAND, D. K. (1986). *Statistical Thinking for Behavioral Scientists.* Boston: Duxbury.

HOEL, P. AND JESSEN, R. J. (1982). *Basic Statistics for Business and Economics.* New York: John Wiley.

HUNTSBERGER, D. V. AND BILLINGSLEY, P. (1981). *Elements of Statistical Reasoning* (5th ed.). Boston: Allyn and Bacon.

MENDENHALL, W. AND OTT, L. (1980). *Understanding Statistics.* N. Scituate, Mass.: Duxbury.

MOSES, L. E. (1985). *Think and Explain With Statistics.* Reading, Mass.: Addison-Wesley.

Less Formal Books on Statistics

HAACK, D. J. (1979). *Statistical Literacy.* N. Scituate, Mass.: Duxbury.

HOLLANDER, M. AND PROSCHAN, F. (1984). *The Statistical Exorcist: Dispelling Statistical Anxiety.* New York: Marcel Dekker.

KIMBLE, G. A. (1978). *How to Use (and Misuse) Statistics.* Englewood Cliffs, New Jersey: Prentice Hall.

MONRONEY, M. J. (1951). *Facts From Figures.* London: Penguin.

MOORE, D. S. (1979). *Statistics Concepts and Controversies.* San Francisco: W. H. Freeman.

References for Measures of Relative Inequality and Applications

ALKER, H. R., JR. (1965). *Mathematics and Politics.* New York: MacMillan.

AUERBACK, C. (1964). The Reapportionment Case: One-Man—One-Vote—One-Value. *Supreme Court Review,* University of Chicago Press.

COOTNER, R. C. (1970). *The Apportionment Cases.* University of Tennessee Press.

DUNCAN, O. D. AND DUNCAN, B. (1955). A Methodological Analysis of Segregation Indices. *American Sociological Review* **20,** 212–217.

GASTWIRTH, J. L. (1984). Measures of Uniformity. In: *Encyclopedia of Statistics* (N. L. Johnson and S. Katz, ed). New York: John Wiley.

HACKER, A. (1964). *Congressional Districting.* Washington, D.C.: Brookings.

LANDES, W. M. AND POSNER, R. A. (1981). Market Power in Antitrust Cases. *Harvard Law Review* **94,** 937–996.

McDONALD, T. (1976) Legislative Apportionment. Unpublished manuscript. (A special statistics project that reanalyzed the data presented in *Baker v. Carr* and related cases.)

SCHMALENSEE, R. (1982). Another Look at Market Power. *Harvard Law Review* **95,** 1789–1816.

SINGER, E. M. (1968). *Anti-trust Economics.* Englewood Cliffs, New Jersey: Prentice Hall.

References for Equity of Real Estate Assessments

BEHRENS, J. O. (1977). Property Tax Administration: Use of Assessment Sales Ratios. *Journal of Educational Finance* **3**, 158–164.

FREEDMAN, D. A. (1985). The Mean Versus the Median: A Case Study in 4-R Act Litigation. *Journal of Business and Economic Statistics* **3**, 1–13. (This article shows how the statute may specify the appropriate measures by the typical assessment—market value ratio in a jurisdiction. The author shows how the measure for 4-R Act cases is a weighted average and gives references to various cases which considered whether the median or weighted mean is the more appropriate measure. The decisions are not consistent. In *ACF Industries, Inc. v. Arizona,* 561 F.Supp. 595 (D. Arizona 1982) *affirmed,* 714 F.2d 93 (9th cir. 1983), the court notes that in *de facto* discrimination cases, such as *Lakeland v. Davidson,* the median was preferred, but in 4-R Act cases the weighted mean had essentially been specified in the act.)

NOTO, N. A. (1978). Uniformity of Assessment: High on the List of Property Tax Reform. *Business Review, Federal Reserve Bank of Philadelphia* May–June, 13–23.

OLDMAN, O. AND AARON, H. (1965). Assessment Sales Ratios Under the Boston Property Tax. *National Tax Journal* **18**, 36–49.

ROBERTSON, J. L. (1977). Problems of Valuation and Equalization in Mississippi Ad Valorem Tax System. *Mississippi Law Journal* **48**, 201–257. (This article by the plaintiff's lawyer describes the *Davidson v. Baird* land assessment case.)

ROCKLEN, J. H. (1976). Equality of Property Taxation—the Law and Practice and Prospects. *New England Law Review* **11**, 627–642.

U.S. BUREAU OF THE CENSUS, CENSUS OF GOVERNMENTS (1972). *Assessment Sales Price Ratios and Tax Rates.* Volume 2, Part 2. Wash. D.C.: U.S. Gov't Printing Office.

U.S. BUREAU OF THE CENSUS. (1975). *State and Local Ratio Studies and Properties Assessment.* Services GSS No. 72. Wash. D.C.: U.S. Gov't Printing Office.

YORK, W. E. (1973). Equality in Taxation—Houston's Constitutional Dilemma. *Houston Law Review* **10**, 656–691.

Chapter 2

Probability and Random Variables

1. Introduction

The theory of probability was developed by mathematicians to analyze the chance of winning various gambling games. One problem that was posed by the French nobleman, the Chevalier de Mere, to Pascal was the following: I am winning money by making an even money bet that I can roll at least one 6 in four throws of a single die, however, I am losing money when I make a similar bet on being able to obtain at least one double 6 in 24 throws of a pair of dice. Why? Implicit in this question is the objective of the gambler who wanted to learn which bets would prove favorable over a *long period of time*.

A modern-day betting problem would occur if you wished to bet a friend on the outcome of the World Series. Suppose team A, from your hometown, and team B, from your friend's hometown, are considered evenly matched. If you bet at the beginning of the series of seven possible games, it is clear that you should make an even money bet, i.e., if team A wins your friend pays you one dollar and if team B wins you pay your friend a dollar. Suppose that you don't get together with your friend until five games have been played and your team has won three of them. Your team now has a better than 50-50 chance of winning the series, so what odds should you give your friend so that the bet would be fair? One approach to the problem would be to calculate the probability of team B winning the series, i.e., team B wins the next two games. Since team B

53

has a 50-50 chance or a probability of 1/2 of winning each game, its chances of winning both games is 1/2 of 1/2 = 1/4. Thus, your team has a probability of 3/4 of winning, which is three times that of your friend's, so a fair bet would call for you to pay your friend $3 if his team wins while you receive $1 if your team wins. Notice that we are using the notion of what would happen in many repetitions of a hypothetical World Series to determine a fair bet in a specific series.

Let us consider another example based on the throw of two dice. Suppose one desired to bet on whether the sum of the two faces showing is a 7 or 11. What are fair, favorable and unfavorable bets for this game?

In order to answer this question we need to know the *fraction* of times in a long series of throws of two dice that a 7 or 11 occurs. This fraction, which we will later calculate to be 2/9, is the *probability* that a single toss of the die results in their sum being a 7 or 11. Thus, probability logically involves the idea of phenomena or experiments that are repeatable or that can be thought of as capable of replication.

Once the probability of a particular outcome is known, a fair bet can be determined. For instance, when the probability of an outcome is .5, a fair bet is even money, i.e., for each $1 you bet you win $1 if the event occurs and lose $1 when it doesn't. In the long run you win $1 half the time and lose $1 half the time, so you expect to break even. A fair bet is characterized as one in which both sides should neither win nor lose money if the game is played many times. If you bet $2 that the sum of two die is a 7 or an 11, how much should you receive when this happens for the bet to be fair? Suppose the game will be played 900 times. Since the probability is 2/9ths that you'll win, you should win about 200 times and lose about 700. Since your losses will be about $1400 (2 × 700), to break even you should receive $w, where w times the expected number of games you win should be equal 1400, i.e.,

$$200 \; w \; = \; 1400$$

or w = $7. In general, if you bet on an event with probability p of occurring you should receive odds according to the ratio

$$1 - p : p,$$

e.g., 7/9 : 2/9, or 7 to 2, for betting that the sum of two die will be 7 or 11.

In this chapter we will discuss probabilities for a large class of experiments which include any type of repeatable process, not just laboratory experiments. Thus, playing card games, betting on sports events, sampling accounts payable, hiring workers from a large pool of applicants and recording whether an airplane accident occurs today are *experiments* in our sense.

Formally, we define an *experiment* as any potentially repeatable process resulting in an observation or measurement. We now discuss how to determine the probabilities of the possible outcomes of an experiment and develop some basic concepts of probability theory.

2. Foundations: Events and Their Probabilities

When we consider an experiment we know that there are a variety of possible outcomes. It is convenient to represent these outcomes geometrically as points e_1, e_2, ... e_k, where k is the total number of possible outcomes. The set of points representing all possible outcomes of an experiment is the *sample space* for the experiment.

To illustrate a sample space consider the possible outcomes of rolling two dice. There are 36 outcomes given below.

(1, 1)	(1, 2)	(1, 3)	(1, 4)	(1, 5)	(1, 6)
(2, 1)	(2, 2)	(2, 3)	(2, 4)	(2, 5)	(2, 6)
(3, 1)	(3, 2)	(3, 3)	(3, 4)	(3, 5)	(3, 6)
(4, 1)	(4, 2)	(4, 3)	(4, 4)	(4, 5)	(4, 6)
(5, 1)	(5, 2)	(5, 3)	(5, 4)	(5, 5)	(5, 6)
(6, 1)	(6, 2)	(6, 3)	(6, 4)	(6, 5)	(6, 6)

where the first number in each pair is the number shown on the first die and the second is the number shown on the second die.

Quite often we are not interested in whether a particular simple outcome happened but in whether a *composite event,* such as the sum of the dice equals 7, happened. Notice that the six sample events on the diagonal connecting (6, 1) to (1, 6) form the event that the sum of the two dice equal 7. If we add the simple outcomes (5, 6) and (6, 5) to the previous six, we obtain all of the simple outcomes forming the event that the sum of the two dice is a 7 or 11.

We next need to assign probabilities to each of the simple events or outcomes in the sample space. Since the probability P(e) of the simple event e corresponds to the *proportion* or *fraction* of times it occurs in a long series of replications of the experiment, we realize that these probabilities must satisfy two conditions:

(1) The probability of any simple event is always between 0 and 1.
(2) The sum of the probabilities of *all* the simple events must equal 1.

The first condition is a consequence of the fact that the fraction of times a simple event occurs in a series of n repetitions is the number (between 0 and n) of times the event occurs divided by n, so the *fraction* is between 0 and 1. As the set of all simple events is the *entire* sample space of the experiment, the sum of all their probabilities must equal one.

To assign probabilities to the 36 simple events in the sample space for the toss of two dice, we assume that each of the six faces on the first has the same chance of being the one showing, i.e., each has probability 1/6 of occurring. If the same is true of the second die, each of the 36 points in the sample space is equally likely to occur, i.e., each has probability 1/36.

Moreover, two distinct simple events cannot both occur in the same realization of experiment, so we define the *probability of a composite event* as the *sum of the probabilities of all the simple events* composing it. Since the event that the sum of two dice is a 7 or 11 is composed of eight simple events, each of which has probability 1/36, the composite event has probability 8/36 = 2/9 of occurring on any toss.

Example 2.1.   Consider the experiment of tossing three fair coins. As each coin has two possible outcomes and the outcome (head or tail) of each toss does not affect the outcome of the other tosses there are eight $(2 \times 2 \times 2)$ simple events which we enumerate as

H	H	H	e_1
T	H	H	e_2
H	T	H	e_3
H	H	T	e_4
H	T	T	e_5
T	H	T	e_6
T	T	H	e_7
T	T	T	e_8

As the coins are fair, i.e., each has probability 1/2 of coming up a head or a tail, each of the eight simple events has the same probability 1/8 of occurring.

Consider the event A: All three coins show the same face. To determine its probability denoted by $P(A)$, we note that it is composed of the two simple events e_1 and e_8. Hence, $P(A) = 2 \cdot 1/8 = 2/8 = 1/4$.

Consider the event B: At least one tail and one head occur in the three tosses. This event is composed of all the simple events except e_1 and e_8, i.e., it consists of six simple events each having probability 1/8 of occurring, so $P(B)$ equals 6/8 or 3/4. Alternatively, B occurs only when A does not so that they are opposite events. Since either A or B must occur we can calculate $P(B)$ by subtracting $P(A) = 1/4$ from 1, again obtaining $P(B) = 3/4$.

In many situations all simple events may *not* have the same probability of happening. To illustrate this we consider

Example 2.2.   An urn (jar) contains 10 balls, 5 of which are blue, 3 are red and 2 are green. A person is blindfolded and draws a ball from the urn. What are the simple events and their probabilities? The simple events are:

e_1—a blue ball is drawn;
e_2—a red ball is drawn;
e_3—a green ball is drawn.

Since the balls are chosen at random (i.e., the color of a particular ball does not affect the chance it is selected), the chance a blue ball is chosen is 5/10, as there are 5 blue balls out of 10 balls. Thus $P(e_1) = .5$. Similarly, $P(e_2) = .3$, as there are 3 red balls among the 10 balls in the urn and $P(e_3) = .2$. Notice that while all 10 balls have the same chance of being drawn, the *color* of the ball is the important characteristic, and the urn contained different proportions of balls of the three colors.

Before discussing sample spaces with more interesting but more complex probability structures, it is convenient to learn a few more concepts and rules for calculating probabilities.

Recall that a general *event* or *composite event* A is a collection of simple events and $P(A)$ is the sum of the probabilities, $P(e_i)$, of the simple events, e_i, forming it. More generally, we define the *union* of two events A and B as the event that occurs when either A or B or both occur when the experiment is carried out. The *union* of A and B is denoted by $A \cup B$. In the dice tossing example, if A denotes the event that the sum is 7, B the event the sum is 11, then $A \cup B$ is the event that the sum is 7 or 11.

A graphical way of presenting the sample space and the events of special interest is the *Venn diagram*. In Figure 2.1, the sample space, S, of the dice tossing experiment consists of all simple events (points) in the rectangle, and each event, e.g., A, is represented by a region containing all the simple events (points) forming it.

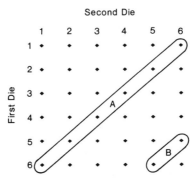

FIGURE 2.1.   Venn diagram of the sample space of two die and the events A, their sum is 7, and B, their sum is 11. Note that the event A ∪ B is the region containing the points of the sample space contained in A or in B.

Sometimes we are interested in an event which occurs when both of two events *A* and *B* occur. This event is called the *intersection* of *A* and *B* because it is composed of the *simple* events which are common to both *A* and *B*. In the die tossing experiment, let *A* be the event the first toss is a one, *B* the event that the second toss is a one. Their intersection *A* ∩ *B* is the event that both tosses yield a one. Their union *A* ∪ *B* is the event that a one *appears* on at least one of the tosses. Figure 2.2 presents the Venn diagram for this example.

From the diagram and the fact that each of the 36 sample points has the

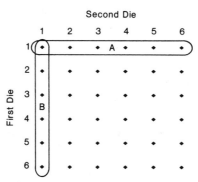

FIGURE 2.2.   Venn diagram for the sample space of two die and the events A, a one occurs on the first toss, and B, a one occurs on the second toss. Notice that the composite event A ∪ B contains the 11 sample events contained in A or in B. One event: a 1 on both die is in A ∩ B.

same probability, 1/36, of occurring, satisfy yourself that the probabilities of the events are given by:

$$P(A) = \frac{1}{6}$$

$$P(B) = \frac{1}{6}$$

$$P(A \cap B) = \frac{1}{36}$$

$$P(A \cup B) = \frac{11}{36}.$$

In your calculation of $P(A \cup B)$ you might have counted all 11 points belonging to A or B *or* you might have noticed that $A \cup B$ consists of all the events in A and all in B but the events in $A \cap B$ (in our example $A \cap B$ is just one simple event $(1, 1)$) are counted twice. This gives rise to a general method of calculating $P(A \cup B)$:

(2.1) $P(A \cup B) = P(A) + P(B) - P(A \cap B).$

Diagrammatically this is pictured in Figure 2.3.

When the events A and B have *no* simple events in common, $P(A \cup B) = P(A) + P(B)$. When this is true we say that the events A and B are mutually *exclusive,* i.e., they have no simple events in common. Exclusive events have the property that if one occurs, the other *cannot* occur (on any single repetition of the experiment).

In the die throwing example, when A = the event, the sum of the two faces is 7; when $A = B$, the sum is 11.

$$P(A \cup B) = \frac{6}{36} + \frac{2}{36} = \frac{8}{36},$$

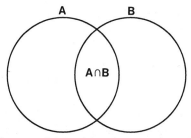

FIGURE 2.3.   Venn Diagram of A B where the area of a region or set corresponds to its probability. Thus, $P(A \cup B) = P(A) + P(B) - P(A \cap B)$.

as A and B are exclusive events. If C is the event that the difference between the die is 1, then C is composed of 10 simple events, the five above and five below the diagonal connecting $(1, 1)$ to $(6, 6)$ in the sample space. As $A \cap C$ consists of two events, $(3, 4)$ and $(4, 3)$, where the face numbers both sum to 7 and differ by 1, $P(A \cap C) = 2/36 = 1/18$. From formula (2.1) we find

$$P(A \cup C) = \frac{6}{36} + \frac{10}{36} - \frac{2}{36} = \frac{14}{36} = \frac{7}{18},$$

which is the probability of the composite event that the sum of the two die is a 7 or 11 and/or that the difference between the faces equals one.

The simplest type of exclusive events are given in the following:

Definition. For every event A, we call the remaining simple events which are not in A, the *complement* of A and denote it by $\overline{A}$.

As every simple event is either in A or $\overline{A}$, we have

$$1 = P(A \cup \overline{A}) = P(A) + P(\overline{A}),$$

so that

(2.2) $$P(A) = 1 - P(\overline{A}).$$

The importance of formula (2.2) is that in some situations $P(\overline{A})$ will be easier to find than $P(A)$. Indeed, this occurred in example 2.1 where it was simpler to obtain $P(\overline{B})$ than $P(B)$, as $\overline{B}$ contained only two simple events, while B was composed of six events.

Problems

1. Suppose two dice are tossed and the following events are observed:
   (A) the sum of the numbers (faces) showing is an even number;
   (B) the sum of the numbers showing is an odd number;
   (C) the sum of the numbers showing is a 7 or 11.
   (a) Find the probability of each of the three events.
   (b) If the event A occurs can the event C occur?
   (c) Are any two of the events complementary? Check your answer by verifying that they have no simple events in common and their probabilities sum to 1.0.
   (d) Find the probability that an odd number, other than a 7 or 11, is the sum of the two numbers showing. *Hint:* Circle the appropriate simple events forming A, B and C on a copy of the sample space given in Figure 2.1.

2. An experiment results in one of four simple events E_1, E_2, E_3 and E_4 with respective probabilities .4, .3, .2 and .1, i.e., $P(E_1) = .4$, $P(E_2) = .3$, $P(E_2) = .2$, and $P(E_1) = .1$

Let $A = E_1 \cup E_2$

$B = E_1 \cup E_2 \cup E_4$ and

$C = E_1 \cup E_3$.

Find $P(A \cap B)$

$P(A \cap C)$

$P(A \cup C)$

$P(B \cup C)$

$P(\overline{A} \cap C)$

$P(\overline{C} \cap E_3)$

$P(\overline{C} \cap A)$

$P(\overline{A} \cap \overline{B})$

$P(\overline{A} \cap \overline{C})$.

3. Independent Events, Dependent Events and Conditional Probability

a. Basic concepts

Intuitively we know that the result of a toss of fair coin on one occasion does not affect the outcome of a subsequent toss. In contrast, if we select two cards from a deck of 52, the event that the first one is an ace *decreases* the probability that the second card is an ace, as there are only three aces among the remaining 51 cards. The coin tossing situation is an example of independent outcomes or events, while the results of drawing cards consecutively is an example of dependent events. In this section we follow our intuition to obtain a probabilistic formulation of the notion of independence and introduce the concept of conditional probability of an event B, given that another event, A, occurs. The concept of conditional probability will enable us to decide whether events are independent or not and is useful in evaluating identification evidence.

From the coin tossing illustration, it is reasonable to consider events to be *independent* if the occurrence or nonoccurrence of one event has *no* effect on that of the other event (or events). For example, in tossing a fair die two times in a row, the chance of obtaining a 1 on the second toss is 1/6, regardless of the face which turned up in the first throw.

How can we define this idea in terms of the probabilities of the occurrence of the individual events? Again we consider tossing a fair coin, i.e., one such that the probability of a head occurring on each toss is 1/2. What is the probability of observing two heads in two consecutive tosses? You probably said 1/4.

Let us explore the reasoning behind your answer. For a fair coin there is probability 1/2 of a head appearing on any toss. Thus, half the time a head will appear on the first toss. Once this event has occurred we still must toss the coin for the second time, and there is probability 1/2 of a head on this second toss. Thus, the chance the coin is a head on the second as well as the first is 1/2 of 1/2, or 1/2 times 1/2 = 1/4. The above intuition gives rise to the following

Definition. Two events A and B are independent if the probability that *both* occur is the *product* of their individual probabilities, $P(A) \cdot P(B)$. Symbolically we express this as

(2.3) $P(A \cap B) = P(A) \cdot P(B).$

Formula (2.3) is often called the multiplication rule, as it says that probability that two *independent* events both occur is the product of their individual probabilities. Moreover, it generalizes to more than two events. If three events are independent, the probability that all three occur is the product of their three individual probabilities. Thus, the probability that three consecutive tosses of a fair coin result in three heads is $1/2 \times 1/2 \times 1/2 = 1/8$. More generally, the probability that in k (any integer) tosses of a fair coin we obtain *all* heads is

(2.4) $$\underbrace{\frac{1}{2} \times \frac{1}{2} \times \ldots \times \frac{1}{2}}_{k \text{ times}} = \left(\frac{1}{2}\right)^k = \frac{1}{2^k}.$$

We emphasize that in order for formula (2.4) and the multiplication rule to be a proper method of calculating the probability that all k events occur together, the events must be *independent* of one another.[1]

Not all events are independent, indeed, we are often interested in the relationship between events. Intuitively, events are *dependent* if the outcome of one *changes* the probability that the other event also occurs. Some examples of dependent events follow:

(a) Suppose you are drawing cards from a deck. What is the chance you obtain an ace on the first draw? Clearly it is $4/52 = 1/13 = .0769$ as there are four aces in the deck of 52 cards. Now suppose you did *not* draw an ace on the first draw. What is the probability you will obtain an ace on the second? Since there are four aces left in a deck, which how has 51 cards, your chance is $4/51 = .0784$. On the other hand, if you *had drawn* an *ace* on the first draw, the probability you would obtain an ace on the second draw would be $3/51 = 1/17 = .0588$, because there are only three aces among the remaining 51 cards.

(b) Another class of events that are dependent are *exclusive* events. For example, let *A* be the event it will be raining at noon tomorrow and *B* the event it will be sunny and clear at noon tomorrow. Since *A* and *B* cannot both happen, they are exclusive, as if one happens the other has a probability of zero of happening.

Our discussion of dependent events leads naturally to the concept of *conditional probability,* the probability that an event *B* will occur *given* the knowledge that another event *A* occurs, written $P(B|A)$. In the case of mutually exclusive events, as in example (b), $P(B|A) = 0$, as both events *cannot* possibly occur together. In the card drawing example, let the event *A* denote an ace appears in the first draw and *B* the event an ace is drawn on the second. Then $P(B|A) = 3/51$ and $P(B|\overline{A}) = 4/51$. (Recall $\overline{A}$ is the complement of *A* and means that an ace was *not* drawn the first time.) Thus, the probability that *B* occurs is affected by the occurrence of the event *A*. On the other hand, if *A* and *B* are *independent* events $P(B|A)$ should equal $P(B)$ and $P(B|\overline{A})$ should also equal $P(B)$, as the chance that *B* occurs, $P(B)$, is unaffected by *whether or not A* occurs.

Another use of the concept of conditional probability is illustrated by the following:

Example 2.3. Suppose you desire to predict whether a randomly selected person is a Democrat (the event *A*) or a Republican ($\overline{A}$). You may not inquire about the person's political views but you may ask: Is the family income of the person greater than \$50,000 (*B*) or not ($\overline{B}$)? Should you take advantage of the knowledge of whether *B* occurred in your prediction about whether *A* occurred too? Using the knowledge that high income people are more likely to be Republican than those with low or average incomes, our prediction of the political preference of an individual should be more accurate using data about their income. In terms of conditional probability the information about income level means that

$$P(A|B) < P(A),$$

i.e., the probability of a person with income over \$50,000 being a Democrat is *less* than the probability that a random member of the general

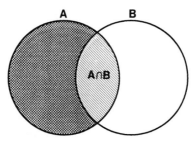

FIGURE 2.4.   Venn Diagram representing the conditional probability $P(B|A)$, that B occurs given A has occurred as the ratio of the shaded area $P(A \cap B)$ to the total marked area, $P(A)$, representing the event A.

population is a Democrat. This application also demonstrates the importance of carefully defining the event, A, of interest, its probability, $P(A)$, and distinguishing $P(A)$ from its conditional probability given the occurrence of another event B.

So far we have used the concept of conditional probability in an intuitive fashion as meaning the proportion of times B occurs where A has occurred. In order to obtain a formula to enable us to calculate conditional probabilities, consider a Venn diagram (see Figure 2.4) in which the *area* of each event is *proportional* to its *probability*.

The probability that the event A occurs, $P(A)$, is its area. How can we represent $P(B|A)$, i.e., the probability that B occurs given that A occurs? If A occurs, the only way that B can also occur is if A and B both occur, i.e., $(A \cap B)$ happens. In Figure 2.4, interpreting $P(A)$ as the area of A and $P(A \cap B)$ as the area of $A \cap B$ means that the ratio

(2.5) $$\frac{P(A \cap B)}{P(A)} = P(B|A)$$

represents the proportion of times that B occurs when A occurs, as it is the fraction of the total area, $P(A)$, that $P(A \cap B)$ forms.

If we cross-multiply in formula (2.5) we obtain

(2.6) $$P(A \cap B) = P(A) \cdot P(B|A).$$

In words, formula (2.6) says that the probability that A and B *both* occur is the probability that A occurs *times* the probability that B occurs *when* A has occurred. The formula is really a modification of the product rule for independent events to account for the *dependence* of the events. Let us illustrate its use on the card drawing problem.

What is the probability we obtain two aces in two consecutive draws?

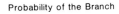

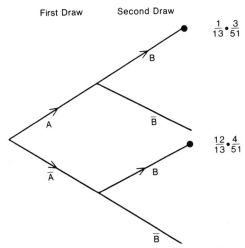

FIGURE 2.5. Tree diagram illustrating the calculation of the event B that the second card drawn from a well shuffled deck is an ace. The top branch is the event that both cards drawn are aces and has probability $P(A \cap B)$. The second branch leading to B is the event $\bar{A} \cap B$.

Let A denote the event that an ace is drawn on the first draw; B an ace is obtained on the second draw. We need to calculate $P(A \cap B)$. Again, $P(A) = 1/13$. However, $P(B|A)$, the probability an ace is drawn on the second draw *given* that an ace is drawn on the *first*, is $3/51$, as there are three aces left among the 51 cards. Thus $P(A \cap B) = 1/13 \cdot 3/51 = .0045$.

The notion of conditional probability allows us to calculate probabilities of events which may, at first glance, not be obvious. Let us consider again the following events:

$A =$ the first card drawn is an ace.
$B =$ the second card drawn is an ace.

Notice that $P(B)$ is the *total probability* that the second card is an ace *regardless* of the first card drawn. Can you guess what $P(B)$ is?

The formal method of obtaining $P(B)$ is to think of the drawings in sequence, either A occurs or it doesn't (i.e., $\bar{A}$ occurs). Then either B or $\bar{B}$ occurs on the second draw. The possibilities are drawn in Figure 2.5, which is called a tree diagram. Notice that B can occur with A (indicated by $>>$) or with $\bar{A}$. The first path means that $(A \cap B)$ occurs, and this event has probability $1/13 \cdot 3/51 = .004525$. The second path is the event

$(\overline{A} \cap B)$, i.e., B occurs when $\overline{A}$ occurs (the first card was not an ace). This probability is

$$P(\overline{A} \cap B) = P(\overline{A}) \cdot P(B|\overline{A}) = \frac{12}{13} \cdot \frac{4}{51} = \frac{48}{13 \cdot 51} = .0724,$$

as $P(\overline{A}) = 12/13$ and $P(B|\overline{A}) = 4/51$, as there are still four aces in among the 51 cards from which the second card will be selected. Since the events $(A \cap B)$ and $(\overline{A} \cap B)$ are mutually *exclusive,* as A and $\overline{A}$ are exclusive (the first card cannot be an ace and *not* an ace), the total probability that B occurs is the sum of the two probabilities, i.e.,

$$P(B) = P(A \cap B) + P(\overline{A} \cap B) = \frac{3}{13 \cdot 51} + \frac{48}{13 \cdot 51} = \frac{51}{13 \cdot 51} = \frac{1}{13}.$$
(2.7)

Thus, $P(B) = 1/13$, a result which you may have guessed because *before* any cards are drawn the chance of any card appearing on any particular draw should be the same as the probability it is drawn first.[2]

There is another way to interpret formula (2.7)

$$P(B) = P(A \cap B) + P(\overline{A} \cap B),$$

namely, the probability that B occurs is the sum of the probability it occurs with A and the probability it occurs with $\overline{A}$. This follows from the fact that the whole sample space is $A \cup \overline{A}$ (see Figure 2.6).

Thus, we obtain the probability of the event B by first finding the probability of its intersection with A, i.e., $P(B \cap A)$, then calculating the probability of its intersection with $\overline{A}$ and adding both probabilities.

Since formula (2.6) implies

$$P(A \cap B) = P(A)P(B|A) \text{ and } P(B \cap \overline{A}) = P(\overline{A})P(B|\overline{A}),$$

$P(B)$ can be calculated from

(2.8) $$P(B) = P(A)P(B|A) + P(\overline{A})P(B|\overline{A}).$$

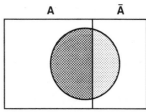

FIGURE 2.6.   Venn diagram illustrating the total probability theorem. The event B, the circular region, is composed of its intersection with event A plus its intersection with $\overline{A}$.

Formula (2.8) expresses $P(B)$ as a *weighted* average of the two conditional probabilities, where the *weights* are the probabilities that the events A and $\overline{A}$ occur. Formula (2.8) is a mathematical formula, which states that *the probability that event B occurs* is the probability that event A occurs times the conditional probability that B occurs when A does, *plus* the probability that the event A does *not* occur, times the conditional probability that B occurs when A does *not* occur. We illustrate the concept on another example:

Example 2.4. Suppose we wish to find the probability that a random member of the population is over 6' tall and are told that 10% of women are 6' or taller and 25% of men are. Assuming each sex is half of the population, what is the chance a randomly selected person is over 6' tall?

Let B be the event a person is over 6' tall and A the event the person is male. We desire to calculate

$$P(B) = P(A \cap B) + P(\overline{A} \cap B) \qquad \text{or}$$

$$P(B) = P(A) \cdot P(B|A) + P(\overline{A}) \cdot P(B|\overline{A}),$$

i.e., P(a person is over 6') $= P$(person is male) $\times P$(male is over 6') *plus* P(person is female) $\times P$(female is over 6'). The data specified in the problem tell us that $P(A) = P(\overline{A}) = 1/2$ and $P(B|A) = .25$, as 25% of the males are over 6' tall. Similarly $P(B|\overline{A}) = .10$. Hence using formula (2.8) we obtain

$$P(B) = .5(.25) + .5(.10) = .175.$$

One can think of this calculation in stages. First find the probability of obtaining a person of each sex. Then, for each sex, find the probability a person of that sex is over 6' tall. Finally, weight these conditional probabilities by the chance of obtaining a person of the respective sex.

The critical idea underlying this approach to finding $P(B)$ is that it is often easier to find $P(A \cap B)$ and $P(\overline{A} \cap B)$ for a suitable event A than to obtain $P(B)$ directly. Notice that the same idea works if the whole space, S, can be split into three events, A_1, A_2 and A_3, such that $S = A_1 \cup A_2 \cup A_3$ and $A_1 \cap A_2 = 0$, $A_2 \cap A_3 = 0$, $A_1 \cap A_3 = 0$, i.e., A_1 and A_3 are mutually exclusive events. Then (see Figure 2.7).

$$(2.9) \qquad P(B) = P(A_1 \cap B) + P(A_2 \cap B) + P(A_3 \cap B),$$

and, using formula (2.8) again, for each $P(A_i \cap B)$ we obtain

$$(2.10) \quad P(B) = P(A_1)P(B|A_1) + P(A_2)P(B|A_2) + P(A_3)P(B|A_3).$$

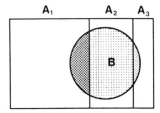

FIGURE 2.7. Venn diagram showing that the probability of the event B, the circular region, is the sum of the probabilities of the events $B \cap A_1$, $B \cap A_2$ and $B \cap A_3$, where A_1, A_2 and A_3 are mutually exclusive events whose union is the entire sample space.

Moreover, if the sample space can be decomposed into k exclusive events whose union is the whole sample space, we can obtain $P(B)$ by this method. The generalization of (2.10) is called the *total probability theorem* and represents the probability an event B occurs as a weighted average of the conditional probabilities $P(B|A_i)$, where the A_i, $i = 1, \ldots k$, are any set of mutually exclusive events whose union is the whole space and the weights are the respective $P(A_i)$. The general formula is

(2.11) $$P(B) = \sum_i P(A_i)P(B|A_i).$$

b. *The use of the total probability theorem in determining the minority fraction of qualified employees in a labor market*

In order to assess whether an employer is recruiting and hiring in a non-discriminatory fashion, one can compare the race-sex composition of its hires for several years with the qualified work force in its labor market.[3] When the qualification for a job can be specified in terms of years of education completed or by experience in a similar occupation, the decennial census data can be used to determine the number of qualified workers and the minority fraction in each county or city in the area from which the employer draws its employees. Because employees typically prefer smaller commutes to larger ones, one would expect that persons living in the counties closer to the firm would be more likely to apply for employment than persons living further away from the plant. We can use this fact and the Total Probability Theorem to determine the probability a qualified applicant belongs to a minority group, i.e., the minority proportion of qualified workers in the relevant labor market. We shall denote the k counties (or other areas) from which job applicants to a firm come by A_1, $A_2, \ldots A_k$; the size of the qualified labor force in the ith area by L_i; and the fraction of each county's qualified labor force that is black by b_i, $i = 1 \ldots, k$.

Let q_i denote the probability an applicant resides in the ith area (A_i), i.e., $q_i = P(A_i)$. (In practice q_i can be determined from residence data on a large number of applicants who have applied for the job in recent years.) Assuming that the recruiting process is fair, if an applicant comes from area A_i, then the probability that applicant is a black is b_i. Then the probability of the event B, an applicant is black (the proportion of qualified workers in the firm's labor market who are black), is given by

$$(2.12) \qquad P(B) = \sum_{i=1}^{k} P(A_i)P(B|A_i) = \sum_{i=1}^{k} q_i b_i.$$

Formula (2.12) calculates the total probability that an applicant is black as the sum over all areas that an applicant comes from that area and is black. Since the conditional probabilities, b_i, that a qualified resident of the ith area is black are often available from census data, the formula is easily applied.

We next show how formula (2.12) was used to determine the minority fraction of the relevant labor pool in *Markey v. Tenneco Oil Co.*[4] The case involved a charge of discrimination in hiring for the job of laborer in the plant. The plaintiff argued that since blacks formed 59.4% of all laborers in the *entire* New Orleans metropolitan area, they should form about 59.4% of Tenneco's new hires. Because the plant site was in St. Bernard parish (county), which is part of the New Orleans metropolitan area, but is not readily accessible by public transportation from the city of New Orleans, the firm introduced the calculation in Table 2.1 below showing that formula (2.12) yields a black proportion of 42.83% among laborers who would apply for jobs. Notice that the weights, q_i, were obtained from residence data of actual applicants not from the residence of employees, which might reflect past hiring practices and residential moves made after a person was hired, rather than the commuting patterns and preferences of people interested in working at the plant.

As blacks formed 48.3% of all hires during the 1970–75 period at issue, the court found that Tenneco did not discriminate in hiring, since this percentage exceeded the expected minority fraction of the appropriate labor pool. Related comparisons are presented in Chapter 4.

c. Bayes' theorem and identification evidence

There is another question that lawyers often face, namely, given certain evidence (the event B), what is the probability that a particular suspect committed the crime (the event A)? Thus, we desire the *conditional* probability $P(A|B)$ *not* the probability $P(A)$, as evidence has changed the origi-

TABLE 2.1.   Calculation of the Probability an Applicant is Black in *Markey v. Tenneco*

Parish	Black Percentage of Laborers (b_i)	Percent of All Applicants From the Parish (q_i)	Contribution to (2.12)
Jefferson	49.29	7.10	3.50
Orleans	71.10	43.10	30.64
St. Bernard	15.21	47.16	7.17
St. Tammany	57.54	2.64	1.52
		Total	42.83

Source: 32 FEP Cases (E.D. La. 1982) 145 at 147.
Note: While b_i and q_i are fractions in formula (2.12), the court used percentages which are 100 times the fraction. Thus, the probability an applicant for the position of laborer is black is .4283.

nal probabilities we had for the possible suspects. Let us reconsider the problem in which we obtained the probability that a person was at least 6′ tall from the conditional probabilities for each sex. Suppose you are now told that a suspect was over 6′ tall, can you make a judgement about the sex of the suspect?

We now desire to calculate the conditional probability

$$P(A|B) = \frac{P(A \cap B)}{P(B)}.$$

Earlier we computed $P(B)$ by the total probability formula and obtained its value of .175. In the course of that calculation we also found

$$P(A \cap B) = P(A)\, P(B|A) = (.5)\,(.25) = .125,$$

so

$$P(A|B) = \frac{.125}{.175} = \frac{5}{7} = .7143.$$

Thus, *given* the fact that the suspect was over 6′ tall, the chance that the suspect is a male is 71%. Notice that *before* we had the knowledge that the suspect was over 6′, we would have said that there was only a 50% chance the suspect was a male. The type of calculation made here is an example of Bayes' Theorem. It is used to ascertain how our original (unconditional) probabilities change after other events are observed and is useful in assessing identification evidence and in evaluating the effect of missing evidence. More involved applications are presented in Chapter 12.

Problems

1. Let A and B be exclusive events. Find $P(A|B)$ and $P(B|A)$.

2. For the same three events, A, B, and C considered in problem 1 of Section 2.2, defined on the sample space for tossing two dice, find
    (a) $P(C|A)$
    (b) $P(C|B)$
    (c) $P(B|A)$
    (d) $P(B|C)$
    (e) $P(A|C)$

3. For any two events A and B, can $P(A|B) = P(B|A)$? Is it *always* true that $P(A|B) = P(B|A)$? *Hint*: Think of examples from the sample spaces we used as illustrations.

4. Your absent-minded professor has 12 socks, all mixed up in a drawer. Two are black, four are tan and six are white. Every morning he reaches randomly into the drawer and selects his socks for the day. What are the probabilities that
    (a) Both socks he draws are tan?
    (b) He draws a matching pair?

5. The adult population of a certain city is made up of white, black and Mexican-Americans in the following proportions: 50%, 30%, 20%. The Board of Education tells you that 80% of the whites have a high school degree (or more) but that only 60% of the blacks and 30% of the Mexicans do. What fraction of the adults in the city have graduated from high school?

Answers to Selected Problems

1. If A and B are exclusive events, $P(A|B) = 0$, as once one of two *exclusive* events occurs, the other cannot occur.

3. If A and B are exclusive, $P(A|B) = P(B|A) = 0$, however, the result is not always true. For example, if

A = the sum of 2 die is 7 and B = the sum of 2 die is 7 or 11, then $P(B|A)$ = 1, as B contains A; i.e., if A occurs B automatically occurs too. On the other hand, $P(A|B)$ = 6/8 = .75.

4. (a) $4/12 \cdot 3/11 = 1/11$
   (b) $1/6 \cdot 1/11 + 1/11 + 1/2 \cdot 5/11 = 1/3$

5. Use the Total Probability Theorem:
   $P(B)$ = (.5)(.8) + (.3)(.6) + (.2)(.3) = .64

4. Random Variables

Almost all the examples we have discussed involved experiments which led to numerical data, e.g., the value of the sum of two fair dice, the average income of males and females in the sample taken by the Census Bureau and the number of heads occurring in repeated tosses of a coin. Often we are not really concerned with the particular simple event that occurred, rather our focus is on a composite event. When two dice are tossed, we were interested in whether the sum was 7 or 11, i.e., what were our chances of winning. By enumerating the sample space of 36 equally likely simple events and realizing that the event 7 or 11 was composed of 8 of these 36 simple events, we found that our probability of winning was 8/36 = 2/9. Rather than keeping the entire sample space in our mind, it is easier to think in terms of the event or events of major interest, e.g., winning or losing. Thus, we might summarize the experiment by defining a function, W, of the possible outcomes of the experiment as follows:

W = 1 whenever one of the eight simple events
(1, 6), (2, 5), (3, 4), (4, 3), (5, 2), (6, 1),
(5, 6), (6, 5) occur

and

W = 0, when any *other* simple event occurs.

Notice that W is defined by assigning a value (in our case 1 or 0) to each simple outcome, and the probability that W takes *each of these values* in any realization of the basic experiment is simply the sum of the probabilities of the simple events for which W is assigned that value. Thus, we can summarize our variable of interest (winning) by noting the values W can assume, 0 (lose) and 1 (win) and their corresponding probabilities of occurrence, 7/9^{ths} and 2/9^{ths}. We express this information in symbols as $P(W = 1) = 2/9$ and $P(W = 0) = 7/9$.

Any function, such as W, defined on a sample space is called a *random variable* because the value it will have depends on the outcome of an experiment with more than one possible simple outcome.

Random variables, such as W, which can take on only two possible values are called simple *binomial* variables. Other such random variables are:

(1) The outcome of a toss of a coin (heads = 1, tails = 0).

(2) Whether a randomly selected adult is unemployed (1) or not (0).

(3) You win (1) a lottery in which 10,000 tickets were sold and you purchased two tickets.

The simple binomial variable is *characterized* by the fact that it takes on only two possible values, usually 0 and 1. The probability, p, that it equals 1 varies with the particular application. In the first example (coin tossing) $p = .5$; in the second p is usually in the range .04 to .10; while in the lottery example p is only .0002.

More generally, we will be concerned with random variables that take on many possible values, $x_1, x_2, ..., x_n$, say, with corresponding probabilities, $p_1, p_2, ..., p_n$. For example, the random variable, S, the sum of the showing faces of two die, can take on the values

$$2, 3, 4, ... 11, 12.$$

By looking at the simple events corresponding to each of values $x_j = j$ ($j = 2, ..., 12$), we can determine the probabilities, p_j, of their occurrence. From the sample space, we see that $S = 2$ only when (1, 1) occurs so that $p_2 = 1/36$. Similarly, $S = 3$ when either (1, 2) or (2, 1) occurs so $p_3 = 2/36$.

The set of possible values ($x_1, x_2, ..., x_n$) of a random variable and their probabilities $p_1, ... p_n$ of occurrence defines the *probability distribution* of the *random variable*. Sometimes p_j is written $p(x_j)$, but it always means $P(S = x_j)$, the probability that the random variable S equals x_j. The reader should verify that the sum, S, of two die has the probability distribution given in Table 2.2.

Another random variable of interest is the number of successes in several trials, say three when there is probability p of success on each one. This is a generalization of the coin-tossing problem where now the probability of a head occurring on each toss is p rather than 1/2. The simple

TABLE 2.2.   Probability Distribution of S, the Sum of Two Die

Values (x)	2	3	4	5	6	7	8	9	10	11	12
Probabilities $p(x)$	$\frac{1}{36}$	$\frac{2}{36}$	$\frac{3}{36}$	$\frac{4}{36}$	$\frac{5}{36}$	$\frac{6}{36}$	$\frac{5}{36}$	$\frac{4}{36}$	$\frac{3}{36}$	$\frac{2}{36}$	$\frac{1}{36}$

events, their probabilities and the probability distribution of S are given in Table 2.3.

The probability of the simple event (TTT) or *no* heads ($S = \emptyset$) is the probability of tail $(1 - p)$ occurring on each toss, i.e., $(1 - p)^3$, because the outcome of each of the three tosses is *independent* of the others.

There are three simple events, (HTT), (THT) and (TTH) which correspond to S having the value 1 (one head occurs). As the results of the three tosses are independent, the probability that the event (HTT) occurs is

the probability a head occurs on the first toss, *i.e., p,*

times

the probability a tail occurs on the second toss or $(1 - p)$

times

the probability a tail occurs on the third toss or $(1 - p)$.

Hence, the probability of the event (HTT) is $p(1 - p)^2$. Similarly, the reader can verify that each of the simple events (THT) and (TTH) also have probability $p(1 - p)^2$, so the probability that exactly one head occurs is

$$p(1 - p)^2 + p(1 - p)^2 + p(1 - p)^2 = 3p(1 - p)^2.$$

TABLE 2.3.   Determination of the Probability Distribution of S, the Number of Heads in Three Tosses of a Coin

Value (x)	Simple Events	Probability of the Simple Events	$P(S = x)$
0	(TTT)	$(1 - p)^3$	$(1 - p)^3$
1	(HTT), (THT), (TTH)	$p(1 - p)^2, p(1 - p)^2, p(1 - p)^2$	$3p(1 - p)^2$
2	(HHT) (HTH) (THH)	$p^2(1 - p), p^2(1 - p), p^2(1 - p)$	$3p^2(1 - p)$
3	(HHH)	p^3	p^3

Note: Recall that we realized that each simple event with the *same* number of heads occurring had the same probability.

The fact that all the simple events with *one* head have the same probability results from the product rule (2.3), since each toss resulting in a head contributes a factor p to the product. Similarly, each toss resulting in a tail contributes a factor $1 - p$. In general, the probability of any *one simple event with k heads* occurring in n tosses is

$$p^k(1 - p)^{n-k},$$

where k is the number of heads and $n - k$ the number of tails in the n tosses. (The probability that the variable S equals k is this probability *times* the number of simple events with exactly k heads, which we discuss later in Section 5.) The right hand column in Table 2.3 presents the probability distribution of the number, S, of heads in three tosses.

By substituting the appropriate value of p, we obtain the probability of obtaining 0, 1, 2 or 3 heads in three tosses of the coin. These probabilities change with p. Indeed, the larger p is, the greater the probability is of obtaining three heads. This can be seen in Table 2.4, which presents the probability distribution of S for various values of p.

Although the number, k, of possible values of a random variable may be quite large, since the probabilities of all the simple events sum to 1 and the random variable can assign each simple event to only one of its possible values, the sum of all the $p(x)$ is 1, i.e.,

$$\sum p(x) = 1,$$

where x ranges over all its possible values. At times, it will be convenient to let $k = \infty$ (infinity) when we may not be able to fix in advance a greatest possible value for k, although we know that the probability of the occurrence of extremely large values (x) will be minute. Example of such *random variables* might be

(a) the number of sales a salesperson makes in a year;

TABLE 2.4. Probability Distribution of the Number of Heads in Three Tosses of a Coin as a Function of p

Value (x) of S	p					
	.05	.10	.25	.50	.75	.9
0	.8574	.7290	.4219	.125	.0156	.0010
1	.1354	.2430	.4219	.375	.1406	.0270
2	.0071	.0270	.1406	.375	.4219	.2430
3	.0001	.0010	.0156	.125	.4219	.7290

(b) the size (in dollars) of the Federal budget or deficit;
(c) the number of cars produced in the world next year.

Random variables whose possible values (x) can be indexed by integers are called *discrete*. The sum, S, of two dice is discrete as is the variable S^2, the square of the sum. S takes on the possible values 2, 3, ..., 12, while S^2 can assume 4, 9, ..., 144.

We now turn to ways of picturing and summarizing the probability distribution of a random variable which are analogous to the methods used to describe data. The similarity is *not* coincidental, as it will often be convenient to consider data as being a sample of many independent realizations of the same random variable (i.e., repeating an experiment many times and recording the observed value of the random variable).

The simplest picture of the probability distribution of the variable R, is to make a graph which represents $p(x)$ as a line of height $p(x)$ over x. A more useful representation, for integer valued random variables, is the *probability histogram*. If we think of the event $R = x$ as the interval $(x - 1/2, x + 1/2)$, then the *rectangle* with height $p(x)$ has area $p(x)$ so that the area over an interval represents the probability that the random variable takes on a value in that interval. In Figure 2.8 we present the probability histograms for the number, S, of heads in tossing a coin three times when $p = .35, .50$ and $.65$. Notice that the histogram shows how the probability of obtaining a large number of heads increases as p increases.

5. The Summary Measures of a Probability Distribution or Random Variable

We have defined the probability distribution of a random variable by listing the possible values, x_1, ..., x_n, the random variable can assume with their respective probabilities, $p_i = p(x_i)$, of occurrence. When thinking about a random phenomenon it is helpful to have an idea of what a *typical* outcome might be as well as a measure of variation about that outcome.

Before proceeding to a general definition let us obtain the typical or expected value of a general binomial distribution, e.g., the number of heads occurring in n tosses of a coin when the probability of a coin coming up heads is p. Suppose, $p = 1/2$ and we flip the coin 10 times. How many heads do you expect to occur? Of course you said five! If we flip the coin 100 times, how many heads do you expect to occur in the 100 tosses?

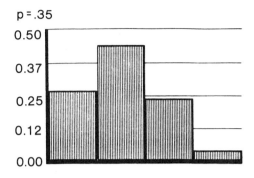

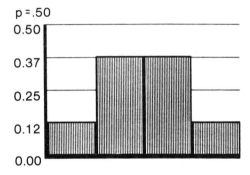

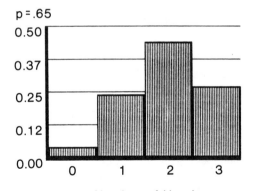

Number of Heads

FIGURE 2.8. Probability histograms of the distribution of the number of heads in three tosses of a coin where the probability p of a head on any toss equals .25, .50 and .75, respectively. Notice how the histogram shifts to the right (gives more probability to the larger possible values) as p increases.

Now, you said 50. Indeed you correctly reasoned that each toss has probability 1/2 of coming up heads, so in n tosses we would expect about half $(n/2)$ of them to be heads.

Similarly, if you learned that the coin had a probability, p, of coming up a head of .7, say, you would expect around 70 heads to occur in 100 tosses and $(.7)n$ heads to occur in n tosses. In general, when we count the number of times an event, with probability p of occurring in any one experiment, occurs in a sequence of n independent repetitions of that experiment, we expect the count to be near np.

In order to define the *expected value* or *mean* of a random variable, we think of repeating the experiment a very large number (N) times. If we take the *average* of the N observed values of the random variable, it should be very close to what we would define as the *theoretical* mean of the random variable or its distribution. This is consistent with the frequency notion of probability, i.e., the definition of the probability of an event as the proportion of times it occurs in a long sequence of independent repetitions. Hence, the *mean* of a random variable is the number that the average of the results of a long series of independent repetitions will approach.

Using these ideas let us obtain the theoretical mean of the random variable, S, the number of heads in three tosses of a fair $(p = .5)$ coin. Since the probability of obtaining 0 heads in three tosses is .125, in 1000 repetitions of tossing the coin three times we expect 0 heads to occur is $Np = 1000 \times .125 = 125$ times.

Similarly, we expect to observe one head among the three tosses in about $1000(.375) = 375$ of the 1000 repetitions, two heads in $1000(.375) = 375$ and three heads in $1000(.125) = 125$ of the 1000 repetitions. Thus, the average of our large sample should be about

$$(2.13) \quad \frac{(125 \times 0) + (375 \times 1) + (375 \times 2) + (125 \times 3)}{1000} = \frac{1500}{1000} = 1.5.$$

This value, 1.5, also agrees with our previous intuition that the expected number of heads in three tosses of a fair coin should be $np = 3 \cdot 1/2 = 1.5$.

By dividing the expected number of times each possible value (x) of the random variable occurs by $N(1000)$, formula (2.13) can be expressed as

$$(2.14) \quad \left(\frac{125}{1000} \times 0\right) + \left(\frac{375}{1000} \times 1\right) + \left(\frac{375}{1000} \times 2\right) + \left(\frac{125}{1000} \times 3\right) = 1.5,$$

where the first part of each term is the *probability that x occurs* and the second is *x*, where *x* ranges over all possible values of the random variable. Thus, the expected value or mean of the random variable is *a weighted average* of the possible values (*x*'s) where the weight given each possible value (*x*) is its probability of occurrence, $p(x)$. This interpretation enables us to define the *mean* or *expected* value, μ, of a discrete random variable by

(2.15) $$\mu = \sum_x p(x)x.$$

Formula (2.15) makes sense when we think of the mean representing a typical observation or realization of the random variable. Those values (*x*) with larger probabilities, $p(x)$, of occurring receive *more* weight in the computation of the mean, μ.

Just as we needed to describe the spread or variation of a data set about its mean, it is useful to measure the amount by which a random variable is spread about its mean μ. Since the variance, s^2, of a data set essentially is the *average* squared distance of the observations from their average $\bar{x}$, it is reasonable to define the variance σ^2, of a random variable as the *expected squared distance* of the outcome of a random variable X from its mean μ. Since the squared distance of an outcome, x and μ is $(x - \mu)^2$, the expected squared distance is

(2.16) $$\sigma^2 = \sum_x p(x)(x - \mu)^2.$$

Notice that the squared distance $(x - \mu)^2$ has the same probability of occurring as x has, i.e., $p(x)$. Formula (2.16) shows that the variance, σ^2, is a weighted average of the squared distances between the possible values x of the random variable, X, and its mean μ, where the weights are the probabilities, $p(x)$. The standard deviation of a random variable is defined as the square root (the positive one) of the variance and is denoted by σ. The standard deviation of the random variable will be measured in units of the same magnitude as the possible outcomes analogous to the sample standard deviation, s. Again, in a large number, N, of observations on the random variable, X, we expect each possible value, x, to occur about $Np(x)$ times, and the sample variance, s^2, calculated from these N observations will be near σ^2. By repeating the same type of calculation we performed in obtaining the mean, μ, for the coin tossing random variable, one can show that the variance, σ^2, of the probability distribution is the *expected* value of the sample variance, s^2, of a large number of observations of the random variable.

TABLE 2.5.   Calculation of the Mean and Variance of the Number of Heads in Three Tosses of a Coin with $p = .25$

(1)	(2)	(3)	(4)	(5)	(6)
x	$p(x)$	$xp(x)$	$(x - \mu)$	$(x - \mu)^2$	$p(x)(x - \mu)^2$
0	.4219	0	$-.75$	.5625	.2373
1	.4219	.4219	.25	.0625	.0264
2	.1406	.2812	1.25	1.5625	.2197
3	.0156	.0468	2.25	5.0625	.0790
Total		$.7499 = .75 = \mu$			$.5624 = \sigma^2$

$\mu = \Sigma \, xp(x) = .75$ (the sum of the third column)
$\sigma^2 = \Sigma \, p(x)(x - \mu)^2 = $ sum of column 6 $= .5624$

To illustrate the calculation of the mean, μ, and variance, σ^2, of a random variable, or equivalently its probability distribution, we calculate μ and σ^2 for the number, S, of heads in three tosses of a coin, with probability $p = .25$ of success on each toss. The first two columns of Table 2.5 give the possible values of x and their probabilities, $p(x)$. Their contributions $xp(x)$ to the mean, μ, are given in column 3.

The sum of column 3 is μ. In our example we obtain .7499, which essentially equals .75. (The difference is due to using only four decimal places for the probabilities $p(x)$.) The fourth column gives the values of $(x - \mu)$ which are obtained by subtracting .75 from each x. The squares, $(x - \mu)^2$, are given in column 5, and the contributions $p(x) (x - \mu)^2$ of each x to σ^2 are obtained by multiplying each $(x - \mu)^2$ by $p(x)$ (from column 2). These are placed in column 6 and their sum is σ^2, which in our example is .5624.

Finally, the *standard deviation* of the random variable or distribution is the *square root* of its variance, σ^2, and is denoted by σ. The standard deviation of the distribution plays the same role as a summary measure of the expected variability of observations from the random variable as the sample standard deviation, s, has in summarizing the variability of a set of data. In our coin tossing example, $\sigma = .5624 = .75$. The fact that it agrees with the mean, μ, in this example is purely a coincidence.

For many data sets, the bulk of the data lies within two standard deviations of the mean. Similarly, for many random variables, especially those whose values, x, at or near the mean have the largest probabilities, $p(x)$, the probability of observing a value, k, within two standard deviations

(2σ) of the mean (μ), is a .9 or more. Symbolically this is written

$$P(|X - \mu| \le 2\sigma) \ge .9$$

and means that the probability that an *observed value* of the random variable X is between $\mu - 2\sigma$ and $\mu + 2\sigma$ is at least .9.

Note. The symbols $\le$ and $\ge$ stand for less than or equal to and greater than or equal to, respectively.

So far we have discussed the distribution of one random variable, however, we are also concerned with the relationship between random variables. The *joint distribution* of two random variables X and Y that have possible outcomes x_i, $i = 1, ..., m$ and y_j, $j = 1, ..., n$ with respective probabilities $(p(x_i))$ and $(p(y_j))$ is specified by the probabilities

(2.17) $P(X = x_i, Y = y_j) = p(x_i, y_j),$

that the events ($X = x_i$) and ($Y = y_i$) both occur, i.e., $X = x_i$ and $Y = y_j$. in particular, two random variables are *independent* if

(2.18) $p(x_i, y_j) = p(x_i)\,p(y_j)$ for all i and j.

Formula (2.18) is the analog of the multiplication rule for independent events and is the mathematical formulation of our intuitive idea that two random variables are independent if knowledge about the particular value one of them, say X, has does *not* affect the outcome of the other variable, Y. Some examples of *independent* random variables are:

(1) The result of the first and second toss of a fair coin.
(2) A person winning a state lottery this year and their winning the lottery next year.

Examples of dependent random variables are:

(1) If X denotes whether (1) or not (0) a red card is drawn on the first selection from a deck of 52 cards and Y denotes whether (1) or not (0) a black card is drawn on the second selection, the random variables X and Y are dependent, as knowledge of the color of the card drawn first affects the probabilities of the second draw.
(2) If X is a random variable with value 2, 3 or 4, depending on whether a student had a grade-point average (GPA) of C, B or A in college, and Y is a similar random variable for the student's high school GPA, our expe-

rience shows that X and Y are related and, hence, are statistically dependent.

We will need two basic facts about expected values and variances of sums of random variables:

(1) If X and Y are random variables with means μ_x and μ_y, the expected value of $(X + Y)$ equals $\mu_x + \mu_y$. For example, if the earnings of husbands has a distribution with mean \$25,000 and the earnings of wives has a distribution with mean \$15,000, then the *mean* income of husband-wife families is \$40,000.

(2) If X and Y are *independent* random variables then

(2.19)   variance $(X + Y)$ = variance (X) + variance (Y),

i.e., the variance of the *sum* of *independent* random variables is the *sum* of their variances.

Formula (2.19) is based on the assumption that knowledge of one random variable does not affect the distribution of the other. For example, if X is far from its mean μ_x, Y can vary any amount from its mean, μ_y. On the other hand, if X and Y were *dependent,* e.g., X is the height of a father and Y the height of his son, then X being far greater than its mean implies that Y also is likely to be above its mean so that knowledge of X affects the distribution of Y. Thus, $X + Y$ probably will be further from $\mu_x + \mu_y$ than formula (2.19) indicates due to the *positive* dependence between X and Y. In the case of two independent random variables, the fact that one, say X, exceeds its mean μ_x does *not affect* the probability of Y exceeding its mean.

Problems

1.   Compute the mean μ and variance σ^2 for the number of heads in three tosses of a fair coin with $p = .75$ of a head on each toss. The distribution was given in Table 2.4. Do you notice any similarity between the values of σ^2 for this distribution and that of the distribution when $p = .25$ given in the text? Explain.

2.   You are assigned to manage a modest trust fund for an elderly widow. You decide to hire a portfolio manager or bank trust officer to assist you and you interview three firms. They report to you that their average rates of return (after their fees are paid) for the last 20 years were 7.2%, 9.8%

and 5.9%, respectively. Are you making the wisest decision by entrusting the funds to the firm with the 9.8% average rate of return? Explain.

3.* In Chapter 1 we described the use of measures of *relative* inequality. Define the analog of the coefficient of variation for a random variable. For what types of problems would this summary measure be useful?

Answers to Selected Problems

1. $\mu = 3(.75) = 2.25$, $\sigma^2 = .5625$. When a head has probability .75 of occurring, a tail has probability .25. Thus, the two variables (number of heads and number of tails) are complements of one another and the distance that one of them differs from its mean must be minus the distance the other differs from its mean, and the average squared distances of the two variables from their means must be equal.

2. Under the circumstances one should be concerned with the *variability* of the rate of return. If the manager with the highest rate of return also had a significantly greater variability, e.g., returns of -20% to $+30\%$, prudence might suggest accepting a lower average rate to achieve greater safety of the principal.

3. One might use the ratio σ/μ in evaluating portfolio managers as well as the accuracy of tax assessments and appraisals of property (land, art) donated to charity, which are used as the basis of tax deductions.

6. The Binomial Distribution

a. The general binomial model

On several occasions we have been concerned with the number of times a success occurs among several repetitions of the same experiment, e.g., the number of heads in three tosses of a fair coin, the number of times we win the game of tossing two dice in n trials and the number of people out of a sample of 1500 who prefer the incumbent in the next election. If we consider a win in the dice game, or a preference for the incumbent a head or a 1, then all three models are basically the same as coin tossing. We make a (n) of repetitions of an experiment in which the probability of a 1 or head occurring each time is p and count the number, S, of 1's among the n repetitions. Indeed, all experiments which are composed of n independent repetitions of a single experiment which has only *two* possible outcomes are called *binomial experiments,* and the distribution of the number, S, of 1's in the n repetitions has a *binomial distribution* which is determined by n and p, the probability of a 1 on each component experiment or trial. We have already seen that the expected number of 1's in a binomial distribution is np, and later we will learn that the variance is $np(1 - p)$.

Let us focus now on the assumptions underlying the binomial model. They are:

(a) The basic experiment consists of n identical trials or replications.

(b) Each trial has two possible outcomes, which are usually denoted by S or 1 (for success) and F or 0 (for failure or nonoccurrence).

(c) The probability p of success on each trial remains the same for all n trials.

(d) The n trials are independent of one another, i.e., the outcome of a trial does not affect the outcome of any other one.

The binomial random variable, S, the number of successes in n trials with probability p of success at each one, can be regarded as the *sum* of n independent simple random variables, X_i, where each X_i has probability p of taking on the value 1, and probability $1 - p$ of a 0. By regarding S as a sum, i.e.,

$$S = X_1 + X_2 + \ldots + X_n,$$

it is intuitively clear that the *expected value* of S should be the sum of the n expected values of X_i. In the binomial model, each X_i has probability p of being a 1, so its expected value, μ, is also p (recall $\mu = p.1 + (1 - p)0 = p$), so the expected value of S is np. Similarly, the *variance*[5] of each simple binomial variable is $p(1 - p)$, and since the component X_i's are *independent,* the variance of S is the sum of the n individual variances or $\sigma^2(S) = np(1 - p)$.

Let us explore the appropriateness of the binomial model in several possible applications. As you read each application ask yourself whether the variable, S, of interest is binomial and whether the four assumptions are valid (or at least approximately).

(1) The number of girls among the next 100 babies born in the United States.

(2) The number of blacks hired by a company which hires 3 persons from 10 qualified applicants, 3 of whom are black.

(3) The number of blacks hired by a company hiring 3 persons from 10,000 qualified applicants, 30% of whom are black.

(4) The number of women among a venire (list of persons who may be selected for jury duty) in a large city.

(5) The number of employees of a pesticide producer who develop cancer.

The first example clearly fits the binomial model, as there is a constant probability of about .5 that the sex of a baby is female and the sex of one baby has no influence on that of the others.

In the second example, the probability that a black is the first hire is 3/10 (assuming all qualified applicants have the same chance of being successful), however, the probability of the second hire being black is 2/9 if the first hire is black and 3/9 if the first hire is not. Thus, the consecutive selections are *dependent* so the independence assumption is violated. Thinking in terms of the representation

$$S = X_1 + X_2 + X_3,$$

where X_i is a 1 when the ith selection is black, we say that the random variables X_1, X_2 and X_3 are *dependent*.

In the third example, there still is a *very slight* dependence among the selections, however, the *change* in the probability of selecting a black is so small that for practical purposes we can use the binomial model with $n = 3$ and $p = .3$. Similarly, the binomial applies to the fourth example, provided that the size of the venire is small compared to the total pool of eligible jurors. If we assume that each worker has the same chance, p, of developing cancer, then the total number of such workers has a binomial distribution with parameters n, the number of employees and p. In this example we need to make sure that the workers were exposed to the pesticide for about the same in order to ensure that they all have the same probability, p, of getting the disease.

So far we have seen that the mean and variance of S are determined by the *parameters* n and p, and now we obtain the entire distribution of S, i.e., the probabilities p or $p(k)$ of the event $P(S = k)$, i.e., the probability that there are exactly k successes among the n independent trials.

The general formula can be developed by observing that when we calculated the probabilities of the eight simple events in the sample space of three tosses of a possibly biased coin, i.e., the probability of a head was given by p, which was not necessarily equal to 1/2, the probability only depended on the *number* of heads occurring in the three tosses. Thus, the three simple events

$$(H, T, T) \qquad (T, H, T) \text{ and } (T, T, H)$$

all had probability $p(1 - p)^2$ i.e.,

$$p^{(\text{number of heads})} \times (1 - p)^{(\text{number of tails})}.$$

This result is true in general, as any simple event with k successes among the n trials has probability

$$p^{(\text{number of successes})} \cdot (1 - p)^{n \text{ minus the number of success}}$$

or

$$p^k(1 - p)^{n-k}.$$

Of course there are many simple outcomes that have exactly k successes, just as we noted that three simple outcomes corresponded to exactly one head occurring in three tosses of a coin. We need to count the *number* of ways one can select k trials out of the n possibilities, for the successes. The other trials will be those on which a failure occurs. The formula[6] for the number of ways to select k objects out of a pool of n is denoted by

(2.20) $$\binom{n}{k}$$

and equals

$$\frac{n!}{(n - k)!k!},$$

where $n! = n \cdot (n - 1)(n - 2) \dots 1$. Thus the probability that there are exactly k successes in n trials is

(2.21) $$P(S = k) = \binom{n}{k} p^k(1 - p)^{n-k}.$$

For small values of n and k, the computation of (2.20) and $P(S = k)$ is relatively easy. Fortunately, there are good approximations when n is large. Before proceeding with our discussion of binomial model, we illustrate some calculations.

Example 2.5.   Find $\binom{5}{2}$.

Here $n = 5$ and $k = 2$, so

$$\binom{5}{2} = \frac{5!}{3!\,2!} = \frac{5 \cdot 4 \cdot 3!}{3!\,2} = 10.$$

Notice that one can simplify the calculation by cancelling. This is always possible, and one should use the *larger* of $k!$ and $(n - k)!$ to cancel out a part of the numerator $n!$.

Example 2.6. Find $\binom{10}{1}$.

Here $n = 10$ and $k = 1$ so

$$\binom{10}{1} = \frac{10!}{9!\,1!} = \frac{10 \cdot 9!}{9!\,1} = \frac{10}{1} = 1.$$

Example 2.7. Find $\binom{5}{5}$.

Here we need to mention a convention $0! = 1$ so that

$$\binom{5}{5} = \frac{5!}{0!\,5!} = 1.$$

Notice that the answer 1 makes sense, as there is only one way to select all five objects from a total of five.

To see the effect the probability, p, of success on any one trial has on the entire distribution, the distribution of the number of successes in 10 trials for various value of p is given in Table 2.6.

Notice that the expected number of successes $np = 10p$ and standard deviation $\sqrt{np(1 - p)} = \sqrt{10p(1 - p)}$ are given, so the reader can see which deviations from the expected value or mean of the distribution are likely and which ones are unlikely.

From Table 2.6 we realize that as p increases, the distribution places more probability on the higher possible values 8, 9 and 10. When $p = .5$, the distribution is symmetric, i.e., the chance that we obtain *one* success less than the expected value (5) (i.e., 4) equals the probability of obtaining *one more* (i.e., 6) success than expected. Similarly, the chance of obtaining any number of successes less than expected equals the probability of obtaining the same number more than expected. This only occurs for the binomial variable when $p = .5$, as an examination of Table 2.6 shows.

b. Application of the binomial distribution to the issue of jury discrimination

We now give a brief introduction to the use of the binomial model in the analysis of data on the composition of jury panels or venires, to assess whether blacks and other groups are discriminated against. The earliest jury discrimination cases dealt with situations where blacks had been

TABLE 2.6.   The Binomial Distribution for the Number of Successes in 10 Trials
for Various Values of the Probability, p, of Successes on Each Trial

$p =$	.1	.2	.3	.4	.5	.6	.9
Number (k) of successes							
0	.3487	.1074	.0282	.0060	.0010	.0001	.0000
1	.3474	.2684	.1211	.0403	.0098	.0016	.0000
2	.1937	.3020	.2335	.1209	.0439	.0106	.0000
3	.0574	.2013	.2668	.2150	.1172	.0425	.0000
4	.0112	.0881	.2001	.2508	.2051	.1115	.0001
5	.0015	.0264	.1029	.2007	.2461	.2007	.0015
6	.0001	.0055	.0368	.1115	.2051	.2508	.0112
7	.0000	.0008	.0090	.0425	.1172	.2150	.0574
8	.0000	.0001	.0014	.0106	.0439	.1209	.1937
9	.0000	.0000	.0001	.0016	.0098	.0403	.3474
10	.0000	.0000	.0000	.0001	.0010	.0060	.3487
Expected	1.0	2.0	3.0	4.0	5.0	6.0	9.0
Std. Dev.	.9487	1.2649	1.4491	1.5492	1.5811	1.5492	.9487

Note: The probability of obtaining k successes when $p = .6$ *equals* that of obtaining $10 - k$ successes when $p = .4$, since the event of k successes with $p = .6$ is *equivalent* to the event of $10 - 1$ failures when we *count* failures as each has probability .4 $(1 - .6)$ of occurring on each trial. This is why the standard deviation for $p = .1(.4)$ agree with those for $p = .9(.6)$.

systematically excluded from jury duty for many years, e.g., *Hill v. Texas* 316 U.S. 400 (1942) and *Norris v. Alabama* 244 U.S. 587 (1935). More recent cases have dealt with the issue of whether the proportion of blacks and other groups on juries or venires reflect their proportion in the community at large since juries should be a cross section[7] of the community.

Since several panels or venires of jurors typically form a small fraction of the entire adult population of the city or county, we realize that any person chosen to serve on the venire has probability, p, the minority fraction of the eligible population. This fraction can be obtained from census data on adults over 21 or between 21 and 65 (if elderly persons are usually excused from jury duty). If blacks form 20% of the eligible population, then the probability that any one juror is black would be .2, and the number of blacks on a jury of size 12 has a binomial distribution with $n = 12$ and $p = .2$. Notice that the binomial model is based on the assumption that each juror's race is independent of the race of the other jurors, i.e., each juror is selected by a system equivalent to selecting one name out of a large box with all the names of eligible jurors in it. In this application this assumption is quite reasonable. Indeed, the expression jury "wheel" suggests that juror selection is analogous to a spin of a roulette wheel. In a fair game, the number occurring on one spin does not affect the result of the succeeding spins.

In Chapter 4, we present a detailed discussion of the use of the binomial model in discrimination cases. For now we illustrate its use on data from *Turner v. Fouche* 396 U.S. 346 (1970). The black residents of Taliafero County, Georgia challenged the methods used to select school board and grand jury members, where 60% of the population of the county was black and only 6 of the 23 grand jury members were black. Assuming that each member had a probability of .6 of being a black, we need to calculate the probability that out of 23 selections six or fewer were black. Without much calculation we know that under the binomial model ($n = 23, p = .6$) we expect $np = 13.8$ black members. Since the standard deviation $\sqrt{np(1 - p)}$ of this binomial variable is 2.35, we realize that the difference between the actual number (6) of blacks and their expected number (13.8) equals 7.8, which is more than two standard deviations ($2 \times 2.35 = 4.7$) from the expected number, suggesting that the outcome is not a likely one. The exact probability of observing six or fewer successes for this binomial distribution is .0017, which is less than one in 500. It indicates that it is very unlikely that the jury selection process was a random choice from the county's population, so the county had the burden of explaining why so few blacks were selected. Typically, it is difficult to justify such a large underrepresentation (here blacks received less than half their expected number of jury assignments).

It should be emphasized that we computed the probability of obtaining six or fewer black jurors rather than the probability of obtaining exactly six jurors, because we certainly would have inferred discrimination was likely to be present had fewer than six jurors been black if we were willing to infer this when six blacks served on the grand jury.

Thus, before accusing the county of discrimination, the probability of observing the actual data (number of minority jurors) or even more convincing data (fewer minorities) calculated under the assumption that a proper selection process was operating should be small. Such an outcome leads us to conclude that the actual selection process differed from a fair one and operated against the interests of the black population.

Problem

Suppose you were trying to defend Taliafero County. How could you attempt to make the evidence presented above less convincing?

Discussion of the Problem

One possible way to mitigate the evidence is to demonstrate the original value of $p = .6$ was too high. For example, you might go to the census data and exclude people under 18 from the calculation had they been included. Also, you might be able to justify excluding a portion of women in the child-bearing and child-rearing ages. Could any other requirements be justified, e.g., should jurors possess a minimum amount of education, not have a criminal record, etc.? In order to prevail along these lines, one would need to justify reducing the black fraction of eligible voters from .6 to .45 or less.

c.   Application of the binomial model to DeMere's problem

At the beginning of the chapter we described a problem which inspired the development of probability. The first part asked for the probability of the event A that *at least one* 6 would occur in four independent tosses of a fair die. This event is the probability that a binomial variable with parameters $n = 4$ and $p = 1/6$ takes on a value *greater* than 0. It is easier to calculate the *probability* of the *complementary* event, that *no* 6 occurs in four throws. From formula (2.21) this is

$$\binom{4}{0} \left(\frac{1}{6}\right)^0 \left(\frac{5}{6}\right)^4 = .482$$

so the probability of A happening is $1 - .482 = .518$. Thus, the nobleman did make money when he accepted an even money bet.

The second part asked why, betting on the event B, at least one double 6 occurs in 24 independent throws of a *pair* of fair dice. Again, the event concerns the outcome of a binomial variable with $n = 24$ and $p = 1/36$ (only one of the 36 possible simple events was a double 6). It is easier to calculate $P(\bar{B})$, the probability that no double 6 occurs in 24 tosses or

$$P(\bar{B}) = \binom{24}{0} \left(\frac{1}{36}\right)^0 \left(\frac{35}{36}\right)^{24} = .5086.$$

Hence, the probability of winning a bet that event B occurs is .4914, which is less than .5 but not much less. Thus, the nobleman must have made a substantial number of bets to notice that it was unfavorable.

7. The Hypergeometric Model

a. Basic concepts

In our discussion of the binomial model we emphasized two basic assumptions: (1) the probability of a success remains the same for all n independent repetitions, and (2) the outcome of one trial does not affect (is *independent* of) the outcome of the others. We have seen two examples, drawing cards randomly from a deck and hiring employees from a small pool of qualified candidates, where the outcome of the first trial changes the probability of success on the next trial. In order to account for the dependence among the outcomes of the repetitions, we need a new model for the situation where we select n items from a set of N items of which n_1 items are of one type (a's) and $n_2 = N - n_1$ are of a different type (b's). The number, S, of a items that are among the n randomly selected from the total pool of size N is a random variable with a *hypergeometric* distribution.

The exact formula for the distribution of the random variable S is derived by noting that we have $\binom{N}{n}$ ways of selecting n items from the set of N just as we had $\binom{n}{k}$ ways of selecting k trials out of the n trials for the successes in the binomial model. In order to obtain exactly k type a items and $n - k$ type b items among the n selected, we may choose any k of the n_1 type a's along with any $n - k$ of the n_2 type b items. There are $\binom{n_1}{k}$ ways of selecting k type a's from the total of n_1 and $\binom{n_2}{n-k}$ ways of selecting the remaining $n - k$ objects in our sample from the n_2 type b items. Since each set of k type a's could be selected in conjunction with any of the sets of $n - k$ type b's, there are

$$\binom{n_1}{k} \cdot \binom{n_2}{n-k}$$

possible ways for the total sample of n items to contain k type a members. Since the probability that $S = k$ is

$$\frac{\text{the number of ways the event, } S = k, \text{ can occur}}{\text{number of ways we can select any } n \text{ items from the total of } N}$$

we have,

$$(2.22) \qquad P(S = k) = \frac{\binom{n_1}{k} \cdot \binom{n_2}{n - k}}{\binom{N}{n}},$$

where k usually ranges from 0 to the smaller of n_1 and n.[8]

Examples of the Hypergeometric Distribution

1. Suppose a jar contains 5 red and 5 blue marbles. If 2 marbles are drawn at random, e.g., if a person is blindfolded and then selects the 2 marbles, what is the probability that both balls are of different colors?

  In this application both n_1 and n_2 are 5, so $N = 10$, while $n = 2$. The event that one marble of each color is drawn means that S, the number of red marbles drawn, is 1. If $k = 1$, then $n - k = 2 - 1 = 1$. Substituting in formula (2.22) yields

$$P(S = 1) = \frac{\binom{5}{1} \binom{5}{1}}{\binom{10}{2}} = \frac{5 \cdot 5}{\frac{(10 \cdot 9)}{2}} = \frac{5}{9} = .555,$$

2. For the above problem, what is the probability distribution of the random variable, S, the number of red balls drawn?

  To find the probability that $S = 0$, no red marbles are drawn, we set $k = 0$ and $n - k = 2 - 0 = 2$ in formula (2.22). Of course, $n_1 = n_2 = 5$ and $N = 10$ as before. Hence,

$$P(S = 0) = \frac{\binom{5}{0} \binom{5}{2}}{\binom{10}{2}} = \frac{\frac{1 \cdot (5 \cdot 4)}{2}}{\frac{(10 \cdot 9)}{2}} = \frac{2}{9} = .222.$$

Similarly, to find the probability that both marbles selected are red, $P(S = 2)$ we set $k = 2$, so $n - k = 2 - 2 = 0$ in formula (2.16) yielding

$$P(S = 2) = \frac{\binom{5}{2} \binom{5}{0}}{\binom{10}{2}} = \frac{\frac{1 \cdot (5 \cdot 4)}{2}}{\frac{(10 \cdot 9)}{2}} = \frac{2}{9} = .222.$$

Thus, we have obtained the probabilities $p(x)$ for the values $x = 0$, 1 and 2 of the number (S) of red marbles drawn. The reader should verify that the mean μ of this random variable equals one.

3.   Suppose that the numbers of red and blue marbles were not equal, e.g., there were $7(n_1)$ red and $3(n_2)$ blue ones. Would the events *no* red marbles drawn and 2 red marbles drawn have the same probability as they did previously?
Intuitively, we now have more red marbles, so the chance of obtaining a blue marble on both drawings should be smaller than before. We obtain the new probability distribution of the number, S^*, of red marbles obtained in two drawings from the jar by substituting $n_1 = 7$, $n_2 = 3$ in formula (2.19). The values of $N(10)$ and $n(2)$ remain as before. Thus,

$$P(S^* = 0) = \frac{\binom{7}{0}\binom{3}{2}}{\binom{10}{2}} = \frac{1 \cdot 3}{\frac{(10 \cdot 9)}{2}} = \frac{1}{15},$$

$$P(S^* = 1) = \frac{\binom{7}{1}\binom{3}{1}}{\binom{10}{2}} = \frac{7 \cdot 3}{\frac{(10 \cdot 9)}{2}} = \frac{7}{15},$$

and

$$P(S^* = 2) = \frac{\binom{7}{2}\binom{3}{0}}{\binom{10}{2}} = \frac{\frac{(7 \cdot 6)}{2 \cdot 1}}{\frac{(10 \cdot 9)}{2}} = \frac{21}{45} = \frac{7}{15}.$$

In order to appreciate the relationship between the hypergeometric and binomial models, note that the *outcome* of the *first* trial among the k selections is a simple binomial and variable with $p = n_1/N$, the fraction of the N balls which are of type a. Before we select any items, what is the probability that the jth selection is an a item? Since we are beginning with the fraction, p, of items and in any sequence of selections of a's and b's each ordering is just as likely to occur as any other, the chance any selection an a item is p. (We saw a special case of this result when we demonstrated that the probability of drawing an ace on the second draw is $1/13$, the same as the probability of drawing an ace on the first draw). This implies that the *expected number* of *a* items among the *n* drawn is *np*, as we are making *n* selections, each of which has probability *p* (before the selection process starts) of being an *a* item. Thus, the *expected number* of *a* items in *n* drawings from a pool of *N* items, *pN* of which are *a*'s, is the *same* as that of a binomial random variable with parameters *n* and *p*. The variance of the hypergeometric variable, *S*, however, is *less* than that of the corresponding *binomial,* because whenever *fewer* than expected number of *a* items are chosen in the early drawings, the *fraction* of *a* items among the items remaining for future selection is *greater* than *p*, so the chance of selecting an *a* item in the later drawings is *greater* than *p*. Similarly, if more *a* items than expected are chosen in the early trials, the fraction of *a*'s among the remaining items is less than *p*. Thus, the changing composition of the pool of possible future selections counterbalance the current deviation from what is expected. This decreases the possible variability of the end result, after all *n* selections have been made, relative to the binomial model. Remember, in the binomial situation the outcome of each selection does not affect the others, so that having fewer than expected successes on the first half of *n* trials does *not* alter the chance of a success on the second half of the trials.

To illustrate the difference, we compare the hypergeometric distribution, S^* with $n_1 = n_2 = 5$ and $n = 2$ with the binomial distribution with the same mean (1) and number ($n = 2$) of repetitions. Thus, $p = 1/2$. This binomial distribution places probability 1/4 on 0 successes, 1/2 on 1 and 1/4 on 2 successes. Notice that the binomial distribution places *less* probability (1/2) on the central (expected) outcome 1 than the correct hypergeometric probability (5/9) and, correspondingly, larger probabilities on the more extreme (0 and 2) outcomes. This implies that the hypergeometric has a smaller variance than the binomial with the same mean. The probability histograms for the two distributions are given in Figure 2.9.

The formulas for the mean, μ, and variance, σ^2, of the general hypergeometric distribution, where $N = n_1 + n_2$ and $p = n_1/N$ are

(2.23) $\mu = np$ and $\sigma^2 = np(1 - p) \dfrac{(N - n)}{N - 1}.$

When we compare the *hypergeometric* to the *binomial* model with the same values of *n* (number of selections or trials) and *p* (probability of success on the first trial), we notice that the *means* are identical but the variance of the hypergeometric model is *smaller* than the binomial variance, $np(1 - p)$, as $(N - n)/(N - 1)$ is never greater than 1. Since the binomial model is easier to work with, whenever the size *N* of the total

Hypergeometric Distribution

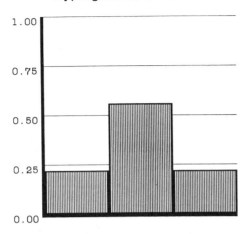

Binomial Distribution

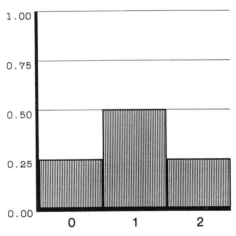

Number of Red Marbles

FIGURE 2.9. Probability histograms of the hypergeometric distribution of the number of red marbles in a sample of two selected from a set of ten marbles, five of which are red, and the binomial distribution with the same mean, i.e., $p = 1/2$ and $n = 2$. Notice that the expected value (1) has a greater probability of occurring under the hypergeometric model.

pool of available items is *large* relative to the number (n) of selections made, we can use the *binomial* distribution to *approximate* the hypergeometric.

To illustrate formula (2.23) we compute the *mean* and *variance* of the number of red marbles obtained in two draws from a jar with five marbles of each color:

$$\mu = np = 2 \cdot \frac{5}{10} = 1$$

$$\sigma^2 = np(1 - p) \frac{N - n}{N - 1} = 2 \left(\frac{1}{2}\right) \left(\frac{1}{2}\right) \frac{10 - 2}{10 - 1} = \frac{4}{9}.$$

Notice that if we forgot that the true model was the hypergeometric and used the binomial model with $n = 2$ and $p = 1/2$, one would have had the correct mean but too large a variance, as the variance of the *binomial* distribution is $np(1 - p) = 2(1/2)(1/2) = 1/2$ or .5, instead of 4/9, which is reflected in the differing probabilities the two distributions place on the expected value (1). On the other hand, if $n = 20$ and $N = 1000$, the extra factor in the variance is

$$\frac{N - n}{N - 1} = \frac{1000 - 20}{1000 - 1} = \frac{980}{999} = .981,$$

which makes a negligible difference. This is why the binomial model can be used to analyze data in jury discrimination cases. The number (n) of jurors on the panel is typically less than 1% of the eligible population (N). Later we will see that courts have erred in using the binomial model, however, when the number of selections formed a significant fraction of the eligible population.

b. Application to assessing discrimination in promotions:
  Jurgens v. Thomas[9]

The major application of the hypergeometric model in law is in the statistical assessment of hiring, promotion, termination and job assignment data in employment discrimination cases. Again, the basic idea is that if *many fewer than the expected number of minorities* are among those hired or promoted, then the firm may be discriminating and should be required to explain or justify its practices. While we will discuss the formal statistical test later in Chapter 5, we illustrate the idea on data from *Jurgens v. Thomas,* showing that the EEOC itself may have discriminated against men in promotion. The data in Table 2.7 reports the number of eligible males and females and the number who were promoted.

TABLE 2.7. Promotion Data from *Jurgens v. Thomas*

	Promoted	Not Promoted	Total Eligible
Males	3	59	62
Females	29	193	222
	32	252	284

Source: Table 1 from 29 FEP Cases 1561 at 1569.

Notice that the number of promotions that men should receive, assuming that all 284 eligibles were qualified, has a *hypergeometric* distribution where $n_1 = 62$, $n_2 = 222$ and $n = 32$. Before calculating the exact probabilities, we note that the *expected* number of males among the 32 promotees is

$$np = \frac{32 \cdot 62}{284} = 6.99, \qquad \text{or about 7,}$$

so that the three promotions men received was less than half the number of promotions a sex-blind system would be expected to yield. In order to decide whether the three promotions received by male employees is small enough to raise doubts about the promotion process of the EEOC, one calculates the probability of obtaining 0, 1, 2 or 3 male promotions in the hypergeometric model. As in our discussion of jury data, the reason we include the probability of obtaining *less than* the actual number of promotions is that these events would be further from the *expected* number (7) than the observed number (3) and that had they occurred, they would have constituted stronger evidence of possible bias. The probability of obtaining *three or fewer* male promotions, i.e., $P(S = 0) + P(S = 1) + P(S = 2) + P(S = 3)$, where S has the hypergeometric distribution with parameters ($n_1 = 62$, $n_2 = 222$, $n = 32$), is .0491,[10] a sufficiently small result that helped convince the judge of potential bias in the system, especially as the pool of eligibles was restricted to those applicants who met the objective certification requirements for the job so that there was no reason to believe that females or males as a group were better qualified.

Problems

In each of the following situations describe whether the binomial or hypergeometric model is most appropriate. If possible, state the parameters n and p of the binomial and n, p (or n_1/N), and $N = n_1 + n_2$ of the hypergeometric. When your answer is the hypergeometric, do you think that the binomial gives a good approximation? Explain your answers.

1. (a) A written examination is given to 100 candidates for a job. Anyone who receives a grade of 60 or more passes. What is the distribution of the number of candidates who pass the exam? *Hint:* You can determine the type of distribution and the parameter n, but the numerical value of p cannot be specified from the information given.

(b) Suppose that 60 of the candidates were male and 40 were female and that historical records show that 40% of persons taking the test score 60 or more. What is the distribution of the number of male candidates who pass; the number of female candidates who pass?

(c) Suppose that *half* the candidates of each sex actually pass the exam. Out of the remaining pool of 30 males and 20 females, 15 persons are chosen on the basis of an oral interview. What is the distribution of the number of females selected from this pool of 50?

(d) In part (c) suppose that two people are selected. What is the distribution of the number of females selected?

2. In order to determine whether a new vaccine helps immunize people against influenza, the government sponsored a study of the vaccine's effectiveness by giving the vaccine to 100 patients. A control group of 100 persons of similar health status was not given the vaccine.

(a) Assuming that 20% of the public get this particular flu each winter, describe the distribution of the number of cases of flu the control group has during that winter.

(b) If the vaccine is *ineffective*, what is the distribution of the number of cases among the 100 persons who were immunized?

(c) Suppose that the vaccine is *ineffective*. At the end of the flu season we observe 38 cases in *both* groups. What is the distribution of the number of control persons who got the flu, i.e., who were among the 38 cases?

(d) Suppose the vaccine was *effective* and reduced one's chances of getting the flu to one half the normal rate. What is the distribution of the number of immunized persons who got the flu? How does this distribution differ from that of nonimmunized (control) group which you obtained in part (a)?

(e) From your answer to parts (a) and (d), do you think this type of experiment would aid the Food and Drug Administration in deciding whether the vaccine was effective?

3. Find the mean and variance of the binomial and hypergeometric distributions you obtained in the previous two questions.

4. (a) Find the distribution of the number of *minorities* among 3 persons hired by a firm from a pool of 12 qualified applicants, 4 of whom are minority?

(b) If it turned out that none of the minority members were among the 3 hires, would this be convincing evidence of bias in the firm's hiring process (Answer probabilistically)?

(c) Would your answer to (b) change if the firm hired 7 persons, none of whom were minority, from the set of 12 qualified applicants? Explain.

Answers to Selected Problems

1. (a) binomial, $n = 100$ and p = probability a candidate has of passing.
(b) binomial $n = 60$, $p = .4$ for the males; $n = 40$, $p = .4$ for the females.
(c) hypergeometric $n_1 = 20$, $n_2 = 30$, $n = 15$.
(d) hypergeometric with $n_1 = 20$, $n_2 = 30$, $n = 2$.

2. (a) binomial $n = 100$, $p = .2$.
(b) same as (a).
(c) hypergeometric $n_1 = 100$, $n_2 = 100$, $n = 38$.
(d) binomial, $n = 100$, $p = .1$.
(e) Yes.

3. For problem 1
(a) mean is $100p$, variance $100p(1 - p)$;
(b) males mean 24, variance 14.4, females mean 16, variance 9.6;
(c) mean $15 \cdot 2/5 = 6$, variance $(3 \cdot 6)(50 - 15)/(50 - 1) = 2.57$;
(d) mean $2 \cdot 2/5 = 4/5 = .8$, variance .470.

4. (a) hypergeometric $n_1 = 4$, $n_2 = 8$, $n = 3$.
(b) the probability of obtaining 0 minorities in 3 hires is $8/12 \cdot 7/11 \cdot 6/10 = .255$, which is not especially small.
(c) The probability of 0 minority hires out of 7 now is

$$\frac{8}{12} \cdot \frac{7}{11} \cdot \frac{6}{10} \cdot \frac{5}{9} \cdot \frac{4}{8} \cdot \frac{3}{7} \cdot \frac{2}{6} = .01,$$

which is quite small. Thus, the outcome has a low probability of occurring by chance (random selection) and is evidence of possible bias in the selection process.

8. Continuous Random Variables and the Normal Distribution

a. Fundamental ideas

So far we have been mainly concerned with discrete random variables which can take on only a finite number of possible values. Some variables, however, can assume any real number on a line or interval. For instance, a person's height can be measured, at least theoretically, to any desired degree of accuracy, because one's possible height is not restricted to units like an inch or half inch or even a tenth of an inch. Other continuous variables are the lifetime of an individual or new automobile, the temperature in a room, and the pressure a fiber or other material can withstand before breaking or tearing. Continuous variables can also be used to *approximate* discrete ones. For instance, family earnings can take on many possible values. If one reports them to the penny, there are 100 possible values per dollar interval, and we saw that the Census Bureau reports earnings near $0 to about $100,000, which implies that there are $100,000 \times 100 = 10^7$ possible values. It is easier to work with a continuous distribution where family earnings can take on any number between $0 and $100,000 than with a discrete one with 10^7 possible outcomes.

The *distribution* of a continuous variable is given by a *curve* with the property that the *area* under the curve within any interval (a, b) is the *probability* of observing a value of the random variable in that interval. In Figure 2.10 we graph two continuous distributions, the first a bell curve

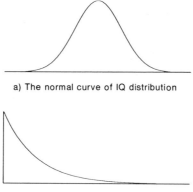

a) The normal curve of IQ distribution

b) An exponential curve for the life of a working machine

FIGURE 2.10.   Two probability functions of continuous random variables. The top curve is represents a normal or bell curve with mean 100 and standard deviation 15. The bottom curve is an exponential distribution, which often describes the useful life of equipment.

which is centered around a typical value (its mean μ); the second, a curve giving the distribution of useful life of a new piece of equipment. In the second example, we are often interested in whether the equipment will last for at least a certain minimum amount of time (T), which is the area under the curve over the region T to infinity (or the largest possible value).

The curve specifying the probability a continuous variable lies in any interval is called a probability *density function* or *frequency function,* and the areas are obtained by the use of calculus. We will not be concerned with how the areas are obtained but will give the resulting areas for the most widely used continuous distribution, the *normal curve.*

The *frequency function* can be thought of as a generalized *histogram,* since the probability of an observation being in any interval is the area under the frequency function in that interval. No longer are we restricted to the particular intervals used to summarize a particular data set. Instead, if one took many independent measurements of the same continuous variable and reported them in grouped form, as in Table 1.7, one would increase the number of intervals used to summarize the data as the sample size (number of observations) increased. The histograms made on the basis of 10, 20, 30, ... group intervals would approach the *frequency function,* since the area over an interval of the histogram is just the fraction of the data in that interval. As the sample size increases, that fraction of all the data in an interval approaches the probability of an observation being in that interval.

Continuous distributions also have a theoretical mean μ and variance σ^2. For our purposes they can be considered as the values that the sample mean $\bar{x}$ and variance s^2 approach as the sample size increases. You probably have had some contact with the bell-shaped *normal* curve, as school grades and IQ scores are examples of variables which follow the normal distribution. Other variables that have a normal distribution are the average of several measurements of the same quantity, e.g., readings of a thermometer, heights of all males in the U.S. and random errors in some billing systems (but not "errors" citizens make in reporting their income to tax authorities).

The normal curve is defined once its mean (μ) and standard deviation (σ) are known. Once these are given, one converts the problem of finding the relevant probability into one of looking up the corresponding area under the frequency function by first *transforming* the normal variable X to standard units or Z scores as follows: For any value X, the Z score

(2.24) $$Z = \frac{X - \mu}{\sigma}$$

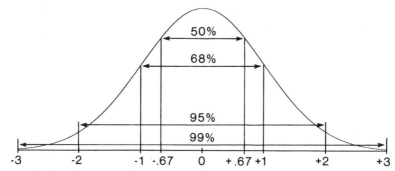

FIGURE 2.11.   Intervals which are symmetric about the mean containing 50, 68,
95 and 99.7% of the area or probability under the normal curve.
The numbers .67, ±1, ±2 and ±3 are distances from the mean
expressed in terms of standard deviations.

tells us how far above or below the mean the value X is, measured in units
of standard deviations.

The Z score enables us to translate any normal variable (X) into the
standard normal form, with mean 0 and standard deviation 1, so that we
only need to familiarize ourselves with the areas under the standard normal curve. In Figure 2.11, we present the intervals which are symmetric about the mean and contain 50%, 68% and 95% of the probability or
area under the curve. Notice that for any normal variable, 95% of the
observations are expected to lie within two standard deviations of the
mean.

In addition to the central or main portion of the curve, we are often
interested in the probabilities of events which are far from the mean or
expected value. Approximate probabilities or areas under the *left* tail
i.e., the probability of observing a standard normal variable with a value
less than z for several values of z (-3, -2.0, -0.1, -1.645, -1, 0) are
given in Figure 2.12. Notice that there is an approximate probability of
.025 of a normal variable assuming a value two standard deviations below
the mean. By the symmetry of the normal curve, the probability of observing a value or exceeding the mean by two standard deviations or more
is also .025.

Before presenting a more complete table of areas, we illustrate the use
of Figures 2.11 and 2.12 in calculating probabilities of interest.

Example 2.8.   A professor is asked by the Dean of Students to advise a
student. Suppose that the IQ's of students at the school have a normal
distribution with mean 125 and standard deviation 15. What is the chance

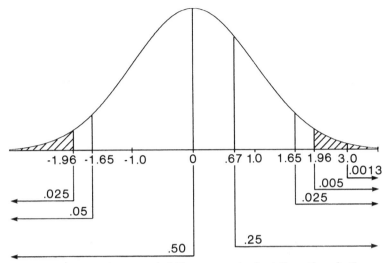

FIGURE 2.12.   Approximate probability or area in the tail portions in the normal curve. The shaded area represents the probability of observing a value 1.96 standard deviations or more from the mean and has area .050. The right half of the figure presents the probabilities of observing a value exceeding the mean by .67, 1.65, 1.96, 2.58 and 3 standard deviations. The symmetry of the normal curve implies that the probability of exceeding the mean by x or more standard deviations equals the probability of being below the mean by x or more standard deviations.

that the professor's advisee will be one of the very bright students with an IQ of 140 or more?

If X denotes the IQ of the student, we need to calculate the probability that X is greater or equal to 140. To convert this to standard units, we subtract the mean (125) from 140 and then divide the standard deviation (15) so that we want the probability that

(2.25) $$Z \geq \frac{140 - 125}{15} \geq \frac{15}{15} = 1,$$

i.e., the area in the right portion (called the tail) in Figure 2.12. Since the normal curve is *symmetric* about 0, the probability that Z is greater than or equal to 1 equals the probability that Z is less than or equal to -1. From Figure 2.12 this probability equals .1587 or about .16. This result also implies that a student with an IQ of 140 ranks at the 84th percentile of all students, since 84% of all students have an IQ less than or equal to that of the student.

Example 2.9. The first woman hired by an accounting firm has been employed for 24 months but has not received a pay raise. She finds out that over the last several years newly hired males typically receive a raise after one year of service. Suppose that the time to first pay raise for males follows a normal law, with mean 12 months and standard deviation 4 months. Should she complain?

The woman's Z score is

$$Z = \frac{X - \mu}{\sigma} = \frac{24 - 12}{4} = +3.$$

The probability of observing a value three standard deviations or more above the mean is only .0013 (see Figure 2.12). This small probability certainly justifies her complaining as 99.87% of the males would have received a raise within 24 months.

Example 2.10. A coffee processer sells 8 ounce jars of coffee. The machine used to fill coffee is set to give 8 ounces, but the amount it actually fills a jar is a normal random variable with mean, $\mu = 8$ ounces and standard deviation $\sigma = .1$ ounce.

(a) What fraction of jars contain less than 8 ounces of coffee?
Answer. Since 8 ounces is the mean, and the normal curve is symmetric about its mean, *half* of the jars contain less than it.

(b) What fraction of jars contain between 7.8 ounces and 8.2 ounces?
Answer. Translating these values into z scores yields

$$z_1 = \frac{7.8 - 8.0}{-1} = -2 \quad \text{and} \quad z_2 = \frac{8.2 - 8}{-1} = +2.$$

We desire the probability that the standard normal, Z, is between -2 and $+2$ standard deviations from the mean. From Figure 2.11, this probability is .95 or about 95% of the jars contain between 7.8 and 8.2 ounces of coffee.

(c) What fraction of jars contain less than 7.9 ounces?
Answer. Translating 7.9 into standard units, yields

$$z = \frac{7.9 - 8.0}{.1} = \frac{-.1}{.1} = -1.0.$$

The probability of observing a value one or more standard deviations *below* mean is (from Figure 2.11) .1587 or about 16%.

(d) The manufacturer is concerned about a competitor or consumer protection agency sampling its product and asserting that *half* the jars of coffee it sells are underweight (i.e., contain less than 8 ounces of coffee). Therefore, it decides to increase the setting of the machine to 8.1 ounces. What fraction of jars will now be underweight?

Answer. Assuming that the standard deviation remains the same, we calculate the probability that an observation from a normal variable with mean 8.1 and standard deviation .1 is less than 8.0. In terms of z scores we calculate

$$z = \frac{8.0 - 8.1}{.1} = \frac{-1}{1} = -1,$$

which we know has probability .1587 of occurring. Thus, by increasing the setting of the machine, the manufacturer has reduced the proportion of underweight jars from 50% to 16%.

(e) Suppose the manufacturer is still unhappy knowing that nearly 16% of its coffee jars are underweight and wants to find the proper setting of the machine so that no more than 5% of the coffee jars it sells will be underweight. What should the setting be?

Answer. This problem is different than the others because the mean of the normal curve is specified. From Figure 2.12 we realize that only 5% of the area under a normal curve is less than -1.645 standard deviations from the mean. In our example we *want* 8 ounces to correspond to this z value, i.e.,

$$\frac{8 - \mu}{.1} = \frac{x - \mu}{\sigma} = Z = -1.645$$

or

$$8 - \mu = (.1)(-1.645) = -.1645$$

or

$$\mu = 8 + .1645 = 8.1645$$

is the setting which satisfies the 5% requirement.

(f) The previous problem was unrealistic, as a consumer protection agency would probably not complain if a jar contained 7.98 ounces of coffee instead of 8.0 but might well complain if they felt that more than 5% of 8-ounce coffee jars contained less than 7.9 ounces. If the manufacturer sets the machine so that $\mu = 8.1$, would the consumer agency be satisfied?

Answer. This problem is similar to part (c), only the mean is 8.1 rather than 8.0. Hence,

$$Z = \frac{7.9 - 8.1}{.1} = -2$$

standard units. From Figure 2.11, this corresponds to a probability of about .025, so the manufacturer would be in compliance with the agency's criteria.

In order to facilitate the use of the normal curve in Table A of the appendix we give the areas in the extreme regions and in the symmetric interval about the mean for the standard normal distribution or z scores. Both the area over the curve and the probability of the event being calculated are given over each column, and we end the section by illustrating the use of Table A.

b.   Using Table A giving the probability content of regions under the normal curve

(1) To find the probability of observing a value exceeding the mean by 1.5 standard deviations or more we look *down* the first column in Table A (as the event of interest is $P(Z > 1.5)$ at 1.5 and find .0668, the desired probability.

(2) To find the probability of observing an event which *differs* from the mean by 2.5 standard deviations or more in either direction, i.e., the observation *exceeds* the mean by at least 2.5 standard deviations or is at least that far *below* the mean, we use *column 3,* as the event of interest is

$$(Z > 2.5) \cup (Z < -2.5).$$

The entry for $z = 2.5$ is .0124.

(3) To find the probability of observing a normal variable which *does not exceed* the mean by more than 1.2 standard deviations, we realize that this *is* the *complement* of the event the observation exceeds the mean by 1.2 standard deviations. The probability of the complement is given in column 1 as .1151, so the probability desired is $1 - .1151 = .8849$.

Problems

1.   Which   of the following random variables are continuous (or essentially continuous)? Of them, which are likely to follow a normal curve?

   (a) grade point averages of first year law students;

(b) the number of students who drop out of school after passing all their courses;

(c) the amount of money lost by all shareholders in a bank that fails;

(d) the noise level generated by a jet plane over a neighborhood in the flight pattern near an airport;

(e) the amount of time it takes workers in a plant to assemble a component;

(f) the lifetime of a newborn female baby in the United States.

2.   Assume that storms in an area produce rainfall which is normally distributed with mean 4 inches and standard deviation 3 inches.

(a) In order to reduce flood damage to low-lying areas, local officials propose to construct a dam that will contain rainfalls up to 7 inches. For what fraction of rainfalls will the dam protect the low lying areas?

(b) If you owned property in the low-lying areas, would you be satisfied with the protection offered by the proposed dam? Answer in terms of probability (i.e., if you are unhappy suggest a more appropriate dam).

(c) Find the amounts of rainfall the dam should be able to contain in order that 99.7% of all storms will not flood the area.

(d) For policymaking purposes are these probability calculations helpful? Are they the only factors that should be considered? Discuss.

NOTES

1.   Since multiplying several probabilities, all of which are less than one, can lead to quite a small number, indicating a very improbable result, one needs to check the independence assumption carefully. In Chapter 12 we will see a misuse of the formula in our discussion of the *Collins* and *Sneed* cases.

2.   In our example one could consider drawing the two cards at once from the deck and then randomly selecting one to be the first. Every possible pair of cards, e.g., ace-jack, ace-ace, etc., yielding an ace as the first card with a probability 1/2 or 1 (in the ace-ace case), also yields an ace on the second draw with the same probability. Hence, the chance an ace is drawn on the second draw is the same as that of an ace being drawn on the first.

3.   The basic idea underlying this approach was stated by the U.S. Supreme Court in *Hazelwood School District v. U.S.* 97 S.Ct. 2736 (1977). The Court noted that if an employer is not discriminating, then over time his work force should mirror the qualified work force in the area. Hence, a large difference between the minority fraction of employees and their fraction of the relevant work force is evidence of possible discrimination. We discuss this application in depth in Chapter 4, as one needs to make a careful determination of the qualified work force.

4.   707 F.2d 172 (5th Cir. 1983) *affirming* 32 FEP Cases (E.D. La. 1982) 141.

5.   The calculation of the mean and variance of the simple binomial variable is given in Table 2.8.

6.   The derivation of this formula is given in several of the statistical texts mentioned at the end of Chapter 1.

TABLE 2.8. Calculation of the Mean and Variance of a Simple Binomial Random
Variable

Value	$p(x)$	$xp(x)$	$(x - \mu)$	$(x - \mu)^2$	$p(x)(x - \mu)^2$
0	$1 - p$	0	$-p$	p^2	$(1 - p)p^2$
1	p	p	$1 - p$	$(1 - p)^2$	$p(1 - p)^2$
Total		$\mu = p$			$\sigma^2 = p(1 - p)$

Note: $\sigma^2 = (1 - p)p^2 + p(1 - p)^2 = p(1 - p)[p + (1 - p)] = p(1 - p) \cdot 1$ or $p(1 - p)$.

7. For a thorough discussion of the major cases and further references to the legal literature, see

DAUGHTREY, M. C. (1975). Cross Sectionalism in Jury Selection Procedures after *Taylor v. Louisiana*. *Tennessee Law Review* **43**, 1–107.

FINKELSTEIN, M. (1966). The Application of Statistical Decision Theory to Jury Discrimination Cases. *Harvard Law Review* **80**, 338–376.

MICHAEL, M. AND ROWEN, J. V. (1975). Challenges to Jury Composition. *North Carolina Central Law Journal* **7**, 1–24.

8. The exact set of possible values of S depends on n, n_1 and n_2. If n is *less* than the minimum of n_1 and n_2, then S can take on any value between 0 and n. If n is $>n_1$, then the largest possible value of S is n_1, while if $n > n_2$, the smallest possible value of S is $n - n_2$.

9. *Jurgens v. Thomas* (N.D. Texas 1982) 29 FEP Cases, 1561.

10. We omit the details which are given in footnote 15 of the opinion, *supra,* note 9.

Chapter 3

Principles of Statistical Inference Illustrated on Binomial and Normal Data

1. Introduction

In Chapter 2 we saw that the number of minority jurors or (hires) can be regarded as a binomial random variable with parameters n, the number of selections, and p, their fraction of the eligible (qualified) population. The binomial model applies to many other situations in which we classify a population into two groups and are interested in the fraction (p) of the total population who belong to one group. Some examples are:

(1) Politicians are interested in knowing the value of p, the fraction of their constituents who favor a particular policy.

(2) The EPA (Environmental Protection Agency) needs to know the fraction, p, of cars of a particular make or model that violate a pollution standard.

(3) In a trademark infringement case, an estimate of the probability (p) of a potential customer being confused by a similar product is helpful in determining whether infringement has occurred.

In these three applications we are not checking to see that the data fits or comes from a binomial model with a known value of p as we did in the analysis of jury data (e.g., $p = .6$ in the *Turner v. Fouche* case). Our problem is to determine or estimate the value of p from data. Indeed that is a major function of opinion polls, especially in election years.

These two types of problems:

(1) Checking that data reflect the correct probability distribution and
(2) Estimating the value of a parameter (usually p, the probability of a success, or μ, the mean or average value),

are problems of *statistical inference*. The first problem requires the testing of an hypothesis, and the second problem requires an estimation. Because we estimate parameters on the basis of a sample, our sample proportion will probably not equal the true value of p. However, it should be reasonably close to it. In this chapter, we discuss the principles of hypothesis testing and estimation and focus on

(a) The types of errors which are inherent in the process of testing an hypothesis with actual data, and

(b) How to develop a measure of reasonable margin of error for a sample estimate of a parameter, thereby generating an interval or range of values of the parameter that are consistent with the data.

We begin the chapter with a useful approximation to the distribution of the sample mean (or sample proportion in the case of data from a binomial model) that will enable us to calculate the relevant probabilities using the areas under the normal curve given in Table A of the appendix.

2. The Distribution of the Sample Mean and Sample Proportion

Suppose you were interested in finding out the true proportion, p, of the electorate who favored the incumbent President and you hired an established polling firm, who took a representative random sample of 2000 eligible voters and reported that 1200 or 60% of these voters favored the incumbent. How confident would you be in betting that the incumbent would win the election, which is to be held on the following day? Would you be nearly as confident, if the pollster had sampled 10 eligible voters and reported that six of them favored the incumbent? Undoubtedly you were quite confident in the first case but were uneasy at reaching a conclusion from a sample of 10 voters, even though both *sample estimates* of the fraction of voters favoring the incumbent were identical (.6). You realized that the accuracy of an estimate of a parameter, in our example the probability, p, that a voter favors the incumbent increases with the size of the sample. Since the sample proportion is just a special case of a sample mean, the sample proportion, $\overline{P}$ can be expressed as

(3.1) $\overline{P} = \dfrac{\text{number of 1's in a sample of } n}{n} = \dfrac{1}{n} \sum X_i,$

where each of the n X_i's is a simple binomial random variable with probability p of being a 1. In the polling example, the X_i for each respondent favoring the incumbent is a 1, while respondents opposing the incumbent have $X_i = 0$. We next discuss the sampling distribution of the mean.

When we take n independent observations of a random variable, e.g., measure a physical quantity, such as temperature or pressure, n times or choose n persons from a *large* population[1] using a random selection process, ensuring that every member of the large population of size N has the same chance ($1/n$) of being in our sample, then the *sample mean,* of the observations, $X_1, X_2 ..., X_n$ is a random variable. The mean and standard deviation of probability distribution of the sample mean $\overline{X} = 1/n \sum_{i=1}^{n} X_i$ is given in the following result:[2]

If the original distribution of the characteristic (X) being measured has *mean μ and standard deviation σ, then the sample mean has a probability distribution with expected value, μ, and standard deviation $\sigma/\sqrt{n}$.*

The previous statement quantifies your earlier intuition that a sample estimate is more reliable, i.e., has a greater probability of being close to the true parameter, when it is based on a large sample, because the standard deviation of the sample mean, $\overline{X}$, *decreases* as n increases. The standard deviation of the distribution of the sample mean, $\overline{X}$, is also called the *standard error of the mean*. The formula is

(3.2)   standard error $(\overline{X})$ = standard deviation $(\overline{X}) = \dfrac{\sigma}{\sqrt{n}}$,

where σ, the population standard deviation, is divided by the square root of the sample size (n).

In order to make careful calculations we need to use the *Central Limit Theorem*, which states that:

When a random sample of n *observations is taken from a large population, the mean of the sample, $\overline{X}$, will have an* approximately normal distribution *centered about the population mean, μ, with a standard deviation equal to the population standard deviation, σ, divided by the* square root *of the* sample size.

The central limit theorem enables us to approximate the distribution of the *sample mean* by using the normal distribution. We now illustrate how closely the sample mean approaches the true mean, μ, as the size of the sample increases.

Example. Suppose heights of college students are normally distributed with a mean of 69″ and a standard deviation of 3″.

(a) What is the probability that a randomly selected student will have a height within 2″ of the true mean (69″)?

(b) What is the probability that the *average* of a random sample of 16 students will be within 2″ of the true mean?

If we let X be the random variable denoting the height of *one* randomly chosen student, we wish to obtain the probability of the event, $67 < X < 71$, i.e., we wish to calculate

$$P(67 < X < 71).$$

This probability is expressed in terms of the standard normal variable Z by subtracting the population mean (69) from both sides of the inequality and dividing by population standard deviation (3). Thus, we desire the probability that

$$\frac{67 - 69}{3} < Z < \frac{71 - 69}{3} \quad \text{or} \quad P\left(\frac{-2}{3} < Z < +\frac{2}{3}\right)$$

$$= P(-.67 < Z < .67).$$

Using Table A in the appendix, this probability is .4972. Part (b) asks for the probability that the *sample mean* based on 16 observations is within 2 inches of the true mean. The sample mean has a probability distribution with mean 69 and standard deviation, $\sigma/\sqrt{n} = 3/\sqrt{16} = 3/4 = .75$. Using the Central Limit Theorem to calculate the desired probability,

$$P(67 < \overline{X}_{16} < 71),$$

We subtract 69 from both sides of the inequality and then divide by .75 (the standard deviation of $\overline{X}_{16}$), obtaining

$$\frac{P(67 - 69}{.75} < \frac{\overline{X}_{16} - 69}{.75} < \frac{71 - 69)}{.75},$$

which equals $P(-8/3 < Z < 8/3)$. From tables similar to Table A we find

$$P(-2.33 < Z < 2.33) = .9802.$$

This calculation shows that the probability of obtaining a sample mean $\bar{x}$ which is close to (i.e., within a preset distance from) the true mean, μ, *increases* with the sample size. Indeed, the Central Limit Theorem implies that approximately 95% of all *sample means* will be in the interval

$$(3.3) \qquad \left(\mu - \frac{2\sigma}{\sqrt{n}}, \mu + \frac{2\sigma}{\sqrt{n}} \right),$$

because 95% of the probability of a *normal* random variable lies within two standard deviations of its mean. Recall that the standard deviation of the sample mean is $\sigma/\sqrt{n}$, where σ is the *standard deviation* of the *characteristic* (variable) *in the population* being samples and n is the number of observations.

Similarly, we know that approximately 68% of all sample means will be in the interval,

$$(3.4) \qquad \left(\mu - \frac{\sigma}{\sqrt{n}}, \mu + \frac{\sigma}{\sqrt{n}} \right)$$

and that approximately 99.5% of all sample means will lie in the interval

$$(3.5) \qquad \left(\mu - \frac{3\sigma}{\sqrt{n}}, + \frac{3\sigma}{\sqrt{n}} \right).$$

As one expects, the *larger the interval about the mean*, the greater is the probability that the population mean will be contained in it. If one desires a high probability, e.g., 99% of obtaining a sample mean within a fixed length, a, say, of the mean, μ, the above results imply that a large sample size (n) may be needed in contrast with the sample size required if only a modest probability, e.g., 80%, was desired.

We have emphasized the role of the sample size, however, the standard deviation, σ, characteristic under study also is an important factor. The larger σ is, the more observations are required to obtain the same probability of a sample mean being no further from the population mean, μ, than a prespecified amount. Had the standard deviation of the distribution of the height of students been 4″ instead of 3″, the probability that the mean of a sample of 16 students would be within 2″ of the true mean would be $P(-2 < Z < +2) = .954$ instead of .98. This decrease in the precision of the sample mean as an estimator of the true mean is due to the fact that the standard error of the sample mean, $\sigma/\sqrt{n}$, now becomes $4/\sqrt{16} = 1.0$ instead of .75.

Since the sample proportion, $\overline{P}$, is a sample average of n simple binomial random variables where each X_i is 1 with probability p, we can use the Central Limit Theorem to approximate its sampling distribution. In Table 2.8 we showed that each X_i has mean p and standard deviation $\sqrt{p(1-p)}$. Hence, $\overline{P}$ is approximately normally distributed with *mean p* and *standard deviation*

$$(3.6) \qquad \frac{\sigma}{\sqrt{n}} = \frac{\sqrt{p(1-p)}}{\sqrt{n}}.$$

In order to distinguish between the concept of a sample proportion as a random variable and the actual value it takes on in a particular sample, formal statistics texts sometimes use $\overline{P}$ for the random variable and $\overline{p}$ for a specific value. In most applications we will discuss this distinction will be clear. Hence, we will use $\overline{p}$. The same considerations will apply to the use of $\overline{X}$ and $\overline{x}$ for the sample mean.

Example. Suppose that 60% of voters favor the incumbent in an election. A pollster decides to take a poll of 100 eligible voters the day before the election and will announce that the incumbent will win the election if 55% or more of the sample favor the incumbent.

(a) What is the probability that the pollster will make the correct call on the eve of the election?
(b) What is the probability that the sample proportion, $\overline{p}$, will be within 5% (.05) of the true proportion (.60).
We need to calculate the chance that the sample proportion is at least .55, i.e.,

$$(3.7) \qquad\qquad P(\overline{p} \geq .55).$$

As the sample proportion, $\overline{p}$, has mean .6 (the true proportion) and standard deviation

$$(3.8) \qquad \frac{\sqrt{p(1-p)}}{\sqrt{n}} = \frac{\sqrt{(.6)(.4)}}{\sqrt{100}} = \frac{\sqrt{.24}}{10} = .049,$$

we use the normal approximation to calculate the probability of the event

$$(3.9) \qquad \left[Z = \frac{\overline{p} - .6}{.049} \geq \frac{.55 - .6}{.049} = \frac{.05}{.049} = -1.02 \right].$$

From Table A in the appendix, we obtain the probability that a standard normal variable, Z *exceeds* -1.0 as .8413, which approximates the desired probability.

Similarly, we calculate the answer to part (b), the probability of the event,

(3.10) $[.6 - .05 < \bar{p} < .6 + .05]$ or $[.55 < \bar{p} < .65]$

by converting it to an event expressed in terms of the Z variable. Subtracting the mean .60 from both sides of (3.10) and dividing by the standard deviation (.049) of $\bar{p}$ we have

(3.11) $P\left[\dfrac{(.55 - .60}{.049} \le \dfrac{\bar{p} - .60}{.049} = Z \le \dfrac{.65 - .60)}{.049}\right]$

or

(3.12) $P(-1.02 < Z < +1.02),$

which (from Table A) is about .683.

The reader may wonder whether the normal approximation to the sample proportion from binomial data is very accurate, because the numerator in the proportion—the number of successes—has a *discrete distribution*. In large samples, this does not have a substantial effect, but we can easily improve the normal approximation if we recall that the probability histogram (Figure 2.9) of the number of successes among the n trials *represents* the *probability* that $S = k$ as an *interval* $k - 0.5$ to $k + 0.5$. In our example, the event of interest,

$$[\bar{p} \ge .55],$$

is the same as $S \ge 55$, since $S = n\bar{p}$. If we use the normal distribution to approximate S and calculate the probability that $S \ge 54.5$ (as 55 is spread over the interval 54.5 to 55.5), we obtain a more accurate approximation. For part (a) of our example, the calculation proceeds as follows. The event of interest $S \ge 55$ now becomes

(3.13) $S \ge 54.5,$

and its probability is obtained by subtracting the expected value, 60, of S from both sides of (3.13) and dividing by the standard deviation of S, $\sqrt{np(1 - p)} = \sqrt{(100)(.6)(.4)} = \sqrt{24} = 4.899$. Thus, the event $S > 54.5$ is expressed in terms of the standard normal Z variable as

(3.14) $Z \ge \dfrac{54.5 - 60}{4.899} = -1.123.$

From Table A, we obtain the probability that $[Z \geq -1.1]$, as .8643, which is slightly larger then .8413, obtained previously. The reason this calculation is more accurate is that the full probability that $S = k$ is now included in the region $S \geq k$, while the first approximation missed about half of this probability.

Since we will often be interested in approximating the distribution of the *number* of successes (minorities hired, persons confused by an imitator's trademark, product failures, etc.), we will use the second method, which makes an adjustment or correction for the fact that we are using a continuous curve to approximate[3] a discrete distribution. In Figure 3.1, we plot the histogram of the binomial distribution with $n = 16$ and $p = .5$ and the *normal approximation,* with *mean np* $= 8$ and standard deviation $np(1 - p) = 16(1/2)(1/2) = 2$. The reader can see that the second method, which spreads each *discrete integer, k,* over the interval $(k - .5, k + .5)$ and uses the *normal* distribution with the same *mean* and *standard deviation* to approximate S, yields a more accurate picture of the original binomial variable.

The normal curve can be used to approximate a variety of distributions that have a modal region, i.e., the possible values of the variable near the mean or median have the highest probability of occurring. One approximates a distribution with mean μ and standard deviation σ by a *normal* distribution with the *same mean* and *standard deviation.* In most of our applications, we shall use the normal curve to approximate the *sampling distribution* of the sum, S, or mean $\bar{x}$ of a sample of n observations and must be *careful* to use the *standard deviation* of the random variable (statistic) being approximated, e.g., the standard deviation of the distribution of $\bar{x}$ is $\sigma/\sqrt{n}$, where σ is the standard deviation of the *population* from which the sample is taken.

The accuracy of the normal approximation of the sample average (or sum or count) depends on the size (n) of the sample and the shape of the distribution of the characteristic in the population sampled. For our purpose we will assume the normal approximation is valid in samples of moderate size (30 or more); however, in serious applications one should check its accuracy. Since we will be primarily concerned with the concepts of statistical inference, we may omit the factor .5 when using the normal curve to approximate a *count* or *discrete* distribution, especially when the samples are reasonably large $(n > 100)$.

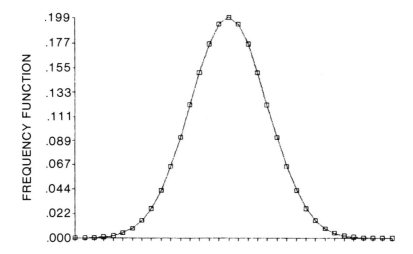

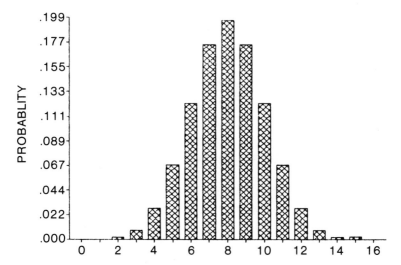

FIGURE 3.1.   Comparison of the binomial distribution with parameters $n = 16$, $p = .5$ with the normal distribution with the same mean, 8, and standard deviation, 2.

Problems

1. A politician believes that his constituents are nearly evenly divided on a controversial issue. In order to check this assumption, he commissions a poll of 100 eligible voters in his district. Before learning the results of the poll he decides that he will

(A) Straddle the issue if fewer than 55% of the voters favor one of the two positions.

(B) Announce he supports position A if more than 55% of the sample favor A.

(C) Announce he supports position B if more than 55% of the sample favor B.

(a) Assuming that his constituency is evenly divided, what are the probabilities that

(1) He will straddle the issue.

(2) He will support *one* of the positions.

(3) He will support position A.

Hint: Define a random variable indicating whether a voter favors A or not.

(b) Assuming that 60% of constituents favor position A, what are the probabilities that, on the basis of the results of the poll,

(1) He will support position A;

(2) He will support position B;

(3) He will straddle the issue.

2. Suppose that a minority group forms 30% of the *eligible* voters in a county. The authorities receive complaints of harassment of minorities at the polls (e.g., long delays and triple checks of identification, registration, etc.). You are part of an investigating team and interview a random sample of 400 eligible voters to ascertain whether they attempted to vote, their minority status and whether they encountered any form of harassment. If it is known that 56.25% of all eligible voters turn out for elections and this figure *applies perfectly* to your sample,

(a) What is the number of actual voters you should find in your sample?

(b) If there really was *no* harassment of minorities, what number of minority voters would you *expect* to find in your sample of *voters who attempted to vote.*

(c) Suppose that 20% of all the voters who actually cast ballots were from the minority group. Could you conclude that their complaints were valid?

(d) Suppose that you learned that only 25% of the eligible voters who went to the polls (attempted to vote) were minority members. Would this affect your answer to part (c)?

3. Estimation and Confidence Intervals (Large Sample)

a. Two-sided confidence intervals

A major purpose of statistics is to *estimate parameters* such as the mean of a characteristic of a population or the probability p of a binomial distribution. Assuming that a proper random sample is taken so that each observation x_i is selected independently of the others, we estimate μ by the sample average x and the probability p by the *proportion* of successes in the sample. Simply reporting these estimates, however, does not give an indication of their accuracy. Therefore statisticians report the *sampling error* of the estimates and/or an interval about the sample mean, called a *confidence interval,* which gives us a *range of possible values for the population mean, μ,* that are consistent with the sample results.

The *sampling error* of an *estimate* is measured in terms of the *standard deviation* of its distribution. Indeed this standard deviation is called the standard error of the estimate. Thus, a sample mean $\bar{x}$ has *standard error,* $\sigma/\sqrt{n}$, and a sample proportion has sampling error, $\sqrt{p(1-p)}/\sqrt{n}$.

To develop the appropriate confidence interval, we recall that sample means and proportions have (approximately) normal distributions. Thus, approximately 95% of all sample means will be in the interval

$$(3.15) \qquad \left(\mu - \frac{1.96\sigma}{\sqrt{n}}, \, \mu + \frac{1.96\sigma}{\sqrt{n}} \right),$$

as 95% of the probability of the standard normal curve lies between -1.96 and $+1.96$. If we know the standard deviation, σ, of the distribution being sampled, then *before* we take our sample we know that there is probability of .95 that the sample mean will lie in the interval (3.15) or, equivalently, that with probability .95, the distance between the sample mean, $\bar{x}$, and the population mean, μ, will be less than $(1.96)\sigma/\sqrt{n}$.

Since we are interested in estimating the population mean by the sample mean, we can regard the interval

$$(3.16) \qquad \left(\bar{x} - \frac{1.96\sigma}{\sqrt{n}}, \, \bar{x} + \frac{1.96\sigma}{\sqrt{n}} \right)$$

as an interval estimate of the population mean in the sense that *before* we took the sample there was a 95% probability that the difference between $\bar{x}$ and μ would be less than (1.96) $\sigma/\sqrt{n}$. Thus,

(3.17) $$P \left(\frac{-1.96\sigma}{\sqrt{n}} < \bar{x} < \frac{+1.96\sigma}{\sqrt{n}} \right) = .95$$

or, subtracting μ from both inequalities,

(3.18) $$P \left(\frac{-1.96\sigma}{\sqrt{n}} < \bar{x} - \mu < \frac{1.96\sigma}{\sqrt{n}} \right) = .95$$

After we take the sample and calculate the sample mean ($\bar{x}$), what is the *probability* that the interval (3.16) contains the population mean (μ) we are estimating? One is tempted to answer .95. However, that was the probability that the mean μ would be in the interval *before* we took our sample. Afterwards, we *cannot tell* whether the interval (3.16) based on a particular sample really contains the true mean, so we *cannot* give a valid answer to the question. We do know that if *many* samples are taken, then 95% of the time the sample mean will differ from the true mean by less than (1.96) $\sigma/\sqrt{n}$. For all these samples the interval (3.16) will contain the true population mean. Unfortunately, we cannot tell whether a particular interval of the form (3.16) based on a single sample will contain the true mean (μ). This is why we call intervals of the form (3.16) *confidence intervals* rather than *probability intervals*. We have 95% *confidence* that an interval of the form

$$\left(\bar{X} - \frac{1.96\sigma}{\sqrt{n}}, \bar{X} + \frac{1.96\sigma}{\sqrt{n}} \right)$$

calculated from a particular sample contains the true value, μ, of the population mean, because we know that in many repetitions of the experiment (similar samples) 95% of such intervals will.

So far we have only discussed 95% confidence intervals. However, the reader will realize that the role played by the value 95% was to determine the factor 1.96 in equation (3.15), as 95% of the area under the standard normal curve lies between -1.96 and $+1.96$. If we desired a greater confidence, say 99%, then we replace 1.96 by 2.58 since 99% of the area under the standard normal curve lies between -2.58 and $+2.58$. In general, we create a $100(1 - \alpha)\%$ confidence interval by obtaining the z value which satisfies the relationship.

(3.19) $$P[-z < Z < +z] = 1 - \alpha$$

From Figure 3.2, we realize that this value, z, is also characterized by the fact that there is probability $\alpha/2$ that a standard normal variable *exceeds* $+z$ or is less than $-z$. Thus, the value of z satisfying equation (3.19) is *labeled* $z_{\alpha/2}$ in Figure 3.2. It is characterized by the fact that the probability that a standard normal variable, Z, exceeds it is $\alpha/2$ or, equivalently, by the probability that Z is less than $-z_{\alpha/2}$ is $\alpha/2$ (by symmetry). Hence, a general $100(1 - \alpha)\%$ confidence interval is given by

(3.20) $$\bar{x} \pm \frac{z_{\alpha/2}\sigma}{\sqrt{n}}$$

For the convenience of the reader, Table 3.1 gives commonly used *confidence* levels, their associated points $z_{\alpha/2}$ on the standard normal curve and the formula for the *lower* and *upper* end points or limits of the confidence interval.

There are several possible notations for confidence intervals. We will often use the terminology 95% CONF or 98% CONF and then give the interval. Sometimes we will include the parameter i.e., we will write

$$95\% \text{ CONF}(\mu; 17.2, 20.1)$$

to mean that the 95% confidence interval for the mean, μ, is 17.2 to 20.1.

The advantage of reporting a confidence interval for a parameter in addition to the basic sample estimate, called a *point estimate,* is that it

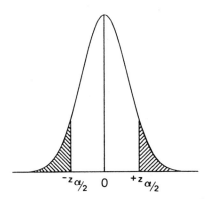

FIGURE 3.2.   Graph of a standard normal distribution indicating the points $\pm z_{\alpha/2}$. These points are defined by the conditions that the shaded area under the curve up to $-z_{\alpha/2}$ is $\alpha/2$ and the shaded area under the curve past $+z_{\alpha/2}$ equals $\alpha/2$. The area between $-z_{\alpha/2}$ and $+z_{\alpha/2}$ also equals $1 - \alpha$. In this picture α is about .14 so $-z_{\alpha/2}$ and $+z_{\alpha/2}$ are 1.5 standard deviations below and above the mean.

gives a range of values of the parameter which are *consistent* with data in the sense that they differ from the point estimate by an amount which *could be* due to the inaccuracy inherent in using a sample. The confidence level $100(1 - \alpha)\%$ for the mean, μ, is interpreted as the proportion of times in many replications the random interval

$$\left(\bar{x} - \frac{z_{\alpha/2}\sigma}{\sqrt{n}}, \bar{x} + \frac{z_{\alpha/2}\sigma}{\sqrt{n}}\right)$$

will contain the true mean in a long sequence of repetitions of the experiment. The half width $z_{\alpha/2} \cdot \sigma/\sqrt{n}$ of the interval is the *margin of error* required to have the specified degree of confidence. From Table 3.1, it is clear that the greater the level of confidence required, the larger the interval must be.

We now illustrate the methodology and its use.

Example 1.   The SEC requires companies to file annual reports concerning their financial status. Due to the large number of accounts receivable, it is impossible to audit every account. Therefore, random sampling is allowed, provided that the sampling average is within a prespecified amount with 95% confidence.

(a) Suppose the accounts receivable of a firm have a true mean of $125 and *historically* are known to have a standard deviation of $50. If the auditor takes a sample of 49 accounts, what is the *possible error* (or half length) of the 95% confidence interval?

(b) Suppose the SEC required that the reported mean from the sample be within $5 of the true mean with 95% confidence. How large a sample should the auditor take assuming that the historical standard deviation is applicable to the current year's accounts?

TABLE 3.1.   Two-Sided Confidence Intervals for a Population Mean

Confidence Level	$z_{\alpha/2}$	Lower End-Point	Upper End-Point
.80	1.18	$\bar{x} - 1.18\,\sigma/\sqrt{n}$	$\bar{x} + 1.18\,\sigma/\sqrt{n}$
.90	1.645	$\bar{x} - 1.645\,\sigma/\sqrt{n}$	$\bar{x} + 1.645\,\sigma/\sqrt{n}$
.95	1.96	$\bar{x} - 1.96\,\sigma/\sqrt{n}$	$\bar{x} + 1.96\,\sigma/\sqrt{n}$
.99	2.58	$\bar{x} - 2.58\,\sigma/\sqrt{n}$	$\bar{x} + 2.58\,\sigma/\sqrt{n}$

Let us construct the 95% interval using formula (3.20) and Table 3.1, yielding

$$\bar{x} \pm (1.96)\frac{\sigma}{\sqrt{n}}$$

or

$$\bar{x} \pm (1.96) \cdot \frac{50}{\sqrt{49}}.$$

The margin of error therefore is $(1.96)(50)/\sqrt{49} = \$14$.

Notice that we were able to calculate the half length of the confidence interval without knowing the observed sample mean, provided we had knowledge, or a good estimate, of σ, the standard deviation of variable in question (accounts receivable in our example).

Part (b) calls for determining the sample size (n) needed to satisfy the SEC requirements. In the expression for the margin of error at the 95% confidence level, n is unknown but must satisfy

$$(1.96)\frac{50}{\sqrt{n}} = \$5$$

or

$$\sqrt{n} = \frac{(1.96) \times 50}{5} = 19.6, \text{ so}$$

$$n = (19.6)^2 = 384.16 \text{ or } 385.$$

Comment. The above calculations assumed that the population standard deviation, σ, was known. In practice, one often can use prior experience or knowledge to set an upper bound (largest possible value) for σ and use that to plan the study. Otherwise, one may take a small preliminary or pilot sample and estimate σ from it, using the sample deviation, s. Then one can use that value, plus an allowance for sampling error, in planning the main sample.

Example 2. When the U.S. government funded employment training programs, it decided the eligibility of a county, city or appropriate sub-area on the basis of the unemployment rate in that area. Although the national census is taken only every 10 years, the Labor Department relied on it to determine the unemployment rates of cities a few years later.

However, an area could qualify for funds on the basis of its own sample survey. Suppose the civic leaders in an area thought it had an unemployment rate greater than the qualifying threshold (6%), even though its rate in the previous census was less than 6%, and contracts for a sample of 400 members of the labor force (persons available for work) to be interviewed using the same questionnaire and unemployment classification as the census.

(a) If the true unemployment rate is 6%, what is the probability that the estimated rate will be at least 6%?

(b) Suppose the actual sample contained 23 unemployed persons among the 400 or a rate of 5.75%. Calculate a 90% confidence interval for the true unemployment rate.

(c) On the basis of the above calculations, was the policy of fixing a threshold rate for eligibility fair in that it treated all areas of the county with the identical unemployment rate similarly?

The answer to part (a) can be calculated once we recall that the sample proportion, $\bar{p}$, is just the *mean* of a sample from a simple binomial distribution with mean $\mu = p$ and standard deviation $\sigma = \sqrt{p(1 - p)}$. By the Central Limit Theorem, the sample proportion, $\bar{p}$, is *normally* distributed about the *true* value $p(.06)$ with standard deviation

$$\frac{\sigma}{\sqrt{n}} = \frac{\sqrt{(.06)(.94)}}{\sqrt{400}} = .0119 \simeq .012.$$

Since the approximate normal distribution of the *sample proportion* is *symmetric* about the true p of .06, we realize without calculation that there is approximately a 50% chance that it will be greater than or equal to the true value. For completeness, we obtain the answer by transforming the probability desired $P(\bar{p} \geq .06)$ into the standard normal, Z, form. To obtain

$$P(\bar{p} \geq .06),$$

subtract the mean of $\bar{p}(.06)$ from both sides of the inequality and divide both sides by the standard deviation of $\bar{p}$ (.012). Thus,

$$P[\bar{p} \geq .06] = P\left[\frac{\bar{p} - .06}{.012} \geq \frac{.06 - .06}{.012}\right] = P[Z \geq 0] = .5.$$

(b) A 90% confidence interval for the sample proportion is obtained from the general formula or Table 3.1 as

$$\bar{x} \pm \frac{(1.645)\sigma}{\sqrt{n}} .$$

Substituting the sample estimate $\bar{p}$ for $\bar{x}$, and $\sqrt{\bar{p}(1 - \bar{p})}$ for σ, yields

(3.21) $.05 \pm (1.645) \dfrac{\sqrt{(.0575)(.9425)}}{\sqrt{400}} = .0575 \pm .0191.$

or

(3.21a)   90% CONF $(p; .0384, .0766).$

(c) Notice that the confidence interval (3.21) ranges from .0384 to .0766, and the eligibility criteria (.06) is well within it. Thus, the citizens of the area are justified in feeling that they *might be eligible* for the program, even though the estimated rate was just under the threshold level. Moreover, from our calculation in part (a) we realize that *half* of the areas with an unemployment rate of 6% will qualify for the progress and *half* won't. Notice that increasing the sample size of the survey to obtain a more accurate estimate or a shorter confidence interval will *not* change this conclusion. Moreover, localities with unemployment rates near 6% will have different probabilities of qualifying depending on the sample size their rates were based on.[4]

From a statistical viewpoint, these results imply that eligibility rules requiring threshold criteria will invariably produce the inequitable treatment of subareas of the nation. Had Congress used an allocation formula which depended on the unemployment rate, e.g. $X(thousand) for each 1% of unemployment, the effect of the inherent uncertainty or sampling error in the statistical data could not have such a drastic *all* or *none* consequence on eligibility for funds.

Technical Comment. Our derivation of the confidence interval for the fraction p using the normal approximation always yields a symmetric interval about the proportion. When p is small (less than .10), the sample size required in order for the normal approximation to be valid becomes quite large, and special statistical procedures may be needed. The reason this problem occurs is that when we estimate a small proportion, say .05, on the basis of a relatively small sample, the most we can possibly *under-estimate* the true value by is .05, however, we can overestimate it by much more (up to .95). Thus, the distribution of the sampling error (the difference between the estimate and the parameter) can be *asymmetric*. We illustrate the possible effect in

Example 3. The state of Michigan adopted no-fault insurance to be effective on October 1, 1973. The act (1972 PA294) required owners of motor vehicles to have insurance in order to drive their car. The law was challenged[5] by plaintiffs (trial lawyers) who asserted that the act violated a citizen's "right to travel" and that it coerced motorists to buy insurance, including "many poor people who had the right to drive but had not the means to buy insurance." Naturally, the number of uninsured motorists who were being coerced became an issue. As there were 4,505,685 passenger vehicles registered in the state, a statistician designed a procedure for taking a random sample of 249 vehicles for which the insurance status was checked. The insurance status of 248 of the sample cars was obtained, as one owner had left the state but data for 15 others were not usable as they had been sold or junked, etc. The final result was that of 233 passenger vehicles operating on the day of the survey, seven were without insurance. A 95% confidence interval for the fraction of uninsured vehicles based on the normal approximation is

$$.030 \pm 1.96 \frac{\sqrt{(.03)(.97)}}{\sqrt{233}} \quad \text{or} \quad 95\% \text{ CONF } (p; .008, .052).$$

The more precise interval, 95% CONF (p; .0132, .0633), which corrected for asymmetry, was used in the proceedings. By multiplying the number of cars on the master file by these fractions, the interval implies that about 59,600 to 285,900 passenger cars were uninsured. On the basis of this confidence interval, the court asked both parties to stipulate that the number of uninsured was between 60,000 and 300,000. The advantage of the confidence interval over a point estimate is that it provided that factfinder with a range of plausible values for the parameter and, therefore, a range of values for the possible effect of the law.

In this application it is implicitly assumed that the missing data was properly omitted and/or random. The randomness assumption is certainly reasonable for persons leaving the state and for cars which were sold but might be questioned for the junked or disabled cars, as poor people probably would be more likely to have owned them. The topic of missing data will be dealt with in Chapter 9, but it is important to understand the assumptions underlying a statistical calculation and what affect deviations from them may have on the ultimate inference.

b. One-sided confidence intervals

So far we have been concerned with estimating a parameter without regard to the direction of the difference between the estimate and the true value. If a manufacturer places an advertisement specifying the average life of a product, then errors of *underestimation* are more important, as consumer groups would only complain if they found out that the product had a lower average life than advertised. Therefore, the manufacturer is concerned with determining an interval for the true mean μ, of the form

$$\mu \text{ is at least } \bar{x} - d,$$

where d will depend on the level of confidence and the standard error $(\sigma/\sqrt{n})$ of the estimate, $\bar{x}$.

In order to obtain a $100(1 - \alpha)\%$ lower confidence interval for μ, we choose d so that

(3.22) $P(\bar{x} - d \leq \mu) = P(\bar{x} - \mu < d) = (1 - \alpha).$

Transforming the probability of the event $(\bar{x} - \mu < d)$ into the standard normal form by dividing by $\sigma/\sqrt{n}$ yields

(3.23) $$P\left[\frac{\bar{x} - \mu}{\frac{\sigma}{\sqrt{n}}} < \frac{d}{\frac{\sigma}{\sqrt{n}}} \right] = 1 - \alpha,$$

where the random variable $(\bar{x} - \mu)/(\sigma/\sqrt{n})$ is a standard normal (Z) variable. We know that

(3.24) $$P[Z < z_\alpha] = 1 - \alpha,$$

where z_α is obtained from Table A. Figure 3.3 shows the region (3.24) and its probability. In order that equation (3.22) is satisfied, $d/(\sigma/\sqrt{n})$ must equal the z_α of equation (3.24). Thus, the general lower confidence interval for μ is

(3.25) $$\mu > \bar{x} - z_\alpha \left(\frac{\sigma}{\sqrt{n}} \right).$$

Example. Suppose a manufacturer desires a 95% *lower* confidence interval on the average lifetime of light bulbs in order to label them properly. One hundred randomly selected bulbs are tested and their *mean life*, $\bar{x} = 867$, and standard deviation, $s = 50$, are observed. As 95% of the area under the standard normal curve lies to left of $z_{.05} = 1.645$, we calculate that

$$d = \frac{z_{.05}\sigma}{\sqrt{n}} = (1.645)\frac{(50)}{\sqrt{100}} = 8.225,$$

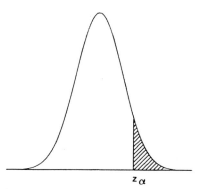

z_α

FIGURE 3.3.   The region under the normal curve defined by z in equation (3.24). The unshaded region has probability or area $1 - \alpha$. The shaded region has area α corresponding to the probability an observation from a normal distribution exceeds $z\alpha$. In the figure α is about .07 and z_α is 1.5 standard deviations above the mean.

and the *lower 95% confidence interval* for μ is

(3.26) μ is at least $(867 - 8.225) = 858.775.$

Thus, we have 95% confidence that the true mean, μ, is at least 858.78 on the basis that the sample mean $(\bar{x})$ was 867.

It is interesting to contrast the one-sided interval (3.26) with the two-sided interval obtained from formula (3.20), i.e.,

$$\bar{x} \pm \frac{(1.96)\sigma}{\sqrt{n}} = 867 \pm \frac{(1.96)50}{\sqrt{100}} = 867 \pm 9.8$$

or

$$95\% \text{ CONF } (\mu; 857.2, 876.8).$$

The lower limit of the two-sided interval is *less* than that of the one-sided interval because the two-sided interval takes the 5% chance that the sample mean will be too far from the true mean and uses half of it (.025) for the possibility of the sample mean being too *low*, and the other half (.025) to allow for the chance the sample mean is *high*. The one-sided *lower* confidence interval places the entire 5% chance that the sample mean is too far from the true value on its being too low, since that is the only risk we are concerned with.

We have described a lower confidence interval for μ, since the application called for a high degree of confidence that μ was *at least as large* as the mean lifetime advertised. The number, $\bar{x} - d$, specifying the lower limit of the confidence interval, can be thought of as the lowest possible value of μ which is consistent (at the level of confidence used) with the data. Similarly, we can derive an upper confidence interval for a parameter. For the mean, μ, of a population, the upper $100(1 - \alpha)\%$ confidence interval is given by

$$(3.27) \qquad \mu \text{ is less than or equal to } \bar{x} + d = \bar{x} + \frac{z_\alpha}{\sqrt{n}}.$$

Upper confidence intervals are used to place an *upper limit* on the value of a parameter that is consistent with observed data. In the present application, a consumer group would create an upper confidence interval from sample data and if the manufacturer advertised an average lifetime *larger* than the *upper limit* of the interval (3.27), they would be justified in complaining.

To illustrate this, suppose the data ($\bar{x} = 867$, $s = 50$, $n = 100$) had been obtained by a state consumer protection agency after it received complaints that the bulbs did not live up to their advertised average lifetime of 900 hours. The agency might develop an upper 95% confidence interval, using (3.27), obtaining

$$\bar{x} = (1.645) \frac{50}{\sqrt{100}} = 867 + 8.225 = 875.225.$$

Since 875.2 is below the advertised lifetime of 900 hours the agency would have sound statistical grounds to cite the manufacturer for misleading or unsupported advertising. Indeed even the upper 99% confidence interval for μ,

$$\bar{x} + (2.33) \frac{50}{\sqrt{100}} = 867 + 11.65 = 878.65,$$

has an upper limit which is *lower* than 900.

Comment. This application shows that one's purpose determines whether a lower or upper confidence interval is appropriate. The manufacturer wishing to be protected from a charge of false advertising should create a lower confidence interval from the sample. The consumer protection agency not only desires to detect fake advertising claims, it also wishes to avoid charges of harassing business. Therefore, it creates an upper confidence interval for the mean lifetime from its sample and accuses the manufacturer of false advertising only when the asserted lifetime exceeds the upper limit of the confidence interval. Both parties use the sampling error to develop margins of safety to protect themselves from false accusations.

Problems

In general, when a confidence interval is called for, the two-sided interval is used. Unless a one-sided interval is asked for or seems appropriate, use the two-sided symmetric interval in your calculations.

1.   Suppose 100 new automobiles are sampled (from all cars sold in a state), and their gas mileage is measured on a fixed course that includes both highway and city driving. The average miles per gallon of the 100 cars equaled 22.3, and the standard deviation was 2. Find
   (a) a 90% confidence interval for the true mean (μ) gas mileage of all new automobiles;
   (b) a 95% confidence interval for μ.
   (c) Suppose you wanted to check whether a car manufacturer was complying with government mileage regulations specifying that μ should be at least 23 miles per gallon. Assume all 100 cars sampled were made by that firm. What would you conclude from the data? Are you satisfied with using the usual two-sided confidence intervals reported in parts (a) and (b) to answer part (c)?

2.   An opinion poll, based on 900 citizens, reports that 52% of them favor a particular viewpoint on an issue. Calculate a 95% confidence interval for the value of p, the true proportion of citizens who favor that viewpoint? Does the result of the poll, by itself, persuade you that majority of citizens favor that viewpoint? Explain. Suppose the sample size had been 10,000 and the result (52%) the same. Would this affect your answer?

3.   Every month the Labor Department reports the unemployment rate for the nation. The Labor Department also presents a 90% confidence interval for the true proportion (p) each month. Assume that a new sample of 50,000 households is taken every month so that each month's rate is an estimate of the proportion, p, of the nation's labor force that is unemployed.
   (a) What is the probability that all 12 confidence intervals reported by the government will be correct, i.e., will contain the true unemployment rate each month?

(b) What is the expected number of monthly reports that will be correct in that the true unemployment rate will be within the reported confidence interval?

(c) After learning of your answer to part (a), suppose the Secretary of Labor consulted you and asked you to suggest a different interval which would have probability greater than .5 of yielding 12 correct confidence intervals next year. What might you suggest?

4. In each of the following situations decide whether a two-sided or a one-sided confidence interval is appropriate. Explain your answer.

(a) The government reports the capacity utilization of all manufacturers (essentially the *proportion* of time plant and equipment are actually used relative to maximum potential use based on a survey of firms.)

(b) The EPA and OSHA estimate the probability (usually small) of an individual contracting a severe illness (e.g., a type of cancer) from exposure to a chemical. They convert this probability into an estimate of the number of persons affected by multiplying the estimate (and the limits of the confidence interval) by the number of people exposed to the chemical.

(c) The Federal Reserve Board estimates the nation's money supply every week using a sample of the nation's banks.

(d) A firm alleges that another company has infringed on its trademark by selling an inferior product that is so similar that potential customers are confused. It takes a survey of potential customers (see Chapter 9 for further discussion of this application) and *reports* the proportion of persons who could not distinguish the two brands.

(e) A city council is considering raising the fare on its public transportation system (subway and/or bus) and takes a sample of its elderly population to assess the probable impact of the increase. The study reports the proportion of the sample who say they cannot afford the increased fare.

Answers to Selected Problems

1. (a) 90% CONF (μ; 21.97, 22.63).

(b) 22.3 $\pm$ .392.

(c) Since 23 exceeds the upper limit of the 95% CONF, we conclude that the cars are not in compliance with the regulation. A one-sided (upper) confidence interval would seem more appropriate. If the specified standard (23 mpg) exceeded the upper end of this interval, we would reach the previous conclusion. Indeed, this is the case in this problem.

3. (a) Since each interval has probability .9 of containing the true mean and each month's sample is independent of the others, the probability that all 12 intervals are correct is $(.9)^{12} = .282$.

(b) $12(.9) = 10.8$.

(c) You need a confidence level γ satisfying $\gamma^{12} = .5$ or $\gamma = .944$. Therefore you might suggest a 95% CONF.

4. Testing Hypotheses

In many applications we have prior knowledge of what the value of a parameter of a probability distribution should be. For instance, the number of minority jurors among a total of n should have the general binomial distribution where the parameter p, the probability any venire person is black, equals the *minority fraction* among the jurisdiction's residents in the appropriate age range. Similarly, EPA regulations specify that the *average miles per gallon* of all cars produced by a manufacturer be no less than a specified number, μ. In this section we discuss the principles of statistical hypothesis testing and illustrate its use in two examples: to check whether a county is providing truly representative venires and to determine whether automobiles from a particular manufacturer are in compliance with the mileage regulation.

The logic underlying hypothesis testing is similar to that used in court trials where an accused person is assumed not guilty unless sufficient evidence is presented to contradict this assumption. In hypothesis testing, we assume that the parameter being tested has the appropriate value μ_0 (e.g., the mean miles per gallon of a firm's cars is $\geq \mu_0$), called the *null hypothesis,* and only reject its validity (analogous to finding the accused guilty) when the data contradict it (e.g., the average miles per gallon of an appropriate sample of cars is below μ_0 by a sufficiently large amount). Thus, the hypothesis being tested is given a preferred status relative to a competing or alternative hypothesis. The special status of null hypotheses stems from science, where one does not wish to reject an accepted theory unless a clearly superior theory has been expounded or new data contradict the original theory.

Before proceeding to discuss the details, we emphasize that there are two types of errors we may make or risks we must take when we rely on sample data (or even population data for a small time period). First we may *reject* the *hypothesis* being tested (null hypothesis), even though it is true, as there is a *small* probability that a *sample* average or proportion differs widely from the hypothesized value by chance (i.e., somehow the cars selected were not truly representative, even though a proper random sample was taken). This type of error is called the type I error, and we denote its probability by α. On the other hand, we may fail to reject the null hypothesis when it is false, e.g., fail to detect that a county listed too few blacks on its jury venires. This error is called the type II error and its probability is denoted by the symbol β. The probability, $1 - \beta$ of correctly rejecting the null hypothesis when it is false is the *power* of the test. Ideally, we would like to make both probabilities α and β small, but this can only be done by taking large samples, which may not be feasible.

When the null hypothesis is true, i.e., the parameter being tested equals its assumed value (p_0 for a proportion, μ_0 for a mean), we know the distribution of the appropriate sample statistics ($\bar{x}, \bar{p}$ or the total count, S). In particular, we consider the *difference* (D) between the *observed statistic* and its *expected value*. The basic idea of hypothesis testing is that when

$$D = \text{observed} - \text{expected}$$

is *large,* we doubt the validity of the hypothesis, since the observed statistic is not consistent with what it is expected to be. The only question remaining is how to decide when the difference, D, is sufficiently large to cause us to seriously doubt or reject the hypothesized value of the parameter.

The answer to the question is obtained from the sampling distribution of the statistic ($\bar{x}$ or $\bar{p}$), as we can use this distribution to determine the chance that D is *greater than or equal to* its calculated value. If this probability is *small,* say, *.05 or less,* then the observed statistic had a low probability of occurrence if the null hypothesis were true, and we reject the idea that the true parameter is the one assumed in the null hypothesis. Indeed, if we agree on a value of this probability (α), usually .01 to .10, before we take the sample we can determine how large D must be (called the critical value) in order for us to reject the hypothesized value of the parameter. If we then take a sample and find that D exceeds the critical value, we reject the null hypothesis and say that we found that the data differed statistically from the assumed value of the parameter.

Let us illustrate these ideas using the EPA mileage problem. Suppose that the average miles per gallon of all cars manufactured this year was required to be 22 (or more). In order to check this, EPA takes a sample of 36 cars in order to test whether μ equals 22 *or is less* than 22. The following three questions arise.

(a) Since EPA does not wish to accuse a complying manufacturer of violating the law it sets $\alpha = .05$. Thus, the EPA is setting the type I error at 5%. Find the value that the sample mean must be *less than* in order for the EPA to accuse the manufacturer.

(b) A group is concerned that the manufacturer really decided to have this year's cars average 21 mpg. What is the probability that if the true mpg of all cars produced by the firm was 21, the EPA's decision rule *would detect* that the manufacturer was in violation? What is the probability (β) that the automaker was in violation and would *not be detected* (type II error)?

(c) Do you feel that the detection system described in (a) is fair to both the firm and the environment? If not, can we design a larger sample which will reduce the probability (β) of failing to detect a violating manufacturer while preserving the low (.05) probability of falsely accusing the manufacturer when its cars are in compliance.

Solution. We need to determine the region of the distribution of the sample mean which is furthest from the expected value, 22, and has probability .05. Suppose the standard deviation of the distribution of miles per gallon of the cars is known to be 4. When the null hypothesis ($\mu = 22$) is true, the sample mean $\bar{x}$ is approximately normally distributed with expected value 22 and standard deviation

$$\frac{\sigma}{\sqrt{n}} = \frac{4}{\sqrt{36}} = \frac{4}{6} = \frac{2}{3}.$$

Hence, we can make the required probability calculation by recalling that $\bar{x} - 22/(2/3)$ has a standard normal (Z) distribution. Since the compliance of the firm will be questioned only if $\bar{x}$ is sufficiently below 22, and we know that the standard normal variable, Z, has probability .05 of being less than -1.645, we would reject the hypothesis that the average mpg of the company's cars is less than 22 only if

(3.28a) $$Z = \frac{\bar{x} - 22}{\frac{2}{3}} \leq -1.645$$

or

(3.28b) $$\bar{x} \leq 22 - \frac{2}{3}(1.645) = 20.90.$$

This value 20.90 is called the *critical value* of a 5% level test because it defines the action we will take. If we observe a sample mean less than 20.9

we will have found a *statistically significant difference* from what was expected and will reject the null hypothesis.

We now ask what is the probability that, if the null hypothesis being tested is *false* and the alternative $\mu = 21$ is *true*, we will reject the null hypothesis and accept the alternative (and accuse the firm of violating the standard)? We must calculate the probability that average mpg of a sample of 36 cars is less than 20.90 when the mpg of the population of cars has a mean of 21 (the alternative) and a standard deviation of 4. Under these assumptions the sample mean ($\bar{x}$) is normally distributed with mean 21 and standard deviation, $\sigma/\sqrt{n} = 2/3$. As before, we calculate

$$(3.29) \qquad P_a(\bar{x} < 20.9)$$

by subtracting the expected value (21) from both sides of the inequality and dividing by the standard deviation (2/3) of $\bar{x}$. The subscript a under the probability, P, in expression (3.29) is to remind us that the probability calculated under the *alternative* rather than the null hypothesis. We next express the probability (3.29) in terms of the standard normal Z variable i.e.,

$$(3.30) \qquad Z = \frac{\bar{x} - 21}{\frac{2}{3}} \leq \frac{20.9 - 21}{\frac{2}{3}} = -.15.$$

From Table A we estimate the probability that $[Z \leq -.15]$ as the average of

$$(3.31) \qquad P(Z < -.1) \quad \text{and} \quad P(Z < -.2),$$

obtaining

$$\frac{(.4602 + .4207)}{2} = .4405.$$

This means that there is a probability of only .44 that an observed sample mean will fall in the critical region:

Reject the null hypothesis $\mu = 22$ if $x < 20.9$,

when the *alternative* $\mu = 21$ is true. An equivalent way of expressing this result is that the probability (β) of a type II error (failing to reject the null hypothesis when it is false and the alternative is true) is

$$1 - .4405 = .5595.$$

or about 56%.

Assuming that an average of 1 mpg below the standard would have serious environmental consequences, we would not be satisfied with such a high type II error probability ($\beta = .56$). Hence, a larger sample should be taken. For example, if $n = 64$, under null hypothesis ($\mu_0 = 22$) the sample average would have expected value (22) and standard deviation

$$\frac{\sigma}{\sqrt{n}} = \frac{4}{8} = \frac{1}{2}.$$

Thus, the standard normal form would be

$$Z = \frac{\bar{x} - 22}{\frac{1}{2}},$$

and the criteria for rejecting the null hypothesis at the .05 level becomes

$$(3.32) \qquad Z = \frac{\bar{x} - 22}{\frac{1}{2}} \leq -1.645 \qquad \text{or} \qquad \bar{x} \leq 21.178.$$

Because of the larger sample size, the sample mean should be closer to the hypothesized value (22) than before. Indeed, there is only a 5% chance that the sample average is less than 21.178 if the firm's cars are in compliance. To obtain the power of the new test criteria (3.32) when the alternative is true, we calculate

$$P_a(\bar{x} < 21.178),$$

recalling that $\bar{x}$ now has expected value 21 and standard deviation 1/2. Proceeding as before this equals the probability that

$$\left[Z = \frac{\bar{x} - 21}{\frac{1}{2}} \leq \frac{.178}{\frac{1}{2}} = .356 \right]$$

or

$$(3.33) \qquad P(Z \leq .356) = .639,$$

which was obtained from detailed tables similar to Table A. (From Table A one could approximate this by averaging the probabilities $P(Z \leq .3)$ and $P(Z \leq .4)$ by weighing them by the factors .44 and .56, respectively.) By increasing the sample size we have reduced the risk, β, to about .36. If a larger sample, say 100 cars, were taken, the critical region (2.33) would become

(3.34) $Z = \dfrac{\bar{x} - 22}{.4} \leq -1.645$ or $\bar{x} \leq 21.34,$

and the *power* becomes $P(Z \leq .85) = .8023$, yielding a type II error risk of just under .2. By increasing the sample size, one can keep the probability (α) of a type I error small and make the risk β of a type II error smaller. If α and β are specified in advance, we can determine the sample size required to assure that these predetermined levels of risk are met.

Comment.   To test the hypothesis that $\mu = \mu_0$ against the alternative $\mu < \mu_0$ at the significance level α, we repeat the same calculation, replacing -1.645 by the appropriate point $-z_\alpha$ satisfying $P(Z \leq -z_\alpha) = \alpha$, so the rejection region for a test at level α is:

(3.35) $Z = \dfrac{\bar{x} - \mu_0}{\dfrac{\sigma}{\sqrt{n}}} \leq -z_\alpha$ or $\bar{x} < \mu_0 - \dfrac{z_\alpha \sigma}{\sqrt{n}}.$

Consequently, we *accept* the null hypothesis that $\mu = \mu_0$ and not the alternative $\mu < \mu_0$ if

$$\bar{x} > \mu_0 - \frac{z_\alpha \sigma}{\sqrt{n}} \qquad \text{or} \qquad \mu_0 < \bar{x} + \frac{z_\alpha \sigma}{\sqrt{n}}.$$

Thus, we accept the null hypothesis $\mu = \mu_0$ *if and only if* it is in the one-sided $100(1 - \alpha)\%$ confidence interval (3.27) based on the observed sample mean $\bar{x}$. While the mathematical manipulations may seem tedious, common sense tells us that if we would *accept* a test of the hypothesis that the parameter μ equals a specific value μ_0 when we observe a particular sample mean, $\bar{x}$, then $\bar{x}$ is consistent with μ_0, i.e., has a reasonable chance of occurring when μ_0 is the population mean. It then follows that μ_0 must be in the confidence interval generated by that particular $\bar{x}$, as the possible values of the parameter μ which can be regarded as consistent with the observed $\bar{x}$ are in the confidence interval.

It should be *emphasized that all* the calculations of critical regions and error probabilities α and β have been carried out *before* the sample was taken. This is a big advantage in the *planning* of a statistical study.

Now assume that the EPA decides to take a sample of 100 cars so that it will have only a 5% chance (α) of rejecting the null hypothesis ($\mu = 22$) when it is true and a 20% chance of failing to reject the null hypothesis when it is false ($\mu = 21$); thus it uses the critical region given by (3.34) and will reject the assumption of compliance if $\bar{x} < 21.34$.

Suppose that the sample average ($\bar{x}$) mpg is 21.14. Of course we would *reject* the null hypothesis, and the EPA presumably would take appropriate action. From a statistical viewpoint we realize that the observed mean (21.14) is *less* than the critical value (21.34), and we can determine the probability that such a low sample mean could occur by chance if the null hypothesis is true. This is done by calculating

(3.36) $P(\bar{x} \leq 21.14)$,

assuming that the sample is taken from a population with mean, $\mu = 22$ and $\sigma = 4$. Then $\bar{x}$ is normal with mean 22 and standard deviation $4/\sqrt{100} = .4$. Transforming (3.36) to its Z form yields

(3.37) $P\left(\dfrac{\bar{x} - 22}{.4} \leq \dfrac{21.14 - 22}{.4}\right) = P(Z < -2.25) = .012.$

Thus, the *probability* of observing a difference (D) between the *observed* sample mean and its *expected* value (under the null hypothesis) is just over 1%, which is convincing evidence that the null hypothesis ($\mu = 22$) is not true and should be rejected. The probability we just calculated is called the *observed significance level,* prob-value or *p*-value of the data and deserves a formal definition:

The *p*-value is the *probability* of obtaining an observed result as extreme (far from expected) or more extreme than the one actually obtained *due to sampling variation or chance.*

From a *p*-value one can immediately decide whether observed data are statistically significant at a preset level (α), since a *p*-value *less* than α is equivalent to rejecting the null hypothesis at the level (α). It is more useful than the concept of testing at a prespecified level, e.g., .05, since it allows the decisionmaker to utilize the actual probability of obtaining data as extreme as the observed data and does not lead to simplistic decision rules such as accepting the null hypothesis when a test of the data yields a *p*-value of .06 or .07. While .06 and .07 are greater than .05, such *p*-values certainly should be considered as casting some doubt on the validity of the null hypothesis, especially in situations where the *power* of the test is low, or in other words, when β is high (say four or more times the value of α). Indeed the *p*-value can be thought of as a scale indicating the weight of the evidence against the null hypothesis. The smaller the *p*-value, the stronger is the evidence that null hypothesis is false.

We now summarize the essential features of hypothesis testing.

The objective of hypothesis testing is to determine the validity of a hypothesis concerning the values of one or more parameters of a characteristic (variable) of a population. It involves the following elements.

(1) A null hypothesis
(2) An alternative hypothesis
(3) A test statistic
(4) A rejection region and the following risks:
    (a) The risk of a type I error, i.e., rejecting the null hypothesis when it is true.
    (b) The risk of a type II error, i.e., failing to reject the null hypothesis when it is false.

The probability of making a type I error is denoted by α. It is the probability of obtaining an observed value of the test statistic in the rejection region when the null hypothesis is true. The *power* of a test is the probability of *rejecting* the null hypothesis when the *alternative* is true. The probability of making a type II error is denoted by β and is *one* minus the power of the test.

It is convenient to summarize the possible decisions and their respective probabilities in Table 3.2. It should be emphasized that the corresponding probabilities in column 4 assume that the null hypothesis is true while the probabilities in column 5 are obtained assuming that the alternative is true.

The basic idea of hypothesis testing is to find a set of outcomes that have a *low probability* of occurring when the null hypothesis is true but have a *high* probability of occurring when the *alternative* is true (and the null hypothesis is false). Intuitively such a set of outcomes forms a good critical region, as they occur rarely if the null hypothesis is true but occur frequently when the alternative is true. In our example, if the hypothesis $\mu = 22$ is true, there should be a low probability of obtaining a sample

TABLE 3.2.   Decision Table With Corresponding Probabilities

Decision	Null Hypothesis (H_0)		Corresponding Probabilities	
	True	False	True (4)	False (5)
Accept H_0	Correct Decision	Type II error	$1 - \alpha$	β
Reject H_0	Type I error	Correct Decision	α	$1 - \beta$

mean much less than 22, e.g., less than 21.5, if an adequate number of observations are taken. Similarly, if the alternative $\mu = 21$ is true, there is a high probability the sample mean will not exceed 21 by more than two standard errors. Hence, critical regions, such as the one reject if $\bar{x} <$ 21.34 which we obtained for a sample of 100, are statistically sensible. This critical region and its probability under both the null and alternative hypothesis are shown in Figure 3.4. The error probabilities (α under the null, β under the alternative) are the areas under the normal curves which approximate the sampling distributions of the mean $\bar{x}$ in each case. Notice that increasing the critical value 21.34 would decrease β, the chance of a type II error at the price of increasing α.

Comment. In the example we assumed that σ, the standard deviation of the variable (mpg) in the population of cars produced was known. If it is not known, then one uses the sample standard deviation, $s = \sqrt{\sum (x_i - \bar{x})^2/(n - 1)}$ to estimate σ and the critical region (3.34) becomes

$$\frac{\bar{x} - \mu_0}{\dfrac{s}{\sqrt{n}}} \leq -z_\alpha \qquad \text{or} \qquad \bar{x} \leq \mu_0 - \frac{z_\alpha \sigma}{\sqrt{n}},$$

where z_α again denotes the point of the normal curve satisfying the formula $P(Z \leq -z_\alpha) = \alpha$.

Before presenting an example with binomial data, we note that the above example dealt with a specific *alternative* hypothesis which was *less* than the *null* hypothesis. Such problems are called one-sided (as in the confidence interval situation), since we are concerned only when the value of the parameter given by the null hypothesis is in error in one direction. This is the typical situation in many legal and policymaking situations. For example, we test whether

(a) The proportion of minority of jurors or hires is *equal to or less than* that fraction (p) in the *eligible* or *qualified* population.

(b) The emission level of a noxious gas is equal to *or* exceeds the appropriate standard.

Sometimes one is interested in alternatives which are two-sided, i.e., a deviation in either direction should lead to a rejection of the null hypothesis. Examples of this situation are:

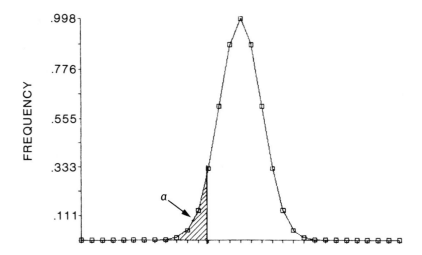

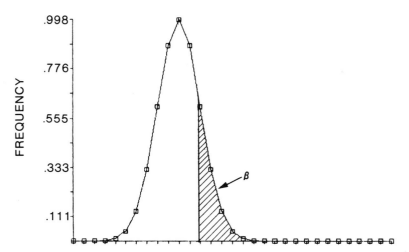

FIGURE 3.4.   The approximate sampling distribution of the sample mean ($\bar{x}$) when the null hypothesis is true (top) and when the alternative is true (bottom). The critical region $\bar{x} < 21.34$ is indicated on the top curve and has probability .05 under the null hypothesis. The complement of the critical region, i.e., $\bar{x} \geq 24.34$ or the *acceptance* region, is drawn on the bottom curve. Its area, *under the alternative*, is β, the type II error probability.

(a) A firm purchases a part that should be 5″ long. It tests a sample of a shipment from a supplier and will not accept it if the sample average length differs from the null hypothesis (length = 5″) in either direction, since parts will be unusable if they are either too large or too small.

(b) In checking a jury panel for *representativeness*, one might want to test whether the fraction of females equals their fraction, say .5, of all eligible jurors and would want to reject the county's selection process if the proportion of females in a sample of venire persons was too low (possible bias against females) or too high (possible bias against males).

(c) In reporting economic data, such as the monthly unemployment rate, we need to test whether a change occurred between the times of the surveys. Technically speaking we compare the difference in rates, which estimates the difference $p_2 - p_1$ between the probabilities p_1 and p_2 of being unemployed during the first and second month, respectively.

Here we wish to detect a change in either direction. In Chapter 5 we discuss methods for testing whether $p_2 - p_1 = 0$ or whether $p_1 \neq p_2$, i.e., $p_1 - p_2 \neq 0$.

We now illustrate the concepts using data from *Turner v. Fouche*,[6] a jury discrimination case in which black residents of Taliafero County, Georgia challenged the methods used by the county. Blacks formed 60% of the population of the county but only 6 blacks were on a grand jury of 23.

Here the number of blacks on the jury should follow a binomial distribution with parameters $p = .6$ and $n = 23$ if the selection process produces a representative sample of the population. Let us develop a *one-sided* test of the null hypothesis, $p = .60$ against the alternative that $p < .60$, as it is unreasonable to believe that a county in Georgia at the time the case was filed discriminated against whites. We shall set α, the risk of type I error at .05.

Under the null hypothesis (the selection process is fair) the binomial distribution can be approximated by a normal variable with

$$\text{mean } \mu = np = 23(.6) = 13.8$$

and

$$\text{standard deviation } \sqrt{np(1 - p)} = \sqrt{23(.6)(.4)} = 2.35.$$

Since a standard normal variable, Z, has probability .05 of being less than -1.645, we make the usual transformation yielding a critical region.

$$(3.38) \qquad Z = \frac{S - 13.8}{2.35} \leq -1.645,$$

where S is the number of blacks among the 23 jurors. Hence, the critical region given by (3.38) is

$$S \leq 13.8 - (1.645)(2.35) = 9.93,$$

which we will round down to

$$(3.39) \qquad S \leq 9.$$

Since the actual number of blacks on the grand jury was 6, we reject the null hypothesis that the county was fair in favor of the alternative that blacks received *less* than their proper representation on the grand jury. From a statistical viewpoint we can ask the following question: Suppose a minority under-representation of one third was considered to be a legally meaningful difference so that we desire a *high* power to detect a system that gave minorities two thirds of their fair share. In the *Turner* case this would be $2/3 \times 60\% = 40\%$ of the jurors. The *alternative* hypothesis now is that grand juries in the county follow a binomial model with $n = 23$ and $p_a = .4$. This binomial variable (S_a) has

$$\text{mean} = 23(.4) = 9.2$$

and

$$\text{standard deviation} = \sqrt{23(.4)(.6)} = 2.35.$$

We calculate the power of the test, i.e., the probability of detecting the discriminatory practice by finding

$$(3.40) \qquad P_a (S_a \leq 9.5),$$

since we are spreading the discrete integer 9 over the interval (8.5, 9.5). Using the normal approximation, (3.40) is equal to

$$P \left[\frac{S_a - 9.2}{2.35} \leq \frac{9.5 - 9.2}{2.35} \right] = P \left[Z \leq \frac{.3}{2.35} \right]$$

$$(3.41) \qquad\qquad\qquad = P[Z \leq 1.28] = .551.$$

Thus, the test has only 55% power or a type II error probability β of .45. The reason the test, based on (3.38) and (3.39), detected the difference between the observed data and its expectation under the null hypothesis ($p = .6$) is that p-value of the data, the probability that a binomial variable with $p = .6$ and $n = 23$ would have a value of 6 or less equals .0017, which is very small.

In Figure 3.5 we plot the histograms of the binomial distributions corresponding to the null ($n = 23$, $p = .6$) and alternative ($n = 23$, $p = .4$) hypotheses and indicate the rejection region.

Comments.   (1) In our analysis of *Turner v. Fouche* data we worked with the sum or total count rather than the sample proportion. They are equivalent statistics as the proportion equals the sum divided by n.

(2) Our power calculations indicated that a larger sample size would have been desirable. In the legal context this problem may not be as easy to remedy as in cases concerning regulatory compliance, as the number of jurors chosen is determined by the need for trials in the area rather than the need to assess whether a discriminatory policy exists. Hence, we are limited to an existing sample size. In the environmental area, we can determine the size of a sample of cars that should be tested. In the next chapter more illustrations of the binomial model in discrimination cases will be given, and factors such as the relevant time frame also operate to restrict the sample size available for analysis.

(3) The basic idea behind most tests of hypothesis is to compare the statistic (calculated from the data actually observed with its expected value). The difference, D, between them is measured in units of the standard error (standard deviation of the distribution of the statistic). Thus, most test statistics can be put in the approximate normal form

(3.42) $$Z = \frac{\text{observed} - \text{expected}}{\text{standard error}}.$$

For one-sided tests, we reject the null hypothesis if the value of (3.42) is too small (or too large). For two-sided tests, which are appropriate if deviations from the null hypothesis in either direction are of concern, we reject if (3.42) is very small or very large. The critical values used to decide whether the statistic (3.42) is too small (large) are determined by the probability α of a type I error that we are willing to tolerate. Once α is set, the appropriate points on the normal distribution are obtained from Table A.

Problems

1.   A state consumer protection agency has received many complaints of short weighing in packaged candy sold in the area. The package should

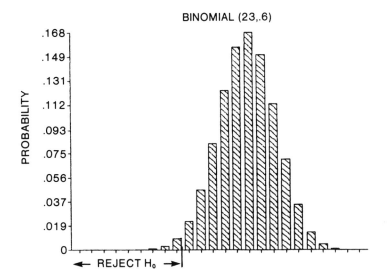

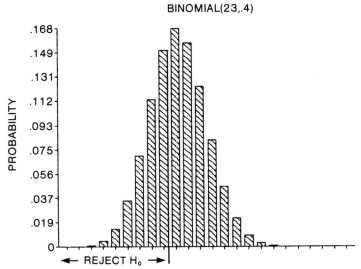

FIGURE 3.5.   Histograms of the binomial distributions with (a) $n = 23$, $p = .6$ (top) and (b) $n = 23$, $p = .4$ (bottom), indicating the critical region of the 5% level one-sided test. Reject the null hypothesis ($p = .6$) if the number of minority juniors is nine or less.

contain 4 ounces of chocolate. A sample of 81 packages are taken and reweighed and a mean weight of 3.8 ounces, with a standard deviation of .3 ounces, is observed.

(a) What is the null hypothesis for this problem?

(b) Define a reasonable alternative hypothesis.

(c) Develop a critical region for a .05 level test of the null hypothesis. Test the observed data.

(d) Calculate the power of the test to detect the alternative hypothesis you chose in part (b).

(e) Calculate the observed significance level (p-value) of the actual data.

(f) On the basis of your answers to (c) and (e), what should the consumer protection agency do?

(g) Would your answer to (f) change if the observed standard deviation had been 3 ounces instead of .3?

2.   Suppose that 4 juries or a total of 48 jury selections are examined in a locality where a minority group forms 40% of the population eligible for jury service.

(a) Find a 5% level one-sided critical region for testing $p_0 = .4$ against $p_a = .2$.

(b) For the critical region you found in (a), calculate the probability (β) of a type II error.

(c) Suppose 4 minority members were among the 48 jurors. Would it be permissible to say that the result is statistically significant at the 5% level (using the one-sided region in part (a))? What more can be said about these data?

5.   Using the Concept of Power to Choose between Two Suggested Procedures

Some commentators[7] have noted that the requirement of establishing a statistically significant difference at the .05 or other predetermined level has led to experts arguing over which test is appropriate and courts[8] have expressed concern over litigation developing into esoteric debates on technical matters. When two (or more) statistical procedures are used to analyze the same set of data to decide whether the null hypothesis should be accepted or rejected, modern statistical theory agrees with common sense—use the *most powerful* test. If one does not use the theoretically most powerful test, then one is increasing the probability, β, of a type II error without any compensating decrease in α, the probability of a type I error. In this section we illustrate the basic issue involved by considering testing the mean (μ) of a *normal distribution*. Then we list some situations where the most powerful statistical test is known and mention a few points that decisionmakers might consider when faced with experts (paid by opposing parties) who advocate different statistical procedures.

We know that the center of any normal curve or distribution is both the population *mean* (μ) and population median, as half the probability lies to the left of μ. Thus, one might decide to use the sample median, M, to make a test about a hypothesized value of μ or derive a confidence interval for it. The reason we use the sample mean ($\bar{x}$) is that the test based on it is more powerful than the one based on M. Similarly, the length of the confidence interval for μ is shorter if the sample mean rather than the sample median is used to estimate μ.

The justification for this assertion when the variable under study has a *normal* distribution, with mean μ and standard deviation, σ, is a consequence of the *sampling distribution* of the two statistics $\bar{x}$ and M which we state in the following

Theorem

(a) The sampling distribution of the mean of n observations from a normal distribution has a normal distribution with expected value μ and standard deviation $\sigma/\sqrt{n}$.

(b) Under the same circumstances, the median, M, of the n observations is approximately normally distributed with mean μ standard deviation $(\sigma/\sqrt{n}) \cdot \sqrt{\pi/2}$.

Since $\pi/2$ equals 1.5699, $\sqrt{\pi/2}$ is 1.253, so the median, (M), has a sampling distribution which is *less* concentrated about the true population mean μ than that of the sample mean, $\bar{x}$. Notice that the standard error of the median is about 1.25 times that of the sample mean.

We explore the consequences of this by returning to our EPA miles per gallon example. We now assume that the miles per gallon of the cars under study follow a normal distribution with mean μ and standard deviation $\sigma = 4$. Suppose a sample of size $n = 100$ is planned. Let us determine the critical region, similar to (3.35), of a 5% test of the hypothesis $\mu = 22$ using the sample median. Then we will compute its power against the alternative, $\mu_a = 21$. Since the standard deviation of the sampling distribution of M is

(3.43) $$1.253 \frac{\sigma}{\sqrt{n}} = (1.253) \frac{4}{\sqrt{100}} = .5012,$$

we obtain a critical region of the form: Reject if $M \leq C$ by transforming to the standard normal, Z. Thus, the critical region is determined from the condition

(3.44) $$Z = \frac{M - 22}{.5012} \leq -1.645 \qquad \text{or} \qquad M \leq 21.176,$$

just as (3.28b) was found using the distribution of $\bar{x}$. Thus, we reject the null hypothesis at the 5% level of significance only if the sample median is less than 21.176.

We obtain the *power* of the test by computing the probability that the sample median is less than 21.176 when the true population mean, μ, equals 21. As before we calculate

$$P_a(M < 21.176)$$

by transforming to the Z variable under the alternative ($\mu = 21$). Proceeding as before shows that we need to obtain the probability of the event

$$\left[Z = \frac{M - 21}{.5012} < \frac{21.176 - 21}{.5012} = \frac{.176}{.5012} = .351 \right],$$

as the standard error of the median (M) was .5012 (see 3.42). From detailed tables (similar to Table A) we obtain

$$P(Z \leq .351) = .637.$$

Hence, the probability, β, of a type II error is $1 - .637 = .363$. This is noticeably larger than the β of .20 of the test *based* on the sample mean, $\bar{x}$. Thus, using the median rather than the mean to make an inference about the population mean (μ) led to a greater type II error for the *same* type I error. This is clearly inefficient. For data from a normal distribution it can be shown that the power and type II error of the test based on the sample median of 100 observations is quite close to that of the sample mean based on only 64 observations. Using the sample median instead of the sample mean in this circumstance is equivalent to wasting about 36 sample observations.

Comments. (1) The same type of calculation using the sampling distribution of M shows that a confidence interval based on M is about 1.25

times as wide as the corresponding one based on $\bar{x}$. Again this is an unnecessarily large uncertainty when one knows that the data comes from a normal distribution.

(2) Fortunately, statistical theory often can determine the most powerful test statistic and an associated most accurate estimate of a parameter when the form of the distribution of the variable under study is known. In particular, we know that

(a) To make statistical inferences about the mean μ of a normal variable, the sample mean, $(\bar{x})$, leads to the most powerful test and the most accurate estimate.

(b) To make statistical inferences about the probability, p, of a binomial model, the sample proportion, or equivalently the sample sum, leads to the most powerful test and the most accurate estimate.

(c) To make statistical inferences about the proportion of the total population that belong to one class (A) in the hypergeometric model, the most powerful test is based on the sample proportion or sum (count) of A's in the sample of n.

Sometimes we may not know the form of the distribution or may believe it is likely to be normal but may wish to hedge a little and not base our inference on the sample mean, which may not be the best statistic if the variable is not normally distributed. There are other procedures which we will learn about in Chapters 7 and 11 which do not depend on the normality assumption but are quite efficient in that they lose the equivalent of only 5% to 10% of the observations in contrast to the 36% lost methods based on the sample median when the underlying variable is normally distributed in the population. These methods enable us to avoid making the assumption that the data are from a normal curve, when they may not be, without losing much statistical information if the variable under study is normally distributed in the population.

How can one avoid being fooled by a statistician who uses a test with low power when a more powerful one is available?

(1) First, ask what is the likely shape of the characteristic (e.g., miles per gallon, height, income, time to promotion, emissions per month) in the population. Is it normal or approximately so or is it skewed like the income data?

(2) If a particular shape is suggested, inquire as to the most powerful test to see whether it is used. If several shapes are used, ask whether a test which has high power across all the shapes exists[9] and if so why

shouldn't it be used. This will avoid two experts selecting the most different or extreme shapes and using the corresponding most powerful tests. (3) Consider the side the expert is testifying for or representing. In a discrimination case, plaintiffs desire statistically significant differences while defendants desire the opposite. If a plaintiff's expert asserts that a variable is known to have a distribution of a specific shape, ask what is the basis of this opinion. Has any check of this assumption been made? Conversely, defendant's experts should be asked about the power of the test they advocate to detect a meaningful difference. If the power is not high, a decisionmaker should raise the question, why should the risk (α) of a type I error be kept so low, say .05, when the risk (β) of a type II error is high, say .4. Would the inference change if the risks were closer, say $\alpha = .10$ and $\beta = .20$?

The above questions are phrased in the context of a legal case but are applicable in deciding whether a study should be carried out. If a preset level of significance must be adhered to, say .05, then why spend substantial funds if the expected power of the test to be used to analyze the data is .5 or less. In the health area, where large sample sizes may not be available, the last part of the third guideline questions the rigid adherence to a low α-level when the power to detect a meaningful risk to public health (say a tripling of one's chance of getting a serious illness) is very low.

NOTES

1.   Technically, selecting a sample from a finite population is analogous to the hypergeometric model, as the probability of selection changes during the sampling process. When the fraction of the total population chosen as the sample is small, this can be neglected and the binomial model used.

2.   The formal proof is based on the following facts: (a) The expected value of a sum of random variables is the sum of their individual expected values, (b) the expected value of a constant times a random variable is the constant times the expected value of the random variable, (c) the variance of the sum of n *independent* random variables is the sum of their respective variances and (d) the variance of a constant times a random variable is the *square* of the constant times the variance of the random variable. This last result says that the standard deviation of a constant times a random variable is the constant times the standard deviation of the random variable. The result that the expected value of a sample mean from a population with mean μ equals μ follows from the first two facts. The expected value of $\sum_{i=1}^{n} X_i$ is $n\mu$ as each X_i has mean μ. When we divide $\sum_{i=1}^{n} X_i$ by n we are multiplying it by $(1/n)$, so the second fact implies that $E(\bar{X}) = E(\sum_{1}^{n} X_i)/n = (n\mu)/n = \mu$.

3.   In the statistical texts this is called the *continuity correction*. It has been used in actual legal cases.

4.   In the decennial census, the unemployment rate is based on a sample of 15% to 20% of the households in an area. For large areas, such a sample yields a highly accurate estimate. For a small town of population 2000 the census estimate would be based on about 400

households. Routine calculation shows that the census sample for such a town with a true unemployment rate of 6.5% has an approximate probability of .342 of yielding an estimated rate of less than 6%. A large city with the same true unemployment rate would be virtually certain of qualifying.

5. For a more detailed description of the case, see the paper by L. Katz (1975).
6. 396 U.S. 346 (1970).
7. Baldus, D. C. and Cole, J. W. L. *Statistical Proof of Discrimination 1987 Supplement,* at 190.
8. *EEOC v Federal Reserve Bank of Richmond* 698 F.2d 633 (4th Cir. 1983) at 645.
9. Such tests are called efficiency robust tests.

REFERENCES

Articles

KATZ, L. (1975). Presentation of a Confidence Interval Estimate as Evidence in a Legal Proceeding. *American Statistican* **29,** 138–142.

KAYE, D. (1983). Statistical Significance and the Burden of Persuasion. *Law and Contemporary Problems* **46,** 13–23.

Books

In addition to the basic texts mentioned at the beginning, the reader might consult:

INGELFINGER, J. A., MOSTELLER, F., THIBODEAU, L. A. AND WARE, J. H. (1983). *Biostatistics in Clinical Medicine.* New York: MacMillan (an excellent discussion of the importance of the power and *p*-value of a statistical test).

MENDENHALL, W. AND REINMUTH, J. E. (1982). *Statistics for Management and Economics,* 4th ed. North Scituate, Mass.: Duxbury.

SMITH, G. (1985). *Statistical Reasoning.* Boston: Allyn and Bacon.

Use of the Binomial
Model in Cases Involving
Discrimination in Jury
Selection or Employment
Opportunity

Chapter 4

1. Introduction

In this chapter we illustrate how the concepts of hypothesis testing and confidence interval estimation are used in the analysis of data in discrimination cases where the number of minority jurors (or hires) in a sample of n should have a binomial distribution with parameters n and p (the minority fraction of the eligible population). It is helpful to think about two distinct stages in applying the binomial model in discrimination cases:

(a) Determining the proportion (p) that minorities form of the population eligible for jury service (or qualified for the job).

(b) Performing the statistical test to assess whether the actual selection process yields results consistent with random sampling of the relevant population.

In this chapter we first review some of the early uses of statistics in jury discrimination cases and then discuss the case of *Castenada v. Partida*.[1] We discuss the use of the binomial model in the equal employment context separately because the first step determining the minority share (p) of qualified persons in the labor market area is more difficult than determining the proportion of the minority population eligible for jury service.

153

2. Historical Uses of Statistics in Jury Discrimination

Since there are few, if any, special skills required of jurors, courts typically determine the minority share of eligible persons from census figures for the appropriate age segment of the population in the relevant jurisdiction (city, county). Sometimes other lists, such as voter registration, are used, and multiple sources[2] may be needed to compile a comprehensive master list.

The earliest cases involved virtual total exclusion of a minority group on jury lists or panels for a long period of time. For example, in *Norris v. Alabama*,[3] blacks formed 7.5% of the eligible population, but none were called in 24 years. In *Hill v. Texas*[4] blacks formed 14% of the eligible population (according to census data), and none had been called in 16 years. We will illustrate the basic statistical concepts with data for one year from the *Hill v. Texas* case. Each year the Dallas County jury commission created four grand jury panels, each of three months duration. They summoned 16 persons for each panel and selected 12. None of those summoned were black. Thus, in *one* year the Commission selected 64 individuals for possible jury service, *none* of whom were black. The opinion described several data sources for the determination of the fraction (p) of potential jurors who were black. We will use the poll taxation list which gives a lower value of p than census population data, although we realize that the poll tax itself was used to exclude blacks from civic and political power. Of the 66,000 poll taxpayers, 8000 were blacks so that $p = 8/66 = .1212$.

Since observing *no* blacks out of 64 persons randomly selected from the poll tax rolls is the same as observing 64 whites out of the 64, and as the fraction q of whites on the poll tax list is

$$q = 1 - p = 1 - \frac{8}{66} = \frac{58}{66},$$

the probability of the actual data occurring by chance is the chance of obtaining whites on *all* 64 independent trials with probability q on each. This probability is

(4.1) $q^{64} = \left(\frac{58}{66}\right)^{64} = .00026,$

which is *less* than one in 1000. Such a small p-value (there is no possible outcome farther from the expected number—.1212(64) = 7.76 or 8 black jurors) for just *one* year of data certainly supports the Supreme Court's finding that "chance or accident could hardly have accounted for the continuous omission of negroes from grand jury lists for so long a period of time", especially when similar data were observed for 16 years.

In our analysis we used poll-tax payers as the population from which jurors could be selected rather than the raw census data, since it yielded a lower value of p. Thus, we are giving Dallas County the benefit of any doubt about the most appropriate data source. When several *reasonable* data sources may yield different values of p, we can test the data for consistency with each p. An equivalent approach is to create a one-sided upper $100(1 - \alpha)\%$ confidence interval for p from the data. If all of the fractions p *exceed* the upper end of the confidence interval, then a test of the data for consistency with any of them would result in rejection at the prespecified level α. We now illustrate the calculation of the one-sided *99% confidence interval for p on the data in Hill* using the binomial distribution.

The 99% confidence interval contains all values of p that give a probability exceeding .01 for the observed data or a more extreme outcome, i.e., these values of p would *not* be rejected by a one-sided test at the .01 level. In the present situation 0 is the most extreme possible value. Since the probability that any juror selected at random is white is $1 - p$, as p is the proportion of blacks in the eligible pool, the probability that all 64 jurors are white is $(1 - p)^{64}$. Hence, p must satisfy

(4.2) $(1 - p)^{64} \geq .01$

in order to be in the 99% CONF. Using a calculator to take 64th roots of both sides of (4.2) yields

$$1 - p \geq (.01)^{1/64} = .93067$$

or

$$p \leq 1 - .93067 = .0694.$$

Thus, the 99% one-sided CONF for p is

(4.3)   99% CONF $(p; 0, .0694)$,

so any value of p *greater* than .0694 or about .07 being tested against the *Hill* data would be rejected as a plausible value of the minority fraction in the population of eligible jurors. Since both data sources mentioned in the case, the census and the poll tax list, had minority fractions[5] exceeding .07, the question of which source was more appropriate would not affect the ultimate statistical inference, using a one-sided test at the .01 level of significance.

The need for more precise statistical analysis arose when courts were asked to examine situations in which some blacks were on jury venires and had to decide whether they received their "fair share". In *Swain v. Alabama*,[6] the U.S. Supreme Court compared the black fraction of grand jurors (about 12%) with their fraction in the community (26%) and decided that the difference of 10–15% was *insufficient* to create a *prima facie*[7] case. Later the Fourth Circuit in *Blackwell v. Thomas*[8] said that if the difference between the black fraction of juries and their fraction (p) in the population is greater than 10% and an opportunity for discrimination exists, then a *prima facie* case of discrimination can be established.

A difficulty with the rote application of the absolute difference ($\bar{p} - p$) criteria stated in *Blackwell* is that minorities who constitute less than 10% of the population in an area could be excluded from juries. This anomaly can be avoided if relative measures such as

(a) the ratio of the proportion ($\bar{p}$) on juries to the proportion in the appropriate population (p) i.e., $\bar{p}/p$, or

(b) the *relative* under-representation, i.e., $(p - \bar{p})/p$, the ratio of the absolute difference in the proportions to the true one

are considered. Notice that the second measure (b) is just *one* minus the first (a), so both relate to the same concept, the fraction of their fair share minorities receive.

The *Swain v. Alabama* case has drawn a number of critical comments,[9] in part because hypothesis testing and confidence intervals were not used by the court at the time. Plaintiff Swain asserted that blacks were under-represented on grand juries in Tallegda County, Alabama and that no black has ever served on a petit jury, in part because their participation on the grand juries was limited and never exceeded their proportion of the population. A nonstatistical legal issue in the case was whether the system of preemptory challenges which prosecutors used to eliminate blacks from petit juries was constitutional. Of more statistical interest are the following facts that will be used as the basis of our analysis:

(1) Blacks formed 26% of the population eligible for jury service.
(2) About four juries are selected each year.
(3) During the 10 year period under consideration, 1953–1962, jury panels averaged between 50 to 60 members.
(4) During the period, 80% of the grand jury panels had at least one

black, the black fraction of jurors ranged from 10–12%, and in 1955 the grand jury panel was 23% black (which was their highest percentage on any panel).

Since the summaries of the U.S. Supreme Court and state court decisions do not give all the required data we will assume that

(a) 40 jury panels were created.
(b) The average panel size was 50.
(c) Blacks formed 12% or 240 of the 2000 jurors selected.

Note that the assumptions are favorable to the state of Alabama.

Let us first find the probability of observing 12% or fewer blacks on juries if the jurors were selected at random from the eligible population (26% black). This probability is obtained using the normal approximation described in Section 3.1 as follows:

$$P(S \leq 240.5) = P\left(\frac{S - (2000)(.26)}{(2000)(.26)(.74)} \leq \frac{240.5 - (2000)(.26)}{(2000)(.26)(.74)}\right)$$

(4.4) $= P(Z - 14.25) \approx .812 \times 10^{-90}.$

Such a minute probability clearly implies rejecting the hypothesis that the jurors were representative of the population at all standard levels of significance.

If one assumed that the fraction of eligible jurors who were black was unknown, from (3.27) we obtain an upper 99% CONF as

(4.5a) $0 \text{ to } .12 + (2.327)\sqrt{\frac{(.26)(.74)}{2000}}$

or

(4.5b) $99\% \text{ CONF}(p; 0, .1428).$

Thus, 14.3% is the largest possible percentage of blacks in the eligible population that would be consistent with the data. Notice that the true proportion (26%) of blacks among eligible persons is much greater than 14.3%.

Although the Court did not perform the above calculation and perhaps was handicapped by lack of precise data on the number of jurors chosen, it could have studied the issue of whether blacks were limited to no more than their fraction of eligibles. Since the maximum percentage of black jurors on any panel was 23%, we know that they were below the expected fraction (26%) either on all 40 panels or on 39 of them (assuming that 23%

equals 26% in view of the rounding inherent in calculating percentages from discrete data). The probability that the number of blacks on any jury panel is below their expected value is approximately[10] 1/2, so the chance that they would be *below their expected value* on all 40 jury panels is $(1/2)^{40} = 0.09 \times 10^{-13}$ and the probability that they would be below 39 times and above once is

$$40 \left(\frac{1}{2}\right)^{40} = 3.638 \times 10^{-11}.$$

Thus, the probability of observing 39 or 40 panels on which blacks had their expected (population) share or *less* out of 40 panels is

$$9.09 \times 10^{-13} + 3.638 \times 10^{-11} = 3.73 \times 10^{-11}$$

or less than *one in a billion*. Thus, the data certainly supports the plaintiff's assertion that the black participation on grand juries was limited. Such a finding might have been helpful in analyzing the effect of preemptory challenges, as they can be used to systematically exclude blacks when black participation on the grand juries is limited to a small number.

We emphasize that *statistics alone* do not determine the ultimate legal decision. Courts also look at the degree of opportunity to discriminate, e.g., the amount of subjectivity in the juror selection process. Indeed, in the *Swain* case the decisions do not indicate that the race of potential jurors was on the master lists used. One way this knowledge can be incorporated into the analysis is in the choice of *level* (α) of significance required to decide that the jury selection process under scrutiny deviated from an unbiased and representative one. Thus, a 5% level one-sided test may be appropriate when racial identifiers are attached to the names of all potential jurors, but a 1% level may be deemed appropriate if the jurisdiction has attempted to design a truly representative selection process. Of course, the specification of the appropriate significance level is a legal rather than statistical decision.

Similarly, measures of the impact of the alleged discrimination, such as the number of venire persons the minority group lost over the time period and measures of relative impact, should also be considered, especially in large samples (exceeding 1000) that can classify small deviations from the null hypothesis as statistically significant at the .05 level that legally might be deemed minimal. The power of the test should also play a role in assessing whether a finding of a nonsignificant difference based on small samples or a barely significant difference based on a large sample is truly informative. We will discuss the role of statistical power in our analysis of employment discrimination cases, as its potential effect is more interesting there. We next discuss some important recent cases.

3. Recent Jury Discrimination Cases Utilizing Statistical Methodology

In *Alexander v. Louisiana*,[11] a black appealed his conviction in Lafayette Parish on the grounds that the grand jury selection procedures were discriminatory against blacks and because women were excluded from jury service by the state. The statistical arguments, of course, involved only the black population. The jury selection process was conducted by a commission who compiled a list of names from a variety of sources, e.g., telephone directories, voter polls and lists provided by the school board and by the jury commissioners themselves. The jury selection process proceeded as follows: A questionnaire was mailed to all persons on the lists that *included* a space to report race. Through this process 7374 questionnaires were returned, of which 1015 were from blacks and 189 had no racial identification. The jury commissioners then rejected about 5000 questionnaires on the grounds that these individuals were not qualified for jury services or were exempted by state law. From the remaining 2000 persons, 400 names were selected, supposedly in a random manner, and placed in a box from which grand jury panels of 20 were selected for the parish. Of these 400 persons, 27 were black. On the venire of 20 persons for the petitioner's grand jury there was one black, but none of the 12 jurors on the grand jury that actually indicted him were black.

In order to analyze the data statistically, we must compute the probability of observing 27 or fewer blacks out of 400 persons from which the grand juries were selected, assuming that blacks constitute $100p\%$ of the eligible pool. The major problem here is determining the appropriate value of p that should be used. Although the case was tried in 1979, only census data for 1970 and voter registration lists were available to the court, in addition to the questionnaire results. In Table 4.1 we present data for a number of reasonable referent (comparison) groups and determine the fraction (p) of blacks in each group.

We now compute the probability of observing 27 or fewer blacks out of the 400 persons who comprise the pool of possible jurors for the proportion (13.76%) of respondents to the questionnaire who were black. If we reject the null hypothesis, $p = .1376$, in favor of the alternative that blacks

TABLE 4.1.   Minority Fraction in Possible Data Sources of Eligible Jurors in *Alexander v. Louisiana*

	Black	Total	Fraction Black
Population 21+ (1960)	9473	44,986	.2106
Voter Registration List	6610	40,896	.1616
Respondents to Questionnaires	1015	7374	.1376

Source: 405 U.S. 625 at 627–628.

were underrepresented for this value of p, clearly a test of any larger value of p would also lead to rejection.

Let S = numbers of black jurors. Under the hypotheses being tested, the random variable (S) is a binomial one with $n = 400$ and $p = .1376$, so its expected value is

$$np = 400 \ (.1376) = 55.04,$$

and its standard deviation is

$$\sqrt{np(1 - p)} = \sqrt{400(.1376)(.8624)} = 6.8896.$$

Using the normal approximation, as in Chapter 3, we obtain the p-value of the observed data (27 black jurors) by calculating

$$(4.6) \quad P(S \le 27.5) = P\left(S \le \frac{27.5 - 55.04}{6.8896}\right) = P(Z \le -3.998),$$

which is less than .001 (one in a thousand) and leads to rejection at the usual .05 or .01 levels. Thus, the data supported the plaintiff's claim.

An important case, *Castenada v. Partida*,[12] involved discrimination against Mexican-Americans. In a 5–4 decision the Supreme Court held that

(1) A *prima facie* case of discrimination against Mexican-Americans in Hidalgo County, Texas was established by the fact that during an 11-year period (1962–1972) only 39% of the 870 persons called for grand jury service had Spanish surnames although the county's population was 79.1% Mexican-American.

(2) The state failed to rebut the *prima facie* case, because it failed to offer evidence about the methods used to determine qualified jurors (e.g., literacy, lack of criminal record) and to justify the criteria used.

(3) The trial judge's conclusion that, because the Mexican-Americans were the "governing majority" in the county it was unlikely that they were subject to discrimination, was not correct.

In addition to the Court's adopting formal hypothesis testing, an interesting aspect of the case was the discussion of the determination of the proportion (p) of eligible jurors who were Mexican-American. In his dissent Chief Justice Burger stressed that *eligible* population statistics not gross population figures should provide the relevant starting point. He noted that only 72% of the adults in Hidalgo County, as of the 1970 census, were Spanish surnamed, rather than the 79.1% of the total population. Secondly he noted that 22.9% of the Spanish surnamed population over age 25 had no schooling and claimed that since one requirement for serving as grand juries in Texas was literacy in English, about 20% of adult age Mexican-Americans would be ineligible on those grounds alone. The actual data used by the Supreme Court is given in Table 4.2.

The majority opinion pooled the data for the 11-year period and calculated the probability of observing 339 or fewer Mexican-Americans in a sample of 870 persons when the fraction (p) of Mexican Americans

TABLE 4.2.   Data on Jury Composition used in *Castenada v. Partida*

Year	Average No. persons on grand jury list	Average No. Spanish surnamed per list	Percentage Spanish surnamed
1962	16	6	37.5%
1963	16	5.75	35.9%
1964	16	4.75	29.7%
1965	16.2	5	30.9%
1966	20	7.5	37.5%
1967	20.25	7.25	35.8%
1968	20	6.6	33 %
1969	20	10	50 %
1970	20	8	40 %
1971	20	9.4	47 %
1972	20	10.5	52.5%

Source: 430 U.S. 482 at 487 n.7.

equalled .791. Using the normal approximation, they found the result *differed from* its expected value (688) under random sampling by 29 standard deviations.[13] Since a difference of even two or three standard corresponds to the usual significance levels (.05 and .01), the Court found the disparity highly significant. Moreover, they noted that the probability of the observed data being 29 standard deviations from its expected value (its *p*-value) is 10^{-140}.

The majority decision rebutted Chief Justice Burger's argument by making the following points:

(a) Under the Texas method of selecting grand jurors an individual's qualifications are not determined until after they appear in the district court. Prior to that time an unbiased selection procedure should result in persons of all educational characteristics appearing on the list. Thus, the Chief Justice's argument was justified only as to the correction for age. Moreover, if the jury commissioners were excluding those persons lacking the ability to read or write, then the state should have explained to the Court how this was accomplished.

(b) Because the definition of "literacy" is imprecise and the census data on educational attainment refers to persons 25 and over, while the age cutoff for jury selection in Hidalgo County was 21 (voter qualification), valid inferences might be difficult to obtain from the census data. In particular, the majority noted that it was not improbable that the educational level of persons in the younger age group would exceed that of their elders so that data for persons age 25 and over would *underestimate* the educational level of persons 21 and over.

(c) The Court used the statistics for persons 25 and over to derive the fraction of persons who had some schooling and were Mexican-American. These data are given in Table 4.3.

TABLE 4.3.   Educational Data Used in *Castenada v. Partida*

	All Persons	Persons with No Schooling	Persons with Schooling
Total population	80,649	13,205	66,844
Spanish surnamed	55,949	12,817	43,132
Spanish fraction	.6937	.9706	.645

Source: The data for the total population are taken from Table 83 of the 1970 Census Vol. PC(1)C45 General Social and Economic Characteristics—Texas and the data for Spanish surnamed are from Table 97.

(d) The Court then changed the null hypothesis to the calculated fraction .645 of all persons who met Justice Burger's age and educational attainment criteria who were Mexican-American. The expected number of minority jurors would be $np = (870)(.645) = 561.15$ and its standard deviation is

$$\sqrt{np(1 - p)} = \sqrt{(870)(.645)(.355)} = 14.1.$$

Hence, the probability of as few or fewer minority jurors as observed is obtained from the normal transform as

$$(4.7) \quad Z = \frac{\text{observed} - \text{expected}}{\text{standard deviation}} = \frac{339 - 561.15}{14.1} = \frac{-226.65}{14.1} = -15.79.$$

(We are ignoring the factor 1/2 here, as it will have a negligible effect).

The probability of observing a standard normal variable 15.79 *standard deviations* below its expected value, i.e.,

$$P(Z \le -15.79)$$

is about 10^{-50}. Thus, assuming Chief Justice Burger's arguments were correct, Mexican-Americans still were significantly underrepresented on the jury panels.

The Court's discussion highlights an important use of hypothesis testing, namely one can *assess* whether an explanation of a statistically significant difference (between the observed data from its expected value) really does reduce the difference to a value that has a reasonable probability of occurring by chance. Here the age and literacy factors were offered as justifying the relatively low share of Mexican-American jurors. After incorporating their effect on the appropriate fraction (p), the Court showed that Mexican-Americans remained underrepresented.[14] The use of the p-value in the opinion is also quite illuminating. When that value is extremely small, a substantial change in the parameter value (p) will be needed in order to reduce the disparity to statistical insignificance. The majority opinion did note the lack of rebutted evidence in the case and stated, "We emphasize, however, that we are not saying that the statistical disparities proved here could never be explained in another case; we are simply saying that the state did not do so in this case." The small p-value indicates that the state faced a very difficult task.

We will now calculate how small p would have to be before the observed data would be accepted as being consistent with it. In the opinion, the Court used a *two-sided* test but did not specify a level of significance (α) for the Type I error. Rather, it said that differences between two and three standard deviations are suspect to social scientists. Thus, they expressed the α-level in terms of the normal approximation. If we interpret the two standard deviations criteria as equivalent to a two-sided test at this .05 level, then the corresponding level of a one-sided test would be .025. A *one-sided* 97.5% confidence interval for p, is obtained from formula (3.27) and has an upper limit

$$(4.8) \quad \bar{p} + z_{.025} \frac{\sqrt{\bar{p}(1 - \bar{p})}}{\sqrt{n}} = \frac{339}{870} + (1.96) \frac{\sqrt{\frac{339}{870} \cdot \frac{531}{870}}}{\sqrt{870}} = .422.$$

Thus, the actual jury composition (39% minority) in the *Castenada* case would lead to rejection of any hypothesized minority fraction (p) of eligible jurors *greater* than .422, using a one-sided test[15] at the .025 significance level.

The above result, that a county in which a minority group composing 43% of all eligible jurors would be declared statistically significantly underrepresented on venires when they form 39% or less of all venire persons, may appear surprising. The difference of 4% between the actual and expected minority proportions seems small, especially when measured in *relative* terms, i.e., they received about 10% (4/43) fewer venire positions than expected. The reason we can detect a comparatively small difference from what would be expected (under random selection from a population, 43% of whom are minority members) is that the sample size (870) is rather large, and the standard deviation of a sample proportion *decreases* as the sample size *increases*. Indeed, we know that as the sample size increases, the sample proportion approaches the true proportion. Thus, it is helpful to discuss two measures of the magnitude of any statistical disparity: the *absolute difference* between the *observed* and expected *number* of jurors (or hires, etc.), which estimates the "loss" for the group (in the *Castenada* case the plaintiffs lost $870 - 339 = 531$ slots if $p = .79$ and $870 - 561 = 309$ positions if $p = .645$, both of which are sizeable differences); and a measure of *relative impact* such as

$$(4.9) \quad \frac{\text{expected proportion} - \text{sample proportion}}{\text{expected proportion}} \quad \text{or} \quad \frac{p - \bar{p}}{p}.$$

In our hypothetical situation ($p = .43$), this measure was only 10%. For the actual data, using the majority opinion's p of .791, the measure (4.9) equals

$$\frac{.791 - .390}{.791} = .507.$$

This implies that Mexican-Americans received slightly less than *half* their expected share of venire positions and *suggests* that an individual Mexican-American had only half the chance a white had of appearing in a jury venire (a more precise measure of their relative probabilities will be given in Chapter 5).

The degree of relative disparity (4.9) that courts may find tolerable is a legal rather than a statistical one. Statistical analysis, however, can aid in determining whether an observed disparity could have arisen by chance, and summary measures of absolute and relative impact may aid in interpreting the results. The absolute disparity or difference between the observed number of minorities and their expected number (np) indicates the total number of juror positions the minority group lost. It depends on both the fraction p minorities form of the eligible population and on the number n of jury selections in the sample. If we assume that during the time period studied minority group members had the same chance of being selected for a jury venire as majority persons but only half the number (870) of venire selections were studied, i.e., 435, we would have observed approximately one half of the former number of minority jurors ($339/2 \simeq 170$) and would have expected half as many (about 281). Hence, the relative measure (4.9) is not affected by the sample size and may be more useful in comparing cases than the absolute measure of disparity. We end this section with a brief discussion of the usefulness and limitations of relative measures and why they should be used in conjunction with statistical testing rather than in place of it.

The United States Commission on Civil Rights proposed that any disparity of 20% or more between the *proportion* of eligible whites selected for a master jury wheel and the *proportion* of eligible minority persons selected should be remedied by supplementation. Under this measure, if 80% of eligible whites are on the voter lists, then at least 64% ($4/5 \times 80$) of the minority population should be eligible for the jury wheel. A *modification* of this idea is to use a 20% deficiency criteria so that a jury selection process would pass the representativeness requirement if minorities actually on juries formed 80% of their fraction in the eligible population, i.e., if

$$(4.10) \qquad \frac{\bar{p}}{p} \geq .8,$$

where $\bar{p}$ is the minority proportion in the actual data, and p is the minority fraction of the eligible population.

There are several problems inherent in this approach. First, in areas where the minority fraction of the eligible population is small, say 5%, a sample (jury venire) proportion of 4% is *not likely* to be statistically significant and may actually be quite close to the expected proportion.[16] Secondly, establishing a specific allowable deviation may diminish the incentive of government officials to compile fully representative master lists. Finally, while determination of the minority share (*p*) of the persons eligible for jury service appears to be straightforward, as the census count includes data on age and education[17] for all cities and counties, there is evidence that a greater fraction of minority individuals are missed in the census than are whites. The issue arose in an equal employment case[18] and may be significant in places where the undercount of minorities is large.

The best practical course is to calculate an appropriate statistical test, including its *p*-value, and measures of relative and absolute disparity. If a statistical significant difference, at the .05 level, say, is obtained from a large sample of data showing a *small* relative disparity, courts might decide that the difference is minimal. Conversely, if a small sample of data showing a large relative disparity is not quite significant at the .05 level, perhaps courts should give that finding some weight, especially if the race of potential venire persons was known to the selecting officials.

Problems

1. Use the normal approximation to the binomial to analyze the data in *Blackwell v. Thomas,* 476 F.2d 443 (1973). Would the Castenada methodology yield a different conclusion than the Fourth Circuit's method did? Use both fractions, *p* = .44 (of the population 21–65) and *p* = .41 (of eligible voters) in your analysis.

2. The relative measure, $\bar{p}/p$, or

$$\frac{\text{minority share of actual jurors}}{\text{minority share of the eligible population}}$$

was used in *Quadra v. Superior Court of San Francisco* 378 F.Supp. 605 (N.D. Ca. 1974). Look up the case and write a short memorandum on the statistical aspects of it.

3. Contrast the concept of relative disparity as in problem 2 with that of absolute disparity or difference between the actual number of minority jurors and their expected number, assuming proper representation. Calculate the values for the *Castenada, Alexander* and *Swain* cases. Discuss the potential usefulness of both types of measures.

Hint: Think about measuring the impact on the class of potential minority jurors and the effect on an individual class member.

4. Use of the Binomial Model in Analyzing Data on Hiring in Equal Employment Cases

There are two approaches that are useful in examining hiring data for evidence of discriminatory practices. When reliable data for the people who actually applied for the job(s) at issue during the relevant time period are available, one can compare the proportion of minority applicants who are hired with the corresponding proportion of majority applicants to see whether hiring practices are fair. Statistical procedures for testing whether the observed hiring rates are fair, i.e., whether an observed difference between the rates might have occurred by chance, i.e., from sampling variability, are described in Chapter 5. That general approach is called the applicant flow method in the EEO literature. When applicant data do not exist or are incomplete (e.g., race or sex designation is miss-ing)[19] or unreliable (only partial records are available or some interested persons were not given written applications), an alternative procedure for determining the fraction (p) of minorities in the eligible (qualified) labor force in the appropriate geographic area must be used to test whether the minority fraction of actual hires is consistent with the value of p. The same test statistic (4.7) used in analyzing jury composition data is then used to analyze the hiring data. This approach is called the demographic method, as the minority share (p) of the eligible labor force[20] is deter-mined from an external data source such as the census.

The demographic method does not rely solely on the applicant data and was originally used by courts when they noticed that minority members might not apply to firms with a history of and reputation for discrimina-tion. Essentially it checks fair recruitment and fair hiring practices in one test. For example, if minorities form 20% of the qualified labor pool in an area, under fair recruiting they should form close to 20% of all applicants. If the hiring rates of minority and majority applicants are equal, then the minority percentage of all hires should equal their share of applicants, about 20%.

The demographic method is useful when courts believe that eligible candidates may have been discouraged from applying, e.g., due to an imposition of an invalid requirement or when minority applicants may form a disproportionately large share of the less qualified applicants due to an employer's affirmative action advertising campaign. Under such circumstances, the actual applicants may not even be an approximation to a random or representative sample of the true qualified labor pool and the demographic method should be used. When reliable applicant data is available, the methods presented in Chapter 5 are considered more appropriate than the demographic method because the minority share (p) is obtained for the actual applicants.

In this section we illustrate the use of the binomial model in several cases of increasing complexity. We will also see that applicant data may be useful in the process of specifying the minority fraction (p), even though it is not sufficiently reliable for use in the applicant flow method (e.g., if the race of non-hired applicants is unknown).

a. Jones v. Tri-County Electric Cooperative:[21]
racial hiring discrimination

This case concerned hiring by a utility company, which employed about 50 people, that had hired only one black (in a janitorial position) from the time the Civil Rights Act became law (July 1, 1965) until the initiation of the suit in 1972. Three plaintiffs applied for a job in December 1971. The firm hired two whites in January and February 1972 without informing the plaintiffs, who then filed the suit in March 1972. The firm offered the data in Table 4.4 as evidence of nondiscriminatory hiring policy, as it shows that 34% of all black applicants were hired in contrast to 22% of the white applicants.

The court noted that virtually all the black hires in the data occurred *after* the commencement of the legal action and that the blacks formed 40% of the population in the area served by the company from which it drew its employees. Therefore, the court found that the fraction of blacks

TABLE 4.4.   Applicant Data from *Jones v.
Tri-County Electric Coopera-
tive*

	Hired	Applicants	% Hired
Black	8	23	34.78
White	35	159	22.01
All	43	182	23.63

Source: The data is given in the text of the opinion
512 F.2d 1 at 2.

among the hires, $\bar{p} = 8/43 = .186$, was sufficiently far from .40 to conclude that the firm discriminated against actual and potential black applicants. We use the binomial model with $p = .4$, $n = 43$ to confirm the court's finding.

To compute the p-value of the data we calculate the probability, $P(S \leq 8.5)$, of obtaining 8 or fewer black hires, assuming S is binomial with parameters $n = 43$, $p = .4$. Because sample size n of 43 is small, we include the continuity correction of 1/2. Transforming to the standard normal form we obtain

$$Z = \frac{\text{observed} - \text{expected} + .5}{\text{standard deviation}} = \frac{8 - 17.2 + .5}{\sqrt{10.32}}$$
(4.11)

$$= \frac{-8.7}{3.2125} = -2.708,$$

as the expected number of blacks is $np = 43 \times .4 = 17.2$ and its variance $np(1 - p) = (17.2)(.6) = 10.32$. A distance of 2.7 or more *standard deviations* of the normal Z *below* its expected value 0 has probability .0034 of occurring, so the data are statistically significant at any level greater than .0034 if a one-sided test criterion is adopted and at any level greater than .0068 if a two-sided test criterion is used.

In addition to calculating the test statistic (4.11), we note that the difference of 8.7 or 9 jobs slightly exceeded the number, 8, of black hires. Although an absolute difference of 9 jobs seems small, notice that it implies that blacks were apparently denied *half* the positions they should have received. Thus, the relative measure observed/expected, which is equivalent to $\bar{p}/p$ or $.186/.4 = .465$, shows that blacks received only 46.5% of their expected number of jobs.

In order to find the highest proportion, p, of the eligible labor pool that blacks could form so that the hiring data (8/43) would not be statistically significant at the .05 level using a one-sided test, we calculate the 95% upper confidence interval (3.27) as

$$(4.12) \quad \bar{p} + (1.645) \sqrt{\frac{\bar{p}(1 - \bar{p})}{n}} = .186 + (1.645) \sqrt{\frac{(.186)(.814)}{43}}$$

or

$$(4.13) \qquad\qquad 95\% \text{ CONF } (p; 0, .283).$$

Thus, if a one-sided .05 level criterion was adopted, the observed fraction of blacks (.184) would not be consistent with any p *greater* than .283 so that even if the firm could demonstrate that the value .40 for p was too large, it would have to justify reducing p to less than .283 in order to affect the ultimate statistical inference.

In the *Castenada v. Partida* case, the Supreme Court used a two-sided test criterion which considers a deviation from the tested p in either direction. In view of the fact that Mexican-Americans were the majority group in the county, that was logically plausible. Given the prior history of the defendant in the instant case, the natural alternative hypothesis is that blacks would continue to be underrepresented, so a one-sided test seems more appropriate.

We now turn to a case where the key issue was the determination of the value of p by specifying the appropriate geographic area from which the firm drew its workers. This area is called the firm's labor market area.

b.   Markey v. Tenneco Oil Corp.:[22] *alleged hiring discrimination*

The black plaintiffs in this case sued Tenneco for discrimination in hiring at its plant in St. Bernard parish near New Orleans. Since the jobs at issue were laborer positions, plaintiffs compared the black fraction (.483) of actual hires to their fraction of persons employed as laborers in the New Orleans SMSA (standard metropolitan statistical area) (.594) and showed that the difference was statistically significant. The SMSA[23] concept was developed by the U.S. Government on the basis of commuting patterns into and around a central city for which economic data is reported by government agencies. It is built up by successively adding counties to the central city area on the basis of the percentage of their employed residents commuting to the city or areas already included in the SMSA. If this percentage exceeds a minimum threshold, then the county is added. Implicit in the process is the notion that residents of close-in suburban areas will have a higher probability of working in the city than the residents of more remote areas, as the commuting patterns of residents of nearby counties are examined first. It should be noted that commuters from the city and close-in suburbs to jobs in the more distant counties also enter into the determination of an SMSA.

The defendant asserted that its plant was not located in the central city but in St. Bernard parish, which is outside New Orleans and not a very convenient commute from the city. It argued that a weighted labor market area based on the Total Probability Theorem (2.11) would reflect the commuting pattern to its location. Since the black fraction in the weighted labor market depends on their fractions, b_i, of laborers in each subarea and their fraction q_i of residents in the ith area who are potential workers (interested in laborer jobs), the proper determination of the q_i is a key step. The employer used weights (q_i) determined from the percentage of new employees, not applicants, residing in each of the four parishes forming the New Orleans SMSA (see Table 2.1 which was derived from applicant data). This calculation yielded a black fraction, p, of potential laborers available to the firm of about .33. As blacks formed 48.3% of all hires, the district court decision[24] found that the firm had not discriminated.

The first appellate decision[25] accepted the notion of weighting the eligible labor forces residing in each of the subareas of a large metropolitan area by their proximity to the plant; however, they questioned the propriety of using the residence of *new hires* to derive the weights. If hiring discrimination were present, then areas with a large proportion of white residents would receive a larger weight in the calculation than they deserve, so the court remanded the case for further consideration of the appropriate labor market. The opinion stated that the residence of applicants would be more indicative of the labor pool the firm could draw on, absent any discriminatory recruitment. The subsequent opinion[26] used applicant data to derive the weights (q_i) given in Table 2.1 and obtained .428 as the appropriate black share of the labor pool. Since the black proportion (48.3%) of all hires exceeded 42.8%, the firm prevailed.

While the ultimate decision was unchanged, notice that the choice of data used to determine the weight of each component area's labor force has a meaningful impact on the value of p. The change from 33% to 42.8% is certainly substantial. The weighted labor market area concept[27] was derived from a probability model, assuming that workers in each of the k areas $A_i (i = 1, ..., k)$ of the larger metropolitan area have differing probabilities of desiring to commute to a specific plant that is located in one subarea, say A_i, and the weights q_i, the fraction of the firm's labor pool residing in the ith subarea, were obtained from the model (see the annotated references for further details). The weights q_i should reflect the actual applications for jobs people make, assuming that no unusual barriers to recruitment or vigorous affirmative action program exists in the labor market area. Under these circumstances, the weights q_i determined from applicant data would be the ideal weights.[28] When these data are unavailable or unreliable, other approximations can be used based on census commuting data; however, these calculations should be based on the commuting pattern of persons with the appropriate qualifications and job skills or similar pay levels.

The weighted labor market concept has been accepted in a number of cases, several of which we list below:

Vuyanich v. Republic National Bank 505 F.Supp. 224, 24 FEP Cases 128 (N.D. Tex. 1980), *vacated and remanded on other grounds.* 723 F.2d 1195 (5th Cir. 1984).

Gay v. Waiter's 489 F.Supp. 282 (N.D. Cal. 1980), *affirmed* 694 F.2d 531, 30 FEP Cases 605 (9th Cir. 1982) (weighted average of central city and rest of SMSA based on residence of applicants).

EEOC v. North Hills Passevant Hospital 19 FEP Cases 200 (N.D. Pa. 1979).

Williams v. Owens-Illinois Corp. 665 F.2d 918 (9th Cir. 1982).

Barker v. City of Detroit 483 F.Supp, 930 at 959 (E.D. Mich. 1979) (greater weight given to city over SMSA based on applicant data).

Berger v. Iron Workers Local 201 42 FEP Cases 1611 (D.D.C. 1985).

When reading the above cases the reader should note that courts properly are more skeptical when the weights (q_i) are determined from the residence pattern of employees or new hires than when they are calculated from applicant data.

A recent case, *U.S. v. Pasadena Ind. School District,* 43 FEP Cases 1319 (N.D. Tex. 1987) noted that the weighted SMSA can yield an underestimate of minority availability when the recruitment process is biased and residential segregation is present. The court preferred a gravity model, which assumes that workers living the same distance from the job site have the same probability of applying. This model is conceptually similar to the weighted labor market area model since one can consider each subarea A_i to be composed of residential streets the same distance from the job. For example, A_1 can consist of locations less than 15 minutes away, A_2 of locations 15–30 minutes away, etc. Variations of the gravity model also incorporate other factors determining residential preference such as housing quality. Guest and Cluett (1976) review these models and note that they fit the commuting patterns for whites better than they fit data for blacks.

c. *Hazelwood School District v. United States:*[29] *alleged hiring discrimination against blacks*

This is one of the most important cases because the Supreme Court adopted statistical hypothesis testing in EEO cases in its decision and discussed the care required in determining the appropriate labor market area from which the minority fraction (p) of the qualified labor pool is calculated. The U.S. Government sued the City of Hazelwood, a suburb of St. Louis, on behalf of black teachers who were not hired by the school system. The Court of Appeals[30] compared the percentage of teachers residing in the SMSA (5.7%) to their percentage (1.7%) of all teachers *employed* by the school system and found a pattern of discriminatory hiring. It also noted that the 5.7% figure might be too low, as about one third of newly hired teachers lived in St. Louis where 15.7% of resident teachers were black.

The Supreme Court first observed that Hazelwood became subject to the Civil Rights Act in March 1972, so comparing the black availability, (5.7%) of all employed teachers living within the SMSA, to the black percentage of all teachers employed by the city in 1974 was unfair to the city, as its employees included many teachers who were hired before the act was imposed. The Court said that the data given in Table 4.5, only including teachers hired in the 1972–73 post-act period, should be used.

The Court noted that the black percentage (3.7%) of hires was closer to the availability figure (5.7%) than their share (1.8%) of all employed teachers. The Court did not accept the 5.7% availability figure, however, and remanded the case for further consideration of the appropriate labor market and instructed the Court to determine whether teacher employment data in St. Louis City or St. Louis County or an "intermediate figure" provided "the most accurate basis for comparison". It also told the lower court to assess the effect of affirmative action hiring in the city of St. Louis might have on the labor pool available to Hazelwood and to see whether data on actual applicants could be used to compare hiring rates.

In his dissent, Justice Stevens noted that if the 5.7% availability figure were correct, then of the 405 hires one expects 23 ($405 \times .057 = 23.08$) to be black and that his clerk made a calculation that the difference of 8 would be significant at the .05 level (using a one-sided test).

TABLE 4.5.   Teachers Hired by Hazelwood School District in 1972 and 1973

	Black	White	Total	% Black
1972	10	272	282	3.55
1973	5	118	123	4.07
Both	15	390	405	3.7%

Source: 433 U.S. 299 at 311 n.17.

Comments. (1) From the test calculated by Justice Stevens' law clerk, we realize that if a value of p greater than .057 is determined by the lower court, then the data will be statistically significant at the .05 level. Indeed, an approximate upper 95% confidence interval obtained from formula (3.27) indicates that the data would be statistically significant at the .05 level (one-sided test) for any p greater than .055.

(2) If a significant fraction of all applicants come from St. Louis, then a weighted labor market will probably yield a black fraction greater than the SMSA figure of 5.7%.

(3) There is a logical error in the Court's statistical comparison. After emphasizing hiring data during the relevant time frame and correctly noting that data on persons employed included many pre-act hires the Court neglected the fact that the census data also refers to all employed teachers not just newly hired ones. Since most new hires are at the entry salary levels, one can use census earnings data in defining the eligible labor pool, i.e., one can exclude persons employed in an occupation who earn more than the entry level salary from the potential labor pool. In doing this calculation one should allow for some lateral movement, so usually the author eliminates persons earning about 10–15% or more than the job pays. Usually this procedure leads to an increased minority availability, relative to their share of all persons employed in an occupation, for entry level jobs and a decreased availability figure for senior positions.

In the three cases discussed we have seen that the critical step in the demographic method is the determination of the minority share (p) of the appropriate pool of potential employees. In addition to geographical and wage considerations, other factors that may be important to consider are:

(1) The proportion of new hires in an occupation who come from different components of the labor force. For example, women form a larger proportion of persons reentering the labor force than they do of new entrants (recent graduates) or the employed.

(2) The previous jobs held and salary earned, as most employed persons do not take paycuts when they change employers. There is a substantial amount of occupational mobility, so relying on data concerning persons currently employed in an occupation may not include all persons qualified for the job in question. A weighted model, analogous to the one used in determining the weighted SMSA, can be developed to account for occupational mobility.

As other commentators[31] have noted, the demographic method develops a proxy or substitute pool of possible applicants from which the employer should draw his workers in the absence of discrimination. The proxy population should reflect persons with the requisite skills, economic incentives to apply and their commuting preferences. While one can invariably raise questions concerning inclusiveness of all possible factors in the determination of p, courts have realized that it is easier to criticize an approach than to develop a superior one and usually accept the most accurate model offered.[32] The use of a confidence interval giving all the value of p which would lead to accepting the data (i.e., accepting the null hypothesis of nondiscrimination) can be used to show that a factor would not have a sufficiently strong effect to reduce a statistically significant result to a nonsignificant one. This was the reasoning used in the *Castenada* opinion to demonstrate that the literacy requirement would not affect the ultimate statistical conclusion. We close this section by showing how a confidence interval was used to prove that alleged defects in a plaintiff's demographic proxy labor pools could not truly explain the disparity.

d.   Capaci v. Katz & Besthoff Inc.:[33] alleged sex discrimination in hiring

This case originated when a female pharmacist filed a charge of discrimination against the defendant asserting that females were not offered managerial posts. The EEOC joined the case and, in one aspect of the case, alleged that females were not hired as managerial trainees, a position which only required applicants to have a high school diploma.

As no applicant data were available for the time between the effective date of the Civil Rights Act (July 1965) and the date of the original charge (January 1973), a variety of referent or comparison groups were used to estimate the female fraction of the eligible labor force. These fractions and the p-value of the test of significance calculated on the actual hiring data, 0 females out of 265 hires during the July 1965–January 1973 time period, are reported in Table 4.6. Persons employed in relevant occupations earning more than the position paid were excluded[34] from some of the referent groups in order to make them more appropriate for trainee positions. The female fractions, b_i, of the potentially interested labor pool residing in each area where the firm had stores were obtained from this refined census data. The weight q_i given to each area was the proportion of all stores located in that area.[35]

Notice that testing the data, 0 female hires out of 265, against the *lowest* female fraction in any of the referent groups in Table 4.6, $p = .1607$, yielded a highly significant disparity, a p-value of 7×10^{-21}. Indeed, one would expect $(265)(.1607) = 42.6$ females hired in contrast with the *zero* hires that occurred. Thus, the court did not need to decide which comparison group was the most appropriate. Of course, one might agree that the entire civilian labor force includes too many persons without the requisite background and an interest in the job, and would overestimate the female fraction (p), while the all managerial group contains persons already employed in higher paying managerial jobs, most of whom are male, so it would yield an underestimate of p. The true value of p, however, is likely to be between the two extremes.

The defendant criticized these comparison groups on grounds that women did not desire these jobs, as they involved night work and unload-

TABLE 4.6. Statistical Test Comparing Manager Trainee Hires With Various Labor Market Referents for the Period July 1, 1965 to January 1, 1973

Referent	Theoretical Fraction	P-value of Observed Data
Civilian Labor Force	.3431	4.338×10^{-49}
Managers Earning Less than $7000 (in 1969)	.2899	3.978×10^{-40}
Experienced Wholesale & Retail Managers Earning Less than $7000 (in 1979)	.2507	6.078×10^{-34}
General Merchandise Retail Store Managers	.2364	9.109×10^{-32}
Department and Sales Manager (Retail Trade)	.2207	2.003×10^{-29}
All Managers	.1607	6.888×10^{-21}

Source: *Capaci v. Katz & Besthoff* 722 F.2d 647 at 652 n.2.

Note: All probabilities are far less than one in a billion. The two and three standard deviations criteria described by the Supreme Court in *Castenada v. Partida*, 430 U.S. 482, 97 S.Ct. 1272, 51 L.Ed.2d 498 (1977), correspond to probabilities of 1 in 20 (.05) and 1 in 100 (.01). The probabilities in the last column are all less than one in a billion.

ing supply trucks, so they would self-select themselves out of the labor pool by not applying. In rebuttal, it was pointed out that women formed about 24% of the employed persons (nationwide) whose job ended at the same time defendants stores closed. Moreover, the 99.5% upper confidence interval for p, i.e., the largest value of p that would be consistent with the data or would be accepted if tested as the null hypothesis on the data, using a two-sided test at the .01 level (a rather stringent criteria), was obtained by solving[36]

(4.14) $$(1 - p)^{265} = .005,$$

yielding

(4.15) $$99.5\% \text{ CONF } (p; 0, .02).$$

Thus, as long as females formed 2% or more of the qualified labor pool for new hires, one would find that 0 of 265 would be a statistically significant disparity at the one-sided .005 or 2-sided .01 level of significance.

Although the lower court accepted the defendant's criticisms of the comparison groups used in Table 4.6, the Fifth Circuit reversed the trial court's decision and found hiring discrimination. Their reasons included:

(a) The referent groups used by the plaintiff were reasonably refined. In particular, by looking at referent groups, including other merchandising, department and sales managers, the self-selection of women out of the eligible labor pool was taken into account (to some extent).

(b) Females formed 19.2% of all applicants in the 1975–76 post-charge era for which applicant data were available. This figure was within the 16–29% range of female managerial availability figures used in Table 4.6 and clearly excludes women who self-selected not to apply.

(c) The fact that the confidence interval (4.15) showed that any female availability fraction greater than .02 would yield a statistically significant result implied that none of the criticisms of the reference groups offered by the defendant would reduce female availability to a sufficiently small fraction so that the actual data would yield a non-significant (statistically speaking) result. Indeed, the female fractions in both the post-charge applicant data as well as the late hours worker census data far exceeded .02.

Problems

1. Suppose that a careful determination shows that a minority group forms 50% of all persons qualified for a position. A firm has hired 225

persons of whom 75 are minority. Perform the test of significance and obtain the p-value. What is your final statistical conclusion?

2.   In the *Jones v. Tri-County* decision, the judge determined the minority availability (their fraction, p, of the available labor force) by calculating their fraction of the population in the labor market area. All members of the general population are not available for work, i.e., retired persons, children, housewives, etc., are not employed nor are they seeking work. Restricting attention to the *labor force* (persons available for work) typically changes the value of p by a small amount for blacks and other racial or ethnic groups but by a larger amount for women. Suppose that the black fraction of the labor force typically equals nine tenths their fraction of the general population.

(a) What affect would this have on the calculation made in (4.11)?

(b) Repeat the calculation of the Z statistic and p-value (observed level of significance) of the actual data. Does this more accurate estimate of p change the ultimate statistical inference (at the .05 significance level)?

(c) Suppose the defendant suggested that proportionately more blacks in the labor force were not qualified for or interested in the jobs in question. How great a disproportion would be needed to make the actual data consistent with the defendant's explanation?

(d) How might the plaintiff rebut the defendant's argument in (c)?

3.   The defendant in the *Capaci* case argued that a statistically significant difference should be present in each year in order for a pattern of statistical significance to be established.

(a) From a logical viewpoint how reasonable is this?

(b) Statistical evidence is used to establish a pattern of discriminatory treatment that was the rule rather than the exception. How important should data from a time period of one year or less be in determining whether a pattern of discriminatory treatment was in effect?

(c) Write a short memorandum on this topic citing several cases. As a starting point you might look at *Teamsters v. United States* 550 F.2d 1343 (4th Cir. 1976) as well as the *Capaci* and *Vuyanich* opinions.

Answers to Selected Problems

1.   We would expect $np = 225(1/2) = 112.5$ hires with a standard deviation of $\sqrt{np(1 - p)} = \sqrt{225 \cdot 1/2 \cdot 1/2} = \sqrt{56.25} = 7.5$. Thus, the difference $112.5 - 75$ or 37.5 jobs corresponds to a Z statistic of $(75 - 112.5 + .5)/7.5 = -4.93$ or a p-value of less than 1 in 10,000. Thus we

would reject the hypothesis that the firm was hiring from a pool which was 50% minority. Notice that the relative measure $\bar{p}/p = 2/3$, which is less than the .8 or four fifths criteria.

2. (a,b) Now $p = .9 \times .4 = .36$, so the expected number of black hires would be 15.48, so the numerator would become -6.98. The denominator would also change slightly, but the result remains statistically significant.

(c) The simplest approach to this problem is to imagine a labor pool of 1000 persons, 360 of whom are black and 640 are white. We wish to eliminate a fraction $(1 - f_1)$ of blacks and $(1 - f_2)$ of whites so that blacks form between 18% and 28% of that pool (18% is their share of the actual hires and 28% is near the upper end of the 95% confidence interval (4.13). We will use the figure 25%, since the explanation should do more than yield a barely nonsignificant result. Thus we need to find fractions f_1 and f_2 (the fractions f_1 and f_2 are the *eligibility* fractions) so that blacks form only 25% (or less) of the eligible pool, i.e.,

$$\frac{\text{blacks in pool}}{\text{total pool}} = \frac{360f_1}{360f_1 + 640f_2} = .25.$$

Note that $360f_1$ blacks and $640f_2$ whites will remain eligible. This means that

$$360f_1 = \left(\frac{1}{4}\right)(360f_1 + 640f_2) = 90f_1 + 160f_2$$

or

$$270f_1 = 160f_2$$

or

$$f_1 = \frac{160}{270}f_2 = (.5925)f_2.$$

Thus, the probability (f_1) that a black member of the labor force is eligible (qualified and interested) for the job must be *60%* (or less) than that of a white in order for the explanation to be reasonable.

(d) The plaintiff might refine the labor force data to eliminate persons in higher paying jobs and professional positions, as we have seen this typically raises minority availability for entry-level jobs.

3. The purpose of this problem is to start the reader thinking about two issues: combining or pooling data and the appropriate time frame, which

will be discussed later. Logically, a year is convenient to use but is simply the amount of time it takes for the earth to make one revolution about the sun. Its relevance to economic phenomena such as the business cycle or legally relevant time periods (back-pay eligibility, statutes of limitations, etc.) is not clear. We will see in Section 6 of this chapter that insisting on statistically significant results for each year of data means that one is using a level (α) of significance much *less* than the usual ones (.05 or .01). In the next section we will see that this increases the type II error (risk of not detecting discrimination when it is present).

5. The Role of the Power of a Statistical Test and the Trade-Off between the Type I and Type II Error Rates

Until now our analyses of jury venire and hiring data have concentrated on calculating the probability of observing as few or fewer minorities than actually appeared on the venire or among the hires. If this probability (the *p*-value) was less than a preset one-sided significance level, say .025 (corresponding to a two-sided 5% level of significance), then we rejected the null hypothesis—that the hires were made from a pool with the assumed minority fraction (*p*)—and concluded that the minority group might have been subject to discrimination.[37] Keeping the preset significance at a low level, α, makes the Type I error (risk to the defendant) very low, i.e., there is only a probability α that if the null hypothesis were true (the firm's hires were like a random sample from the appropriate labor pool), we would infer discrimination may well have occurred.

What about the risk to the plaintiff or type II error? Suppose the firm's hiring practices did operate to limit minorities to half or two thirds of their appropriate share (*p*) of hires. What is the probability that we would detect this? In statistical terminology we are asking, "What is the power of the test to detect the alternative hypothesis". This is important because the risk to the plaintiff is one *minus* the power, i.e., the probability, β, of failing to reject the null hypothesis when the alternative (minorities are given less than their fair share) is true. In this section we illustrate the following idea: When courts place too stringent a requirement on keeping the significance level very low (e.g., α at .01 or .025), they may make the plaintiffs' burden of establishing a *prima facie* case unduly difficult, as this practice implies that the risk of failing to detect possible discrimination when it exists can be quite large.

Let us re-examine the *Jones v. Tri-County Electric Coop.* data from this viewpoint. Recall that blacks formed 40% ($p = .4$) of the appropriate labor pool but received only 8 of 43 or 18.6% of the jobs. Before doing any calculations, one should think about what would be a legally meaningful or important difference from the expected fraction, .4. Common sense suggests that if 38% of the firm's hires had been black, the firm should not be labeled a discriminator, especially as the assumed value of p, .40, may not be a perfect estimate of the true availability of the minorities. This also makes sense from the notion of a relative measure of impact, as .38 is 95% of .40 so that the two measures of relative impact mentioned previously are

$$(4.16) \qquad \frac{\bar{p}}{p} = \frac{.38}{.40} = .95$$

and

$$(4.17) \qquad \frac{\bar{p} - p}{p} = \frac{.38 - .40}{.40} = \frac{-.02}{.40} = -.05,$$

respectively, which are close to their ideal values of 1.0 and 0. Thus, had 38% of the defendant's hires been black, the 5% shortfall implied by formula (4.17) would not be considered substantial or indicative of a race-conscious hiring policy.

If the relative measures indicate a 50% or even $33\frac{1}{3}$% shortfall, i.e., blacks received only one half to two thirds of their expected share of hires, then most people would regard this as a serious matter and significant evidence of discrimination. Various government guidelines[38] suggest a shortfall of 20% or more, i.e., the minorities receiving less than 80% (four fifths) of their expected share would be meaningful evidence of possible discrimination. In Table 4.7, we report the power of the binomial test to detect various alternative policies of discriminatory hiring. We assumed various values f of the fraction of their fair share p (which we set at .4 as the court did) of jobs due blacks to which an employer might desire to limit them. Thus, an f of .5 means that the employer desired to give blacks half of their fair share. For the *Jones* case this is $.5p = .5 \times .4 = .2$. The last column in the table gives the corresponding type II error probability, which is the risk that the plaintiff will fail to detect the alternative (the firm tries to give minorities the smaller fraction, fp, rather than their fair fraction, p, of the jobs).

Notice that using the one-sided test criteria—reject if Z in formula (4.11) is < -1.96, corresponding to a one-sided test at level .025—implies that if the defendant had a policy limiting blacks to *half* of their fair share

TABLE 4.7. Power of the Binomial Test to Detect Various Alternatives to Fair Hiring in *Jones v. Tri-County* and the Corresponding Risk to the Plaintiff

Significance Level $\alpha = .025$			
Minorities Held to a Fraction, f, of their Fair Share	Corresponding Alternative Value of $p(p_1)$	Power of the Binomial Test	Plaintiff's Risk or Probability (β) of a Type II Error
.8	.32	.138	.862
.75	.30	.203	.797
.60	.24	.512	.488
.50	.20	.755	.245
Significance Level $\alpha = .05$			
.8	.32	.224	.776
.75	.30	.312	.668
.60	.24	.655	.345
.50	.20	.856	.140

Note: The power was obtained by using the normal approximation to the distribution of the number of hires, p, assuming that the alternative value p_1 holds and the number, n, of hires is 43.

of jobs ($p_1 = .20$), by examining a sample of 43 hires, we have a probability of about .25 (.245) of *failing* to detect the discriminatory practice. By increasing the type I error to .05, i.e., giving the defendant a 5% chance of having to justify the data, we decrease the plaintiff's risk to .14 from .245, which is a substantial reduction. In the *Jones* case this is a reasonable trade-off, as the plaintiff's risk remains larger than the defendant's.

It should be emphasized that the power calculations underlying Table 4.7 can be carried out *before* looking at the number of minority hires in the data. All that is needed is the total number, n, of hires, the value of p corresponding to the null hypothesis being tested (in our example, $p = .4$ is the minority fraction in the appropriate labor pool) and the value of the parameter p_1 corresponding to an alternative minority share which would suggest discrimination. Several values of p_1, all of which were fractions of

p, were considered in Table 4.7. The results show that the probability (β) of a type II error declines as the distance between the alternative and null hypothesis *increases*. Thus, when $\alpha = .05$, the risk of a type II error is only .14 if one is concerned with detecting a practice corresponding to minorities receiving half their fair share but increases to .776 if one desires to detect a practice corresponding to minorities receiving four fifths of their fair share.

In the equal employment and jury discrimination applications, the number of hires (the number (n) of trials in the binomial distribution) is determined by external factors such as the relevant time period, the economy and employee turnover. Because of this, the sample size available for analysis may be too small to detect a meaningful alternative without making the type I error (risk to the defendant) too high. For example, in the *Jones* case, if the four fifths alternative, $p_1 = (.8) \times .4 = .32$, was deemed meaningful, a one-sided .05 level test only had power of 22.4%, so plaintiffs risk was 77.6%. Most statisticians would be reluctant to increase the level (α) of a one-sided test to much more than .05, perhaps to a maximum of .10. Even this would still entail a risk to plaintiffs of about 50%. Hence, the available sample of 43 hires in *Jones* would have been too small to detect a 20% shortfall if both the type I and type II error rates should be smaller than .25, say.

When the sample size is too small to enable both risks of error to be low, it is reasonable to keep the type I error at the .05 or .10 level but not give as much weight to a *non*significant result, as one would if the type II risk was small, say .25 or less. In the *Jones* case, the fact that a statistically significant result (p-value of less than .01) was obtained when the type II error rate was high at meaningful alternatives, such as $p_1 = (.75)p$ relative to a type I error rate of .05, makes the evidence more meaningful than in a situation where the type II error rate was less than the preset type I error rate of .05. This can occur if a very large sample of hires is examined and a small difference, in terms of percent, is observed.

The only way to resolve the trade-off between the two types of errors inherent in analyzing data is to determine reasonable alternatives to the value of p and calculate the power of the test and corresponding type II error rates, as in Table 4.7. Then one can balance the two risks of error involved. While it may be tempting to assert that the two error rates, α and β, should be equal,[39] this does not consider the size of the sample or the magnitude of the risks. When the sample size will not allow both risks to be reasonably small, the data may not be useful in the decisionmaking process.[40]

Sometimes courts are faced with different experts advocating the use of different statistical tests. One criterion that should enter into the decision as to which one is appropriate is the power the competing procedures have to detect a reasonable alternative. This problem does not occur with binomial data, as there is only one reasonable test statistic (4.11), but we will see an example of a court accepting a test with absolutely no power, i.e., it could never find a statistically significant difference, in Chapter 7. In most uses of statistical analysis in law and regulatory analysis, it is clear which party involved desires a significant result and which partly prefers a nonsignificant result. Courts and policymakers should consider these factors in assessing the positions advocated by the respective parties. In the EEO context, defendant's desire a nonsignificant result and may advocate a test with low power (high type II error rate). Plaintiffs desiring a significant result may ignore violations of the assumptions underlying a statistical procedure in order to make the p-value as small as possible.

For example, in *Minnis v. Brinkerhoff*[41] the plaintiffs considered a sample of about 40 job evaluations on 9 employees as independent observations. If one considers an employee's rating as a binomial variable with two values, 1 = satisfactory and 0 = unsatisfactory, then the fact *that each employee was rated several times* suggests that the evaluations of a particular employee are *dependent,* e.g., an employee who is a good worker during one period is likely to remain so during the next. By ignoring the dependence in the data, the plaintiffs obtained a more significant (lower p-value) than was truly justified. The judge, however, understood the statistical problem immediately.

6. Combining Results of Statistical Tests on Related Binomial Data Sets

When examining hiring data for possible discriminatory treatment, the data for different occupations should be considered separately if they require different degrees of skill and prior experience. Typically, the minority share (p) of the qualified labor force will be different for the various job categories, and the sample sizes for each category can be so small that meaningful analyses[42] are virtually impossible to make. Nevertheless, the totality of the data should be examined to ascertain whether it reflects a consistent pattern of fair hiring or one of minority underrepresentation. This section describes a procedure for combining the subcategory analyses into an overall test. It can be used to combine hiring data for different types of jobs, for different plant locations or over several years if the minority availability, p, changed during the period. We begin the section by discussing the problem of fragmenting a large sample and show why requiring a statistical significant result in each category means that a much more stringent level of significance is required than the usual .05 one. We then describe a test based on the difference between actual and expected number of hires in all categories that generalizes the usual binomial test statistic (4.11) and illustrate its use. Finally, we discuss the determination of the appropriate job categories to be combined.

a. The fragmentation problem

This problem occurs when a large sample of data is broken down into smaller subsamples and statistical tests are conducted on the subsamples rather than on the total data set. It is illustrated by the data in Table 4.8, which reports hypothetical data on jury composition for ten 12-member juries in an area where a minority group forms 40% of eligible jurors.

Notice that if a .01 significance level for a one-sided test were required,

TABLE 4.8. Hypothetical Jury Composition Data

Jury Number	Number of Minority Jurors	Minority Proportion of Jurors	P-value of Binomial Test
1	2	.167	.0835
2	3	.250	.2254
3	2	.167	.0835
4	2	.167	.0835
5	3	.250	.2254
6	1	.083	.0196
7	2	.167	.0835
8	3	.250	.2254
9	1	.083	.0196
10	2	.167	.0835
Total	21	.175 = 21/120	9.7×10^{-8} (less than one in a million)

the binomial test analyzing each *one* of the individual juries does *not* yield *one* significant result. This is due to the small sample size (12) of each jury. When all 120 juror selections are examined, the minority fraction, .175, of jurors is *less* than half of its expected value of .40, and the resulting test statistic is not only significant at the .01 level, it is significant at a level of one in a million. Indeed the chance of 21 or fewer minority members appearing among a total of 120 jurors when they form 40% of the eligible pool is about 1 in 10 million.

The fragmentation problem occurs in lower court decisions when judges are presented data one year at a time[43] or separately by occupation,[44] even though the Supreme Court combined 11 years of data into one sample in *Castenada v. Partida*. As long as one is analyzing the same statistical population over the time period, as the Supreme Court was in *Castenada*, all the data sets can be considered as a single large one. In the fair hiring area, however, one needs to analyze data in several occupations with different minority availabilities (p's). We now describe an appropriate method.

b.   Combining related binomial data sets

Before presenting the generalized binomial test, it may be useful to look at some data from an actual case, *Cooper v. University of Texas at Dallas*.[45] In that case, the plaintiff charged the defendant university with sex discrimination in hiring and submitted the data in Table 4.9, comparing hires by the university during 1976–1977 with data on persons receiving doctorates in the appropriate disciplines in 1975. Since PhDs in English are not eligible for mathematics professorships and vice versa, one cannot consider all 178 hires as being a sample from a common population. Thus, the data in Table 4.9 is organized by division, e.g., Humanities, Social Science, etc. The sex-ratios of new PhDs available to the departments in each division are probably similar, in contrast to the difference between Humanities and Natural Science.

The logical way to study the hiring practices across the university is to compare the *total number of female hires* with *their expected number,* just as we did in the ordinary binomial case (3.41 and 4.11). Since the number of female hires, A_i, in the ith division (here i ranges over five divisions) is a binomial variable with parameters n_i (the number of hires) and p_i the female fraction of the available qualified labor pool, the expected value of A_i is $n_i p_i$ and its variance is $n_i p_i (1 - p_i)$. The total of female hires across all divisions is the sum of the binomial variables, A_i,

TABLE 4.9.   Plaintiff's Hiring Data in *Cooper v.*
University of Texas at Dallas

University Division	Availability (p_i)	Total Hires (n_i)	Actual Female Hires (A_i)
Arts-Humanities	.383	48	14
Human Development	.385	32	12
Management-Administration	.043	26	0
Natural Science	.138	38	1
Social Science	.209	34	6
Total		178	33

Source: 482 F.Supp. 187 at 196.

and has expected value $\Sigma n_i p_i$ and variance $\Sigma n_i p_i(1 - p_i)$, since the hires in one division are independent of the hires in the others.[46] Assuming the normal approximation is valid, we can use the statistic

$$(4.18) \quad \frac{\Sigma A_i - \Sigma n_i p_i + \frac{1}{2}}{\sqrt{n_i p_i(1 - p_i)}} = \frac{\text{observed} - \text{expected}}{\text{standard deviation}}$$

in the same way we used (4.11) to analyze jury composition data. Again, the factor 1/2 or .5 in (4.18) is added to improve the accuracy of the normal approximation to the distribution of the sum of the discrete binomial variables. The application of formula (4.18) to the data in Table 4.9 is given in Table 4.10. In Table 4.10, we give the difference between the observed and expected number of female hires ($A_i - n_i p_i$) for each category and then *add* them to obtain the total difference between the observed and expected number of female hires. This enables us to see that the differences were in the same direction, all negative, although the differences in the Human Development Division is essentially 0, i.e., females apparently received their expected number of positions in that division. When combining the results of binomial data sets, it is not necessary that all the differences be in the same direction, but differences opposite to the majority of the ones combined should *not be too great* in magnitude. In particular, a statistically significant difference in the *oppo-*

TABLE 4.10.   Calculation of the Generalized Binomial Test for the Hiring
Data From *Cooper v. University of Texas at Dallas*

Division	Actual Female Hires (A_i)	Expected Female Hires ($n_i p_i$)	Difference ($A_i - n_i p_i$)	Variance $n_i p_i (1 - p_i)$
Arts-Humanities	14	18.38	−4.38	11.340
Human Development	12	12.32	−.32	7.577
Management-Administration	0	1.12	−1.12	1.072
Natural Science	1	5.24	−4.24	4.517
Social Science	6	7.11	−1.11	5.624
Total	33	44.17	−11.17	30.13

Standard deviation = $\sqrt{\text{variance}}$ = 30.13 = 5.489
Formula (4.18) = (−11.17 + .5)/5.489 = −1.94

site direction to the others is an indication that a different process may be operating in that category, so it usually should be considered separately.

We note that in the *Cooper* data, formula (4.18) yields a Z of −1.94, corresponding to a one-sided p-value of .026. Ordinarily, such a value indicates a statistically significant result; however, we used the plaintiff's values for the female availabilities, p_i, which were determined from recent PhDs and therefore are appropriate for assistant professorships but not for associate and full professorships. As a reasonably large portion of the hires in the sample were for more senior jobs for which female availability is less than that for entry level professorships,[47] the defendant successfully rebutted the charge. *Decreasing* the p_i *reduces* the expected number, $\Sigma\, n_i p_i$ of female hires. Consequently, the magnitude of the calculated Z of −1.94 in formula (4.18) is also smaller, so the p-value increased to a nonsignificant level.

When applying the generalized binomial procedure (4.18), it is important to focus on a *relevant* set of job titles or occupations. In the *Cooper* case, only faculty members with the same general qualifications were appropriate, as the plaintiff was an unsuccessful applicant for an assistant professorship. Hiring in clerical or administrative jobs is usually carried out in a different manner than in faculty positions. Moreover, the labor market for clerical jobs is a local one, while faculty are recruited nationwide.[48] If, on the other hand, one limited the universe of study to hires in the department to which Ms. Cooper applied, then the sample would be too small to find significance. Whether the whole university, the school (Arts and Sciences, Law, etc.) or the division is the most relevant universe is a question involving legal considerations as well as statistical ones (sample size). A judge might need to consider the administrative organization to uncover the people who truly affect the hiring process.

We next illustrate the use of the generalized binomial test in *Vuyanich v. Republic National Bank*.[49] The opinion contains an excellent discussion of the factors that should play a role in determining the fraction (p) of minorities from the labor pool available for a job as well as the degree of refinement that the plaintiffs' and defendants' data should meet at various stages of a case.[50] We will discuss a portion of the defendant's submission. First, the 3500 jobs were grouped into families of jobs. Each family of jobs was similar with respect to required skill level, salary, opportunity for advancement and geographical area of the labor market. The availability of persons for each job type was determined by a weighted average of the minority proportion of persons in the census data with the same educational level or prior job experience as the actual hires. The calculation is similar to the one we used in Chapter 2 to determine the weighted geographic labor market. The weights now are the fraction of all hires with the appropriate background (education and/or experience), and the labor pools are defined in terms of qualification (high school and job experience, college but no experience, etc.) rather than by geographic region of the labor market.[51] We now discuss the data used in the case and reported in Table 4.11 along with the calculation of the generalized binomial test (4.18). The test yielded a

$$(4.19) \qquad \frac{observed - expected}{standard\ deviation} = \frac{-16.9926}{8.9938} = -1.89,$$

a result which has a one-sided p-value of about .03 and would be significant at the .05 significance level if a one-sided test was adopted but not if a two-sided test was deemed appropriate. More important than whether the difference is deemed statistically significant is the actual p-value, which indicates that even if a two-sided test were used the result is close to the .05 level.

Continuation (Optional)

In the opinion, Judge Higginbotham noted that analyzing the data for each category separately, as defendants had done, made it difficult to find an

TABLE 4.11. Data Concerning Female Hires in 1970–1974 From *Vuyanich v. Republic National Bank*

Job Group	Availability	Hires	Female	Expected	Difference	Variance
Managers	.2076	31	1	6.4356	−5.4356	5.0996
Accountants	.2115	85	20	17.9775	+2.0225	14.1753
Securities Analysts, etc.	.2239	89	24	19.927	+4.0729	15.4654
Commercial Loan	.1522	135	13	20.547	−7.547	17.4197
Data Processing	.1432	81	11	11.5992	−.5992	9.9382
Trust	.1726	48	7	8.2848	−1.2848	6.8548
Internal Service	.1398	18	2	2.5164	−.5164	2.1646
Oper. Services	.2310	55	5	12.705	−7.705	9.7701
Total					−16.9926	80.8877

Source: 505 F.Supp 224 at 368 n.189.

Note: We omit the correction factor .5 in the total difference column to make our discussion comparable to that in the opinion. Thus, the MH test yields a Z = (difference)/standard deviation = $-16.99/8.994 = 1.89$, as the standard deviation is $\sqrt{80.8877} = 8.994$.

overall pattern of statistical significance. In many job categories *no* female (or black) hires were in the *acceptance* region of the usual binomial test statistic (3.38) so that the test could not conclude that discrimination might be present in situations where no blacks were hired. Clearly, such a "statistical test" is not a true test of the hypothesis of no discrimination against an alternative of discrimination. This is a good example of the fragmentation problem mentioned earlier. In order to combine the results in each category, the judge formed a different summary statistic that typically is more conservative statistically than (4.18). He assumed that all 542 hires came from a single binomial distribution with parameter p^*, a weighted average of the group availabilities (p_i) where the weights given each p_i were proportional to their share $n_i/n(n = \Sigma\ n_i)$ of hires. Thus, he set

$$p^* = \sum \frac{n_i}{n}\,(p_i) = \frac{31}{542}\,(.2076)$$

$$(4.20) \qquad\qquad + \frac{85}{542}\,(2115) + \ldots + \frac{55}{542}\,(.2310) = .1845$$

and tested the total number of female hires (83) against their expected number, $542 \times .1845 = 99.99$. Since the standard deviation of the binomial variable (number of female hires) is $\sqrt{542(.1845)(.8155)} = 9.03$, he computed

$$(4.21) \qquad Z = \frac{\text{actual} - \text{expected}}{\text{standard deviation}} = \frac{83 - 99.99}{9.03} = -1.88$$

and concluded that the difference of 17 jobs between the actual (83) and expected (99.99) number of female hires was statistically significant at the .06 level (two-sided).

In his discussion, Judge Higginbotham also discussed flaws in the weights used by the bank. They were determined from the bank's data on hires, so the proportion of persons with prior experience in the eligible pool may be overstated, as persons not currently employed in a particular job may still be qualified for it. Moreover, we know that determining availability from census figures on persons currently employed in a job tends to understate the number of persons qualified for entry- and lower-level jobs in that occupation. Thus, a more defined calculation of the availability fractions (p_i) probably will increase black and female availabilities and hence yield a more significant value of the test statistic.

In comparing his result with ours, we first note that the judge did not use the continuity correction of 1/2 in his calculation. Had he done so, he would have obtained

$$(4.22) \qquad Z = \frac{-16.49}{9.03} = 1.826,$$

which would be significant at the .07 level and, probably, would not have affected his inference.[52] The results obtained by Judge Higginbotham agreed quite closely with ours because both statistics have the same expected value, $\Sigma n_i p_i$, under the assumption of fair hiring from the relevant labor pools. The standard deviation of his test statistic, however, will always exceed ours.[53] Thus, his procedure is statistically conservative in that it allows for a slightly wider variation from the expected number of hires than is necessary. The reason the difference between the procedures is quite small in our specific example is that the availability fractions (p_i) vary over a relatively small range. If the availability values (p_i) in all the categories happen to be identical, say p, then both methods reduce to the single binomial test statistic (4.11), as one can consider all $n = \Sigma n_i$ hires to be replications of the same binomial experiment with the same probability, p, of a minority hire on each one.

Problems

1. In order to illustrate the effect of the plaintiffs overestimation of female availability in *Cooper v. University of Texas at Dallas*, reduce the p_i's used in Table 4.9 as follows: .383 to .333; .385 to .35; .043 to .03; .138 to .09; and .209 to .16. Recalculate the test statistic (4.15) and its p-value using these availability fractions. Assuming the new availability figures are correct, does the data indicate a statistically significant under-hiring of female professors (use the .05 level)?

2.* Suppose that the plaintiff's availability figures in *Cooper* were correct. Show that there is a statistically significant disparity, indicating females received less than their fair share of professorships in the natural sciences.

(a) Would it be proper to use this result to conclude that female applicants received too few positions in the university as a whole?

(b) Dr. Cooper applied to the Management Science Division of the university. How relevant would a statistically significant disparity between actual and expected female hires in the Natural Science Division be to her individual claim?

(c) Suppose Dr. Cooper had applied for a post in the Natural Sciences Division. Would your answer to (b) change? Explain.

3. Read the hiring section of the opinion in *Coser v. Moore*, 587 F.Supp. 572 (1983), a case involving a charge of sex discrimination in which the court had to choose between availability fractions (p_i) that were determined from national data and fractions determined from regional data, i.e., about 70% of new hires came from a five-state region suggested by the plaintiff. Do you think a weighted labor market, analogous to *Markey v. Tenneco* would be more appropriate? Discuss how this *might* have affected the ultimate decision concerning the hiring issue.

4.* The data in Table 4.12 on hires in various job categories were analyzed in *EEOC v. United Virginia Bank* 615 F.2d 147 (4th Cir. 1980).

(a) Assuming that the availability fractions used in the analysis by the court are correct, should a combination test have been used? In particular, note that black hires in the service category exceeded their expected number.

(b) If you answered yes to (a), which job categories should have been combined?

TABLE 4.12.   Hiring Data From *EEOC v. United Virginia Bank*

Occupation	Black Avail- ability	Total Hires in post-act Era	Expected Number of Blacks	Observed
Officials and Managers	.048	53	2.55	2
Clerical	.140	301	42.14	30
Operatives	.454	3	1.36	1
Service	.496	6	2.98	6

Source: 615 F.2d 147 at 151.

(c) The availability fractions were obtained from the 1970 census data on all persons employed in the job in the SMSA, while the data refer to new hires. Using the results in *Capaci v. Katz and Besthoff* (Table 4.6) as a guide, make realistic adjustments to the availability fractions and test the bank's hires against these availability figures. Does your statistical inference, especially in clerical jobs, differ from that in the decision?

(d) Read the district and appellate court opinions. In view of the discussion of the individual plaintiffs, does the wage cut-off adjustment you used in (c) appear justified?

7.   Summary

This chapter discussed how the binomial model can be used to analyze the composition of jury venires or hires to determine whether the data can be considered as a random sample from a large population of which minorities form $100p\%$. The determination of the minority fraction, p, is a crucial step in these applications. As there are no special qualifications for jury service, the value of p usually can be obtained from the decennial census data for the jurisdiction. On the other hand, the calculation of p in the employment discrimination context may be quite involved, as background skills, the salary the job pays and commuting patterns of workers are factors that play a role in specifying the appropriate labor pool from which eligible applicants should be selected. Usually the process of determining p is more important than the calculation of the formal test statistic

(4.11), since the expected number of minority hires depends critically on the value of p.

In addition to deciding whether data are statistically significant at a preassigned level, α, typically .05, we emphasized that the p-value of the data should be calculated as the smaller the p-value is, the less likely that the actual data can be considered to be a sample from the appropriate population. We also discussed the concept of power and the trade-off between the probabilities, α and β, of type I and type II errors, respectively. Simply reporting whether a statistical test yields a significant result at the .05 or another preset level ignores the possibility that the sample size (number of hires or venire persons) was too small to detect a meaningful difference from the assumed value of p, as well as minimizing the implication of statistical tests with much smaller p-values.

The last section dealt with a new topic, namely, splitting up a sample into relevant subcategories and then combining the statistical calculations into one summary statistic. When the data are broken into subcategories but not recombined, it is possible for defendants to make the size of some of the categories so small that a statistically significant result could never occur.[54] Alternatively, plaintiffs might find a statistically significant result in one subcategory and ignore the fact that the total picture shows that minorities received their fair share of all relevant jobs.

When using combination methods the decision as to which data sets (e.g., job categories) should properly be combined involves statistical, labor market and legal considerations. In the *Cooper v. University of Texas at Dallas* case, the combination of hiring data, especially at the assistant professor level across disciplines, is appropriate as all positions are similar. Some judgement is needed in determining positions that are sufficiently similar to the one(s) at issue to be relevant. The organizational structure is an important factor as are the nature of the legal action (class action or individual claim) and legal theory being argued. We will return to some of these issues when we discuss other combination procedures. Finally, we note that there are several measures of *relative impact* for summarizing data grouped into relevant categories. The simplest one is

$$(4.23) \qquad \frac{\text{actual number of hires in all categories}}{\text{expected number of hires in all categories}}.$$

It is the precise analog of the measure $(\bar{p}/p)$ used for a single data set. In the *Cooper* case this ratio is $33/44.17 = .747$, which suggests a meaningful difference under the four fifths criteria if the female availability fractions were correct. That guideline is formulated in terms of the ratio of the hiring rate of minority applicants to that of majority applicants. Hence, it is not exactly equivalent to the measure (4.23), however, it is reasonable to consider a minority underrepresentation of 20% as meaningful too.

NOTES

1. 430 U.S. 482 (1977).
2. See Kairys, D., Kadane, J. and Lehosczky, J. (1977), cited in the references.
3. 294 U.S. 587 at 590–592 (1932).
4. 316 U.S. 400 (1942).
5. The technique of using several reasonable estimates of the parameter of interest, the minority fraction of eligible jurors, is called *triangulation* by Mosteller in Assessing Unknown Numbers: Order of Magnitude Estimation in *Statistics and Public Policy* (1977) ed. by Mosteller, F. and Fairley, W. Reading, Mass: Addison-Wesley. In our example, the poll tax roles are more likely to underestimate the true p than the census data so that the census figure is more appropriate.
6. 380 U.S. 202, 85 S.Ct. 824 (1965).
7. The term *prima facie* means that the evidence appears (on its face) to indicate that a discriminatory practice was operating. If plaintiffs demonstrate a *prima facie* case, often by showing a statistically significant or meaningful disparity exists, then the burden of proof shifts to the defendant who now must explain or justify it. This can be accomplished by a more careful statistical analysis or by showing that the original data were inaccurate. The process will be illustrated in our discussion of actual cases in this chapter and the next one.
8. 476 F.2d 443 (4th Cir. 1973).
9. See the following articles listed in the references: Finkelstein (1966), Kuhn (1968), Comment (1973) and Kairys, Kadane and Lehosczky (1977).
10. The probability 1/2 is correct for the normal variable. In Chapter 3 we learned that the binomial distribution can often be approximated by the normal. This is why we now say approximately 1/2.
11. 405 U.S. 625, 92 S.Ct. 1221 (1972).
12. 430 U.S. 482, 97 S.Ct. 1272 (1977).
13. This calculation is the same one we used in Chapter 3, formula (3.38) and in our discussion of *Alexander v. Louisiana*. It means that the Z value (difference)/standard deviation is -29. Notice that an outcome this far from expected is much less likely to occur than the Z value of -4 we calculated in *Alexander*.
14. This is an example of the plaintiffs establishing a *prima facie* case, the defendants (in this instance, the argument of Chief Justice Burger) offering an explanation and the plaintiffs (or Court majority) then showing that the explanation fails to adequately explain the statistical disparity.
15. In the *Castenada* case, the Court used a two-sided test. For such a test the two standard deviation criteria corresponds approximately to a .05 level test. The corresponding one-sided test then has level $(1/2)(.05) = .025$. The one-sided test and corresponding one-sided confidence interval for p makes more sense in this application as the consequence of rejecting the null hypothesis is concluding that discrimination may be present and requiring the defendant to explain it. Thus, we need to find the *smallest* minority fraction (p) that is consistent with the actual data. This p value is the upper end point of a one-sided confidence interval (3.27).
16. Indeed, using tables of the binomial distribution one finds that the probability of observing *exactly* 4 blacks among 100 venire persons when $p = .05$ (remember we expect $np = 100 \times .05 = 5$ blacks) is .1782.

17. Actually the data on education is obtained from a sample of the population. However, the census sample is quite large, so for many applications one can ignore the sampling error.

18. *Rios v. Steamfitters, Local 38* 542 F.2d 579, 13 FEP Cases 705 (2d Cir. 1976).

19. In the past some employers may not have asked applicants their race and/or sex in order to make the application form nondiscriminatory. Such data are collected for all new hires (employees), however.

20. The labor force consists of all persons working or available for work. The subset of the total labor force which is qualified and presumably potentially interested in a specific job is often called the eligible labor pool.

21. 512 F.2d 13 (5th Cir. 1975).

22. 707 F.2d 172 (5th Cir. 1983), affirming 32 FEP Cases 145 (E.D. La. 1982).

23. The SMSA (standard metropolitan statistical area), now called MSA, was the term used by the U.S. Government for an economically integrated area, consisting of a central city (or pair of cities) and the surrounding counties. One of the major factors in determining that a county belongs to an SMSA is the commuting pattern of its residents. The official definition is given in Metropolitan Statistical Area Classification (1980) *Federal Register 45*, 956–963.

24. 439 F.Supp. 219 (E.D. La. 1977).

25. 635 F.2d 497 (5th Cir. 1981).

26. 32 FEP Cases 145 (E.D. La. 1982) *affirmed* 707 F.2d 172 (5th Cir. 1983).

27. The idea of weighting the areas by their proximity to the location of a firm was thought of by many people. The *Stamps v. Detroit Edison* case may have been the first one to incorporate the geographic aspect in an opinion. The author's 1976 paper with Haber may have been the first presentation of a formal mathematical model.

28. This term was used in Haber and Gastwirth (1978), cited in the references to the chapter, and implicitly assumes that the residence pattern of the applicants reflects the residence pattern of applicants to a nondiscriminatory employer. As Judge Higginbotham noted in *Vuyanich v. Republic National Bank,* 505 F.Supp. 224 (N.D. Tex. 1980), the determination of the appropriate weights is a factual question to be made on a case-by-case basis.

29. 433 U.S. 299, 97 S.Ct. 2736 (1977).

30. 534 F.2d 805 (8th Cir. 1976).

31. See Baldus and Cole, (1980) in the references for this chapter.

32. In *Capaci v. Katz & Besthoff* 711 F.2d 653 (5th Cir. 1983) the Court notes that a perfect statistical model is not required. Similarly, reasonable matching of job titles with available census data was accepted in *Hartmann v. Wick* 36 FEP Cases 622 (D.D.C. 1984).

33. 711 F.2d 647 (5th Cir. 1983).

34. Since the 1970 census data referred to income in 1969, and manager trainees earned between $5980 and $6580 a year at that time, persons employed in managerial jobs paying $7000 or more were excluded from the potential labor or applicant pool by plaintiffs.

35. Since the defendant had stores in New Orleans, Baton Rouge and the rest of Louisiana, the census data for each referent group in each of the three areas was weighted in accordance to the number of stores in the area. Since the fraction of stores in each area varied during the 1965–1972 period, the weighting yielding the *lowest* female availability fraction was used by plaintiffs.

36. The idea is to find that value p such that the probability of no female hires in 265 repetitions, which is $(1 - p)^{265}$, is only .005.

37. Recall that statistical evidence is used to show a *prima facie* case of discrimination, which shifts the burden of producing contrary evidence to the defendant.

38.   Uniform Guidelines on Employee Selection Procedures (1978). *Federal Register 13,* 38,295–38,309.

39.   This position was advocated by Dawson (1980) but is not generally accepted in statistical practice. Interested readers should also consult the paper by Kaye (1983) in the references to this chapter.

40.   The adequacy of a sample depends on the problem being studied, the risks of error that are tolerable and the magnitude of the difference between the null and alternative hypotheses being compared. It is preferable to perform a power analysis (Table 4.7) before rejecting a sample as too small than to create an arbitrary rule that samples must contain at least n observations. In our discussion of epidemiological studies, we will see that the concept of statistical power can be used to plan a study of adequate size.

41.   *Minnis v. Brinkerhoff* Civil Action 80–206 (D.D.C.) unpublished opinion.

42.   By a meaningful analysis we mean a test of significance with small type I and type II errors, e.g., $\alpha < .10$, $\beta < .20$.

43.   See *Vuyanich v. Republic National Bank* 505 F.Supp. 224 (N.D. Tex. 1982) *vacated and remanded* on other grounds 723 F.2d 1195 (5th Cir.); *Wheeler v. City of Columbus Miss.* 686 F.2d 1144 (5th Cir. 1982) and *Capaci, supra,* note 33.

44.   See *Wheeler, supra* note 42, and *EEOC v. United Virginia Bank* 615 F.2d 147 (4th Cir. 1980).

45.   482 F.Supp. 187 (N.D. Tex. 1979).

46.   Recall that the expected value of the sum of several random variables is the sum of the expected numbers of the individual variables. As the random number, A_i, of minority selections in the ith category is a binomial variable with parameters n_i and p_i, the expected number of minority hires in the ith category is $n_i p_i$, and the variance of A_i is $n_i p_i (1 - p_i)$. Thus, the expected number of the total number, ΣA_i, of hires in all k job categories is $\Sigma n_i p_i$. The *variance* given for the sum of the individual binomial variables does depend on the assumption of independence in the different categories (i.e., who is hired in one division does not affect who is hired in other divisions). Under the independence assumption the variance of the sum (ΣA_i) is just the sum of the individual variances, i.e., $\Sigma n_i p_i (1 - p_i)$.

47.   It is common knowledge that more and more women have continued their education and their careers in the last 10 or 20 years. In actual litigation this can be verified by examining the data on new degrees received during the relevant time periods. For instance, most persons eligible for full professorships in 1975 probably received their doctorates prior to 1965.

48.   In actuality, this is an over-simplification. While faculty positions are advertised nationally, there is some evidence that geographic preferences have an important role. In particular, two career couples may prefer jobs in large metropolitan areas where there are several potential employers for both spouses to jobs in small towns with only one possible employer. For a case which touches on this topic but did not pursue it in depth, see *Coser v. Moore,* 587 F.Supp. 572 (E.D. N.Y. 1983) affirmed 739 F.2d 746 (2nd Cir. 1984).

49.   See *supra* note 42.

50.   Recall that once plaintiffs establish a *prima facie* case, the defendant can rebut it by showing the data or calculated availability fractions were erroneous, as in *Cooper*. Plaintiffs then have the opportunity to show that defendants explanation is a pretext and does not provide an adequate explanation. The use of the confidence interval in *Capaci* showed that the reasons offered by defendant could not reduce female availability to 2% in light of the fact that they formed 19% of post-charge applicants. A comprehensive analysis of reasons courts have accepted or rejected explanations given by defendants and the arguments used by plaintiffs to demonstrate the inadequacy of those explanations is given in Section 2 of the current supplement to *Baldus and Cole*.

51. Mathematically, the same calculation based on the Total Probability Theorem in Chapter 2 is used.
52. See his discussion of significance levels (p-values) as a sliding scale. Thus, he properly considers the p-value as indicating the strength of the statistical evidence. Moreover, the bank's availability fractions were likely to be underestimates.
53. This is a mathematical result beyond the scope of our text. Indeed, it is known that any time our procedure leads to rejection of the null hypothesis (one-sided test) so will (4.19). See Hoeffding, W. (1956). On the Distribution of the Number of Successes in Independent Trials. *Annals of Mathematical Statistics 27*, 713–721.
54. This point was emphasized by Judge Higginbotham in his opinion in *Vuyanich, supra* note 28, and Judge Greene in *Trout v. Hidalgo*, 517 F.Supp 873 at 833 n.35 (D.C. Cir. 1980).

REFERENCES

Books

BALDUS AND COLE, J. W. L. (1980). *Statistical Proof of Discrimination.* Colorado Springs: Shepard's/McGraw-Hill. (This is the basic reference for statistical methods used in analyzing data arising in discrimination cases. We will refer to it as Baldus and Cole. Although we will offer some alternative methods and analyses of the data in a few cases, anyone involved with the EEO area should be acquainted with it.)

CONNOLLY, W. B. JR. AND PETERSON, D. W. (1980). *Use of Statistics in Equal Employment Opportunity Litigation.* New York: Law Journal Seminars Press.

Articles

BRUAN, L. (1980). Statistics and the Law: Hypothesis Testing and its Application to Title VII Cases. *Hastings Law Journal 32*, 59–79.

COMMENT. (1973). The Civil Petitioner's Right to Representative Grand Juries and a Statistical Method of Showing Discrimination in Jury Selection Cases Generally. *U.C.L.A. Law Review 20*, 581–654.

DAWSON, D. (1980). Are Statisticians Being Fair to Employment Discrimination Plaintiffs? *Jurimetrics Journal 20*, 1–20.

DORSEANO, W. V. (1975). Statistical Evidence in Employment Discrimination Litigation: Selection of the Available Population, Problems and Proposals. *Southwestern Law Journal 29*, 859–875.

FINKELSTEIN, M. (1966). The Application of Statistical Decision Theory to the Jury Discrimination Cases. *Harvard Law Review 80*, 338–376. (The original article proposing the use of the binomial model to analyze data on the racial composition of jury venires.)

GASTWIRTH, J. L. AND HABER, S. E. (1976). Defining the Labor Market for Equal Employment Standards. *Monthly Labor Review 99*, 32–36. (Develops a probability model which yields the weighted SMSA model described in the text and used in *Markey v. Tenneco*.)

GASTWIRTH, J. L. (1981). Estimating the Demographic Mix of the Available Labor Force. *Monthly Labor Review* **101**, 26–29. (Noted the incorrect use of unadjusted census data when all persons employed in an occupation are used to derive the minority fraction of the labor pool available for entry level (new) hires and suggested earnings data to eliminate the more senior members of an occupation from the referent data.)

GASTWIRTH, J. L. (1984). Statistical Methods for Analyzing Claims of Employment Discrimination. *Industrial and Labor Relations Review* **38**, 75–86.

GUEST, A. AND CLUETT, C. (1976). Workplace and Residential Location: A Push–Pull Model. *Journal of Regional Science* **10**, 399–410. (This paper discusses the gravity and related models of commuting patterns.

HABER, S. E. AND GASTWIRTH, J. L. (1978). Specifying the Labor Market for Individual Firms. *Monthly Labor Review* **101**, 26–29. (Discusses extensions of the methods used in their 1976 paper in order to handle special problems that arise when a firm has several plants in an area. Various approximations to the ideal applicant weighting of the subareas are presented.)

KAYE, D. H. (1983). Statistical Significance and the Burden of Persuasion. *Law and Contemporary Problems* **46**, 13–23.

KAYE, D. H. (1985). Statistical Analysis in Jury Discrimination Cases. *Jurimetrics Journal* **25**, 274–289.

KAIRYS, D., KADANE, J. AND LEHOSCZKY, J. (1977). Jury Representationess; A Mandate for Multiple Source Lists. *California Law Review* **65**, 776–827. (Discusses the need to use multiple sources such as voter registration, drivers licenses, etc. in order to obtain a fully representative pool from which venire persons may be chosen.)

KUHN, R. S. (1968). Jury Discrimination: The Next Phase. *Southern California Law Review* **41**, 235–328. (This article provides a helpful discussion of the way juries were selected in the past. It documents the problems inherent in relying on volunteers or key persons and the relevant cases.)

MONTLOCK, K. (1973). Using Statistical Evidence to Enforce the Laws Against Discrimination. *Cleveland State Law Journal* **22**, 259–280. (One of the earliest articles concerning the use of statistical evidence in employment discrimination. It cites a number of cases where the demographic method was adopted due to the lack of minority applicants to firms with a history of discrimination.)

ROSENBLUM, M. (1977). The Use of Labor Statistics and Analysis in Title VII Cases: Rios, Chicago, and Beyond. *Industrial Relations Law Journal* **1**, 685–710. (A useful discussion of the problems and pitfalls involved with the use of labor statistics in EEO cases.)

Chapter 5

Statistical Procedures for Comparing Proportions

1. Introduction

In the previous two chapters we developed statistical tests and estimates for a *proportion* or *probability* and applied them in the context of alleged discrimination. An alternative approach to analyzing the issue of fair hiring is to compare the hiring rates of the minority applicants for a job with that of majority applicants. We must determine whether the probability, p_1, a minority applicant has of being hired is equal to the corresponding probability, p_2 of a majority applicant from the actual hiring proportions, $\bar{p}_1$ and $\bar{p}_2$. In this chapter we develop tests to ascertain whether the underlying probabilities are equal and derive a confidence interval for the difference $p_1 - p_2$ between two probabilities based on the difference, $\bar{p}_1 - \bar{p}_2$ between the corresponding sample proportions. The problem of comparing two probabilities or rates occurs in many applications of statistics. Some examples are:

(a) In the Department of Transportation's consideration[1] of the relative merits of air bags and seat belts data (see Table 5.1) showing the effect of Canada's passing a mandatory seat belt use law were used to justify the potential benefit of the states passing similar laws. Here the proportions being compared relate to the probability a driver uses the seat belt, so p_1 is the probability of use before the law went into effect and p_2 is the probabil-

201

TABLE 5.1.   Percentage of Drivers Using Seat Belts Before and After the Canadian Provinces Enacted Mandatory Seat Belt Laws

Province	Effective Date of the Law	Use Before	Use in 1983
Ontario	1/76	23	60
Quebec	8/76	18	61
Saskatchewan	1/77	32	54
British Columbia	10/77	37	67
Newfoundland	7/82	9	76
New Brunswick	6/83	4	68

Source: Table 12 from Department of Transportation (1984). Preamble to NHSTA Rule on Automatic Occupant Restraint (1984). *Product Liability and Safety Reporter* **12,** 545–596 at 580.

ity of use afterwards. The data in Table 5.1 clearly indicate that Canadians obeyed the law.

In this example, the two rates being compared refer to the same population (drivers in Canada) at *different* points in time.

(b) The Department of Transportation (DOT) is also concerned with comparing the severe injury rates of drivers using seat belts with those whose cars are equipped with air bags. Here the basic probabilities being compared are the probability, p_1, a driver using a seat belt in an accident and is severely injured and p_2 is the corresponding probability for a driver whose car has an operating air bag mechanism.

The car driving public can be divided into three subpopulations—those who use seat belts only, those whose cars have an operating air bag device and those who don't use any safety restraint. The DOT wishes to compare the severe injury probabilities of the first two subpopulations to evaluate which of two strategies,

(1) requiring airbags in all cars or

(2) encouraging states to pass laws making the wearing of seatbelts mandatory

will lead to the least number of severe injuries to the driving public.

(c) In medical studies, which often play a role in deciding whether to regulate exposure to a chemical, one compares the probability, p_1, an exposed person gets a disease with the probability, p_2, a nonexposed person gets the disease. In proving a drug is effective, one compares the probability of cure (or remission) of a new drug with that of a placebo or pre-existing drug.

(d) Since cancer and other diseases resulting from exposure to carcinogens (tobacco, dioxin, etc.) take a long time to develop (have a long latency period), rather than follow a sample of exposed persons and another sample of unexposed individuals for many years until the cancer develops, an alternative approach to assessing whether a chemical is associated[2] with a disease is a retrospective or case-control study. Here we compare a group of persons with the disease (cases) with persons of similar age and previous general health status (controls) who don't have the disease and ask whether the exposure rates of the two groups to the chemical are equal or not. If the exposure rate of the cases significantly exceeds that of the controls, then we conclude that exposure to the chemicals increases one's chances of getting the disease.

All the applications mentioned are primarily concerned with deciding whether two probabilities or proportions are the same and the basic data used can be summarized in a 2 × 2 table of the form given in Table 5.2. An example of a 2 × 2 table concerning the initial placement of new hires, who did not have prior job experience, was used in *Marsh v. Eaton Corporation*.[3] The data given in Table 5.3 shows that about 47% of the men were placed in the better jobs while 0% of the women were.

Another example of the occurrence of 2 × 2 tables in EEO cases is in assessing whether a test has a disproportionate impact on minority applicants because their pass rate is less than that of majority applicants. The data in Table 5.4 reports the results of the test which was the subject of controversy in *Teal v. Connecticut*.[4] In this application we implicitly assume that the applicants are a sample of the population of potential workers so that if we determine that the pass rate of minorities is significantly

TABLE 5.2. Format of Data Used to Compare Two Proportions

	Success	Non-success	Total	Fraction of Success
Group I	a	b	$a + b = n_1$	$\dfrac{a}{n_1}$
Group II	c	d	$c + d = n_2$	$\dfrac{c}{n_2}$
Total	$a + c = m$	$b + d = N - m$	$n_1 + n_2 = N$	$\dfrac{(a + c)}{(n_1 + n_2)}$

TABLE 5.3.   Initial Placement Data from *Marsh v. Eaton*

	High Level Job	Low Level Job	Total	Fraction in High Level
Female	0	27	27	0
Male	8	9	17	.4706
Total	8	36	44	.1818

Source: Data cited in the opinion 639 F.2d 328 (6th Cir. 1981) at 329.

less than that of majority persons, the conclusion inferred is generalizable to future applicants.

In assessing the possible effect of hazardous chemicals in the vicinity of Love Canal,[5] scientists compared the incidence (rate) of low birth weight in families living in the swale area of the canal (the area located on the natural drainage pathways from the canal) to the rest of the Love Canal region. Part of this data is summarized in the 2 × 2 table, Table 5.5.

In this chapter we first discuss several measures of the difference between two probabilities or proportions and introduce the odds ratio, which is technically the most convenient measure of relative disparity. In Sections 3 and 4 we describe two procedures for testing whether the underlying probabilities p_1 and p_2 are equal by comparing the two sample proportions and a method for obtaining a confidence interval for the difference $p_1 - p_2$. The first method is based on the assumption that the data are random samples of each group and is most appropriate for the analysis of the Teal data (Table 5.4). The second method, Fisher's exact test, is used when the overall number of successes in both groups is fixed and is

TABLE 5.4.   Black and White Applicants and the Number of Each Group Who Passed the Test in *Teal v. Connecticut*

	Pass	Fail	Total	Fraction Passing
Black	26	22	48	.5417
White	206	53	259	.7954
Total	232	75	307	.7557

Source: Data cited in the opinion 102 S.Ct. 2525 (1982) at 2529 n.4.

TABLE 5.5. Total Live Births and Babies Born of Low Birth Weight in the Swale and Non-swale Areas of Love Canal

	Low Birth Weight	Normal Birth Weight	Total	Fraction of Babies With Low Birth Weight
Swale Area	21	153	174	.1207
Non-swale Area	32	411	443	.0722
Total	53	564	617	.0859

Source: Table 1 from Vianna, N. J. and Polan, A. K. (1984). Incidence of Low Birth Weight Among Love Canal Residents. *Science* **226**, 1217–1219.

most appropriate for the analysis of the *Marsh v. Eaton* data (Table 5.3). In large samples both methods are equivalent, but they may yield slightly different results in small samples.

Section 5 deals with combining several related data sets, such as hiring, in a variety of occupations (analogous to Section 6 of Chapter 4) or rates of disease in various age groups in the population. Chapter 6 will discuss further uses of these procedures in equal employment cases and introduce the reader to their use in health studies.

Problems

1.* In EEO cases one must evaluate whether a test, which can be a formal written one or a requirement such as possession of a high school diploma or being at least 5'8" tall, has the effect of excluding a disproportionate number of minority applicants.

(a) Describe this problem in terms of comparing two proportions or probabilities.

(b) Should the total number of persons who pass the test during a year be considered as a fixed preset number or is it a random variable itself depending on the results of the test?

2.* We shall learn in Chapter 10 that the concept of a rate is slightly different than that of a probability, because rates refer to a fixed time period. Formulate illustrations (b) and (c) in the text more carefully in terms of probabilities by incorporating a realistic time period in the definition of the two probabilities being compared.

3.* In examining case-control data (d) a simple comparison of the proportion of cases exposed to the chemical with the proportion of controls who were not exposed may not utilize all of the available information, as different people may be exposed to different amounts of the chemical or for different periods. How might one incorporate such factors in a careful study?

4.* Two measures of the difference between probabilities are:
 (a) the difference $\delta = p_1 - p_2$ and
 (b) the ratio $SR = p_1/p_2$.
  (1) For each of the data sets in Tables 5.3, 5.4 and 5.5, compute estimates of both measures using the appropriate fractions as estimates of the true probabilities.
  (2) Can you think of situations in which one of the measures is more appropriate than the other?

Answers to Selected Problems

1. (a) Let $p_1(p_2)$ denote the proportion of minority (majority) members in the labor market area who are potentially interested in the job at issue and satisfy the requirements. If the actual applicants can be regarded as a sample of these individuals, we are comparing two proportions.
 (b) When the cutoff score or requirement is set prior to the evaluation of the applicant, the number of persons who pass is a random variable. *Note:* In our discussion of actual cases, special problems can arise, as people in the local area may know that an employer has a requirement, so persons not satisfying it may not apply. In such cases the actual applicant pool may not be a representative sample of interested applicants, so the effect of the questioned requirement is evaluated on census data.

2. Assessing the Difference between Two Rates or Proportions

Before examining or even collecting data, it is helpful to think about how the results will be interpreted and used. When comparing proportions, e.g., pass rates of blacks and whites on an exam or disease rates of persons exposed to those not exposed to a toxic substance, the method of analysis and ultimate inference may depend on the choice of statistical measure. For example, let $\bar{p}_1$ and $\bar{p}_2$ be the hire rates of black and white applicants, i.e., we can regard them as estimates of the probability a white (black) applicant is hired. The simple difference $\delta = p_1 - p_2$ measures how much smaller or larger the probability a black applicant has of being hired than a white has and is a measure of the absolute difference without consideration of the magnitude of p_1 and p_2. An alternate measure, the *selection ratio, p_1/p_2 = SR,* expresses the probability, p_1, a black has of being hired as a fraction of that (p_2) of a white.

The two measures, δ and SR, have different meanings and both can be useful. To illustrate this, consider two pairs of probabilities (.8, .9) and (.1, .2). Notice that δ equals $-.1$ for *both* pairs while the selection ratios are .8/9 = .89 and .1/.2 = .5, respectively. Common sense suggests that if we are concerned with the chance an *individual black* has of being hired relative to that of a white, the disparity between the second pair of probabilities (.1, .2) is more meaningful than the disparity between the first pair (.8, .9). However, if we wish to estimate the number of *additional blacks* who would have been hired had they *enjoyed* the *same hire rate as whites*, we would multiply the number of black applicants by δ (.1 in our example) in both situations.

The difference, δ, however, possesses a nice mathematical property that the selection ratio, R, does not have. Suppose we compared the non-hire or rejection probabilities $(1 - p_1, 1 - p_2)$, i.e., the rejection rates for our two pairs of probabilities which are

$$(.2, .1) \quad \text{and} \quad (.9, .8).$$

The difference measured in both cases is just $.2 - .1 = +.1$ $(.9 - .8 = +.1)$, so its *absolute magnitude* (.1) *remains* the *same.* Just its sign changes, since the group possessing the larger hire probability has the smaller non-hire probability. On the other hand, the selection ratio changes dramatically. For the first pair of numbers, the selection ratio of the non-hire probabilities is $.2/.1 = 2$, in contrast with the selection ratio .8/.9 computed for the hire probabilities. Thus we can say that a black applicant has 89% of the chance a white has of being hired or twice the white's chance of not being hired. This asymmetry can lead to conflicting conclusions as to the meaning and significance[6] of a difference in two rates. Therefore, we introduce the *odds ratio,* which is a ratio measure like the selection ratio but has the same meaning whether we consider success (hire) rates or failure (non-hire) rates.

Recall that if an event has probability p of occurring, then the probability it will *not* occur is $1 - p$, and we say that the odds of the event occurring are p to $1 - p$. In betting language, this means that if you bet money on the occurrence of the event (e.g., horse A wins the race), the ratio of your bet to your potential winnings should be $p/(1 - p)$. For instance, if $p = 1/3$, then $1 - p = 2/3$ and $p/(1 - p) = 1/2$, or the odds are $1:2$ against the event happening. Thus, a fair bet would offer you \$2 for every \$1 you wager on the occurrence of the event. This agrees with our intuition, as the chance that A does *not* occur is twice as large as the chance that it does.

If we consider two different probabilities (e.g., promotion or hiring), p_1 and p_2, for the minority and majority groups, respectively, then the odds faced by a minority member are $p_1/(1 - p_1)$, while those faced by a majority member are $p_2/(1 - p_2)$. Their ratio is called the odds ratio (OR).

$$(5.1) \qquad \frac{\dfrac{p_1}{(1 - p_1)}}{\dfrac{p_2}{(1 - p_2)}} = \frac{p_1(1 - p_2)}{p_2(1 - p_1)}.$$

In words, the odds ratio (5.1) comparing the odds of success for members of group I relative to those of group II members is

$$\frac{\dfrac{\text{success rate in group I}}{\text{failure rate in group I}}}{\dfrac{\text{success rate in group II}}{\text{failure rate in group II}}} = \frac{\text{success rate in group I}}{\text{success rate in group II}} \times \frac{\text{failure rate in group II}}{\text{failure rate in group I}}.$$

Thus, the OR is related to the selection ratio (ratio of success rates), as it is the product of the selection ratio and the failure ratio (of group II relative to group I). When the odds ratio is *less* than one, minorities have less of a chance for promotion (or hire) than majority members. The reverse is true if the odds ratio is greater than one.

Computing the odds ratio from formula (5.1) for the pair (.1, .2) yields

$$\frac{\dfrac{.1}{.9}}{\dfrac{.2}{.8}} = \frac{.1}{.9} \times \frac{.8}{.2} = .444,$$

indicating that the odds a black applicant has of being hired are 44.4% of those a white has. Calculating the odds ratio based on nonselection rates (.8, .9) one obtains

$$\frac{\dfrac{.9}{.1}}{\dfrac{.8}{.2}} = 2.25,$$

which is the *reciprocal* of .444 ($1/.444 = 2.25$), i.e., the odds of a black applicant not being selected are about $2\frac{1}{4}$ times that of a white. Thus, the basic meaning of the odds ratio measure is the same regardless of whether hire (pass) or non-hire (fail) probabilities are used, as the odds ratio is symmetric in that using failure probabilities ($1 - p$) instead of passing probabilities (p) yields the same conclusion. In our numerical example, blacks had slightly less than half the odds a white had of being hired and slightly more than twice the odds a white had of not being hired.

Comments. (1) Although statisticians usually prefer the odds ratio to the selection ratio, the selection ratio is the basis of the four-fifths rule used by government agencies in assessing employment practices for possible discriminatory impact. If the minority pass (hire) rate is *less* than four fifths (or .8) of the majority rate, then the practice is said to have a disparate or disproportionate impact on the minority group, and employers are required to justify its job relevance. We shall see that this type of analysis is mainly used when a specific employment practice, such as requiring the passing of a written or physical test or possession of a diploma, are at issue. Measures of comparative disparity are quite useful in summarizing the overall effect of a hiring or promotion process in situations without specific requirements, since they directly compare the probability or odds of success of minority candidates to those of majority candidates.

(2) When the success probabilities p_1 and p_2 are small, the selection ratio and odds ratio are essentially the same (calculate them when $p_1 = .01$, $p_2 = .02$). Since epidemiologic studies deal with the probability, which is usually quite small, of getting a specific disease, the two ratios are sometimes used interchangeably. In this application the *selection ratio* is called the *relative risk* (of getting the disease), and the odds ratio is an accurate approximation to it.

The formula for computing the *estimated* odds ratio from data in the format of a 2×2 table (5.2) is obtained by substituting the sample proportions for the corresponding probabilities. Thus, p_1 is replaced by $\bar{p}_1$; p_2 by $\bar{p}_2$, ($1 - p_1$) by $1 - \bar{p}_1$; and $1 - p_2$ by $1 - \bar{p}_2$. Thus, the second formula for the odds ratio in (5.1) becomes

$$(5.2) \qquad \frac{\bar{p}_1}{\bar{p}_2} \cdot \frac{(1 - \bar{p}_2)}{(1 - \bar{p}_1)} = \frac{\dfrac{a}{n_1}}{\dfrac{c}{n_2}} \cdot \frac{\dfrac{d}{n_2}}{\dfrac{b}{n_1}} = \frac{\dfrac{ad}{n_1 n_2}}{\dfrac{cb}{n_1 n_2}} = \frac{ad}{bc}.$$

For the birth-weight data in Table 5.5, the odds a family residing in the swale area has of having a low birth-weight baby are

$$\frac{(21)(411)}{(32)(153)} = 1.76$$

times those of families living in the non-swale area. Of course, 1.76 is an estimate of the *true* odds ratio (5.1), since it is based on data. Had a different time period been studied, the result might have been different from 1.76. Notice that the selection ratio or risk of having a Swale area resident having a low birth-weight baby relative to that of a non-swale area resident is

$$.1207/.0722 = 1.67,$$

again illustrating that when comparing small rates or probabilities the odds ratio is a good approximation to the selection ratio or relative risk.

Problems

1.   For the Canadian seat-belt-use data (Table 5.1) compute the estimates of the difference, δ, and selection ratio, R, measures for several provinces.

   (a) Which measure seems most sensible to use in assessing the effect of the law?

   (b) Which measure seems more consistent as a measure across all provinces?

2.   Compute the three measures, δ, SR and the odds ratio (OR) for the *Teal v. Connecticut* data.

3.   Compute the selection ratio (SR) and odds ratio (OR) for the following pairs of success probabilities. When is OR a good approximation to SR?

Success Probabilities	
Group I	Group II
.04	.02
.20	.10
.40	.20
.80	.40

4.* One of the earliest attempts to use statistical data in jury discrimination cases may well have occurred in the trial of John Mitchell in England in 1848. After he was convicted for violating the Government Security Act, Mitchell asserted that the jury had been stacked against him, as Catholics were underrepresented. The basic data for the venire selections follows:

	Eligible for Jury Service	Selected
Catholic	3426	28
Protestant	1235	122

(a) Calculate the jury selection probabilities for members of the two faiths and the associated odds and selection ratios.

(b) Is it really necessary to calculate a formal statistical test to determine whether a petitioner's claim is supported by the data?

Historical Note: This case is from the *Monthly Law Reporter,* September 1848, p. 193–203. The Crown (prosecution) eliminated all 28 Catholics on the venire with their challenges. The Court did not find discrimination on the basis of religion as the Crown would not do such a thing. (I am indebted to Prof. Daniel Kleitman of MIT for this example.)

Answers to Selected Problems

1. The computations are straightforward, e.g., for Ontario SR = .60/.23 = 2.61, while δ = .60 − .23 = .37. Neither measure is consistent over all the provinces, but the selection ratio (SR) seems to vary more, i.e., its smallest value is .54/.32 = 1.688, while its largest value is .68/.04 = 17.

2. δ = .5417 − .7957 = −.2537, i.e., the pass rate of blacks was 25% lower than the white rate. SR = .5417/.7954 = .681, or the black pass rate was 68% of the white rate. OR = 26/22 × 53/206 = .304 or blacks faced odds only 30% of those faced by whites.

3. The selection ratio is two for all pairs. The odds ratio is 2.042 for the first pair (.04, .020), which is a close approximation to 2.0; is .25/.111 = 2.25 for the second pair (.2, .1); a fair approximation to 2.0; and 4/.6666 = 6 for the last pair (.8, .4), a very poor approximation to 2.0.

3. Comparing Two Sample Proportions

The data in each row of a 2×2 table can be regarded as arising from a binomial distribution. If each member of group I (II) has success probability $p_1(p_2)$, then the number of successes of group I (II) members is a binomial variable with parameters $n_1(n_2)$ and $p_1(p_2)$. We have realized that data in the format of Table 5.2, the natural estimates of p_1 and p_2, are their respective success fractions or proportions. Even when the true underlying probabilities, p_1 and p_2, are equal, the sample proportions (success fractions), $\bar{p}_1$ and $\bar{p}_2$, in a particular set of data usually are not exactly equal, due to chance fluctuations (sampling error). Their difference, $\bar{p}_1 - \bar{p}_2$, is a random variable with expected value 0, as under the null hypothesis ($p_1 = p_2$) both sample proportions *estimate* the same probability, which we label p_c (c is used to denote a *common* value for p_1 and p_2).

If the *null hypothesis* is true, then an obvious estimate of p_c from data in the format of Table 5.2 is the fraction of successes in the total data set, i.e.,

$$(5.3) \qquad \bar{p}_c = \frac{(a + c)}{(n_1 + n_2)},$$

since all $n_1 + n_2$ observations would be from the same binomial distribution with success probability p_c.

Under the null hypothesis, the *standard deviation* of the difference $\bar{p} - \bar{p}_2$ between the two sample proportions is given by

$$(5.4) \qquad \sqrt{\bar{p}_c(1 - \bar{p}_c)\left(\frac{1}{n_1} + \frac{1}{n_2}\right)}.$$

In words, formula (5.4) for the standard deviation of $(\bar{p}_1 - \bar{p}_2)$ can be expressed as the square root of

$$(5.4a) \qquad \sqrt{\left(\begin{matrix}\text{overall}\\ \text{success}\\ \text{rate}\end{matrix}\right) \times \left(\begin{matrix}\text{overall}\\ \text{failure}\\ \text{rate}\end{matrix}\right) \times \left(\frac{1}{\begin{matrix}\text{size of}\\ \text{group I}\end{matrix}} + \frac{1}{\begin{matrix}\text{size of}\\ \text{group II}\end{matrix}}\right)}.$$

Notice that formula (5.4) is similar to the standard deviation of a sample proportion from a single binomial variable

$$(5.5) \qquad \sqrt{\left(\begin{matrix}\text{success}\\ \text{rate}\end{matrix}\right) \times \left(\begin{matrix}\text{failure}\\ \text{rate}\end{matrix}\right) \times \frac{1}{\text{sample size}}}.$$

Now the sample sizes of both groups enter into the calculation.

If the sample sizes are adequate for the central limit theorem or normal approximation to apply, we can develop an analog to the one sample procedure (3.38) by expressing the actual difference, $\bar{p}_1 - \bar{p}_2$, between the two sample proportions and its expected value, 0, under the null hypothesis that $p_1 = p_2$ in units of standard deviations of the random variable, $\bar{p}_1 - \bar{p}_2$. Thus, we obtain the approximate test statistic,

$$(5.6) \qquad Z = \frac{\bar{p}_1 - \bar{p}_2}{\sqrt{\bar{p}_c(1 - \bar{p}_c)\left(\dfrac{1}{n_1} + \dfrac{1}{n_2}\right)}},$$

which has a standard normal distribution. In words, the statistic (5.6) is

$$(5.6a) \qquad \frac{\text{the difference in ``success'' fractions in the two groups}}{\substack{\text{the standard deviation of the difference between} \\ \text{the sample success fractions}}}.$$

Let us apply the test statistic (5.6) to the data in Table 5.5. Here $\bar{p}_1 = .1207$, $\bar{p}_2 = .0722$ and $\bar{p}_c = .0859$, while $n_1 = 174$, $n_2 = 443$. Hence, (5.6) becomes

$$\frac{.1207 - 0722}{\sqrt{(.0857)(1 - .0859)(1/174 + 1/443)}} = \frac{.0485}{\sqrt{(.0859)(.9141)(.0080)}}$$

$$(5.7) \qquad\qquad\qquad\qquad\qquad = \frac{.0485}{.0251} = 1.935.$$

The difference of 1.935 standard deviations from expected is statistically significant if a one-sided .05 level test is used and just misses significance if a two-sided .05 level criteria is adopted. As the one-sided p-value is .0265 and the two-sided p-value is .053 (2 × .0265), it is reasonable to conclude that residents of the swale area had a statistically significantly higher chance of having a low birth-weight baby than other residents of the Love Canal area.

In most examination or testing situations, whether or not an individual passes is not affected by the test results of other candidates. Thus, the Teal data in Table 5.5 can be regarded as testing whether the probability (p_1) a black applicant passes the test is equal to that (p_2) of a white. Applying the test statistic (5.6) to the data in Table 5.4 yields

$$(5.8) \qquad \frac{.5417 - .7954}{\sqrt{(.7557)(.2443)\left(\dfrac{1}{48} + \dfrac{1}{259}\right)}} = \frac{-.2537}{.0675} = -3.76.$$

This difference of 3.76 standard deviations from that expected clearly is statistically significant at commonly used levels of significance (.05 or .01). Indeed, the one-sided p-value is about .001.

The ratio of the odds a black candidate has of passing the test in *Teal* to that of a white candidate is [from (5.2)]

$$(5.9) \qquad \frac{26 \times 53}{206 \times 22} = .304.$$

Thus, black candidates had only 30% the odds of passing that a white had. The estimate of $(\bar{p}_1/\bar{p}_2)$ the selection ratio (p_1/p_2) from the data is

$$\frac{.5417}{.7954} = .68,$$

which is less than the four-fifths (.8) criteria, indicating that the difference is a meaningful one. Notice that if the ratio of the rejection fraction proportions were used, then the blacks failed at a ratio

$$\frac{.4583}{.2046} = 2.24$$

times that of whites. There is no simple relationship between the ratio of pass rates to the ratio of failure rates, except that if one is less than one, the other is greater than one. If we compute the ratio of the odds a black fails to those of a white, we obtain (by interchanging the pass and fail columns in Table 5.4)

$$(5.10) \qquad \frac{22 \times 206}{26 \times 53} = \frac{4532}{1378} = 3.289,$$

which is the *reciprocal* of .304. This illustrates the point made in the previous section that the meaning of the odds ratio is the same regardless of whether pass or fail rates are considered. The fact that blacks had about one third the odds of whites of passing or, equivalently, had about three times the odds of failing as whites again indicates that the difference in the pass rates in *Teal* is meaningful in a practical sense as well as being statistically significant.

We close this section by obtaining a *confidence interval* for the *difference $p_1 - p_2$* between two probabilities using the sample proportions $\bar{p}_1$ and $\bar{p}_2$ as estimates of p_1 and p_2. It is based on the fact that each sample proportion is approximately normally distributed with

$$(5.11) \qquad \text{mean } p \text{ and variance } \frac{p(1 - p)}{n},$$

where p is the true probability of success and n is the sample size. Unlike the testing situation where we assume (under the null hypothesis) that the true values of p_1 and p_2 are the same, we now believe they may differ and desire to estimate $p_1 - p_2$ by $\bar{p}_1 - \bar{p}_2$. From the fact that the variance of a difference of two independent statistics is the sum of the two variances, the difference between the two proportions $\bar{p}_1 - \bar{p}_2$ has

(5.12)   mean $p_1 - p_2$ and variance $\dfrac{p_1(1 - p_1)}{n_1} + \dfrac{p_2(1 - p_2)}{n_2}$,

where n_1 and n_2 are the respective sample sizes.

Assuming that the sample sizes are large enough for the normal approximation (Central Limit Theorem) to be valid, a $100(1 - \alpha)\%$ confidence interval for $p_1 - p_2$, analogous to that in (3.20), is

(5.13) $(\bar{p}_1 - \bar{p}_2) \pm z_{\alpha/2} \sqrt{\dfrac{\bar{p}_1(1 - \bar{p}_1)}{n_1} + \dfrac{\bar{p}_2(1 - \bar{p}_2)}{n_2}}$,

where we substitute the sample proportions for the unknown true probabilities p_1 and p_2 in the formula for the standard deviation.

Example.   We now illustrate the use of formula (5.13) by finding a 95% confidence interval for the *difference* in the pass rates of blacks and whites in *Teal v. Connecticut*. From the data in Table 5.4, we realize that

$$\bar{p}_1 = .5417, \qquad \bar{p}_2 = .7957, \qquad n_1 = 48 \qquad \text{and} \qquad n_2 = 259.$$

Substituting these values in (5.13) yields

$$p_1 - p_2 = (.5417 - .79570) \pm (1.96) \times$$

(5.14) $\sqrt{\dfrac{(.5417)(.4583)}{48} + \dfrac{(.7957)(.2043)}{259}}$

$$= (-.2514) \pm (1.96)(.0762)$$

(5.15) $= -.2514 \pm .149$,

or

(5.16)   95% CONF $(p_1 - p_2; -.403, -.105)$.

This means that we are 95% confident that the probability a black applicant passes the test is *less* than that of a white applicant by at least .1 but not more than .4. Of course, our *estimate* of the difference, $\delta = p_1 - p_2$ is $-.254$. As before, the confidence interval provides a range of possible values of the true difference in pass rates which are consistent with the observed data in that, even accounting for the fluctuations of random sampling (the potential pool of test takers), the actual data has a reasonable probability of occurring only if the true difference lies in the confidence interval.

Problems

1.* Suppose the Love Canal data (Table 5.5) had been based on a larger number of observations, so all entries were *twice* those of Table 5.5.
    (a) Write out the new data set and compute the fractions of low birth-weight babies in each group.
    (b) Does the odds ratio change? Explain.
    (c) Does the result of our test of significance change?
    (d) Does the confidence interval (5.13) change?
    (e) What do your answers to (c) and (d) imply?

2.* In our interpretation of the Teal data we considered the applicants who took the test as a sample of the pool of potential applicants. When is this assumption reasonable? Are there circumstances where it may not be reasonable? Suppose the only individuals who will be affected by the legal decision are those who took the questioned exam. Does the result of our statistical test showing a difference of -3.76 standard deviations between the pass rates aid our understanding of the impact of the exam on the actual black candidates?

Answers to Selected Problems

1. (a,b) The fraction of low birth-weight babies will be unchanged so that our estimated odds ratio remains the same.
    (c,d,e) The statistical test will yield a more significant result (smaller p-value) and a narrower confidence interval. This happens because the sample sizes are larger (doubled), so the sampling errors are *smaller*. Hence, we are more confident that the observed difference is real and not due to sampling fluctuation than we were before (using the data in Table 5.4).

2. This assumption is reasonable as long as the job opportunity was well advertised in the community. Yes, if there were special economic circumstances, such as a major layoff of highly qualified workers from a nearby local, they would distort the representativeness of the applicant pool. If

the affected persons are the actual test takers, the statistical inference could be considered more relevant, since we need not be concerned with the representativeness of the sample. Of course, we would be interested in checking that background qualifications were similar in both groups of test takers. If this is true, then the statistically significant result would be quite helpful in interpreting the effect of the exam.

4. Comparing Proportions or Success Rates When the Total Number of Successes Is Fixed: The Fisher Exact Test

Sometimes the data reported in a 2×2 table is not based on two independent samples. For example, in the job assignment data (Table 5.3) the number of better jobs may be determined by conditions external to the discrimination issue being studied, as the state of the economy and employee turnover affect the total number of available positions. Thus, the firm can only place $(a + c)$ or 8 (for the data in Table 5.3) persons in the better jobs and must select those 8 from the pool of 44 new hires, consisting of 27 women and 17 men so that the hypergeometric model of Section 2.7 is appropriate. Similarly, when one analyzes hiring data, the total number of hires is usually a fixed value, M, and they are elected from the pool of applicants. Thus, the hiring process typically fits the hypergeometric model.

From the hypergeometric distribution (formula 2.22), the probability of the observed data in Table 5.2 is given by

$$(5.17) \qquad p(a) = \frac{\binom{n_1}{a}\binom{n_2}{m - a}}{\binom{n_1 + n_2}{m}}.$$

For the *Marsh v. Eaton* data (Table 5.3), the probability that 0 women would have been placed in the higher level job is

$$\frac{\binom{27}{0}\binom{17}{8}}{\binom{44}{8}} = \frac{1 \cdot \dfrac{17!}{8!9!}}{\dfrac{44!}{8!36!}} = \frac{17! \, 36!}{9! \, 44!}$$

$$(5.18) \qquad = \frac{17.16.15.14.13.12.11.10}{44.43.42.41.40.39.38.37} = .00014,$$

quite a small probability, supporting the Sixth Circuit's ruling that the plaintiffs had shown a *Prima facie* case, partially on the basis of the data, even though the opinion did not carry out the formal statistical test.

In the *Marsh* data, 0 was the most *extreme* possible outcome. In general, a one-sided test of size α is obtained by computing the probability of the observed value a and *smaller* values and seeing if this probability is less than α. Notice that we are computing the p-value of the data. A two-sided test can be obtained by doubling the p-value of the one-sided test or by developing an appropriate two-sided region. We will simply double the p-value of the one-sided test.

We now illustrate the use of the test on data from *Johnson v. Perini*,[8] where the concern was whether blacks were discharged at a higher rate than whites. The concept of a discharge seems clear enough, however, there are two ways one can be discharged. First, the employer may fire an employee for poor work performance or insubordination or any other cause where there is room for a substantial degree of subjective evaluation on the employer's part. On the other hand, an employee may be terminated because of excessive absenteeism, showing up for work intoxicated or for other reasons which are primarily under the control of the employee. When analyzing termination data it may be preferable to separate out the terminations in which the *employer's* judgement has the major role in determining whether the worker is discharged, especially when the motivation of the employer is being scrutinized.

The data for terminations for cause is reported in Table 5.6. The probability of the observed data is given by

$$(5.19) \qquad \frac{\binom{9}{1}\binom{47}{1}}{\binom{56}{2}} = \frac{9.47}{\frac{56.55}{2}} = \frac{18.47}{56.55} = .2747.$$

The only more extreme table than Table 5.6 would have both terminees black. This table is given in Table 5.7.

The probability of the data in Table 5.7 is

$$\frac{\binom{9}{2}\binom{47}{0}}{\binom{56}{2}} = \frac{9.8}{\frac{56.55}{2}} = \frac{72}{3080} = .023,$$

so the overall probability of observing as many or more blacks terminated

TABLE 5.6.   Black and White Employees Classified by Whether or Not They Were Terminated for Cause in *Johnson v. Perini*

	Terminated (Cause)	Not Terminated	Total	Fraction Terminated
Black	1	8	9	.111
White	1	46	47	.021
Total	2	54	56	.036

Source: Defendant's exhibit filed in the district court.

for cause than in the actual data is .2747 + .023 = .278, which is not close to significance. Notice that simply relying on the selection ratio, .111/.021 = 5.38, in Table 5.6 would suggest the blacks were five times as likely as whites to be terminated. The reason for the sharply contrasting conclusions of the formal statistical test and the simple comparison of the termination rates is that the sample consisted of only two terminees.

While rates and proportions calculated from small samples are less reliable than those derived from larger samples, it is still useful to calculate the formal statistical test. Had the actual data been the more extreme Table (5.7), the court might have required more explanation from the defendants about their procedures for evaluating job performance.

In the actual case, there were a total of four discharges for any reason. Not only was the difference between the discharge rates for black and white employees not significant, the judge also questioned the reliability of such a small sample. Implicitly, he is questioning the validity of the hypergeometric model, i.e., each person in the pool (employees) has the same chance of being terminated. If a *few* employees were less qualified and were terminated, they would have a major impact on the statistical inference derived from such a small sample but a negligible one in large samples, e.g., 100 terminations from a work force of 2500.

TABLE 5.7.   More Extreme Data Than in Table 5.6 for Use in Calculating Fisher's Exact Test

	Terminated (Cause)	Not Terminated	Total	Fraction Terminated
Black	2	7	9	.222
White	0	47	47	0.00
Total	2	54	56	.036

As an illustration of the wide applicability of Fisher's exact test, consider the data in Table 5.8 which reports the results of a diagnostic test given to children in an early stage of Reye's Syndrome in order to predict whether the disease will progress to a more serious stage (coma and possible brain damage and/or death). The test predicted further progress if the patient's ammonia count exceeded 100 mg/deciliter and prothrombine time was greater than 3 seconds.

In order to determine whether the diagnostic procedure is an effective predictor, we test the hypothesis that the probability of a patient with a high score proceeding to a more serious stage equals the probability of a patient with low scores proceeding to a more serious illness against the alternative that the high (low) scores have a greater (lesser) probability of becoming sicker. Using formula (5.17) we find the probability that all five patients who progressed to a more serious stage came from those who had high scores in the diagnostic test is

$$
\frac{\binom{7}{5}\binom{76}{0}}{\binom{83}{5}} = \frac{\left(\frac{7 \cdot 6}{2}\right) 1}{\frac{83 \cdot 82 \cdot 81 \cdot 80 \cdot 79}{5 \cdot 4 \cdot 3 \cdot 2 \cdot 1}} = \frac{(7 \cdot 3)120}{83 \cdot 82 \cdot 81 \cdot 80 \cdot 79} = .000000723.
$$

a minuscule probability, indicating that the results of the diagnostic procedure cannot be due to chance but are due to the intrinsic relation between the chemical test and the progression of Reye's Syndrome.

In this application, the data were generated by a process *in between* that of sampling two binomial populations and selecting a fixed number of objects from a large pool consisting of two types. At the time the test is

---

TABLE 5.8.   Progress of Patients to More Serious Stage of Reye's Syndrome Classified by Diagnostic Test

	Progressed	Did Not Progress	Total
High Ammonia Levels and Prothrombine Time	5	2	7
Low Levels of Ammonia, etc.	0	76	76
Total	5	78	83

Source: Table 2 from Heubi, J. E., Daugherty, C. C., Partin, J. S., Partin, J. C. and Shubert, W. K. (1984). Grade 1 Reye's Syndrome Outcomes and Predictors of Progression to Deeper Coma Grades. *New England Journal of Medicine* **311**, 1539–1542.

administered, each patient has probability p_1 or p_2 of proceeding to a more serious stage, depending on the test results, so the model in Section 3 is appropriate. However, the data was analyzed after several years of observation in order to accumulate a reasonable number of cases which progressed. Thus, at the time of analysis, we know that five patients progressed to the very serious stages. Because the data was originally generated by two binomial populations, but we waited until a sufficiently large number of serious cases (total number of events in both categories) occurred before analyzing the data, it is not clear which test is appropriate. Fortunately, when the number of events (successes, selections) are small relative to the total sample ($n_1 + n_2$), both test statistics, Fisher's and (5.6), give similar results.

The exact calculation of the probability of the observed data and more extreme ones required by Fisher's test becomes quite tedious in larger samples, and we now present an approximate test which is analogous to the normal approximation for binomial data.

If we denote the number of minority successes by the random variable, A, then from formula (2.23), A has expected value

$$(5.20) \qquad \mu = \frac{n_1}{N} m = \frac{n_1}{N} (a + c)$$

and variance

$$(5.21) \quad \sigma^2 = \left(\frac{n_1}{N}\right)\left(\frac{n_2}{N}\right) \frac{m(N - m)}{N - 1} = \frac{(a + b)(c + d)(a + c)(b + d)}{N^2(N - 1)},$$

where $n_2 = N - n_1$ and m is the total number of successes: $a + c$, in Table 5.2.

In words, the expected number of the $m = a + c$ successes from group I is their proportion: (n_1/N) of the total pool *times* the number, m, of successes and the variance of the number of successes in group I is

$$\frac{\left(\begin{array}{c}\text{group I's}\\\text{fraction of}\\\text{the total}\end{array}\right) \times \left(\begin{array}{c}\text{group II's}\\\text{fraction of}\\\text{the total}\end{array}\right) \times \left(\begin{array}{c}\text{number of}\\\text{successes}\end{array}\right)\left(\begin{array}{c}\text{number of}\\\text{failures}\end{array}\right)}{(\text{total number})^2 \times (\text{total number minus 1})}.$$

Expressing the variable A in its standardized form, i.e., measuring the difference between the actual and expected value of A in units of the standard deviation of A, yields

$$(5.22) \qquad \frac{\text{actual data } (A) - \text{expected value of } A}{\text{standard deviation of } A},$$

and the test statistic corresponding to (5.22) is

$$(5.23) \qquad Z = \frac{a - m\left(\frac{n_1}{N}\right)}{\sqrt{\frac{n_1}{N} \cdot \frac{n_2}{N} \cdot \frac{m(N - m)}{N - 1}}},$$

which has an approximate standard normal distribution.

Let us now use the approximate test to analyze the data from *Jurgens v. Thomas* in Table 2.7. Now $a = 3$, $m = 32$, $n = 62$, $n = 222$ and $N = 284$. Hence, from (5.20) we find that the expected number of male promotions is

$$(5.24) \qquad \frac{m - n_1}{n} = \frac{32 \cdot 62}{284} = 6.986,$$

and the variance, obtained from formula (5.21), is

$$(5.25) \qquad \frac{62}{284} \cdot \frac{222}{284} \cdot \frac{32}{283} \cdot 252 = 4.863;$$

so the standard deviation equals $\sqrt{4.803} = 2.205$.

Thus, the normal approximate test statistic (5.23) is

$$(5.26) \qquad Z = \frac{3 - 6.986}{2.205} = \frac{-3.986}{2.205} = -1.807,$$

i.e., the difference between the actual (3) and expected number (6.98) of such promotions is -1.807 standard deviation units and has a p-value of about .036, which is a reasonable approximation to the exact value, .0491.

For our purposes, it is important to note that there exist relatively simple procedures available to test whether two sample proportions can be regarded as coming from a common population when the total number of successes is random (Section 3) or when the total number of successes is fixed. Moreover, it can be shown that in large samples the tests become virtually identical regardless of how the data was generated. This is a useful result, because in some situations we may not know the mechanism generating the data or the data may be from a mixture of the binomial and hypergeometric models. For example, someone grading a test might notice that too many (too few) people were passing and become stricter (more lenient) during the grading process. It also means that for the purpose of discussing the basic concepts, we may use the formula for the confidence intervals given in Section 3 in the present context.

It is important to realize that the basic comparison of the *actual data* to its *expected value* which was used in the binomial model also applies to tests comparing two proportions. We saw this in the normal approximation (5.23) to Fisher's test, and we now show it for the test (5.6) used to compare samples from two binomial distributions. Consider the usual formal (Table 5.2) of the data. If both populations had the same probability (p) of success, we would estimate p by $(a + c)/(n_1 + n_2)$, the fraction of successes in the total number, $n_1 + n_2$, of trials. We would expect that

$$(5.27) \qquad \frac{n_1}{n_1 + n_2} (a + c)$$

members of group I be successes. The *difference* between actual number, a, and the expected number of successes from group I is

$$(5.28) \qquad a - \frac{n_1}{n_1 + n_2} (a + c).$$

Some algebra shows that (5.28) becomes

$$(5.29) \qquad \frac{a(n_1 + n_2) - an_1 - cn_1}{n_1 + n_2} = \frac{a(c + d) - c(a + b)}{n_1 + n_2} = \frac{ad - bc}{n_1 + n_2}.$$

In words, the difference between the actual and *expected number* of *successes from group I* is

$$(5.29\text{b}) \qquad \frac{\left[\left(\begin{array}{c}\text{group I}\\\text{successes}\end{array}\right) \cdot \left(\begin{array}{c}\text{group II}\\\text{failures}\end{array}\right)\right] \text{ minus } \left[\left(\begin{array}{c}\text{group I}\\\text{failures}\end{array}\right) \cdot \left(\begin{array}{c}\text{group II}\\\text{successes}\end{array}\right)\right]}{\text{total of group I eligibles and group II eligibles}},$$

where the $\cdot$ indicates the adjacent terms are multiplied.

The numerator $\bar{p}_1 - \bar{p}_2$, of formula (5.6) is

$$(5.30) \qquad \bar{p}_1 - \bar{p}_2 = \frac{a}{a + b} - \frac{c}{c + d} = \frac{ad - bc}{(a + b)(c + d)} = \frac{ad - bc}{n_1 \times n_2}$$

or formula (5.30b)

$$\frac{\left[\left(\begin{array}{c}\text{group I}\\\text{success}\end{array}\right) \cdot \left(\begin{array}{c}\text{group II}\\\text{failures}\end{array}\right)\right] \text{ minus } \left[\left(\begin{array}{c}\text{group I}\\\text{failures}\end{array}\right) \cdot \left(\begin{array}{c}\text{group II}\\\text{success}\end{array}\right)\right]}{\text{the number of group I members times the number of group II members}}.$$

The *numerators* of (5.29) and (5.30) are the *same*, but the denominators differ because the statistic (5.29) deals with the difference between the *count* or number of group I members and its expected value, while (5.6) and (5.30) consider the proportions. Since the count (total number of successes) is just the number of trials times the proportion of successes, the *basic concept* underlying both test statistics is the same. Both numerators have *expected* value *zero* under the null hypothesis of equal success probabilities in the two groups, but measure the difference from the expected value in different *scales*. It should be noted that when either statistic (5.29) or (5.30) equals the expected value 0, $ad = bc$, so the estimated odds ratio equals 1. This agrees with our common sense, as $p_1 = p_2$ and the OR $= 1$ are equivalent statements.

We close this section by giving another *interpretation* of Fisher's test for a difference between proportions when we have the whole *population* rather than a sample. For concreteness, consider the *Marsh v. Eaton* job assignment date in Table 5.3. In order to interpret the observed data, we impose a probability model on it by asking the question, "Suppose the selection (for the better jobs) were done by a random device giving each new employee the same chance of receiving the better job, what is the probability that the observed or more extreme data could have resulted?" If this probability is *small*, we draw the logical conclusion that a random or chance process was *very unlikely* to have generated the data, so a difference in the success rates of the two groups should be regarded as a real one. If this probability is high, as in the *Johnson v. Perini* data, then we realize that the difference in termination proportions could be due to chance. Another advantage of using the probability calculation and formal statistical test is that the effect of the sample size (the number of selections) is incorporated in the calculation, so we do not have to concern ourselves with the issue of how large a sample is needed before a test can be made. However, we need to check that the qualifications of the groups being compared are similar in order that the assumption of random selection is applicable.

The above interpretation can be used to justify the use of Fisher's exact test or the test (5.23), which is an approximation to it, in situations such as *Teal* (see Problem 3.2) if the only persons eligible for relief are those who took the test. While we did not discuss the statistical power of the tests presented in Sections 3 and 4, the lessons learned in Chapter 3 still apply. A test which is not statistically significant at the .05 level should not be given great importance when the power to detect a reasonable alternative, e.g., $\delta = .1$ or SR $= .667$, is low. The size of the sample or universe may simply be too small for statistical analysis to shed light on the issue. Similarly, a statistically significant result at the .05 level based on a large sample may not reflect a meaningful difference. Use of the measures in Section 2 in conjunction with formal statistical tests and their p-values should enable one to reach sensible conclusions. We will illustrate these ideas in the EEO and public health areas in Chapter 6.

Problems

1.*   Answer the following questions for each of the data sets described below.

   (a) Which procedure is most appropriate to analyze this data set? Why?

   (b) Carry out the appropriate computation to determine whether the difference in the proportions is statistically significant using a one-sided 5% level test. Report the approximate p-value.

   (c) Calculate an appropriate measure (or measures) of the difference between the proportions. Explain why you chose the measure(s) you calculated.

   (1) This data concerns applicants and hires for a legal assistant position.

	Hired	Not Hired	Total	Fraction Hired
Male	50	150	200	.25
Female	2	18	20	.10
Total	52	168	220	.236

(2) This data concerns the number of people who passed a height requirement for a security occupation.

	Pass	Fail	Total	Fraction of Passing
Male	60	40	100	.60
Female	15	35	50	.30
Total	75	75	150	.50

(3) This data concerns the number of people who were promoted from a set of eligible employees.

	Promoted	Not	Total	Fraction Promoted
Black	40	160	200	.20
White	80	120	200	.40
Total	120	280	400	.30

(4) This data is adapted from a study[9] used to assess whether persons living near an airport have more psychiatric problems, due in part to the noise level, than people living away from airports.

	Total Population in Area	Psychiatric Hospitalizations	% Affected
Near Airports	100,000	2,000	2%
Away from Airports	150,000	1,500	1%

2.* An employer gives a test to black and white applicants. The data is reported below.

	Pass	Fail	Total	Fraction Passing
Black	5	19	24	.2083
White	11	10	21	.5238
All	16	29	45	.3556

(a) Is the government's four-fifths rule violated?

(b) Calculate the odds ratio between black and whites (i.e., what are the odds a black passes relative to a white?)

(c) In order to test (statistically) the data to see whether the difference in pass rates could have occurred by chance, define the *underlying probability model*.

(d) Carry out the procedure your answer to (c) implies is proper.

3.* In a reverse discrimination suit, *Murray v. District of Columbia*,[10] the plaintiff submitted the data in Table 5.9 on the proportions of white and black applicants who were interviewed.

TABLE 5.9. The Number of Black and White Applicants and Fraction of Each Group Who Were Interviewed in *Murray v. D.C.*

Race	Interviewed	Not	Total	Fraction
White	4	70	74	.054
Black	7	29	36	.1944
Total	11	99	110	.100

Source: Data given in the opinion 34 FEP Cases 644 (D. D.C. 1983) at 646.

(a) Using the test statistics (5.23) determine whether the two observed interview fractions can be regarded as being samples from the same population (i.e., are the rates equal?). Use the .05 level of significance.

(b) Compute the selection and odds ratios of the white rate relative to the black one. Do they suggest a meaningful difference to you?

(c) The judge decided that the statistical significance of the data (your answer to part (a)) was diminished by the fact that a switch of one black interviewee to white might have yielded a nonsignificant result at the .05 level.

(1) What is the p-value of the data, assuming the judge's procedure was correct (i.e., five blacks and six whites could be assumed to have been interviewed)? More importantly, if one requires statistical significance to remain valid after a switch, how does this affect the level of significance actually being used by the court? How does this affect the type II error?

(2) The data in Table 5.9 was just statistically significant but failed to satisfy the judge. Write out a possible data set which would have satisfied the judge's criteria. Perform the test (5.23) and calculate the p-value.

(3) On the basis of your analysis was the judge correct from a statistical standpoint? Read the opinion and see whether this issue might have altered the ultimate outcome of the case.

(4) Look up the following cases and comment on the use of statistical analysis:

(A) *Harrell v. Northern Electric Co.* 672 F.2d. 444 (5th Cir. 1982)

(B) *EEOC v. American Nat'l Bank* 30 FEP Cases 906 (4th Cir. 1982)

(C) *White v. San Diego* 605 F.2d. 455, 401 (9th Cir. 1979)

(D) *Schmid v. Frosch* 515 F. Supp. 1260 (D. D.C. 1981)

(E) *Pennsylvania v. Rizzo* 466 F. Supp. 1219 (E.D. Pa. 1979)

5. On the Assumptions Underlying the Methods of Testing whether Two Probabilities Are Equal

The two statistical procedures, (5.6) and Fisher's test (5.23), assume that all members of each group have the same probability of success, e.g. passing the test, buckling the seatbelt, or having a low birth weight baby.

In actual applications it is unrealistic to assume that everyone in a group has the identical probability of success, yet the methods are still

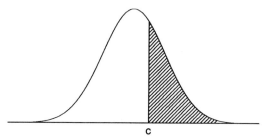

FIGURE 5.1.   The shaded area under normal curve of ability denotes the fraction of individuals where ability level exceeds the threshold c. In the figure c is chosen so that about 30% of the population possess the requisite ability.

applicable. When the success probability varies among individual members of the groups, the null hypothesis, that the success rates are equal, is equivalent to assuming that the distribution of ability to pass or be selected is the same for both groups. Essentially, we are equating the probability of a success as the probability that a member of the group has an ability exceeding threshold value, c, say. Thus, the probability, p, of a success is just the area, in Figure 5.1, corresponding to the portion of the population whose ability exceeds c.

Before we select the sample, each member of the sample has the probability p (the probability that their "ability" exceeds c) of passing, since the sample member will be randomly selected from the population which has a distribution of ability. When the null hypotheses H_0—the ability to pass (be a success) is the same in both groups—is true, it follows that the success probabilities of the members of both samples are expected to be equal, the difference between them is due to sampling variability.

So far we have discussed the general applicability of the procedures for comparing two proportions from sample data. The hypergeometric model and Fisher's exact test also apply when the distribution of likelihood of success varies among members of each population, but the distribution of ability is the same for both populations. Under this null hypothesis all $n_1 + n_2$ observations come from the same distribution of ability, and we can order the observations in terms of their relative rankings $n_1 + n_2$ for the top (highest ability) down to 1 (lowest). The chance that a member of group I has any specific ranking is their proportion, $n_1/(n_1 + n_2)$, of the total number of observations. The hypergeometric probability (5.17), the basis of Fisher's exact test, calculates the probability that a or fewer members of group I are among the top m ranks in the total of $n_1 + n_2$.

Thus, we do not require that every member of each population have the identical probability of being successful in order for the methods discussed in Sections 3 and 4 to be applicable. We are testing the hypothesis that the distribution of the likelihood of success or ability to succeed is the same for both groups and the observations can be considered as random samples from each population.

Quite often we know that other factors such as educational background are related to the success probability. If the groups being compared have the same proportion of persons with elementary school, high school and college educations, then reasonably large samples from both groups should have approximately the same proportions of persons in each level, and the statistical tests (5.6) and (5.23) can be used. If these factors are *not* distributed equally in the two groups, then the data should be subdivided into subgroups which are homogenous with respect to them. For example, the success rates of members of the two groups with the same education will be compared. Combination methods, described in the next section, can be used to compare the success rates of the two groups, adjusting for these relevant factors, which are called influential variable factors or covariates.[11]

6. Combining Results from Related 2 × 2 Tables

The focus of comparative studies often is whether members of one group have a higher probability of an outcome or event (e.g., hire or disease) than members of another group. In order to obtain a pure estimate of any difference that is due to group membership, other factors related to the likelihood of the occurrence of the event need to be controlled for. As we saw in our discussion of combining binomial data sets in Chapter 4, one may stratify the total data set into appropriate subsets such that the members of the sample (or population) in each of the subsets have similar values of the relevant factors. In this section we will be concerned with data organized into several 2 × 2 tables, e.g., hiring data categorized by job applied for (occupation), termination data categorized by length of service (seniority), or disease incidence by amount of exposure or by exposure to another agent that may cause disease.

Before discussing the methodology it is helpful to look at two examples. Table 5.10 presents the promotion data used in *Agarwal v. McKee*,[12] which Judge Orrick decided helped plaintiffs establish a *prima facie* case of discrimination (later rebutted) without the benefit of formal statistical

TABLE 5.10.   Promotion Data for Minority and Majority Group Employees From
Agarwal v. McKee for the Period 1970–74

Level	Lowest Salary	Minority Employed	Promoted	Rate	Majority Employed	Promoted	Rate
7	$21,360	19	3	15.8%	238	35	14.7%
8	19,704	39	7	17.9%	147	45	30.6%
9	17,628	87	17	19.3%	235	54	32.0%
10	15,660	143	34	23.8%	242	77	31.8%
Total		288	61	21.2%	862	211	24.5%

Source: 19 FEP Cases 503 (N.D. Cal. 1977) at 513.

analysis. Notice that the difference between black and white promotion
rates in levels 8, 9 and 10 is lost if promotion rates are compared in the
aggregate, i.e., ignoring the importance of job level.

In our previous discussion of the toxic effects of chemicals near Love
Canal, we looked at the aggregate data in Table 5.5. Since a mothers'
smoking is known to be potentially harmful to a fetus, the data for smokers and nonsmokers should be studied separately. We report this data in
Table 5.11. Notice that both smoking and exposure to chemical wastes
(Swale area) appear to increase the probability of having a low birth-
weight baby.

While one can calculate the test (5.6) for the difference between the
success rates and the associated estimate (5.2) of the odds ratio from the
2 × 2 table for each category, one really desires a summary procedure
combining results from all the categories or strata. In this section we

TABLE 5.11.   Births and Low Birth Weight Children in the Swale and Non-swale
Areas by Smoking History of the Mother

	Swale Area			Non-swale Area		
	Low Birth Weights	All Births	Fraction	Low Birth Weights	All Births	Fraction
Never Smoked	7	70	.100	7	174	.040
Smoked	13	102	.127	25	265	.094

Source: Table 1 from Vianna, N. J. and Polan, A. K. (1984). Incidence of Low Birth Weight
Among Love Canal Residents. *Science* **226,** 1217–1219.

describe the Mantel-Haenszel test statistic and the Mantel-Haenszel estimator[13] of the overall odds ratio and illustrate its use on promotion data from an EEO case. The MH test procedure is analogous to the procedure (4.15) used to combine binomial data sets, as it is based on the sum of the *differences* between *actual* and *expected* number of successes from group I across *all categories* divided by the *standard deviation* of this sum.

Recall that for a single 2 × 2 table (see Table 5.2), when members of both groups have the same probability of success, the expected number of successes from group I is

$$\text{(5.31)} \qquad \frac{(a + c)(a + b)}{N} = \frac{(a + c)n_1}{N}.$$

If the hypergeometric model is valid for the data, the variance of the number of successes (the variable A) is given by

$$\text{(5.32)} \qquad \frac{n_1}{N} \frac{n_2}{N} \frac{m(N - m)}{N - 1} = \frac{(a + b)(c + d)(a + c)(b + d)}{N^2(N - 1)},$$

where $m = (a + c)$ is the total number of successes in both groups and a, b, c and d are the entries in Table 5.2.

The differences between the actual and expected number of successes in each of the k tables (indexed by i) are given by

$$\text{(5.33)} \qquad a_i - \frac{(a_i + c_i)n_i}{N_i},$$

and the difference for the ith table has variance

$$\text{(5.34)} \qquad \frac{(a_i + b_i)(c_i + d_i)(a_i + c_i)(b_i + d_i)}{N_i^2(N - 1)}.$$

The *total difference* is the sum of (5.33) computed for each table, and the *variance* of this total is the sum of the *individual variances*. Since the standard deviation or standard error is the *square root* of the *variance*, the normal form of the MH-statistic is

$$Z = \frac{\left(\begin{array}{c} \text{total number of successes} \\ \text{in all tables} \end{array} \right) \text{ minus } \left(\begin{array}{c} \text{expected number of} \\ \text{successes in all tables} \end{array} \right)}{\left(\begin{array}{c} \text{standard deviation of the} \\ \text{total number of successes in all tables} \end{array} \right)}$$

(5.35)

The formulas make the calculation appear more formidable than it really is. We illustrate the computation by analyzing the data in Table

TABLE 5.12.   The 2 × 2 Table Classifying Minority and Majority Persons Employed in Level 10 Jobs by
Whether or Not They Received a Promotion

	Promoted	Not Promoted	Total
Minority	34	109	143
Majority	77	165	242
Total	111	274	385

Source: 19 FEP Cases 503 (N.D. Cal. 1977) at 513.

5.10. First, we consider one 2 × 2 subtable (level 10) and report it in the
standard format of a 2 × 2 table in Table 5.12.

From (5.31) we see that the expected number of minority promotions is

$$\frac{(143)(111)}{385} = 41.23,$$

so the difference between actual and expected promotions for level 10
minority employees is $34 - 41.23 = -7.23$. This result means that level
10 minorities received 7.23 fewer promotions than expected, assuming
both groups had the same promotion rate. From equation (5.34), the
variance of the number of minority promotions equals

$$\frac{(11) \times (274) \times (242) \times (143)}{[385 \times 384]} = 18.49.$$

Repeating these calculations for each table yields the results reported in
Table 5.13. The normal form (5.35) of the MH test, incorporating the

TABLE 5.13.   Mantel-Haenszel Analysis of *Agarwal v. McKee* Promotion Data
Given in Table 5.10

Level	Expected Minority Promotions	Actual Minority Promotions	Difference	Variance
7	2.81	3	+.19	2.225
8	10.90	7	−3.90	6.242
9	19.18	17	−2.18	10.947
10	41.23	34	−7.23	18.492
Total			−13.12	37.906

continuity correction (1/2) is

$$\frac{\text{actual number of successes } - \text{ expected } + .5}{\text{standard deviation}} = \frac{\text{difference } + .5}{\sqrt{\text{variance}}}$$

$$= \frac{-13.2 + .5}{\sqrt{37.906}} = \frac{12.62}{6.156} = -2.05.$$

Hence, the difference of about 13 jobs between the actual and expected number of minority promotions in all grade levels is statistically significant at the .05 level. If a one-sided alternative is considered relevant, i.e., the most reasonable alternative to equal promotion probabilities is that minorities would have less chance than majority members, the p-value of the data is

$$\Pr[Z < -2.05] \simeq .02,$$

implying that if blacks and whites had the same probability of promotion from each level, the chance of observing as few or fewer black promotions as occurred is 2%. Thus, the judge's assessment is confirmed by the MH test.

The data in Table 5.10 display two important characteristics that affect the MH test statistic. The promotion rates vary by level (usually declining as salary rises), and the distribution of minorities among the levels differs from that of non-minorities (proportionally more minorities are in the lower levels). If one ignores these aspects of the data and compares the overall promotion rates of 21.2% and 24.5%, one would not find the difference in the rates observed by Judge Orrick to be statistically significant (see problem 1).

In order to obtain an overall estimate of the odds ratio for all tables being combined, the Mantel-Haenszel procedure uses a weighted average of the odds ratios of the component tables. Indexing each 2×2 table by i, and recalling that the odds ratio for the ith table is

$$\frac{(a_i d_i)}{(b_i c_i)},$$

the MH estimate of a common odds ratio is

(5.36)
$$\sum_{i=1}^{k} w_i \frac{a_i d_i}{b_i c_i} = \frac{\sum_{i=1}^{k} (a_i d_i) N_i^{-1}}{\sum_{i=1}^{k} (b_i c_i) N_i^{-1}},$$

TABLE 5.14.   Calculation of the Mantel-Haenszel Estimate of the Overall Odds Ratio Illustrated on the Data from Table 5.10

Group	Promoted	Not	Total	Individual Odds Ratio	Numerator $(a_i d_i)$ N_i	Denominator $(b_i c_i)$ N_i
Level 7 I	3	16	19	$\frac{3(203)}{(16)35} = 1.0875$	$\frac{(3)(203)}{257} = 2.3696$	$\frac{(16)(35)}{257} = 2.179$
II	35	203	238			
All	38	219	257			
Level 8 I	7	32	39			
II	45	102	147			
All	52	134	176	.4958	4.0568	8.181
Level 9 I	17	70	87			
II	54	181	235			
All	71	251	322	.8140	9.5599	11.739
Level 10 I	34	109	143			
II	77	165	242			
All	111	274	385	.668	14.5714	21.800
Total (Numerator and Denominator)					30.5537	43.869

$$MH = \frac{Numerator}{Denominator} = \frac{(30.5537)}{43.8699} = .6965 \approx .70$$

Note: We calculated the odds ratios of each table in the fourth column to enable us to check (a) that the summary measure lies between the smallest and largest of them and (b) that the odds ratios are not contradictory, i.e., all are near the null hypothesis of equality (1) or less than it.

where the weights, w_i, are given by

$$w_i = \frac{(b_i c_i)N_i^{-1}}{\sum\limits_{i=1}^{k} (b_i c_i)N_i^{-1}}.$$

Formula (5.36) may appear complex, but once the data for each table is displayed in the format of Table 5.2, the calculation of the numerator and denominator of the right side of (5.36) is straightforward. In Table 5.14 we present the calculation in detail for the *Agarwal v. McKee* data. Notice that we rearranged the data in Table 5.10 into four 2 × 2 tables.

The overall odds ratio of about .70 indicates that minority members had only 70% of the odds majority members had of being promoted, which is a meaningful disparity.[14] Thus, the odds ratio measure is consistent with the finding of a statistically significant difference between the promotion rates. We should mention that each job level consisted of a variety of

TABLE 5.15.   Hypothetical Data From *Caston v. Duke University*

	Hires	Not Hired	Total	Fraction Hired
		Job A		
Black	0	4	4	0.00
White	4	4	8	.50
		Job B		
Black	2	38	40	.05
White	0	4	4	0.00
		Simple Addition		
Black	2	42	44	.0455
White	4	8	12	.3333
All	6	50	56	.1071

Source: 34 FEP Cases 102 (N.D. N.C. 1983) at 107.

occupations having different rates of promotion and proportionately more minorities were employed in the slower promoting occupations so that the defendant was able to explain the statistically significance.

Courts have often failed to use combination methods (probably because they weren't used by the parties in the case) when they could clarify matters. For example, in *Caston v. Duke*,[15] the court had to choose between analyzing the several 2 × 2 tables individually or adding up the applicants and hires in all the tables to form a single table. The court correctly noticed that when the success probabilities (hire or promotion rates) differed greatly from table to table, simply adding up the tables can lead to an erroneous result. By considering the hypothetical data in Table 5.15, the court noted that white applicants seemed to have the advantage in job A, but blacks did better in job B. If one combined the data into one table (simple additive table), the normal approximation to Fisher's exact test yields a significant result, i.e., from formula (5.23) we obtain

$$(5.37) \qquad Z = \frac{2 - 4.714 + .5}{.9583} = \frac{-2.214}{.9583} = -2.31.$$

On the other hand, Fisher's exact test applied to Table A, shows that the difference between the actual (0) and expected (1.33) black hires is not statistically significant. Indeed, the probability of no blacks in four selections from the 12 person pool is .1414, a nonsignificant one-sided *p*-

value.[16] Similarly, Fisher's exact test applied to Table B shows that observing no whites in two selections has probability .82. Because the selection probabilities and racial composition of eligibles (applicants) are substantially different in each table, the simple addition method leads to an erroneous inference. Common sense suggests that when Table A, showing a nonsignificant black disadvantage, is combined with one showing a nonsignificant black advantage, a proper combination method should yield a nonsignificant difference. We next show that the MH procedure gives this result.

The MH statistic, computed as in Table 5.13, has the value

$$(5.38) \qquad Z = \frac{2 - 3.151 + 5}{\sqrt{.6465 + .1614}} = \frac{.651}{.8988} = -.7243.$$

This value ($-.7243$) reflects a difference *less* than one standard deviation from expected and does not indicate a significant difference in selection rates. Indeed, the one-sided p-value is about .2654, which is larger than the p-value, .14, of Table A. This result agrees with our intuition, as the data in Table B was favorable to blacks, so when it is combined with Table A, the disparity between black and white selection rates should be lessened. The *increase* in p-value means that the disparity in the totality of data is *less* than the disparity in Table A, by itself.

The advantage of using a proper combination method is that one avoids the problem of *fragmentation* and its resultant loss of statistical power (increased risk of failing to reject the null hypothesis when it is false) and the error involved with simple aggregation noted by the judge in *Caston* and Judge Orrick in *Agarwal*. We emphasize that one needs to carefully consider the appropriate method of subdividing the total data set into strata. Nonstatistical factors, such as the similarity of job groups, the legally relevant time frame, etc. play important roles. It is useful to look at the data in each of the strata or subgroups to make sure that the general pattern of the odds ratios or differences from expected values are similar. In the *Agarwal* case, minorities received less than their expected share in three of four job levels and received their expected share in only one, where few were employed. Had minorities received a significant excess of promotions in one category, usually one should not routinely combine this data with that of the three strata showing an underrepresentation. One should investigate the reason for the apparent anomaly. In the next chapter we illustrate the use of the methods of this chapter in EEO cases and public health policy.

Problems

1. Suppose one *ignored* the grade levels of employees in Table 5.10 and analyzed the promotion rates in all levels from the combined table given in the last row of Table 5.10.

(a) Show that the difference in rates is not significant at the .05 level (one-sided test).

(b) Under what conditions is it reasonable to ignore the subcategories and just analyze the pooled data (total of all subcategories)?

2.* Show that the data in Table 5.11 enables us to calculate

(a) The odds a resident of the Swale area has of having a low birthweight baby relative to those of a nonresident, adjusting for the smoking history of the mother and

(b) The odds a smoking mother has of having a low birth-weight baby relative to those of a nonsmoker, adjusting for residence in the Swale area.

Based on your calculations, which factor, smoking or exposure to chemical waste, has a stronger effect?

3. In order to organize data on terminations to study possible discrimination against female employees, which of the following factors might be used to form strata?

(a) Seniority
(b) Occupation
(c) Education

Should all three be used to form the subgroups?

Answer to Selected Problem

3. Perhaps seniority is the most relevant factor, and occupation may play a role depending on the firm's policy. Since education and occupation are related, it may not be necessary to use both in forming strata. When the data set is over-stratified, i.e., classified into too many subgroups, one loses power to detect the overall pattern.

APPENDIX 5A

The Sampling Error of the Odds Ratio of a 2 × 2 Table and the Associated Confidence Interval

Most of the applications of the odds ratio we considered in this chapter concerned testing the hypothesis that two sample proportions were equal and then using the odds ratio as one measure of the relative difference between the rates. When the odds ratio is not equal to 1.0, its sampling distribution is more complicated than when the null hypothesis (OR = 1) is true, and we now describe some useful approximations. Further details and references can be found in Fleiss (1981).

Using large sample approximations, it can be shown that the standard error (S.E.) of the estimated odds ratio, OR, from a 2 × 2 table in the format of Table 5.2 is

$$(5A.1) \qquad \text{S.E.} \ (\widehat{OR}) = \widehat{OR} \ \sqrt{\left(\frac{1}{a}\right) + \left(\frac{1}{b}\right) + \left(\frac{1}{c}\right) + \left(\frac{1}{d}\right)}.$$

For a table with small values of one or more of the counts (a, b, c or d), one half is added to each of them. To illustrate its use, we calculate $\widehat{OR}$ and its standard error for the data in Table 5.2 from the *Teal* case. Recalling that $\widehat{OR} = .304$, we obtain

$$\text{S.E.} \ (\widehat{OR}) = (.304) \ \sqrt{\left(\frac{1}{26}\right) + \left(\frac{1}{22}\right) + \left(\frac{1}{53}\right) + \left(\frac{1}{206}\right)} = .0997 \simeq .10.$$

(5A.2)

One would like to make confidence intervals for OR from (5A.2) using a normal distribution to approximate its sampling distribution so that a 95 CONF for OR would be

$$(5A.3) \qquad\qquad \widehat{OR} \pm (1.96) \ \text{S.E.} \ (\text{OR}).$$

Unfortunately, this formula requires quite a large sample to be valid because the odds ratio does *not* have a sampling distribution which is symmetric about the true odds ratio, OR, even when OR = 1.0. The reason this asymmetry occurs is that sample odds ratios below 1.0 must range between 0 and 1, while those above 1.0 can be arbitrarily large. For example, consider the situation where the data shows that the first group has twice the odds of success as the second group, with the situation where the first group has one half the odds of success of the second. In the first case $\widehat{OR} = 2.0$, and the difference between $\widehat{OR}$ and 1.0 is 1.0. In the second case $\widehat{OR} = 1/2$, and the difference between OR and 1.0 is .5. As far as measuring a difference from 1.0, odds ratios of 2.0 and .5 really have the same meaning, namely, that one group has twice the odds of success of the other.

In order to account for this asymmetry, statisticians consider the logarithm of the OR, which we denote by LO. Notice that an OR of *one* is transformed to an LO of *zero*, an OR of 2.0 is transformed to an LO of log $2 = .693$ and log $(1/2) = -.693$. Thus, log $(1/2)$ and log (2) are equally distant from $\ln(1) = 0$, which corresponds to the equality of the two proportions. A good estimate of the standard error (S.E.) of the estimate $\widehat{LO}$ of LO from a 2×2 table is

$$(5A.4) \quad S.E.\ (\widehat{LO}) = \sqrt{\left(\frac{1}{a + .5}\right) + \left(\frac{1}{b + .5}\right) + \left(\frac{1}{c + .5}\right) + \left(\frac{1}{d + .5}\right)}.$$

For the Teal data we have $\widehat{LO} = \log(.304) = -1.1907$ and

$$S.E.\ (\widehat{LO}) = \sqrt{.1059} = .3254,$$

a 95% CONF for LO, therefore, is

$$LO = -1.191 \pm (1.96)(.3254) = -1.191 \pm .6378$$

or 95% CONF (LO; $-.553$, $-.253$).

To convert this to a 95% CONF for the odds ratio (OR), we exponentiate[17] the limits of the interval obtaining

$$(5A.5) \qquad\qquad 95\% \text{ CONF (OR; .161, .575).}$$

Notice that this interval is *not* symmetric about $\widehat{OR} = .304$, as the upper endpoint, .575, is further from .304 than the lower endpoint, .161, is. This is a consequence of the asymmetry we mentioned previously.

Problems

1. Compare the 95% CONF for the OR we obtained in equation (5A.5) with one that ignored the asymmetry of the sampling distribution of $\widehat{OR}$ and added $\pm(1.96)$ times S.E. $(\widehat{OR})$, given in (5A.2) to $\widehat{OR}$. Is the difference potentially meaningful?

2. Calculate the standard error of the estimated odds ratio of the data in Table 5.4.

Answers to Selected Problems

1. Equation (5A.3) yields a 95% CONF for OR of $.304 \pm .196$ or (.108, .500). This interval exaggerates the difference between $\widehat{OR}$ and 1.0, relative to the more appropriate interval (.161, .575). In the present context this would not have a serious impact; however, in another application it

might have an impact, as the test of the null hypothesis OR = 1 is equivalent to ascertaining whether the corresponding 1.0 is contained in the corresponding confidence interval.

APPENDIX 5B

Analogs of the Overall Odds Ratio for the Binomial Model

In Chapter 5 we assumed that the complete 2 × 2 table was available for analysis, i.e., both the number of applicants and the number of hires from each group are known, and obtained a measure of relative disparity, the odds ratio, in addition to the test based on the difference between actual and expected hires. For the single 2 × 2 table, the estimate of the summary odds ratio is $(ad)/(bc)$, and when the data is stratified the Mantel-Haenszel estimator (5.36) of the overall odds ratio is used. In this appendix we derive the analogs of these estimators for the binomial model by using the fact that the binomial model approximates the hypergeometric when the number of selections or successes is *small*. For ease in exposition we discuss the formulas in the context of fair hiring.

In the single 2 × 2 table, the expected number of hires (5.27) from group I is their *fraction* of all applicants *times* the *total number of hires*. When the applicant data is not known but the minority fraction, p, of persons qualified for and potentially interested in the job can be determined from external data, as discussed in Chapter 4, it is reasonable to use p in place of the minority fraction of the actual applicants. In the EEO context this is sensible, because fair recruitment practices should lead to an applicant pool with a minority fraction near p. Then the number of minority hires, under the assumption of fair recruitment and fair hiring, will have a binomial distribution with parameters t (number of hires) and p (minority availability). This binomial distribution can be regarded as an approximation to the hypergeometric (Section 2.7) and is quite accurate when the number of hires is small relative to the number of applicants.

In order to develop the analog of the odds ratio $(ad)/(bc)$ for the complete 2 × 2 table in the format of Table 5.2, we rewrite the odds ratio as

$$(5B.1) \qquad \frac{ad}{bc} = \frac{a(n_2 - c)}{c(n_1 - a)} = \frac{a\left(\dfrac{n_2}{n_1 + n_2} - \dfrac{c}{n_1 + n_2}\right)}{c\left(\dfrac{n_1}{n_1 + n_2} - \dfrac{a}{n_1 + n_2}\right)}.$$

Although the actual numbers n_1 and n_2 of applicants from each group are unknown, we know that $n_1/(n_1 + n_2)$ is close to p, and $n_2/(n_1 + n_2)$ is near $1 - p$. If $n_1 + n_2$ is very large compared to a or c, $a/(n_1 + n_2)$, and $c/(n_1 + n_2)$ are both *small*, so as an approximation we can set them equal to zero. Then the right side of (5B.1) becomes

$$
(5B.2) \qquad \frac{a(1 - p)}{cp} = \frac{\dfrac{a}{t - a}}{\dfrac{p}{(1 - p)}},
$$

where $t = a + c$ is the total number of hires. Formula (5B.2) can also be obtained by replacing the unknown numbers, n_1 and n_2, of applicants by the large number of potential applicants, N_1 and N_2, of each group in the large external qualified population. Now $N_1/(N_1 + N_2) = p$, $N_2/(N_1 + N_2) = 1 - p$, while $a/(N_1 + N_2)$ and $c/(N_1 + N_2)$ are both very small, so they can be set equal to 0 in formula (5B.1) as before.

Although the derivation of formula (5B.2) used some approximations, the formula itself has an intuitive meaning. The *numerator* $a/(t - a)$ is the odds of selecting a minority (group I) member from the t persons *actually* hired while the *denominator*, $p/(1 - p)$, is the odds of selecting a minority member from the large external pool of eligible persons. Thus, formula (5A.2) is the ratio of the odds of selecting a minority member from the persons actually hired *relative* to the odds of selecting a minority member from the large external pool of qualified individuals. Under the null hypothesis of fair recruitment and fair hiring this odds ratio should equal 1.0.

The analog of the Mantel-Haenszel summary estimator (5.36), when data for several binomial data sets needs to be combined into an overall odds ratio, can be obtained by the same methods used to derive (5B.2), which yields

$$
(5B.3) \qquad \frac{\sum a_i(1 - p_i)}{\sum (t_i - a_i)p_i},
$$

where a_i is the observed number of minority hires out of the total t_i in the ith data set (strata), and p_i is the minority fraction in the external pool of persons qualified for jobs in the ith strata. The calculation of formula (5A.3) is illustrated in Table 5.16 on the data from the *Cooper v. University of Texas at Dallas* case discussed in Section 4.6. In all likelihood, the overall odds ratio of about .66 would have been deemed a meaningful difference had the availability figures not been flawed.

TABLE 5.16.   Illustrative Calculation of the Overall Odds Ratio for Combined Binomial Data Sets: The Ratio of the Hiring Odds Female Applicants Faced Relative to Male Applicants in *Cooper v. Univ. of Texas at Dallas*

Division	Avail-ability (p_i)	Total Hires (t_i)	Female Hires (a_i)	Components of Numerator $a_i(1 - p_i)$	Components of Denominator $(t_i - a_i)p_i$
Arts	.383	48	14	8.638	13.022
Human Development	.385	32	12	7.380	7.700
Management	.043	26	0	0.0	1.118
Natural Sciences	.138	38	1	.862	5.106
Social Sciences	.209	34	6	4.746	5.852
TOTALS		178	33	21.626	32.798

Overall odds ratio (5B.3) $= \dfrac{21.626}{32.796} = .659$

Source: The basic data was given in Table 4.9.

Finally, it should be noted that the sampling variability of the estimated odds ratio (5B.2) obtained by sampling a binomial distribution can be large, especially when the number (t) of hires is less than 100. One reason for this is that the factor $p/(1 - p)$ in the denominator of (5B.2) is small (recall that p is the minority share of the qualified labor pool) so that small changes in the observed number (a) of hires can lead to relatively large changes in the ratio. Therefore, the estimated odds ratio should be used in conjunction with an appropriate statistical test such as the one in conjunction with an appropriate statistical test such as the one discussed in Section 4.6. The sampling error and associated confidence interval for the summary odds ratio (5B.3) are given in Gastwirth and Greenhouse (1987).

NOTES

1. National Highway Traffic Safety Administration's Rule on Automatic Occupant Restraint 49. (1984). Reported in *Product Safety and Liability Reporter* **12**, 28, 545–596.

2. By a statistical association between two variables we mean that knowledge that one factor is present affects the probability that the other also is present. If exposure to a chemical is associated with a disease, then the probability, p_e, of an exposed person getting the disease exceeds the corresponding probability, p, of an unexposed person. Not all *statistical associations* are due to causal relationships, as there can be a third factor which

underlies the association we observe in a set of data. In the present context, smoking is known to be strongly associated with lung cancer. If the exposed population has a greater proportion of smokers, then one would observe more cases of lung cancer in the exposed population, even if the chemical has no effect on a person's chances of developing cancer.

3.   25 FEP Cases 57 (N.D. Ohio 1979), *affirmed in part* and *reversed in part,* 639 F.2d 328, 25 FEP Cases 64 (6th Cir. 1981).

4.   645 F.2d 133 (2nd Cir. 1981), *affirmed,* 102 S.Ct. 2525, 29 FEP Cases 1 (1982).

5.   Vianna, N. J. and Polan, A. K. (1984). Incidence of Low Birth Weight Among Love Canal Residents. *Science* **226**, 1217–1219.

6.   In addition to formal tests of statistical significance, one is concerned with practical significance or real word effect. If an employment practice eliminated 2% of the majority applicants and 4% of the minority applicants, the selection ratio of hire rates .96/.98 = .9796 would indicate a minimal effect, while the selection ratio of the non-hire rates would be .04/.022 = 2.0, which suggests a serious effect. The selection ratio based on hire rates is more relevant in the present context, especially when the success rates are large.

7.   The *variance* of the sum or difference of *independent* random variables is the sum of their variances. Under the null hypothesis, $p_1 = p_2 = p$, so p_1 has variance $[p(1 - p)]/n_1$, p_2 has variance $[p(1 - p)]/n_2$ and their sum has variance $[p(1 - p)](1/n_1 + 1/n_2)$.

8.   No. 76-2259 (D.C. D.C. June 1, 1978).

9.   Meecham, W. C. and Smith, H. G. (1977). Effects of Jet Aircraft Noise on Mental Health Admissions. *British Journal of Audiology* **11**, 81–85.

10.   34 FEP Cases 644 (D. D.C. 1983).

11.   The term "covariate" conveys the idea that both variables usually move or vary in a systematic fashion. Later we will measure the strength of this covariation by the correlation coefficient. A major concern of statistical analysis is to separate those correlations or associations which are real and reflect causality or other scientific reasons for the observed association from those which are caused by another factor which was not considered in the analysis.

12.   19 FEP Cases (N.D. Ca. 1977). 503 at 513, *affirmed* 644 F.2d 803, 25 FEP Cases 1565 (9th Cir. 1981).

13.   The procedure was developed by Mantel and Haenszel (1959), who modified a previous method of Cochran (1954). It is now the established method for combining the results of subgroup comparisons, as done in Baldus and Cole, *Statistical Proof.*

14.   Since the odds ratio is less than the selection ratio, a 70% odds ratio might be used as a rough approximation to an 80% selection ratio. In my examination of cases, odds ratios of about 70% seem to occur in statistically close situations, e.g., see the appellate opinion in *Agarwal* (footnote 12).

15.   34 FEP Cases 102 (D.C. N.C. 1983).

16.   Recall the *p*-values less than .05 imply that the data is significant at the .05 level.

17.   Exponentiation is the inverse of taking logarithms. Recall that log 10 = 2.3026 means that $e^{2.3026} = 10$, where e is the mathematically natural base (2.71828) for logarithms. It is often convenient to work in the logarithmic scale and then convert the answer to the original scale of measurement by exponentiating the answer.

REFERENCES

General Statistical Texts

CONOVER, W. J. (1980). *Practical Nonparametric Statistics,* 2nd. ed. New York: Wiley. (This book gives a nice treatment of Fisher's exact test.)

FLEISS, J. (1981). *Statistical Methods for Rates and Proportions*, 2nd. ed. New York: Wiley. (A useful and readable discussion of the basic procedures including combination methods with illustrative examples from medical statistics.)

SIEGEL, S. (1956). *Nonparametric Statistics for the Behavioral Sciences*. New York: McGraw Hill.

Articles

BICKEL, P. J., HAMMEL, E. A. AND O'CONNELL, J. W. (1975). Sex Bias in Graduate Admissions: Data from Berkeley. *Science* **187**, 398–404. (Perhaps the first article emphasizing the importance of stratifying data appropriately in the study of discrimination. The authors show that an apparent bias against women in the aggregated data is explained when the data is stratified by department. The anomaly occurred because women formed a higher fraction of applicants to departments with low acceptance rates than they did to departments with higher acceptance rates.)

COCHRAN, W. G. (1954). Some Methods for Strengthening the Common Chi-Square Tests. *Biometrics,* **10**, 417–451.

GASTWIRTH, J. L. (1984). Statistical Methods for Analyzing Claims of Employment Discrimination. *Industrial and Labor Relations Review* **38**, 75–86. (Section 5 of this chapter and several examples in Chapter 6 come from this article, which provides further references to the literature.)

GASTWIRTH, J. L. AND GREENHOUSE, S. W. (1987). Estimating a Common Relative Risk: Application in Equal Employment. *Journal of the American Statistical Association* **82**, 38–45.

MANTEL, N. AND HAENSZEL, W. H. (1959). Statistical Aspects of the Analysis of Data From Retrospective Studies of Disease. *Journal of the National Cancer Institute,* **22**, 719–748.

MEIER, P., SACKS, J. AND ZABELL, S. L. (1984). What Happened in Hazelwood: Statistics, Employment Discrimination and the 80% Rule. *American Bar Foundation Research Journal* **1984**, 139–186.

SHOBEN, E. (1978). Differential Pass Fail Rates in Employment Testing: Statistical Proof Under Title VII. *Harvard Law Review* **91**, 793–813. (This important article describes Fisher's exact test, which it recommends for use in Title VII cases concerned with testing the equality of pass rates. The article has been cited in many legal cases. The author does not consider the Fisher's test as applicable to data on the entire population of interest because there is no sampling error. However, we note that the concept of randomization does allow one to utilize it in such cases to assess whether a chance assignment process could have yielded the observed data, and analyze the *Marsh v. Eaton* and *Johnson v. Perini* data in that framework.)

SMITH, A. B. JR. AND ABRAM, T. G. (1981). Quantitative Analyses and Proof of Employment Discrimination. *University of Illinois Law Review* **1981**, 33–74.

WITTES, J. AND WALLENSTEIN, S. (1987). The Power of the Mantel-Haenszel Test. *Journal of the American Statistical Association* **82**, 1104–1109. (This paper summarizes recent research on the power of the MH test. These results should enable courts to require power calculations similar to those described for the binomial model in Section 4 to be provided when the MH test is used.)

Application of the
Statistical Methods for
Comparing Proportions in
Equal Employment Cases
and the Assessment of

Chapter 6   Health Risks

The statistical methods for comparing proportions and measures of the difference between proportions (or probabilities) are used extensively in the EEO and health areas. In this chapter we discuss some of the relevant subject matter background which should be incorporated into a statistical analysis in order that it be most relevant to the basic issues. A variety of actual data sets will be presented to illustrate how data should be properly organized and analyzed. Several common errors will be illustrated.

1. Some Background to the Use of the Methods in Equal Employment Cases

In 1977[1] the Supreme Court distinguished cases involving the impact or effect of an apparently neutral requirement, such as passing a written test or possessing a high school diploma, that eliminates proportionately more minority members than majority members from possible employment or advancement, from cases alleging a general claim that the defendant purposely treated minorities less favorably than others. The first type of case involves the possible disparate impact of a specific employment practice.[2] The potential disparate impact of a particular practice is usually assessed by comparing the proportions of minority and majority applicants who pass the test or satisfy the requirement. When the difference between these proportions is statistically significant, and/or the selection ratio (ratio of the minority pass rate to the majority pass rate) is less than four fifths[3] (.8), the employment practice at issue may be deemed to have a disparate or disproportionate impact. Recently, courts have tended to rely more on plaintiffs showing a statistically significant difference exists rather than on the four-fifths rule. In many situations both criteria are satisfied. For example, the data in Table 5.4 from *Teal v. Connecticut* show a selection ratio of .68, and we obtained a highly significant result (two-sided *p*-value less than .001) using a formal statistical test.

The second category of cases concern the disparate treatment of similarly qualified minority and majority employees. Comparative data on hiring, promotion and termination rates are used to study whether the difference in these rates is statistically significant. The reason for this is that the employer's motive is the focal point at issue in a disparate treatment case. As the U.S. Supreme Court said in *Teamsters v. U.S.*,[4] "the ultimate factual issues are thus simply whether there was a pattern or practice of such disparate treatment and, if so, whether the differences were racially premised." In a footnote[5] the court noted that "disparate treatment ... is the most easily understood type of discrimination. The employer simply treats some people less favorably than others because of their race, color, religion, sex or national origin. Proof of discriminatory motive is critical, although it can in some situations be inferred from the mere fact of differences." The role of statistical data and analysis is to summarize and interpret the facts of the case, since imbalance between a defendant's work force and the pool of qualified available workers "is often a telltale sign of purposeful discrimination."[6]

Several cases[7] suggest that a more substantial disparity between the minority and majority success (e.g., hire, promotion) rates may be needed to demonstrate a pattern of disparate *treatment* than to show a disparate impact of a particular employment criteria. Thus, courts typically require plaintiffs to show a statistically significant difference at the .05 level or less in order to substantiate their allegations of discrimination. In order to appreciate the role of statistical evidence, we need to understand the order of proof or submission of relevant evidence in these cases. The Supreme Court outlined this in the seminal *McDonnell-Douglas v. Green*[8] case.

In Title VII litigation the plaintiff has the burden of ultimately persuading the court that he or she was discriminated against. The complainant has the initial burden of establishing a *prima facie* case of discrimination. This may be accomplished by showing:

(1) The plaintiff belongs to a protected (minority) group,
(2) The plaintiff was qualified for the job sought and the job was available,
(3) In spite of the plaintiff's qualifications he or she was denied the job, and
(4) The job remained open or was filled by a non-minority person with lesser qualifications.

Statistical data is most pertinent to the third aspect. If a specific qualification is at issue, plaintiffs may show that it has a disparate impact. Since it is difficult to evaluate an explanation of why a particular person was or was not hired, a statistically significant difference in the treatment of similarly qualified persons can be used by a plaintiff to demonstrate that they were probably denied the job for discriminatory reasons. Logically, if members of the minority group are treated unfairly as a class, it is more likely than not that an individual minority member would receive unfair treatment. If the plaintiff establishes a *prima facie* case, then the burden of production (of suitable evidence) shifts to the employer, who needs to articulate a legitimate nondiscriminatory reason for the complaintant's rejection. When the employer presents such evidence, the burden shifts back to the plaintiff, who has the opportunity to show that the employer's explanation was a pretext. Of course, employers can use statistical evidence showing that the minority and majority group receive equal treatment (e.g., have the same hire rates) as part of their rebuttal of a *prima facie* case established on nonstatistical grounds. Indeed, when the Supreme Court, in *Cooper v. Federal Reserve Bank of Richmond,*[9] allowed a small subgroup of a class to proceed with their *individual* claims, even though the bank prevailed in a prior class action, it noted that the "prior adjudication may well prove beneficial to the Bank in the Baxter action: the determination in the Cooper action that the Bank had not engaged in a general pattern or practice of discrimination would be relevant on the issue of pretext. See *Green v. McDonnell Douglas,* 411 U.S. at 804-805, 5 FEP Cases at 970."

In the *Green* case, which involved a charge of failure to rehire a worker who had participated in a "stall-in", the Supreme Court noted that the plaintiff might show that the employer's reason for not hiring him, his past participation in a "stall-in", was a pretext by introducing:

(1) Evidence that white employees involved in similar acts were retained or rehired, or

(2) Facts as to employer's treatment of the employee during his previous term of employment and/or his activities on behalf of Civil Rights in general, and

(3) Information about the employer's general policies and practices with respect to minority group employment.

The use of this framework in disparate treatment cases was clarified in *Texas Department of Community Affairs v. Burdine,*[10] which emphasized that the plaintiff's proof in the first and third phases must be by a preponderance of the evidence, while the defendant's burden of production *need not persuade* the court that it was motivated by the offered reason. The defendant's evidence should raise a *genuine issue of fact* as to whether they discriminated against the plaintiff.

In actual practice the defendant often meets its burden of rebutting statistical evidence by showing that the data is basically unreliable or the plaintiff's analysis was incomplete and that a more thorough analysis shows that any remaining difference between the treatment of minority and majority members is *not* statistically significant. The plaintiff then has the opportunity to demonstrate flaws in the defendant's analysis.

Before examining data from specific cases, we need to emphasize that simply comparing the status (e.g., salaries) of minority employees with majority employees *without considering* their *qualifications* fails to separate the behavior of the employer from other historical, labor market and social factors which are not in the defendant's control. The relevance of statistical data, especially when used in disparate treatment cases, involves such questions as:

(1) What is the composition of the available pool of potential hires or promotees? Typically, promotions are made from current employees in lower level jobs who possess the necessary *skills*. The available pool for new hires consists of the actual applicants (when the data is reliable and recruitment is not an issue) or an external labor pool consisting of persons with the appropriate qualifications, residing in the labor market and potentially interested in the job.

(2) What period of time do we consider? If a current imbalance in an employer's work force is a result solely of pre-act discrimination, then the employer cannot be held liable in the post-act period.[11]

(3) What actually happened during the liability period—the time frame for which the defendant is legally responsible? Did the employer treat all

groups fairly in this period, or did he continue a previous pattern of discriminatory treatment?

(4) What was the impact of the filing of the original charge, the filing of the civil suit, possible intervention by an agency of the government or other interest groups and/or the actual trial on the behavior of the employer or on the class of potential employees?

Statistical evidence should be tailored to the facts and circumstances of the particular case, even though the *same methods of analysis* are used to draw inferences. When we discuss and re-analyze data from actual cases, we will sometimes see that the parties or the court itself failed to focus on the relevant time frame or to properly assess the impact of the complaint or to define the appropriate labor pool carefully. In addition, we shall see how combination methods could have been used to clarify the issues and how the concept of statistical power[12] should replace rough guesses as to the adequacy of the size, sample or weight that should be given to a finding of nonsignificance based on a small sample or a barely significant result in a very large sample.

A problem that often arises in cases is whether a one-sided or two-sided test should be used. A two-sided test is appropriate when the alternative to fairness is a bias against or in favor of a minority group while a one-sided test is appropriate when the only realistic alternative is discrimination. Recent cases, such as *Craik v. Minnesota State Univ. Bd.*, 731 F.2d 465 (8th Cir. 1984) and *Palmer v. Shultz* 815 F.2d 84 (D.C. Cir. 1987) tend to require a statistically significant result from a two-sided test at the .05 level in order for a plaintiff to establish a *prima facie* case solely in the basis of statistics. A significant result at the .05 or even .10 level using a one-sided test can be used to support other evidence of potentially discriminatory practices. Indeed, in *Craik* the majority found that the fact that no females were elected chairperson when they competed against males was evidence of discrimination even though a careful calculation of the probability that no women would win any of the five elections is .1325, which is not significant at the .10 level (one-sided test). However, other evidence of animosity towards women in these positions strengthened the plaintiff's case.

We will present the test that seems appropriate as the reader can double the *p*-value of a one-sided test in order to convert it to a two-sided test. Consideration of the power of the test will also aid our interpretation of data. When the occurrence of *no* minorities in the job at issue does not lead to rejection of the null hypothesis of equality courts, may discount a non-significant result. In *Craik* the majority realized that the test had no power, i.e., discrimination could never be found. In conjunction with the non-statistical evidence the data helped establish a *prima facie* case.

2. Data from Specific Equal Employment Cases

In this section we discuss data from actual cases, which will be categorized by the success or failure of the data and analysis to support the position of the offerer and by the failure of one party to use the most appropriate methods of analysis.

a.   Cases in which plaintiff's data was inadequate to help establish a prima facie *case or was readily rebutted*

1) *Pirone et al. v. Home Insurance Co.:*[13] Alleged Age Discrimination

This case dealt with a charge of age discrimination in terminations. To buttress their case, the plaintiffs introduced data comparing the proportion of persons in the age range 40–65 (protected by the Age Discrimination Act) among *terminees* with their *proportion of new hires.*

The judge noted that the fact that entry-level employees are uniformly younger than terminees has no special import as "logic suggests that this will be the natural order of things" and quoted the Sixth Circuit's opinion in *Langeson v. Anaconda Co.*[14] that stated, "It is apparent that in the usual case, absent any discriminatory intent, discharged employees will more often than not be replaced by those younger than they, for older employees are constantly moving out of the labor market while younger ones move in. For this reason hiring data which is contrasted with termination data is virtually useless in any realistic analysis of a claim of disparate treatment because of age. It is only logical to assume any institution that wants to survive will be constantly acquiring young new hires and losing old employees through termination or retirement." We note that the above analysis is consistent with our discussion concerning the definitions of the labor pool for entry-level jobs in Section 4.4, where we eliminated persons in the occupation earning more than the job in question paid from the potential labor pool. As earnings tend to rise with age and experience, the labor pool available for entry-level jobs will be younger than the total labor force.

In addition to pointing out the inadequacy of the plaintiff's comparisons, Judge Carter went on to describe a more relevant statistical comparison stating, "Statistical data comparing the age of the terminated employees in the New York office with the age of those retained in that office, *Schwager v. Sun Oil Company of Pennsylvania,* 591 F.2d 58, 59 (10th Cir. 1979), or comparison of the percentage of employees between 40 and 65 terminated with the percentage of 40- to 65-year-olds retained in the defendant's work force might have been relevant, *Marshall v. Sun Oil Co.* (Delaware), 605 F.2d 1331 (5th Cir. 1979), reh. denied, 610 F.2d 818 (5th Cir. 1979), but no such credible data was offered." The methods of Chapter 5 could have been used to compare the termination fractions of employees in the protected class with that of employees under 40 had such data been offered in evidence.

2) *Freeman v. Lewis:*[15] Alleged Race and Sex Discrimination

A white female alleged that she had been discriminated against with respect to opportunities for promotion because of her race and sex by the Office of Civil Rights in a subagency of the U.S. Department of Transportation. To support her claim she compared the race-sex composition of the 25 employees who served in the office during the relevant time period to the race-sex mix of the 4642 employees of the subagency.

The race-sex mix of the total subagency[16] was black males 4%, black females 7.7%, white males 65% and white females 18.5%, while the Office of Civil Rights consisted of 8 black males, 9 black females, 3 white males and 3 white females. Plaintiff's expert compared the composition of the office to that of the entire subagency and found that *whites* were statistically significantly underrepresented.

The trial judge realized that the plaintiff's calculation depended on the assumption that each race-sex group had the same distribution of requisite training and experience for the job as well as similar levels of interest in working in the area of civil rights. Indeed, he noted that proportionately fewer whites, relative to blacks, had interest and experience in the equal employment area, so the above assumption was incorrect. The district court opinion also expressed doubt about the validity of the small sample size, however, a larger sample per se would not have been more reliable had plaintiffs made the same simple comparison. On the other hand, if the assumption that the race-sex composition of the subagency equaled that of the appropriate pool for the job in question were reasonable, then the sample size would have been adequate. Indeed, the chance of obtaining 6 or fewer whites in a sample size of 25 when the white fraction of the qualified pool was .835 is *less than* one in 10,000.[17]

3) *Eison v. City of Knoxville:*[18] Alleged Disparate Impact
of a Test on Women

A female candidate at the Knoxville Police Academy claimed that the
physical qualification tests, designed to establish that a person had sufficient strength and endurance, had a disparate impact on females, as the
pass rate of females in her class (1982) was less than four fifths that of
males. While the district court agreed that the EEOC used the four-fifths
rule as a rule of thumb for establishing adverse impact, the opinion noted
that the plaintiff restricted her evaluation of the physical test to persons in
her class instead of examining the results for all persons who took the
exam.

In Tables 6.1 and 6.2 we present both data sets and their selection
ratios. Since the four-fifths rule is a guideline, it is preferable to augment it
by a proper test of the hypothesis that the pass rates are equal. Using the
test statistic (5.6), we find that the data in Table 6.1 would *not* be significant if a two-sided, .05 level were required but would be if a one-sided test
were accepted, as

(6.1) $$Z = \frac{.11312}{60662} = -1.708.$$

In contrast, the difference in the pass rates in the plaintiff's class alone
would be significant at the .05 level, even if a two-sided test criteria were
adopted, as the test statistic (5.6) yields

(6.2) $$Z = \frac{-.25225}{.12515} = -2.015.$$

The main point is that Judge Taylor is statistically correct in his insis-
tence on examining the total universe of persons taking the test, not on
subsets.[19] Furthermore, if one divides a data set into subgroups of suffi-

TABLE 6.1.   Pass Rates for all Persons in *Eison v. Knoxville*

	Pass	Fail	Total	Fraction Passing
Female	16	3	19	.842
Male	64	3	67	.955
Total	80	6	86	.930

Source: 570 F.Supp. 11 at 12, 33 FEP Cases 1141 (E.D. Tenn. 1983).
Note: The selection ratio .842/.955 = .882 exceeds the four-fifths rule.

cient size, where statistical significance at the .05 level can be found, then the probability that *at least one subgroup* will show a significant difference is *greater*[20] than .05. This error can be considered as the opposite of fragmentation, because it subjects the data set to multiple statistical tests. When the data should be considered in subgroups, a suitable combination procedure, such as the Mantel-Haenszel procedure given in Chapter 5, can be used.

The application of a formal statistical test (5.6) in relatively small samples (note that only 19 women ever took the test) relies on the assumption that the test takers can be considered as representative of the pool of potential candidates. In the case at hand, the opinion mentioned that all failures occurred in the plaintiff's class. Perhaps the reasons for this might have been explored further by the parties in the case. If the physical fitness test or its administration changed during the period, then the plaintiff's data would be more relevant. On the other hand, the plaintiff's class was the largest of the three and may have included persons of lesser agility than usual.

This case also indicates the importance of calculating measures of the disparity. The selection ratio of .882 in Table 6.1 is consistent with the notion that the test was not designed to exclude females. The odds ratio, however, shows that women had only 25% the *odds* of *success* that males had. This results from the fact that the odds of success, $p / (1 - p)$, become very large if p is close to 1. Thus, the selection ratio may be preferable as a measure of relative disparity when high success rates are being compared. Had the pass rates in Table 6.1 been based on larger samples, the difference between them would be statistically significant (see problem 6.1) and the low odds ratio of .25 would indicate that the difference in male/female odds ratios was real. The selection ratio of nearly .9 suggests that a *small real* difference may not be *meaningful* in the context of this application.

TABLE 6.2.   Pass Rates for Persons in Plaintiff's Class in *Eison v. Knoxville*

	Pass	Fail	Total	Fraction Passing
Female	6	3	9	.666
Male	34	3	37	.919
Total	40	6	46	.870

Source: 570 F.Supp. 11 at 12, 33 FEP Cases 1141 (E.D. Tenn. 1983).
Note: The selection ratio .666/.919 = .725 is less than .8.

4) *Davis v. City of Dallas:*[21] Alleged Race and Sex Discrimination

In this case the city of Dallas was charged with both race and sex discrimination in its hiring process, and the court had to choose between the analysis of actual applicant data and the demographic method described in Section 4.4. We will see that Judge Higginbotham carefully evaluated the relative merits of the analyses submitted by both parties.

As the opinion noted, "Despite the usual array of statistical exercises, the inescapable conclusion is that liability here turns on one relatively simple question ... In order to measure the discrepancy between actual and potential hires, what figures should properly be compared to the actual number of hires? ... the question is how the actual record compares to what it presumably would have been in a sex or race neutral hiring process." The plaintiffs advocated that the court rely on an applicant flow analysis to evaluate black hires (blacks formed 22% of all applicants and 12% of the area's labor force) but on the demographic method to evaluate female hires (females formed 39% of the area's labor force, according to census data, and 17.5% of all applicants. The defendant naturally took the reverse position.

Here we will consider the hiring data for females. The plaintiffs calculated the female percentage of the total labor force in the local area (SMSA). They did not attempt to incorporate any of the age, education or physical requirements of the job nor any measure of interest level. In fact, the city recruiter testified that a substantial number of women decided not to apply after learning that assignment to patrol duty was mandatory. The court then examined the applicant data to make sure that females were not discouraged from applying due to unnecessary job requirements. Since the height and weight requirements differed for the two sexes and were not very stringent[22] and the education requirement did not adversely impact on females, the judge decided that the applicant data was more reliable and relevant. It is important to note that the court checked that the recruitment process was fair and that females would not be deterred from applying due to overly restrictive job requirements before accepting the applicant data as the preferred data source. Since plaintiffs failed to develop a refined availability figure,[23] the court's choice is undoubtedly correct.

As far as the formal statistical inference is concerned, the court calculated that females formed 17.5% of the applicants during the 1973–1978 period, during which the police department hired 945 persons, 147 of whom were female. The binomial model[24] was used and the test statistic

(4.4) calculated to yield

$$(6.3) \quad Z = \frac{\text{actual} - \text{expected}}{\text{standard error}} = \frac{147 - (945)(.175)}{11.68} = \frac{-18.375}{11.68} = -1.57,$$

a nonsignificant result at the .05 level.
The measures of disparity we have used indicate that females lost about

$$\text{difference} = \text{actual} - \text{expected} = 18.374$$

jobs or, proportionately,

$$(6.4) \quad \frac{\text{difference}}{\text{expected}} = \frac{18.375}{165.375} = .111,$$

which is less than the 20% shortfall (from expected) criteria which we used earlier to approximate the EEOC's four-fifths rule. The analog of the odds ratio (5.1), given by (5B,2) is

$$(6.5) \quad \frac{\dfrac{.1555}{.8445}}{\dfrac{.175}{.825}} = \frac{.1841}{.2121} = .868,$$

as $p_1 = 147/945 = .1555$, while $p = .175$. Again, .868 seems quite near 1.0 and is far from the odds ratio of .70 which occurred in the statistically close *Agarwal v. McKee*[25] case.

Although the measures of absolute impact (6.4) and relative disparity between the hiring odds do not indicate a substantial effect on females, the p-value, .0582, of a one-sided test (6.3) barely missed statistical significance if the one-sided .05 level criteria is used. Indeed if *one* less female had been hired, the difference between actual and expected hires in (6.3) would have been -19.375 and division by the standard error, 11.6805, would equal -1.659, yielding a statistically significant result at the one-sided .05 level.[26] Why are seemingly small differences in treatment so close to statistical significance? The answer is the relatively *large* sample size, which allows us to detect small deviations from the null hypothesis being tested, even if they are not very meaningful, and the neglect of the concept of the power of the test or, equivalently, the type II error. In Table 6.3 we present the approximate power and type II error for the analysis of the odds ratio for the binomial data (see Appendix B to Chapter 5) from the *Davis* case.

Notice that the alternative, .133, is about 75% that of the null value of $p = .175$ and probably is sufficiently different from it to be practically

TABLE 6.3.   Approximate Power and Type II Error Rate (β) for the Binomial
Model Used to Analyze Female Hires in *Davis v. Dallas*

Alternative Odds Ratio	Corresponding Fraction (r) of Females	Statistical Power	(Type II Error)
.8	.145	.81	.19
.75	.133	.977	.023
.667	.124	>.999	<.01
.50	.096	>.9999	<.0001

Note: The sign (>) means greater than and (<) means less than. The null hypothesis is that
the odds ratio is 1 and the female fraction of eligibles is .175. The alternative that the odds
ratio is less than 1.0 is equivalent to an alternative that the female fraction (p) of eligibles is
less than .175. We approximated the critical region of a .05 level one-sided test of the null
hypothesis and obtained a cutoff value of 146, i.e., 146 or fewer female hires would be
sufficiently far from the expected 165.38 to reject the null hypothesis (p = .175). The power
is the probability that the actual number of hires would be less than 146 when the alternative
value of p is true and 945 hires (observations) are made. One minus the power, the type II
error rate, is the probability of failing to detect discrimination when the employer appears to
be giving females a lower fraction (r) of positions.

important. The type II error rate, the probability of failing to reject the
null hypothesis when this alternative is true, i.e., the chance of failing to
detect a statistical indication of discriminatory treatment when females
have 75% the hiring odds as males, is .025, which is one half of the type I
error (.05) or chance of finding statistical discrimination when the defendant is hiring fairly. This is the reverse of the small sample problem, noted
previously, where the large possible sampling fluctuating does not allow
one to conclude that a statistically significant disparity exists, even when
the raw numbers suggest a meaningful difference. In small samples, the
power will be low, hence, a nonsignificant result cannot be interpreted as
evidence that no discrimination occurred.

Comments.   (1) By deciding on what a *meaningful difference*[27] that
should be detected is *prior* to accepting the result of a formal hypothesis
test, a court could ask for the *power* of the test to detect a meaningful
alternative. This calculation can be accomplished without knowledge of
the actual number of minority hires (or promotions), as it depends only on
itself and the expected value and standard deviation of the number of
hires, calculated under the assumed alternative and null hypotheses. In
most scientific applications the type I error rate, α, is kept less than the
type II error rate, β. If β is less than α, as in the *Davis* case, it is sensible

to increase β to at least α. Thus, perhaps we should require a significant disparity at the .03 level,[28] say, rather than at the .05 level. The Z-value of -1.57 would not have been close to the critical value of -1.9 defining statistical significance at the .03 level.

(2) Making an analysis of the probabilities of the two types of errors and weighing them carefully requires more thought than using a fixed rule such as always requiring significance at the .05 level or always requiring a sample size of at least 50. By doing these power calculations we keep in mind the possible errors that can occur and give less weight in our ultimate decision to small but statistically significant differences in large samples or to nonsignificant differences but apparently meaningful ones in small samples. Again, notice how both the measure of effect or impact and the p-value and power of a statistical test aided our understanding of the data and are consistent with the court's ultimate conclusion.

5) *EEOC v. Datapoint:*[29] Alleged National Origin Discrimination

This case originated when the defendant discharged a Mexican-American from employment in December 1970. The EEOC intervened on behalf of the plaintiff and expanded the charge to include hiring discrimination with respect to Mexican-Americans and females. The EEOC based its proof of a *prima facie* case on a comparison of the defendant's work force, by job category, with the minority work force in the two nearby counties during the years 1970, 1971 and 1973. In addition, the minority proportion of applicants and hires for *some* positions in 1973 and 1974 was also presented to the court. An extract of the data is given in Table 6.4.

Although the trial judge did not determine whether the plaintiff's data had established a *prima facie* case, the defendant rebutted the plaintiff's evidence by demonstrating that:

(a) The geographical location of its plant as well as its inaccessibility by public transportation would diminish its minority applicant flow.

(b) The applicant data was incorrectly computed because several related job categories were excluded (e.g., engineers), while others (e.g., test technicians) were included. Furthermore, the plaintiff's applicant data in 1971–73 was not organized by job applied for[30] nor were applicants divided according to the two possible locations they applied to.

The appellate court noted, "Isolating the categories of officials, managers and programmers, plaintiff's evidence might be sufficient to infer discrimination in these job categories. But, while statistics are an appropriate

TABLE 6.4.   Work Force and Applicant Flow Data From *EEOC v. Datapoint*

Positions	Minority Percentages					
	1973 Area Work Force	1973 Company Employment	1973 Applicants	1973 Hires	1974 Applicants	1974 Hires
Office/Cleri- cal	40.0	8.6	25.5	13.2	22.6	17.8
Operatives	50.0	31.0	59.3	50.1	—	—
Officials and Managers	25.0	4.0	15.5	2.9	13.5	3.3
Programmers	18.5	2.8	10.0	4.9	21.6	5.4
Test Techni- cians	45.6	22.2	—	—	28.6	15.5

Source: Extracted from the opinion, 17 FEP Cases 281 at 285. We note that the opinion reported only a portion of the data submitted at the original trial.

method of proving a *prima facie* case of racial discrimination, such statistics must be relevant, material and meaningful, not segmented and particularized and fashioned to obtain a desired conclusion.''

In this case the plaintiff's demographic statistics were inadequate because the employment data in the labor market areas were not adjusted for geographic preferences, and its applicant flow data failed to reflect the *totality* of positions under scrutiny. A further flaw in EEOC's statistical presentation was that it attempted to prove discrimination in the 1971– 1973 period on the basis of applicant flow data for 1973–74. Obviously, data for 1971–1973 would be more relevant. This case is of interest, as the data in Table 6.4 is suggestive of a statistical difference in treatment and a more careful statistical presentation might have assisted the plaintiffs.

Comment. The issue of the relevant time frame is quite important in this case. Almost all the data used by both parties was *subsequent* to the date of the original charge. Indeed, the defendant initiated an affirmative action plan in 1973 and showed that its minority employee percentage subsequently increased by about 3% a year. Logically, data preceding the time of the alleged act of discrimination would be more relevant in determining the defendant's intentions at that time than data referring to a later time period, especially the period *after* a formal complaint or charge of discrimination was filed.

We now discuss cases where the plaintiff's data established a strong *prima facie* case. In these cases we will see that the plaintiffs focused their data on the issue at hand, considered all the appropriate positions and tried to incorporate the qualifications of the actual or potential applicants in their comparison of hiring or promotion rates.

b. Cases in which statistical data aided plaintiffs in establishing a solid prima facie *case*

1) *Griggs v. Duke Power Co.*[31] and Disparate Impact Cases

In this seminal disparate impact case a black plaintiff challenged the requirement that applicants possess a high school diploma or pass a standardized intelligence test. The disparate impact of this requirement was demonstrated by submitting census data[32] showing that in 1960, 34% of white males in North Carolina had completed high school while only 12% of black males had and that the EEOC in another case[33] found that 58% of whites but only 6% of blacks passed the intelligence test used by the defendant. Once a *prima facie* case of disparate impact has been shown, the employer must show that the practice is necessary for business purposes, i.e., persons satisfying the requirement are superior workers. Thus, the Supreme Court examined the issue of the relationship of the requirements to job performance and found that the company had not submitted a meaningful study demonstrating such a relationship. Indeed, the opinion noted that during the period from July 2, 1965 to November 14, 1966, white non-high school graduates had almost the same promotion rate as white graduates, which is inconsistent with the defendant's claim that the education requirement is necessary for satisfactory job performance.

Other major cases involving the issue of the impact of a specific employment practice are *Dothard v. Rawlinson*[34] and *Teal v. Connecticut.*[35] We note that disparate impact in the Teal case was established using actual applicant data (Table 5.4), demonstrating that minority pass rate was statistically significantly less than the majority rate (one-sided *p*-value of .0003) and a selection ratio of .681. When applicant data is not available or reliable, the effect of a requirement can be assessed as the court did in *Griggs*. Note that the selection ratio in *Griggs* was 12/34 = .353, indicating a very substantial impact on blacks.

An interesting disparate impact case occurred in Arizona[36] where a female biology teacher asserted that the school district discriminated against females when it coupled a vacancy for a biology teacher with that of an assistant football coach. Although 10 applicants (all male) were selected for the final selection panel from a total of 85 applicants (54 male, 31 female), the appeals court said that the lower court's statement "that plaintiff has failed to provide any relevant statistical evidence" asks too much. The effect of coupling the two jobs was clear to the appellate court. Had it proceeded to analyze the 10 selections for the finals, with Fisher's exact test (Section 5.4) it would have obtained a one-sided p-value of about .01, which substantiates its conclusion concerning the effect of coupling. The court noted that the defendant school district failed to show that its practice of coupling extracurricular activity contracts with regular teaching posts satisfied the criteria of business necessity that employment practices with a disparate impact must meet but implied that in other situations a school district might be able to do so.

We now turn to two cases involving the issue of discriminatory treatment.

2) *Boykin v. Georgia Pacific Corporation:*[37] Racial Discrimination in Job Assignments

Two black plaintiffs, employed at defendant's sawmill, complained that blacks were primarily assigned to low level jobs and were denied promotions.[38] Plaintiffs presented the data in Tables 6.5 and 6.6 to demonstrate a significant disparity in the initial jobs given to blacks and whites.

Applying the normal approximation (5.23) to Fisher's exact test to the data in Table 6.5 to determine whether blacks received their expected share of the 112 better job assignments, we find

$$(6.6) \qquad Z = \frac{295 - 649\left(\frac{317}{761}\right)}{\sqrt{\frac{317}{761} \times \frac{444}{761} \times \frac{(649)(112)}{760}}} = \frac{-24.654}{4.82} = -5.11,$$

corresponding to a one-sided p-value of less than 1 in 10,000, a highly significant result. (We should mention that the appellate opinion used the binomial model rather than the hypergeometric one and obtained a corresponding disparity of -4.8 standard deviations.) We used the hypergeometric model, since the job assignments are not independent (once the better jobs are assigned the remainder of the new hires must be given the utility posts), and the favorable selections constituted more than 10% of the total pool. In the present case the court's statistically conservative[39] method did not affect the ultimate inference.[40]

TABLE 6.5. Number and Percentage, by Race, of Employees by Initial Job Assignment in *Boykin v. Georgia Pacific*

Race	Assigned To Non-Utility Job	Assigned To Utility Job	Total	Fraction
Black	22	295	317	.069
White	90	354	444	.203
Total	112	649	761	.147

Source: Table I from the opinion, 706 F.2d 1384 at 1387.
Note: The non-utility job is the more desirable.

The measures of absolute and relative disparity also indicate the meaningfulness of the difference in job assignment rates. Blacks received 22 jobs out of an expected 46.7 or only 47% of their expected share. The selection ratio of .34 and the odds ratio of .293 also indicate that any individual black had approximately one third the chance of a white of being assigned a better (non-utility) job.

In *Boykin* the plaintiffs also submitted job assignment data (Table 6.6) for persons who had relevant prior experience for non-utility jobs. The data clearly reflects a statistically significant difference at the usual .05 level (see problem 4a) and the selection ratio of about one half indicates that blacks with prior experience also were treated differently than similarly qualified whites.

This second data set is very important, because it shows that prior job experience cannot fully explain the statistically significant difference in Table 6.5. Indeed, plaintiffs might have further strengthened their analysis by also considering the initial job assignment data for new employees without any relevant prior experience by subtracting the data in Table 6.6

TABLE 6.6. Number and Percentage, by Race, of Employees Who Had Prior Experience for Non-Utility Jobs by Initial Job Assignment

Race	Assigned To Non-Utility Job	Assigned To Utility Job	Total	Fraction
Black	13	107	120	.1215
White	61	184	245	.2490
Total	74	291	365	.2027

Source: Table II from the opinion, 706 F.2d 1384 at 1388.

from Table 6.5 and using this data in conjunction with Table 6.6 in a combined analysis (see problem 4b).

In rebuttal the defendant asserted that

(a) the number of employees involved was too small to permit a statistical analysis, because the firm's total employment fluctuated between 60 and 110 workers, while the job assignment data (Table 6.5) consisted of 761 employees hired over a number of years, and

(b) the data was inadequately standardized for the qualifications of the new hires.

The appellate opinion noted the irrelevance of the defendant's first assertion when a charge of discrimination over several years is under study. Employee turnover is a normal part of our economy, and the court is examining the placement of newly hired workers. The opinion emphasized that the dispositive point is the statistical significance of the data as determined by using methodology approved by the U.S. Supreme Court in *Castenada* and *Hazelwood*.

The defendant's second explanation was rejected, because plaintiffs "used all information listed" on the employment application. If more experience or education was truly needed, then one would expect that the application form would ask for this information. Since the plant manager had testified that the skills needed for most jobs could be learned on the job, it was difficult for the defendant to justify other factors as relevant for deciding the initial job assigned to an employee.

This case is important because it indicates that plaintiffs should incorporate job-related qualifications that are available to them, but they need not account for all conceivable job-related factors. The D.C. Circuit has also recognized that the degree of refinement that a plaintiff's statistical analysis should have depends on the quality of the available data[41] and that a plaintiff's initial evidence needs to account for the minimum objective qualifications needed for the job.[42] In *Segar v. Smith*[43] the court held that plaintiffs need not account for the U.S. Civil Service's "amorphous criteria" of "specialized experience" in addition to seniority and education. Of course, the more qualifications plaintiffs can include in their analysis, the more difficult it will be for defendants to show flaws in the analysis or incorporate other relevant explanatory factors.

The promotion data used in *Boykin* appears in Table 6.19 (problem 5). The defendant attempted to rebut a statistically significant difference in promotion rates by presenting evidence concerning a few specific positions but did not present a statistical analysis incorporating new factors or eliminating persons originally hired before the appropriate statute of limitations period.[44] The court did not accept this explanation and stated that to rebut statistical evidence "one must either show flaws in the plaintiff's statistics or provide a nondiscriminatory reason or explanation of the results." The logical flaw in defendant's concentrating on a few promotions and not on all of the qualified labor pools and relevant job categories is similar to the flaws we noted in analyses submitted by plaintiffs in *Eison* and *Datapoint*.

3) *Hogan v. Pierce:*[45] Race Discrimination in Promotion

In promotion cases, the population of potential promotees consists of the defendant's employees in lower level jobs who possess the requisite qualifications for higher level jobs. Usually data on persons who applied for or asked to be considered for the position should be used to evaluate the relative merits of the individuals. When this data is not available because the applicant files were destroyed or because the job announcement was not made known to all eligible employees, one may be able to reconstruct the pool of eligibles and consider them as applicants. This was done in *Hogan v. Pierce* where the plaintiff, a black male employed as a GS-13 computer specialist, had been denied a promotion to a GS-14 position. The plaintiff helped his case by analyzing promotions from Grade 13 to Grade 14 from March 1972, the effective date of the amendments extending the Civil Rights Act to the government sector, through the date of the administrative complaint in 1977. At the time of each promotion during this period, all employees who possessed the minimal qualifications according to the Civil Service regulations, i.e., were employed in computer-related occupations and had served for at least one year at the previous grade (13), were considered the eligible pool. The dates of promotion and the racial mix of the eligible pool are reported in Table 6.7.

Plaintiff's expert applied the MH test to the data in Table 6.7 obtaining

$$(6.7) \qquad Z = \frac{\text{observed} - \text{expected} + .5}{\text{standard deviation}} = \frac{-4.517}{1.837} = -2.46.$$

Thus, if black and white eligible candidates had the same chance of promotion, the probability that no blacks would be promoted is about .007, a statistically significant result.[46] In his opinion accepting plaintiff's analysis, Judge Robinson also noted that the analysis demonstrated that the pool of eligibles was large enough that "zero" promotions could not have occurred by chance, even though the total number of promotions over the relevant time period was relatively small (18).

TABLE 6.7. Promotion Data, by Race, from *Hogan v. Pierce*

Date of Promotion	Whites		Blacks	
	Eligible	Promoted	Eligible	Promoted
July 1974	20	4	7	0
August 1974	17	4	7	0
September 1974	15	2	8	0
April 1975	18	1	8	0
May 1975	18	1	8	0
October 1975	30	1	10	0
November 1975	31	2	10	0
February 1976	31	1	10	0
March 1976	31	1	10	0
November 1977	34	1	13	0

Source: Plaintiff's exhibit on file with D.C. District Court.

From a statistical viewpoint, we mention that this application of the test is slightly different than our previous uses of the method as we followed[47] the employees over a period of several years. Those persons who left GS-13 level jobs were replaced by others who eventually acquired the necessary experience (one year). Looking at the data in Table 6.7, one might surmise that seniority might explain why whites received the early promotions. By 1977, however, the average black GS-13 had more seniority than the typical white. Thus, seniority could not be the job-related factor justifying the promotion decisions, as blacks did not receive more of the later promotions. In fact, the defendant did not question the plaintiff's finding of a nonsignificant difference in years of service. Rather the government submitted post-charge data comparing the grade levels held by blacks employed in the computer area in the defendant agency with the levels they held in other government agencies. This data was not focused on either the specific type of promotion (GS-13 to 14) at issue or the time period before and around the time[48] of the promotion decision and subsequent charge.

In the next section we discuss two cases in which more refined statistical methods might have aided the plaintiffs either in establishing a *prima facie* case or in showing that the defendant's statistical evidence did not really explain the statistical disparity shown by plaintiffs. The third case tells how a court accepted a defendant's nonstatistical explanation of a significant difference in hiring rates, even though it rejected its statistical submission. The reader will notice that our reanalysis of the data in these cases will tend to support the plaintiff's claim. This is not necessarily the situation.[49]

3.   More Complex Statistical Cases

a.   Bazemore v. Friday:[50] *Alleged racial discrimination in pay raises*

We will consider the fairness of the merit pay system used by the North Carolina Agricultural Extension Service aspect of the case. Merit pay increases were given to agents who received ratings in the top *three* quartiles but were not given to agents who ranked in the lowest quartile. The appellate opinion noted "that if there were discrimination and black employees were assigned to a lower quartile, especially the fourth quartile, because of their race there would be a salary disparity resulting on account of race." The court then analyzed the quartile ranking data given in Table 6.8. The data is reported by district as the quartile rankings were made by the respective district chairmen.

   Since only agents ranked in the lowest quartile were denied a raise, the court combined the data in the first three quartiles and considered the data as a set of 2 × 2 tables, i.e., persons in the top three quartiles received a raise while the remaining employees did not. The court then tested the data in each district *separately* for statistical significance. Thus, the court

TABLE 6.8.   Quartile Rankings of White and Black Employees, by District and Race, in *Bazemore v. Friday*

District	Quartile							
	I		II		III		IV	
	W	B	W	B	W	B	W	B
NC	17	5	16	7	14	12	12	9
NE	12	2	13	3	10	5	8	3
NW	19	1	21	1	17	3	9	4
SE	22	1	18	9	14	6	10	7
SW	20	3	21	2	18	2	12	4
W	16	0	16	0	15	0	13	0
Total	106	12	105	22	88	28	64	27

Source: 751 F.2d 662 at 673.

fragmented the data and noted that *only* in the northwest district was statistical significance approached.

Since the court's approach decreases the sample size available for each test, its procedure has very low power. Moreover, requiring a significant difference at the .05 level in each of the five districts with employees of both races really means that the court actually tested the total data set at the level of

$$(.05)^5 = .0000002,$$

since the rankings in one district were independent of those in the other districts. Hence, it is not surprising that a significant disparity was not found by the court.

In Table 6.9 we present the basic data and the result of the *Mantel-Haenszel* test. In the present context a significant *excess* over the expected number of blacks in the fourth quartile indicates possible discrimination. The test yields a normal Z of

$$(6.8) \qquad Z = \frac{\text{difference} - .5}{\text{standard error}} = \frac{9.10 - .5}{10.597} = 2.80,$$

or a one-sided p-value of about .003. Such a low p value implies that the data in Table 6.9 would be significant at both the .05 and .01 levels even if a two-sided test were deemed appropriate.[51]

The data in Table 6.9 is also consistent, as blacks are below or just at their expected number of low-ranked employees in all districts. Thus, the data can properly be combined.[52] The MH summary odds ratio estimate (5.30) for the data is 2.166, indicating that the odds a black employee had

TABLE 6.9. Mantel-Haenszel Test for a Difference in the Probability Black and White Employees had of Being Ranked in the Fourth Quartile in *Bazemore v. Friday*

District	Black		White		Black Expected in 4th Quartile	Difference	Variance
	Employed	4th Quartile	Employed	4th Quartile			
NC	33	9	59	12	7.533	1.47	3.769
NE	13	3	53	8	2.167	.83	1.472
NW	9	4	66	9	1.560	2.44	1.150
SE	23	7	64	10	4.494	2.51	2.691
SW	11	4	71	12	2.146	1.85	1.514
Total	89	27	313	51		9.10	10.597

Source: The data is from Table 6.8 and the calculations follow the format given in Section 5.6.

of being ranked in the lowest quartile were twice those of a white. Alternatively, blacks had odds $(2.166)^{-1} = .462$ or about one half the odds whites had of receiving a merit pay raise. This is a much lower odds ratio than we found in other cases,[53] which held that plaintiffs had established a *prima facie* case.

The MH analysis focuses on the issue of whether blacks were represented in the lowest quarter (or upper 75%) of the agents in proportion to their representation in the respective district agent populations and avoids the error of fragmentation in the opinion. It should be mentioned that there may be a legal question concerning the appropriate universe for analysis, as each county made its salary decisions separately, however, the quartile ranking system for determining whether an agent was eligible for a raise was the same for all districts. Furthermore, in its discussion of the fairness of the selection process for county chairman posts, the court indicated that all the data should be aggregated into a single 2 × 2 table and should include the situations where all applicants were of the same race. Had the court done this for the data in Table 6.9, it would have analyzed the data in Table 6.10 and obtained a Z-value of the normal approximation to Fisher's test statistic of $+2.528$, corresponding to a one-sided p-value of .0057. While this method is not as statistically sound as the MH analysis, in the present context the ultimate conclusion would be the same. In general the data in separate 2 × 2 tables should not be simply aggregated into a single table, unless the differences are similar in each component table as happened here.

Comment. The data does raise an interesting and important statistical issue. The MH analysis uses only the data from districts[54] having both white and black applicants, but excluded the district (West) in which no blacks were employed. In contrast, the simple aggregate data in Table 6.10 included the West district. Is it correct for the MH analysis to neglect one of six regions? Most statisticians would prefer the MH analysis, as it

TABLE 6.10. Simple Aggregation of Quartile Data in Table 6.8 for All Regions

	In Fourth Quartile	In Upper Three Quartiles	Total	Fraction in Lower Quartiles
Blacks	27	62	89	.303
Whites	64	299	363	.176
Total	91	361	452	.201

focuses on how blacks fare in comparison to similarly situated whites, however, there are instances where the data in racially homogenous categories are important. For instance, if we are considering promotions from a work force in which current employees apply for advancement, the employees may know the person amongst them who is best qualified and only that person, and perhaps one or two others, may apply. If most of these special cases consist of all minority (or all majority) applicants, then one should consider this fact in interpreting the results of the MH analysis rather than simply aggregating the data. For example, if the data in Table 6.9 had referred to promotions, e.g., being in the fourth quartile the equivalent of not being promoted, the statistical excess of about four blacks not receiving a promotion *might* be explained by supplementary data showing that four blacks but no whites were promoted in special circumstances.

b.   Allen v. Prince George's County, MD:[55] *Alleged racial discrimination*

This case was a class action alleging the county had discriminated against blacks in hiring and promotion. We will focus primarily on the hiring issue but will show how a more careful analysis than presented in the case indicates that plaintiff's statistical evidence of possible discrimination in hiring was stronger than their promotion data.

   The plaintiff's hiring case was made on the basis of a static comparison of the county's employment pattern with that of its geographic labor market, as discussed in Chapter 4. The racial composition of the 1980 work force in various EEO categories was compared to the 1980 census data on the racial mix of persons employed in the appropriate occupations. The plaintiff's data included pre-act hires in both the employer's work force and the census data. Because one third of the defendant's current employees were hired prior to the effective date (March 1972) of the Civil Rights Act, the court did not accept the conclusion of the plaintiff's expert that the data showed significant underrepresentation of blacks.

   In addition to criticizing the plaintiff's inclusion of pre-act hires, the defendant introduced the applicant flow data and analysis given in Table 6.11. The defendant properly reported the applicant data by job category, however, their expert analyzed each category separately and did not combine the results. Notice the small sample sizes (number of selections) in several categories, which virtually preclude finding a statistically significant difference.

TABLE 6.11. Hiring Data from *Allen v. Prince George's County*

EEO Category	Total Applicants	Black Applicants	Black% of Applicants	Total Hires	Black Hires	Black % of Hires	Z-value	P-value
Off./Admin. (1)	215	27	12.56	12	2	16.67		.8209
Professional (2)	1010	374	37.03	78	28	35.90	-.22	
Technician (3)	401	114	28.43	36	4	11.11	-2.41	
Prof. Serv. (4)	1023	573	56.01	103	44	42.73	-2.87	
Para-Prof. (5)	961	448	46.62	62	16	25.81	-3.40	
Off./Cler. (6)	2428	919	37.85	238	72	30.25	-2.54	
Skilled Crafts (7)	274	83	30.29	35	11	31.43	.16	
Serv./Maint. (8)	154	85	55.19	20	8	40.00		.1107

Source: 538 F.Supp. 833 at 851.

Note: The submission used the normal approximation (Z-value) in categories of sufficient size for its applicability. The *p*-value of Fisher's exact test were given for the two categories (1, 8) with a small number of hires. For the convenience of the reader we include the *p*-value corresponding to the normal approximations (Z-values).

The court asserted that the four statistically significant disparities in Table 6.11 would not be sufficient evidence to establish a *prima facie* case of discrimination, as they would be isolated bits of statistical information. While the court probably was unaware[56] of the concept of statistical power, we remind the reader that by requiring a statistically significant underrepresentation at the two standard deviation level (two-sided 5% level test) in all eight job categories, it was requiring a one-sided *p*-value of about[57]

(6.9) $(.025)^8 = 1.53 \times 10^{-13}$,

which corresponds to a difference of more than eight standard deviation units, far in excess of the usual criteria of two to three standard deviations.

On the other hand, in its discussion of the individual categories, the opinion discussed special recruitment problems in the protective service category and a more refined analysis of the office-clerical category, which reduced the statistical disparity to -2.18 standard deviations instead of the -2.54 shown in Table 6.11. The opinion stated "although the statistical disparities in the para-professional and technician categories exceed the two or three standard deviation level, consideration of the number of individuals involved does not indicate to the court that there are "gross statistical disparities ... As Dr. Bloch testified, a shift[58] of eight individuals in the para-professional category from white hires to black hires and a shift of at most three individuals in the technician category from white hires to black hires would result in the elimination of any statistical disparity." By focusing on a measure of absolute impact which depends on the sample size,[59] the court missed the fact that the black technician hiring rate (.0351) was less than half that of the white rate (.1115). Similarly, the black para-professional hiring rate of .0357 is less than half the white rate of .0897. Thus, the statistical disparities in both categories easily satisfy the four-fifths rule for a meaningful difference as well as being statistically significant.

Before presenting the MH analysis of the data in Table 6.11, we note that the actual number of black hires is about equal to its expected number (in categories 1, 2, 7) or below its expected number (in the remaining categories). In no category did blacks substantially exceed their expected number. This intuitive examination of the data is corroborated by the MH test, calculated in Table 6.12, which shows that blacks received about 55 fewer jobs than their expected number, 240, or a deficit of 23%, and the

MH statistic (5.35) is

(6.10) $Z = -4.81.$

The probability of observing a standard normal variate 4.8 or more standard deviations from its expected value is less than .0001. Moreover, the summary odds ratio is .637, implying that blacks faced hiring odds of less than two thirds of those faced by whites.

In order to evaluate the effect of the defendant's rebuttal, which reduced the disparity in clerical jobs to −2.18 standard deviations, and the assertion that minority protective service workers were difficult to recruit, we can delete the protective service category[60] and increase the number of black clerical hires to 75, say. The MH test then yields

$$Z = -3.86,$$

and the estimated summary odds ratio becomes .668. While the MH test is less significant, it remains statistically significant at the two-sided .01 level (p-value < .001), which suggests that the defendant's explanation does not fully explain the underhiring of blacks.

It should also be emphasized that one of the named plaintiffs was allegedly interested in a clerical job. For her individual case, the data in this category might be given more weight. The choice of job categories most

TABLE 6.12.   Mantel-Haenszel Analysis of the Hiring Data in *Allen* Reported in Table 6.11

Category	Minority Applied	Minority Hired	Majority Applied	Majority Hired	Exp. Min. Hires	Difference	Variance
1	27	2	88	10	2.817	−0.82	1.948
2	374	28	646	50	28.600	−0.60	16.745
3	114	4	287	32	10.234	−6.23	6.684
4	573	44	450	59	57.692	−13.69	22.845
5	448	16	513	46	28.903	−12.90	14.449
6	919	72	1509	166	90.083	−18.08	50.519
7	83	11	191	24	10.602	0.40	6.470
8	85	8	69	12	11.039	−3.04	4.332
Total		185			239.97	−54.97	123.991

Note: The MH test $Z = \dfrac{(-54.97 + .5)}{\sqrt{123.991}} = -4.89.$

TABLE 6.13. Promotion Data from *Allen v. Prince George's County*

EEO Category	Total Applicants	Black Applicants	Black % of Applicants	Total Promoted	Black Promoted	Black % of Promotions	Z-value	P-value
(1)	100	8	8.0	23	0	0.0	-1.78	.1131
(2)	207	65	31.40	33	6	18.18	-.47	
(3)	142	28	19.72	30	5	16.67		.9789
(4)	34	7	20.59	4	2	50.00		.3232
(5)	105	32	30.48	21	5	23.81		
(6)	378	101	26.72	86	21	24.42	-.55	
(7)	179	120	67.04	50	30	60.00	-1.25	
(8)	10	2	20.00	2	1	50.00		.9778

Source: 538 F.Supp. 833 at 851.
Note: The *p*-values were given in the opinion for categories (1, 4, 5, 8).

relevant to a particular claim of discrimination first depends on the legal issue. Then a careful labor market analysis to determine the set of jobs of similar skill and the labor supply for them and the availability of statistical data enter into the analysis. Finally, a powerful statistical test should be used.

The promotion data introduced by the defendant is reported in Table 6.13. Notice that there is only one category (2) in which a statistical disparity at the .05 level (one-sided test) exists, although the fact that 0 blacks were promoted in the official category (1) might suggest unfair treatment. On the other hand, blacks in category (4) fared better than expected in the promotion process, and the two standard deviation criteria of significance was not met in any job category. Although there still is an approximate pattern of blacks receiving less than or equal their expected number of promotions, the differences are smaller than in the hiring data. These visual observations are confirmed by the MH analysis given in Table 6.14. The summary test statistic, $Z = -2.03$, has a one-sided p-value of about .02, which is statistically significant but not as low[61] as the hiring data. The MH summary odds ratio estimate is .697, which exceeds that of the hiring case.

While we discuss the promotion data to contrast it with the hiring data, one may ask why did the defendants introduce it, as, properly analyzed,[62] it reflected a statistically significant disparity between the number of promotions received by blacks and their expected number in all job categories.

TABLE 6.14. Mantel-Haenszel Analysis of the Promotion Data in Table 6.13

| Category | Minority | | Majority | | Expected Minority Promotions | Diff. | Variance |
	Applied	Promoted	Applied	Promoted			
1	8	0	92	23	1.840	−1.84	1.317
2	65	6	142	27	10.362	−4.36	6.00
3	28	5	114	25	5.915	−0.92	3.772
4	7	2	17	2	1.167	0.83	0.719
5	32	5	73	16	6.400	−1.40	3.594
6	101	21	277	65	22.979	−1.98	13.042
7	120	30	59	20	33.530	−3.52	8.007
8	2	1	8	2	0.600	0.40	0.373

Note: The MH test statistic is $Z = \dfrac{(-12.79 + 5)}{\sqrt{36.824}} = -2.03$.

c. *Capaci v. Katz and Besthoff:*[63] *Alleged post-charge
hiring discrimination*

We close this section with a discussion of the issue of managerial trainee
hires in the post-charge period in the *Capaci* case as we analyzed the pre-
charge data in Section 4.4d. The plaintiff, a female pharmacist, filed her
first promotion discrimination charge against the defendant in January
1973, and the formal suit was filed on October 8, 1974. The EEOC was
permitted to intervene on behalf of the claims of the class (women who
were denied managerial or supervisory positions) in late 1976 or early
1977. The sexual composition of all persons appointed to managerial
trainee positions, by year, from the effective date of the Civil Rights Act
(July 1965) to a few months prior to the trial is given in Table 6.15.
Applicant flow data was not available until 1976 and 1977, and the plaintiff's data is reported in Table 6.16. The defendant contended that the
data should have been broken down by locality, as a person applying in
one location should not be regarded as an applicant for a job at another
location. This data, for 1977, is reported in Table 6.17.

As we noted in Section 4.4, the district court did not accept plaintiffs'
labor force comparison of the pre-charge data, 1965 thru 1972, as it felt
that the external labor pools were inappropriate; however, the appellate
court reversed the district court on this issue. A cursory examination of
the data in Table 6.15 suggests that women received their first appointment to a managerial traineeship in 1974, the year following the original
complaint, and fared extremely well in 1978, just prior to the trial. Before
we formally analyze the data in Table 6.16 and 6.17, the reader should
look at Table 6.15 and ask the following questions:

(1) Was there a change in the employer's employment policy subsequent to the filing of the original charge?

(2) If so, when did the change result in women receiving their fair share
of traineeships?

(3) How relevant is the applicant flow data in Table 6.16 and 6.17 to the
time period 1973–1975?

Plaintiffs analyzed the post-charge data in two ways. The hiring rates in
the combined applicant flow data in Table 6.16 was analyzed[64] by the test
statistic (5.6), which yielded a Z of -3.96, a statistically significant result
at the two-sided .01 level (p-value $= .000064$). Note that the odds ratio is
.318 and the selection ratio is $.1596/.3737 = .427$, which support the statistical test, as they indicate that female applicants had a meaningful

TABLE 6.15.   Sex of Managerial Trainees Appointed by Katz and Besthoff from July 1965 thru 1978

Year	No. of Males	No. of Females
1965	12	0
1966	20	0
1967	28	0
1968	31	0
1969	32	0
1970	42	0
1971	47	0
1972	54	0
1973	71	0
1974	93	1
1975	55	3
1976	67	5
1977	85	8
1978	1	11

Source: 525 F.Supp. 317 at 326.
Note: The data for 1965 are for the part of the year (July 1 thru December 31) when the Civil Rights Act was applicable. The 1978 data covers the first 6 or 8 months of the year. The trial was originally scheduled for the fall of 1978 but was held in January 1979. The data includes hires from the external labor market as well as from advancements from within the firm. Over 90% of the appointments were hires from outside the firm.

disadvantage relative to males. Plaintiffs also analyzed the 1973–1977 post-charge data using the external labor market pools in Table 4.6 and showed that the chance that 17 or fewer females would be among the 371 hires was less than 1 in 10,000 when females formed 16% of the external labor pool. It is clear from Table 6.15 that females had an advantage[65] over males in 1978. This point was ignored in both opinions.

The defendant tested the hiring data in Table 6.15 separately for each year at the .01 level of significance, using a variety of labor force referents, the lowest of which was the female fraction (.114) of all officials and managers reported in the EEOC data for Louisiana. Defendant's expert found *no pattern* of disparate treatment over all the years at this level. Similarly, he analyzed the data in Table 6.17 separately for each location and found a statistically significant difference only in New Orleans, the

TABLE 6.16.   Plaintiff's Hiring Data for 1976 and 1977

	Hires	Non-Hires	Applicants	Fraction Hired
		1976		
Females	5	7	12	.4166
Males	64	36	100	.6400
Total	69	43	112	.6161
		1977		
Females	10	72	82	.1220
Males	84	212	296	.2838
Total	94	284	378	.2487
		Both Years Combined		
Females	15	79	94	.1596
Males	148	248	396	.3737
Totals	163	327	490	.3327

Source: 525 F.Supp. 317 at 323, reorganized and aggregated to facilitate our treatment.

only area in which there were 20 or more hires. Although the district court noted that defendant's approach reduced the possibility of the statistical test to find a significant result,[66] it accepted the defendant's analysis. In addition to the statistical evidence, the defendant also produced live testimony from several women who left the managerial trainee program due to the hours of work required. The district court accepted this explanation of females self-selecting themselves out of the potential applicant pool as rebutting both the pre- and post-charge data, while the appellate opinion noted that the managerial labor force referents used by plaintiffs were corrected, at least partially, for self-selection, as all managers face hours and responsibilities that would not appeal to all women.

In its discussion of the defendant's data in Table 6.17, the appellate opinion stated[67] that the defendant "attempted to demonstrate that there was no statistically significant evidence of discrimination when the data was broken down by city or year or both. In our view, this was an unfair and obvious attempt to disaggregate that data to the point where it was difficult to demonstrate statistical significance." However, the court did not overturn the district court's finding of no discrimination in hiring either during the post-charge period or the 1973–1975 sub-period[68] prior to the EEOC's intervention in the case. It is interesting to contrast the Fifth

TABLE 6.17. Defendant's Exhibit Organizing Hiring Data by Location *Capaci v. Katz & Besthoff*

LOCATION	SEX	APPLICANTS	HIRES	S.R.	STAT. TEST
Alexandria	M	26	1	3.8%	N.S.
	F	4	0	0.0%	
Baton Rouge	M	25	14	56.0%	N.S.
	F	11	4	36.4%	
Bogalusa	M	5	2	40.0%	N.S.
	F	1	0	0.0%	
Gulfport	M	7	0	0.0%	N.S.
	F	3	0	0.0%	
Gonzales	M	1	1	100.0%	N.S.
	F	0	0	N/A	
Hattiesburg	M	22	1	4.5%	N.S.
	F	5	1	20.0%	
Houma	M	8	3	37.5%	N.S.
	F	1	1	100.0%	
Lafayette	M	33	2	6.1%	N.S.
	F	3	0	0.0%	
Lake Charles	M	12	3	25.0%	N.S.
	F	7	0	0.0%	
Long Beach	M	5	3	60.0%	N.S.
	F	2	0	0.0%	
Laurel	M	1	0	0.0%	N.S.
	F	0	0	N/A	
Mobile	M	25	3	12.0%	N.S.
	F	11	0	0.0%	
Monroe	M	1	1	100.0%	N.S.
	F	1	0	0.0%	
McComb	M	1	1	100.0%	N.S.
	F	0	0	N/A	
Morgan City	M	5	1	20.0%	N.S.
	F	1	0	0.0%	
Natchez	M	2	1	50.0%	N.S.
	F	0	0	N/A	
New Orleans	M	51	39	76.5%	.01
	F	6	0	0.0%	
Opelousas	M	2	2	100.0%	N.S.
	F	0	0	N/A	
Pascagoula	M	8	1	12.5%	N.S.
	F	9	0	0.0%	

Continued

Statistical Reasoning in Law and Public Policy

TABLE 6.17.   (Continued)

LOCATION	SEX	APPLICANTS	HIRES	S.R.	STAT. TEST
Ruston	M	2	1	50.0%	N.S.
	F	0	0	N/A	
Shreveport	M	50	3	6.0%	N.S.
	F	15	1	6.7%	
Thibodaux	M	3	1	33.3%	N.S.
	F	0	0	N/A	
Sulphur	M	1	0	0.0%	N.S.
	F	0	0	N/A	
Slidell	M	0	0	N/A	N.S.
	F	1	1	100.0%	
Vicksburg	M	2	2	100.0%	N.S.
	F	0	0	N/A	
No Area	M	3	0	0.0%	N.S.
	F	1	0	0.0%	

Source: 722 F.2d 637 at 655.
Note: S.R. stands for selection ratio and N.S. means not significant.

Circuit's acceptance of data from 1976 and 1977 as relevant to the entire post-charge period, 1973–1977, in *Capaci,* with its previous decision in *Datapoint.*

Although the Mantel-Haenszel combination test was not used to combine the results of the defendant's tests in each location, we present it in Table 6.18. The results are consistent with the simpler aggregation used by plaintiff, as the MH test yielded a Z of -3.21, slightly less significant than -3.96. On the other hand, the MH summary odds ratio, .266, is less than that (.318) obtained from the simple aggregation in Table 6.16. It should be noted that only 14 of the 26 locations (including no area) enter into the MH analysis in Table 6.18. This occurs because only strata (locations) containing applicants of both sexes and in which there was at least one hire enter into the MH analysis. The fact that no hires occurred in several locations in Table 6.17 raises some doubt as to whether applicants were only interested in local area jobs.

Comments.   The *Capaci* case highlights several important issues.

(1) The choice of the most relevant time frame to determine whether the employer did discriminate at the time of the original charge. Common sense suggests that pre-charge data bears more directly on this issue than

TABLE 6.18. Mantel-Haenszel Test Combining Defendants Hiring Data in the Separate Locations from *Capaci v. Katz & Besthoff*

Region	Female Applicants	Hires	Male Applicant	Hires	Expected Female Hires	Difference	Variance
Alexandria	4	0	26	1	.133	−.13	.116
Baton Rouge	11	4	25	14	5.500	−1.50	1.964
Bogalusa	1	0	5	2	.333	−.33	.222
Hattiesburg	5	1	22	1	.37	.63	.290
Houma	1	1	8	3	.444	.56	.247
Lafayette	3	0	33	2	.167	−.17	.148
Lake Charles	7	0	12	3	1.108	−1.11	.620
Long Beach	2	0	5	3	.857	−.86	.408
Mobile	11	0	25	3	.917	−.92	.600
Monroe	1	0	1	1	.5	−.50	.250
Morgan City	1	0	5	1	1.167	−.17	.139
New Orleans	6	0	51	39	4.105	−4.11	1.181
Pascagoula	9	0	8	1	.529	−.53	.249
Shreveport	15	1	50	3	.923	.08	.677
Total						−9.05	7.112

Note: The MH test (5.29) is $Z = (-9.05 + .5)/7.112 = -3.21$ (one-sided *p*-value = .001. The MH estimate of the summary odds ratio is .266.

post-charge data (especially if there are indications that a change of policy occurred). Whether one should go back as far as the effective date of the Civil Rights Act or just rely on data for two or three years prior to the charge, say, is open to question, since the Supreme Court stated in *United Airlines v. Evans,* 431 U.S. 553 (1977), that a "discriminatory act which is not made the basis for a timely charge is the legal equivalent of a discriminatory act which occurred before the statute was passed. It may constitute relevant background evidence in a proceeding in which the status of a current practice is at issue, but separately considered, it is merely an unfortunate event in history which has no present legal significance."

That statement has raised questions concerning the time period for which statistical data are relevant to the Court's ultimate finding. In *Teamsters v. United States,* 431 U.S. 324 (1977), the Court utilized data from July 2, 1965 until January 1, 1969 in its analysis of a suit filed in May 1968, because the challenged practices had gone unchanged until January 1969.

If the firm changed a discriminatory policy prior to the statute of limitations period, so it was hiring fairly at the time of the charge, the earlier post-Civil Rights Act data probably should not be given much weight. If the data from these two periods is statistically similar, e.g., indicates the same hiring pattern (fair or unfair), then it is statistically proper to combine them in a proper analysis.

(2) How much weight should be given to an explanation of a statistical disparity that is not buttressed by a statistical analysis? In *Capaci,* the district court accepted the defendant's explanation that women self-selected not to apply for managerial jobs due to evening/night duty and some lifting duties, even though they formed 19.2% of the post-charge applicants and a Labor Department survey showed that females formed 24% of the nation's workers who left work at the time (10 p.m.) that the defendant's store closed. If it is not possible to make a statistical adjustment, e.g., by using data on work schedules or hours worked during a week, then one might look at the female share of recent applicants in comparable systems.[69] For example, females formed about 17% of applicants for police jobs in *Davis v. Dallas,* an occupation which is less traditional for women than store managers.

(3) When an employer has been found liable for discrimination in the pre-charge period, is it logically proper to assume, as the null hypothesis, that the employer is fair, when we analyze the post-charge data? The problem arises because statistical hypothesis testing gives the null hypothesis special status, as we keep the probability, α, of falsely rejecting it, low (usually less than .05). Once a court has found that discriminatory practices were in effect during the pre-charge period, it seems more reasonable to assume that these practices would continue, rather than to assume that the employer has changed and to find that discrimination remained the operating policy until the data indicates that fair hiring was in operation. A glance at the data in Tables 6.15 and 6.16 should convince the reader that a change occurred sometime after January 1, 1976 and a sharp change occurred around 1978.

The author is not aware of a large body of statistical literature on this problem. A possible way of dealing with it is to continue to test the null hypothesis of fair hiring (hire rates are equal or the hires follow the binomial model with p equal to an appropriate availability figure) but place greater emphasis on keeping β, the risk of failing to reject the null hypothesis when it is false, low than on keeping α low. Thus, one might require that β be less than .05. Of course, one needs to define an appropriate alternative, such as the selection ratio is .8 or odds ratio is .7, to make this calculation. An equivalent way of expressing this strategy is to interchange the roles of the null and alternative hypotheses. Thus, we now test the null hypothesis that the OR is less than or equal to .75 or .80, say,[70] against the alternative that is is greater than .75 or .80.

Problems

1. Double the entries in the 2×2 table 6.1 from *Eison v. Knoxville*, i.e., assume that 6 males failed and 128 passed, and 6 females failed while 32 passed.

    (a) Show that selection and odds ratios remain the same as before, while the formal statistical test (5.6) is now statistically significant at the two-sided .05 level.

    (b) Why is this important?

2. The Datapoint Corporation began operation in 1968.

    (a) Assuming that the 1973 employment data was similar to that of 1970, how might the plaintiffs have presented a more convincing demographic analysis of the situation near the time of the charge?

    (b) Do you think that minority applicants might have fared better in the job categories omitted by the EEOC in their submission?

    (c) Since the named plaintiff had complained of being discriminatorily terminated, how relevant would the hiring data (even if current) be in resolving her individual case?

3. In the *Civil Rights Division v. Amphitheater* case,

    (a) Verify that the Fisher exact test would yield a significant result at the two-sided .05 level. (You may use the binomial approximation which we know is conservative.)

    (b) Suppose you represented the defendant. Could you raise statistical objections to the analysis of the selection process discussed in the text? What data might you have analyzed to ascertain whether its submission into evidence would have assisted your client?

4. (a) Verify that the data in Table 6.6 indicates that blacks had a significantly lower probability of being assigned to the non-utility jobs in *Boykin*. Calculate the one-sided p-value and the two-sided p-value.

    (b) Create the new 2×2 table corresponding to Tables 6.6 and 6.5, specifying the job assignments given to persons without prior experience. Perform the Mantel-Haenszel analysis (5.35), combining the results in

Table 6.6 with this data. Your result will compare the initial job assignment proportions, accounting for differences in prior experience. Do you expect your end result to give a more or less significant result than we obtained in our analysis (6.6) of the data in Table 6.5?

5.* The data in Table 6.19 reports the number and fraction of non-probationery employees (by race) who were initially assigned to a utility job and were promoted.

(a) What is the appropriate statistical model underlying the data and the corresponding statistical test?

(b) Carry out this analysis.

(c) Compare your results with those in the opinion. The opinion used the binomial approximation, i.e., it assumed that blacks formed the fraction, $p = 157/335 = .469$, of the utility workers and compared their actual promotions (42) with their expected (59) and obtained a Z-score (4.4) of -3.04 standard deviations.

(d) Compute the odds ratio of the actual data and the approximation (5.B2) suitable for the binomial model. Are they in agreement?

(e) Why are your calculations in parts (c) and (d) of potential importance?

6.* Since persons applying in one year might not really be available or interested in the job a year later, the hiring data in Table 6.16 should have been analyzed by using the MH test combining the two yearly differences. Carry out this procedure and compute the summary odds ratio. Does this change the ultimate inference? Why is this problem logically important?

TABLE 6.19. Number and Percentage by Race of Non-probationary Employees Initially Assigned to Utility Positions and the Promotions They Received (from Boykin)

Race	Promoted	Not Promoted	Total Initially Assigned to Utility Jobs	Fraction Promoted
Black	42	115	157	.2675
White	84	94	178	.4719
Total	126	209	335	.3761

Source: 706 F.2d 1384 at 1389.

Answers to Selected Problems

1. (b) This emphasizes the effect that the sample size has on whether a difference is statistically significant at a fixed, e.g., .05 level.

2. (a) In addition to correcting the census data used in the comparison for commuting patterns, some highly paid employed persons in the various occupations might be excluded from the census data, as most of the firm's employees were recent hires. A better analysis would be to compare the new hire data to refined census data. The most appropriate analysis would analyze the actual applicant data, after including all relevant jobs, by the combination procedures described in Chapter 4. The refined demographic data could be used to assess whether the applicant data was consistent with a fair recruitment policy.

(b) This is a nonstatistical issue, however, common sense suggests that a party would offer as much evidence favorable to their case as possible.

(c) Comparative data on discharges as in *Johnson v. Perini* (Table 5.6) would have focused on the main issue. If minorities had a meaningful, but not statistically significantly higher, termination rate then hiring data might be relevant, as hiring discrimination might have limited the size of the sample of minority workers available to assess the discharge policy. It does not seem proper for an employer who discriminates in hiring to be protected from a claim of discrimination in termination or promotion policy because of the small number of minority employees. Similarly, an employer who affirmatively hires minorities should not be penalized if, due to the large number of minority employees, a statistically significant but substantively small difference in termination rates is shown.

3. (a) The binomial approximation sets the female fraction at $p = 31/85 = .365$. We calculate the probability that 0 females were hired as $(1 - .365) = (.635) = .01068$, which is less than .025, implying significance at a level even less than .05 (two-sided). The exact hypergeometric probability is

$$\frac{\binom{32}{0}\binom{54}{10}}{\binom{85}{10}} = .0076.$$

(b) One could question whether the analysis of the applicants for a single position yields an accurate picture of the employment process or the effect of job coupling. One might study applicant data for all coupled jobs during several years prior to the charge to see whether coupling truly had a disparate impact. The fact that defendants did not offer such data suggests that it would not have been helpful.

6. The MH test still gives a statistically significant result, even at the two-sided .01 level. As the estimated OR of .361 is quite meaningful, the ultimate inference is not changed by incorporating the yearly stratification. The problem reminds us of the importance of checking a possible explanation of a disparity by a proper statistical analysis.

4. Introduction to the Analysis of Epidemiologic Data

There are two broad classes of epidemiologic studies, follow-up or prospective studies, in which the subjects are followed for a period of time, or retrospective studies, which look for events or circumstances that occurred prior to the onset of a disease to ascertain whether they may have caused the illness. A typical prospective study is the birth-weight study near Love Canal in which births were observed for several years for an exposed population (Swale area residents) and a comparable nonexposed population (non-Swale). In a retrospective study, the fraction of cases who were exposed to a chemical is compared with the corresponding exposed fraction of a control group, consisting of persons of similar age and prior health status.

In an ideal prospective or cohort study, the same persons are followed for the entire time period. In the real world, however, people move away from the site of the study and sometimes cannot be located. In a study such as the Love Canal one, a substantial amount of moving into or out of the area can lead to wide variations in exposure levels among the Swale area residents. Thus, it is preferable to follow people who left the area to see whether babies born subsequently were affected and to stratify the data by amount of exposure. We then look for a pattern of *dose-response,* i.e., the risk of getting the disease or potential health problem should increase with the degree of exposure.

The methods described in Chapter 5 are directly applicable to prospective studies. When disease status refers to whether or not a subject acquired the disease within a set number of years, the data can be arranged in the usual format of 2×2 tables, as displayed in Table 6.20. The parameter of major interest is the *relative risk,* the ratio of the probability an

TABLE 6.20. Format of Prospective or Cohort Study Data

	Disease Status		Total	Fraction With Disease
	Present	Absent		
Exposed Group	a	b	$n_1 = a + b$	$\dfrac{a}{n_1}$
Control Group	c	d	$n_2 = c + d$	$\dfrac{c}{n_2}$
Total	$a + c$	$b + d$	N	

exposed person gets the disease to that of a nonexposed person. We learned in Chapter 5 that when these probabilities are small, the *relative risk* or *selection* ratio is closely approximated by the *odds ratio,* so we will use the *odds ratio* in our discussion, since the probability of getting a specific disease is usually small. When other factors such as smoking, called confounders in the epidemiologic literature and covariates in the statistical literature, affect one's chance of getting the disease, one can stratify the data by the presence or absence of this factor, as was done for the Love Canal data (Table 5.11).

A disadvantage of the prospective approach is that toxic chemicals often cause or promote only one or a few diseases, each of which is relatively rare. If a disease affects only 1 in 10,000 people a year, and exposure to a substance triples the risk, then only 3 cases are expected to occur among 10,000 exposed subjects. To obtain a modest sample of 12 to 15 cases, one needs to follow 10,000 people for four to five years or 50,000 people for one year. Such a study is very expensive. Moreover, if one desires to follow workers from the time of their first exposure, to avoid the possibility that they were exposed to other chemical hazards in previous jobs, then one may need to wait 20 to 30 years before health problems appear.

The idea underlying a retrospective study is seen by looking at the prospective study data (Table 6.20) at the end of the study when we now know who got the disease and who did not and asking the question, did these two groups have the same rate of exposure to the substance under study or were a higher fraction of the persons who contracted the disease (cases) exposed to the substance.

The format of this retrospective view of the data is given in Table 6.21. Notice that the *fraction* of cases (disease present) who were exposed,

TABLE 6.21. Retrospective Format of Cohort Data

		Exposed	Not Exposed (Control)	Total	Fraction Exposed
Disease	Present (Case)	a	c	$a + c$	$\dfrac{a}{(a + c)}$
Status	Absent (Control)	b	d	$b + d$	$\dfrac{b}{(b + d)}$
Total		$a + b$	$c + d$		

$a/(a + c)$ in Table 6.21 does *not* equal

$$(6.11) \qquad \frac{a}{(a + b)},$$

the fraction of exposed persons who became diseased in the retrospective study (Table 6.20). However, the odds ratio

$$(6.12) \qquad \frac{ad}{bc}$$

of Table 6.21 is the same as the odds ratio in Table 6.20. This means that *The odds a diseased person was exposed relative to the odds a nondiseased person was exposed* (odds ratio from the retrospective view) = *The odds an exposed person gets the disease relative to the odds a nonexposed person* (odds ratio from prospective view).

Let us reconsider the birth-weight data in the Love Canal area (Table 5.5) from this retrospective view. After classifying each newborn baby into the low or normal weight category, we ask his or her parents where they reside, since we desire to compare

(a) the probability (p_1) that a low birth-weight baby came from the Swale area

with

(b) the probability (p_2) that a normal birth-weight baby came from the Swale area.

The data in Table 5.5 organized in the format of Table 6.21 is given in Table 6.22. The odds ratio of the data in Table 6.22 is

$$(6.13) \qquad \frac{21 \times 411}{32 \times 153} = 1.762,$$

identical to that of Table 5.5 given in Section 5.2, illustrating that we obtain the same odds ratio estimate whether we look at the data from the retrospective or prospective view.

TABLE 6.22. Retrospective Format of the Love Canal Data in Table 5.5

	Residence		Total	Fraction Residing in Swale Area
	Swale	Non-swale		
Low birth weight	21	32	54	.396
Normal birth weight	153	411	564	.271
Total	174	443	617	.282

It is now natural to ask whether there is a relationship between the corresponding tests for equality of the proportions in Table 5.5 and 6.22. Let us apply the test statistic (5.6) to the data in Table 6.22. Remember that these probabilities now refer to residence of the families of low- and normal-weight babies. The resulting test statistic is

$$(6.14) \qquad Z = \frac{.396 - .271}{\sqrt{(.282)(.718)\left(\frac{1}{53} + \frac{1}{564}\right)}} = \frac{.125}{.0646} = 1.935,$$

which precisely agrees with our previous result. Again we conclude that the difference in the incidence of low and normal birth-weight babies is not due to chance.

Common sense suggests that if a chemical is toxic then the fraction of exposed people getting the disease should be greater than normal, and a higher fraction of cases (persons with the disease) should have been exposed. What may be surprising is that the odds ratios of the two views of the data and the corresponding tests of equality of the proportions are equivalent.

The major advantage of the retrospective view is that it enables us to carry out studies now instead of having to follow a cohort for a long time. On the other hand, since we have not followed an exposed cohort and a control group to compare the exposure rate of the cases, we need to find a suitable control group. Usually, one first obtains almost all the cases diagnosed in an area or in several hospitals and then obtains a comparable sample of the population in the area to serve as the control group. One tries to find controls with the same age and sex distribution as the cases. Cases and controls answer questionnaires concerning their history of exposure to the substance under study and information on potential confounding factors such as smoking,[71] diet, etc. If both groups are balanced with respect to the confounders, e.g., the proportion of smokers is the same in both the cases and controls, then the data can be analyzed in the form of Table 6.21. Otherwise, the data is stratified and the MH analysis is utilized. Some studies use several types of controls, e.g., the population-based controls described above and persons who visited a hospital emergency room during the same time the case was diagnosed,[72] to insure that the odds ratio is similar in both case-control comparisons. Other studies use a matched design in which we match each case to one or more controls of the same age, sex, race, smoking pattern, etc. We will discuss the analysis of matched studies and problems in selecting a suitable control group in Chapter 11.

We now discuss an actual case control study[73] used in a legal case[74] concerning the environmental impact of the U.S. Navy's proposed expansion of an extremely low frequency (ELF) submarine station, because new information concerning biological effects of ELF electromagnetic radiation had been ignored by the Navy in their environmental impact analysis. Thus, the legal issue in the case dealt with the adequacy of the Navy's study of the possible effect of an expanded station rather than on the scientific issue.

Since major power lines, called high current configurations (HCCs), emit ELF, the study compared the residence (near to or far from a power line or HCC) of children who died of cancer (cases) with those of the control group. All persons dying of cancer before age 19 during the years 1950–1973 who were born in Colorado and lived in the Denver area formed the population of cases. The controls were selected from persons born in Colorado near the birth date of the cases. The ideal control was the next birth certificate (by date) in the files. Several comparisons of the fractions of cases and controls who were exposed to HCC were made because people may move several times during their lifetime and the *amount of exposure to high power is only approximately* measured by their address at birth or death. In Table 6.23 we present a subset of the data for which the birth and death addresses of the cases sex and birth and current address of the controls was identical so that it is reasonable to assume that they lived in the same house their entire life. In order to test whether the fraction of cases (.44) exposed to high current lines was equal to the fraction of controls (.20), we apply the test statistic (5.6), obtaining

$$(6.15) \qquad Z = \frac{\bar{p}_2 - \bar{p}_1}{\sqrt{p_c(1 - p_c)\left(\frac{1}{n_1} + \frac{1}{n_2}\right)}} = \frac{.2373}{.0604} = 3.93,$$

indicating that the two rates are significantly different (approximate *p*-

value = .00001). Moreover, the odds ratio equals

$$\frac{ad}{bc} = \frac{48 \times 102}{61 \times 26} = 3.087,$$

which is quite meaningful.

When interpreting an odds ratio of 3 from a retrospective study, we must remember that it means the relative risk of a child living continuously near high power lines of being a victim of cancer is three times that of an unexposed child. Of course, the probability of childhood cancer is quite small.

In such *observational* studies one must be concerned with possible *confounders*, variables which also *influence* one's chances of getting the disease under study. Because prior studies had suggested that living near heavy traffic might increase one's chances of getting cancer, the data was stratified according to the traffic pattern. This data is reported in Table 6.24 and refers to all cases and controls (not just those with stable addresses).

Cursory examination of the stratified data in Table 6.24 suggests that *exposure* to HCC is associated with getting cancer. The odds ratios for the two subtables are 2.71 and 2.03, respectively, and the corresponding Z scores of the test (5.6) of significance are 2.49 (two-sided p-value = .0128) and 4.53 (p-value less than .00001). The MH test combining both data sets yields a $Z = 5.3$ (p-value $< .0001$) and an estimated overall odds ratio of 2.16. The fact that the odds ratio for the heavy traffic strata is *greater* than the odds ratio for the other location strata *indicates* that living near a heavy traffic pattern (and presumably being exposed to exhaust fumes, etc.) also affect ones chances of getting cancer. Moreover, there may be an interaction or promotion effect of exposure to heavy traffic and exposure to HCC. The advantage of stratifying the data by proximity to heavy

TABLE 6.23. Wiring Configurations at Homes of Cases and Controls with Table Residence: Colorado 1976–1977

	HCC Home	LCC Homes	Total	Fraction Exposed
Cases	48	61	109	.4404
Controls	26	102	128	.2031
Total	74	163	237	.3122

Source: Extracted from Table 3 of Wertheimer, N. and Leeper, E. (1979). Electrical Wiring Configurations and Childhood Cancer. *American Journal of Epidemiology* 109, 273–284.

TABLE 6.24.   Wiring Configurations at Homes of all Cases and Controls Stratified by Traffic Level

	HCC	LCC	All	Fraction Exposed
	Heavy Traffic Areas			
Cases	39	35	74	.527
Control	14	34	48	.298
Total	53	69	132	.434
	Other Areas			
Cases	146	271	417	.350
Control	87	335	424	.210
Total	235	606	841	.279
	Simple Aggregation of the Data Ignoring Traffic Level			
Case	185	306	491	.377
Control	103	359	462	.223
Total	288	665	953	.302

Source: Table 9 of Wertheimer, N. and Leeper, E. (1979), the source of Table 6.23.

traffic is that the odds ratio 2.16 is a more accurate estimate of the effect of exposure to HCC. It should be mentioned that the association found in the study is in dispute. A study[75] in Rhode Island did not find a similar association, while two other case-control studies[76] and several other health studies[77] did.

This particular study illustrates several basic issues in case control studies:

(a) Finding all cases or a representative sample of them.

(b) Finding a suitable (comparable) control group.

(c) Assessing the exposure status (for this study exposure to ELF was not directly measured, proximity to HCC wiring was used).

(d) Accounting for possible confounders or alternative explanation of the observed elevated risk of exposed individuals.

As a general principle it is best to rely on more than one epidemiologic study (of either or both types) before concluding that exposure to a substance is related to getting a particular disease. In chapter 10 we will discuss statistical techniques which are useful in analyzing data counting the number of events, each of which has a small probability of occurring, that happen over a period of time and will apply them to cohort or prospective studies. We close this chapter with a fundamental result,[78] due to Cornfield, concerning the potential effect of a possible confounder that is not considered in a study.

Suppose we compare the disease rate of an exposed group (II) with a control group (I) and find a relative risk of R (e.g., 3). A skeptic asserts that a new factor (confounder) X really caused the observed relative risk and that really there is no association. If the new agent X acts on the disease producing mechanism independently of exposure, then in order for it to fully explain the observed relative risk of R (which is greater than 1) two conditions must hold

(a) The relative risk (RX) associated with factor X must exceed R (the risk found in the study), and

(b) The fraction (F) of persons in the exposed group (II) on whom factor X operates (e.g., who were exposed to X or inherently possess it if it is age, sex) must be *at least R times* the corresponding fraction of the control group.

Suppose we observe a relative risk of 5 when studying the association of a chemical exposure and a worker subsequently getting cancer of the renal pelvis after stratifying the data to account for smoking behavior of the study groups. A trade association challenges this conclusion asserting that a greater proportion of the exposed population drank alcoholic beverages, which caused the disease, rather than the chemical. The previous result implies that in order for this assertion to fully explain the result of the study:

(a) Drinking alcoholic beverages increases one's chance of getting the cancer by 5 (which is not the case), and

(b) The fraction of persons who drink in the exposed group is at least 5 times that of the control group.

Notice that if more than 20% of the control group drinks alcoholic beverages then (b) implies that alcohol consumption *cannot* explain the observed risk of 5, since the fraction of exposed persons who drink would have to exceed 1.0, which is impossible.

Therefore, large and statistically significant values of odds ratios estimated from studies which account for the major potential confounding variables (e.g., age, smoking) usually indicate a real effect of exposure on one's chances of getting the disease studied. The magnitude of the estimated association (relative risk) may change somewhat when other factors which have a small influence are included.

On the other hand, had our hypothetical study on cancer of the renal pelvis estimated a relative risk of 2.0 but failed to adjust for smoking, which has a relative risk of about 7.6 for males and 5.8 for females,[79] then condition (a) is satisfied and it is conceivable that 20–25% of the control group smoked while 45–50% of the exposed group smoked. Thus, the observed relative risk of 2.0 might have been due to the different smoking patterns of the cases and controls rather than exposure to the chemical.

Problems

1.* When we stratified the case control data to account for the effect of living near heavy traffic, we noticed the risk of cancer was higher for persons exposed to HCC and living near heavy traffic than for persons only exposed to HCC, as the odds ratios were 2.72 vs. 2.03. On the other hand, the p-values of the test for the equality of the exposure fractions gave a smaller and hence more significant p-value for the data referring to persons not living near heavy traffic. Is there an error in our calculations? If not, explain our results.

2.* Suppose one used the data in Table 6.24 to estimate the relative risk of exposure to HCC for persons in high traffic areas by computing

$$\frac{\text{fraction of cases exposed}}{\text{fraction of controls exposed}} = \frac{.527}{.298} = 1.77.$$

Why is this computation incorrect?

3. Suppose that probability of a child getting cancer before 19 is 1 in a 1000 and that the relative risk due to living near a high current power line is 2.0.

(a) What other information would you need to decide whether these power lines pose a serious public health problem?

(b) Find some relevant data and/or make some reasonable assumptions to enable you to estimate the number of childhood cancers that might be due to exposure to high current power lines.

(c) Suppose it were possible to reroute the major power lines in the nation which would lead to half as many children being exposed as are today. How many lives would be saved each year? What factors might enter into the ultimate decision?

4.* It is usually possible to suggest an extra factor or variable that might be related to success which was not used in an analysis. Show that Cornfield's observation on how strong and prevalent this factor must be in the exposed group relative to the control group applies in the following EEO settings to support the findings made:

(a) In *Boykin,* plaintiff's showed (Table 6.6) that blacks had half the probability of whites of receiving the better initial assignments after consideration of prior experience. Suppose the defendant asserted that a higher proportion of whites had a college education and this meant they had more promise as an employee. Is it plausible that this omitted factor could explain why whites had *twice* the chance of blacks of receiving the better job?

(b) In *Agarwal,* we noted that minorities had 70% of the odds of promotion as majority employees. How plausible is it that differences in the occupations held by the two groups could explain this difference?

Answers to Selected Problems

1. Remember that statistical significance depends on the sample size. Only 132 subjects in the study lived near high traffic routes, while 841 lived in other locations. Therefore, the statistical fluctuation or standard deviation of the difference between the exposure fractions is much smaller for the second set of data, enabling us to detect a smaller difference as significant.

2. The relative risk, R, we are interested in is the

$$R = \frac{\text{probability an exposed person gets cancer}}{\text{probability an unexposed person gets cancer}},$$

not the ratio of the exposure probabilities. Because the probabilities of getting a particular disease are small, the R is well approximated by the odds ratio and the odds ratio (and only the odds ratio) is the same for the prospective and retrospective organization of the data in a follow-up study.

4. The jobs at issue in *Boykin* were relatively low-skilled blue collar jobs which usually are not sought after by college graduates. Thus, the fraction of applicants who completed college was probably quite small. Moreover, college education is not likely to double one's chances of being a capable employee, especially among persons who had prior job experience. Thus, this explanation lacks credibility.

APPENDIX. **Cornfield's Condition for a New Factor to Explain an Observed Association**

This appendix presents a formal proof of the result of Cornfield (1959), which stated that a new agent or factor, X, which was not considered in a study that found a relative risk, $R_0 > 1$, between persons exposed to the agent studied relative to an unexposed or control group would need to possess a relative risk,

(6A.1) $R_X \geq R_0$

and prevalence ratio, $\theta > R_0$, in order to have caused the observed relative risk, R_0. Recall that the prevalence ratio is the ratio of the fraction, f_2, of persons exposed to the original study agent who were also exposed to agent X to the fraction, f_1, of persons in the control (unexposed) group who were exposed to agent X.

Let p denote the small probability a person not exposed to the study agent or new agent X has of contracting the disease. Now, the $100 f_1\%$ of the control group who were exposed to agent X have probability pR_X of getting the disease, while the remaining fraction $(1 - f_1)$ have probability p.

By the total probability theorem (2.11), the probability a member of the control group contracts the disease is

(6A.2) $P_I = f_1 R_X p + (1 - f_1)p.$

Similarly, the probability a member of group II contracts the disease is

(6A.3) $P_{II} = f_2 R_X p + (1 - f_2)p.$

Notice that in deriving expressions (6A.2) and (6A.3), we assume that the study agent has no effect, so persons who are not exposed to agent X have the natural probability, p, of contracting the disease.

Now the observed relative risk, R_0, is

(6A.4) $R_0 = \dfrac{P_{II}}{P_I} = \dfrac{f_2 p R_X + (1 - f_2)p}{f_1 p R_X + (1 - f_1)p} = \dfrac{R_X f_2 + (1 - f_2)}{R_X f_1 + (1 - f_1)}.$

The *largest* possible value of R_0 occurs when the numerator $R_X f_2 + (1 - f_1)$ is large and the denominator $R_X f_1 + (1 - f_1)$ is small. Since $R_X > 1$, this happens when $f_2 = 1$ and $f_1 = 0$. Thus, the *largest* possible value of R_0 is R_X, i.e., $R_0 \leq R_X$.

Next we need to determine the ratio θ of the fraction, f_2, of persons exposed to the study agent (group II) who were also exposed to agent X to the corresponding fraction, f_1, of persons not exposed to the study agent but were exposed to agent X, that would be required for agent X to have caused the observed relative risk. Letting $f_2 = \theta f_1$, expression (6A.4) becomes

(6A.5) $$R_0 = \frac{\theta f_1 R_X + 1 - \theta f_1}{f_1 R_X + (1 - f_1)} = \frac{\theta f_1 (R_X - 1) + 1}{f_1 (R_X - 1) + 1}.$$

Multiplying both sides of (6A.5) by $[f_1(R_X - 1) + 1]$ yields

$$R_0 f_1 (R_X - 1) + R_0 = \theta f_1 (R_X - 1) + 1$$

or

$$R_0 - 1 = (\theta - R_0)(R_X - 1)f_1,$$

and, finally,

(6A.6) $$\theta = R_0 + \frac{R_0 - 1}{(R_X - 1)f_1}.$$

Since both R_0 and R_X are greater than 1, as we found an association between the original agent studied and the disease, the second term

$$\frac{(R_0 - 1)}{(R_X - 1)f_1}$$

is positive, so the prevalence ratio, θ, must exceed R_0.

Formula (6A.6) then tells us more than the statement of Cornfield, as it enables us to calculate the prevalence of agent X in the original exposed group that is required to explain the observed association from its prevalence, f_1, in the control group.

Note that in formula (6A.6) the prevalence ratio, θ, decreases as R_X increases. This makes sense because the greater the association between the new factor X and the disease, the less prevalent it needs to be in order to cause the observed disease rate.

Problems

1. Show that in order for a new agent to explain an observed relative risk, R_0, its prevalence ratio lies between R_0 and $R_0 + 1/f_1$.

2. Show that if $R_0 = 3$ and f_1 is at least 1/3, then *no* new agent X can explain the observed association.
Hint: Show that f_2 would have to exceed 1.0, which is impossible.

NOTES

1. *Teamsters v. United States* 431 U.S. 324, 14 FEP Cases 1514 at 1519 (1977).
2. The first major disparate impact case was *Griggs v. Duke Power Co.* 401 U.S. 424 (1971). 3 FEP Cases 175, which analyzed the effect of requiring a high school diploma for a semi-skilled job.
3. The four-fifths rule was formulated as an EEOC guideline and adopted for general government use in Uniform Guidelines on Employer Selection Procedures. *Federal Register* (1978) **13**, 38315 at 38309.
4. *supra*, footnote 1 at 335.
5. *supra*, footnote 1 at 335, footnote 15.
6. *supra*, footnote 1 at footnote 20, 339–340.
7. *Rivera v. City of Wichita Falls* 665 F.2d 531, 27 FEP Cases 531 (5th Cir. 1982).
8. 411 U.S. 792, 5 FEP Cases 965 (1973).
9. 35 FEP Cases 1 (1984).
10. 101 S.Ct. 1089 (1981). 25 FEP Cases 113.
11. See *United Airlines v. Evans* 431 U.S. 553 (1977) for a discussion of this issue.
12. See Section 3.6 and the discussion of the power study, Table 4.7 of the *Jones* case in Section 4.5.
13. 559 F.Supp. 306 (S.D.N.Y. 1983).
14. 510 F.2d 307 at 313n.4 (6th Cir. 1975).
15. 28 FEP Cases 574 (D.D.C. 1980) subsequently *reversed* on nonstatistical grounds. 675 F.2d 398, 28 FEP Cases 833 (D.C. Cir. 1982).
16. The percentages don't add to 100, as some employees were Hispanic.
17. The exact probability, obtained from the binomial distribution rather than the normal approximation, is 8.64×10^{-11}, which is less than one in a billion. Of course, this calculation depends critically on the value of p. Had the value .835 for p been correct, the data would have been strong evidence supporting the plaintiff's claim.
18. 33 FEP Cases 1141 (E.D. Tenn. 1983).
19. This statistical error has also been made by defendants, e.g., in *Worthy v. U.S. Steel Corporation*, 616 F.2d 698 (3d. Cir. 1980) 22 FEP Cases 102, a case involving a demotion of an employee for several safety violations. The defendant submitted evidence that two white employees were similarly disciplined. However, other whites were not. The appellate opinion remanded the case noting that "the district court was obliged to conduct a thorough inquiry into the treatment of comparable employees."
20. For example, assume that each of 10 years of hiring data is analyzed separately, that the employer is hiring fairly and each year's applicants form a new independent sample of the pool of eligibles. By chance, there is probability .05 that in any year significantly fewer minority members are hired. The probability that statistical significance will not be found in one year is .95, but the probability that statistical significance will *not* occur in all 10 years is $(.95)^{10} = .5987$, implying that that the probability is .401 (1.0 minus .599) that in at least one year a fair employer would be found to have a statistical imbalance.
21. 483 F.Supp. 45 (D.C. Tex. 1979), rehearing denied 487 F.Supp. 389 (D.C. Tex. 1980).
22. Here women were required to be taller than 5'6". This was contrasted to the situation in *Dothard v. Rawlinson*, 433 U.S. 321, 97 S.Ct. 2720 (1977), where all persons had to meet the same height requirement which had a disparate impact in females.
23. The use of demographic method without adjusting or refining it for relevant factors has increasingly been rejected by courts. For further discussion and references to the literature on availability see the references given in Chapter 4.
24. Had the numbers of applicants been available, the hypergeometric model would have been more accurate, since hires are made from a finite set of applicants. Since the applicants

differ in each year, perhaps the MH procedure (Section 5.6) combining hiring data in all years would be the most accurate method. If the female fraction of applicants did not vary widely during the period and only a small fraction of all applicants are hired, then the binomial model is a good approximation to the hypergeometric.

25. 19 FEP Cases 503 (N.D. Cal. 1977), *affirmed* 644 F.2d 803, 25 FEP Cases 1565 (9th Cir. 1981).

26. While the sensitivity of statistical analysis to the change of one or two observations is interesting, it really focuses our attention on the importance of considering the *p*-value as a sliding scale. We use the instant case to remind the reader of this point (see Problem 3 of Section 5.4).

27. The determination of the magnitude of difference that is meaningful depends on the area of application. The four-fifths rule is one such determination.

28. This level was chosen to bring the two error rates α and β close to one another.

29. 570 F.2d 1264, 17 FEP Cases 281 (5th Cir. 1978).

30. Implicit here is an interesting legal issue, namely, what is expected of plaintiffs who must rely on data kept by the defendant. In the case under discussion, the plaintiffs could have stratified the data by geography so that they failed to utilize all the information available to them.

31. 401 U.S. 424, 91 S.Ct. 849, 3 FEP Cases 175 (1971).

32. U.S. Bureau of the Census, *U.S. Census of Population: 1960*, Vol. 1, Part 35, Table 47.

33. Decision of the EEOC, *Commerce Clearing House Employment Practice Guide* 17304.53 (Dec. 2, 1966).

34. 433 U.S. 321, 97 S.Ct. 2720, 15 FEP Cases 10 (1977).

35. 102 S.Ct. 2525, 29 FEP Cases 1 (1982).

36. *Civil Rights Division v. Amphitheater District*, Arizona Court of Appeals, 33 FEP Cases 1135 (1983).

37. 706 F.2d 1384, 32 FEP Cases 25 (5th Cir. 1983).

38. The original complaint also included a claim of discriminatory hiring practices which was not pursued on appeal.

39. Recall that the standard deviation of the hypergeometric random variable is less than that of the binomial variable with the same mean (Section 2.7). Hence, the test statistic which measures the difference from expected in terms of standard deviation units is slightly lower in magnitude, as the difference is being divided by an overestimate of the true hypergeometric standard deviation.

40. In statistically close cases, the failure to use the proper statistical model can make a difference. See the discussion of *EEOC v. Federal Reserve Bank of Richmond*, 698 F.2d 633, 30 FEP Cases 1137 (4th Cir. 1983) in Baldus and Cole (1984 Supplement at 109 and Gastwirth, J. L. (1984), cited in the references to Chapter 5).

41. *Trout v. Lehman*, 704 F.2d 1094 at 1101, 34 FEP Cases 286 (D.C. Cir. 1983), vacated on other grounds, 104 S.Ct. 1404, 34 FEP Cases 76 (1984).

42. See *Davis v. Califano*, 613 F.2d 957 at 964 (D.C. Cir. 1980) and *DeMedina v. Reinhardt*, 686 F.2d 997 at 1003, 29 FEP Cases 1084 (D.C. Cir. 1982).

43. 738 F.2d 1249, 34 FEP Cases 31 (D.C. Cir. 1984).

44. Deleting pre-act hires had a substantial effect in *EEOC v. United Virginia Bank*, 615 F.2d 147, 21 FEP Cases 1405 (4th Cir. 1980).

45. *Hogan v. Pierce*, 31 FEP Cases 115 (D.C. D.C. 1983).

46. In rebuttal, plaintiffs also submitted a calculation of the exact probability, which was .003. The exact calculation is more complex because many hypergeometric data sets are being considered and the normal approximation used in the MH test is usually sufficiently accurate for most purposes. In borderline situations, the exact calculation needs to be made.

Clearly, the judge was primarily concerned with the p-value being sufficiently small to conclude statistical significance.

47.   This area of statistics is called "survival analysis" and the first use of the MH method in this context appears in Mantel, N. (1966). Evaluation of Survival Data and Two New Rank Order Statistics Arising in its Consideration. *Cancer Chemotherapy Report* **50,** 163–170.

48.   At the trial the judge made the point that a window around the time of the charge would be more helpful.

49.   Since plaintiffs have the ultimate burden of persuasion, it is more common for their analyses to be less than convincing so that the defendant can raise doubts about the plaintiff's evidence. Hence, it is easier to illustrate the advantage of more complex statistical analyses on cases in which plaintiffs did not use them.

50.   751 F.2d 662, 36 FEP Cases 834 (4th Cir. 1984).

51.   Since the Supreme Court used a two-tailed test in Castenada and Hazelwood, some lower courts require that degree of significance. Other courts have accepted one-tailed tests. As we have noted, the p-value should be regarded as a sliding scale, with lower p-values implying greater evidence of a disparity or difference.

52.   Sometimes one or two strata may show a statistically significant difference opposite to the remaining strata. Then one should examine the data to determine whether some special circumstances might be affecting the strata that do not conform to the general pattern. We shall see an instance of this in our discussion of the *Capaci* case, when the data for the year just before trial displays a different pattern than the years before and right after the charge.

53.   In *Agarwal*, the odds ratio was just under .7. In *Reynolds*, the odds ratio was .62.

54.   In the MH analysis strata consisting solely of members of one group will always have the observed data equal its expected value, so the difference is 0 and its variance is also 0. Hence, these strata can be deleted.

55.   538 F.Supp. 833 (1982), *affirmed* 737 F.2d 1299 (4th Cir. 1984).

56.   The opinion does not mention power or statistical power.

57.   Since the court is concerned with disparities on the low side, it really requires a one-sided p-value of .025 in each category. As the hiring process (under the null hypothesis of random selection from the appropriate pool) in each category is independent of hiring in other categories, we use the multiplication rule (2.3) to obtain (6.9).

58.   In problem 4 of Chapter 5 we learned to be suspicious of changing the data, especially when the change is made in only one direction and the power of the test is not considered. Notice that blacks were expected to obtain 28.9 para-professional jobs but received only 16. By allowing a shift of 8, the expert, and the judge, were allowing a shift of over one fourth of the expected number of positions. While it may be reasonable to examine the effect of changing one or two positions to explore the sensitivity of the p-value (significance level) and the measures of disparity to small errors in the data, this large shift of eight hires does not have a sound statistical basis.

59.   The absolute impact is the difference between the observed and expected number of hires or promotions. It depends on the black fraction of eligibles and the number of selections made.

60.   A nonstatistical aspect of the discussion of the protective service issue in the opinion it is the court's acceptance of the defendant's assertion of a recruitment problem in the sheriff's department. In Table 6.11, the protective service category had the highest fraction of black applicants. The defendant's procedure of eliminating applicants with poor work records, background checks, etc. seems to have been accepted without an analysis of data concerning the effect of these criteria on black applicants. Of course, the record of the case may have established that these criteria are necessary for an effective sheriff's office.

61. Recall that the smaller the p-value, the stronger the evidence contradicts the null hypothesis.

62. In the opinion, the stratification by job category was ignored as it states, the "evidence indicates that blacks constituted 31.72% of all applicants and were promoted in 31.77% of the cases, producing a black promotion rate of 21.1% and a white promotion rate of 21.06%." We note that the odds ratio of this simply aggregated data is virtually 1.0, while in the properly analyzed data the OR was about .7. The reason that the simple aggregation or pooling of the data into a single 2 × 2 table led to an incorrect analysis of the data in Table 6.13 is that proportionately more blacks were employed in job categories 6 and 7, which had higher than average promotion rates. This phenomenon also occurred in the *Agarwal v. McKee* data discussed in Section 5.6.

63. 525 F.Supp 317, 30 FEP Cases 1541 (E.D. La. 1981) *affirmed in part, reversed in part,* 711 F.2d 647, 32 FEP 961 (5th Cir. 1983).

64. In the actual case the chi-square test, which is based on the square of the test statistic (5.6), was used. Both procedures yield equivalent results, however, (5.6) is more convenient for testing one-sided alternatives.

65. Indeed, plaintiffs showed that even if the largest availability fraction in Table 4.6 was used, the probability of females obtaining 11 or more of the 12 hires was less than .01. This means that if we tested the null hypothesis of fair hiring against the alternative that men received less than equal treatment, we would reject the null hypothesis and infer that in 1978 males received significantly fewer jobs than they were expected to. The author sometimes refers to such sudden changes as the "Something Happened on the Way to the Courtroom" phenomena.

66. 525 F.Supp. 217, footnote 11 at 325.

67. 711 F.2d 647 at 654–655.

68. We choose this period by simply looking at the data in Table 6.15. Females did not receive even half the share (19.2%) of hires that they formed of the post-charge applicant pool.

69. See Chapter 4 of Baldus and Cole (1980) for a related discussion.

70. Since several statistically close cases, such as the promotion data in *Agarwal* and *Allen,* had ORs of about .7, this seems to be a borderline odds ratio. To be sure that an employer who discriminated in the past is now hiring fairly, one might use a higher OR, say .75 or .80, to ensure that the policy truly has changed.

71. The determination of other important factors that affect the disease process belongs to medical and epidemiologic experts. We use smoking and diet, as they are known to affect one's probability of getting lung cancer and/or heart disease. They are called confounding factors, because the failure to consider them can lead to a seriously biased estimate of the effect of the agent under study. For example, if in a lung cancer study the exposed population contained a higher fraction of smokers, which was ignored in the analysis, the estimated relative risk of exposure to the agent would include the effect of the extra fraction of smokers and would be an overestimate of the risk of the agent. Conversely, if the control group had a higher fraction of smokers, the relative risk of the agent under investigation would be underestimated.

72. Since cases and their relatives are often under more stress than controls and this may affect their ability to accurately recall past events, controls who have recently had a stressful situation may be a useful comparison group.

73. Wertheimer, N. and Leeper, E. (1979) Electrical Wiring Configurations and Childhood Cancer. *American Journal of Epidemiology* **109**, 273–284.

74. *Wisconsin v. Weinberger,* 578 F.Supp. 1327 (W.D. Wisc. 1978), *reversed* on other grounds 745 F.2d 412 (7th Cir. 1984).

75. Fulton, J. P., Cobb, S., Preble, L., Leone, L., and Forman, E. (1980). Electrical

Wiring Configurations and Childhood Leukemia in Rhode Island. *American Journal of Epidemiology* **111**, 292–296.

76.   See Wertheimer, N. and Leeper, E. (1982). Adult Cancer Related to Electrical Wires Near the Home. *International Journal of Epidemiology* **11**, 345–355; Tomenius, L., Hellstrom, L. and Enander, B. (1982). Electrical Construction and 50 HZ Magnetic Fields at the Dwelling of Tumour Cases (0–18 years of age) in the County of Stockholm. In *Proceedings of International Symposium on Occupational Health and Safety Mining and Tunnelling* (Prague).

77.   e.g., Colemen, M., Bell, J. and Skeet, R. (1983). "Leukemia Incidence in Electrical Workers." *Lancet* (1) **8331**, 982–983.

78.   Cornfield, J., Haenszel, W., Hammond, E. C., Lillienfeld, A. M., Shimkin, M. B. and Wynder, E. L. (1959). Smoking and Lung Cancer: Recent Evidence and a Discussion of Some Questions. *Journal of the National Cancer Institute* **22**, 173–203. The result is in an appendix to the paper and is due to Cornfield.

79.   McLauglin, J. K., Blot, W. J., Mandel, J. S., Schuman, L. M., Mehl, E. S. and Frauemeni, J. F., Jr. (1983). Etiology of Cancer of the Renal Pelvis. *Journal of the National Cancer Institute* **71**, 287–291.

REFERENCES

In addition to the references given in Chapters 4 and 5 concerning the statistical methods used in discrimination cases, we mention some useful texts is epidemiology.

BRESLOW, N. E. AND DAY, N. E. (1980). *Statistical Methods in Cancer Research, Volume 1. The Analysis of Case-Control Studies.* IARC Scientific Publication No. 32, Lyon, France, International Agency for Research on Cancer. (The major reference for the statistical methods used to analyze case-control studies.)

KLEINBAUM, D. G., KUPPER, L. L. AND MORGENSTERN, H. (1982). *Epidemiologic Research: Principles and Quantitative Methods.* Belmont, Ca.: Wadsworth.

LILIENFELD, A. M. AND LILIENFELD, D. B. (1980). *Foundations of Epidemiology,* 2nd ed. New York, Oxford University Press.

MACMAHON, B. AND PUGH, T. F. (1970). *Epidemiology: Principles and Methods.* Boston: Little Brown. (The above two books are probably the most cited texts in epidemiology).

MAUSNER, J. S., BALIN, A. K. AND KRAMER, S. (1984). *Epidemiology: An Introductory Text,* 2nd ed. Philadelphia: W. B. Saunders.

MICHAEL, M., BOYCE, W. T., AND WILCOX, A. J. (1984). *Biomedical Bestiary: An Epidemiologic Guide to Flaws and Fallacies in the Medical Literature.* Boston: Little Brown. (A readable discussion of the types of errors that can occur in epidemiologic studies.)

SCHLESSELMAN, J. J. (1982). *Case Control Studies,* New York: Oxford University Press. (The most readable textbook dealing with all aspects of case control studies.)

Chapter 7

Comparing Two Distributions

1. Introduction

Many applications of statistics involve comparing two sets of data to determine if they can be considered to be from the same population or whether they differ in a systematic manner, e.g., are the numbers in one set significantly larger than those in the second set? For example, the Equal Pay Act requires that females and males performing the same tasks receive equal pay. Thus, we need to determine whether the wages received by employees of both sexes are the same, or do persons of one sex receive less than the other. Similarly, in medicine, one studies whether one treatment is superior to another (e.g., does a new drug cure patients faster than the currently used drug).

In this chapter we will discuss two procedures, the Wilcoxon-Mann Whitney test and the t-test, and demonstrate their use in a variety of situations. After describing both procedures, we give several illustrations of their actual use. We then interpret the results of the tests when the data analyzed consist of both entire populations or are random samples from them. Section 5 discusses procedures for combining the results of several Wilcoxon tests. This is important when it is necessary to stratify (subdivide) a population into similar subgroups (e.g., employees by occupation or persons exposed to a possible toxic chemical by duration of exposure), but an overall test for a possible difference between the groups being compared is required. The final section discusses some of the limitations and potential misuses of combination methods.

2. The Tests and Their Interpretation on Complete Population Data: The Randomization Model

Let us consider the problem of comparing wages received by male and female employees performing the same job. Suppose that males receive salaries x_1, x_2, ..., x_m and females receive salaries: y_1, ..., y_n. For concreteness will analyze the following data:

Male salaries: 5100, 8700, 8750, 10,900, 11,100, 11,300, 12,000, 12,500

Female salaries: 4200, 4800, 5200, 6600, 7000, 8900.

If the same wage setting mechanism was used to determine all the salaries, the wages in both data sets would look as though they were drawn from a common population, while if the persons of one sex were typically better paid, they would have salaries coming from a distribution with a larger mean or median than the other sex. In Figure 7.1 we draw the wage distributions under the alternative (H_a) hypotheses. Notice that under the alternative hypothesis (H_a), one distribution is *shifted* to the *right* of the other by an amount Δ. Under the null hypothesis (H_0), $\Delta = 0$ and both curves are the same.

One way of comparing the male and female salaries is to compare each

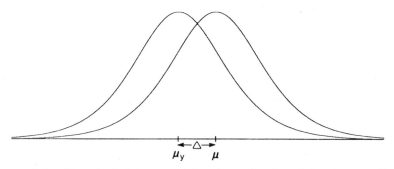

FIGURE 7.1.   Hypothetical frequency functions of male and female wage distributions which are symmetric about their respective means μ_x and μ_y, where $\mu_x - \mu_y = \Delta$.

female salary with every male salary and count the number of times the female earns more than the male. Notice that each female is compared with m males. Since there are n females, we have a total of mn comparisons, and we can calculate the *proportion* $(\overline{P})$ of them in which the female earns more than the male. Intuitively, if male and female employees had the same chance of receiving each salary (i.e., the distribution of qualifications and underlying ability is the same for males and females), one would expect about *half* of the salary comparisons to show the female earning more than the male and about half the opposite. Conversely, if females typically earned less than males, this proportion would be less than 1/2. Since proportions correspond to probabilities, we are using the *probability* (P) a female earns more than a male to indicate whether the two sexes have the same salary distribution (P near 1/2) or different ones. This probability measure is the basis of the Wilcoxon test and can be used to compare any two sets of numbers such as length of time to promotion, grade level of initial job assignment or test scores of two groups.

Since the most commonly used measure of the typical or central value of a data set is the mean, another natural measure of the difference between the two sets of wages is $\overline{y} - \overline{x}$ the difference between the means of the two groups. This measure is the basis of the t-test.

So far we have just described two measures summarizing how data from two populations may differ, and we need a criteria to assess whether an observed difference is significant. We do this by imposing a probability model upon the data by assuming that the $m + n$ salaries are assigned at random to the employees, i.e., we suppose that each employee has the same chance of receiving each possible salary. By introducing this *random* assignment model we introduce possible variability in the two measures $\overline{y} - \overline{x}$ and $\overline{P}$, i.e., each of them is now a random variable. If the null hypothesis that the salary generating mechanism for employees of both sexes is the same is true, then $\overline{y} - \overline{x}$ should have a sampling distribution centered about 0, its expected value (under random assignment each group mean is expected to equal the average of all $m + n$ salaries). Similarly, the expected value of $\overline{P}$ will be 1/2.

Another way of describing the randomization model is analogous to Fisher's exact test discussed in Chapter 5. Suppose that all $m + n$ (8 + 6 = 14 in our example) salaries are put into an urn and employees select their salaries at random (blindfolded). Then each employee has the same chance of obtaining any salary. Although we know that employees do not draw their salaries out of an urn (or hat), the underlying idea of the randomization model is that under the null hypothesis membership in either group (males or females) should have no effect on the wage received. Under this assumption the sex of the employee is like a label which should not affect the outcome. Thus, one is suspicious of the validity of the null hypothesis when a reasonable measure such as $\bar{P}$ or $\bar{y} - \bar{x}$ differs significantly from its expected value, because an unusually large fraction of one group receive low salaries.

When comparing data for two populations, e.g., salaries for males and females, and a statistically significant difference is found, this does not *necessarily* imply that group membership is the cause of the observed difference. Perhaps another factor such as seniority or educational background is the cause and the members of group II, say, have lower seniority or educational levels. One way of exploring the effect of related factors is to stratify (subdivide) the total data set into subgroups of similar characteristics, e.g., educational level and seniority status, calculate the Wilcoxon test for each subgroup and then combine the results into an overall summary measure as described in Section 5. Another approach to assessing the influence of other factors on an observed difference between two groups is regression analysis discussed in Chapter 8. For our present purposes we assume that the 14 salaries in our example are for employees in the same occupation with similar lengths of service.

In order to develop statistical tests based on $\bar{P}$ and $\bar{y} - \bar{x}$, we need to determine their probability distributions under the randomization model. We then can decide whether the measure calculated on the actual data differs significantly from its expected value. Since the exact distributions of both test statistics—the Wilcoxon, which is based on $\bar{P}$, and the t-test based on $\bar{y} - \bar{x}$—are complicated, we will describe the usual normal approximations. This has the advantage of expressing both statistical tests in the familiar form,

$$(7.1) \qquad Z = \frac{\text{observed} - \text{expected}}{\text{standard error}},$$

where the standard error is the standard deviation of the sampling distribution of the statistic. Indeed, sometimes we will use the term "standard deviation" for "standard error."

a. The Wilcoxon test

Formally, we define the statistic, $\bar{P}$, in terms of the *mn* comparison variables:

$$W_{ij} = \begin{cases} 1 & \text{if } x_i < y_j \\ \dfrac{1}{2} & \text{if } x_i = y_j \\ 0 & \text{if } x_i > y_j \end{cases}$$

i.e., w_{ij} is 1 when the jth y is greater than the ith x, 1/2 when they are equal, and zero otherwise. Notice that i ranges from l to m while j ranges from l to n. The proportion of the mn comparisons for which the y member is $\geq$ the x member is

(7.2) $$\bar{P} = \frac{1}{mn} \sum w_{ij}$$

and is an estimate of the parameter, P, the probability a member of the y group receives a salary at least as large as a member of the x group.

Under the null hypothesis, $P = 1/2$ and $E(\bar{P}) = 1/2$. When all the salaries are distinct so that no ties ($w_{ij} = 1/2$) are possible, the *variance* of $\bar{P}$ is given by

(7.3) $$V(\bar{P}) = \frac{(m + n + 1)}{12mn},$$

and the null distribution of $\bar{P}$ is well approximated by the normal distribution with mean 1/2 and standard deviation $\sqrt{V(\bar{P})}$. Formula (7.3) is still accurate when a small proportion of the mn comparisons are ties. Otherwise, one should consult the book by Lehmann (1975) cited at the end of the chapter for the correct formula. We now illustrate the procedure on the wage data given earlier. First, arrange all the data in increasing order, as in Table 7.1.

For each y, the number of comparisons in which it is larger than the x is given in the far column on the right. This number can range from 0 to m (the total number of x's), as each y *could* be smaller than all the x's (yielding a value of 0) or larger than all the x's (yielding the value m). The reader should verify the counts in the column. For our data, the total 6 is the number of the $mn = 48$ ($m = 8$, $n = 6$) comparisons in which the y was larger than the x. Thus,

(7.4) $$\bar{P} = \frac{6}{48} = \frac{1}{8}.$$

To test whether a value of $\bar{P}$ this far away from its expected value of 1/2 could have occurred by chance, we perform the two-sided test using the

TABLE 7.1. Illustrative Wage Data Organized in Increasing Order by Sex and the Calculation of the Wilcoxon Measure $\bar{P}$

X (Male Wages)	Y (Female Wages)	# times $y > x$
	4200	0
	4800	0
5100		
	5200	1
	6600	1
	7000	1
8700		
8750		
	8900	3
10,900		
11,100		
11,300		
12,000		
12,500		
	Total	6

$$\bar{P} = \frac{6}{48} = .125.$$

normal approximation. As

$$(7.5) \qquad V(\bar{P}) = \frac{(m + n + 1)}{12mn} = \frac{(8 + 6 + 1)}{12 \times 48} = \frac{15}{576} = .026,$$

the standard error of $\bar{P}$ $\sqrt{V(\bar{P})} = \sqrt{.026} = .1613$. Thus, the normal form (7.1) of the Wilcoxon test becomes

$$Z = \frac{\text{observed } \bar{P} - \text{expected value } \left(\frac{1}{2}\right)}{\text{standard error of } \bar{P}} = \frac{\frac{1}{8} - \frac{1}{2}}{.1613} = \frac{-.375}{.1613} = -2.32.$$
(7.6)

From Table A, a Z-value of -2.32 corresponds to a two-sided p-value of .0222. Thus, the probability of observing as large a deviation from the expected value of 1/2, in either direction, is about 2%. Since the actual significance level (2%) is quite small and the estimated probability that a woman earned more than a man is 1/8 instead of 1/2, the data indicate both a meaningful and a statistically significant difference. This example also illustrates the importance of calculating the actual significance level of the data (the p-value) instead of simply using the fixed levels of .01 and .05.

Comments. (1) In the above analysis we used the normal approximation, although our sample sizes were rather small. There are tables of the distribution of the statistic P or an equivalent version based on the sum of the ranks of the y's in the combined ordered array presented in Table 7.1. Although the normal approximation is usually accurate, in important applications (with small sample sizes) these exact tables should be used, especially when the p-value of the observed data is close to a predetermined significance level which is of special relevance (e.g., .05 or .01).

(2) We noted that a value of $\overline{P}$ of 1/8 was meaningfully different from the value 1/2 expected under the assumption that both sets of numbers come from a common population. There is no simple rule for deciding what difference from expected is meaningful. The same is true for the measure $\bar{y} - \bar{x}$, although it probably would be difficult to justify a $\bar{y}$ more than 5% or 10% less than $\bar{x}$. The determination of a meaningful difference or disparity depends primarily on the subject matter area but also on the quality of the data.[1]

b.   The t-test based on $\bar{y} - \bar{x}$

In order to develop a test of equality of two group means under the randomization model, we imagine that the y's are a random sample from the total population of $m + n$ values. Notice that the mean of the total population is

$$(7.7) \qquad \mu = \frac{\Sigma y_i + \Sigma x_i}{m + n} = \frac{\bar{n}y + m\bar{x}}{m + n} = \frac{m}{m + n}\,(\bar{x}) + \frac{n}{m + n}\,(\bar{y}),$$

and the variance σ^2 is

$$(7.8) \qquad \sigma^2 = \frac{\Sigma(x_i - \mu)^2 + \Sigma(y_i - \mu)^2}{m + n - 1}.$$

Assuming that the y's are a random sample of size n from the $m + n$ values, $\bar{y}$ is a random variable with expected value μ and variance

$$(7.9) \qquad \frac{\sigma^2}{n} \cdot \frac{N - n}{N - 1},$$

where $N = m + n$. This formula differs from the variance of a sample mean taken from a large population, i.e., σ^2/n, by the factor $(N - n)/$

$(N - 1)$. This is the same factor that appeared in our discussion of the variance (2.20) of the hypergeometric variable. It is a correction term adjusting for the fact that the random selections from a small finite population are not completely independent of one another. Fortunately, the sampling distribution of $\bar{y}$ can still be approximated by the normal distribution provided we use the correct standard deviation. Thus, the statistic

$$(7.10) \quad Z = \frac{\text{observed mean } (\bar{y}) - \text{expected } (\mu)}{\text{standard deviation}} = \frac{\bar{y} - \mu}{\sqrt{\dfrac{\sigma^2}{n} \cdot \dfrac{N - n}{N - 1}}}$$

has a standard normal distribution.

In our situation notice that

$$\bar{y} - \mu = \bar{y} - \left[\frac{m}{m + n} \bar{x} + \frac{n}{m + n} \bar{y} \right] = \frac{m}{m + n} (\bar{y} - \bar{x}),$$

so that (7.10) becomes

$$(7.11) \qquad \frac{\dfrac{m}{m + n} (\bar{y} - \bar{x})}{\sigma \sqrt{\dfrac{1}{n} \cdot \dfrac{m}{m + n - 1}}} .$$

Since $m + n - 1$ essentially equals $m + n$ if we replace $m + n - 1$ by $m + n$ in the last expression in (7.11), and cancel and collect terms, we obtain the t-statistic

$$(7.12) \qquad \frac{(\bar{y} - \bar{x}) \sqrt{\dfrac{mn}{m + n}}}{\sigma} = \frac{\bar{y} - \bar{x}}{\sigma \sqrt{\dfrac{1}{n} + \dfrac{1}{m}}} = t,$$

as $1/n + 1/m = m + n/mn$. The formula on the right of (7.2) is referred to as the t form. It is essentially equal to the normal form in the present application, but later we will have to estimate σ^2, because data for the entire population will not be available.

For the data in Table 7.1, $\bar{y} = 6116.6$, $\bar{x} = 10043.75$ and σ is calculated using formula (7.8) and equals 2630.62. Hence, the test statistic (7.12) is

$$(7.13) \qquad t = \frac{6116.66 - 10043.75}{\sigma \sqrt{\dfrac{1}{6} + \dfrac{1}{8}}} = \frac{-3927.09}{(2630.62) \sqrt{.1666 + .1250}}$$

$$= \frac{-3927.09}{(2630.62)(.540)} = -2.76,$$

a result which is significant at the .01 level (one sided). The one-sided prob-value is .003, and if a two-sided test was appropriate, the two-sided prob-value of .006 still implies that the difference is significant at the .01 level.

Although the t-test yielded a slightly more significant result than the Wilcoxon on the wage data, the results are essentially consistent since both p-values are quite small. The advantage of using tests based on the randomization model is that a statistically significant result implies that the observed disparity is very unlikely to have occurred by chance.[2] Thus, some other factor is needed to explain the observed salary difference between the sexes observed in the data.

Problems

1. Suppose the data on male and female wages given in the text were for persons employed by a firm in the same occupation. What legitimate (nondiscriminatory) factors might explain the difference we observed?

2. Suppose that the women had less previous experience than the men and that this experience should be worth $500 a year. How could you modify the procedures used in the text to test the null hypothesis that the typical female employees was paid $500 *less* than the typical male, indicating fair treatment, against the alternative that they were paid less than comparably qualified men. Carry out the test on the data in the text. Why might this null hypothesis be of interest?

3. Use the Wilcoxon and t-tests to determine whether the following hourly wage data sets can be considered as having the same distribution:

   Blacks: $3.58, 3.60, 3.63, 3.79, 4.16, 4.61

   Whites: $3.48, 3.79, 4.16, 4.36, 4.46, 4.61, 4.91, 4.97

Answers to Selected Problems

1. Seniority with the current employer is the easiest factor to justify. Other factors would be prior experience, highest degree of formal education or amount of special training classes taken while on the job.

2. The easiest way would be to subtract $500 from each male salary (or add $500 to each female salary) and test the adjusted data as before. This type of hypothesis would be of interest if a contract called for set salary

increments on the basis of seniority or courses completed in job-related areas in addition to negotiated or assigned pay raises.

3. Applications to Data from Actual Cases

In this section we illustrate the use of the Wilcoxon test in promotion and assignment cases. The first application will be to compare the length of time male and female employees stay in a job position before being promoted. The second will be to examine the status of female employees relative to males when the positions are in a graded system. This analysis can be used to evaluate the fairness of initial assignment policy or the current assignments.

a. The time to promotion issue: Capaci v. Katz and Besthoff, Inc.[3]

In this case, a female plaintiff alleged that she had been denied a promotion on account of her sex. In a deposition, the defendant's expert presented an analysis of the time taken between the initial hire and a promotion to the position of chief pharmacist for all pharmacists promoted in the period from the date of the Civil Right Act *to the end* of the year in which the charge was filed and claimed that there was *no* difference between the two distributions. The plaintiff's expert analyzed the following data, which is limited to all promotions *up to the time* of the charge (January, 1973).

Females: 453, 229

Males: 49, 192, 14, 12, 14, 5, 37, 7, 69, *483*, 34, 18,
            25, 125, 34, 22, 25, 64, 14, 23, 21, 67, 47, 24

Notice that there were two females and 24 males promoted to the position, so we can make $2 \times 24 = 48$ comparisons. The estimate ($\bar{P}$) of the probability, P, a female took *less* time than a male to be promoted is $2/48 = 1/24$, as only *one* male took longer than both females. This probability is far less than its expected value (1/2), and we need to check for statistical significance. To use the normal form of the Wilcoxon statistic (7.6) we first calculate the variance of $\bar{P}$ using formula (7.5), i.e.,

$$V(\bar{P}) = \frac{m + n + 1}{12mn} = \frac{27}{12(48)} = \frac{9}{4(48)} = .047.$$

Thus, the standard deviation of $\overline{P}$ is $\sqrt{.047} = .217$, so (7.6) becomes

$$(7.14) \qquad Z = \frac{\frac{1}{24} - \frac{1}{2}}{.217} = -2.11.$$

From tables of the normal curve (Table A) we see that a Z-value of -2.11 means that the one-sided p-value of this data is .0174. Hence, we would reject the null hypothesis that males and females have the same distribution of time to promotion if the usual .05 significance level[4] is adopted. Since the normal approximation which is used in obtaining the p-value of expression (7.14) is a large-sample result, and our sample size is under 30, at the trial the exact one-sided p-value .0123 obtained from available tables[5] was used.

This data set is of statistical interest because (1) it shows that the normal approximation for the Wilcoxon test statistic is reasonably accurate in small samples, however, the exact calculation of the p-value is desirable for small samples, especially when the p-value obtained from the normal approximation is close to .05 or .01. (2) It shows that the choice of the significance level can be quite critical in small samples. Indeed, if the three standard deviation criteria had been adopted by the court, it could *never* have been satisfied, even if both females had taken longer than *all* the males. The three-standard deviation criteria would have required a difference of $3(.217) = .65$ from .5, which is impossible as the maximum deviation of a probability from 1/2 is 1/2 (as all probabilities are between 0 and 1). (3) Although the total sample size (26) in the Capaci case was greater than the example in the text (14), the number of possible comparisons (mn) was the same (48), and the standard deviation of $\overline{P}$ was larger for the Capaci case data than for the data in the text. This apparent inconsistency is due to the fact the sampling variability of a statistic used to compare two data sets depends on *both* sample sizes as well as on their total. For data generated in experiments which are designed in advance, it can be shown that for a fixed total sample size ($m + n$) the standard deviation of ($\overline{P}$) is smallest when $m = n$. Unlike laboratory experiments, in many applications one cannot prespecify these sample sizes, e.g., the numbers of men and women who are hired and stay with the company long enough to be eligible for promotion depends on personal preferences as well as the firm's employment policy.

Comments. (1) In this case the small number, two, of female pharmacists who were promoted between the time of the Civil Rights Act and the filing of the charge, was the main issue. The length of time to promotion is another indicator of disparate treatment.[6] Because of the significant difference in time to promotion they obtained plaintiffs then compared the promotion rates of pharmacists hired after the effective[7] date of the Civil Rights Act. This procedure eliminates the lingering effect of pre-act discrimination and seniority considerations from the comparison of promotion rates. Thus, the seniority levels of the male and female pharmacists hired after the Civil Rights Act should be similar so fair employment practices should lead to equal promotion rates in the post-act era. The defendant's expert rebutted the analysis by using a different test, the median test, which counts the number of y's (females) above the median of the combined sample. He did not obtain a significant result at the .05 level, because the median test has *no* power with a sample of only two y's. An intuitive reason for this is the following: The probability that a single random observation exceeds the median of the population is 1/2, so the probability that two independent selections[8] both exceed the median is $1/2 \times 1/2 = .25$. Notice that no matter what the difference between the two sets of times to promotion was, the median test would *never* find the difference significant. In addition to stating that the median test had low power, the plaintiffs asked the defendant's expert whether his procedure would detect a difference in time to promotion of one million years. Of course, the answer was no. The concept of power did not, however, play a role in the decision, as the judge accepted the defendant's analysis. Another aspect of the different analyses presented to the court was that the defendant's expert studied the period from 1965 through the *end* of 1973, which included three post-charge promotions of females in the analysis. This data is presented in Table 7.2 along with data for the 1974 through 1978 period. The appellate opinion also accepted the defendant's analysis, although one wonders how the apparent *change* in promotion policy after the charge was filed (three in one year after the charge, in contrast with two during the $6\frac{1}{2}$ year pre-charge period) and the fact that in the post-charge era women were promoted in less time than men was was not noted.[9]

(2) The Capaci data, properly analyzed, again points out the need to distinguish between practical and statistical significance and to remind us that statistical significance also depends on the sample size. In view of the obvious difference (11/24) between the observed P-measure (1/24) and its expected value (1/2), the difference between the two averages and the small sample size, it seems reasonable for a court to use a significance level somewhat higher than .05, e.g., .10, provided that the type II error

TABLE 7.2. Time to Promotion to Chief Pharmacist for
Pharmacists Promoted in 1965–1973 or in
1974–1978

Months	1965–1973 Female	Male	1974–1978 Female	Male
Over 200	2	1	0	3
190–199	0	1	0	0
180–189	0	0	0	0
170–179	0	0	0	1
160–169	0	0	0	0
150–159	0	0	0	0
140–149	0	0	0	0
130–139	0	0	0	0
120–129	0	1	0	1
110–119	0	0	0	0
100–109	0	0	0	1
90–99	0	0	0	1
80–89	0	0	0	0
70–79	1	0	0	2
60–69	0	4	0	4
50–59	0	1	0	2
40–49	0	2	0	4
30–39	1	4	0	3
20–29	1	8	0	5
10–19	0	8	2	8
1–9	0	2	1	5
Total	5	32	3	40

Source: The district court opinion 527 F.Supp. 317, 30 FEP
Cases 1541 (D.C. La. 1981).

rate at a reasonable alternative, such as a difference of two or three years, remained at least as large as the type I error.

(3) Baldus and Cole refer to this case[10] and mention that courts often are confused when two statistical tests yield conflicting conclusions, so they suggest that the role of tests be given less weight and the raw disparity e.g., the difference between the medians, be given more weight. The theory of statistics tells us to use the most powerful test which is appropriate for the problem, and this principle may help guide the judicial system in assessing such conflicts. If a disparity, e.g., an average of 163 months

until promotion for females versus 29.10 for males, appears meaningful and there is a conflict between tests, the court should inquire about the power of the tests advocated by both parties.

(4) Another nonparametric procedure was suggested by Harper (1981). Although he prefers the Wilcoxon test for general use, it is mentioned in the recent book by Wehmhoefer. This method arranges all $m + n$ numbers in increasing order, finds the rank, r, of the smallest y and then asks what is the probability that all n y's would be among the largest $m + n - (r - 1)$ members of the combined sample. These authors note that one difficulty with this method is that one first examines the data to locate the smallest y. Actually there is a way to do this without looking at the data, namely, to use the rank of the smallest y as the test criteria and use its probability distribution[11] to accept or reject the null hypothesis. The major statistical qualm with this method is that the extreme values are often subject to error or special circumstances so that it is preferable not to use statistical methods emphasizing them. Indeed, faced with a similar time to promotion issue in *Lewis v. Nat'l Labor Relations Board*,[12] the court rejected a finding of a statistically significant difference, because it was due to a few unusually slow promotions (of minority members). One of the advantages of the Wilcoxon method is that it only uses the ranks of the data, not the actual numbers, so it gives less weight to the extreme values (large or small) than the t-test does. If there are a few special situations, it might be preferable to have the parties involved agree to treat them separately and then proceed to analyze the remaining data. Finally, both the Wilcoxon and t-tests are based on well-established measures of the impact or effect of the employment practice or process on the minority group. The test using the rank of the smallest y is not based on such a measure.

b. *Comparing the grade levels of black and white employees in computer-related occupations in the Department of Housing and Urban Development: Hogan v. Pierce*[13]

Recall that *Hogan v. Pierce,* discussed in Section 6.2, involved a claim of discrimination in promotion to a fairly high level, GS-14, Civil Service job. In order to provide background information on the status of black employees in computer-related positions relative to white employees, the data in Table 7.3, reporting the grade levels they held at various times, was submitted to the court. The first year, 1972, reports the situation when government agencies were covered by the Civil Rights Act and the last year, 1977, reports the data at the time of the complaint. In Table 7.4

TABLE 7.3.   Grade Levels Held by Black and White Persons Employed in Computer Related Positions at HUD in the Years 1972, 1975 and 1977

	1972		1975		1977	
Grade	Black	White	Black	White	Black	White
1	0	0	0	0	0	0
2	0	0	0	0	1	0
3	0	0	0	0	0	2
4	0	0	2	0	0	0
5	9	3	7	1	8	1
6	3	1	6	1	7	0
7	3	1	5	1	11	3
8	3	1	5	1	5	1
9	1	6	4	4	7	4
10	0	5	2	0	2	2
11	7	9	5	14	7	6
12	5	23	7	36	8	39
13	4	17	10	39	14	55
14	1	8	0	15	0	19
15	0	5	1	6	1	11
16	0	1	0	1	0	1
	36	80	54	119	72	144

Source: The data is extracted from a plaintiff's exhibit submitted during the *Hogan v. Pierce* trial. The exhibit reported the data for each year during the 1972–1977 period.

the results of the Wilcoxon test applied to the yearly data in the exhibit from which Table 7.3 was taken shows that the probability a black employee held as high a position as a white ranged from .24 to .18 during the period, and the difference from its expected value (1/2), expressed in terms of standard deviations, always exceeded 4 and the p-values were less than one in 100,000. Thus, we conclude that blacks had a different and less favorable grade distribution than whites.

From our analysis thus far, we cannot conclude that illegal discrimination was the reason blacks typically held lower grades than whites. The data in Table 7.3 reflects pre-act as well as post-act employment decisions and includes several types of jobs in the computer field. Thus, the assumption underlying the Wilcoxon test that all employees (regardless of race) have the same chance of being at each grade level may not be

TABLE 7.4.   Results of Applying the Wilcoxon Test to
the Data in the Exhibit Underlying Table
8.3

Year	$P(8.2)$	$Z(8.6)$
1972	.2434	−4.465
1973	.2178	−5.448
1974	.2420	−5.459
1975	.2066	−6.306
1976	.1825	−7.406
1977	.1926	−7.544

Note: Because the grade levels are discrete, there are a number of ties, i.e., some blacks and whites have the same grade level. The variance used in calculating (8.5) and, therefore, in the standard deviation in (8.6) incorporated the correction for ties.

entirely justified. On the other hand, the occupations included in Table 7.3 all involved the computer series, and none of the official job descriptions required more than a high school diploma. Moreover, the fact that the probability measure *declined* from .24 to .19 during the period under consideration in *Hogan* is consistent with a claim of discrimination in promotion, especially as the minority fraction of all employees remained nearly constant (ranging from 31.03% to 34.6%) during the period so that affirmative action hiring at lower grade levels during the post-act period probably could not explain the decline.

It should be emphasized that courts are often dubious of statistical analyses of data which include many different occupations requiring much different educational backgrounds and varying amounts of prior experience.[14] Recall that the randomization assumption requires that the distribution of these factors is the same in each of the two groups being compared, as we noted in our discussion of Fisher's exact test in Chapter 5. This assumption is weaker than the original assumption used to derive the randomization tests, namely, that each individual has the same chance of receiving each job.

When there is a difference in the distribution of relevant job skills between the groups, the aggregate data should be stratified into subgroups which are comparable with respect to the major factors and the summary *P* measure and test of significance discussed later in Section 5 is utilized.

Courts are correct in questioning inferences derived from data aggregating many job types, especially when plaintiffs have access to more accurate or refined data. However, when highly significant differences, such as those obtained in Table 7.3, on data limited to jobs that are reasonably related to the one at the issue, then a more careful refutation of the statistical inference should be required than simply saying that the data may include a small fraction of pre-act hires or jobs of lesser (or greater) skill than the ones under scrutiny. This is where the estimated measure, $\bar{P}$, or $\bar{y} - \bar{x}$ and the p-value of a powerful test play a role. One can assess the possible impact of the inclusion of some data of doubtful relevance on the ultimate conclusion.

In the *Hogan v. Pierce* case, these considerations did not arise, as the defendant had the opportunity to redo the analysis excluding pre-act hires and/or introduce other factors but chose to rely on data beginning at the time of the charge. Judge Robinson asked the defendant's expert whether it would be more appropriate to have a window of time around the charge. The judge had already seen the data in Table 6.7 and the Mantel-Haenzel analysis in addition to Tables 7.3 and 7.4 and was aware of the limited relevance of post-charge data to what occurred at the time the plaintiff was denied the promotion.

The type of data and analysis presented in Tables 7.3 and 7.4 are more relevant to a claim of discrimination in initial job assignment, when the positions can be ordered by their desirability (e.g., grade or pay levels) than to a claim of discrimination in promotion, because the analysis of the status of employees at one fixed time cannot distinguish between employees who started at lower grades and perhaps advanced and those who were hired directly in the higher grades.

c. Brief description of other actual applications

In our discussion of the acceptance of statistical analyses by courts we have emphasized the concern that another factor or variable might explain the conclusion that there is a statistically significant difference between minority and majority salaries or promotion rates. The Wilcoxon test has been used to demonstrate that both groups have the same distribution of a possible explanatory factor, e.g., similar fractions of both groups have high, moderate and low levels of it. Therefore, the observed difference between the groups cannot logically be explained by one group possessing a higher average level of the influential factor.

In *Hogan v. Pierce,* the eligible pool for the promotions to grade 14 reported in Table 6.7 was defined in terms of the minimum tenure in the previous grade 13 required by the Civil Service rules. Since seniority exceeding this minimum amount might enhance one's chance of promotion, plaintiffs applied the Wilcoxon test to the seniority levels of black and white employees in the eligible pool for the particular promotion Mr. Hogan was denied. It showed no significant difference between the seniority levels, although black employees had a higher average level (about one year more) than whites. Since that promotion was made in January 1977, towards the end of the time frame of the data, one might ask whether the same situation held throughout the period. Since the same individuals were common to many of the eligible pools, it is unlikely that the seniority patterns could have been that much different, and the issue never was raised at the trial.

In *Berger v. Iron Workers Local 201*,[15] a union administered a practical exam for admission. Before taking the exam applicants had to satisfy a job experience requirement which they did by serving as an apprentice or by working on jobs as part of an auxiliary labor pool which was called upon when demand for labor exceeded the formal union membership. Common sense suggests that more practical experience should increase a person's performance on the exam, so plaintiffs used the Wilcoxon test to demonstrate that blacks had a significantly higher amount of prior experience. Thus, a previously demonstrated difference in admission rates could not be explained by blacks possessing less prior experience and, indeed, was reinforced by the fact that blacks had more experience than whites.

In a claim for damage to oil while it was transported because some incompatible oils were mixed together causing a reaction leading to sediment formation, the Wilcoxon test was used to establish a significantly increased level of sedimentation in the holds of the tanker with the mixed oils than in the holds with only one oil or with known compatible oils. Thus, one concluded that chance or accidental factors could not explain the increased sedimentation in the holds with the mixed oils and that it was caused by the mix of oils. We shall discuss this claim in Chapter 8, as another factor (temperature) was suggested and shown to have had much less influence on sedimentation than the oil mix.

Comment.   When the Wilcoxon, t-test or any other statistical test is used to show that an explanatory variable such as seniority or prior experience is distributed similarly in the two groups being compared, a borderline result, e.g., a one-sided *p*-value in the range .05 to .10, should still raise a question as to whether that factor might have influenced the result of the simple comparison or at least biased the estimated effect $\bar{P}$ or $\bar{y} - \bar{x}$. In Section 5 we shall see that a seemingly balanced covariate (related variable) was not really similarly distributed in the two groups, and its effect was so strong that the data should have been stratified according to its presence or absence.

Problems

1. Compute the mean and median time to promotion of females and male pharmacists from the *Capaci* pre-charge data. Does the difference between the means and/or the medians seem meaningful to you?

2.* In the Capaci case, pharmacists were promoted to one of two positions—chief pharmacist or assistant store manager.

(a) Would the data presented in the text be evidence of discrimination *had* 5 of the 19 pharmacists promoted to assistant manager been female and their average time to promotion been about two years?

(b) In analyzing the promotion issue in *Capaci,* which of the following two approaches makes more sense to you?

(1) Consider all pharmacists employed in the appropriate time period and test whether the promotion rate of both sexes to chief pharmacist was the same; then test whether or not the promotion rates to assistant manager were equal.

(2) Consider promotion to either job as an advancement and test whether the advancement rates were the same.

(c) What method of analysis or modification might be preferable to the ones described in part (b)?

3. Perform the t-test on the Capaci pre-charge data using the normal approximation in the text, recognizing that your calculation is approximate due to the small sample size. Would you say that your result confirms the Wilcoxon test or the median test procedure?

4.* One may properly criticize the data in Table 7.3 as being biased against the defendant, as it included pre-act employment decisions, i.e., the data reports the status of all employees as of the beginning of the year.

(a) From the results of the analysis reported in Table 7.4 do you think that limiting the analysis to all employees in 1977 who were hired after the effective date of the Civil Right Act (March 1972) would have made a substantial impact? Explain the reasoning behind your answer.

(b) Which of the two statistical analyses the plaintiffs presented in *Hogan v. Pierce* do you feel is more supportive of the plaintiffs claim of discrimination? Why?

(c) Suppose the grade distributions in Table 7.3 had been closer, so that the $\bar{P}$ measures in all three years were in the range .4 to .45 and the Z-form (7.6) of the Wilcoxon was about -1.0, corresponding to a one-sided p-value of about .16. Would it have been proper for plaintiffs to assert that the three tests were statistically *independent* so that the overall prob-value should be $(.16)^3 = .004$, because the probability that several independent events occur is the product of their probabilities? Explain your reasoning.

5. The overaggregation issue arose in the case of *Ste Marie v. Eastern Railroad Association* 458 F.Supp. 1147, 18 FEP Cases 671 (D.C.N.Y. 1978), *rev'd* 650 F.2d 395, 26 FEP Cases 167 (2nd Cir. 1981). Read the statistical portion of the appellate opinion. What major assumption underlying the plaintiff's analysis was suspect and contributed to the reversal of the district court's finding of discrimination in job assignments?

Answers to Selected Problems

2. (a) Obviously this data should be included in the analysis. The easiest way is to consider time to promotion (to either position). In all likelihood the result of a formal test would be a finding of a nonsignificant difference between the sexes in time to advancement.

(b) The second method is preferable, as in the first method pharmacists who are promoted to one job are still included as eligible for the other, which is unreasonable.

(c) One should consider doing an analysis similar to that in the *Hogan v. Pierce* case, where the eligible pools at the time of every promotion (to either position) are analyzed by the MH method.

3. Your result will confirm the Wilcoxon test.

4. (a) It is difficult to answer this with complete confidence. Although the $\bar{P}$ measure declined during the period, we cannot distinguish between several possible explanations: discrimination in promotion, discrimination in placement of new hires or fairness in initial placement, and promotion at low levels but discrimination in promotion at higher levels.

(b) The analysis in Chapter 6 is more convincing, as it focuses on promotions at the appropriate grade from the eligible pool and a time frame appropriate to studying the defendant's compliance with the equal employment law at the time of the questioned promotion.

(c) Since many employees remained throughout the entire period, the observations in each year are *highly* dependent. In Chapter 12 we will see that in such situations the p-value obtained by multiplication typically *underestimates* the true *p*-value, thereby exaggerating the statistical significance of the data.

5. The plaintiff's analysis assumed that all employees were equally likely to be assigned to each of three types of jobs: managerial, technical or clerical. Even a weaker assumption that the women had similar educational and related skills as the men is probably invalid, so the reasoning in the appellate opinion is statistically sound, especially as plaintiffs have the duty to present a *prima facie* case.

4. Comparing Two Random Samples from Different Populations

When studying whether a particular firm's salaries are awarded fairly, the randomization model applies because we are limiting our statistical inference to the specific population studied. If a significant difference between the wages of female and male employees is found, the persons eligible for relief are precisely those used in the analysis. However, we are often interested in comparing wages of male and female workers in an entire industry or occupation or in comparing the efficacy of a new drug relative to a currently used one for the general population. Since the total population of workers in an industry or possible patients is quite large, we can only study a random (or at least representative) sample in order to draw an inference which is valid for the entire population. Note that analysis of a convenient small population may not lead to an inference generalizable to the entire population of interest. Could one fairly generalize our conclusion about the difference in time to promotion of the pharmacists employed at K and B during the period of July 1965 through January 1973 to the entire pharmaceutical industry? Obviously not, as this particular firm was the subject of a specific claim of discrimination. Thus, the most reliable method of establishing a conclusion about an entire population is from taking a carefully defined random sample and analyzing the data. In this section we describe how the Wilcoxon test applies to random samples from the two populations being compared and indicate the additional assumptions needed to make the t-test valid in small random samples ($m, n < 30$).

Recall that the hypothesis we are testing is that the distribution of the *y*'s is the same as that of the *x*'s, i.e., we know that there is variability among the *y*'s (and *x*'s) internally but are concerned that there may be a systematic shift of the *y*'s downwards (or upwards) from the *x*'s (see Fig. 7.1). Formally, we assume that $x_1, ..., x_n$ are a random sample from a population with a characteristic of interest, say annual salary, with a density function $f(x)$ or cumulative distribution (ogive) $F(x)$ and y_1, ..., y_n are a similar random sample from a population in which the same characteristic has a density function $g(x)$ or cumulative distribution $G(x)$. The null hypothesis is that the two distributions F and G are the same, i.e., $F(x) = G(x)$. A one-sided alternative is that $G(x) = F(x - \Delta)$, which means that the y's are shifted to the left of the x's. For example, suppose the male salary distribution, $F(x)$ was normally distributed, with mean \$20,000 and standard deviation \$2000. If $\Delta = \$2000$, then females salaries are normally distributed with a mean of \$18,000 and a standard deviation of \$2000. We graph the cumulative distributions when the alternative $G(x) = F(x - \Delta)$ holds in Fig. 7.2. Under the alternative, the *fraction* of females earning less than \$$x$ *equals* the fraction of males earning less than \$$(x - \Delta)$. Again, when $\Delta = \$2000$, the fraction of females earning \$20,000 or less is *equal* to the fraction of males earning \$22,000 or less, so that a higher fraction of women than men earn *less than* \$20,000. This holds for any salary level (\$20,000 was chosen for convenience).

The logic underlying the validity of the Wilcoxon test of the null hypothesis $F(x) = G(x)$ carries over to the analysis of two independent random samples of size m and n from the respective populations. The theory underlying the sampling distribution of $\bar{P}$ only required the probability that a y observation assumes any specific rank, say the largest among the total sample of $N = n + m$ equals $n/(n + m)$, the fraction of y's in the total sample. Now suppose that the x's and y's have the same distribution, what is the probability that the largest ranked observation is a y? Under the null hypothesis that the two distributions (F and G) are the

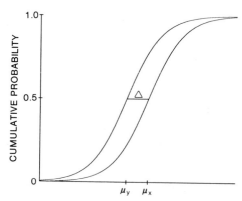

FIGURE 7.2.   The ogives or cumulative distributions for the hypothetical male and female wages in Figure 8.1. Note that the difference between their medians (the values on the x-axis where the ogive equals .5) is $\Delta = \mu_x - \mu_y$.

same, the whole set of $m + n = N$ random observations can be considered as one large sample of size N. Before the sample is taken, each of the N observations has the same probability $(1/N)$ of being the largest (or of having any specified relative rank). Thus, the chance a y observation is the largest is just the fraction of y's (n/N) in the total sample. When the alternative $G(x) = F(x - \Delta)$ is true, the y's will be shifted down from the x's (see Figs. 7.1 and 7.2) so the probability that a y observation will have one of the lower ranks will exceed n/N. This is why the Wilcoxon test helps us distinguish between the null and alternative hypotheses. When the *alternative is true*, in more than half the pairwise comparisons the y will be less than the x.

More generally, under the null hypothesis that $F(x) = G(x)$, the ranks of the y observations in the combined sample of $N = n + m$ observations can be regarded as a random selection of n ranks from the integers 1, ..., N, because under the null hypothesis we can't distinguish an x observation from a y observation (without their label) so that before we take the sample each observation has the same probability $(1/N)$ of being any specific rank, i.e., being the 1st, 2nd, ..., N[th] largest. The reader may recognize that this is equivalent to the assumption of the randomization model, where we replace the values of the y's by their ranks. Thus, the Wilcoxon test, which is based on comparing each y with each x, i.e., finding how the y observations rank relative to the x's, can be used on sample data without change.

Since the distribution of the Wilcoxon measure $\bar{P}$ (7.2) and its approximate normal form (7.6) remain the same, we would perform the same calculations as done in Section 2, had the 8 male and 6 female salaries been based on random samples from employees of both sexes. We would conclude that the probability of observing a $\bar{P}$ so far from its expected value (1/2), in either direction, is .02 and would reject the null hypothesis that the salary distributions are the same if a two-sided .05 level test criteria were used.

The adaptation of the t-statistic for the *randomization* model,

$$(7.15) \qquad t = \frac{\bar{y} - \bar{x}}{\sigma \sqrt{\left(\frac{1}{n} + \frac{1}{m}\right)}},$$

where σ^2 is given by (7.8), is more involved, because we no longer know the numerical value of σ, the standard deviation of the total population, and need to estimate it as well as the two population means from the sample data. To do this we use the fact that under the null hypothesis when both distributions are equal, they also have a common variance, σ^2. A safe way to estimate σ^2 is to average the sample variances s_x^2 and s_y^2 from the separate samples in proportion[16] to the sample sizes on which they are based. Thus, we estimate the common variance σ^2 by

(7.16)
$$s^2 = \frac{(n-1)\, s_y^2 + (m-1)\, s_x^2}{m + n - 2}$$

where

$$s_x^2 = \frac{1}{m-1} \sum (x_i - \bar{x})^2 \quad \text{and} \quad s_y^2 = \frac{1}{n-1} \sum (y_i - \bar{y})^2.$$

Replacing σ in (7.15) by s, the square root of s^2 in formula (7.16) yields the t-statistic:

(7.17)
$$t = \frac{\bar{y} - \bar{x}}{s \sqrt{\dfrac{1}{n} + \dfrac{1}{m}}}.$$

Using the estimates of σ^2 based on both sample variances, s_x^2 and s_y^2, and s^2, also gives us the opportunity to check that the assumption that both distributions have the same variance is not grossly violated.[17]

In *large samples* the t-statistic (7.17) has a standard normal distribution when the null hypothesis is true. When the alternative is true, say the mean of the variable in the y-population is less than μ_x, the mean value of the variable in the x-population, the difference $\bar{y} - \bar{x}$, between the sample means will estimate the difference $\mu_y - \mu_x$ between the population means and the t-statistic (7.17) will be centered around the value,

(7.18)
$$\frac{\mu_y - \mu_x}{\sigma \sqrt{\dfrac{1}{n} + \dfrac{1}{m}}},$$

as s^2 will approach the common variance, σ^2. Notice that when n and m increase, the denominator of (7.18) gets quite small. Thus, when the alternative (μ_y is less than μ_x) is true, if the sample sizes are sufficiently large we will detect the difference $\mu_y - \mu_x$, as the t-test (7.17) will exceed ± 1.96. This fact is useful in determining the sample sizes m and n that should be taken in order to detect a difference of $\Delta = \mu_x - \mu_y$ which is deemed to be important.

We now illustrate the use of the statistic on an example: In order to check whether a construction union is complying with a consent decree and is now assigning work fairly, a sample of 100 black and 100 white union members is taken and data on the total hours they worked last year are obtained from the union's records. If the union is assigning workers to jobs with no consideration of race, then the population means μ_b and μ_w of black and white members would be equal. Thus, we are testing

$$H_0: \mu_b = \mu_w$$

against the alternative hypothesis

$$H_a: \mu_b < \mu_w.$$

We choose a one-sided alternative because we are monitoring compliance with a consent decree of a union whose former employment practices were questionable. We will use the t-test statistic (7.17) and will reject the null hypothesis if $t < -1.645$, since a standard normal variable has only a 5% chance of being less. Suppose that the sample means and standard deviations are:

$$\text{Whites} \quad \bar{x} = 2100, \ s = 150$$

$$\text{Blacks:} \quad \bar{y} = 1900, \ s = 125.$$

Now $\bar{y} - \bar{x} = -200$ and we find the estimate s^2 of the common variance from (7.16), i.e.,

$$s^2 = \frac{99(125)^2 + 99(1500)^2}{198} = \frac{1}{2}((125)^2 + (150)^2)$$

$$= \frac{15625 + 22500}{2} = 190625.$$

Thus, $s = \sqrt{190625} = 138.07$ and the t-statistic (7.17) is

$$(7.19) \quad \frac{-200}{138.07 \sqrt{\frac{1}{100} + \frac{1}{100}}} = \frac{-200}{(138.07)(.1414)} = \frac{-200}{19.52} = -10.24,$$

which is much less than -1.645. Indeed, its p-value is less than one in a billion.[18] Thus, we conclude that the union is assigning black members less work, as the difference of 200 hours between the sample means was too great to have occurred by chance if black and white members had the same distribution of hours worked.

In our discussion of the test statistic (7.17) we substituted an estimate s of the standard deviation, σ, in formula (7.15). In large samples, s is an accurate estimate, and the usual normal approximation applies. In *smaller samples* (m, $n \leq 30$) an allowance needs to be made for the fact that σ is unknown and our estimate s includes some sampling error. This added uncertainty means that there is a greater probability than .05 under the null hypothesis, that the t-statistic will be less than -1.645, and we need to develop appropriate tables for the new sampling distribution of the t-statistic. In Appendix B we present more details and illustrate the necessary modifications for determining the p-value of the t-test. Fortunately, the ideas of hypothesis testing and the formulas for confidence intervals remain the same. The only change is that the critical values -1.645 or -1.96 etc. from the standard normal table are replaced by their analogs from the t-distribution which correspond to the same probabilities, i.e., -1.645 is replaced by the point, $t_{.05}$, defined by the fact that only 5% of the time will an observation from the t-distribution be *less* than it. It is important to note that the *small sample* tables of the t-distribution given in the appendix are derived under the assumption that the characteristic studied has a *normal* distribution. Thus, the t-test in *small examples* may not be valid if the data comes from a non-normal curve, which is why the Wilcoxon method may be preferable for legal and policy purposes. We close this section by presenting the formula for a $100(1 - \alpha)\%$ confidence interval for the difference, $\mu_y - \mu_x$, of the two population means based on the sample mean. The idea is the same as the one-sample case (Section 3.3), the only change is that the estimated standard deviation of $\bar{y} - \bar{x}$ is now $s \sqrt{1/m + 1/n}$ instead of $s/\sqrt{n}$. Hence, the $100(1 - \alpha)\%$ confidence interval for $\mu_y - \mu_x$ is given by

$$(7.20) \qquad \mu_y - \mu_x = (\bar{y} - \bar{x}) \pm t_{\alpha/2}\, s\, \sqrt{\frac{1}{m} + \frac{1}{n}}.$$

For example, the 95% confidence interval for the difference in average hours worked by the union members is

$$-200 + (1.96)(138.07) \sqrt{.01 + .01} \qquad \text{or} \qquad -200 \pm 38.27$$

$$\text{or} \qquad 95\%,\ \text{CONF}(\mu_b - \mu_w;\ -238.27,\ -161.73),$$

so we can be 95% confident that the true difference between the number of hours worked by black and white union members is between 161.73 and 238.22.

Comments. (1) Remember it is important to report the estimated difference of 200 hours in addition to the formal statistical test, as it indicates the magnitude of the disparity, enabling one to assess its practical meaning. In the example, a difference of 200 hours translates into a difference of about 10% in annual earnings, assuming a typical work week of 40 hours for 50 weeks, which certainly is of practical importance.

(2) One can also obtain an estimate of the difference Δ between the population means (μ_y and μ_x) from the Wilcoxon test. This estimate is precisely the amount, Δ, one has to subtract from the original x sample values so that the Wilcoxon statistic has value $1/2$, i.e., when we compare the y-sample to the adjusted x-sample, $x_i^* = x_i - \Delta$, the y_i's are less than x_i's in exactly *half* of the comparisons. The intuitive idea is that after subtracting Δ from the x's, there should be no difference in the two populations, so the Wilcoxon statistic, $\overline{P}$, should now be at its expected value of $1/2$. Since a confidence interval for any parameter consists of those values consistent with the null hypothesis, a confidence interval for Δ contains all values of Δ which lead to accepting the hypothesis of no difference between the y sample and the modified x sample, $x_i^* = x_i - \Delta$.

The above description appears to be based on a trial and error approach, as one must guess the size of the difference Δ, calculate the Wilcoxon test, and increase or decrease the value of Δ depending on whether $\overline{P}$ is greater or less than $1/2$. Simpler computational approaches are available, and it turns out that the estimate $\hat{\Delta}$ of Δ associated with the Wilcoxon procedure is the *median* of all the mn differences $\{y_j - x_i\}$. A formula for the standard deviation of $\hat{\Delta}$ is available, and we refer the reader to the references (Hollander and Wolfe, Lehmann) for details.

(3) The formulas for the standard error of both the Wilcoxon and t-test statistics were calculated under the assumptions that the underlying distributions were the same. Sometimes one desires to test whether two populations have the same mean (μ), even though they may have different variances. When the variances do not differ very much the methods we discuss can be used. Otherwise they need to be modified. One approach to accomplish this is to calculate the standard error of $\overline{P}$ or $\overline{y} - \overline{x}$ under these more general conditions and then estimate it from the data, just as we used the sample standard deviation, s, to estimate σ in the t-test statistic (7.17). Further information about methods for this situation, called the Fisher-Behrens problem in the statistical literature, can be found in the more advanced reference books.

Problems

1. You are part of a team of economists, statisticians and lawyers reviewing the salary records of a large employer for possible race discrimination in a job with approximately 2000 black and 10,000 white incumbent

employees. Rather than work with all 12,000 records, it is reasonable to take a sample of 400. Which of the following sampling strategies makes the most sense to you? Assume, you will use the Wilcoxon test to analyze the data.

(a) Select a random sample of 400 employees from the totality of employee records.

(b) Select two separate random samples of 100 black and 300 white employees.

(c) Select two separate random samples of 200 black and 200 white employees.

Explain your answer.

2. (a) Suppose two random samples of 100 male and 200 female teachers in the nation yield average male earnings of \$17,000 and average female earnings of \$15,000. Assuming both wage distributions have the same standard deviation σ, equal to \$4000, construct a 95% confidence interval for the *difference* $\mu_m - \mu_f$ between the population male mean wage (μ_m) and the female mean (μ_f).

(b) Does your answer to part (a) also imply that the difference between the average pay of male and female teachers is statistically significant at the 5% level (use a two-sided test criteria)? Find the p-value of the t-test.

(c) If your answer to (b) is yes, could this finding be due to discrimination? What other factors might explain the difference?

(d) Suppose that the sample average for female teachers was \$16,750, and the male average (is still \$17,000) but that the sample sizes had been 10,000 of each sex. Is there a statistically significant difference between male and female earnings? Use a two-sided .05 level test. Compare the p-values of the test on this data with that of part (b). Which is smaller, implying a higher degree of statistical significance? Why?

Answers to Selected Problems

1. (c) Because the variance of $\overline{P}$, under the null hypothesis ($P = 1/2$), is $(m + n + 1)/12mn$, if the total $m + n$ is fixed, as it is in our example, this variance is *smallest* when $m = n$.

2. (a) The confidence interval is $\mu_m - \mu_f = 2000 + (1.96)$ $4000\sqrt{1/100 + 1/200} = 2000 \pm 960.20$.

(b) Yes, $Z = 2000/4000\sqrt{.015} = 4.08$, p-value $\cong 0.0001$.

(c) While the result could be due to discrimination, it could also be due differences in seniority and conceivably due to differences in assignment (teachers of specialized high school subjects might be paid more than elementary school teachers). The validity of these explanations should be verified by proper statistical analyses.

(d) Now, the t-test statistic (7.17) is $(250)/(4000\sqrt{2/10000})$ or $250/56.57 = 4.42$, which is also statistically significant. The p-value of this test is *less* than that of part (b), implying a greater degree of statistical significance even though the difference between the group averages is much less. The reason this occurs is that the sample sizes are much larger, implying that the standard error in the denominator of (7.17) is very small. Hence, even a small difference in the sample averages being tested will be deemed statistically significant. This reminds us that statistical significance depends on sample size as well as on the true difference between both population means.

5. Combining the Results of Several Wilcoxon Tests

As we learned in Chapters 5 and 6, one often needs to summarize the results of several statistical tests applied to appropriate subgroups of the population (or sample) studied. In the equal pay setting it is sensible to compare male and female salaries in each occupation separately and then combine the results into one summary statistic. Similarly, in assessing the possible effect of a chemical on workers, it is reasonable to classify the workers into age or general health categories, compare lifetimes of exposed and unexposed workers in each category separately and then combine the results. In this section we present the methodology in subsection a and illustrate its use in two examples in subsections b and c.

a. Statistical procedures for combining Wilcoxon test statistics

Suppose we analyze data stratified into k classes by the Wilcoxon test, i.e., we have calculated the value of $\bar{P}_i$ for each of the k strata. Denote these statistics by $\bar{P}_1, \bar{P}_2, ..., \bar{P}_k$. Under the null hypothesis of *no* effect or difference between the groups, each of the $\bar{P}_i$ is estimating a common value 1/2, but the variability of each $\bar{P}_i$ is different, as the sample sizes m_i and n_i of the two groups vary among the data sets. If the alternative hypothesis is true, e.g., females are paid less than males for similar work, then the $\bar{P}_i$ are all estimating a number less than 1/2. Assume that this number, π, say, is the *same* for all data sets. We then wish to combine the different estimates, $\overline{P}_i$ of π from the k data sets. Common sense suggests that we give greater weight to the $\overline{P}_i$'s, which are based on a greater number of pairwise comparisons, since they will be more accurate (recall that the sampling variance of $\overline{P}_i$ is proportional to $(m_i + n_i)/(m_i n_i)$). Technically speaking, we weigh each $\overline{P}_i$ inversely to its variance, as the smaller its variance, the more precise an estimate of the common is $\overline{P}_i$.

The formula for the combined estimate of $\hat{P}$ is

(7.21) $$\hat{P}_i = \sum w_i \overline{P}_i,$$

where w_i is proportional to $1/\mathrm{Var}(\overline{P}_i)$. When each data set consists of data with no (or few) ties, $\mathrm{Var}(\overline{P}_i)$ is $(m_i + n_i + 1)/12 m_i n_i$ (from (7.3)) so that

(7.22) $$w_i = \frac{\dfrac{12 m_i n_i}{m_i + n_i + 1}}{\displaystyle\sum_{i=1}^{k} \dfrac{12 m_i n_i}{m_i + n_i + 1}} = \frac{\dfrac{m_i n_i}{m_i + n_i + 1}}{\displaystyle\sum_{i=1}^{k} \dfrac{m_i n_i}{m_i + n_i + 1}}.$$

The reason we divide each $1/\mathrm{Var}(\overline{P}_i)$ by the sum over all k, i.e., $\sum_i^k [\mathrm{Var}(\overline{P}_i)]^{-1}$, is to make the weights, w_i, add to 1.0. Thus, the estimated summary $\hat{P}$ is a weighted average of the estimates $\overline{P}_i$ in the individual strata.

Thus, $\hat{P}$ (7.21) provides a summary measure of the probability a randomly selected Y(female) receives at least as much as a randomly selected X(male) when the comparisons are restricted to comparable members of the other group (persons in the same category or strata such as occupation). If the null hypothesis that all $P_i = 1/2$ (i.e., in each data set the x's and y's have the same distribution) is true, then $\hat{P}$ has variance

(7.23) $$\left[\frac{1}{12} \cdot \frac{1}{\displaystyle\sum_{i=1}^{k} \dfrac{m_i n_i}{m_1 + m_i + 1}} \right],$$

so the standard normal for m analogous to (7.6) used to carry out a test which combines all the data sets is

(7.24) $$Z = \frac{\left(\hat{P} - \dfrac{1}{2} \right)}{\sqrt{\dfrac{1}{12}} \sqrt{\displaystyle\sum \dfrac{m_i n_i}{m_i + m_i + 1}}}$$

While the computations are somewhat tedious to carry out, the summary measure and the formal test yield measures of the meaningfulness of the disparity as well as its statistical significance or p-value. We next apply the combination method to some hypothetical wage data given in Table 7.5.

The $\bar{P}_i$'s for each occupation are calculated from formula (7.2) and a format for combining them is presented in Table 7.6.

The weight w_i given to the data set in Table 7.6 is the fraction its factor (reciprocal of its $V(\bar{P}_i)$) forms of the total of the factor column and reflects the variance of $\bar{P}_i$ calculated from that data set. Thus, the weight given to the managerial data is $3.125/11.087 = .2819$. The total of the last column is the overall $\hat{P}$ (7.21). The denominator of the standard normal test (7.24) is obtained by multiplying the total of the factor column by 12, and taking its reciprocal and square root. In our example, 12 times the factor total $(11.087) = 133.04$. Its reciprocal is .007516, which has square root .0867. Thus, the normal form of the combined Wilcoxon test (7.24) is

$$Z = \frac{(\hat{P} - .05)}{.0867} = \frac{.3962 - .5}{.0867} = \frac{-.1038}{.0867} = -1.197.$$

TABLE 7.5. Annual Salary for Male and Female Employees in Three Occupations

Male		Female
$(m = 10)$	Managers	$(n = 5)$
		34,300
36,600		
		38,200
38,900		
39,100		
41,800		
		42,000
45,700		
		46,100
47,400		
49,200		
50,000		
		51,000
51,250		
55,500		

Continued

TABLE 7.5.   (*Continued*)

Male ($m = 10$)	Programmers	Female ($n = 10$)
		24,500
		24,900
25,100		
		25,200
25,450		
25,800		
		26,000
26,300		
		28,000
28,500		
		29,400
29,700		
		30,600
30,800		
31,000		
		31,100
		31,800
		32,700
33,200		
35,900		
($m = 8$)	Sales Representatives	($n = 8$)
		19,500
		20,000
20,100		
21,500		
21,700		
		21,800
21,900		
		22,700
23,000		
		23,500
23,800		
25,000		
25,100		
		25,400

TABLE 7.6.   Format for Combining Wilcoxon Tests Comparing Two Groups on Stratified Data Illustrated on the Data in Table 8.5

Data Set	m	n	Factor $\left(\dfrac{m_i n_i}{m_i + n_i + 1}\right)$	Weight	$\bar{P}_i$	Weight $\times \bar{P}_i$
Managers	10	5	= 3.125	.2819	.34	.0958
Programmers	10	10	= 4.762	.4295	.42	.1801
Sales Rep.	8	6	= 3.200	.2886	.4167	.1203
		Total	11.087			$P = .3962$

Note: The reciprocal of the variance of each $\bar{P}_i$ is called its factor (column 4) and the weight given to each $\bar{P}_i$ is the fraction its factor is of the total of all factors. The sum of the last column $(w_i x \bar{P}_i)$ is the desired weighted average of the individual $\hat{P}_i$.

This difference of approximately -1.2 standard deviations corresponds to a *one-sided* p-value of about .115, which is not statistically significant. Although the females were paid somewhat less than the males in each occupation (all $\bar{P}_i$'s were less than .5), the combination procedure shows that these differences could have occurred by chance.

When using a combination procedure to analyze several sets of data, it is important to assure oneself that all the data sets are indeed related to the issue at hand. The analysis we carried out on the hypothetical data in Table 7.5 is appropriate to rebut a charge of unequal pay for equal work if those occupations constitute the totality of relevant occupations in the appropriate unit(s) of the firm, although one could question whether the test had a reasonable power in view of the small sample sizes.

The analysis using (7.24) is based on the *assumption* that there is a common value, P, which each $\bar{P}_i$ estimates. The format for the calculation given in Table 7.5 enables us to check that the estimates $\bar{P}_i$ are similar. When there is a wide variation among the $\bar{P}_i$'s one should question whether the data sets (e.g., occupations) should be combined, as they have different statistical characteristics. In our example, this might occur if the salaries in some occupations or job categories were determined by a union contract emphasizing seniority, while in others salaries were determined by individual negotiation or a merit pay system.

The potential for an error of over-combination occurs when some of the $\bar{P}_i$ are quite small, while most $\bar{P}_i$ are around 1/2, but the p-value of (7.24) is just below .05. Then a highly statistically significant result in one or two strata may be causing the combination procedure for the entire data set to be significant at the .05 level. Conversely, the results in the other strata (where $\overline{P}_i$ is near 1/2) may be combined with the significant one(s) to diminish their significance.[19] To avoid these errors one needs to examine the data carefully to make sure that only appropriate strata are being used and that data from different time periods or locations[20] with different statistical characteristics have not been inadvertently combined.

Since the estimate, $\hat{P}$, in (7.21) is a weighted average of the individual $\overline{P}_i$'s, it provides a summary measure of the overall disparity, which is still useful when the individual $\overline{P}_i$'s vary among themselves. If the variation among the $\overline{P}_i$'s is sufficiently great as to question the assumption that all of them are estimating a common value, then an alternative procedure is to simply average the $\overline{P}_i$'s, ignoring the sample sizes in each category. This statistic,

$$(7.25) \qquad\qquad P^* = \frac{1}{k} \sum_{i=1}^{k} \overline{P}_i,$$

can be used as the summary measure of disparity and its normalized form,

$$(7.26) \qquad Z = \frac{k\left(P^* - \frac{1}{2}\right)}{\sqrt{\sum \frac{(m_i + n_i + 1)}{12m_i n_i}}} = \frac{k\sqrt{12}\left(P^* - \frac{1}{2}\right)}{\sqrt{\sum \frac{m_i + n_i + 1}{m_i n_i}}},$$

can be used to test the null hypothesis. For the data in Table 7.5, $k = 3$, $p^* = .3922$ and $Z = -1.22$ so that both methods give similar results.

When the individual $\overline{P}_i$'s are of a similar magnitude, the first method using formulas (7.21) and (7.24) is superior, as it incorporates the variability inherent in the separate $\overline{P}_i$'s. It is reassuring, however, to calculate both statistics $\hat{P}$ and P^* and obtain similar, not necessarily equal, results. We will not discuss methods for combining several t-tests, which are more complex, but note that when the standard deviations of the distributions of the characteristic under study are approximately equal for both groups in all strata, a summary measure of the overall average difference is

$$(7.27) \qquad\qquad \sum w_i(\overline{y}_i - \overline{x}_i),$$

where the w_i are again given by formula (7.22). We now illustrate the use of combined Wilcoxon procedure on data arising in an equal employment case and on data considered in determining the limits on occupational exposure to a chemical.

*b. Application to the quartile rank data in Bazemore v. Friday:
assessing possible discrimination in job evaluations*

When we previously analyzed the job evaluation (ranking) data in Table
6.7 from *Bazemore v. Friday*, the data was further compressed into several 2 × 2 tables in Table 6.8. The four quartile classifications were
grouped in two classes, *in* or *not in* the fourth quartile, because employees
in the lowest quartile did not receive a pay raise. This dichotomy of the
ranking data may oversimplify the issue of fair treatment if

(1) the amount of a pay raise was related to the quartile rank *or*
(2) the quartile ranks were used in judging an employee's suitability for
a future promotion *or*
(3) the overall fairness of the job evaluation system was an issue.

In order to study the data to resolve the above issues, the distribution of
blacks among all the four quartiles should be compared with the corresponding distribution of whites.

The Wilcoxon measure, $\overline{P}$, and its associated test are well suited to
compare the rankings in *each region,* because it is computed by comparing the ranks of every pair of black and white employees and gives value
1/2 to any pair when both members receive the same quartile rank. Since
the basic data in Table 6.7 was naturally stratified by region, and each
employee was ranked against employees in that region, the combined
Wilcoxon measure (7.21) and test statistic (7.24) are appropriate tools to
analyze the complete data presented in Table 6.7.

The calculation of the combined Wilcoxon procedure, following a format similar to that of Table 7.6, is presented in Table 7.7. Because of the
sizable fraction of ties inherent in data organized into quartile ranks, the
variances of the stratum (regions) $\overline{P}_i$'s are calculated using the appropriate
refined formula.[21] The summary estimate of the probability a black employee received at least as high a quartile rank as a white one equals $\hat{P} =$
.3534, and the standard deviation (square root of (7.23)) of the sampling or
randomization distribution of $\hat{P}$ is .03476. The standard normal form
(7.24) of the combined Wilcoxon test is

(7.28) $$Z = \frac{\hat{P} - \dfrac{1}{2}}{\text{standard error }(\hat{P})} = \frac{.5 - .353}{.03476} = -4.23.$$

If a two-sided test criteria was adopted, a Z of -4.23 corresponds to a

TABLE 7.7. Calculation of the Combined Wilcoxon Test for the *Bazemore v. Friday* Quartile Ranking Data in Table 6.7

Region	$\bar{P}_i$	Var $\bar{P}_i$	Factor	Weight (w_i)	$w_i \times \bar{P}_i$
NC	375	.00375	266.667	.3223	.1209
NE	.381	.00794	125.881	.1521	.0580
NW	.259	.00997	100.271	.1212	.0314
SE	.323	.00466	214.500	.2592	.0872
SW	.385	.00832	120.192	.1452	.0559
Total			827.511		289.489

Note: Each factor is the reciprocal of the variance of $\bar{P}_i$. Due to the many ties the data Var ($\bar{P}_i$) was obtained from formula (1.35) from the book by Lehmann.

p-value of .000016, a highly significant result. Thus, the null hypothesis that black and white employees have the same grade distributions is rejected in favor of the alternative that blacks received lower rankings.

Notice that the combined Wilcoxon analysis yielded a more significant difference than the MH analysis presented in Chapter 6. The reason for this is that restricting the examination of the data to whether or not an employee received a rank in the lowest (4th) quartile does not use the information about the relative ranks of blacks and whites within the other three quartiles. Even if the plaintiffs had offered this analysis, the outcome of the case might have been the same, as the appellate opinion required a significant difference at the .05 level for a two-sided test in each region. The increased sensitivity of the Wilcoxon procedure using the full quartile data relative to the dichotomized data (Table 6.8) discussed in the opinion is illustrated by the fact that significant differences are now found in three (NC, NW, SE) regions in contrast with only one region using the test for a difference between the proportions of employees receiving a rank in the lowest quartile.

c. *Assessing the effect of occupational exposure to ethylene oxide in order to set OSHA standards*

The chemical ethylene oxide (ETO) is known to be mutagenic and is suspected to be carcinogenic. Hence, OSHA limits the average concentration of ETO over an eight-hour workday that a worker can be exposed to a maximum of 50 ppm. In recent deliberations[22] the issue of whether to limit the maximum short-term exposure in addition to a daily total or cumulative exposure arose. We will not discuss the many studies considered and evaluated in the policymaking process but will examine the data from one study which was used to support limiting short-term exposures and show that the smoking effect appears to be four times as great as exposure to low cumulative doses. Thus, smoking is an important covariate which probably should be considered in future studies.

Since it is often easier to detect mutagenic effects than carcinogenic ones, the study determined the average number of sister chromatic exchanges (SCE), which is a sensitive measure of chromosomal effects of mutagens, as they are visual manifestations of an exchange in the DNA. The study compared SCE counts occurring in exposed and nonexposed workers in two hospitals.

The basic data is reported in Table 7.8, where the exposed group was further categorized by low and high exposure levels. It should be noted that the individual cumulative dose levels (D) in Table 7.8 were obtained by multiplying the average dose per task involving exposure to ETO by the estimated number of times workers performed these tasks over a six-month period.

The investigators compared the average number of SCE's per cell between the control and all exposed persons by the Wilcoxon test and obtained a significant difference at the .05 level (one-sided test). They noted that the control and exposed groups were well matched on a number of factors, such as age, sex, recent illnesses and smoking, which might affect the SCE count. There were five smokers in each group, although the controls smoked more (an average of 21 cigarettes per day) than the exposed (9 per day). Although the study notes that smokers in each category had a higher average SCE count, the effect of smoking was not estimated. Rather the average SCE count in the high exposure group was shown to significantly exceed that of the control or low exposed group. Thus, the study presents strong evidence that cumulative dose levels in the range of 500 ± 300 mg, which includes almost all of the highly exposed group, increase the SCE count. Their conclusion that "these data suggest that ETO elicits an increase in SCE frequency at average levels of exposure that are low in comparison with the current OSHA standard of 50 ppm" was based on 30 measurements of exposure in hospital A, which had a time weighted average of .92 ppm. The investigators controlled for smoking by checking that the proportion of smokers in each group was similar. We now show that smoking is a more important risk factor than low exposure to ETO.

TABLE 7.8.   The Number of SCEs Per Cell for Hospital Workers Classified by their Cumulative 6 Month Exposure to ETO

Group	Hospital	Smoker	Estimated Dose Per Task	Estimated Number of Tasks	Estimated Total Dose	Average Number of SCEs Per Cell
C	A	N				6.80
C	A	N				8.22
C	A	N				7.20
C	A	N				5.50
C	A	N				7.46
C	A	S				9.38
C	A	S				6.82
C	A	S				7.16
C	A	S				7.52
C	A	S				8.30
C	A	S				8.90
C	A	S				7.96
C	A	S				7.04
			Control Group Average		0	7.56
L	A	S	0		0	7.50
L	A	S	0		0	8.16
L	A	S	0		0	9.62
L	B	N	.1	96	10	7.24
L	A	S	.26	48	12	7.76
L	A	S	.26	48	12	6.60
L	A	S	.26	48	12	8.54
L	B	N	.1	120	12	8.28
L	A	N	9.6	6	58	6.16
			Low Exposed Group Average		13	7.76
H	A	S	9.6	18	173	9.64
H	A	N	9.6	40	384	8.00
H	A	S	9.6	48	461	12.98
H	A	S	15.5	48	744	11.66
H	A	N	15.5	48	744	11.66
			High Exposed Group Average		501	10.69

Source: This Table is taken from Table 2 of Yager, J. W., Hines, C. J. and Spear, R. C. (1983). Exposure to Ethylene Oxide at Work Increases Sister Chromatid Exchanges in Human Peripheral Lymphocytes. *Science* 219, 1221–1223.

It is convenient to rearrange the data in Table 7.8 in increasing order of SCE count within each exposure and smoking category, and this is done in Table 7.9. Although there is a slight (just under .20) average increase in SCE count between the low exposed and the control groups, it is not statistically significant. More interestingly, the difference in SCE counts between smokers and nonsmokers in both the control and low exposed groups was about .80 or roughly *four* times the average difference between the control and low exposed persons. To investigate the role of smoking further, we performed a combined Wilcoxon test for smokers versus nonsmokers using the test statistic (7.24) on the SCE counts of the smokers and nonsmokers in each of the three groups. The result was statistically significant if a one-sided .05 level is adopted (p-value = .041). Considering the small sample sizes involved and the magnitude of the smoking effect, it appears that smoking is a major factor and should be studied further.

Although our analysis does not affect the conclusion that relatively high

TABLE 7.9. ETO Data of Table 8.8 in Increasing Order of SCE Count, Stratified by Smoking and Exposure Categories

	Control		Low-Exposure		High-Exposure	
	Nonsmoker	Smoker	Nonsmoker	Smoker	Nonsmoker	Smoker
	5.50		6.16		8.00	
	6.80			6.60		9.64
		6.82	7.24*			11.16
		7.04		7.50	11.66	
		7.16		7.76		12.98
	7.20			8.16		
	7.46		8.28			
		7.52		8.54		
		7.96				
	8.22			9.62		
		8.30				
		8.90				
		9.38				
AVG.	7.036	7.885	7.226	8.030	9.83	11.26
DIFF.		.849		.804		1.43

Source: Adapted from Table 2 of Yager, Hines and Spear (1983). Exposure to Ethylene Oxide at Work Increases Sister Chromatid Exchanges in Human Peripheral Lymphocytes. *Science* 219, 1221–1223.
Note: The observations indicated with an * were from Hospital B while the rest were from Hospital A.

levels of exposure to ETO are related to an increased SCE count, it does raise a question as to whether low exposure carries a meaningfully increased risk, especially for nonsmokers. The study was one of several used in support of a short-term exposure limit, perhaps because it noted that if SCE induction was a function of dose rate, as indicated by some animal studies, then short-term exposure levels might need to be controlled. Examining the data in Table 7.9, the reader will see that only two exposed workers came from hospital B and their pattern of exposure was quite different than the others; they had many exposures to a very low dose, so they were in the low total dose category. In light of the fact that they were nonsmokers whose SCE counts were somewhat elevated, the pattern of exposure should also be considered in further studies. It should be noted that recent studies have supported the relationship between exposure to ETO and an increased SCE count.

This data set illustrates how difficult it is to obtain definitive results with a relatively small sample, especially when there are potentially important factors such as smoking and the pattern of exposure whose effects cannot be fully considered. Finally, we emphasize that we examined the data before suggesting that the pattern of exposure might play a role.[23] It is possible that this observation occurred by chance (sample size is only two) or it is due to something related to the hospital (other chemical exposures in the hospital or geographic area). When data from several separate sites are used, it is wise to examine each data set separately to see whether they all have a similar pattern before considering the data as one large data set. For example, suppose the three exposure levels in Table 7.9 were three sites A, B and C and our object was to *estimate* the effect of smoking on SCE counts. Since the estimates from sites A and B (control and low) are quite close, it is sensible to pool them. On the other hand, the data in area C (high) not only yielded a higher difference, the SCE counts were higher for both nonsmokers and smokers. Thus one might feel that the workers or conditions in area C were different than those in areas A and B, so we should not present a common estimate for all three populations. On the other hand, if one's primary objective is to test whether smoking increases the SCE count then one could still use the combined Wilcoxon test to discern a common direction or tendency across all areas. The point here is that the degree of similarity required to make an *estimate of a common effect* is greater than that required to test for a *common direction* of an effect.

By now it is apparent to the reader that the proper degree of stratification and the decision as to which covariates or factors should be considered in an analysis is a mixture of statistical science, art and knowledge of the subject matter area. One should be guided by the same principles we discussed in Chapter 6. Evidence should be presented that a factor has a substantial effect, as we did with smoking, before a study should be questioned because it did not incorporate that factor. Similarly, the possible effect of an omitted covariate should be assessed from related studies which included it to determine whether its omission is important. Again, before pooling data from different sources into one large sample, checks for consistency of the results[24] in the separate strata should be made.

We end this chapter with a section illustrating some of the limitations of the method of stratification and combination as well as some of the misuses and abuses of combination techniques. Quite often the misuses do not appear in the formal calculations, rather they are due to a failure to accurately specify the main issue to be studied and the major covariates which should be controlled for *prior* to the data collection process.

Problems

1.* (a) When the appellate opinion in *Bazemore v. Friday* insisted on finding significant difference at the .05 level (two-sided) in each of the five districts with employees of both races, what is the true level of significance the judges were requiring? Assume the rankings were done independently by different regional managers in each division.

(b) Do the estimated P_i's in Table 7.7 appear to indicate a consistent pattern of blacks receiving lower job ratings? Why does this *logically* support combining the results of the separate regional Wilcoxon measures into a summary one?

2. Suppose the *Bazemore v. Friday* data in Table 6.7 had been dichotomized at the median rather than the lowest quartile, i.e., employees were classified as in the lower half (third or fourth quartile) or upper half. Compute the MH summary statistic of the five 2 × 2 tables corresponding to this summarization. Before doing the calculation, do you think that your result will be as significant as that obtained from the combined Wilcoxon test? Why?

3. (a) Use the Wilcoxon test to verify that the difference in SCE counts of the control and low exposure groups in the data reported in Tables 7.7 and 7.8 is *not* statistically significant at the .05 level (two-sided test). Find the approximate *p*-value and decide whether your previous inference

would change if a one-sided test at the .05 level had been specified. In this problem ignore the smoking factor.

(b) Verify the finding in the original study that the SCE counts in the highly exposed group significantly exceeded that of the low exposed group.

4. Verify the result of the combined Wilcoxon procedure on the data in Table 7.9. Remember that we are comparing the SCE counts of smokers versus nonsmokers within each exposure category.

5.* The SCE study also reported that smokers in the control (nonexposed) group smoked more cigarettes per day on average (21) than smokers in the exposed groups (9).

a. How might this be reflected in the results presented in Table 7.9?

b. Could this yield a bias in our estimate of the possible increase in SCE counts due to exposure to ETO? If so, in which direction would this bias be?

Answers to Selected Problems

1. (a) Since they required that the blacks have significantly *lower* ranks than the whites in each region, they actually were using a one-sided .025 level test in each region. So their level of significance was $(.025)^5 = 9 \times 10^{-9}$. If you answered $(.05)^5 = 3.12 \times 10^{-7}$, you understood the major point.

(b) Since the $\overline{P}_i$ in all regions are less than 1/2, there appears to be a consistent pattern. Logically we are assessing the fairness of the process of evaluation. As the pattern is similar in all regions, they all provide information relevant to determining whether a general pattern exists.

2. The dichotomy at the median typically will provide less information than the Wilcoxon procedure. In each region (strata) the Wilcoxon test is usually more powerful than the median test, as differences between black and white pairs of employees both of whom are above (or below) the median, are considered in the Wilcoxon test but ignored in the median test.

5. (a) Since smoking increases SCE counts, the heavier smokers are likely to have larger SCE counts than other smokers. Thus, the smokers in the control group probably had a somewhat elevated increase in SCE

counts relative to smokers in the exposed group. Using the differences between average SCE counts in the exposed and control groups may yield an underestimate (bias) of the effect of ETO since the effect of the excess smoking among the control group smokers is missed.

6. Potential Problems Arising in the Use of Stratified Analyses

In this section we review and illustrate some common mistakes that occur when data is stratified into comparable subgroups and then examined to determine whether there is an overall difference between the groups. The proper amount of stratification requires careful thought prior to collecting and analyzing the data. Failure to incorporate a major factor such as smoking in a study of a possible carcinogen or mutagen can lead to a substantial bias in the estimated effect. Similarly, aggregating over too many dissimilar job types or mixing promotion and hiring decisions may exaggerate or mask a real difference. On the other hand, because stratified analyses only compare members of the two groups in the same strata, one needs to avoid using too many characteristics, some of which are highly related, to form the strata, as the power of the summary test decreases as more small strata replace a few large ones. It is rather easy to suggest a new factor which may influence a statistically significant difference observed in a data set, however, most of the possible effect of the new factor may already be accounted for by criteria already used in the stratification. This is especially true if the new factor is distributed similarly among both groups (within each strata). Overstratification can occur in a study of fair promotion policy when prior experience and firm specific seniority are used along with current grade level and occupation to form strata. Presumably the current grade level already reflects these factors, and perhaps only tenure at the present grade[25] is needed. Similarly, in a health study, weight and dietary habits may be highly related, especially if height and age are already being used to form the strata.

   A third error that occurs too often in the analysis of stratified data is to require statistical significance at some fixed level, e.g., .05, for the comparisons in *every* strata, rather than using a summary test. Notice that if the data were stratified into four groups which were independent of one another (e.g., employees in different occupations), then the probability of observing *four* significant differences at the .05 level, assuming there truly was *no* difference, is $(.05)^4 = .00000625$.[26] In no serious application of statistics is such a minute level of significance commonly used. A less blatant misuse of statistics is the failure to use a statistically efficient combination method, i.e., one with low power or one designed for use on a different type of data.

The effect of the passage of time on the phenomenon under study needs to be accounted for. In longitudinal health studies such as the Framingham study in Chapter 10, people age and will naturally have increased rates of some diseases. In equal employment cases the minority fraction of the qualified pool may change over time.[27] In some analyses the creation of more strata may suffice, while in others more sophisticated statistical methods such as regression (discussed in Chapter 7) will be needed to account for these gradual changes.

Finally, in longitudinal studies people leave the area or the employer. In health studies we may know when people drop out, but in promotion cases the only data available may be for persons who are currently employed or who were employed around the time the charge was filed.[28] In analyzing such data, the fact that the study is *retrospective, i.e.,* looks back in time, must be kept in mind, as the characteristics of the persons who left employment may be different from those who remain. This is especially relevant to the analysis of promotion data, as qualified minority employees may leave if they perceive diminished opportunity and in crime victimization studies, where crimes that occurred a few years ago are reported as happening in the last year or so. If this happens, the comparison suffers from retrospective bias[29] and one should try to judge its potential effect on the statistical analysis.

We now illustrate some of these problems and assess their impact on data from employment discrimination cases.

a.   Boykin v. Georgia Power:[30] *a case of promotion discrimination and its effect on salaries*

The wage data from *Boykin v. Georgia Power,* given in Table 7.10, was introduced to support plaintiffs claim of discrimination in promotion. Since new hires were typically placed in entry level positions[31] and advanced as they learned on the job, under a system of equal opportunity the salaries of all employees should increase over time, and salaries of black and white employees should increase at the same rate. Due to the natural variation in ability among employees, we do not expect all employees to progress at the identical rate, but the average rates of increase for both groups should be similar.

As background, we note that the firm opened in 1970 and the original

TABLE 7.10. Average Wage as of 2/11/76 For Employees (by Race) of the Georgia Power Company

Year of Hire	White		Black		Difference in Averages
	Number	Average	Number	Average	
1970	5	3.88	6	2.79	.89
1971	3	3.90	2	2.82	1.08
1972	5	3.11	3	2.75	.36
1973	4	3.55	3	2.91	.64
1974	2	3.43	2	2.78	.65
1975	10	3.59	11	2.77	.82
1976	2	2.65	7	2.65	0

Source: Table IV from 706 F.2d 1384 at 1388.

charge was filed in 1972, while the data relates to persons employed in 1976. Although no formal statistical analysis was carried out, the data indicate a systematic differential showing that blacks earned less than whites and served to bolster other statistical evidence concerning differences between the races in initial assignment and time to promotion submitted by plaintiffs. The data in Table 7.10 show an additional pattern of unequal pay which the combination procedures cannot detect; blacks in each cohort not only received less than whites in the same cohort but less than whites in cohorts of lesser seniority.[32]

In order to assess whether there was a substantial amount of retrospective bias, i.e., of a magnitude sufficient to explain the systematic difference reflected in the data, it would be desirable to have data on the turnover rate of employees by race for each year during the period. Since this data was not available, let us examine the number of employees of each race by year. As fair hiring was not an issue on appeal and as blacks form about half of the employees remaining from those hired in each year, the data is consistent with the assumption that employees of both races left at random.[33] Thus, the degree of retrospective bias is likely to be small. Moreover, we can ask what type of process could create the retrospective bias of a magnitude large enough to create the differences evident in Table 7.10. Either a much higher fraction of the more capable blacks, relative to capable whites, would have left the firm or a much higher fraction of the less qualified whites relative to both blacks and the more capable whites would have had to leave. The first possibility implies that other employers in the area (Mississippi) preferred hiring capable blacks to capable whites, which is not credible. The second possibility is more plausible if whites had more job opportunities in the area. However, there is no reason to believe that only the less able whites would have these opportunities and, consequently, a high turnover rate relative to more capable whites. Thus, labor market considerations also undercut retrospective bias being the cause of the observed black-white pay disparities in Table 7.10.

Retrospective bias also occurs in occupational health studies when the health status of current employees is ascertained. Some employees who were adversely affected by the agent under study may have sought alternative employment. Therefore, the observed estimates of relative risk may not increase as much with duration (years) of exposure to a toxic chemical as one would normally expect. The problem is inherent in all historical studies, even those where we try to develop the past history (health or employment) from currently available records. Typically, the data on employees who left a number of years prior to the time of the study are less accurate, and often a substantial portion of the records are missing. Again an assessment of the magnitude of the possible effect the missing data could realistically have on the ultimate inference should be made. The effect of missing data is discussed further in Chapter 9.

b. Pouncy v. Prudential:[34] *alleged racial discrimination in salary*

In this case the plaintiffs attempted to demonstrate salary discrimination by comparing the average wage of black and white current (1978) employees by their year of hire. These differences in average salaries were $31.72 per week for 1973 hires, $4.45 for 1974 hires, $23.92 for 1975 hires, $17.71 for 1976 hires and $20.62 for 1977 hires. The district court noted that these simple comparisons failed to account for skill level, education and training so that no meaningful conclusions could be drawn concerning the effect of race. The appellate opinion agreed with this analysis and did not even review the defendant's rebuttal evidence. That analysis showed that black and white employees holding jobs at the same level with the same tenure were paid the same.

The plaintiff's evidence in this case suffered from so much overaggregation that they failed to establish a *prime facie* case. Both analyses might have been affected by retrospective bias, but this issue was not discussed in either opinion, presumably because neither party raised it at the trial. Had the data been available, the plaintiffs might have stratified employees hired in each year by initial level at hire (within similar occupations) and then compared their salary raises. Then the 1974 and 1975 salaries of persons hired in 1973 and who left during 1976, say, could have been used and might have clarified the situation.

c. *Segar v. Civiletti:*[35] *racial discrimination in salaries*

In this case the defendant, the Drug Enforcement Agency (DEA), presented an approximation to a full prospective study, which they called cohort analysis, in order to rebut the plaintiff's allegations of a salary disparity between black and white employees. They divided the work force into groups of agents based on the year the agents joined DEA and the grade level they received at that time. The average salaries of black and white agents were compared as of October 1978 in each of 15 strata, presumably using the t-test (8.12 or 8.17), and the defendants found a significant difference in only four of the 15 groups[36] and apparently interpreted this as *not* indicating a pattern of discrimination.

Judge Robinson's opinion properly rejected this analysis. First, he noted that only two subgroups contained more than 31 agents and the differences were quite significant in them (*p*-values .01 and .002) and that the small sample sizes in the other groups diminished the power[37] of the statistical test. Secondly, he noted that agents who left DEA prior to October 1978 were excluded (possible retrospective bias).

Although the statistical interpretation of observing four significant differences at the .05 level (one-sided) among the 15 strata was not discussed, in the opinion we now show that it is consistent with a pattern of pay disparity. Under the null hypothesis of nondiscrimination, the probability of observing a significant difference in any subgroup is .05. Assuming that the 15 subgroups are independent,[38] the number of significant differences that would arise by chance has a binomial distribution with parameters $n = 15$ and $p = .05$, so we expect

$$np = 15 \times .05 = .75$$

or less than *one* of the individual strata comparisons to show a significant result. A rough calculation using the normal approximation (Section 3.1) with a continuity correction yields

$$Z = \frac{\text{observed number of significant results} - \text{expected}}{\text{standard deviation}}$$

$$= \frac{4 - .75 - .5}{(15)(.05)(.95)} = 3.26,$$

indicating a statistically significant excess number of strata differences.

This approximation[39] is confirmed by obtaining the exact probability that a binomial random variable with these parameters would equal 4 or more, which is .0055. Of course, this simple method relies only on whether or not there was a significant difference in each subgroup and does not use the magnitude of the differences in each cohort or their p-values. Thus, the fact that the p-values in the larger groups were .01 and .002 is not given full weight in this calculation. Nevertheless, this analysis confirms Judge Robinson's opinion and reminds us again of the fallacy of requiring significant differences to be shown in all subgroups.

The opinion also questioned the propriety and relevance of the criteria used by the defendant in forming the strata. In particular, the use of the grade level at initial assignment may bias the promotion analysis against plaintiffs when there is evidence of discrimination in these assignments, as there was in *Segar*. Also special qualifications of the individual agents, e.g., education and experience, were not incorporated, i.e., all "agents entering at the same grade in the same grade were treated as if they had equal qualifications". Had there *not* been a question concerning the fairness of the initial assignments, the distribution of these characteristics probably would be similar among agents of both races, as the requirements for government jobs are often expressed in terms of the minimum education and experience necessary for the position. Hence, grade level initially assigned would incorporate a substantial amount of the information contained in the education and prior experience characteristics so it might not be necessary to control for these in addition to initial grade received. If a substantial difference in pay existed, then reasoning similar to Cornfield's result suggests that small differences between blacks and whites in education and experience, not captured by initial grade assignment, are very unlikely to explain the large pay differential. Indeed, the appellate opinion, *Segar v. Smith*,[40] noted that a different statistical analysis, based only on persons the DEA itself hired, ensured that the groups analyzed would possess relatively similar composite of skills and experience.

The next case we discuss illustrates how by ignoring the effect of time, allowing promotion and hiring decisions to be combined, and not noticing that extra strata were added in some job categories, a court may have glossed over evidence of hiring discrimination.

d. Adams v. Gaudet:[41] *alleged discrimination in hiring and promotion*

This case concerned possible discrimination in both hiring and promotion in several job categories. The original complaint was filed on August 31,

1976 and the class was defined as all black employees or applicants as of, or after, August 30, 1975. The court did note that the school board had a prior history of discrimination and had been ordered to desegregate the system in 1970.

The trial judge accepted that the plaintiff's evidence showing that few blacks had been hired or promoted between 1970 and August 1976 in some jobs—e.g., 2 blacks and 24 white assistant coaches, 1 black and 17 white clericals were chosen, and 0 black and 10 white teachers were promoted to principal—together with the history of racial discrimination, sufficed to establish a *prima facie* case.

The analysis offered by the defendant and accepted in the decision

TABLE 7.11. *P*-values of Fisher's Exact Test in the Separate Job Categories in *Adams v. Gaudet*

Test	*P*-values
Promotions	
Administrative Staff, Principal and	
Assistant Principal	
Certified vs. Applied (123,113)	.504
Applied vs. Promoted	
Administrative Staff (41,6)	.705
Principals (61,11)	.8869
Assistant Principals (22,9)	.834
Lunch Room Managers	
September (1976) (10,2)	.800
September (1978) (11,1)	1.000
September (1980) (10,3)	1.000
Hires	
Coaches (224,53)	.0895
Music Teachers (94,12)	.510
Clericals (193,15)	.04897

Source: 515 F.Supp. 1086 at 1138–1139.
Note: The numbers in parentheses denote the total of all applicants and the number of selections (when applicable). All *p*-values are one-sided, corresponding to testing the hypothesis of equal rates against the alternative that the black rate is less than the white one.

concerned the time period August 30, 1975 through September 1980. The relevant portion is reproduced in Table 7.11. First the defendant showed that no one-sided test was significant at the level $\alpha = .0227$, which corresponds precisely to the two-sided two-standard deviation criteria. Indeed all the one-sided p-values in Table 7.11 exceed .05. Then a combined or overall summary statistic based on the distribution of the product of the p-values was presented.[42] Notice that results of analyses of data *concerning promotions* (principals, lunch room managers, etc.) *were combined with data on hiring,* although courts typically examine these issues separately. Moreover, the hiring data for all years combined in each job category was considered as one strata, while each year's data on promotion to lunchroom manager was considered as a separate strata. Similarly, the promotion data for administrators was broken down in two steps. First the black and white proportions of state-certified persons who applied were compared, and then the success rates of those who applied for promotion were compared. From the p-values in Table 7.11, it is clear that blacks were not adversely affected at either stage.

If one examines the hiring data, reproduced in Table 7.12, it appears that black applicants for coaching or clerical positions faired worse than white. The odds ratios are less than 1/2, however, statistically significant differences at the two-sided .05 level were not found due to the small sample sizes (number of hires). No discussion of power appears in the opinion. If one analyzes the hiring data for all three jobs (it would be unfair to the defendant to exclude music teachers where the hiring rates were equal) the MH procedure (Section 5.6) yields a Z of -2.14 and a summary odds ratio of .47. This suggests that the hiring process might have been discriminatory and perhaps a further explanation should have been required of defendants. This case is also interesting, because the

TABLE 7.12.   Hiring Data From Adams v. Gaudet for the Period August 1976 to September 1980

Position	Minority			Majority		
	Applied	Hired	Rate	Applied	Hired	Rate
Coaches	51	8	15.69	128	45	35.16
Music Teachers	20	2	10.00	74	10	13.51
Clericals	71	2	.028	128	13	10.16

Source: 515 F.Supp. 1086 at 1137. We calculated the hiring rates.

pre-charge data showing discrimination from 1970 until August 1976 was rebutted by primarily post-charge data (August 1975 until September 1980). Common sense suggests that the pre-charge period is the more relevant one for ascertaining the situation at the time the charge was filed. Furthermore, if a minority group was discriminated against in the past, the current pool of eligibles may contain a higher fraction of highly qualified persons than the current pool of majority eligibles, so even when the promotion rates of both groups in the second time period are the same, discrimination may be present. For example, suppose a firm has 100 lower level employees of each race in the first period and promotes 50 whites and 0 blacks, although 50% of the employees of each race are qualified for promotion and another 100 lower level employees of each race are added due to expansion. Assuming the employer only promotes qualified persons, among the current 350 lower level employees there are 100 qualified blacks and 50 qualified whites. Thus blacks form 66.67% of the qualified pool rather than their share (200/350 = 57.14%) of all lower level employees. Thus, if they receive 57% of all the promotions in the second period they still would be getting less than their proper share.

There are no well-established procedures for adjusting the post-charge data for pre-act or pre-statute of limitations period discrimination. With large data sets, one can analyze promotions given to persons hired within a three-year or other relevant period prior to the charge, as in *Segar v. Civiletti.* In situations such as *Adams v. Gaudet,* one could require that the test statistic have reasonably high power (80% or more) to detect an odds ratio of .5, even if the type I error has to be increased to .1 or .2.

It is interesting to contrast this lower court opinion (in the Fifth Circuit) accepting primarily post complaint data to rebut a *prima facie* case based on pre-complaint data, with the Ninth Circuit's rejection of a "cohort analysis," similar to the defendant's analysis in *Segar,* in *O'Brien v. Sky Chefs Inc.*[43] Their opinion states, "However, the 'cohort group' study covered advancements in years from 1976–1979 but the named plaintiffs left Sky Chiefs in 1976. The asserted individual claims encompassed the period from 1968–1976, and the class claims appear to cover the years 1964–1978. Hence, any inference from defendants 1976–1979 study would seem to have little probative value for the class' pre-1976 claims on the individuals 1968–1976 claims. In addition, this action was filed in 1977 and later changes in promotion policies could not erase liability for earlier discrimination. *Teamsters* 431 U.S. at 341-342."

Another interesting aspect of the defendant's exhibits reproduced as an appendix in the *Adams v. Gaudet* opinion is that the raw data for most of the promotions (including the year) is given, but corresponding data is not given for the hires. If almost all of the blacks were hired *after* the date of the charge, common sense would suggest that the pre-charge era discrimination found earlier had persisted at least for a while into the post-charge period. In situations where there are many hires, rather than give the applicant pool for each hire, one can consider the data by six-month or yearly intervals. This still enables one to ascertain whether the process changed and if so which data sets can properly be combined.

We have emphasized the importance of examining the data for a change in policy after critical events occurred because post-charge data is often introduced to rebut pre-charge data in equal employment cases. While such a change may not be sufficient to establish a *prima facie* case by itself,[44] from a statistical view, data or statistical analyses for the different periods should *not* be routinely combined if the characteristics of the data sets differ substantially. The logical importance of the time to promotion data in the *Capaci* case was that until the charge was filed females waited much longer for a promotion than males. Thus, to make a fair comparison of comparable employees, persons of similar seniority levels should be compared. In Table 7.13 we reproduce an exhibit comparing the promotion rates of all pharmacists hired after the effective date of the Civil Rights Act and before the filing of the complaint. The appellate opinion did not accept this and similar exhibits, as it did not accept the necessity to control for seniority since it did not reverse the lower court's preference for the median test analysis over the Wilcoxon procedure.

Comments. (a) To be fair to the appellate court we must mention that we do not know whether the plaintiffs emphasized the total lack of power of the median test on appeal.

TABLE 7.13. Promotions Received by Pharmacists Hired by Katz and Besthoff between July 1, 1965 and January 1, 1973

	Promoted	Not Promoted	Total
Males	28	148	176
Females	0	20	20
Total	28	168	196

Source: Author's copy of plaintiff's exhibit submitted to the court.
Note: Promotions to either chief pharmacist or assistant manager are counted.

(b) Recall that in *Capaci* the defendant rebutted the plaintiffs' time to promotion analysis, in part, by submitting the data in Table 7.2, which includes three promotions received by females *after* the charge was filed. Since the two senior females who were promoted in the pre-charge period were appointed chief pharmacist in 1968, the year the position was created, and no females were promoted to either assistant manager or chief pharmacist from that time until several months after the charge was filed,[45] how reasonable is the assumption, needed to justify combining the first post-charge year's of data with the pre-charge data, that the promotion process was unaffected by the filing of the charge?

In addition to sharp changes in response to specific circumstances, the process under study may change gradually due to changes in society or the economy as a whole. For example in a major study[46] concerning the relationship between cholesterol and other dietary factors to heart problems in men, an experimental group of men were given a cholesterol-reducing drug while the control group was not. Both groups were followed for a number of years. The sample sizes of the study groups were chosen so that the study would have sufficient power of detecting a difference of 1.5 in the relative risk of a heart attack. During the period when the study was carried out, however, more American men began exercising regularly and watching their diet. Hence, the control group reduced their cholesterol consumption, although they still had higher cholesterol levels than the experimental group. As a result, the study may not find a statistically significant difference in heart attack rates, although the results still suggest that lowering cholesterol intake and other risk factors reduces one's risk of a heart attack.

Problems

1. Read the *Adams v. Gaudet* opinion focusing on the statistical appendix. In the 1976–1977 years, how many supervisory jobs were filled? How many of these did blacks receive? How might one have analyzed the data? Given the history of discrimination, what does your common sense tell you about the time discrimination against blacks ended?

2. Read the opinion in *U.S. v. Page Industries* 726 F.2d. 1038, 34 FEP Cases 430 (5th Cir. 1984).
   (a) Discuss how the fact that the time needed for promotion *declined* for all workers from the 1960s to the 1970s affected the defendant's exhibit 193.

(b) How might the plaintiffs have improved their statistical presentation?

3. Read the paper by Harper in the references. What other factors might properly be incorporated in a termination case? What modification of the simple Wilcoxon test should then be used?

4. (a) Use the approximate formula given in (7.27) to calculate the overall black-white wage differential for the data in Table 7.10.

(b) Does this summary measure reflect the totality of the discrimination in promotions and initial job assignments that the court ultimately found?

5. Do the biases in cohort analysis as it has been used in Title VII cases tend to disadvantage the plaintiff or defendant when they are used to analyze salary data? How might one reduce these potential biases?

6. Assume that the reasoning in the *Capaci* decision allowing the pooling of the 1973 post-charge time to promotion data with the pre-charge data is logically correct. Using similar logic, should the court have found sex discrimination in the hiring of management trainees (Table 6.15) in part of the post-charge period? Explain your reasoning.

NOTES

1. The difference between group averages that will be considered meaningful depends on the use of the results. This is similar to the situation we encountered in Chapters 5 and 6 when we compared two proportions. Since it is practically impossible to control for all conceivable covariates (influential factors), experience with the data used in a particular field of application will lead to reasonable criterion, similar to the four-fifths rule. In the equal pay context, for persons performing the same job and having similar experience levels and educational backgrounds, a difference of 5% might well be meaningful. If the data consisted of wages for all persons in the job regardless of seniority, then a 5% difference might well be due to seniority pay differentials. Thus, the quality or degree of refinement of the data will play a role in determining whether an observed difference should be considered a substantive one.

2. At first glance it may appear redundant to make a test of significance on data for the complete population, since one can say that the difference between the averages equals a known number. However, in most applications we wish to conclude that the difference is due to some action or cause, e.g., a discriminatory policy, better educational opportunities or exposure to a substance, and there may be some slight variation among the subjects in both groups in their level of a covariate. The randomization test enables us to infer that even if this influential variable was distributed at random in the two groups, it is unlikely to have such a lopsided distribution that it would explain the observed difference. Another justification of the randomization test is that our data typically consists of persons available at a

particular time, e.g., employees as of the end of the year or persons living in an environmentally-impacted area at the time of study. While we may have data on all these people, they might be regarded as a sample from a larger population, e.g., persons employed during a 10-year period or persons ever living for a year or more in the area. A significant result obtained from a suitable randomization test indicates that it is unlikely that characteristics of the population studied at one time could differ enough from those of the larger possible populations to explain the results. Thus, critics of the conclusion should be required to show that the changes in the larger possible populations were dramatic enough to explain the observed disparity.

3. 711 F.2d 647, 32 FEP Cases 961 (5th Cir. 1983).

4. Even if the two-sided test was deemed appropriate, the data would be significant at the .05 level, as the two-sided p-value is twice the one-sided one, i.e., .0344, which is less than .05. In the actual case the judge required significance at the .01 level, which could never be attained with such a small sample.

5. See any of the elementary texts in the references. Mosteller and Rourke give the exact formula when one group is of size 2.

6. In *Pouncy v. Prudential Insurance Co.*, 668 F.2d 795, 28 FEP Cases 121 (5th Cir. 1982) the opinion notes, "We previously have suggested that the mean length of time between promotions may be relevant in proving discrimination. *Wilkins* 654 F.2d at 402, 26 FEP Cases at 1242."

7. Other courts have used this method to eliminate the effect of pre-act discrimination, e.g., *Segar v. Civiletti,* 508 F.Supp. 690 sub nom *Segar v. Smith* 738 F.2d 1249, 35 FEP Cases 31 (D.C. Cir. 1984).

8. Since we have a small finite population, the two selections are not exactly independent. If one considers the median of the combined samples as the 13th observation, the probability that both females are among the largest 13 observations is .24, which is well in excess of .05.

9. In fairness to the court, we do not know what issues were emphasized in the post-trial and appellate briefs. On the other hand, the pre-charge and post-charge periods were examined separately for evidence of discrimination in the hiring of managerial trainees (Section 4.4). This enables the fact finder to distinguish between the initial determination of liability and the possible subsequent determination of the period in which discrimination occurred.

10. See their 1984 supplement at 124.

11. The probability that the smallest y has rank r or higher is $\binom{N-r+1}{n}/\binom{N}{n}$. This is the p-value of a one-sided test against the alternative that the y's are larger than the x's. On the Capaci data, this one-sided p-value becomes $\binom{3}{2}/\binom{26}{2} = .0092$, as the smallest y (229) has rank 24 among all 26 numbers, so $N - r + 1 = 26 - 24 + 1 = 3$.

12. 750 F.2d 1266, 36 FEP Cases 1388 (5th Cir. 1985) affirming 36 FEP Cases 1386 (D.C. Tex. 1979).

13. FEP Cases 115 (D.D.C. 1983).

14. It is hard to discern a precise rule for determining the largest amount of aggregation that plaintiffs are allowed in their initial statistical exhibits with which they try to establish a *prima facie* case. The degree of specialized knowledge and skill needed to perform the various jobs and how clearly they have been specified by the employer are important. When a wide variety of occupations are aggregated, courts may simply disregard plaintiff's data in the form of Table 7.2. For instance, in *Fridge v. Statts* 30 FEP Cases 216 (D.D.C. 1982), data reporting the grade levels held by black and white employees in the General Accounting Office (GAO) employed in job levels 12 through 15, which include a wide variety of professional positions, was given no weight due to this over aggregation. On the other hand, in *Pouncy v. Prudential* 499 F.Supp. 427 (D.C. Tex. 1980) *aff'd* 688 F.2d 795, 28 FEP Cases 121 (5th Cir. 1982), a case involving a number of occupations but not as specialized and diverse as in *Statts,* the plaintiffs were allowed to establish a *prima facie* case of discrimina-

tion in promotions, in part, using similar data. The defendants rebutted any inference of discrimination by focusing on promotions occurring in the relevant time period and considering the eligible employees in the next lower grade as the pool of qualified persons. This type of analysis is usually the most persuasive statistical exhibit in a promotion case. The view expressed in *Maddox v. Claytor*[38] FEP Cases 715 (11th Cir. 1985) that static descriptive summary statistics provide a backdrop for more sophisticated evidence but, by themselves, are not sufficiently focused on employment practices under scrutiny to present a reliable picture is an appropriate description of role of static data such as that in Table 7.2, especially when a variety of occupations are included.

15.   42 FEP Cases 1161 (D.D.C. 1985), 843 F.2d 1395 (D.C. Cir. 1988).

16.   Actually, we weight them in proportion to the number of observations in each sample *minus* one because of the fact that we have only $n - 1$ independent measures of the spread (see Chapter 1) or variability of the data about its average.

17.   Although there exist tests for the problem of determining whether two sample variances can be regarded as being from a common population, we will not discuss them here. Rather, we will suggest a simple rule that if the ratio of the larger sample variance to the smaller one is 4 or less, the t-test will be reasonably accurate.

18.   When the number of standard deviations from expected is so large (10), the normal approximation to such a minute probability in moderate sample sizes is not that accurate. We will use less than one in a billion for situations where the number of standard deviations from expected exceeds 6 or 7.

19.   In the discrimination context, plaintiffs may attempt to widen the scope of their complaint by combining a highly significant result in one job category or time period with nonsignificant differences in others, while defendants may attempt to hide a significant difference by combining it with less relevant data in order to obtain a nonsignificant summary statistic.

20.   The effect of different sites may occur in health studies, as one hospital may follow a different treatment protocol than the others or the pattern of exposure to a chemical may differ in different plants. If the results in the various strata point in the same direction, then it is appropriate to combine them into a summary test.

21.   See formula (1.35) on page 30 of Lehmann's *Nonparametrics*.

22.   The original rule requiring both a reduction in the eight-hour average exposure and imposing a short-term exposure limit of 7.5 ppm was issued in the *Federal Register* (1984) *49*, 25734. The final rule which eliminated the short-term limit was published in the *Federal Register* (1984) *50*, 64. The short-term limit was reinstated in *Public Citizen Health Research Group v. Tyson* 796 F.2d 1479 (D.C. Cir. 1986).

23.   The procedure of first formulating an hypothesis after examining a data set and then testing it on the same data has an inherent bias towards confirmation. Remember that one often desires to reject the null hypothesis in favor of finding an effect. Suppose one saw the ETO data on the control and highly exposed groups and checked to see whether the groups differed in proportions of people

(a) with blond hair;

(b) under 5'8";

(c) who were Republican;

(d) who went to college, etc.;

and found that those with high SCE counts were mainly Republicans, and then compared the SCE counts of Republicans and Democrats and found a significant difference. Would this really imply that one's party affiliation causes SCEs? Of course not. Since even a random sample cannot be perfectly balanced with respect to all conceivable characteristics, when one examines data for many characteristics one has a high probability of finding one that will yield a significant difference at the .05 level. Thus, one should think about the major factors that are likely to affect the phenomena under study. In this example, one might have considered that exposure pattern was an important factor based on prior animal studies. If one only has some preliminary ideas, one should use one data set to formulate hypotheses and another independent data set to test them out.

24. This error can be avoided by following our discussion of the data in Table 5.10 from *Agarwal v. McKee*, where ignoring the grade level obscured a statistical indication of possible discrimination in promotions and of the data in Table 5.15 from *Caston v. Duke*, where the court noticed that simple addition of both 2 × 2 tables was misleading.

25. This assumes that the initial job assignments were given out fairly and that one is carrying out a prospective analysis, so current grade level does not reflect earlier discrimination in promotion.

26. Recall that the probability of obtaining a significant result at the .05 level by chance (i.e., of the null hypothesis true) is .05. Thus, the probability that four successive *independent* trials each with probability .05 of success would all show success is $(.05)^4 = 00000625$.

27. As discrimination in educational opportunity declines, one expects the minority fraction of persons eligible for entry-level technical and professional jobs to increase. This might be accompanied by a decline in the minority fraction of the labor pool available for unskilled jobs.

28. There are some EEOC guidelines for record keeping. In particular, once a charge is filed employment records should be kept. It might be preferable to encourage employers to keep records for two or three years before they are thrown out. Then one could obtain an accurate picture of the situation at the time of the charge.

29. Retrospective bias refers to statistical problems that may arise in studies when data pertaining to past events is collected currently. In our example the remaining employees may not be a representative of the original ones. Another form of retrospective bias occurs when people are asked today to recall events occurring several years ago. Often people can recall that an event happened but not the precise time it occurred, usually telescoping time so that it is reported as happening more recently than it actually did. Also, the farther in the past an event occurred, the more likely it is that it will be forgotten. Thus, people will report more visits to doctors' offices this year than three years ago, which might lead one to erroneously infer that the health of the population declined when it really did not change.

30. 706 F.2d 1384, 32 FEP Cases 25 (5th Cir. 1983).

31. Recall that the data in Tables 6.5 and 6.6 showed that proportionally more whites than blacks were placed above the lowest level.

32. This occurs because the individual Wilcoxon tests being combined compare members in a cohort or strata to one another and illustrates why one should avoid using related criteria to form separate strata. This loss of relevant comparisons did not occur when we used the Mantel-Haenszel test to combine data on hires or promotion in different occupations or years as there was no competition among members of the different strata.

33. Here we are implicitly assuming that all employees have the same probability of leaving in any one year period for reasons unrelated to discrimination, e.g., a better job offer or personal preference. Then the fractions of employees of both races who remain should be about the same.

34. 668 F.2d 795, 28 FEP Cases 121 (5th Cir. 1982) *affirming* 499 F.Supp. 427, 23 FEP Cases 1349 (S.D. Tex. 1980).

35. 508 F.Supp. 690 25 FEP Cases 1452 (D.C. 1981).

36. They subsequently refined the analysis in the four subgroups, and we refer the reader to the opinion for details.

37. The opinion does not use the term "power" but notes at page 698, "The size of the sample affects the statistical significance of a study. The smaller the sample is, the greater the disparity has to be before it can be considered statistically significant."

38. Essentially, this assumes that the members of each strata compete for promotions and pay raises only among themselves. While this may not be completely accurate, it is a reasonable assumption, as we have complete population data. Thus, one could argue that given the pay increases or promotions received by the entire strata, they should be distributed at random among the members of that strata or cohort, as all employees in a cohort possessed similar qualifications.

39. Remember that the normal approximation was derived for large samples, while $n = 15$ here, as each cohort comparison counts as *one* binomial outcome.

40. 738 F.2d 1249, 35 FEP Cases 31 (D.C. Cir. 1984).

41. 515 F.Supp. 1086, 30 FEP Cases 1258 (W.D. La. 1981).

42. The idea underlying this procedure, due to Fisher, is that the overall p-value summarizing the result of *independent* tests is the product of the individual p-values. Under the null hypotheses of no difference, each p-value should be near 1/2, so the product of the p-values should be near $(1/2)^k$. The exact calculation of these probabilities is due to R. A. Fisher, and the procedure is described in the reference by Rosenthal.

43. 670 F.2d 864, 28 FEP Cases 1690 (9th Cir. 1982).

44. *Worley v. Western Electric Co.* 26 FEP Cases 1708 (N.D. Ga. 1981).

45. Recall that the charge was filed at the end of January 1973 and that the EEOC is required to notify an employer of the filing of a charge within 30 days. The *first female* promotion occurred in April 1973. Had this promotion occurred before the employer had been notified of the charge, its exclusion by plaintiffs would not have been justified.

46. Newton, J. D., Broste, S., Cohen, L., Fishman, E. L., Kjelsberg, M. O. and Schoenberger, J. (1981). The Multiple Risk Factor Intervention Trial. *Preventive Medicine* 10, 519–543.

REFERENCES

Elementary Statistics Texts

CONOVER, W. J. (1971). *Practical Nonparametric Statistics*. New York: Wiley.

DANIEL, W. W. (1978). *Applied Nonparametric Statistics*. Boston: Houghton Mifflin.

HOLLANDER, M. AND WOLFE, D. A. (1973). *Nonparametric Statistical Methods*. New York: Wiley.

HOLLANDER, M. AND PROSCHAN, F. (1984). *The Statistical Exorcist: Dispelling Statistical Anxiety*. New York: Marcel Dekker. (This book also discusses the promotion data from the *Capaci* case.)

MOSTELLER, F. M. AND ROURKE, R. E. K. (1973). *Sturdy Statistics*. Boston: Addison Wesley.

SIEGEL, S. (1956). *Nonparametric Statistics*. New York: McGraw Hill.

More Advanced Statistics Texts

HETTMANSPERGER, T. P. (1984). *Statistical Inference Based on Ranks*. New York: Wiley. (An up-to-date account of recent developments and extensions of the Wilcoxon and related tests to analyze data fitting more complex statistical models, such as regression, which we discuss in Chapter 8.)

LEHMANN, E. L. (1975). *Nonparametrics: Statistical Methods Based on Ranks.* San Francisco: Holden Day. (An intermediate level text stressing the Wilcoxon procedure and its extensions, written by one of the founding fathers of the modern approach to the subject.)

Articles and Books

AUSTIN, S. G. AND SIELKEN, R. L., JR. (1988). Issues in Assessing the Carcinogenic Hazards of Ethylene Oxide. *Journal of Occupational Medicine* **30**, 36–45.

GASTWIRTH, J. L. AND WANG, J. L. (1987). Nonparametric Tests in Small Unbalanced Samples: Application in Employment Discrimination Cases. *Canadian Journal of Statistics* **15**, 339–248. (This article develops a more powerful version of the median test for use in unbalanced samples but shows that the Wilcoxon test is usually even more powerful. The new median test does reject the null hypothesis on the *Capaci* data.)

GOLDBERG, L. ED. (1986). Hazard Assessment of Ethylene Oxide. Boca Raton: CRC Press.

HARPER, G. L. (1981). Statistics as Evidence of Age Discrimination. *Hastings Law Journal* **32**, 1347–1375. (This article describes the use of the Wilcoxon test to study claims of age discrimination in termination. The age distribution of the terminees is compared to that of those retained. It also discusses the alternative procedure which we describe in the text. That method is related to statistical tests based on exceedances. The article is the basis of Sections 6 and 7 of Chapter 11 in Wehmhoefer, R. A. (1985). *Statistics in Litigation*. Colorado Springs: Shepards/McGraw Hill.)

ROSENTHAL, R. (1978). Combining Results of Independent Studies. *Psychological Bulletin* **85**, 155–193. (Discusses several tests which are useful in combining independent statistical tests, emphasizing the importance of providing an overall estimate of the *effect* or *difference*.)

STOLLEY, P. D., SOPER, K. A., GALLOWAY, S. M., NICHOLS, W. W., NORMAN, S. A., AND WOLMAN, S. R. (1984). Sister Chromatid Exchanges Associated with Occupational Exposure to Ethylene Oxide. *Mutation Research* **129**, 89–102. (A paper published after the deliberations on ETO that corroborates the effect of exposure to ETO and smoking on SCE counts.)

Chapter 8

Measuring the Relationship between Variables

1. Introduction

In many applications we are not only interested in the distribution of a variable (e.g., hourly wage or annual salary) in a population but also desire to understand the factors (e.g., education, father's income, seniority) which explain why the earnings distribution presented in Chapter 1 has such a large variation. To explore the influence of one factor, e.g., education, we can study the data in Tables 1.13 and 1.16, which report wage distributions by educational category. Notice that the *average* college graduate earned more than the *average* high school graduate, although some persons with only a high school education earned more than the average salary of college graduates.

The data in Tables 1.13 and 1.16 do *not prove that education caused* the difference in salary between the two groups, as there are other factors that influence education and earnings. Establishing a meaningful association or relationship between variables, however, is quite helpful in discovering the underlying causal process, as well as an aid to prediction.[1] In this chapter, we first discuss the correlation coefficient, which is a measure of the degree of linear association between two variables, and the regression line, which enables us to make predictions of one variable from

363

knowledge of the other (e.g., law schools use LSAT scores to predict an applicant's likelihood of success in class).

Since there are often several factors influencing the distribution of the variables of interest (e.g., earnings are affected by seniority, years of formal education, specific occupational training and, possibly, by race or sex), a more general method of combining the influence of several characteristics on the variable under study, multiple regression, is discussed. Through its use, we are often able to discover which variables influence the outcome variable and their relative weight or influence.

Before we become immersed in the details of investigating the relationship between variables, some historical background may clarify the type of studies which can be made with the methods of this chapter. During the late nineteenth century, Galton was concerned with the influence of heredity on human attributes. In 1899 he published the results of his study about the relationship between the heights of fathers and sons—very tall fathers had tall sons; however, as a group, the sons were not as tall as their fathers. Similarly, very short fathers had short sons, but on the average, the sons were taller than their fathers. The average height of sons of fathers in the medium range was closer to that of their fathers. Thus, one could use the height of a father to predict the height of his son, but one could not simply use the height of the father as a predictor of his son's height. Rather, one had to allow for the tendency of the sons of very short or very tall fathers to be between the height of their father and the average of all men. This phenomenon was called the *regression effect* or *regression toward the mean*. Galton denoted the relation between the heights of father and son by the symbol, r, for regression. Today we call r the correlation coefficient. Roughly speaking, it means that if the height of a father is x standard deviations above average, the best prediction of his son's height is rx standard deviations above average. Thus, if $r = .6$, sons of very tall fathers who are *two* standard deviations above average (the 97.5th percentile of the distribution of male heights) should have an average height of $.6 \times 2 = 1.2$ standard deviations above average (the 88.5th percentile). The formula for making the prediction is based on fitting a line to data on the heights of fathers and sons. Hence, we begin with reviewing the mathematical properties of the line.

2. The Linear Relationship

Many relationships one studied in school were expressible as linear equations. For example, the circumference (C) of a circle of radius R equals 2π

times R, i.e., $C = 2\pi R$. Thus, given the *radius* of a circle, we can determine its *circumference*. Similarly, if a car goes at a constant speed, say 55 miles per hour, if we know the time, X, spent travelling, then the distance D covered during the time equals 55X.

Suppose a firm pays *new* employees an annual salary of $15,000 and gives them a raise of $1000 at the end of each year of service. Then, if we know the length of service (X), we can determine an employee's yearly salary (Y) from the equation: $Y = 15,000 + 1000X$.

Equations of this type are called linear and are represented in the form

(8.1) $Y = a + bX$

because the relationship between the variables Y and X on a graph of the points (x, y) is a straight line. Notice that when $X = 0$, $Y = a$, and the value, a, is called the *intercept* of the line. When $X = 1$, $Y = a + b$, when $X = 2$, $Y = a + 2b$ and, in general, whenever X *increases* by 1 unit Y increases by b units. The constant b is called the slope of the line and determines the *change* in Y corresponding to a *change* in X. Because we will use such equations to determine the value of Y from the value of X, Y is called the *dependent* variable and X is considered the *independent* variable.

Example 8.1.   Consider the values of X and Y satisfying the equation $Y = 2 + 1.5X$:

X	0	1	2	3	4	5	6
Y	2	3.5	5	6.5	8	9.5	11.

Notice that the intercept is 2, which is the value of Y, when $X = 0$, and the slope, $b = 1.5$. The line thru the points is given in Figure 8.1. Also, the average values of the X's and the Y's are 3 and 6.5, respectively, and this point $(\overline{X}, \overline{Y}) = (3, 6.5)$ *lies on the line.*

Although the linear relationship seems quite a special one, many apparently more general relationships can be expressed in terms of linear ones. For example, the *area* (A) of a circle equals πR^2 where R is the radius. The relation between A and R is *not linear*, but the relation between A and R^2 is. By considering a new *variable*[2], $X = R^2$, we can express the area of the circle as a *linear equation* $A = \pi X$. Alternatively, one can consider the variable $Y = \ln A$, formed by taking the logarithm[3] of the area. Then the equation $A = \pi R^2$ becomes

(8.2) $\ln A = \ln \pi + 2 \ln R.$

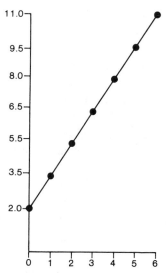

FIGURE 8.1.   The line $y = 2 + 1.5x$ which connects the points in example 8.1.

Hence, if we call ln R the variable X from which we will predict the logarithm (Y) of the area (A), we have a linear relation $Y = a + bX$, where $a = \ln \pi$ and $b = 2$.

Problems

1.   Given the equation $Y = 1 + 3X$,

   (a) Calculate the values of Y corresponding to each of the following values of $X =$

$$X \quad 1 \quad 2 \quad 3 \quad 4 \quad 5$$
$$Y \quad 4$$

   (b) Plot the 5 pairs of points (X, Y) on a graph paper and draw the line.

   (c) Calculate the average values of X and Y and verify that the point (X, Y) lies on the lines (i.e., verify that $Y = 1 + 3X$).

2.   Let Y be the area of a circle with radius, R. i.e.,

$$R = 1 \quad 2 \quad 3 \quad 4 \quad 5$$
$$Y = \pi \quad 4\pi \quad 9\pi \quad 16\pi \quad 25\pi$$

Let $X = R^2$ and plot the relation $Y = \pi X$ on graph paper. If your calculator doesn't have a value of π, use $\pi = 3.14$.

3. The Correlation Coefficient

In Tables 1.13 and 1.16, we saw that for both sexes education is associated with increased earnings; however, there were some persons who had only completed elementary school who earned more than the average college graduate. This suggests that a measure of the strength of the relationship between two variables should be defined in terms of an average over the data. The definition of the correlation coefficient, Y, is based on the idea that if X and Y are *positively related,* then usually, or on average, when X is large (small), Y is large (small).

When is a particular value of X_1 large relative to the whole distribution of possible X values? If we think of normal data, we might say X is large if it is at least one standard deviation above average and very large if it is two or more standard deviations above the average. Thus, we can consider an observation X_1 to be large or small according to the size of

$$(8.3) \qquad \frac{(X_1 - \overline{X})}{S_x},$$

where $\overline{X}$ is the mean and S_x the standard deviation of the X's. Formula (8.3) expresses the difference between X_1 and the average $(\overline{X})$ in terms of standard deviation units.

In order to assess the relationship between a pair of measurements (X_1, Y_1) notice that if both members of the pair are above their respective means $(\overline{X}$ and $\overline{Y})$ the product

$$(8.4) \qquad \frac{(X_1 - \overline{X})}{S_x} \cdot \frac{(Y_1 - \overline{Y})}{S_y}$$

is positive. Similarly, if both X_1 and Y_1 are below their respective means, the product (8.4) is positive. On the other hand, when one member of the pair (X_1, Y_1) is above the mean of its group, while the other is below, the product (8.4) is negative. If we average (8.4) *over all* pairs, then if the two variables typically are positively related, this average should be positive, while the reverse is true when they are negatively related. If there is no relationship, e.g., the variables X and Y are independent of one another, approximately half of the pairs (X_i, Y_i) will yield positive values of (8.4), while the other half will yield negative values, so the average of (8.4) over all pairs should be close to zero. We now give the formal *definition*:

Let $(X_1, Y_1), \ldots (X_n, Y_n)$ be n observations on the variables X and Y.

The correlation coefficient, r, is defined as

$$(8.5) \quad r = \frac{1}{n-1}\left\{\frac{(X_1 - \overline{X})}{S_x}\frac{(Y_1 - \overline{Y})}{S_y} + \cdots + \frac{(X_n - \overline{X})}{S_x}\frac{(Y_n - \overline{Y})}{S_y}\right\}$$

or

$$(8.6) \quad r = \frac{1}{n-1}\sum_{i=1}^{n}\frac{(X_i - \overline{X})}{S_x}\frac{(Y_i - \overline{Y})}{S_y} = \frac{1}{n-1}\sum_{i=1}^{n}\frac{(X_i - \overline{X})(Y_i - \overline{Y})}{S_x S_y},$$

where $\overline{X}$ and $\overline{Y}$ are the means of the X and Y values and S_x and S_y are their standard deviations. Notice that we divided the sum of the products of the form (8.4) by $n - 1$ rather than n to obtain their average. This is a technical point similar to using $n - 1$ instead of n in calculating the variance of n observations and is due to the fact that we estimate the average value of the X's and Y's by their sample means $\overline{X}$ and $\overline{Y}$.

Expression (8.6) is obtained from (8.5) by factoring out $S_x S_y$ from the denominator of each term in (8.5) and is easier to work with, as we now divide the sum of the cross products $(X_i - \overline{X}) \cdot (Y_i - \overline{Y})$ only once by $S_x S_y$, instead of dividing each cross product term by it.

Example 8.2. Suppose that we have the following data on X = LSAT scores and Y = GPA of law students

$$
\begin{array}{ccccccc}
X & 500 & 600 & 700 & 500 & 600 & 700 \\
Y & 2.3 & 3.2 & 3.6 & 2.7 & 2.8 & 3.4
\end{array}
$$

It is easily seen that $\overline{X} = 600$ and $\overline{Y} = 3.0$, and we now calculate S_x, S_y and r by using the format in Table 8.1. Now S_x^2 is obtained by dividing the total of column (6), which is 40,000, by one less than the number of observations, i.e., $6 - 1 = 5$, yielding 8000, so S_x, the standard deviation of the X's, equals $\sqrt{8000} = 89.4427$. Similarly, the standard deviation, S_y

---

TABLE 8.1.   Format For Calculating r

	(1)	(2)	(3)	(4)	(5)	(6)	(7)
	X	Y	$X - \overline{X}$	$Y - \overline{Y}$	$(X - \overline{X})(Y - \overline{Y})$	$(X - \overline{X})^2$	$(Y - \overline{Y})^2$
	500	2.3	-100	$-.7$	$+70$	10000	.49
	600	3.2	0	$+.2$	0	0	.04
	700	3.6	$+100$	$+.6$	$+60$	10000	.36
	500	2.7	-100	$-.3$	$+30$	10000	.09
	600	2.8	0	$-.2$	0	0	.04
	700	3.4	$+100$	$+.4$	$+40$	10000	.16
TOTALS			0	0	200	40000	1.18

of the Y's is $\sqrt{(1.18)}/5 = \sqrt{.236} = .4858$. The numerator of (8.6) is the total of the products in column 5, divided by 5, i.e., 200/5 = 40. Putting these values in (8.6) along with the values for S_x and S_y yields

$$r = \frac{40}{(89.4427)(.4858)} = .9206.$$

Since the correlation coefficient, r, takes on values between -1 and $+1$, the value .92 in the example indicates a strong relationship between the LSAT score (X) and GPA (Y) of the students. This high degree of association in the data is confirmed by plotting the data (Figure 8.2).

In general, the correlation coefficient, r, measures how close the plot of points (X_i, Y_i) are around a straight line. In Figure 8.3, we present several plots of samples of 20 with varying values of r. Notice that the extreme values of r equal to $+1$ on -1 indicate a perfectly straight linear relation between the variables X and Y, where the sign ($+$ or $-$) of r corresponds to the slope of the line. When $r = .5$, the points vary quite a bit about the line, while when $r = +.25$, only a slight association about the line is evident.

The interpretation of the correlation coefficient, r, as a measure of how close the variables X and Y fit a straight line is of fundamental importance because it implies that r doesn't measure all possible relationships be-

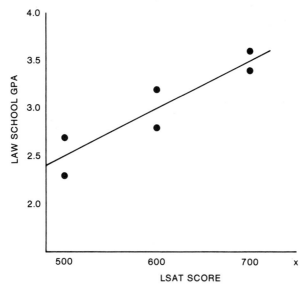

FIGURE 8.2.   A graph of the 6 data points in example 8.2.

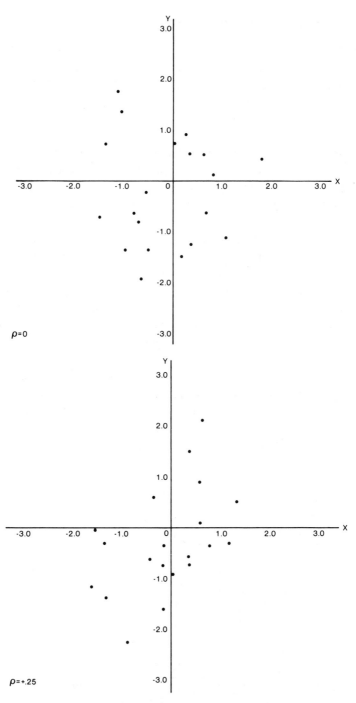

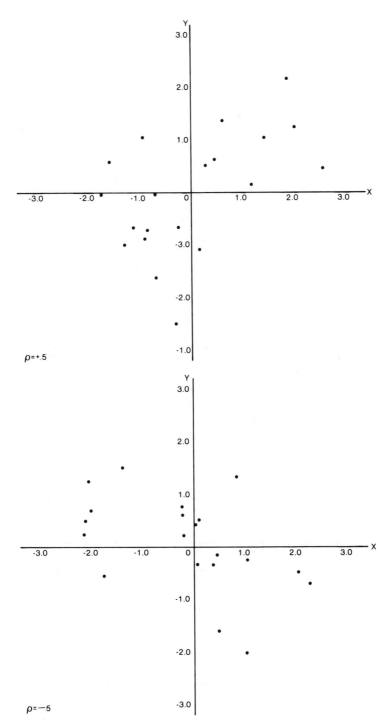

FIGURE 8.3. *Continued*

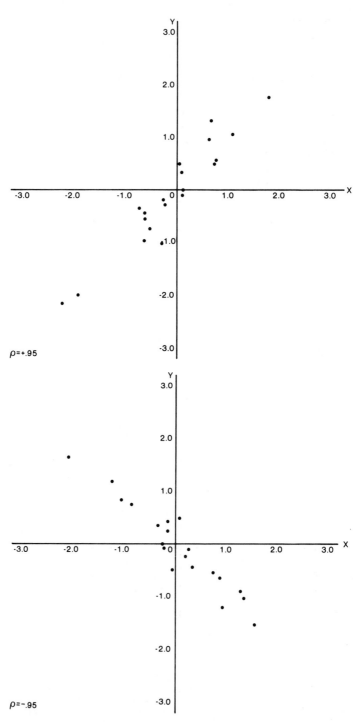

FIGURE 8.3. *Continued*

372

tween the variables X and Y but only their linear (straight line) relationship. It suggests that we will be able to use the line about which sample points (x_i, y_i) fall to predict the values of one variable (Y) from the other (X).

Later we will describe a more formal method of deriving the line used to predict the y values from the corresponding x's; however, we can guess the answer from the idea used in defining r. Recall that r measures how closely $(X_i - \overline{X})/S_x$ and $(Y_i - \overline{Y})/S_y$ move together. Indeed, if X and Y always move together, i.e., $r = 1$, then

$$(8.7) \qquad \frac{(Y_i - \overline{Y})}{S_y} = \frac{(X_i - \overline{X})}{S_x},$$

i.e., Y_i and X_i both *differ* from their group mean by the *same distance, measured* in *standard deviation units.* Since r measures the degree of the relationship between X and Y, if we wanted to predict a value of Y from the corresponding value of its X, we might expect that $(Y_i - \overline{Y})/S_y$ should be near $r(X_i - \overline{X})/S_x$, differing from it only by a random amount which is unrelated to the value X_i. Thus replacing 1 by r in (8.7) gives us the equation for the line that we expect the points (X_i, Y_i) to be centered around, i.e., the line enabling us to predict Y_i from X_i is given by

$$(8.8) \qquad \frac{(Y_i - \overline{Y})}{S_y} = \frac{r(X_i - \overline{X})}{S_x}.$$

After some algebraic manipulation, this line has two useful expressions

$$(8.9) \qquad Y_i = \overline{Y} + \frac{rS_y}{S_x}(X_i - \overline{X})$$

and

$$(8.10) \qquad Y_i = \left[\overline{Y} - \left(\frac{rS_y}{S_x}\right)\overline{X}\right] + r\left(\frac{S_y}{S_x}\right)X_i.$$

Formula (8.9) tells us that if $r > 0$ and $X_i > \overline{X}$ then we expect Y_i to be larger than $\overline{Y}$ by $r(S_x/S_y)$ times the amount X_i exceeds $\overline{X}$. If both X and Y have the same variance (or are standardized variables) then $S_y/S_x = 1$ and (8.9) tells us that when $X_i > \overline{X}$, the expected value of Y_i is greater than Y by an amount $r(X_i - \overline{X})$ which is *less* than $(X_i - \overline{X})$. This is the mathematical expression of the regression towards the mean phenomenon described in the introduction to the chapter. The second formula (8.10) expresses the line in terms of its slope $b = r(S_y/S_x)$ and intercept $a = (\overline{Y} - (r\,S_y/S_x)\,\overline{X})$.

The linear relation (8.9) or (8.10) expressing the correlation between the variables X and Y leads to another way of viewing the degree of association between the variables, namely, how well can we predict an observation Y_i knowing the regression line (8.9) or (8.10), and its X_i.

In order to appreciate the value of the predictions from the regression line, suppose that we only knew $\overline{Y}$ and had to guess each value Y_i. We would guess (predict) each Y_i to be $\overline{Y}$. If we measured the error of our prediction by the square of the difference between the prediction ($\overline{Y}$) and Y_i, our average error would be

$$\frac{1}{n} \sum_{i=1}^{n} (Y_i - \overline{Y})^2 = S_y^2 \left(\frac{n-1}{n} \right).$$

With the regression line (8.9), our prediction of Y_i can be regarded as

(8.11) $$\overline{Y} + \frac{rS_y}{S_x} (X_i - \overline{X}) + e_i,$$

where e_i is a random error which has mean 0. The average squared error of the predictions based on (8.11) is $(1/n) \sum_{i=1}^{n} e_i^2$. To calculate it we note that

(8.12) $$Y_i - \overline{Y} = r \left(\frac{S_y}{S_x} \right) (X_i - \overline{X}) + e_i,$$

so that

(8.13) $$(Y_i - \overline{Y})^2 = r^2 \left(\frac{S_y}{S_x} \right)^2 (X_i - \overline{X})^2 + e_i^2 + 2r \left(\frac{S_y}{S_x} \right) (X_i - \overline{X}) e_i.$$

Adding the n terms in (8.13) yields

(8.14) $$\sum (Y_i - \overline{Y})^2 = r^2 \left(\frac{S_y}{S_x} \right)^2 \cdot \sum (X_i - \overline{X})^2 + e_i^2,$$

where we delete the sum of the cross product term in (8.13) as the $\sum e_i$ will be near 0. Dividing (8.14) by $n - 1$ yields

$$\frac{1}{n-1} \sum (Y_i - \overline{Y})^{-2} = r^2 \left(\frac{S_y^2}{S_x^2} \right) \frac{1}{n-1} \sum (X_i - \overline{X})^2 + \frac{1}{n-1} e_i^2.$$

As $\sum (X_i - \overline{X})^2 = (n - 1) S_x^2$, (8.14) becomes

(8.15) $$S_y^2 = r^2 S_y^2 + \frac{1}{n-1} \sum e_i^2.$$

Thus, the average square of the errors, e_i, is

(8.16) $$\frac{1}{n} \sum e_i^2 = \frac{n-1}{n} \frac{1}{n-1} \sum e_i^2 = \frac{n-1}{n} (1 - r^2) S_y^2.$$

Formula (8.16) means that the average squared error of the predictions of Y based on the correlation between Y and X are *smaller*, by the factor $(1 - r^2)$, than the average squared error, $S_y^2(n - 1)/n$, not using the relationship. In other words, using the correlation between Y and X enables us to reduce the variability of predictions of Y without using knowledge of X, by r^2. Thus, r^2, the square of the correlation coefficient, can be regarded as the proportion of the variation of the variable Y that can be explained statistically by its linear relation with X.

Indeed, expression (8.14) is often described as follows. The total sum of squared deviations of the Y's about their mean is the sum of two components: (a) the portion predictable or explainable by its relation with X and (b) a portion that is completely unrelated to X.

Let us now illustrate the use of the regression or prediction line on the data in our example. Since $r = .92$, $S_x = 81.65$, $S_y = .4435$, $\overline{X} = 600$ and $\overline{Y} = 3.0$, equation (8.11) giving the expected value of Y corresponding to a particular X becomes

(8.17) $Y = 3.0 + .005 (X - \overline{X}) = 3.00 + .005 (X - 600)$

or

$Y = .005X.$

Using (8.17) we can compare the actual Y's to their predicted values (which are labeled $\hat{Y}_i$) determined from the regression line: $Y = .005X$. Each difference $Y_i - \hat{Y}_i$ can be regarded as an observation on the error e_i and is called the ith *residual*. By averaging the squares $(Y_i - \hat{Y}_i)^2$, we estimate the variance of the errors, e_i, which have the mean 0. This is done in Table 8.2. Notice that $1/n \sum e_i^2 = (.18)/6 = .03$. We can check our calculation of r^2 by using (8.16), which expressed r^2 as $1 - $ [average square error]/S_y^2. For the data, $r^2 = 1 - (.03)/.19667 = .8475$, which equals $(.9206)^2$, the square of the value of r we calculated in Table 8.1.

Remark. We have developed the regression line for predicting Y on the basis of X. This was natural for our example, as the LSAT score is available before one attends law school and receives grades. Sometimes the variables X and Y are available at the same time, so one might desire to predict X from Y. To obtain this line one does *not* solve (8.9) for X in

TABLE 8.2. Comparison of Predictions From the Fitted Regression Line With the Original Observations

	Actual	Predicted	Difference		Squared Difference (e_i^2)
X	Y	$\hat{Y}_i$	$Y_i - \hat{Y}_i$		$(Y_i - \hat{Y}_i)^2$
500	2.3	2.5	$-.2$		.04
600	3.2	3.0	$+.2$		.04
700	3.6	3.5	$-.1$		.01
500	2.7	2.5	$+.2$		.04
600	2.8	3.0	$-.2$		.04
700	3.4	3.5	$-.1$		.01
				Total	.18

The estimated average squared error is $\left(\frac{1}{6}\right)(.18) = .03$.

terms of Y. Rather, one *interchanges* the role of X and Y, and fits the line

$$(8.9a) \qquad X = \overline{X} + r\left(\frac{S_x}{S_y}\right)(Y_i - \overline{Y})$$

to the data. Carrying out this calculation for our data set yields

$$(8.17a) \quad X = 600 + (.92)\frac{(81.65)}{(.4435)}(Y - 3) = 91.87 + 169.38Y,$$

which clearly *differs* from what would obtain solving (8.17) for X, i.e., $X = 200Y$.

The reason for this seeming discrepancy is that the correlation coefficient measures the linear relation between the *standardized variables,* so our equation for predicting Y from X, given in (8.12), is

$$\frac{(Y_i - \overline{Y})}{S_y} = \frac{r(X_i - \overline{X})}{S_x} + \text{error}\,(Y),$$

while the corresponding equation for predicting X from Y is

$$\frac{(X - \overline{X})}{S_x} = \frac{r(Y - \overline{Y})}{S_y} + \text{error}\,(X).$$

Notice that the residual errors relate to the variable that will be predicted and will have variance $(1 - r^2)$ times the variance of that variable. Thus, we should not expect the two regression lines fitted to a set of data to be the same.

4. The Use of Correlation Analysis

In Chapter 5, we noted that plaintiffs may support a claim that a test has a disparate impact on minority applicants by showing that the difference in pass rates is statistically significant. If plaintiffs are successful in their claim, the defendant must show that the test is job-related. This is accomplished by demonstrating a meaningful and statistically significant correlation between the test scores and productivity in the job at issue. Although this may appear to be an easy or routine task, a number of special issues arise in this area.

a. The standard test of significance

Suppose we have complete data on the test scores (X) and (Y) of a sample of n individuals, e.g., the data on LSAT score and GPA in example 8.2. When the variables X and Y both have a normal distribution, and there is *no* correlation between them, then the sample correlation, r, will be near 0. Indeed, r has expected value 0 and standard deviation $\sqrt{(1 - r^2)/(n - 2)}$. When n is *large* (50 or more) the distribution[5] of r is approximately normal, and we convert this normal to a standard normal Z, as we did earlier for the tests based on the sample mean $(\overline{X})$. Thus, under the *null hypothesis* of no correlation

$$(8.18) \qquad Z = \frac{r}{\sqrt{\dfrac{1 - r^2}{n - 2}}} = r \frac{\sqrt{n - 2}}{\sqrt{1 - r^2}}$$

is a standard normal variable. It is used to make tests of significance at any desired level. For example, a 5% level test is carried out by rejecting the null hypothesis when

$$|Z| > 1.96.$$

Example 8.3 Suppose a sample of 51 students yields a sample correlation coefficient $r = .3$. To test the null hypothesis at the 5% level, compute

$$z = \frac{r}{\sqrt{1 - r^2}} \sqrt{n - 2} = \frac{.3}{\sqrt{1 - (.3)^2}} \times 7 = \frac{.3 \times 7}{.954} = 2.20,$$

which is larger than 1.96, leading to rejecting the null hypothesis of zero correlation at the 5% level (two-sided test). Again, we mention that in *large* samples, a small value of *r* (e.g., 02) may be statistically significant, i.e., not zero, but may *not* be practically useful or meaningful. Thus, before a study is carried out, the degree of correlation that will be deemed meaningful should be determined by examining the results of related studies. The magnitude of *r* that is meaningful will vary with the area of application and may also depend on relevant cost factors. For example, if workers in a chemical plant handling compound A are found to have more absences than other workers and the number of days absent is slightly correlated (*r* = .3) with the proportion of time the worker is exposed to the chemical, the ultimate regulatory decision may hinge on the nature of the illness and the availability of a substitute compound that has similar chemical properties with no relation to a disease and does not sustantially increase production costs. If the correlation is much higher (e.g., *r* = .7) and the illness very severe, then the risk to the workers may justify a ban on the use of the chemical regardless of costs. (This topic will be considered later in Chapters 13 and 14.)

A precise formulation of this type of reasoning is called decision theory and incorporates cost and other factors, such as risk to workers and the public, as well as statistical concepts. We will see that some of the opinions in the EEOC cases involving employment tests incorporate these trade-offs, especially in cases where there is a substantial risk to the public such as airline pilots, police officers, health professionals and bus drivers.

b. Complications arising in the validation of tests

In theory, it seems easy to decide whether a personnel test or requirement[6] is a reasonable predictor of productivity by using the statistical test (8.18). In practical application the following problems, among others, arise:

(1) What is a proper measure of job productivity or skill?

(2) How much of a correlation between a test and job skill should be required in order to decide whether a test that has a disparate impact is valid?

(3) Should a test have approximately the same predictive ability (r^2) for all subgroups of the population or is it all right for a test to be a better prediction for one group (e.g., whites) than other groups (Hispanics)?

(4) If a test has been used, persons with low scores on the test (*X*

variable) were not hired. How can one calculate the correlation coefficient when their productivity (Y) scores aren't available?

Although these questions are not purely statistical in nature, we shall briefly discuss the issues, and refer the reader to the EEO testing guidelines,[7] Arvey (1979) and the readings in Part 1 of Dreher and Sackett (1983) for further references.

The issue of measuring job productivity in a fair manner often arises when ratings of supervisors are used as the productivity criterion, especially when the supervisors are white males. Moreover, the uniformity of the grading system across all supervisors, should be demonstrated by documenting that the same criteria were used by all supervisors. This is related to the issue of the reliability[8] of the rating system used to assess productivity. Two cases that have dealt with these issues are *Albermarle Paper Co. v. Moody*[9] and *Scott Paper v. Watkins.*[10]

Although the *Uniform Guidelines* (1978) tend to treat the second topic as a combined statistical and practical one, the earlier 1970 EEOC guidelines incorporated other considerations, such as the number of persons affected, risk to the public of a lesser qualified worker, etc. In our discussion of actual cases, we will see that judges do give these factors some weight in their evaluation of the usefulness of a test.

The third issue is called differential validity, and a substantial literature has been developed on methods for adjusting the results of tests to make the final decisions fairer. We note that statistical tests, analogous to the one for the difference in two means, based on the difference between two sample correlations, r_1 and r_2, exist to test for differential validity.

The fourth question has two interesting statistical aspects. There are statistical techniques for estimating the correlation coefficient for data which is restricted in range, i.e., for which no (Y) score is available when the X variable (test score) is below a threshold or cutoff value X_0. They depend on the assumption that the two variables have a full bivariate normal distribution. When these methods aren't used and the standard, r, (8.6) is calculated from the pairs (X, Y), with complete data one will *underestimate* the true correlation between the variables. The reason for this can be seen by examining the formula (8.6) for r. Notice that cross-products, $(Y_i - \overline{Y})/S_y \times (X_i - \overline{X})/S_x$, that will contribute most to the estimate of r are the ones with large differences between Y_i and $\overline{Y}$ and/or X_i and $\overline{X}$. When we eliminate the small X values from the calculation, not only do we change $\overline{X}$, we also eliminate *all* the *low* values of X_i which also have large (negative) values of $(X_i - \overline{X})$. To assess the effect of using the ordinary formula (8.6) for r on data similar to that in Figure 8.3, we started with 100 observations from standardized normal variables with $r = .732$ and then restricted the X's to lie above the 20th percentile, then above the median, and finally to be in the top quarter. The resulting r's calculated from the data were as follows:

full sample	$r = .732$
upper 80% sample (X's)	$r = .633$
upper half sample	$r = .563$
top 20% of the sample	$r = .467$

Notice that the estimated correlation, r, decreased with the amount of missing data and that when only 20% of the y values corresponding to the lowest X scores were missing, an underestimate occurs. The reason that this relatively small amount of missing data causes such a serious bias is that the missing Y scores were *not* random but depended on their corresponding X scores.

When one can assume that the variable X and Y have a joint normal distribution, i.e., both X and Y have a normal distribution, and the correlation between them is given by a regression line of the form (8.10), psychometricians developed the following modified estimate r of the true correlation to compensate for the restricted range:

(8.19)
$$\hat{r} = \frac{r \left(\dfrac{\sigma_x}{S_x} \right)}{\sqrt{1 - r^2 + r^2 \left(\dfrac{\sigma_x}{S_x} \right)^2}},$$

where S_x is the standard deviation of the X values of the *restricted data* for which both (X_i, Y_i) are observed, σ_x is the standard deviation of the entire X distribution and r is the correlation coefficient calculated from the *restricted* data.

For the data in the previous example, formula (8.19) yields the following estimates for the true correlation: .704 for the 80% sample, .692 for the half sample and .637 for the data restricted to the upper 20%. In all cases these modified estimators are nearer the value $r = .732$ of the complete data.

c.   Cases involving test validation

The Supreme Court has considered the testing issue in *Griggs v. Duke Power*,[11] *Albemarle Paper Co. v. Moody*[12] and *Connecticut v. Teal*.[13]

Once the plaintiff demonstrates that the requirement or test at issue excludes a disproportionate share of minorities from an employment opportunity, the defendant can demonstrate its job relatedness by showing that persons with high tests scores or who satisfy the requirement are more productive workers. The defendant need not show that a particular requirement is related to *all* aspects of job performance but only to an important aspect. After the defendant has validated the test as job-related, the plaintiff may show that the employer's legitimate interest in obtaining skilled, competent workers could be satisfied by another selection procedure which has less of an exclusionary effect (on minorities).

1) *Albemarle v. Moody*

In the late 1950s applicants for hire at the firm's plant in the line of progression for skilled jobs were required to score 100 or more on the Beta test of nonverbal intelligence and 18 or more on the Wunderlich test of verbal ability. Each cutoff score was the national norm (average). After the Civil Rights Act was passed in 1964, the company allowed blacks to enter the skilled job category provided they passed these tests, but few succeeded in doing so. The white incumbents in skilled jobs who were hired prior to the use of the tests were not required to pass them in order to retain their jobs. Indeed, in the validation study, some of them scored quite low on the tests.

The opinion relies quite heavily on the 1970 guidelines established by the EEOC as well as standards of the American Psychological Association. These guidelines discussed the appropriateness of content and criteria-related validity[14] of the tests, the selection of subjects to insure they represent potential applicants including minorities, the gathering of measures of job performance or other job-related criteria *after* the test scores were obtained, as well as statistical methods. Moreover, the guidelines cautioned about the use of subjective evaluation of supervisors and the need to ensure that when the test is given to current employees in order to validate it, all had similar opportunities to acquire on-the-job skills, as well as ensuring that when several jobs are grouped together in the study they require similar skills. Also, when current employees are studied to validate a test, one must check that they remain representative of the pool of potential applicants.

The defendant's validation study calculated a different correlation measure, the Phi coefficient,[15] between an employee's test score and the average of their *rankings* relative to their coworkers assigned by two

TABLE 8.3. Results of the Validation Study Submitted in *Albemarle v. Moody*

Job Group	N	Beta	Test W–A	W–B
1. Caustic Operator, Lime Kiln Operator	8	.25	1.00**	.47
2. C. E. Recovery Operator, C. E. Recovery 1st Helpers & Evaporator Operators . . .	12	.64**	.32	.17
3. Wood Yard: Long Log Operators, Log Stackers, Small Equipment Operators & Oilers.	14	.00	1.00**	.72*
4. Technical Services: B Mill Shift Testmen, Additive men, General Lab. Testmen, General Lab. asst., A Mill Testmen, Samplemen .		.50*	.75**	.64*
5. B Paper Mill: Machine Tenders and Back Tenders	16	.00	.50**	.34
6. B Paper Mill: Stock Room Operator, Stock Room 1st Helper	8	−.50	.00	.00
7. B Paper Mill: 3rd Hands, 4th Hands & 5th Hands	21	.43	.81**	.60**
8. Wood Yard: Chipper Unloader, Chipper Operator, No. 2 Chain Operator	6	.76*	−.25	1.00**
9. Pulp Mill: Stock Room Operator, Stock Room 1st Helpers	8	.50	.80*	.76*
10. Power Plant: Power Plant Operator, Power Plant 1st Helper, Power Plant 2nd Helper.	12	.34	.75**	.66*

Source: The appendix to the opinion 422 U.S. at p. 405.
Note: The sample size is denoted by N. The results of the two forms of the Wunderlich test are denoted by W–A and W–B and a single (double) asterisk means that the phi coefficient was significantly different from 0 at a, the .05 (.01) level of significance (two-sided test).

supervisors. The study dealt with 10 job groups at the *upper* end of the nine lines of progression, and the jobs were grouped by their proximity in the line of progression. The results of the study are given in Table 8.3. The opinion noted the following flaws with the study:

(1) For some of the job groups in Table 8.3 the tests did not yield a statistically significant relationship at the .05 level (two-sided). Moreover, for the two forms of the Wunderlich A and B tests, which are supposed to be interchangeable tests of verbal ability, significant correlations were obtained for one form but not the other in four groups. Neither test yielded a significant result in two groups (2, 6).

(2) The study was based on a subjective supervisor's evaluation which did not assess the person's job performance against a *set standard,* only relative to other employees. Indeed, specific criteria for evaluating job performance were not established. Furthermore, the study was conducted by plant officials without neutral on-scene oversight just prior to litigation.

(3) The jobs were all near the top of the skill line, and the guidelines noted that such a procedure is reasonable if new employees typically will proceed to these job levels in a reasonable period of time, but not otherwise. The firm did not submit data on the promotion rate, demonstrating the appropriateness of validating a test on top-of-the line jobs.

(4) The validation study was given to current employees, not new applicants, as the American Psychological Association's standards recommend.

(5) Only four blacks were among the 105 employees studied, implying that possible differential validity could not even be examined.

On these grounds the Court agreed with the Court of Appeals decision which reversed the district court's finding that Albemarle had demonstrated the job-relatedness of the tests.

Comments. (1) It is difficult to question the Court's reluctance to accept vague supervisory evaluations, presumably by white supervisors, under the circumstances the study was conducted. Had this not been a major issue, the pattern of statistically significant results in Table 8.3 would suggest that the tests were related to job performance, at least in some job groups (4, 7, 9, 10). Indeed, if some of the job groups required similar skills, a proper combination method could be used.

(2) Another problem with the *ranking* or *employee comparison* approach is that more experienced employees may do better because they

have had more time to learn the job skills or they had really found a job they were both good at and interested in, so they remained on the job for a long time, or the supervisors know them better. Some adjustment needs to be made to account for seniority, especially when incumbents rather than applicants are studied. Indeed, it is preferable to validate a test by a predictive study, which first gives it to people and then assesses their subsequent job performance. Courts, however, have split on whether concurrent studies based on incumbent employees are as suitable as predictive or prospective ones, e.g., *Black Law Enforcement Officers* v. *City of Akron*, 40 FEP Cases (N.D. Oh. 1986) accepted a concurrent study of test scores and job performance measures, in part because of the time required to validate a predictive test, as one would have to hire a number of people as police sergeants and then assess them on the job performance later. Other cases concerning this issue are *U.S.* v. *City of Chicago* 549 F.2d 415 (7th Cir. 1977) *cert. denied* 434 U.S. 875 (1977), and *Worthy v. U.S. Steel* 616 F.2d 698 (3rd Cir. 1980).

(3) The *power* of the study was not considered. To use such small samples does not make sense from the point of view of the employer who desires to find a statistically significant correlation.

(4) In any particular application, the specific criteria of job performance being used in the study, as well as the apparent relevance of the test at issue, undoubtedly should play a role in deciding whether a concurrent validation study is reasonable, especially as the truncation in range problem will remain in either type of study since persons scoring poorly on the test typically are not hired. There is another potential problem in the use of incumbent employees, however, as the less interested or less able persons may leave the work force. Thus, the performance ratings of the remaining employees may be better than one could expect from a set of applicants. On the other hand, in situations where there are many opportunities for further advancement, long-term employees may only be performing at the satisfactory level, rather than at higher levels, again complicating the analysis. Because of the possibility that present incumbents are not truly representative of the pool of potential applicants, statisticians generally would prefer predictive or prospective studies. Some checks of representativeness, such as those discussed in Chapter 9, will be useful in assessing the potential seriousness of the problem of representativeness when incumbent employees are tested in lieu of applicants. In *Albemarle* the paucity of blacks in the validation study implied that using incumbent employees would not be remotely representative of the pool of potential applicants.

2) *Craig v. County of Los Angeles*[16] and *Blake v. City of Los Angeles:*[17] The Impact of Height Requirements and Tests on Minority Applicants

These two cases concern the effect of requirements on height, passing a physical abilities test, and a paper and pencil test on women and Mexican-American applicants, respectively, for police jobs. In *Blake*, a class action suit charging the city with sex discrimination in employment on the police department, plaintiffs easily demonstrated that the requirement that applicants be at least 5'6" tall excluded proportionately more women than men. They also challenged a physical abilities test in which only half of the female applicants passed, in contrast to 97.4% of the males. In *Craig*, plaintiffs challenged a height requirement and two written examinations. Since only one exam had a disparate impact (33% of the Mexican-American applicants failed compared to 13% of whites), only that exam and the height requirement needed validation as job-related.

We first discuss the studies submitted by the police department in *Blake*. After asserting that taller officers could more easily control resisting suspects with a minimum use of force and that they had better capacities to observe field situations, the city offered two studies to validate the height requirement. Using questionnaires returned by arresting officers, the study concluded:

(a) There is no relationship between officers' height and suspect resistance, and

(b) Shorter officers use strong force more than taller officers do.

The second conclusion was based on the following percentages of arrests using strong force: 5% by officers 5'8" to 5'9", 4.5% by officers 6' and 6'1", and 3.8% by police 6'2" and over. Furthermore, the difference between the 5% and 3.8% figures was statistically significant at the .05 level.

Another study was based on simulations of police subduing suspects concluded that taller officers perform the bar-arm control hold better than shorter officers. Plaintiffs attacked the studies because

(a) No officers under 5'6" were included.

(b) There was unreported data showing that persons 5'7" in height use strong force less frequently than persons 5'8" to 5'11".

(c) As the height requirement has been lowered from 5'9" to 5'8" in 1954, long-term police officers were taller, so one needed to control for seniority in the data analysis.

(d) The definition of "strong force" used in the study was ambiguous.

(e) The second bar-arm study could be affected by rater bias, since the rater was aware of the litigation and purpose of the study.

In addition, plaintiffs discovered that the city had made *four* other studies which demonstrated *no statistically significant* relationship between height and police job performance, including one concerning the frequency with which an officer drew a weapon.

Since the *Blake* case involved an appeal of the district court's summary judgement in favor of the city, the appellate opinion did not address the issue of whether the city might be able to demonstrate the business necessity of the height requirement at the trial, it simply stated that the evidence did not justify the height requirement.

Comments. (1) The fact that four other studies which failed to show a relationship were not submitted by the city is very important. In Chapters 5 and 6 we discussed the importance of combination methods for independent statistical tests (or groups) and mentioned the *multiple comparison problem*, i.e., when many studies are made the chance that at least one will be statistically significant at the .05 level is greater than .05, so an adjustment must be made for this. As the studies were not described in detail, we cannot assess them statistically, but note that it would not be surprising to obtain one or two significant results by chance out of five studies. More importantly, we cannot decide whether the aspects of the job they were concerned with were more (or less) basic tasks than the studies the city did offer into evidence.

(2) The analysis of the strong force study which compared the rates of the shortest and tallest categories is *not* the appropriate statistical analysis. In Section 7 we describe a procedure, based on the idea of a positive correlation, for this type of data. The omission of the data on officers 5'10" to 5'11" is also bothersome.

(3) Even if the strong force study were correct, is a difference of 5% versus 3.8% meaningful in this context? Only if it could be demonstrated that innocent persons (bystanders) were likely to be hurt when officers used strong force and that this small difference could translate into a meaningful effect would this result be convincing. In view of the study showing no relationship between the drawing of a weapon and height, the topic of safety to the public does not appear to have been an issue in the case.

We will not discuss the components of the physical abilities test, but note that the tests were instituted (or reinstituted) when women were first permitted to apply for police jobs. Persons failing the test were not hired, so their job performance was not measured and the correlations between test scores and successful performance in the police academy (e.g., peer evaluation, shooting skill) were modest, with most less than .30. The strongest correlation was between the pretraining physical abilities and a during-training physical abilities test. The court noted that this was insufficient unless the during-training physical tests were independently shown to be job-related. Indeed, the court noted,[18] "If employers were permitted to validate selection devices without reference to job performance, then non-job-related devices could always be validated through the simple expedient of employing them at both the pre-training and post-training stage." The possibility of discrimination in this manner is diminished when the test concerns training or education given by independent institutions prior to employment rather than training under the employer's control.

In *Craig*, the height requirement could not be validated, however, the written test, which was used to determine an applicant's likelihood of success in the academic training program for the position of deputy sheriff, was. The test measured reading, writing and reasoning skills, which were deemed essential to acceptable performance in courses in constitutional and criminal law and procedures given at the academy.

Since there was no dispute that the training of officers in these areas of the law was job-related, the issue focused on the appropriateness of the level of verbal and cognitive ability required of applicants. The study at issue yielded a statistically significant correlation of .60, substantially greater than the typical correlation (.3) in *Blake*.

The plaintiffs criticized the study because of the restriction in range issue, i.e., applicants who failed the test did not attend the academy, so the EEOC guideline stating that validation studies should include some persons who would be excluded by the selection criteria was violated. The plaintiffs also cited the *Blake* case, which noted the absence of persons 5'6" and under in the defendant's study and asserted that the test was not shown to correlate with other elements of the job.

The opinion distinguished the present study from *Blake* because the correlation was high. There were no serious flaws such as the vague definition of "strong force" or lack of control for experience that affected the *Blake* study, nor could plaintiffs demonstrate the existence of other data indicating a lack of correlation between the test and what it was designed to measure. The opinion noted that the correlation was sufficiently strong to support the inference of the trial court that persons excluded would not be likely to succeed in the academic training program. Indeed, the opinion states,[19] "We perceive no reason at this point to require the sheriff's department to hire and train a sample of failing applicants with the attendant expense to the county and potential unfairness to the candidates so hired, in order to provide statisticians with more certain results." The opinion also noted that when a selection device is a strong predictor of, or is significantly correlated with, important aspects of work or academy performance, it need not demonstrate a significant correlation with *all* aspects of work or training.

The panel opinion did remand the case for further findings on the second link of the validation process, i.e., the county needed to demonstrate that the level of academic training given new recruits manifestly relates to the knowledge that deputy sheriffs must possess to do the job properly. In particular, they should establish that the after-training exam fairly measures the trainees' mastery of the subject matter taught in the academy.

Comments. (1) Other courts have found that training program validation may be sufficient. In particular, national teacher examination test scores were validated by correlating them with academic teacher training program results rather than job performance in *NEA v. South Carolina,* 434 U.S. 1026, 98 S.Ct. 765 (1978) affirming *U.S. v. South Carolina,* 445 F.Supp. 1094 (D. S.C. 1977). The *Craig* court noted that both the qualifying test and the academic program were not under the control of the state so that the case was not directly applicable to the situation in *Craig.* Therefore, it required the county to show that performance in the academy was related to an important aspect of job performance.

(2) In situations where there is some restriction in range, it is important to know whether the ordinary formula (8.6) or the corrected formula (8.19) was used. The ordinary formula yields an underestimate of the true correlation so that if it were used in *Craig* the true correlation would exceed .6, which would provide more statistical support for the decision.

3) *Easley v. Anheuser-Busch*[20]

In *Easley,* a written test was shown to have a disparate impact on minority applicants for bottling jobs, and the defendant submitted a validation study to show that it was job-related. The opinion did not present the statistical results such as correlations and *p*-values, however, it accepted the plaintiff's criticism of the test. First, the job analysis carried out to determine the major skills involved in the work did not consider all of the jobs bottlers were assigned, nor did it rank the various work factors, which should correlate with the test in order of importance. The test purported to measure 6 of the 13 work factors (criteria), but the most important factor affecting job performance, identified by the defendant as vigilance, was among the seven unmeasured factors. Also, the test supposedly measured the ability to learn on-the-job, but a follow-up validity study, which should have correlated the test scores with work skill after the people were employed for a while, was not conducted.

The opinion also noted that before the test was instituted, bottlers were hired after a review of their application and one or more interviews. Under that system blacks formed twice the proportion of new hires than they did under the new system (36% versus 18%). The defendant asserted that there had been problems with some of the bottlers hired under the old system, but one of its employees testified that it had been satisfactory.

Comments. (1) This case is of interest as the data on disparate impact and disparate treatment were quite clear. In addition to the difference in the racial mix of hires under the two systems, black applicants waited an average of 214.2 days prior to being tested, while whites waited an average of 101.6 days.

(2) The test validation study in *Easley* illustrates why concurrent validation on current employees is more subject to statistical bias than a prospective or predictive one, especially when the test is supposed to measure aptitude for the job.

(3) The written test in *Easley* emphasized following instructions and writing on the basis that they would predict an applicant's ability to tend a production line, identify problems and take appropriate action, but the questions did not closely approximate production line work. As noted earlier, the most important work factor was not considered.

(4) It is interesting to contrast the *Easley* decision with those in *NEA v. South Carolina* and *Craig*. Although the latter cases accepted less than full compliance with the EEOC validation guidelines, the tests measured important job-related knowledge. In *Easley,* the basic job analysis conducted to identify the major factors was deficient. In such circumstances it is virtually impossible to validate a test or requirement, as one cannot correlate it with the variable it is supposed to predict.

4) Related Issues and Cases

When reading the decisions in these cases we realize that the propriety of a requirement or test is not simply an issue of whether it is statistically significantly correlated with a productivity related characteristic. Issues include the magnitude of the correlation, the importance of the ability or skill to the job and to the safety and well-being of the public, as well as the background of the specific case, e.g., when the requirement was instituted or does other evidence of discriminatory treatment exist. Other topics that needed consideration were:

(1) Whether a requirement that had a disparate impact on a minority group could be offset by another one in which the minority group had an advantage so that neither test should require validation.

(2) Is it permissible to validate a pre-employment test with tests given after a training period rather than on-the-job productivity?

(3) How does one assess the possible disparate impact of a requirement or test when people who don't think they will satisfy it don't apply for the job?

In *Washington v. Davis*,[21] a case filed on constitutional grounds rather than the Civil Rights Act, the Supreme Court accepted a validation study which showed a significant relationship between a test used in the hiring process and scores police trainees received in a 17-week training course. Although it is important to hire people who will successfully complete a training course, one might also wish to know that high scoring trainees are better than average performers on the job before accepting training school scores as valid predictors. On the other hand, an employer who provides a long period of training at full pay is making a substantial investment in each hire. This issue can be viewed in the framework of decision theory, which attempts to quantify the risks (i.e., failure to hire a qualified minority, the loss in training costs and possible public safety) with the gains (i.e., a fairer hiring system and a better image of the employer with the minority community, a more efficient work force) by expressing the possible gains and losses in dollar terms and weighing them by their probability of occurrence.

While courts have not analyzed cases precisely in these terms, this view underlies a number of decisions. In *Ensley Branch, NAACP v. Seibels*,[22] Judge Pointer indicated that although one test showed a statistically significant relationship, its *low* correlation of .21 rendered it inappropriate for practical use. Similarly, in *Shield Club v. City of Cleveland*[23] an *r* of .20 was deemed insufficient. In cases involving significant risk to the public, a small relationship may have a meaningful potential effect. The first significant case which discussed this topic was *Spurlock v. United Airlines*[24] in which the airlines' requirement of a college degree was challenged. The court wrote

> "When a job requires a small amount of skill and training and the consequences of hiring an unqualified applicant are insignificant, the courts should examine closely any pre-employment standard or criteria which discriminate against minorities. In such a case, the employer should have a heavy burden to demonstrate to the court's satisfaction that his employment criteria are job-related. On the other hand, when the job clearly requires a high degree of skill and the economic and human risks involved in hiring an unqualified applicant are great, the employer bears a corresponding lighter burden to show that his employment criteria are job-related. Cf. 29 C.F.R. & 1607.-5(c)(2)(iii) ... The courts, therefore, should proceed with great caution before requiring an employer to lower his pre-employment standard for such a job. 475 F.2d at 219."

Many other circuit court decisions have upheld this view that the magnitude of the relationship of a pre-employment test to a productivity factor required to demonstrate its validity should depend on the responsibility of the employer for the safety and well-being of the public. In *Pennsylvania v. O'Neill*,[25] a correlation of .21 was found acceptable for a predictive validation of a police promotion exam. Age at hiring limits were sustained for bus drivers in *Usery v. Tamiami Trail Tours,* 531 F.2d 224 (5th Cir. 1976) and *Hodgson v. Greyhound Lines Inc.* 499 F.2d 859 *cert. denied* 95 S.Ct. 805 (1975), and educational requirements for law enforcement jobs in *Davis v. Dallas* 777 F.2d 205 (5th Cir. 1985). However, in *Watkins v. Scott Paper Co.*,[26] a high school diploma requirement for employees who desired to move to certain job lines in a paper mill required validation, even though the company stated that some workers would be in charge of the boiler room and would have responsibility for the safety of everyone in the plant. This situation is readily distinguished from the airline and police officer cases, as relatively few workers were assigned to the boiler room, while all workers in the more desirable job lines were subject to various educational requirements.

On the other hand, a strict age requirement that new police officers must be 29-years-old or under was found to be inapplicable to persons between 40 and 70 in *Hahn v. City of Buffalo* 770 F.2d 12 (2d Cir. 1985) because of the Age Discrimination Law, but the city could exclude persons between 29 and 39. *Doyle v. Suffolk County* 786 F.2d 523 (2d Cir. 1986) also considered the constitutionality of the age requirement. Again, the specific statute a case is concerned with affects the nature of the evidence the parties need to submit in order to prevail. An important recent case, *Western Airlines v. Criswell* 105 S.Ct. 2743 (1985), concerned the use of age as a proxy for safety-related factors. It indicates that employers need to demonstrate a factual basis, e.g., from accident statistics or health studies, that all or virtually all persons over the particular age would be unable to perform the job safely. Alternatively, the employer can show that it is impossible or impractical to assess employees on an individual basis. The court noted that the defense that a job criteria which excludes a protected class on the basis that the criteria is a bonafide occupational requirement is a narrow exception.

The data establishing the disparate impact of a written exam on the promotion process in *Connecticut v. Teal,*[27] was presented in Table 5.4. The main import of that decision was that the defendant argued that the *overall* result of the selection process, which also considered past work experience, supervisor's recommendations and seniority, did not have a disparate impact. Indeed, 22.9% of the black candidates were promoted, while only 13.5% of the whites were. The district court accepted the state's assertion that the bottom line showed no evidence of discrimination, but the Second Circuit reversed, noting that where "an identifiable pass-fail barrier denies an employment opportunity to a disproportionately large number of minorities and prevents them from proceeding to the next step in the selection process, the barrier needs to be validated in and of itself." The Supreme Court affirmed the appellate opinion, noting that the bottom line result may assist an employer in rebutting a charge of discrimination but that a racially balanced work force could not immunize an employer for other specific acts of discrimination. A dissenting opinion criticized the majority, asserting that it confused the aim of the EEOC law, which was to provide all individuals with a nondiscriminatory work environment, with the methods of proof used in these cases, which involve statistical data on groups.

Comment. The *timing* of the events may have played a role in the majority opinion. The exam was given on December 2, 1978, and the results announced in March 1979. The plaintiffs filed suit in April 1979. More than a year later, one month before the original trial, the promotions were made. The Court of Appeals characterized the results as an affirmative action program, but the Supreme Court decided not to assess the correctness of that description, which the defendant contested. As we have noted previously, actions taken subsequent to a formal charge or suit should be scrutinized with great care, as they are at least as likely to be a response to the charge as they are to be a continuation of the previous policies.

Usually the impact of a requirement or test is evaluated by comparing the success rates of actual applicants. The major exception to this is in the evaluation of height requirements, as short persons may simply not apply so that courts rely on national data as in *Dothard v. Rawlinson*.[28] It should be noted that height requirements which do not exclude a disproportionate fraction of a protected class are permissible even though one might doubt their job relatedness. For instance different height ranges for men and women were allowed in *Smith* v. *Eastern Airlines* 44 FEP Cases 1690 (E.D. Tex. 1986) as the same fraction of each sex satisfied them. Other recent cases which have questioned the validity of applicant data in disparate impact cases are *Moore v. Hughes Helicopters, Inc.* 708 F.2d 475 (9th Cir. 1983) and *Kligo v. Bowman Transport*.[29] In *Moore,* the effect of a high school education requirement was assessed by examining census data rather than actual applicant files, because individuals who lack a diploma could self-select not to apply for the job. Similarly, a requirement of one year's over-the-road truck driving experience in *Kilgo* was shown to have a disparate impact on females, since women formed 1.27% of job applicants while they formed 1.96% to 4.06% of several reasonable labor pools. In *Kilgo,* the difference between the hiring percentages 56% and 87% of female and male applicants would also have satisfied the EEOC four-fifths rule. Furthermore, 60 males who did not satisfy the experience requirement had been hired in contrast to *no* women, which indicated that the requirement might well be a pretext for discrimination against women.

When the applicant data is deemed unreliable because potential applicants are inhibited from applying because of the requirement, a proper validation study becomes far more difficult to make. For some jobs, such as truck drivers or police officers, one might be able to obtain data from similar employers who do not use the requirement. In almost all cases where applicant data was unreliable, satisfactory validation of the requirement at issue has not been accomplished.

Problems

1. Read the opinion in *Black Law Enforcement Officers v. City of Akron* 40 FEP Cases 323 (N.D. Oh. 1986), focusing on its treatment of issues of correlation and statistically significant difference. Consider the following questions:

    (a) What are the proper statistical procedures to determine the significance of the data showing that the performance appraisals given detective and investigative policemen exceeded those given uniform officers by about eight points?

(b) How objective were the performance ratings?

(c) How carefully were the written tests used, developed and validated?

2. Rank the following jobs in order of their responsibility for public safety and well-being: correctional officer, bank teller, bank computer programmer, school teacher, credit investigator, Internal Revenue Service auditor, nurse assigned to surgery. How might the criteria you used in your rankings affect the standards used to justify the imposition of an educational requirement or passing a polygraph test in a case alleging disparate impact?

3. In the *Easley* case, the difference in the average time between application and the opportunity to take the test was clearly meaningful, so a formal test of significance was not used. What procedures are available to consider the issue in situations which are less clear cut?

4. Read the article by Booth and Mackay (1980) and discuss the relationship between the public's well-being and the magnitude of the correlation coefficients courts require to validate a test.

5.* How much of an effect on the validation study in *Craig* could the fact that persons under 5′6″ were excluded have had?

Answers to Selected Problems

1. (a) The t-test (if the data were normal) or the Wilcoxon test (see Chapter 7).

1. (b, c) The senior officers apparently favored members of the investigative units, which were virtually closed to blacks. The grading criteria were not uniformly applied. Indeed, there was no check of inter-rater reliability, which can be carried out by having two or more raters assess a sample of candidates and studying the correlation between their ratings.

3. Same as 1a.

5.* As height and general academic performance are not related, it is unlikely that this would seriously bias the estimated correlation.

5. Regression Analysis

So far, we have derived the regression line, enabling us to predict our variable (Y) from another variable (X) from their correlation. The theory used to test the significance of the relationship between X and Y assumed both variables had normal distributions. In this section, we shall show that the same regression line can be used when the variable Y is predicted from a characteristic X which need not have a normal distribution (i.e., X is a known quantity). Sometimes we are concerned with predicting the value of a variable (Y), e.g., law school grades from several variables, e.g., LSAT scores, undergraduate grade point average and academic standing of the undergraduate school attended. In other contexts, we are interested in whether a characteristic such as race or sex affects wages after several legitimate factors such as educational background and seniority have been accounted for. These more general questions can be analyzed with the aid of multiple regression analysis, which not only provides a test of whether the characteristic (race or sex) affects the variable (Y = wages) but also estimates the magnitude of the effect of the characteristic.

a. Simple linear regression

Suppose we wished to predict the annual wage (Y) of employees in a union from their seniority (X), assuming that the union is supposed to assign the better (longer-lasting) jobs according to seniority. Although the union strictly follows seniority, its job assignments cannot be expected to be in complete accord with seniority, as the length of each prospective job cannot be assessed perfectly and there is inherent variation in the effect of weather on days worked, as well as the days each union member misses for illness and other personal reasons.

Thus, a reasonable approximation to the process generating the wage data might be

$$Y = a + bX + e,$$

where e is an error term incorporating the random effects mentioned above. In this model, a can be interpreted as the average annual salary of new union members, b the average increment in earnings for *each* year of seniority and e is a random error. This error should have mean 0, since there is no reason to believe that one union member should miss more days of work for illness than another or that the union would misjudge the desirability of a prospective job in a nonrandom fashion.

TABLE 8.4. Hypothetical Wage Data for Male and Female Employees and the Predictions Yielded by the Simple Regression Model

Seniority	Wage	Predicted	Difference
1	13,938	15,141.77	−1203.77
2	16,743	15,645.25	1097.75
3	17,617	16,148.73	1468.27
4	17,926	16,652.21	1273.79
5	15,913	17,155.69	−1242.69
6	18,851	17,659.17	1191.83
7	16,498	18,162.65	−1664.65
8	18,343	18,666.13	−323.13
9	17,459	19,169.61	−1710.61
10	20,552	19,673.09	878.91
11	19,609	20,176.57	−567.57
12	23,353	20,680.05	2672.95
13	18,487	21,183.53	−2696.53
14	22,148	21,687.01	460.99
15	22,355	22,190.49	164.51
16	22,060	22,693.97	−633.97
17	23,200	23,197.45	2.55
18	22,742	23,700.93	−958.93
19	22,936	24,204.41	−1268.41
20	27,767	24,707.89	3059.11

Note: The seniority for each employee is measured in months. The predictions were obtained from the regression equation $Y = 14638.29 + 503.48X$. In practice one may round the coefficients to 14638 and 503.5. The differences between the actual wages and the predictions are given in the last column. These differences are called the residuals.

In Table 8.4 we report annual wage and seniority data for 20 workers. In the third column, we report the predicted earnings derived from a regression line. The fourth column reports the difference between the actual wage (Y) and its predicted value (Y) from the line. We now describe the method used to fit the line. Recall that when we used the correlation between LSAT scores and law school grades to obtain a linear formula for predicting grades from the LSAT scores, we saw that these predictions yielded a smaller average *squared error* than the original grades had about their average $(\overline{Y})$. This suggests that a general measure of accuracy of any prediction model is to use the average (or total) of the squared deviations between the actual observations and their predicted values obtained from the regression line. If we plotted the pairs (X_i, Y_i) in Table 8.4 on graph paper, one might draw several lines that seemed to fit the data; however, statisticians use the line that yields the *minimum* average of the squared deviations between each observation Y_i and its prediction, $\hat{Y}_i$.

For the data in Table 8.4, this line is

$$(8.20) \qquad Y = 14{,}368.3 + 503.48X$$

and is called the least squares line. Notice that the prediction of each Y_i derived from the line is obtained by substituting the value of X_i associated with it in equation (8.20). Thus, for the union member with $X = 1$, $Y = 15{,}142$. Similarly, for the member with $X = 7$, $Y = 18{,}163$. Fortunately, the least squares line is given by the same formula (8.9) or (8.10) that we obtained in our derivation of the prediction line in our discussion of correlation. Indeed, statisticians call both lines regression lines. The formula for the slope $\hat{b}$ of the fitted line is

$$(8.21) \qquad \hat{b} = \frac{\sum (X_i - \overline{X})Y_i}{\sum (X_i - \overline{X})^2},$$

and the formula for the intercept a is

$$(8.22) \qquad \hat{a} = \overline{Y} - \hat{b}\overline{X}.$$

The reason we write the values of a and b specifying the linear relation (8.22) between Y and X with hats over them is that they are not the values of the true line but are estimates obtained from data and are subject to error.

As in our discussion of statistical analysis involving the success probability, p, of a binomial distribution and the mean, μ, of a normal distribution, we can test hypotheses concerning the true value of the parameters a and b, as well as estimate them from the data and present the associated 95% (or any other level) confidence intervals. In legal applications, we may be interested in whether the slope parameter, b, is different from zero (e.g., are wages related to seniority?) or whether two estimates of b, derived from data for male and female employees, respectively, are equal. Rather than present more complex formulas, we discuss the interpretation of a typical computerized regression analysis.

For the data similar to that in Table 8.4, the following statistics should be reported:

Fitted line $Y = 14.638.3 + 503.48X$
Standard error   (720)   (60.1)
t-ratio   20.33   8.38

Under each coefficient, we report its standard error, (the standard deviation of the sampling distribution of the estimates $\hat{a}$ and $\hat{b}$ of b). This can be used to obtain a confidence interval. For samples of 25 or more, an *approximate* 95% CONF allows a margin of error *twice* this standard deviation, i.e., for our data, we have 95% confidence that the true b (seniority coefficient) lies between

$$(8.23) \quad 503.5 - 2(60.1) \quad \text{and} \quad 503.5 + 2(60.1) \quad \text{or} \quad \text{CONF } (b; 443,563),$$

as the standard error, $s_{\hat{b}}$, of $\hat{b}$ is 60.1.

The t-ratio is used to test whether the coefficient is zero. It is similar to the Z score. For our data the test for $b = 0$ is

$$(8.24) \qquad t = \frac{\hat{b} - 0}{s_{\hat{b}}} = \frac{503.5}{60.1} = 8.38,$$

which is highly significant, as the chance of obtaining data eight standard deviations from expected is *very* small (less than one in a million).

Two other statistics are also reported. An *F-test*[30] measures the significance of the entire relationship between Y and the factor X used to predict it, and it will be quite significant for our data. The *R-square* (R^2) for our data is .796 and is interpreted as the square of the *correlation* between the observations and the *predictions* made from the line using knowledge of the variable X. Although X is not a random variable, the interpretation of R^2 as the proportion of the variability of Y we can explain by using knowledge of X to predict the value of Y, which we discussed in Section 3, remains the same.

There are several assumptions which concern the nature of the error term in the regression model. They are:

(1) The random errors in each of the observations are *independent* of one another.

(2) The random errors in each of the observations have a common distribution with mean 0 (i.e., there is no systematic component in the errors) and a common variance, σ^2.

(3) The magnitude of the random error does not depend on the value of X, i.e., the larger deviations from the regression line are not related to small or large values of X (seniority). Although this assumption follows

from the previous one, it is quite important. If the magnitude of the errors (their standard deviation) varies with X, there are generalizations of least squares that can be used to properly fit the data.

(4) The error terms follow a normal distribution. This assumption underlies the validity of the t-tests for the significance of the coefficients and the associated confidence intervals. It is less critical in large samples where a suitable generalization of the central limit theorem applies.

The variance of the error term e in the simple linear regression is estimated by $s_e^2 (1/n - 2) \sum_{i=1}^{n} (Y_i - \hat{Y}_i)^2$. The reason $n - 2$ is used in place of the factor $(n - 1)$ used in the definition of s^2 for a set of data is that now *two* parameters, a and b, have been estimated from this data, while previously only *one* parameter, the mean μ, was estimated.

The lack of validity of any of the first three assumptions can cast doubt on the results of a regression study. If the errors are not independent of one another, the standard errors of the estimated coefficients, which are calculated under the assumption of independence, are incorrect. In practice, this problem can occur when data collected over a period of time, e.g., monthly, is analyzed and the errors in consecutive data points are positively correlated. When this happens, the true standard error of the estimated coefficient is *larger* than the one calculated by the least squares methodology. Hence, one has a *less accurate* estimate of the coefficients than one would have if the errors were independent.

Problems

1. Suppose you had the following data on salaries (Y) and length of service (X) of eight employees of a firm in the same occupation:

X	9	14	18	20	24	30	36	39
Y	8	9	9	9	10	10	11	11

Here salary (Y) is in dollars per hour, while seniority is in months of employment.

(a) Calculate the correlation coefficient, r, between Y and X and the regression line predicting Y for a given X.

(b) Calculate the residuals ($Y_i - \hat{Y}_i$) between the actual Y_i's and their predictions based on the line you calculated in (a) and calculate R^2 from the usual correlation (r) between two variables (X, Y).

(c) Are you satisfied with the regression predictions you calculated in (b)?

(d) Suppose that the actual system in use at the company was to give $9 per hour to starting employees and increase their wage by $1 after each year of service. Does the data fit this system?

(e) Comment on the statement: When a system [e.g., (d)] for wage increases is not known, or may not be followed precisely, the regression line may yield a reasonable approximation to it.

2. Suppose an employer pays male clerical workers an average of $400 a week and female workers an average of $300 a week. The sample standard deviations for the two groups are $60 for the 100 males and $55 for the 100 females.

(a) Using the normal approximation to the two-sample t-test, determine whether females and male clerical employees are paid according to the same wage scale. Use a two-sided test at the 5% level.

(b) Suppose the employer explains the difference you found in part (a) on the basis that males had greater seniority. Without running a regression analysis on the raw data (which we omit), assess the credibility of this explanation under the following assumptions:

(1) The males all had 10 to 15 years of seniority and the females 0 to 5 years.

(2) The males had an average of 10 years of seniority with a standard deviation of 2 years, while the females had an average of 8 years of seniority with a standard deviation of 2 years.

b. Multiple regression

In the previous sections we developed a regression line to enable us to predict the value of one variable (Y) from knowledge of another factor (X) which was correlated with it (Y). In real life many variables may influence the dependent variable. For example, in a discrimination case, one might wish to assess whether sex influenced salaries, after accounting for any differences in other productivity characteristics, such as education and seniority. In a situation in which goods were damaged in shipment, one might have to determine whether the nature of the packaging or the temperature in the transport vehicle caused the damage. To accomplish this task, one needs to predict the percentage of the shipment which was damaged as a function of the packaging (done by the shipper) and the temperature (set by the transporter). In this section, we describe the techniques of multiple regression, which is a generalization of the ideas of correlation and regression, to allow several independent variables (X_1, X_2, ..., X_k) to influence the dependent variable (Y).

The basic model becomes

(8.25) $Y = a + b_1X_1 + b_2X_2 + \ldots + b_kX_k + e,$

where we predict an observation Y from the values of k independent (X) variables associated with it. Again, there is a random error term, e, in the model, as measurement errors and other random phenomena still affect the data. As in simple regression, the major assumptions underlying the least square multiple regression fit to (8.25) are

(1) The random errors e_i in each observation are *independent* of one another.

(2) The random errors e_i have a common distribution, with mean 0 and the same variance, σ^2.

Although it is difficult to graph the relationship between Y and the set of k independent variables, the formulas for obtaining equation (8.25) are easily handled by computers, which determine the value of the coefficients a, $b_1, b_2, \ldots, b_k$, which yield the predictions $\hat{Y}_i$ of the original set of n Y-observations with the *minimum* sum of squared deviations of the original data from the values Y_i predicted from the model. Formally,

(8.26) $$\sum_{i=1}^{n} (Y_i - \hat{Y}_i)^2$$

is made as small as possible by choosing the estimates of $a, b_1, \ldots, b_k$ appropriately. The estimates of the coefficients in (8.25) obtained in this manner are called least squares estimates.

In addition to determining the best predictor for the variable Y of the form (8.25), tests of the significance of each predictor variable (X_j) and confidence intervals for each coefficient are available. The overall explanatory power of the model is again assessed by the proportion of the total variation in the dependent variable (Y) which is explained by the model, i.e., R^2. The value of R^2 which can be expected from a reasonable model is not solely a statistical problem, as it will vary with the subject matter area.

Remarks. (1) The fraction of the variation in Y predicted or explained by the model is called R^2 because there is a generalization of equation (8.14) which expresses the total $\sum_{i=1}^{n} (Y_i - \overline{Y})^2$ as the sum of the explained part plus the unexplained or residual sum of squares $\sum_{i=1}^{n} (Y_i - \hat{Y}_i)^2$ as before.

(2) When we fit any set of data by a model using k predictors X_1, X_2, ..., X_k, it is almost always possible to suggest another factor X_{k+1}, say, which might improve the fit of the model to the data. One difficulty with using R^2 as a criteria of how well a model fits a data set is that when the new model using the extra factor X_{k+1} is fit to the same data, R^2 can only increase, even when X_{k+1} really does not help in predicting the dependent variable (Y). The reason for this is that the least squares method now chooses the set of coefficients b_1, b_2, ..., b_k, b_{k+1} in (8.25) which minimize the sum of squares of the residuals (8.26). Even if the true b_{k+1} equals zero, meaning that there is no additional information added by using X_{k+1}, on a set of data, a *small* value of b_{k+1} almost always yields a slightly smaller value of (8.26). To account for this, statisticians use an *adjusted* R^2 measure, called adj(R^2), which is based on the fact that the average of the squared residuals is an estimate of the variance, σ^2, of the error term. However, when k variables are used, the residual sum of squares is divided by $n - (k + 1)$ to obtain the estimate of σ^2, because $k + 1$ parameters are estimated. When a new predictor variable is added, the residual sum of squares is divided by $n - (k + 2)$. The adj(R^2) will increase only if the *new* estimate of the variance of the random error component of the model (8.25) is less than the estimated error variance of the model which did not use X_{k+1}.

Deviations from the assumptions on which regression models are fitted can sometimes be corrected by more sophisticated econometric techniques; however, one must be careful in relying on computerized statistical packages to make the adjustments automatically. For example, if the reason the residuals, $Y_i - \hat{Y}_i$, from the multiple regression appear to be dependent is due to the fact that an *important* dependent variable (X_{k+1}) has been omitted from the model, this omission can only be corrected by incorporating this variable or a highly correlated substitute or proxy into the model. The adj(R^2) measure should then increase.

1) An Example of the Use of Multiple Regression

Suppose one wished to study whether female union members were earning the same amount of money as comparably situated male union members. If the only economically and legally justifiable factor explaining the earnings differential is seniority, one could fit a model

$$Y = a + bS + cF + e$$

to the earnings data, where F is an indicator[31] variable equaling 1 if the union member is female and 0 if the member is male. Typically, we are interested in testing the hypothesis $c = 0$ (sex makes no difference) against the two-sided alternative $c \neq 0$ (sex has an effect) or the one-sided alternative $c < 0$ (females earn less than similarly qualified males).

Graphically we are asking whether the two lines on Figure 8.4 can be considered as being from a common population, i.e., whether $c = 0$ or is statistically significantly different from 0.

Suppose there were 10 female and 10 male union members. In the data given in Table 8.5, the females are indicated by a 1 and the males by a 0. The statistical summary of the regression analysis of the data in Table 8.5 as given in Table 8.6 shows that seniority remains a significant factor ($t = 9.98$, corresponding to a two-sided p-value of less than one in 10,000) but that sex is also significant $t = -3.05$, corresponding to a two-sided p-value of .007. The fitted model

$$Y = 15{,}656 + .490S - 1{,}757F$$

indicates that females, on the average, earned \$1757 less than males, and the t-test indicates that this difference was *unlikely* to have occurred by chance.

Suppose the union wishes to explore the data more carefully to rebut the above inference of sex discrimination and uses the data on absences

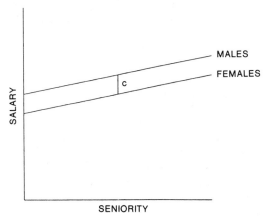

FIGURE 8.4. Graph of the regression lines relating wages to seniority for males and females separately. The difference, c, between the two intercepts reflects the difference in wages at all levels of seniority under the model $y = a + bS + cF + e$. The model assumes that every employer receives the same seniority increments. When $c = o$ the levels coincide.

TABLE 8.5.   Hypothetical Wage Data for Male and Female
             Employees

Seniority (S)	Sex (F)	Days Absent (A)	Wage (Y)
1	1	18	13,938
2	0	8	16,743
3	1	12	17,617
4	0	2	17,926
5	1	13	15,913
6	0	3	18,851
7	1	17	16,498
8	0	7	18,343
9	1	19	17,459
10	0	9	20,552
11	1	11	19,609
12	0	1	23,353
13	1	17	18,487
14	0	3	22,148
15	1	13	22,355
16	0	7	22,060
17	1	12	23,200
18	0	8	22,742
19	1	18	22,936
20	0	2	27,767

Note: The seniority, days absent and sex (females are denoted by 1).

for sickness and/or personal reasons. It could fit the model

(8.27) $Y = a + bS + cF + dA + e,$

where the number, A, of days absent, also given in Table 8.5, is now included. Fitting this model yielded the results reported in Table 8.7.

Notice that the coefficient d for days absent (A) is -2.88 and is statistically significant ($t = -3.98$, corresponding to a two-sided p-value of about .001), while the coefficient, c, of the sex indicator no longer is statistically significant. Indeed, females are estimated to earn *more* than males, but the difference is not significant (two-sided p-value $= .20$). The reason the addition of the variable, $A =$ days voluntarily absent, explained the apparent sex discrimination shown in the previous model is that the female and male members of the union had different absenteeism

TABLE 8.6. Regression Analysis of the Data in Table 8.5 Salaries as a Function of Seniority and Sex (F = female)

Fitted Model (in thousands of dollars)	$Y = 15.6555 + .4903S - 1.7570F$;$R^2 = .868$		
Standard error	(.6821)	(−0499)	(−.5753)
t-ratio	(22.95)	(9.83)	−(3.05)
(two-sided p-value)	<.0001	<.0001	.0072

Detailed Analysis of the Residuals

Observed Value	Predicted Value	Residual
13.938	14.389	0.451
16.743	16.636	0.107
17.617	15.369	2.248
17.926	17.617	0.309
15.913	16.350	0.437
18.851	18.597	0.254
16.498	17.330	0.832
18.343	19.578	1.235
17.459	18.311	0.852
20.552	20.558	0.006
19.609	19.291	0.318
23.353	21.539	1.814
18.487	20.272	1.785
22.148	22.519	0.371
22.355	21.253	1.102
22.060	23.500	1.440
23.200	22.233	0.967
22.742	24.480	1.738
22.936	23.214	0.278
27.767	25.461	2.306

patterns. In the data in Table 8.5, males averaged 5 days of voluntary absence while females averaged 15.

For didactic purposes we developed our multiple regressions by adding new predictor variables in sequence; however, in developing a regression model, it is preferable to base the model on a sound theory (e.g., economic and legal) and include the relevant variables in the equation at the start. One should then be cautious about incorporating suggested addi-

TABLE 8.7.   Regression Analysis of the Data in Table 8.5 Predicting Salaries as a
Function of Seniority, Sex and Days Absent

Fitted Model (in thousands of dollars)	$Y = 17.1915 + .4815S + 1.1143F - 0.2880A$ $;R^2 = .934$			
Standard error	(.6305)	(.0366)	(.8351)	(.0724)
t-ratio	(27.27)	(13.19)	(1.33)	(−3.98)
(two-sided p-value)	.0001	.0001	.2008	.0011

Detailed Analysis of the Residuals

Observed Value	Predicted Value	Residual
13.938	13.603	0.335
16.743	15.851	0.892
17.617	16.294	1.323
17.926	18.542	0.616
15.913	16.969	1.056
18.851	19.217	0.366
16.498	16.781	0.283
18.343	19.028	0.685
17.459	17.168	0.291
20.552	19.415	1.137
19.609	20.435	0.826
23.353	22.682	0.671
18.487	19.670	1.183
22.148	23.069	0.921
22.355	21.785	0.570
22.060	22.890	0.820
23.200	23.036	0.164
22.742	23.555	0.813
22.936	22.271	0.665
27.767	26.246	1.520

tional variables because they may introduce the problem of multicollinearity in the model, i.e., several productivity characteristics may be
highly interrelated, so using one or two of them essentially captures their
total effect. The inclusion of closely-related predictor variables makes
their estimated coefficients quite imprecise (large standard error) and
quite sensitive to a slight change in the data. For example, had we used
age (years over 18) in addition to seniority in equation (8.27), it is clear
that age and seniority would be highly related. Sometimes one incorpo-

rates two measures of seniority such as

(a) seniority with the employer, and
(b) prior job related experience.

These may be *negatively* related, but the correlation is often not of sufficient magnitude to create a problem. If age is also included, then multicollinearity is quite likely, as the sum of the two experience measures will often equal age (years over 18). This problem need not always render a regression defective when it is used to predict a value of a new observation, since the predictions will still be accurate provided the model is sound. In many uses of regression in law, however, we are concerned with estimating the effect of *one* of the predictor variables (X_j) on the variable Y *after controlling* for the influence of the other predictor variables. Multicollinearity becomes important when one of these variables is so highly correlated with variable (X_j) of interest that the estimate of the effect of variable (X_j) may have a large standard error. One must be aware of the fact that some degree of multicollinearity is inevitable. The reason days absent explained the apparent difference in wages between the sexes is that sex and days absent were related. Thus, concern over possible multicollinearity should not outweigh developing an appropriate model. It should make us cautious about accidentally including the effect of the same predictor more than once.

One indicator of multicollinearity among the variables in a regression model is a high R^2, indicating the model is explaining much of the variable (Y) of interest, but some of the coefficients of predictors which should be used are not close[32] to statistical significance. These may be highly related to other predictors or to one another so that large changes in the coefficients do not change the predictions $\hat{Y}_i$ very much. This means that the standard errors of the coefficients of these collinear or highly correlated predictors will be large, so the t-test of whether they equal 0 may accept the null hypothesis.

There are several issues related to the development of a regression which concern how the relationship between Y and the predictor variables, $X_1, \ldots, X_k$, is expressed. This is called model specification. Quite often salary raises are given in percentages rather than fixed dollar increments. A more appropriate model than equation (8.27) would be

$$(8.28) \qquad Y = a.b^S.c^F. \left(\frac{1-A}{T}\right),$$

where a is the initial salary, b is the average annual pay raise, c is the fraction of male pay females receive (if $F = 0$, $c^D = c^O = 1$ for males; if $F = 1$, indicating a female, then c enters into the calculated pay) and A/T is the proportion of total work days (T) the worker was absent. This multiplicative relationship is transformed into an additive one by taking logarithms, as we did in expressing the area of a circle in Section 2. The model then becomes

$$(8.29) \qquad \ln Y = \ln a + b \ln S + F \ln c + \ln \left(\frac{1 - A}{T} \right) + \text{error},$$

and the data is fitted to the model and the results analyzed. In our discussion of actual cases, we will see that model specification is an important issue.

A related issue is the *interaction* of several predictor variables. Health studies are a good example of this, as simultaneous exposure to several environmental agents may increase one's risk of cancer more than the sum of the separate risk increases. Suppose a particular cancer is indicated by a test using a count (Y) of chromosome effects. If smoking and alcohol affect Y additively, we would model the relationship as

$$(8.30) \qquad\qquad Y = a + b_1 S + b_2 C + e,$$

where S is the number of cigarettes and C the ounces of alcohol the individual usually consumes each day. If alcohol and smoking *interact*, increasing the likelihood that a person who is both a heavy smoker and heavy drinker will develop the cancer under study, a better model might be

$$(8.31) \qquad\qquad Y = a + b_1 S + b_2 C + b_3 CS + e,$$

where the coefficient b_3 measures the *additional joint effect* that smoking and alcohol consumption have on the variable Y over and above their *separate* effects captured in equation (8.30).

In equal employment cases, interaction effects may arise when minorities are required to wait longer for a promotion. Then an interaction term for minority status and time employed in the salary regression model will reflect this. This joint effect might be missed if just an indicator of minority status were used, as the data for recent hires who are being paid the same would essentially be combined with data on the employees who did suffer discriminatory treatment.

The wage example illustrates the importance of developing a model incorporating the major covariates *before* collecting much less analyzing data. Failure to consider days absent led us to find a spurious relationship between sex and earnings. This type of error is called *omitted variable bias*, because the effect of the omitted variable may be attributed to one or more of the other predictor variables and/or to random error. If the omitted variable is correlated with one of the predictor variables, as in the example, the estimate of the coefficient of that variable (e.g., sex) will be *biased*,[33] as the model is estimating the direct effect of sex *plus* part of the effect of the omitted variable, namely, that part which is correlated with sex. When an omitted variable is not related to the other predictor variables, its effect contributes to the *error* term, increasing its standard deviation and decreasing the explanatory value (R^2) of the model. It will not lead to a bias in the coefficients of the other predictors, but these estimates will have a larger standard error than they would under the complete model. Therefore, when a model which incorporates the major covariates as predictors and finds the sex or race coefficient significant is criticized for omitting a variable, one needs to assess the magnitude of its possible effect on the estimates of the coefficients of the predictor variables. In the wage equation example, the sex indicator variable is of primary interest. If another characteristic was deemed relevant, it would have to be highly correlated with sex to change the conclusion of our analysis as days absent was. Moreover, if it were related to one of the other variables such as seniority, part of its effect would already be incorporated in the estimated effect of seniority. Hence, the remaining influence of the variable would have to be related to sex to cause serious bias in the estimated effect of sex in a model which did not include it.

Comments. (1) The above discussion assumed that the major factors were included in the basic model. When a factor which is uncorrelated with sex and influences Y (salary) is omitted, the estimated s_e^2 is too large. Adding the variable will lead to a lower s_e^2 and may yield lower standard errors of the other estimated coefficients. This may increase the significance of these coefficients.

(2) Quite often several predictor variables will be related to each other. If there are sound reasons for each of them to be included in the model, they should be. A modest amount of collinearity will not be severe when the sample studied is of reasonable size. Indeed, the days absent variable used in equation (8.27) had to be correlated with sex in the data in order to explain the previous result. The objective of a model is to account for the major predictors so that the effect of each one can be estimated. In some applications the available sample may not be sufficiently large. This might

happen in the discrimination context if the firm or division of the firm under scrutiny was small.

6. Potential Problems in Regression Analyses and Their Effect on the Judicial Acceptance of the Results

As we have seen, regression analyses can aid our understanding of the joint influence of several predictors on the dependent variable (Y). Before giving further illustrations of regression methods, we review some of the potential problems and indicate how one might check to see whether they seriously affect a particular regression. We discuss how these issues were treated in several EEO cases and then illustrate them on a simple data set concerning the relationship between the price of a glass and a bottle of various wines in a first class hotel.

a. Potential problems

Some basic questions one should ask about a regression are:

(1) Were the predictor variables used based on a sound theory? Can the choice of each one be justified on empirical, theoretical or legal grounds? In the wage example, seniority is known to affect wages from empirical studies of lifetime earnings and is cited[34] in the Title VII law.

(2) Are there any omitted variables which should *add* to the predictive value of the model? Why are they not incorporated?

(3) Are proxy variables used for the ideal predictors, e.g., is age used as a substitute for seniority? If so, how reliable is the proxy variable, e.g., is it a better substitute for one portion of the data than the other? If so, how might this affect the ultimate inferences drawn?

(4) How accurate is the basic data? Are the errors random and what are their likely magnitudes? Is there a sizeable portion of missing data and, if so, is it randomly missing or is it concentrated in an important subset?

(5) Is the model properly specified in terms of the functional form and possibility of interaction effects? What statistical diagnostic checks were carried out to assure that the basic assumptions underlying the fitting of regression models to data such as independent errors are satisfied?

(6) Are inappropriate variables included? In our example had there been a significant sex effect and the union then incorporated race as a factor in an equation and this diminished the effect of sex (which could

occur if many of the female members were black), one might not accept this explanation in the context of a discrimination case.

(7) Is there a feedback between the dependent variable (Y) and one or more of the predictor variables? Does this violate the assumption that the dependent variable is affected by changes in the predictors but not conversely? Indeed, the regression model (8.27) does not allow for a feedback effect, although other mathematical models do.

(8) Are there any observations which exert a strong influence on the estimated coefficients fitted by least squares? If so, would their exclusion seriously change the conclusions?

The second, third and sixth questions concern the appropriateness of the predictor variables used. If a variable is omitted, was this done because it is known to be highly correlated with other predictors so it would not add much explanatory force to the model but could reduce the precision of the estimated coefficients of the other variables due to multicollinearity? Was it excluded because it would likely reflect discrimination rather than explain salaries, or because the employer did not collect the appropriate data? This issue is especially pertinent in the discrimination context and arose in our discussion of supervisory evaluations when all the supervisors were white men. Similarly, job assignments or job level has been questioned in decisions[35] concerned with discrimination in initial assignment and promotion. Obviously, if the defendant promotes minorities at a slower rate than majority employees, the grade level reflects this and the effect of the discrimination on wages will be masked if current grade level is used to predict salaries. If the promotion process has been found to be fair,[36] then it is proper to include job level.

When a proxy variable is used in a discrimination case, one needs to check that it is equally reliable for both the majority and minority group. In the *Vuyanich*[37] case, plaintiffs used age (in months minus 72) as a substitute for experience in the labor force. The defendant demonstrated that while the typical age of female employees was about 90% that of the average male employee, the ratio of their average years of experience was only 70%. The potential impact of this difference between the proxy and the proper predictor was shown to be serious enough to cause a bias, as experience had a strong effect on salaries. In this instance the error in the proxy was systematically related to the variable (sex) which was of primary interest.

The accuracy of the data is always relevant and we will discuss missing data in Chapter 9. Since there are invariably some errors in any data set, one needs to assess the amount and possible impact they would have on the conclusions reached. A modest amount of random errors in the measurement of a predictor variable typically causes its influence to be underestimated, since the added error weakens the explanatory force of the variable. This can result in an *underestimate* of the effect of that predictor, which may lead to a bias in the estimates of the coefficients of the other predictors, especially those which are correlated with the predictor which was measured with error.

The issue of feedback is best illustrated by the following example in Rubinfeld (1985, p. 1076):

> Consider an employment situation in which one of the explanatory variables is the score attained by applicants during the interviewing process. If interview scores accurately measure ability to perform on the job, then the multiple regression procedure for testing for wage discrimination is appropriate. If the employer scores women lower than men for inappropriate reasons, however, then the interview score variable will become a good predictor of the wage, and the sex variable will become less insignificant.

The appropriateness of a regression model is an issue which can be studied by considering not only its explanatory value, adj(R^2), but also the plot of the standardized residuals.[38] Since the standardized residuals should look like normally distributed random variables, a disproportionate share of large residuals or other nonrandom patterns indicates that the model and data should be checked. Sometimes there are several reasonable ways to model the effect of a predictor variable. In a wage equation one might believe that each year of seniority is reflected in a fixed *percentage* salary raise rather than a fixed dollar amount. Then a more appropriate model for salaries would be $c \cdot (1 + r)^S$, where r is the annual rate of increase, c is the starting salary and S is years of seniority. Taking logarithms we have

(8.32) $$\ln W = \ln c + S \ln(1 + r),$$

so one should fit an equation using (ln wage) $= a + b$ (seniority). This is why wage equations are often fitted in logarithmic form. When an employer has a set policy, such as reviewing each employee on the yearly anniversary of their hire, a regression model should incorporate this by measuring seniority in terms of complete years of service rather than months.

The examination of residuals is important in detecting possible unusual observations. This is not always easy to do because the effect of an observation in a regression model *depends on the location* of the values of its predictor variables among the values of the predictors of the entire data set. In fitting a regression model, the observations at the *extremes* have the greatest impact on the estimated coefficient. This can be seen from formula (8.21) for the estimated slope, $\hat{b}$, in a simple linear regression where the weight w_i of the ith observation is

$$\frac{(X_i - \overline{X})}{\sum_{j=1}^{n}(X_j - \overline{X})^2}.$$

Thus, the observations with the smallest ($X_i - \overline{X}$ most negative) and largest ($X_i - \overline{X}$ most positive) values of the predictor X will have more influence on the fitted line than the other data points.

One way of examining a fitted regression for possible undue influence of a few data points is to refit the equation to the observations, deleting the questionable ones. If the estimated coefficients ($\hat{a}$, $\hat{b}$) change substantially, then one needs to check the basic data and see whether the deleted observations were accurate or really should follow the same model as the other observations.

The above questions should serve as an introduction to checking the propriety of a regression model that is fitted to a set of data. The model should make sense from a subject matter point of view and the data should satisfy the basic assumptions underlying the regression model. We should note that it is easy to criticize a model for *not* being perfect. Hence, before rejecting a reasonable model because there is a possible flaw (omitted variable, unsuitable proxy or possible measurement error in one of the predictors), one should assess the possible effect the flaw might have, as in *Vuyanich,* rather than immediately concluding that the regression analysis should be discarded. Thus, some judgement and experience is required in evaluating the results yielded by a regression analysis.

Before illustrating how courts have dealt with some of these issues in several employment discrimination cases, we illustrate the topic of model specification and checking residuals on a simple data set consisting of 10 data points.

b. *Using regression to explore the relationship between the price of a glass and the price of a bottle of wine*

In Table 8.8 we report the prices of a glass and a bottle of various wines served in a first class hotel.[39] Two possible models suggest themselves to us. There could be a fixed relationship, i.e., a glass could cost a set

TABLE 8.8. The Price of a Glass and a Bottle of Various Wines

Price of a Glass (Y)	Price of a Bottle (X)
3.75	15.00
3.75	15.00
3.75	15.00
5.00	20.00
6.25	25.00
4.25	25.50
5.00	30.00
5.00	30.00
8.00	48.00
14.00	84.00

fraction of a bottle, or there could be a fixed service charge plus a set
fraction. As the second model is more general and enables us to test
whether the *constant a* is needed, we fit the data to an equation of the
form

$$Y = a + bX,$$

where a is a constant and b is the coefficient (fraction) of the price (X) of a
bottle of the wine. The resulting equation is

$$Y = 1.42 \quad + \quad .1455X$$

(8.33)   (.4197)   (.0114)   standard error
                          (3.39)   (12.68)   t-statistic

and $R^2 = .953$, adj$(R^2) = .947$, and the standard deviation (s_e) of the
residuals is .727. The coefficient b takes on a value near 1/7, which is both
sensible and statistically significant. Also, the constant term is significant,
which suggests that a fixed service charge of about $1.50 was built into the
price. In order to check on the validity of the assumption that the errors
have an approximate normal distribution, a plot of the standardized residuals is given in Figure 8.5. Because each of the residuals $Y_i - \hat{Y}_i$ obtained
from the *fitted regression* do *not* have the same standard deviation, we
divide each residual by its own estimated standard deviation to create a
standardized residual, and these should have a standard normal distribution. They are not quite independent, but their correlation typically is
small, especially in large samples. Figure 8.5 does not indicate any unusually large deviation, although three points seem to be fitted perfectly,

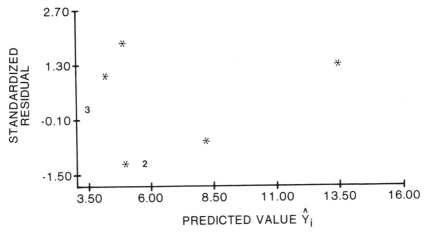

FIGURE 8.5.   Plot of the standardized residuals corresponding to the predicted values y from equation (8.32). These residuals should be approximately normally distributed with mean 0 and standard deviation 1.

which is unusual. The point (84,14) was identified as having a large influence, as we would expect, since the extreme observations are given more weight in estimating $\hat{b}$.

Using many of the criteria in elementary text books, e.g., a high R^2 value, a balance of positive and negative residuals, the model (8.32) seems adequate. Let us look more closely at the data and compute the ratio of the glass and bottle prices. The first five ratios equal 1/4, while the last five are 1/6. This suggests that there are tow types of wine being sold. Indeed, the ratio 1/6 corresponds to champagne, while the ratios of 1/4 are for red or white table wines. This suggests that we fit a model incorporating an indicator variable, $I = 1$ or 0, according to whether the wine is a champagne or not. Thus, the model becomes

(8.34) $Y = a + bX + cIX.$

The reason we use the multiplicative term IX rather than the simple indicator I is because the *price ratios* are affected by the type of wine.

The resulting regression fit to the data is now perfect, i.e., we obtain

(8.35) $Y = .25X - .0833(IX),$
                                    $(0.0) \quad (0.0)$

where the standard errors are 0. Equation (8.35) says that to find the price of a glass of wine if $I = 0$ (table wine), $I \times X = 0$, so use the formula $Y = .25X$. If $I = 1$, use $Y = (.25 - .0833)X = .1667X$ or $(1/6)X$.

This example illustrates the fact that a model with a high R^2 may still be incorrect. One reason the simple model fit fairly well is that all but one of the table wines were in the low price range, while the champagnes had higher prices. The multiplier 1/7 in the simple equation is closer to the value 1/6 for champagne and the constant term, 1.42, helped adjust it to fit the lower-priced dinner wines.

In order to illustrate the effect of a rather unusual observation, we fit the *correct model* (8.34) to the same data, changing only the price of a bottle of Dom Perignon from $84 to $70. The resulting equation is

$$Y = -1.17 + .312X - .04(IX)$$

(8.36)   (.457)   (.0265)   (.0187)   standard error

                              (-2.57)   (11.8)   (-5.57) t-statistic

with $R^2 = .985$ and adj(R^2) = .98. The estimated standard deviation of the error term is

$$(8.37) \qquad s_e = \sqrt{\frac{1}{n-2} \sum (Y_i - Y_i)^2} = .444,$$

which is much less than the standard deviation $3.15 of the original data, reflecting the good fit of equation (8.36) to the data. Of course, we began with a perfect relationship and altered only one data point.

A graph of the predictions and the standardized residuals corresponding to them is given in Fig. 8.6. The reader can see that the standardized

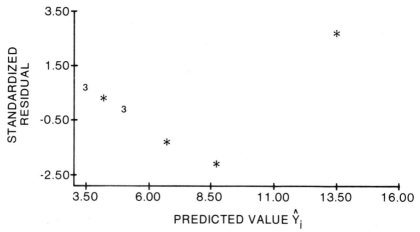

FIGURE 8.6.   Plot of the standardized residuals corresponding to the predicted values y from the regression equation (8.35).

residuals gradually decline until the last observation, which has a value of 2.65. Moreover, the standardized residual of the next to last observation is -2.13. Since the standardized residuals are approximately normally distributed, it is surprising to see two such large residuals in a data set of 10 points (only about 1 in 20 observations from a standard normal distribution should exceed 2 in absolute value) as well as the pattern of steady decline and a compensating jump. Thus, the plot in Figure 8.6 indicates that there is something unusual in the data, which we know to be the case.

Typically, one cannot determine from examining the residuals whether the problem is an error in the data, as in this last example, or a misspecification of the model (omitted variable or incorrect functional form). A plot of the standardized residuals with unusual features is a signal to do some checking of the accuracy of the data and the appropriateness of the model.

Comments. (1) Notice how an error in one observation (chosen on purpose to be an extreme and influential one) changed the estimated coefficients. The importance of having a sound theoretical model can also be seen from this example. Both price structures, a basic charge plus a fraction of the price of a bottle, or a simple ratio varying with the type of wine, make sense. Equation (8.36) with a *negative* estimate of the basic service charge does not. Often an estimate of a coefficient which seems far out of line with what one expects from theory indicates a potential problem. Thus, a wage equation should yield reasonable figures for the effect of an extra year of seniority or the completion of further training.

(2) Since the basic relation between the prices was a multiplicative one, it can also be expressed as

$$Y = aX^{b_1} \cdot e^{b_2 I}$$

or

$$\log Y = a + b_1 \log X + b_2 I,$$

where Y is the price of a glass, X the price of a bottle and $I = 1$ indicates a champagne. The fitted equation becomes

(8.37) $$\log Y = -1.3863 + 1.0 \log X - .4055 I$$

and again is a perfect fit.

Exponentiating equation (8.37) to put it in terms of prices rather than logarithms of prices yields

(8.38)
$$Y = \frac{1}{4} X, \quad \text{if } I = 0$$

$$Y = \frac{1}{4} X \times \frac{2}{3} = \frac{1}{6} X, \quad \text{if } I = 1,$$

which gives the true relationship.

c. Examples of regression analyses submitted in discrimination cases

1) *Segar v. Smith:*[40] Regression Analysis Accepted as Showing a Salary Disparity Between the Races

In support of their claim of discrimination in initial placement and promotion, the plaintiffs introduced a regression analysis of annual salary predicted by the following background characteristics of drug enforcement officers: education, years of prior federal experience, years of prior nonfederal experience and race. As all persons had been hired by the Drug Enforcement Agency (DEA), all had some experience in the enforcement area. In order to control for the possible effect of pre-act discrimination, for which the defendant would not be liable, the regression was also fitted to data for employees hired after 1972. The race coefficients and t-statistics are reported in Table 8.9 for several years of data. The dollar value of the race coefficient is both meaningful and statistically significant in almost all years. As half of the persons included in the 1975 study on post-1972 hires were hired in 1974, it is unreasonable to expect that promotion discrimination could be reflected in the following year, as the Civil Ser-

TABLE 8.9.   Plaintiff's Regression Estimates of the Effect of Race on Salary in *Segar v. Smith*

	All Special Agents		Agents Hired Post 1972	
Date	Race Coefficient	t-Statistic	Race Coefficient	t-Statistic
1/1/75	−$1,628	−4.65	−$ 378	−.84
1/1/76	−$1,744	−5.37	−$1,864	−2.54
1/1/77	−$1,119	−5.15	$1,119	−3.18
1/1/78	−$1,934	−5.15	$ 866	−2.07
1/1/79	−$1,877	−4.50	−$1,026	−2.30

Source: 738 F.2d 1249 at 1262.

vice usually requires one year of service in the previous grade in order for an employee to be eligible for promotion. The defendant criticized the plaintiff's regression analysis on the following grounds:

(1) The significance level of the t-test was not sufficient to sustain an inference of discrimination.

(2) The experience variable did not incorporate a second year of specialized experience, which was required for placement at a grade 9 level instead of grade 7.

(3) The R^2 values of plaintiff's regression were low, ranging from .42 to .52 for those fitted on all employees and from .21 to .37 for those fitted on data for post-1972 hires.

Both the District and Appeals courts rejected these arguments. First, the court noted that the .05 level (which corresponds to a t-statistic of about 2.0 in large samples) is used in social science and that the Justice Department itself adopted that level in the *Uniform Testing Guidelines*.[41] The estimated race coefficient met this criteria in virtually all years. Since all employees had general experience in areas related to the job, the assertion that the experience variables were inadequate hinged on whether blacks had less "specialized experience" than whites. The appellate opinion observed that the definition of "specialized experience" was vague and the suit concerned persons in similar jobs, all of whom had at least one year of prior criminal investigative experience, so it was reasonable to assume that the proportion of blacks possessing several years of "specialized experience" was similar to the proportion of whites.

Comment. We emphasize the difference between the defendant's criticism of regression in *Segar* from that in *Vuyanich*. There the bank demonstrated that using age rather than seniority systematically over estimated the seniority of women. In *Segar,* defendants apparently did *not* submit data demonstrating a meaningful difference between the races in "specialized experience". In order to legitimately criticize a regression model, one should offer evidence that the flaw could have a serious impact on the ultimate inference.

The district court's finding that the R^2 values were "not so low as to adversely affect the veracity of plaintiff's studies" 508 F.Supp. at 697, was upheld. The explanatory value of a model should not be confused with the statistical significance of an estimated coefficient. Indeed, R^2 values in the range of these results occur quite often in wage equations based on the human capital theory[42] when census data is used. As long as the residuals, $(Y_i - \hat{Y}_i)$ are random so that there is no evidence of an effect of an omitted variable which might be correlated with race, the estimate of the race effect is statistically unbiased. Again we note that the value of R^2 which yields an adequate model varies according to the area of application, and the ones in *Segar* were typical of wage equations. Moreover, the R^2 for the model, when fitted to data on all employees, was higher than when recent hires were considered. This should be the case, as the range of possible values for years of experience among the recent hires would be *restricted* relative to the range for all employees, and we know that correlations calculated from such data are less than the correlations based on the full range.

Finally, we note that rather than offer an alternative regression study, the defendants submitted a "cohort analysis". As we showed elsewhere,[43] when properly analyzed, their study was consistent with the plaintiff's claim.

2) *Sobel v. Yeshiva University*:[44] A Careful Critique of Plaintiffs' Regression Renders it Unacceptable

In June 1975, Drs. Sobel and Clutario filed a charge of employment discrimination against the University's Medical School with regard to salary levels and other conditions of employment. Plaintiffs designed a regression model which predicted salary as a function of medical specialty (but not subspecialty), publication rate, years of experience, etc. They studied all faculty members and those hired after 1972 in order to avoid the problem of including any discrimination remaining from the pre-act or pre-statute of limitations period. The data for each year from 1969 to 1979 were analyzed. The sex coefficient was negative and statistically significant at the .05 level for all faculty members in 1970 and the years 1973 through 1978. The plaintiffs' experts concluded that the salary disparity was greater for female members of the class who were hired prior to March 24, 1972, the date Title VII became applicable to universities.

The defendant pointed out that the plaintiffs' regression did not incorporate sufficiently many productivity variables such as subspeciality, whether the faculty member was primarily in research or was a clinician, the amount of research grants or revenue generated through private and affiliated practice, the quality of the research papers or clinical practice, etc. The defendants asserted that academic rank, which was not included in the plaintiffs' regression, would reflect some of these productivity characteristics.

Comment. A substantial literature and case law surrounds the use of rank in a graded system. When promotion is at issue, a salary regression study including rank may be inappropriate unless the court has found the promotion process to be fair. As Finkelstein (1980) states, "the finding that a promotion process is fair should require more than the defendant's employer showing that the promotion rate of minorities is not statistically significantly less than majority employees using a two-sided .05 level test." The judge in Sobel discussed this point and was convinced that the independent faculty committees made the decision on merit.

When rank was included in the plaintiffs model, the sex coefficient was significant in only one year (1975). The defendant also pointed out the following problems:

(1) The plaintiffs used 14 variables to control for experience. Several of them, the square of the total prior experience, total medical experience, job tenure, age and age squared, are obviously collinear, making it difficult to accurately estimate the effect of years of related experience, which is a legitimate factor.

(2) A model using log-salary provided a better fit than the plaintiffs' one based on salary. This was demonstrated by showing that the size of the residuals, the observed *minus* predicted values, increased with salary. Thus, the assumption that the errors have the same variance was not satisfied.

(3) The sign of some of the coefficients changed from year to year, indicating that the plaintiffs' model was unstable. This argument was buttressed by demonstrating the large influence of a few observations. Removing one faculty member, presumably a high paid male, decreased the estimated sex coefficient from 2378 to 1957 and the t-statistic from 2.13 (two-sided p-value = .033) to 1.77 (p-value = .076). Although one might describe this change as moving the sex variable from statistical significance to nonsignificance, that is too simplistic. The doubling of the p-value does diminish the strength of the plaintiffs' evidence, especially in light of the other flaws in their model.

(4) When the defendants included rank, subspecialty and other productivity measures, the explanatory value measured by adj(R^2) increased. Of more relevance is the fact that males had a higher average level on 10 of the 14 predictors the plaintiffs used to measure productivity. This suggests that they are likely to have a higher average level of true productivity so that the components of productivity not fully measured or reflected in the plaintiffs' predictor variables is likely to be related to sex. Hence,

their model will attribute these components to sex, thereby making that coefficient more negative than it truly is.

Comment. The only criticism of the plaintiffs' regression analysis that *may* not be justified concerned the *multicollinearity* between the plaintiffs' predictors of seniority and experience. The effect of multicollinearity is to possibly shift some of the effect of one variable to another predictor with which it is highly related. This need not cause a serious error in the estimate of the coefficient of a predictor variable to which it is *not highly related*. The number of highly related experience variables in the plaintiffs' model in *Sobel* would cause concern, but the effect of multicollinearity might have been examined further. For example, the correlations of the predictors could have been calculated, and their values shown to be high enough to create a problem.

One diagnostic check for a possible multicollinearity problem is due to Theil (1978). By fitting the model to the data but deleting each predictor variable (one at a time), we obtain a measure of the *incremental* effect of the variable from the difference $R^2 - R_j^2$, where R_j^2 is the R^2 of the model *without* the jth predictor (X_j). If the variables are uncorrelated with each other, the total of all increments

$$(8.39) \qquad \sum (R^2 - R_j^2)$$

would be near R^2 because the jth variable would explain ($R^2 - R_j^2$) of the total variation in (Y), and no predictor would also include information contained in the others. Typically, predictors will be somewhat related, e.g., due to the post-war trend to continue in school, educational level and seniority of a work force may be slightly negatively correlated. Only when there is high correlation among the predictors is this problem serious. If the total of all increments (8.39) is much smaller than R^2, e.g., one fourth or less, a serious multicollinearity problem may exist. The predictors with the smallest increments are the ones which are related to one or more of the others. A more refined version of this procedure is due to Swamy, Mehta, Thurman and Iyengar (1985).

3) *Craik v. Minnesota State Univ. Board.*[45] Defendant's Criticisms Were Not Accepted, as their Effect on the Estimated Sex Coefficient Was Not Shown

A regression analysis submitted by the plaintiffs in *Craik* was criticized by the defendants because the data base included some administrators such as deans who held academic rank. The opinion noted that such appointees constituted about 4% of the total data base so that their inclusion could not severely affect the result. Moreover, the defendant did not fit the regression model to the same data excluding them. It is hard to disagree with the majority opinion on its assessment of the potential bias due to a small proportion of the data; however, in fitting a regression, the extreme values receive more weight. Since administrators are often paid more than faculty members, if they were primarily male, including them could have affected the estimated sex coefficient. Nevertheless, the defendant should have rerun the plaintiffs' equation without these employees and obtained the effect that including the administrators had on the significance of the sex coefficient in the plaintiffs' regression.

A related issue that may arise in similar cases is the effect of past administrative service on faculty salaries. Since administrative salaries are higher, when the individual returns to his or her department after a period of years as an associate dean, say, their salary probably will exceed that of a comparable faculty member. Often the person retains the administrative salary and receives lower pay raises until the departmental salaries return to their appropriate relationship. Had this occurred in *Craik* and had women been underrepresented in administrative posts, then a greater fraction of the data might be deemed irrelevant. Of course, any past or present underrepresentation of women in administrative jobs might also indicate discriminatory treatment.

7. Further Applications of Regression Analysis in Law, Dispute Resolution and Public Policy

Regression methods are used in antitrust, utility rate and discrimination cases to determine the economic value of various factors, as well as to determine whether or not a particular variable (X) has an effect on the outcome variable (Y) of interest. Since some of the data sets used in these applications are quite large, we will first describe the use of the ideas of this chapter on two small-sample data sets, the first involving the cause of a chemical reaction causing sedimentation in an oil shipment. The second will be to further explore our study of the effect of smoking on chromatid exchanges in the data set given in Tables 7.8 and 7.9. We then discuss another sex discrimination case. From general knowledge of health effects, smoking is a natural covariate to consider in studies concerning cancer and heart disease because of its known carcinogenic character and the fact that carcinogenic substances are often mutagenic. Similarly, in antitrust applications, economic theory indicates that there will be greater price competition when there are more firms in an industry. Hence, we will need to use multiple regression methods to remove the effects of these related factors on our estimate of the effect of the characteristics of interest.

a. Assessing the influence of smoking and exposure to ethylene oxide on SCE counts

In Section 7.5 we analyzed data on the SCE counts of hospital employees who had been exposed to varying amounts of ethylene oxide (ETO) and observed that the original analysis of the data in Table 7.8 might have neglected the effect of smoking. Now we explore the data set further. The data was first[46] analyzed by classifying each person in one of three exposure categories: 0, low or high. The analysis of covariance used by the original investigators is equivalent to fitting a multiple regression model of the form

$$(8.40) \qquad Y = a + b_1 I_1 + b_2 I_2 + e,$$

where $I_1 = 1$ if a person is in the low exposure category, 0 otherwise, and I_2 indicates whether a person is in the high (1) category. Employees who are in the control group (no exposure) have a zero for both I_1 and I_2. Essentially, the constant a is the average SCE count of the controls, b_1 measures the difference between the SCE counts of the low and unexposed (control) persons, and b_2 measures the difference between the highly exposed and the control categories.

A computerized regression analysis of the data in Table 7.8 yielded the following estimated regression model of the form (8.40):

$$Y = 7.5585 + .2038 I_1 + 3.1295 I_2$$

(8.41)   (.5287)   (.6416)   standard error

                     (.385)   (4.878)   *t*-statistic

with coefficient of determination, $R^2 = .516$, and adj(R^2) = .476. The estimate $\hat{b}_2 = 3.13$ is statistically significant (two-sided *p*-value = .0001) and presumably meaningful, as the SCE count increases from 7.56 to 10.69. On the other hand, the estimated effect $\hat{b}_1 = .204$ of low exposure was not statistically significant and may not be practically meaningful.

Notice that the estimates $\hat{b}_2$ ($\hat{b}_2$) are precisely the difference between the averages of the low (high) categories and the unexposed one. This occurs because the least squares estimate of the mean of each category is

the sample average, so the least squares estimate of the difference between groups is the difference between their averages.

We next include the variable S indicating whether a person smokes
($S = 1$) or not ($S = 0$). The fitted regression model now is

$$Y = 6.977 + .155I + 3.144I_2 + .946S$$
(8.42)   (.496)   (.602)   (.456) standard error
                   (.313)   (5.225)   (2.072) t-statistic

and $R^2 = .592$, while adj(R^2) $= .539$. Equation (8.42) fits the data better,
because the adj(R^2) has increased from .476 to .539. Furthermore, the
smoking variable is statistically significant. Its estimated effect, .95, is
only about one third of that of high exposure but is six times that of low
exposure.

Previously we noted that the two employees from hospital B had a
different pattern of exposure (more frequent exposure to a low dose). If
we delete these employees so the model is fit on the data for employees
from hospital A, we obtain

(8.43) $Y = 6.848 - .075I_1 + 3.147I_2 + 1.156S,$

where the standard errors and R^2 values were similar to those reported for
equation (8.42). Again, the estimate of the effect of low exposure is not
statistically significant, but now it is slightly negative. This suggests that
when smoking is controlled for, the effect of low exposure to ETO is
essentially zero, at least for workers whose exposure pattern is similar to
those in hospital A. Of course, research is needed on persons with the
exposure pattern in hospital B, as deleting these two nonsmokers had an
impact on the estimates of the effect of both low exposure and smoking,
and the SCE counts of the two workers were higher than comparable
workers from hospital A.

The analysis of the data by exposure category is sensible in the present
application because the exposures were estimated and were subject to
error. However, one should explore a regression model using the form

$$Y = a + b_1X + b_2S,$$

where X denotes an individual's estimated exposure and S indicates
whether or not the person smokes. The resulting fitted model is

$$Y = 6.95 + .0058X + 1.099\ S$$
(8.44)   (.00095)   (.424)   standard error
                 (6.1)   (2.6) t-statistic

and $R^2 = .634$, adj(R^2) = .604. This model assumes that SCE counts increase with the amount of exposure and that the lines for smokers and nonsmokers are parallel, differing only by about 1.1, the estimated smoking effect. This model fits the data better than the previous one; however, one might wish to explore other functional forms such as

$$Y = a + b_1X + b_2X^2 + b_3S,$$

which would enable us to see whether higher levels of exposure increase the incidence of SCEs at more than a linear rate (which would be indicated by a significant positive value of b_2).

At this point we will stop analyzing this small data set and summarize our conclusions.

(1) Smoking is an important covariate which should be incorporated in the analysis of similar data sets.

(2) The pattern of exposure may be quite important, as deleting just two observations affected our estimated effect of low exposure.

(3) Further thought needs to be given the appropriate functional form of the relationship between SCE count, exposure to ETO and smoking.

Comments. (1) As this data was used to support further regulation of exposure to ETO, the model used and the value of the estimated coefficients can be quite important. For hospitals whose workers are subject to the exposure pattern of hospital A, equation (8.43) indicates that they should not suffer a serious effect from low exposure, say, at exposure levels no greater than the average of the low-exposure group. Equation (8.44), on the other hand, estimates that each unit of exposure produces an expected increase in SCEs of .006. This can have an impact on the determination of a safe level of exposure. For example, if an increase of .05 SCEs was deemed potentially harmful on the basis of medical evidence, then one might wish to limit the cumulative six-month exposure levels to no more than 8 mg.

(2) A thorough analysis of the data for other possible influential data points besides the hospital B employees might suggest other possible covariates.

(3) Detailed data on the number of cigarettes smoked would also improve our understanding of the role of smoking and enable us to investigate a possible smoking and exposure *interaction*.

b. *Statistical assessment of the relative influence of possible factors that produced sediment in an oil shipment*

A substantial portion of a large shipment of oil was damaged due to sedimentation in some of the tanks or holds. Oil chemists thought that the sedimentation could have been caused by the shippers neglecting to make sure that a particular type of oil (A, say), which mixes well with other types of oil, was *not* present in all the tanks which carried several types of oil which mixed during transit. On the other hand, chemical reactions are often induced or accelerated by high temperature, so the temperature the oils were exposed to could also affect the sedimentation process. Since one company (the shipper) determined which oils were placed in which tanks, while another firm (the carrier) controlled the temperature at which the oil was loaded and discharged (as well as exposed to en route), liability for the damage was partially dependent on which of two factors, mix of oil *or* temperature, had a greater influence on sediment formation.

The basic data for each of the 13 tanks of the oil tanker is presented in Table 8.10. If one examines the data, it is apparent that the tanks which contained type A oil ($I = 0$) had less sediment. There is some indication

TABLE 8.10. Sedimentation in the Holds of an Oil Tanker and the Oil Mix and Temperatures in the Holds

Sediment% (Y)	Absence (1) or Presence (0) of A Oil (I)	Discharge Temperature (D)	Loading Temperature (L)
0.29	0	82	103
0.00	0	87	99
4.09	1	88	114
0.77	0	90	103
3.08	1	92	107
4.09	1	92	125
0.00	0	94	105
4.24	1	101	125
0.95	0	103	107
1.10	0	108	122
0.00	0	114	108
4.33	1	126	126
5.77	1	128	124

that the higher temperatures are associated with higher sediment percentages, but the relation does not appear to be as clear. To make the interpretation of the fitted equation easier, we denote the predictor variables by D for discharge temperature and L for loading temperature, while $I = 1$ indicates that type A oil was in a tank and $I = 0$ indicates that there was no type A oil in the tank. The multiple regression model used to fit the data was

$$Y = a + b_1 I + b_2 D + b_3 L + e,$$

where a is a constant. The resulting equation and standard errors are:

$$Y = -4.973 - 3.1954I + .0144D + .0377L$$

(8.45)		(7.4422)	(.0141)	(.0277)	standard error
		(−7.227)	(1.022)	(1.359)	t-statistic

Notice that the only statistically significant variable was the indicator of type A oil. Its coefficient of -3.2 indicates that it is negatively related to sediment occurrence. The adjusted R^2 of the fitted equation (8.45) was about .93, indicating quite a close fit of the data.

As neither temperature coefficient was statistically significant, while the presence or absence of type A oil was quite significant (p-value = .0005), we conclude that the oil mix was the most important factor. Indeed, the arbitration panel decided, based upon all the facts in the case, that the party responsible for the oil mix should pay the damages.

c. The salary studies submitted in Chang vs. University of Rhode Island[47]

Regression analysis was used to study the effect sex had on the salary of new appointees and all employees in *Chang,* as discrimination was alleged in initial salary assignments, salary raises and promotions. Plaintiffs studied the salary of 222 of a total of 258 new hires throughout the relevant time period. The missing observations were due to incomplete data in the personnel files. Using the logarithmic form of a wage equation, which expresses the effect of each variable in percentage terms, they found that newly hired women had a statistically significant (p-value = .012) disparity of 5.7% in initial pay after controlling for the following predictors: possession of a PhD, years since the highest degree was earned, year of hire by the university, years and type of prior experience, and departmental group. The last category controls for variations in the

TABLE 8.11. Defendant's Regression Analysis of Salaries Received By New Hires from *Chang v. Univ. of Rhode Island*

Rank	Estimated Effect of Sex	*t*-Ratio	Statistical Significance	R^2	Sample Size
Associate	−135.9	0.15	No	.85	49
Assistant	−412.2	1.53	No	.86	252
Instructor	+30.2	0.02	No	.78	99

Source: 40 FEP Cases 3 at 46.
Note: The opinion reported the *t*-ratios in terms of the number of standard deviations of the estimated coefficient of the sex effect from its expected value (0) under the hypothesis of no sex effect.

demand for faculty by broad subject areas, e.g., computer scientists and engineers have more nonacademic opportunities than history professors.

The defendant did not use type of experience, rather they relied solely on years since highest degree and the individual's rank at hire, and analyzed the data in each rank separately. Their results are presented in Table 8.11 and do not demonstrate a significant effect of sex, although the estimated coefficient for assistant professors is not far from significance if a one-sided .05 level criteria had been set.

The opinion noted that the defendant's analysis implicitly assumes that persons were appointed to the appropriate rank. As fairness in initial assignment was also an issue in the case and as such misranking would put some women in the higher pay range of the lower rank rather than in the lower pay range of their appropriate rank, defendants within rank comparison could be biased against the finding of discrimination in pay. Examining the results in Table 8.11, one sees that moving a few women from the assistant professorship category and from instructor to assistant professor could probably make the estimated sex coefficient negative in each rank, and the sex effect for assistant professors would probably reach statistical significance. Also, the defendant did not use the logarithmic form, which is usually more appropriate in salary studies, and apparently did not demonstrate that the residuals were approximately random. Finally, the opinion questioned the defendant's failure to incorporate the type of experience in addition to years of experience. Thus, the plaintiffs' study was closer to a proper comparison of persons with similar experience and credentials, and they prevailed on their charge of discrimination in initial salaries.

Comments. (1) The defendant argued that the high R^2 values in Table 8.11 supported the soundness of their model. However, even within rank, the department and years of experience typically determine a substantial proportion of the variation in academic salaries.

(2) There was another difference between the studies. The defendants included persons hired from 1971 through the 1982–83 academic year. As the original charge was filed in early 1977, and other charges were filed in 1979 and in early 1983, one can question the relevance of using so much post-charge data. This is particularly true of the data for 1981–82 and 1982–83, as the litigation already was in process. We have seen several instances of employers changing their practice subsequent to a charge of discrimination and before the trial date, e.g., in *Teal* (Section 8.4c) and *Capaci* (Section 4.4d and 7.3a).

In their analysis of salaries of all faculty members, the plaintiffs used the same variables as in their initial hiring study, plus longevity at the university, to assess the fairness of advancement practices. They did not use rank, either at time of hire or currently attained, claiming that it might be affected by discrimination, or any measure of productivity such as number or rate of publications while individuals were on the faculty. The defendant used current rank, rank at hire and longevity at the university, in addition to the predictors in their initial pay study. Neither study incorporated post-hire productivity measures, such as publications, receipt of research grants or professional honors, or considered the changes in the salary setting process resulting from a collective bargaining agreement. The court felt that the defendant's studies were more sound than those offered by the plaintiffs, but neither one was truly adequate. In particular, the plaintiffs were criticized for not utilizing post-hire productivity measures in a study which was supposed to demonstrate that discrimination occurred while the plaintiffs were employed by the university.

Comment. These regression studies should be contrasted with those in *Sobel.* There plaintiffs at least attempted to use some post-hire productivity measures. A major problem in the regression analysis of wage data is obtaining an accurate description of the process of salary determination and the data used by the employer in this process. Once the factors are enumerated by the employer, it is reasonable to require the plaintiffs to incorporate data on them which was made available by the employer or explain why they did not, e.g., the data were inaccurate or the system of codes used in the computer system changed from year to year, rendering the data difficult to work with, or the factor itself was under attack as discriminatory and/or irrelevant to productivity. On the other hand, a defendant cannot justifiably criticize the plaintiff's model for not incorporating factors such as "getting along with peers" (which are quite subjective and may reflect discrimination) or quantitative factors, such as research publications or attendance at meetings, when the defendant did not record this data, so it is questionable that these criteria really were used in the promotion or salary setting process. Of course, the burden of proof in these cases is on the plaintiff, so a glaring omission of a pertinent variable, such as productivity while in the employ of the defendant, weakens their case. On the other hand, the Supreme Court recently noted in *Bazemore v. Friday* 106 S.Ct. 3000, 41 FEP Cases 92 (1986) that plaintiffs do not have to incorporate *all* measurable variables. This agrees with our assertion that the major influential variables should be considered. Only in situations in which the estimated coefficient which reflects discrimination is of borderline significance (two-sided p-value between .05 and .10, say) and is of a modest magnitude could minor factors affect the conclusion.

d. Other applications and issues

Regression methods have been used to study the effect of possible conspiracy or collusion in the setting of prices in antitrust cases, e.g., *In re Corrugated Container Antitrust Litig.* 441 *F.Supp.* 921 (S.D. Tex. 1977), the effect of exclusive licensing agreements on prices as possible violation of antitrust laws, e.g., *In re Ampicillin Litig.* 88 F.R.D.174 (D.D.C. 1980) and 526 F.Supp. 494 (D.D.C. 1981), the estimation of profits lost by dealers whose franchises were discontinued, e.g., *Rea v. Ford Motor Co.* 355. F.Supp. 842 (E.D.D.Pa. 1973) and the effect of the institution of area-wide voting on diluting black voting strength as the race of candidates affects the electorate, e.g., *Kirksey v. City of Jackson* 461 F.Supp. 12821 (S.D.Miss. 1978), *Bacon v. Moore* 428 F.Supp. 1123 (S.D.Ala. 1976), *aff'd.mem.,* 575(5th Cir. 1978).

These applications are discussed in the references by Finkelstein, Rubinfeld and Rubinfeld and Steiner, so we will not dwell on the details, as the statistical issues are similar to those in our examples. The main points to consider when assessing a regression analysis are the determination of the appropriate underlying theory, the accuracy of the data on the major predictor variables, the specification of the model and checking that the assumptions of the regression technique are satisfied.

Recently, regression analysis has become more accepted as a way to isolate the effects of several variables. Plaintiffs have been criticized for failing to use it to assess the joint effect of education and experience on salary, *Coble v. Hot Springs School District No. 6*, 682 F.2d 721 at 731 (8th Cir. 1981), and a judgement favoring the plaintiffs' challenge to an at-large system of representation on the basis of a simple correlation study of racial voting patterns by district was barely upheld in *Jones v. City of Lubbock* 730 F.2d 233 (5th Cir. 1984). In a special concurrence, Judge Higgenbotham noted that other factors, such as the candidate's name recognition, party identification, income, etc., should have been included to isolate the effect of race or national origin on "bloc voting."

Two important topics which have both statistical and legal aspects require our attention. The first concerns the accuracy of the measurements on the predictor variables, and the second deals with a reasonable protocol for the discovery process and presentation of regression results.

At first glance, the errors-in-measurement issue appears to be a technical one, which is illustrated by considering a simple linear regression Y on X, e.g., log salary on years of experience *or* math aptitude on verbal aptitude. In both applications, the variable X is not a perfect measure of the desired predictor. Rather than years of experience, we might prefer a measure of on-the-job learning or a measure weighting the type of experience by the length of that experience. Similarly, one's score on one particular verbal test is not a perfect measure of verbal ability. Suppose that the *true* variable, e.g., on-the-job learning, is Z and that the variable, X, we use to estimate or substitute for Z can be represented as

$$(8.46) \qquad\qquad X = Z + e_2,$$

where e_2 is an independent error. Thus, we regard X as a measurement of Z subject to a random error e_2. For simplicity we will assume that all measurement errors are independent normal variables with the same variance σ^2. The proper regression model is

$$(8.47) \qquad\qquad Y = a + bZ + e_1,$$

as Z is the true predictor variable. However, we are fitting the model

$$(8.48) \qquad Y = a + bX + e_1 = a + bZ + be_2 + e_1,$$

as each observation on X includes a random measurement error e_2. From equation (8.48) we see that there is *more error* in the model (8.48) than in the ideal model (8.47). This indicates that we will have lower explanatory value adj(R^2) from the fitted regression, which uses data on X as the residuals $Y_i - \hat{Y}_i$; now estimate $e_1 + be_2$ rather than just e_1 and R^2 equals one minus the proportion of variation due to the error term. This is called the *underadjustment* phenomenon or *errors-in-variables* problem. In addition, the coefficient *b* enters into the error formula, making it harder to disentangle the effect of the random error from that of the predictor variable. Indeed, if the variables are measured in standardized units from their mean, the greater the true correlation between Y and Z in (8.47), the larger the coefficient *b* will be so that the underadjustment problem increases with the strength of the relationship between Y and Z. While there are techniques for mitigating this problem, the fact that the complete effect of the real predictor variables is not being accounted for can lead to a lower explanatory value, adj(R^2), of the model so that in a multiple regression model some of the effect of the important valid predictors can be reflected in the estimated sex or race coefficient. This is likely to occur when one group has higher scores on most of the predictors than the other group as in the *Sobel* case.

While there is no doubt as to the existence of the underadjustment phenomenon and the fact that measurement error does inevitably occur, there *sometimes* is a logical problem in asserting that it causes regression methods to underestimate the effects of productivity variables in disparate treatment cases. Suppose the employer initially assigns newly hired college graduates, including MAs, etc., to jobs according to their years of education and major area of study, and the salaries of the positions correspond to their desirability.

A proper regression model relating salary to years of education and major would seem to capture the employer's initial assignment process. The fact that years of school and major are incomplete measures of a new employee's knowledge and interest may not really matter from the point of assessing the *treatment* the employer gave to similarly situated new hires, especially when the data used are sufficiently accurate for the employer's use in job assignment. If after a discrimination charge is filed, the employer asserts that the academic reputation of the college and the grade-point average were also factors considered, it seems logical to make sure that they really were used and that the plaintiffs as a class had a lower average score on these factors. In particular, one can determine whether job applicants were required to submit transcripts. Thus, the existence of the underadjustment phenomenon by itself should not be used to discredit a regression study using the data the employer relied on in the actual decisionmaking process.

On the other hand, if a defendant employer did utilize other information about the applicants and the plaintiff ignores it, relying on simpler predictors such as education and major area of study, criticism of the plaintiff's study is proper. Similarly, one should be more receptive to the underadjustment argument when an employer is producing a regression model in which the minority group status coefficient is of borderline significance and notes that there still is likely to be a degree of underadjustment, even after they used all the major reasonably available measures of potential productivity, such as past experience, education, grade-point average and school quality. The point here is that the purpose of the statistical analysis in a discrimination case is to assess whether a difference in *treatment* of comparable minority and majority persons occurred, not whether the employment criteria or data the employer used in its decisionmaking were the most appropriate and accurate. Indeed, the court in *Craik* noted that if the employer mismeasured the plaintiff's qualifications, that by itself would *not* be evidence of discrimination. Of course, if the qualifications of females were systematically underestimated relative to males, presumably this would constitute evidence of discriminatory treatment. On the other hand, severe errors in variable or mismeasurement problems could mean that persons with the same measured characteristics may vary so much in ability that they are not truly comparable. The ramifications of measurement error in the qualification variables used in regression analyses in the discrimination context has been the subject of a number of recent articles, which are listed in the references. We have emphasized the importance of minimizing this measurement error by evaluating the effect of using proxy (substitute) variables and obtaining as much information as possible about the actual decision process of the employer, rather than some of the important technical issues, e.g., estimating the potential effect of the underadjustment, which are treated in the references.

Comment. The statistical literature on the errors in variable problems indicates that the errors typically lead to an overestimate of the relative qualifications of the group with lower values of the predictors. Indeed, this was demonstrated by the defendants in *Sobel*. We now give a brief explanation of this effect in the EEO context. Suppose salary (Y) is related to Z but we measure Z by X as in (8.46). When we examine the data for evidence of discrimination by fitting the model

$$(8.47a) \qquad Y = a + bZ + cI + e_1,$$

where $I = 1$ denotes a female employee and $I = 0$ denotes a male, we really are fitting

$$(8.48a) \qquad Y = a + bX + be_2 + cI + e_1$$

to the data. Cochran (1968) showed that the usual estimator (8.21) of b, which ignores the effect of the new error component be_2 is an underestimate of the true b. In fact, it estimates fb, where $f = \sigma_1^2/(\sigma_1^2 + \sigma_2^2)$, the ratio of the variance of the random error variable e_1 in the true model to the sum of the variance of e_1 and the measurement error e_2. Furthermore, the estimate of c, the sex coefficient, has expected value

$$(8.48b) \qquad c + b(1 - f)(\overline{X}_f - \overline{X}_m),$$

where $\overline{X}_m$ denotes the average value of the proxy variable (X) of the male employees while $\overline{X}_f$ denotes the corresponding average for females. When the majority group has higher levels of the productivity characteristic, i.e., $\overline{X}_f < \overline{X}_m$, equation (8.48b) implies that even if the null hypothesis $c = 0$ is true, the estimated sex coefficient will be centered around $b(1 - f)(\overline{X}_f - \overline{X}_m)$, which is negative when $\overline{X}_f$ is less than $\overline{X}_m$. In any single analysis, one needs to assess the degree of mismeasurement to determine whether the degree of bias is sufficient to affect the ultimate inference. In the *Sobel* case where the p-values apparently were only slightly below .05, e.g., .03, the bias due to measurement error could well have caused the significant result. Had the p-value been .001, the defendant would need to demonstrate a large measurement error in order to explain the significant result. This may be an issue at the retrial.

A recent article by Schafer (1987) presents a method for assessing the potential effects of errors in other predictors on the esimated minority group coefficient. The paper by Dempster (1988) and the accompanying commentary provides further insight into the effects of mismeasured and omitted variables in regression models.

The second area of contention in complex cases is the selection of an appropriate data base and appropriate model. Thus, Finkelstein (1978) suggested several protocols. They are:

(1) At the outset, the decisionmaker should specify the data believed to be of most relevance and importance. Both parties' presentations should start with this data and incorporate other data on a separate basis only when necessary for purposes of accuracy or refinement.

(2) A party objecting to the regression results introduced by another party should demonstrate the numerical significance of its objections whenever possible.

(3) In any situation in which the decisionmaker makes significant use of econometric findings, the most useful among the competing ones should be selected, and findings should be made on the basis of that model.

(4) A finding that rests on data that has been analyzed by a regression model should be no more precise than the finding which the decision-maker can make on the basis of the analysis.

The purpose of the above protocol is to minimize the amount of argument between the parties concerning the data base and the appropriateness of the predictor variables. Moreover, once a particular model is selected as being the most appropriate, the uncertainties inherent in the results should be reflected in the findings. The adoption of the second protocol would mean that the procedures used in *Vuyanich* and *Sobel* would be followed by critics of a model, i.e., they would need to demonstrate that an omitted variable or a violation of the assumptions is likely to have a meaningful impact on the results.

In the context of discrimination litigation, there may be a problem with the strict adoption of the first protocol. Through the discovery process, the plaintiffs have access to all the defendant's files that are used in the normal course of business. Quite often, computerized personnel records do not include all the information in the employee files, and the employer may create a more comprehensive data base for use in the litigation itself. This data base may not be open to discovery, especially if it is carried out for the lawyers under the work product rule. Nevertheless, some agreement on the discoverable personnel data base and a common procedure for editing it for errors could be agreed on. If this is done, at some set time prior to the trial and before each side deposes the other's experts about their findings, the data base should be fixed.

Comment. The reason for stopping corrections to the data prior to the depositions of expert witnesses, who will report their analyses of the data, is that missing data and errors in the data base that occurred *prior* to the charge or lawsuit presumably were random. Once litigation commences, the employer has an interest in making sure that all favorable material is in the file. Thus, they might check the files of all minority employees who received a promotion in the last year to make sure that the promotion was recorded. If this is not done for majority employees, the errors in the promotion data will *not* be random. Similarly, plaintiffs might attempt to ensure that all demotions of minorities were recorded, although the employer usually has greater control over the original data. The potential for data base bias may increase after the opposing party's expert has been examined in a deposition, as the theory underlying the planned data analysis will be discovered. The need to finalize the data base at a set time prior to the proceedings applies to all statistical data bases used in litigation and public policy, whether or not they will be analyzed by regression methods.

Finally, we should emphasize the fact that we have described regression models fitted on micro-data, i.e., both the dependent and predictor variables are measured on each subject (individual person in a salary regression, each hold of the oil tanker, etc.). With regression models fitted to earnings data on humans, the values of R^2 which indicate a useful degree of relationship can be modest, e.g., .3 to .6 in wage regressions. In some studies, regression models are fit to *averages* (or medians) of groups, e.g., median wage by educational level. The values of R^2 for regression models fitted to *grouped* data typically are *substantially higher* than when the identical model (using the same predictors) is fit to data on individuals. The reason for this is that the *variation between the individuals* in each group is missing from the grouped data and, therefore, *need* not be explained by the predictors used in the regression model when it is fitted to the grouped data.

This phenomenon can be illustrated by examining some of the regressions in the papers published in *Comparable Worth* (1984). Polachek fitted a wage equation incorporating education, experience, hours worked in the year, number of children, etc. to data for males and females and obtained R^2 values of .38 and .32, respectively. Other regression models he discussed had lower values of R^2. On the other hand, his Table 6 reported results from a study of Fuchs, who fitted the *average* earnings by sex of workers in 46 industries to a regression using the age profile of the workers, unionized proportion of the industry, etc. and obtained R^2 values of about .9. The reason, again, is that the *variation* in salary between workers employed in each industry, which is quite substantial, is excluded. Thus, one cannot say that the predictor variables used in the second study were superior to those in the first one which used data on individuals.

8. Testing whether There Is a Relationship between Variables when One Is a Binomial Variable

In the previous section, the dependent variable was essentially continuous, i.e., it ranged over a continuum of possible values as grade-point averages and wages do. Many applications of statistics are concerned with 0–1 or binomial variables, such as whether a person or animal exposed to a chemical becomes ill or whether an employee is promoted (1) or not (0). This section will describe a procedure for assessing whether there is a relationship between the probability, p of a "1" occurring and a variable which may cause or be related to its occurrence, such as the amount of exposure in testing the toxicity of a chemical or seniority in the promotion situation. In this section, we will use the notion of correlation and regression to describe a test for a relationship between the probability, p, that an event A occurs and a measure of the magnitude of the variable that may influence p. A model analogous to regression will be described in the next section, enabling us to estimate the relationship.

The statistical procedure is easiest to describe in terms of tests used to determine whether a chemical substance may be a potential carcinogen to humans. A variety of strains of mice are exposed to several dose levels of the substance, and the proportion of mice at each level that develop a tumor is reported. If the chemical is not carcinogenic, then these proportions should be about the same, i.e., whether or not a mouse was exposed to the chemical or the amount of exposure will not affect the chance of a tumor developing. If the substance is toxic, then the proportion of mice with a tumor should *increase* with the *level* of exposure (dose level).

The results of a typical animal study are reported in Table 8.12, which reports the total number of mice exposed to each of several dose levels of ethylene dibromide (EDB) as well as the number of mice at each level that developed a tumor. Notice that data is reported for each sex, so we first describe a test for one set of data and then show how to combine the results for both sets or strata.

A general format for the presentation of dose-response data is given in Table 8.13, which allows for any number (k) of dose levels. At each dose level, d_i, $i = 1, ..., k$, there are n_i mice exposed and x_i respond (develop a

TABLE 8.12. Proportion of Mice Developing Tumors From Inhalation of EDB by Dose Level

Sex of Mice	Exposure Level		
	0	10 ppm	40 ppm
Males	0/41	3/48	23/46
Females	4/49	11/49	41/50

Source: Table 2 of the Occupational Health and Safety Administration proposed rulemaking regulating ethylene dibromide. *Federal Register* (1983) *48*, 45969.

tumor). The observations at each level can be considered a *binomial* random variable with parameters (n_i, p_i), where p_i represents the probability that a response (1) occurs at the ith level.

Under the null hypothesis that the chemical has no effect, we can consider each observation as coming from a common binomial distribution with parameters $n = \Sigma\, n_i$ and p, the probability a mouse develops cancer under normal conditions. The parameter p is estimated by

$$(8.49) \qquad \bar{p} = \frac{\displaystyle\sum_{i=1}^{k} x_i}{n}$$

the fraction of *all* exposed animals who develop tumors. Thus, if there is *no effect,* each x_i would essentially[48] have a binomial distribution with mean $n_i\bar{p}$ and variance

$$(8.50) \qquad n_i\bar{p}(1 - \bar{p}).$$

If the alternative (of a positive relationship) is true, then the observed x_i at *low* dose levels should be *below* their expected values $n_i\bar{p}$, calculated under the null hypothesis, as $\bar{p}$ includes the observed responses at high exposure levels. Similarly, the observed x_i at *higher* dose levels should be *above* their corresponding values of $n_i\bar{p}$. Thus, we can *correlate* the deviations, $x_i - n_i\bar{p}$, with the dose levels, d_i, to test whether there is a positive (or negative) relationship. Since we only wish to test whether there is *no* relation versus the alternative that there is one, we can use the numerator

$$(8.51) \qquad T = \sum_{i=1}^{k} (x_i - n_i\bar{p})(d_i - \bar{d})$$

of the correlation coefficient (8.6) as our test statistic.

TABLE 8.13. General Format of Dose Response Data

Dose Level	Number Exposed	Number of Responses	Sample Proportion
d_1	n_1	x_1	$\bar{p}_1 = \dfrac{x_1}{n_1}$
d_2	n_2	x_2	$\bar{p}_2 = \dfrac{x_2}{n_2}$
d_k	n_k	x_k	$\bar{p}_k = \dfrac{x_k}{n_k}$

Since the dose levels are known constants, and the number (x_i) of responses at the ith level is a binomial variable, it follows from (8.50) that under the null hypothesis of *no* relationship, T has *mean 0* and *variance*

$$(8.52) \qquad \bar{p}(1 - \bar{p}) \sum_{i=1}^{k} n_i(d_i - d)^2.$$

The standard normal form of the test statistic

$$Z = \frac{\text{observed minus expected}}{\text{standard deviation}}$$

is

$$(8.53) \qquad \frac{\sum_{i=1}^{k} (x_i - n_i\bar{p})(d_i - \bar{d})}{\sqrt{\bar{p}(1 - \bar{p}) \sum_{i=1}^{k} n_i(d_i - \bar{d})^2}}.$$

The details of the calculation of (8.53) for the female and male mice data sets are presented in Tables 8.14 and 8.15 at the end of the section. For the female mice, (8.53) becomes

$$(8.54) \qquad\qquad Z = 8.03,$$

which is a highly significant result with a p-value of less than one in a million. For the male mice,

$$(8.55) \qquad\qquad Z = 6.50,$$

again a highly significant result. In both cases, the statistical test confirms our common sense reaction to the data. Notice that even though the dose response of the male mice does not look linear (there were relatively few responses at the low dose level (10 ppm), the test statistic still detects the upward trend in response, as exposure levels increase.

In the present application, the test statistic T assumes that under the alternative, the response probabilities would increase in proportion to the increase in dose levels. Sometimes the biochemical process generating the responses is known and suggests that the response probabilities increase more (less) rapidly with exposure levels. Then one should use the appropriate function of the levels, e.g., d_i^2 if the response probabilities increase faster than linearly or $\log d_i$ if the response probabilities increase slower than linearly. Fortunately, the test statistic (8.53) often gives similar results for most reasonable choices of scores (functions of d_i) which increase with the exposure level.

In some applications we do not know the exposure levels d_i; however, one may be able to classify the subjects into categories such as no exposure, light, medium and substantial. Often the simple choice of scores $d_1 = 1$, $d_2 = 2$, $d_3 = 3$, etc. is satisfactory. Thus one may use the test statistic (8.53) to analyze data on illness rates by category of exposure (or possible exposure) when the exact exposure each subject received is not precisely measured. The methodology described in this section is useful in a variety of other areas, e.g., the analysis of hiring rates by educational level to see whether increased education affects an applicant's chances of hire, voter preferences by income level or socioeconomic status, and layoff rates by years of seniority. After one determines that a dose-response relationship exists, one would like to obtain an estimate of its effect which is analogous to the regression coefficient. There are several models of response probabilities which have been developed for doing this. The most common of which is called the logit or logistic model and is described in the next section.

We close our discussion of testing for a dose relationship by describing the combination of several test statistics of the form (8.51), analyzing data stratified into appropriate categories, e.g., different species of mice, age or sex categories. Just as in the Mantel-Haenszel method (Chapter 5) when there are J strata, we add the individual statistics (8.51), which we denote by T_j, $j = 1, ..., J$, and divide them by their standard deviation, which is the square root of the *sum* of the individual variances, V_j, given by formula (8.52). Thus, combining the results of the calculations given in

TABLE 8.14. Calculation Of The Test For Dose Response For Data For Female Mice In Table 8.12

Dose Level (1)	$d_i - \bar{d}$(2)	n_i(3)	x_i(4)	$n_i\bar{p}$(5)	$x_i - n_i\bar{p}$(6)	$(d_i - \bar{d})(x_i - n_i\bar{p})$(7)	$n_i(d_i - \bar{d})^2$(8)
$d_1 = 0$	−16.667	49	4	18.542	−14.542	242.372	13611.656
$d_2 = 10$	−6.667	49	11	18.542	−7.542	50.283	2177.996
$d_3 = 40$	−23.333	50	41	18.920	22.08	515.193	27221.444
Total 50		148	56			807.848	43011.096

$$\bar{d} = \frac{50}{3} = 16.667 \qquad \bar{p} = 56/146 = .3784$$

Variance $= \bar{p}(1 - \bar{p})\,43011.096 = 10116.79$ and $s = \sqrt{\text{variance}} = 100.58$, so $Z = 807.85/1005.8 = 8.032$.

Note: The value of the statistic (8.51) is the total in column 7 and equals 807.848. Its variance (8.52) is $\bar{p}(1 - \bar{p})$ times the total in column 8 and equals $(.3784)(.6216)(43011.096) = 10116.79$. Its standard deviation is $\sqrt{10116.79} = 100.58$ so formula (8.53) is $807.85/100.58 = 8.03$.

TABLE 8.15. Calculation Of The Test For A Dose Response For The Data For Male Mice In Table 8.12

Dose Level (1)	$d_i - \bar{d}$ (2)	n_i(3)	x_i(4)	$n_i\bar{p}$(5)	$x_i - n_i\bar{p}$(6)	$(d_i - \bar{d})(x_i - n_i\bar{p})$(7)	$n_i(d_i - \bar{d})^2$(8)
$d_1 = 0$	−16.667	41	0	7.893	−7.893	131.55	11389.34
$d_2 = 10$	−6.667	48	3	9.240	−6.240	41.60	2133.55
$d_3 = 40$	+23.333	46	23	8.85	14.145	330.05	25043.73
Total 50		135	26		.012*	503.2	38566.62
average							

$\bar{d} = 16.67$ $\bar{p} = .1926$

Note: The variance (8.52) is given by (.1926)(.8074)(38566.62) = 5997.31, and the denominator (8.53) = 77.44 (so (8.53) is 503.2/77.44 = 6.50). The total of the $x_i - n_i\bar{p}$ column (6) indicated by an * should equal 0, except for rounding errors, which is a useful check on one's calculation. Similarly, the total of the $n_i\bar{p}$ (column 5) should equal the total number of responses or the total of column 4.

Tables 8.14 and 8.15 for the female and male mice one gets

$$(8.56) \quad Z = \frac{807.85 + 503.2}{\sqrt{5997.31 + 10116.79}} = \frac{1311.05}{126.94} = 10.33,$$

which is more significant evidence of a positive relationship than either data set provided alone.

9. Logistic Regression: A Technique for Understanding the Factors Influencing Binary Variables

So far we have used regression to study the factors related to continuous variables, e.g., explaining the variation in wage data as a function of skill level, seniority and perhaps the sex or race of employees. Issues such as who is hired or promoted, or even who joins the labor force, are described by binary variables, taking the value 1 or 0 according to whether or not a person is hired or promoted, etc. In this section we first show why the linear regression model described previously is not suited for the problem and then proceed to describe a more appropriate model (logistic regression).

In Table 8.16, we report data on whether or not an employee has been promoted as a function of length of service. Since seniority usually increases the likelihood of being promoted, one might wish to describe the data by ordinary linear regressions, i.e.,

$$(8.57) \qquad\qquad p_i = a + bX_i,$$

TABLE 8.16. Promotion Data as a Function of Seniority

Seniority (Months)	Promoted (1) or Not (0)
3	0
4	0
5	0
6	0
7	0
8	1
9	0
10	1
12	0
14	1
16	0
17	1
18	0
18	1
20	1
22	1
24	1
26	1
28	1
30	1

Note: The data refer to employees who were hired in the entry level position and whether (1) or not (0) they have been promoted.

where p_i is the probability that the ith individual has received a promotion. Thus, the expected probability of promotion increases linearly with seniority (X).

Fitting equation (8.57) to the data in Table 8.16 yields

$$(8.58) \qquad p_i = \begin{array}{cc} -.0524 & + \quad .0406X \\ (.1828) & (.0108) \quad \text{standard error} \\ (-.287) & (3.758) \quad t\text{-statistic} \end{array}$$

The equation has an $R^2 = .440$, and the variable X is statistically significant. Indeed the p-value of the t-test is .0014, which confirms our notion that seniority affects the probability of promotion. When we interpret the coefficient $b = .0406$ as the expected increment in an employee's probability of promotion due to an additional month of service, however, we run into some difficulties. An employee who has worked one month has an expected probability of $-.0524 + .0406 = -.0118$ or about -1%, while an employee with 30 months of seniority has an expected probability of having been promoted of

$$-.0524 + 1.218 = 1.1656,$$

which is *greater* than one. Thus, predictions from the regression line (8.58) can yield probabilities which we know are impossible.

In order to avoid such problems of interpretation, statisticians model the logarithm of the odds of promotion. Recall that if p is the probability a person is promoted $p/(1 - p)$ is the odds they face. The variable $p/(1 - p)$ can range from $0(p = 0)$ to infinity (as p approaches 1) and $\log(p/(1 - p))$ ranges from minus to plus infinity, so it is a continuous variable ranging over all possible real numbers. If

$$(8.59) \qquad \log(p/(1 - p) = a + bX,$$

we can solve for p as follows: Taking exponentials (or antilogs),

$$\frac{p}{1 - p} = e^{a+bX}$$

or

$$(8.60) \qquad p = \frac{e^{a+bX}}{1 + e^{+(a+bX)}} = \frac{1}{1 + e^{-(a+bX)}}.$$

Equation (8.60) relates the probability p of receiving a promotion to X, seniority, and is therefore a function of X. This function is called the logistic function and is graphed in Figure 8.7. If b is positive, then p increases with X. The logistic model is based on this concept and might be considered as

$$(8.61) \qquad \log \frac{Y_i}{1 - Y_i} = a + bX_i + \text{error},$$

where $Y_i = 1$ (if promoted), 0 otherwise.

Since each observation Y_i is a 0 or 1, their logarithm cannot be calculated ($\log 0 = -\infty$, $\log 1 = +\infty$) so the expression (8.61) is not well defined. Hence the logistic model (8.59) is fitted to the data by a more general method than least squares called maximum likelihood. Since we are primarily concerned with interpreting statistical analyses, we describe the results of fitting the logistic model to the data in Table 8.16. These

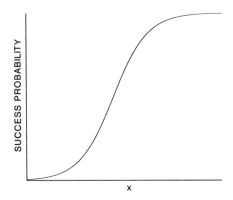

FIGURE 8.7. The logistic curve $p(x) = [1 + e^{-(\alpha+\beta x)}]^{-1}$, relating the probability of "success" to the value of the variable or factor x possessed by an individual.

statistics are similar to those obtained from ordinary regression and are reported below:

Estimate	Standard Error	95% CONF
$a = -3.3482$	1.5265	$(-6.555, \ -.1411)$
$b = \ \ \ .2570$	.1072	$(\ \ .0317, \ \ .4822)$

We report the 95% confidence interval to give the reader an idea of the range of plausible values of the parameters. The t-statistic, the ratio of the estimate to its standard error, can be calculated as in ordinary regression.

Since 0 is *not* included in either confidence *interval*, both parameters a and b are different from zero. Moreover, $\hat{b}$ is positive as expected. To estimate the probability an employee with 10 months of seniority has been promoted, we use formula (8.61) with the estimates of a and b as follows:

(8.62)
$$p_i = \frac{1}{1 + e^{(-3.3482+2.57)}} = \frac{1}{1 + e^{.7782}}$$

$$= \frac{1}{1 + 2.1775} = \frac{1}{3.1775} = .3147.$$

Similarly, the probability an employee with 20 months of service would have received a promotion is estimated as

(8.63) $$p_i = \frac{1}{1 + e^{-(-3,3482+5.24)}} = \frac{1}{1 + .166} = .857.$$

These estimated probabilities certainly agree with the data and avoid the potential problem of estimating a probability outside the range of 0 to 1, as ordinary regression may do.

Because the logistic model (8.59) is *linear* in the logarithm of the odds, the coefficient b can be interpreted as the *expected increase* in the *log-odds* of receiving a promotion due to an additional month of service. Unfortunately, most of us are used to thinking in terms of probabilities or odds, not the logarithms of odds, so we must think carefully about the meaning of the coefficient b. In particular, e^b is the average increase in the odds ratio of having received a promotion for one extra month of seniority. In our example

$$e^b = a^{.2570} = 1.293.$$

Thus, a person who stayed 11 months would have an odds of 1.293 times .4592, the odds of a person employed 10 months (.4592 is the odds corresponding to the probability .3147).

Although we have described the logistic regression model involving only a single variable (X), it can be extended to allow multiple predictors just as in multiple regression. One can test for the significance of each coefficient and obtain predictions for the expected probability of a success or 1 from the analog of (8.60)

(8.64) $$p_i = \frac{1}{(1 + e^{a+\Sigma_1^k b_i X_i})},$$

where the X_i are the various explanatory or predictor variables. Again p_i is now a function of $X_1, X_2, ..., X_k$.

Problems

1.*   For the ordinary regression and logistic regression models fitted to the data in Table 8.16, calculate the *predicted* p_i and compare them to the actual data. Which makes more sense to you?

2.   Each of the following situations describe potential applications of ordinary and/or logistic regression. What data would you collect and which model would you fit? (You can use multiple regression with both models)? Mention any special complications which might arise.

(a) You are working at the Federal Reserve Board and are asked to investigate complaints that a minority group is being turned down for auto loans more frequently than whites.

(b) Suppose veterans who served in Vietnam and were exposed to agent orange are suspected of having reproductive problems, i.e., lower sperm counts, investigate this problem.

(c) Suppose the same Vietnam veterans are suspected of having a having a higher rate of cancer of the skin.

Answers to Selected Problems

1.*   The predictions from each model are given in Table 8.17 at the end of the answer below. Notice that the ordinary line which rises by about .04 each month under predicts the promotion probability after 20 months,

TABLE 8.17.   Predictions to the Data in Table 8.16 Derived From the Ordinary Least Squares Line and the Logistic Model

Seniority	Promoted (1) or Not (0)	Prediction From	
		Linear Model	Logistic Model
3	0	0.0694	0.0706
4	0	0.11	0.0895
5	0	0.1506	0.1127
6	0	0.1912	0.1411
7	0	0.2318	0.1752
8	1	0.2724	0.2155
9	0	0.313	0.2621
10	1	0.3536	0.3147
12	0	0.4348	0.4343
14	1	0.516	0.5621
16	0	0.5972	0.6822
17	1	0.6378	0.7351
18	0	0.6784	0.7821
18	1	0.6784	0.7821
20	1	0.7596	0.8571
22	1	0.8408	0.9094
24	1	0.922	0.9437
26	1	1.0032	0.9656
28	1	1.0844	0.9791
30	1	1.1656	0.9874

Note: The least squares line is $Y_i = -.0524 + .0406X$, while the logistic equation is determined by the parameters $a = -3.3482$ and $b = .2570$.

when all persons received a promotion. This happens because the rate of increase of the logistic curve varies with X, so it usually fits this type of data better. Although the line only predicted one value of a probability outside 0 or 1, the logistic model yields a better fit and more reasonable predictions.

Comment. The ordinary line can yield poor predictions of future observations when the value of X lies *outside* the range of the data used to fit the model e.g., $X = 40$ even when the linear model is appropriate. The use of a model in this way is called *extrapolation* beyond the range of the data. Such extrapolations from virtually all regression models are subject to large uncertainties. In the statistical texts in the references, formulas for such predictions are given, including the *standard error* of such predictions, which assume that the model remains valid. The standard error *increases* with the distance from the central value $(\overline{X})$ of the predictors in the data set used to fit the model to the observation. Thus, even extrapolations from the logistic model for data outside the range of the X-values of the fitted data should be regarded with caution.

10. Applications of Logistic Regression

In this section we describe the use of logistic regression models which are used to analyze data in equal employment litigation, evaluation of public programs and in health studies. It is important to emphasize that there may be different objectives in each application. For example, an epidemiologic study is typically designed to estimate the relative risk a person exposed to an agent has of contracting a particular disease after accounting for other characteristics or factors which also are related to one's chance of becoming ill. Logistic analyses in the equal employment area are designed to assess whether race, sex or other prohibited factors have a negative impact on one's probability of being hired, promoted or being assigned a better job, after accounting for bonafide qualifications or factors such as seniority and education. Thus, factors such as initial job assignment, which would normally affect current job level, may properly be omitted when evidence has *shown* that the initial job assignments were given out in a discriminatory fashion. Notice that the propriety of including such factors is similar to our previous discussion of grade level or rank in regression analyses used in salary or promotion cases.

a. Alleged discrimination in job assignment: Greenspan v. Automobile Club of Michigan[49]

This class action claimed that the defendant discriminated against women in hiring, promotion, job assignment and sick leave policy (women could not use leave for pregnancy-related absence). We will discuss the analysis used to study the issue of whether there was discrimination in the current (1978) job assignments. The plaintiffs introduced two types of regression analysis, ordinary regression of wages and a logistic analysis of job level, high (grades 7–27) or low (grades 1–6). The dependent variable in the logistic regression was whether one held a high (1) or low (0) grade job at the end of 1978. The plaintiffs built successively more complex models, starting with a simple model using as predictor variables sex, age and tenure with the defendant. They added other productivity-related variables, such as education, prior work or military experience, interruptions in work history, etc., as the objective is to estimate the effect, if any, of *gender* on grade assignment, accounting for the effect of these other productivity variables. For all the models developed, the coefficient of the variable indicating a female employee was negative and statistically significant. In order to emphasize the effect of sex, the plaintiffs also estimated the grade level female employees would be in had they been a male with the same qualifications by setting the coefficient of the sex variable equal to 0 and predicting the probability each female now would have of being in the high job level category. The average probability was about 67%, in contrast with the 12% of women who actually were in these jobs.

The defendant criticized the plaintiff's model for not including company-related variables such as job assignment and promotions. The plaintiffs argued that these factors are tainted, as they reflect a discriminatory policy, so they should not be used to explain current job level or salary. In addition, the defendant constructed an ordinary regression model to explain the current (1978) salary of employees. Their predictor or independent variables included tenure with the club, tenure in the present position, 1974 year-end salary (as the class was certified as of January 8, 1974) and gender. The model was fit to each of the 10 EEO job categories, and statistical significance only occurred in one of the 10 categories. Moreover, by incorporating full or part-time status into the model, they reduced the coefficient of the sex indicator variable to nonsignificance. The defendant's expert concluded that there was no difference in salary progression between employees of both sexes during the 1974–78 period. The defendant's model had a high R^2, indicating that it gave an accurate prediction of current salary, however, the use of year-end 1974 salaries accounted for much of the explanatory value of the model. The opinion noted that the defendant's model was useful in determining what salary an employee would receive from the available personnel data. However, Judge Feikens realized that the use of the year-end 1974 salaries incorporated any discrimination in initial job assignment, transfer and promotion that occurred before[50] the class certification data as well as up to a year later. Thus, the plaintiff's model was more relevant for the objective of the case, to assess whether a particular factor, gender in this instance, played a significant role in determining the job level or salary of an employee.

b. Academic rank of initial appointment: Chang v. University of Rhode Island[51]

The logistic model was used to estimate the effect that sex had on the rank newly hired professors received. Both sides introduced models, and we describe the predictor variables they incorporated.

Plaintiffs compared persons hired as instructors, assistant professors, associate professors and full professors, controlling for

(1) years for which the faculty member had been hired,

(2) years since receipt of the highest degree the new faculty member possessed at time of hire,

(3) amount and nature of prior experience, and

(4) the departmental group or field.

These factors account for varying demand for subject matter experts over time (1) and area (4) and the achievement of the person since they received their formal education (2,3). The opinion did not reproduce the results of the entire *logistic* regression equation, as it was concerned with the statistical implications of the estimated coefficient of the indicator variable for sex. The plaintiff's results are given in Table 8.18.

The results in the table are one-sided p-values, testing $b = 0$ versus $b < 0$, where b is the coefficient for the sex indicator (female = 1). Notice that the instructor versus assistant professor and assistant professor versus associate professor comparisons would be significant at the .05 level if a two-sided .05 level criteria were adopted. To appreciate the effect of sex, we express the coefficients in terms of the *odds* females faced relative to males. The plaintiffs estimates are $e^{-1.473} = .229$, $e^{-2.084} = .125$ and $e^{-2.787} = .062$, all of which indicate a meaningful difference. Notice

TABLE 8.18. Coefficient of the Sex Indicator Variable in Plaintiff's Logistic Regression for Rank at time of Hire in *Chang v. Univ. of Rhode Island*

Comparison	Estimated Gender Coefficient	*t*-statistic	Prob-value (one-sided)	Sample Size
Instructor vs. Ass't. Prof.	−1.473	−2.128	.017	199
Ass't. Prof. vs. Assoc. Prof.	−2.084	−1.961	.025	176
Assoc. Prof. vs. Full Prof.	−2.787	−1.483	.069	43

Source: 606 F.Supp. 1161 at 1203.
Note: The gender coefficient estimates the effect of being female.

that the estimated effect at the full professorship level (third comparison) apparently was the largest; however, the estimate was not statistically significantly different from zero because of the small sample size (most academic hiring is done at the assistant professor level). Ordinarily, one would question the appropriateness of requiring a significant result in each comparison, but the plaintiff's analysis of associate and full professor appointments also suffered from missing data on the possession of the doctorate at hire and years since the PhD was received, and had to combine some departmental groups.[52] Thus, the explanatory value of the predictor variables probably was less for these comparisons. In particular, if the women had fewer years of postdoctorate experience, which is reasonable given the increase in female enrollment in graduate programs in recent years, the effect of the time since degree would be partly reflected in the sex indicator, making it a negatively biased estimate of the true sex effect, i.e., the estimated coefficient of the female indicator would be a negative estimate even if it were truly 0 (no effect), since the time factor could not be used.

The defendant's logistic regression, summarized in Table 8.19, incorporated year of hire, highest degree and year earned, departmental group, and degree at hire and included all persons hired since 1971. Judge Selya noted,[53] "statisticians can manipulate numbers to such a degree that sustenance can be found for an otherwise unsupportable position" and then discussed the differences between the models. In particular, the defendant used the variable years since degree as a proxy for prior experience.

TABLE 8.19. Coefficients of the Indicator Variable in Defendant's Logistic Regression in *Chang v. Univ. of Rhode Island*

Comparison	Estimated Gender Coefficient	*t*-statistic	Statistical Significance at the .05 level (two-sided)	Sample Size
Instructor vs. Ass't Prof.	−.04	−.11	No	304
Ass't. Prof. vs. Assoc. Prof.	−.70	−2.11	Yes	289
Assoc. Prof. vs. Full Prof.	−2.93	−.83	No	71

Source: 606 F.Supp. 1161 at 1205.
Note: The gender coefficient estimates the effect of being female.

Although the plaintiff's measure of prior experience did not take into account the quality of experience (e.g., whether prior teaching was at Harvard or a lesser known institution), it still was preferable to the defendant's more simplistic proxy. Secondly, the model used by the defendant's expert assumed that rank placement depended on the receipt of the PhD or other terminal degree, but a number of colleges at the university gave assistant professorships to new faculty members who did not possess the PhD. Although there was possibly some multicollinearity in the plaintiff's model, as types of prior experience and years since degree might be correlated and some of the missing data might have been obtained, the logistic regression submitted by the plaintiff was more plausible, especially as the defendant excluded individuals who received their highest degree subsequent to their initial hire on the unverified assumption that all such people were hired as instructors. Thus, the plaintiffs established a *prima facie* case of discrimination in placement at the assistant and associate professor level that the defendant failed to rebut.

Comment. It is instructive to compare the discussion of regression analysis in *Chang* with that in *Vuyanich*. In both cases, the adequacy of the proxy variables, i.e., time since degree or age for the main variable of interest, prior experience or seniority were assessed and it was determined whether or not the results obtained were accepted. In *Chang,* the plaintiffs used a closer approximation to the true variable, while in *Vuy-*

anich the defendant demonstrated that the use of age instead of seniority systematically overstated the seniority of females relative to males by an average of two years.

An interesting aspect of the *Chang* case concerned the use of logistic analysis in the promotion process by plaintiffs. Here their analysis included the same experience and credentials prior to hire that they used in their rank at hire model but did not consider any measure of post-hire achievements in teaching, research or service to the university or profession. Hence, they did not address the main issue, whether the standards for promotion, typically described in terms of post-hire accomplishment, were applied differently to women. Furthermore, the time taken until promotion was not considered. This was important, because a higher fraction of women were among the more recent hires, many of whom would not have received a promotion, as they had not served a reasonable time (e.g., five years) prior to the time the study was carried out. Thus, a greater percentage of females than males would appear to have been denied promotion, while, in reality, most of the recent hires might not have been ready for consideration for a promotion.

Logistic regression has been used successfully in other discrimination cases, e.g., *Jurgens v. Thomas*[54] and *Melanie v. Board of Higher Education of the City of New York*[55]. We will not discuss these cases, as the major issues are similar to the use of ordinary regression in discrimination cases, namely:

(1) How adequate is the model? Are the major relevant predictor variables considered?

(2) How reliable is the data or a proxy variable used for the ideal predictor variable?

(3) Has the model been checked for validity in a reasonable way and have unusual observations been examined for the corrections of their information and appropriateness for inclusion in the analysis?

(4) Is there a substantial degree of multicollinearity? If so, does it affect the estimated coefficient of primary interest?

c. Evaluating the effectiveness of a preschool program

In Chapters 13 and 14 we will use logistic regression to analyze health data, but we now turn to a potentially controversial application of the method to the evaluation of data on the achievement of preschool children enrolled in the Head Start program.[56] In Table 8.20 we present the raw

TABLE 8.20.   Raw Pass/Not Passed Data for Children at Time of Enrollment

Group	Passed	Did Not Pass	Total	Proportion Passed
Head Start	36	61	97	.371
Not in				
Head Start	97	274	371	.261
Total	133	335	468	

Source: Table 9.1 from Anderson, Auquier, Hauck, Oakes, Vandaele and Weisberg (1980). *Note:* The estimated odds ratio = (36)(274)/(61)(97) = 1.667. The test (5.6) yields $Z = -2.14$.

data, without covariates, reporting whether or not children passed the preschool inventory test when they entered the formal school system, categorized by their participation in the Head Start program.

The data in Table 8.20 and the reported significance test indicates that the Head Start program had a positive effect on the children. However, one might wish to assess the effect of other variables, in particular the educational level of the child's parent or guardian, which might play a role in the encouragement a child received at home after learning. Fitting the model

(8.65) $$\log \frac{\text{pass}}{1 - \text{pass}} = a + cI + bX,$$

where I indicates (1) whether the child participated in a Head Start program and X denotes the education level of the household head, yielded the estimated coefficients

$$a = -2.931, \ c = .325, \ b = .186$$

(the standard errors of the estimates were *not* reported). Since equation (8.65) is in units of the log odds, we express the result in terms of the *odds* of passing by computing $e^c = 1.384$, which is the ratio of odds of passing of head start participants relative to nonparticipants, controlling for the educational level of the head of household, which also has a positive effect. Since children had to be enrolled in a Head Start program, it is possible that parents with more education went out of their way to enroll their children. This implies that there may be a statistical interaction between enrollment in a Head Start program and the child's home environment. This was explored by fitting a model

(8.66) $$\log \frac{\text{pass}}{1 - \text{pass}} = a + b_1I + b_2X + b_3IX,$$

where the variable (IX) is the educational level of the household head, if the child was in Head Start and 0, otherwise. Essentially b_3 reflects any extra joint effect of or interaction between the home environment and participation in the Head Start program. The estimated coefficients for the model (8.66) are

$$a = -2.609, \quad b_1 = -2.522, \quad b_2 = .155, \quad b_3 = .253.$$

Notice that b_3 exceeds b_2, suggesting that the educational level of the household has a greater positive effect on a child's learning when the child is enrolled in a Head Start program than it has for other children.

Comments. (1) The above result agrees with common sense as the interaction may reflect both the education and interest in the child's education of the household head.

(2) Model (8.66) yields an interesting interpretation of the effectiveness of Head Start programs as a function of the educational level (X) of the household head. For children in households with the same value of X, there is a difference of

(8.67) $\qquad\qquad\qquad -2.522 + .253X$

in the log odds of passing between a child who participated and who did not. Notice that (8.67) is about 0 when $X = 10$. Thus, Head Start programs appear to be effective for children who are in households headed by persons with at least 10 years of education. If the model (8.66) is correct, then future programs might consider ways of getting the parents and other adults in the household involved in the educational process. Incorporating the interaction term not only helps us determine where the program was successful but also suggests how it might be improved.

(3) In a discrimination case a similar interaction term might reflect that minorities with lower (or higher) educational levels are facing discrimination in promotion relative to similarly situated majority employees.

(4) In a medical application, a treatment might be more effective at an early stage of a disease than at a later one. Thus, if passing is interpreted as cure (or remission), the variable X might be time since diagnosis or time since the patient noticed some symptoms.

Problems

1. Read the discussion of logistic regression in *Jurgens v. Thomas.* Which predictor variables seem most relevant to the issue in the case?

2. Calculate the estimated effect being female had on the odds of receiving an associate professorship rather than an assistant professorship using the defendant's regression in *Chang*. Why might the defendant's analysis of the instructor versus assistant professor issue be flawed?

3.* Can using logistic regression avoid the potential problems of multicollinearity or errors in the measurement of the predictor variables that occur in multiple regression?

Answers to Selected Problems

2. $e^{-.7} = .496$. Thus, a woman had half the odds of a man of receiving an assistant professorship after accounting for the factors used by the defendant. The defendant's expert assumed that all persons who were hired without the PhD were given instructorships.

3.* No. Logistic regression provides a more appropriate model to fit binary data, which incorporates the effect of predictor variables. Problems such as multicollinearity among the predictors, inaccurate data, etc., still can diminish the quality of logistic analysis. One needs to ascertain whether one or two unusual observations are having undue influence on the estimated coefficients, evaluate the correlation among the predictors, and assess the quality of the data.

Remark. While this book was in press the lower court decision in *Sobel* was vacated and a new trial ordered. The appellate opinion 45 FEP Cases 1785 (2nd Cir. 1988) interpreted the Supreme Court recent *Bazemore* decision to mean that legal pre-act discrimination which carried over into the post-act period was a violation of the act. Hence, the trial court's concern with plaintiff's failure to separate out the effect of pre-act discrimination was no longer appropriate. The opinion is in agreement with the general theme that alleged deficiencies in a reasonably sound regression analysis should be supported by evidence of their potential effect rather than by mere assertions of a possible omitted or mismeasured predictor variable. Thus, defendant's criticizing a regression should follow the approach in *Vuyanich* where the bias due to the use of age in place of seniority was demonstrated.

From a technical view, the appeals court may have given the defendants, showing that male faculty members had higher average values on 16 of the 20 variables used by plaintiffs, too little weight as the variables which positively affect productivity often are positively correlated among themselves. As noted previously, a regression model only misses the effect of an omitted variable which is not related to the included variables. Hence, the court is reasonable in its request for more evidence. On the other hand, the indirect effect of an omitted variable on the included predictors may lead to a statistical bias in their estimates which was the point the defendant was asserting. In the future, courts might require the correlation matrix of the predictors used in a regression analysis to be submitted into evidence. Using the results of Hocking (1976) and Dempster (1988) relevant models of correlation structures could be studied to assess the potential effect of omitted and imperfectly measured variables.

NOTES

1. In many applications the objective is to use knowledge available today to predict future outcomes. Thus, we use aptitude tests to predict success in college and professional schools and build models of the economy to predict the rates of unemployment and inflation that are likely to prevail next year. Using the relationship between variables to make predictions is somewhat easier than discovering the basic causal process, as there may be several characteristics which are related to the underlying mechanism. For example, the motivation and commitment to the job of an employee may be difficult to assess from a pre-employment interview, but studies of highly motivated employees may show that they take fewer absences (especially for nonmedical reasons) than other employees. Thus, attendance data may prove a valuable predictor of future on-the-job success.

2. Here we change the focus of interest from R to R^2. This is called a transformation of the original variable, R, to the new variable, R^2.

3. The logarithm of a number expresses the number as a power of another number called the *base* of the system. In high school, logarithms to the base 10 were used. For example, the logarithm of $100 = 2$ as $10^2 = 100$. Now, scientific or natural logarithms which refer to the base $e = 2.71828 \ldots$ are used. They are denoted by log or ln. For example, $\log 100 = 4.60517$.

4. In the EEOC field, requirements such as the possession of a high school diploma or college degree or being at least $5'10''$ tall are considered *tests* because they must be satisfied in order for a person to be eligible for the job. If they have a disparate or adverse impact on a protected class, then they need to be validated.

5. For small samples, the statistic (8.18) has a t-distribution with $n - 2$ degrees of freedom and the table in Appendix B, mentioned in Chapter 7 should be used. The accuracy of the normal approximation is better for modest significance levels, e.g., $\alpha = .05$ than external ones. Thus a larger sample size is needed if $\alpha = .001$ than if $\alpha = .05$. Indeed, for testing at the .05 level, a sample size of 30 is usually considered adequate for use of the normal approximation to the t.

6. As in footnote 4, the term *test* denotes any requirement used to determine a person's suitability for a job.

7. The first guidelines were issued in 1970 in the *Federal Register 35*, 12333 by the EEOC. They were superseded by the *Uniform Guidelines for Employer Selection Procedures* (1978) published in 29 C.F.R. (1979) 1607, which are used by all relevant government agencies.

8. Reliability concerns the replicability of the result of a test rather than its validity or

correlation. Often reliability is assessed by having test papers graded by more than one person. This topic is discussed in Chapter 11.

9.   422 U.S. 405, 95 S.Ct. 2362 (1975).

10.   530 F.2d 1159 (5th Cir. 1976), *cert. denied* 429 U.S. 824 (1976).

11.   91 S.Ct. 849 (1971).

12.   *supra,* note 9.

13.   457 U.S. 440, 102 S.Ct. 2525 (1982).

14.   Criterion-related validity means that a predictor (e.g., test score) is related to a criterion (a measure) of job performance. In the work setting, the criteria might be supervisory ratings (assuming they are fair) or a measure of output (dollar value of sales made during a year). The correlation between the LSAT and GPA in law schools is an example of criterion-related validation. Content validation is concerned with testing the knowledge, skills and abilities required to perform the job. Such a study begins with a careful job analysis to determine the needed skills. In *Kirkland v. N.Y. Dept. of Corrections* 7 FEP Cases 700 (E.D. N.Y. 1974), the court noted that the attributes selected for a content-related examination must be essential to job performance, the parts of the exam should be weighted to reflect the relative importance of the job attributes and the level of difficulty of the exam must match that of the job. Originally, criterion-related tests were favored by the EEOC, but now both types of validation studies have been accepted, provided they are done in a thorough and bias-free manner.

15.   The Phi coefficient is a measure of association that has been used to summarize the information in a 2×2 table. It is calculated by the formula

$$\phi = \frac{bc - ad}{\sqrt{(a + b)(a + c)(b + d)(c + d)}}.$$

While it has a long history of use, most statisticians now prefer the odds ratio. For further discussion see Lindeman, Merenda and Gold (1980), and Mosteller (1968).

16.   626 F.2d 659 (9th Cir. 1980).

17.   595 F.2d 1367 (9th Cir. 1979).

18.   *supra,* note 17 at 1382 n.17.

19.   *supra,* note 16 at 665.

20.   572 F.Supp. 402, 34 FEP Cases 304 (E.D. Mo. 1983) *affirmed* in relevant part 758 F.2d 251, 37 FEP Cases 549 (8th Cir. 1985).

21.   426 U.S. 229 (1976).

22.   14 FEP Cases 670, 681 (N.D. Ala. 1977).

23.   13 FEP Cases 533, 545 (1974) *modified* 13 FEP Cases 1355 (N.D. Ohio 1975) *affirmed* 538 F.2d 329 (6th Cir. 1976).

24.   475 F.2d 216 (10th Cir. 1972).

25.   465 F.Supp. 451, 460, 464 (D. Pa. 1979).

26.   *supra,* note 10.

27.   *supra,* note 13.

28.   433 U.S. 321, 97 S.Ct. 2720 (1977).

29.   40 FEP Cases 1415 (11th Cir. 1986).

30.   The F-test is used to determine whether the variances of two normal distributions are equal by checking whether the ratio of their sample variance is near 1. In the regression contest, it can be thought of as a comparison of the variance of the residuals $Y_i - \hat{Y}_i$ obtained from the regression line to the variance of the original observation (Y_i). If the model does not aid in prediction, the two variances should be equal. When the model is good, the variance of the residuals should be substantially *less* than the variance of the original Y_i. The F-test checks for the predictive ability of the regression model as a whole rather than each variable separately.

31. We use the term indicator, as it seems more descriptive of the role of the variable than the term "dummy variable" used in econometric texts.

32. While one might prefer a simple rule, such as test each coefficient for significance at the .05 level, we know that statistical significance also depends on sample size and the variability of the basic data. Hence, some judgement is required, which is why we use the expression "close to significance".

33. An estimator is *unbiased* if its sampling distribution is centered about the true value of the parameter it is estimating. Rigorously, we say that the expected value of the estimator equals the parameter. If the sampling distribution of the estimator is centered about a value which is always less (greater) than the true parameter, the estimate is biased on the low (high) side.

34. Section 703 g.2(h) Equal Employment Opportunity Act of 1972.

35. See Finkelstein (1980) for a discussion of this issue. Cases which accepted the use of rank or level include *Presseisen v. Swarthmore College* 442 F.Supp. 593, 616 (E.D. Pa. 1977), *affirmed.*, 582 F.2d 1275 (3d Cir. 1978). Cases which courts questioned its use include *Valentino v. United States Postal Service* 674 F.2d 56 (D.C. Cir. 1982).

36. Finkelstein (1980) notes that "fair" should mean more than any difference in promotion rates is not statistically significant at the .05 level. This is especially true in the present application, as salaries are highly related to rank or grade level.

37. 505 F.Supp. 224 at 315–315.

38. The residuals $Y_i - \hat{Y}_i$ can be regarded as an estimate of the error term e_i; however, the fitting procedure affects them, so they are not truly independent. They have different variances, in part because the slope coefficient (8.21) weights the Y_i differently. One can estimate the standard deviation, S_i of $Y_i - \hat{Y}_i$. Then $(Y_i - \hat{Y}_i)/S_i$ should be close to a standard normal variable. These are the standardized residuals.

39. The Four Seasons Hotel in Washington, D.C.

40. 738 F.2d 1249 (DC Cir. 1984).

41. *supra* footnote 7.

42. The human capital theory that the education background, general work experience plus firm specific knowledge etc., determine wages. Basic works in the area are Becker (1964) and Mincer (1970).

43. See Section 7.6c.

44. 556 F.Supp. 1166, 33 EPD. 34,030 (S.D. N.Y. 1983).

45. 731 F.2d 465, 33 EPD 34,252 (8th Cir. 1984).

46. See the original article cited in Chapter 7.

47. 606 F.Supp. 1161, 40 FEP 3 (D.R.I. 1985).

48. If the chemical has no effect, all the responses would be 0–1 variables, with the same probability p of equalling 1. Here we replace p by its estimate $\bar{p}$, made under the assumption of no effect.

49. 495 F.Supp. 1021 at 1063 (E.D. Mich. 1980).

50. This was actually the second suit filed against the defendant. The first was filed in December 1972. The date of the original charge filed with the EEOC were not given in the opinion.

51. *supra*, note 47.

52. 495. F.Supp. at 1203.

53. 495. F.Supp. at 1206. Actually the predictor variables, rather than the numbers, are being manipulated. Unfortunately, reliable data on employment decisions is often not kept by employers, and both sides naturally gravitate to experts whose subject matter theories, e.g., labor economics, present their cases in the best light. Hopefully, readers will ask questions about the theoretical basis for a regression model, the choice of data and *why* certain desirable data elements were not used or are unavailable.

54. 29 FEP Cases 1561 (N.D. Tex. 1982).
55. 17 FEP Cases 1618 (D.C. N.Y. 1976).
56. This example is taken from Chapter 9 of Anderson, Auquier, Hauck, Oakes, Vandaele and Weisberg (1980).

REFERENCES

Books

AMERICAN PSYCHOLOGICAL ASSOCIATION (1974). *Standards for Educational and Psychological Tests.* Washington, D.C.
ANDERSON, S., AUQUIER, A., HAUCK, W. W., OAKES, D., VANDAELE, W. AND WEISBERG, H. (1980). *Statistical Methods for Comparative Studies.* New York: John Wiley.
ARVEY, R. D. (1979). *Fairness in Selecting Employees.* Reading, MA: Addison-Wesley.
BALDUS, D. C. AND COLE, J. W. L. (1980). *Statistical Proof of Discrimination.* Colorado Springs, CO: Shepard's/McGraw Hill.
BECKER, G. S. (1964). *Human Capital.* New York: National Bureau of Economic Research.
CRONBACH, L. J. AND GLESER, G. (1965). *Psychological Tests and Personal Decisions.* Urbana, Ill.: University of Illinois Press.
DREHER, G. F. AND SACKETT, P. R. (1983). *Perspectives on Employee Staffing and Selection: Readings and Commentary.* Homewood, Ill.: Irwin.
LINDEMAN, R. H., MERENDA, P. F. AND GOLD, R. Z. (1980). *Introduction to Bivariate and Multivariate Analysis.* Glenview, Ill.: Scott Foresman.
PINDYCK, R. AND RUBINFELD, D. (1981). *Economic Models and Economic Forecasts.* New York: McGraw-Hill.
THEIL, H. C. (1978). *Introduction to Econometrics.* Englewood, N.J.: Prentice Hall.
U.S. CIVIL RIGHTS COMMISSION (1984). *Comparable Worth; Issue for the 80's.* (This is a collection of papers concerning the issue of comparable worth. A number of the papers utilize regression methods, while others discuss the job comparability systems and legal issues.)
WONNACOTT, J. J. AND WONNACOTT, T. H. (1979). *Econometrics,* 2nd ed. New York: John Wiley.

Articles

BARRETT, R. S. (1981). Is the Test Content Valid: Or Does it Really Measure a Construct? *Employee Relations Law Journal* **6,** 459–475.
BARRETT, R. S. (1981). Is the Test Content Valid: Or Who Killed Cock Robin? *Employee Relations Law Journal* **6,** 584–600. (These two articles provide useful background in the area of test construction and validation criteria.)

BELSON, W. A. (1956). A Technique for Studying the Effects of a Television Broadcast. *Applied Statistics* **5**, 195–202. (An interesting paper which suggested the method of assessing an effect by comparing the data of one group to predictions made from a regression fitted to the other group. The paper by Scott describes further developments of the idea and its use in EEO litigation.)

BERK, R. A., SUMMERS, A. A. AND WOLFE, B. L. (1976). Statistical Data in School Court Cases: An Interchange. *Journal of Human Resources* **11**, 328–341 and 401–409. (An illuminating dialogue concerning the usefulness of statistical methods, especially regression in the legal context. The interpretation of confidence intervals is questioned by Berk. The rejoinder defends the standard methods as opposed to Bayesian ones, which we discuss in Chapter 12. When looking at the original article, the reader will notice that when individual schools rather than school districts are the unit of analysis, the R^2 from the fitted regression models are lower, reflecting the difference between using micro or grouped data.)

BOOTH, O. AND MACKAY, J. L. (1980). Legal Constraints on Employee Testing and Evolving Trends in the Law. *Emory Law Journal* **29**, 121–194. (A comprehensive survey of virtually all aspects of the role of testing in discrimination cases.)

BLUMROSEN, W. W. (1983). The "Bottom Line" After *Connecticut v. Teal*. *Employee Relations Law Journal* **8**, 572–586. (This article advocates the usefulness of the bottom line approach when several tests or requirements are used in filling a position. The author is aware of the timing issue we have stressed, and he notes, "There is a conceptual problem in allowing the employer to alter the adverse impact of a practice after litigation has begun.")

BUFORD, J. A., JR. AND NORRIS, D. R. (1981). A Salary Equalization Model: Identifying and Correcting Sex-Based Salary Differences. *Employee Relations Law Journal* **6**, 406–421. (A nice review of the literature concerning the reasons for male and female pay differences for the same type of job. A regression model for accounting for legitimate factors is used to illustrate how an employer can correct any remaining discriminatory differentials. The interested reader should also consult the papers by Gray and Scott.)

CLUNE, W. H. (1973). Wealth Discrimination in School Finance. *Northwestern Law Review* **68**, 651–695. (A review of the school finance decisions in which regression methods were used, typically with districts as the unit of analysis.)

EGLI, C. P. (1981). Judicial Refinement of Statistical Evidence in Title *VII* Cases. *Connecticut Law Review* **13**, 515–548.

FINKELSTEIN, M. O. (1973). Regression Models in Administrative Proceedings. *Harvard Law Review* **86**, 1442–1475.

FINKELSTEIN, M. O. (1980). The Judicial Reception of Multiple Regression Studies in Race and Sex Discrimination Cases. *Columbia Law Review* **80**, 737–754.

FINKELSTEIN, M. O. AND LEVENBACH, H. (1983). Regression Estimates of Damages in Price Fixing Cases. *Law and Contemporary Problems* **46**, 145–169.

FISHER, F. (1980). Multiple Regression in Legal Proceedings. *Columbia Law Review* **80**, 702–736. (This article and the one by Finkelstein in the same issue are "must" readings.)

FLORKOWSKI, G. U. (1983). Alternative Selection Procedures and the Uniform Guidelines: Improving the Quality of Employer Investigations. *Employee Relations Law Journal* **8**, 603–617. (A review of the personnel testing literature in light of the guidelines thrust of minimizing adverse impact. The author notes that too much emphasis may have been placed on the finding of a statistically significant relationship between a test and a criterion measure, as job performance is really a function of many characteristics.)

GRAY, M. W. AND SCOTT, E. L. (1980). A "Statistical" Remedy for Statistically Identified Discrimination. *Academe* **14**, 174–181.

KAYE, D. H. (1980). Searching for Truth About Testing. *Yale Law Journal* **90**, 431–457. (A review of three studies of admission tests, which presents a careful overview of the basic issues.)

KILLINGSWORTH, M. R. AND RIEMES, C. (1983). Race, Ranking, Promotions and Pay at a Federal Facility: A Logit Analysis. *Industrial and Labor Relations Review* **37**, 92–107.

LEVIN, B. AND ROBBINS, H. (1983). Urn Models for Regression Analysis with Applications to Employment Discrimination Studies. *Law and Contemporary Problems* **46**, 247–267. (An interesting article proposing an analog of the Mantel-Haenszel procedure for combining a regression type of analysis with stratification. Being new, the method is not as well studied as ordinary regression but has some desirable characteristics.)

MANLEY, R. E. (1974). Legal Aspects of Financing Education. *The Urban Lawyer* **6**, 337–370.

MCCABE, G. (1980). The Interpretation of Regression Analysis Results in Sex and Race Discrimination Problems. *American Statistician* **34**, 212–215.

MINCER, J. (1970). The Distribution of Labor Incomes: A Survey. *Journal of Economic Literature* **8**, 1–26.

MOSTELLER, F. (1968). Association and Estimation in Contingency Tables. *Journal of the American Statistical Association* **63**, 1–28.

NOTE (1975). Beyond the *Prima Facie* Case in Employment Discrimination Law: Statistical Proof and Rebuttal. *Harvard Law Review* **89**, 387–422.

OAXACA, R. L. (1976). Male-Female Wage Differentials in the Telephone Industry. In: *Equal Employment Opportunity in the Telephone Industry* (P. A. Wallace, ed). Cambridge, MA: MIT Press. (The use of regression analysis in the settlement of the AT&T case is described. Many other issues, such as job segregation, are carefully discussed in this book, which is devoted to a pathbreaking case.)

ROTHSCHILD, M. AND WERDEN, G. (1982). Title VII and the Use of Employment Tests: An Illustration of the Limits of the Judicial Process. *Journal of Legal Studies* **11**, 261–280.

RUBINFELD, D. L. AND STEINER, P. O. (1983). Quantitative Methods in Antitrust Litigation. *Law and Contemporary Problems* **46**, 69–141.

RUBINFELD, D. L. (1985). Econometrics in the Courtroom. *Columbia Law Review* **85**, 1048–1097. (A very useful discussion stressing the use of econometric models in the legal setting, emphasizing antitrust cases.)

SCHASTER, M. H. AND MITLER, C. S. (1981). Performance Evaluation as Evidence in ADEA Cases. *Employee Relations Law Journal* **6**, 561–583. (Describes the importance of a careful, unbiased evaluation system in justifying the discharge of an employee.)

SCOTT, E. L. (1979). Linear Models and the Law: Uses and Misuses in Affirmative Action. *Proceedings of the American Statistical Association.* (In addition to the basic material, Professor Scott describes a procedure of estimating female salaries using an equation fitted to males and vice versa. A systematic overprediction of the female salaries using the male regression and a similar underprediction of male salaries using the female equation indicates discriminatory treatment, assuming the model is appropriate.)

SHOBEN, E. (1977). Probing the Discriminatory Effects of Employee Selection Procedures with Disparate Impact Analysis Under Title *VII*. *Harvard Law Review* **91**, 793–813. (This is one of the most referenced articles. Statisticians might disagree with the statement that any difference found in the entire population rather than in a sample is significant. Indeed, the randomization model of Chapter 5 is a way of assessing a difference between groups when relevant data on the entire population is available. Nevertheless, this article is well worth reading, as it integrates legal concepts with statistical ones.)

SWAMY, P. A., MEHTA, J. S. AND IYENGAR, N. W. (1985). A Generalized Multicollinearity Index for Regression Analysis. *Sankhya B* **47**, 401–431.

THOMPSON, D. E. AND CHRISTIANSEN, P. S. (1983). Court Acceptance of the Uniform Guidelines Provisions: The Bottom Line and the Search for Alternatives. *Employee Relations Law Journal* **18**, 587–602. (Discusses the effect of the *Teal* decision on the *Uniform Guidelines* which allowed for a bottom line analysis and related cases. The authors remark that once a test has been validated, rarely have plaintiffs been able to suggest alternative procedures which accomplish the task of selecting qualified employees but have less of an adverse impact.)

Articles on Reverse Regression and Errors in Variables

ASH, A. (1986). The Perverse Logic of Reverse Regression. In: *Statistical Methods in Discrimination Litigation,* (D. H. Kaye and M. Aickin, eds). New York: Marcel Dekker, 85–105.

BIRNBAUM, M. H. (1979). Procedures for the Detection and Correction of Salary Inequities. In: *Salary Equity: Detecting Sex Bias in Salaries Among College and University Professors* (T. Pezzullo and B. Brittingham, eds.). Lexington, Ma: D. C. Heath, Lexington Books.

COCHRAN, W. G. (1968). Errors of Measurement in Statistics. *Technometrics* **10**, 637–656.

CONWAY, D. A. AND ROBERTS, H. V. (1983). Reverse Regression, Fairness, and Employment Discrimination. *Journal of Business and Economic Statistics* **1**, 75–85.

DEMPSTER, A. (1984). Alternative Models for Inferring Employment Discrimination from Statistical Data. In: *W. G. Cochran's Impact on Statistics* (P. S. Rao and J. Sedransk, eds.) New York: Wiley, 309–330.

DEMPSTER, A. (1988). Employment Discrimination and Statistical Science. To appear in *Statistical Science*. (An important paper deriving an expression enabling one to adjust an estimated sex or race coefficient for the possible effect of an omitted variable or measurement error. Thus, it complements Cornfield's result for data which should be analyzed with regression methods.)

GLESER, L. J. (1981). Estimation in a Multivariate "Errors in Variables" Regression Model: Large Sample Results. *Annals of Statistics* **9**, 24–44. (An excellent technical review paper providing many references to the literature on errors in variables.)

GOLDBERGER, A. S. (1984). Reverse Regression and Salary Discrimination. *Journal of Human Resources* **19**, 293–318.

HOCKING, R. R. (1976). The Analysis and Selection of Variables in Linear Regression. *Biometrics* **32**, 1–49. (A basic technical review paper with a good discussion of the effect omitting a variable can have on a fitted regression.)

LEVIN, B. AND ROBBINS, H. (1983). A Note on the Underadjustment Phenomenon. *Statistics and Probability Letters* **1**, 137–139.

PETERSON, D. W. (1986). Measurement Error and Regression Analysis in Employment Cases. In: *Statistical Methods in Discrimination Litigation,* (D. H. Kaye and M. Aickin, eds). New York: Marcel Dekker, 107–132.

SCHAFER, D. W. (1987). Measurement-error Diagnostics and the Sex Discrimination Problem. *Journal of Business and Economic Statistics* **5**, 529–528. (This article presents a method for assessing whether measurement errors are serious enough to alter the basic conclusions drawn from a regression analysis.)

WOLINS, L. (1978). Sex Differentials in Salaries: Faults in the Analysis of Covariance. *Science* **200**, 723. (Perhaps the first article raising the errors in variable issue in the context of measuring discrimination.)

Other Applications of Regression Methods in Law and Public Policy

FEENEY, F., DILL, F. AND WEIR, A. (1983). *Arrests Without Conviction: How Often They Occur and Why*. National Institute of Justice, U.S. Department of Justice, Washington, D.C. (This study explored the role of various evidentiary characteristics and other factors such as type of crime, whether or not a weapon was used, and race on whether or not a trial resulted in a conviction. Many references to studies on what happens after an arrest, plea bargaining and other aspects of the criminal justice system are discussed.)

RUTTENBER, A. J. AND LUKE, L. J. (1984). Heroin-Related Deaths: New Epidemiologic Insights. *Science* **226**, 14–19. (This study of heroin deaths in Washington, D.C. included a case-control study to find the major risk factors involved in heroin-related deaths. Relative to natural or accidental deaths, the number of deaths over each three-month period was correlated with the concentration, weight and price of heroin. Only the linear correlations are given. A multiple regression model might have been useful, especially as the price of heroin was negatively related to the number of deaths, while the concentration was positively related (but not as strongly as price)).

SCHUCKER, R. E., STOKES, R. C., STEWART, M. L. AND HENDERSON, D. P. (1984). The Impact of the Saccharin Warning Label on Sales of Diet Soft Drinks. *Journal of Public Policy and Marketing* **2**, 45–56. (This article analyzes soft drink sales and shows that the growth in sales of diet drinks slowed considerably after the government required a lable warning of a possible association between saccharin and cancer (of the bladder). Multiple regression was used to control for price variations and the strong seasonal effect on demand for soda.)

SOUTH, S. E. AND COHEN, L. E. (1985). Unemployment and the Homicide Rate: A Paradox Resolved? *Social Indicators Research* **17**, 325–344. (This study shows that homicide rates increase when the unemployment rate increases, however, the homicide rate is also negatively related to the unemployment rate. The authors note that these results appear to be inconsistent with each other, although one can offer some plausible theories. They also comment on the high degree of multicollinearity in their model.)

Case Index

M

Maddox v. Claytor, FEP Cases 715 (11th Cir. 1985), 358

Markey v. Tenneco Oil Co., 707 F.2d 172 (5th Cir. 1983) *affirming* 32 FEP Cases (ED. La 1982), 69–70, 170, 192, 198

Marsh v. Eaton Corporation, 25 FEP Cases 57 (N.D. Ohio 1979) *affirmed and reversed in part*, 639 F.2d 328, 25 FEP Cases 64 (6th Cir. 1981), 203–205, 217, 224, 244

Marshall v. Sun Oil Co., (Delaware), 605 F.2d 1331 (5th Cir. 1979), 253

Maryland Commission for Fair Representative v. Tawes, 377 U.S. 656 (1964), 29

McDonnell-Douglas v. Green, 411 U.S. 792, 5 FEP Cases 965 (1973), 248

Mehan v. Howell, 412 U.S. 315 (1973), 29

Melanie v. Board of Higher Educ. of the City of New York, 17 FEP Cases 1618 (S.D. N.Y. 1976), 31 FEP Cases 648 (S.D. N.Y. 1983), 453

Minnis v. Brinkerhoff, 80-0206 (D.D.C. Dec. 8, 1980), xv, 184, 197

Moore v. Hughes Helicopters Inc., 708 F.2d 475 (9th Cir. 1983), 393

Murray v. District of Columbia, 34 FEP Cases 644 (D.D.C. 1983), 226

N

NAACP v. Seibels, 14 FEP Cases 670, 681 (N.S. Ala. 1977), 39

NEA v. South Carolina, 434 U.S. 1026, 98 S.Ct. 765 (1978), 388–389

Norris v. Alabama, 294 U.S. 587 (1935), 88, 154

O

O'Brien v. Sky Chefs Inc., 670 F.2d 864, 28 FEP Cases 1690 (9th Cir. 1982), 353

P

Palmer v. Shultz, 815 F.2d 84 (D.C. Cir. 1987), 251

Pennsylvania v. Rizzo, 466 F.Supp. 1219 (E.D. Pa. 1979), 227

Pennsylvania v. O'Neill, 465 F.Supp. 451 (D. Pa. 1979), 391

People v. Collins, 68 Cal. 2d. 319, 438 P.2033 (1968), 107

Pirone et al. v. Home Insurance Co., 559 F.Supp. 306 (S.D. N.Y. 1983), 252

Pouncy v. Prudential, 668 F.2d 795, 28 FEP Cases 121 (5th Cir. 1982) *affirming* 499 F.Supp. 427, 23 FEP Cases 1349 (S.D. Tex. 1980), 348, 357

Presseisen v. Swarthmore College, 442 F.Supp. 593, 616 (E.D. Pa. 1977) *affirmed* 582 F.2d 1275 (3d Cir. 1978), 459

Public Citizen Health Research Group v. Tyson, 796 F.2d 1479 (D.C. Cir. 1986), 358

Q

Quadra v. Superior Court of San Francisco, 378 F.Supp. 605 (N.D. Ca. 1974), 166

Name Index

Subject Index